$10.90
B&T

Microeconomic Theory and Functions

Microeconomic Theory and Functions

Thomas E. Holland
The University of Texas at Arlington

New York
APPLETON-CENTURY-CROFTS
EDUCATIONAL DIVISION
MEREDITH CORPORATION

to Doris

Copyright © 1973 by

MEREDITH CORPORATION

All rights reserved

This book, or parts thereof, must not be used or reproduced in any manner without written permission. For information address the publisher, Appleton-Century-Crofts, Educational Division, Meredith Corporation, 440 Park Avenue South, New York, N.Y. 10016.

73 74 75 76 77 / 10 9 8 7 6 5 4 3 2 1

Dec. 10, 1973

Library of Congress Card Number: **72-94286**

PRINTED IN THE UNITED STATES OF AMERICA

IBM code: 390-45045-6

Preface

> *The Theory of Economics does not furnish a body of settled conclusions immediately applicable to policy. It is a method rather than a doctrine, an apparatus of the mind, a technique of thinking, which helps its possessor to draw correct conclusions.*
>
> (J. M. Keynes, Cambridge Economic Handbook series)

This textbook contains an introductory-level presentation of microeconomic theory. The pervasive theme of this presentation is that economic theory is an apparatus of the mind which helps its possessor to draw correct conclusions. This apparatus consists essentially of the application of the function concept to economic problems of resource allocation. Explanations of these problems are called principles of economics. At the introductory level, each principle of economics is a verbalization of an economic function or an inference drawn from an operation on a set of economic functions. In short, economic theory consists of drawing conclusions from assumptions using mathematics. Economics as a body of knowledge consists of these principles. They are less than concrete explanations of economic problems, but they are analyzed in the same way via the function concept. They are thus harmoniously related to one another, and analogies and similarities exist between them. Economic theory is therefore a pure and abstract science, with its own logic, that is symmetrical in nature. Lastly, to complete this theme, economic theory is studied because of its content (principles of economics), which is to applied economics (accounting, finance, management, and marketing) as physics is to engineering, and because of its methodology (functions), which is the methodology of science. In accordance with this theme, each principle of microeconomic theory is presented systematically and thoroughly via graphs and algebra according to the function concept. Moreover, as seen on the next page, the function concept is applied to a new classification of microeconomic principles. The end result is a new synthesis of microeconomic theory.

T.E.H.

PRINCIPLES OF MICROECONOMIC THEORY

Principles of Value Theory

Principles of the Theory of Demand for a Product
  law of constant marginal expenditure
  law of decreasing marginal utility
  law of decreasing marginal rate of substitution
  equimarginal principle of equilibrium of a purchaser
  law of demand of a purchaser
  law of market demand

Principles of the Theory of Supply of a Product
  law of constant marginal revenue
  law of constant marginal factor cost
  law of increasing marginal input
  law of increasing marginal cost
  equimarginal principle of equilibrium of a seller
  law of supply of a seller
  law of market supply

Principles of the Theory of Determination of Price and Quantity in a Product Market
  laws of market equilibrium and disequilibrium price and quantity
  principles of period equilibrium of a perfectly competitive seller
  principles of period equilibrium of a monopolistic seller
  principles of period equilibrium of a monopolistic-competitive seller
  principles of equilibrium of an oligopolistic seller

Principles of Distribution Theory

Principles of the Theory of Demand for a Factor of Production
  law of constant marginal factor cost
  law of constant marginal revenue
  law of decreasing marginal output
  law of decreasing marginal revenue-output
  equimarginal principles of equilibrium of a purchaser
  law of demand of a purchaser
  law of market demand

Principles of the Theory of Supply of a Factor of Production (Labor)
  law of constant marginal income
  law of decreasing marginal utility
  law of decreasing marginal rate of substitution
  equimarginal principle of equilibrium of a seller
  law of supply of a seller
  law of market supply

Principles of the Theory of Determination of Price and Quantity in a Factor Market
  laws of equilibrium and disequilibrium price and quantity in a competitive product market and of product sellers
  principles of structural equilibrium of a factor purchaser

Principles of General Equilibrium Theory

Principles of Optimum Allocation of Products
Principles of Optimum Allocation of Factors of Production
Principles of General Equilibrium of all Markets

Contents

Preface

Introduction 1

Model of an Economic System, 2. Microeconomic Theory, 3. Value Theory, 3. Distribution Theory, 4. Theory of the Household and Theory of the Business Firm, 4. Partial and General Equilibrium Theory, 5. National Product Identity, 6. National Income Identity, 6. Aggregate Supply and Demand Functions for Output, 7. Macroeconomic Theory, 7. Summary, 8.

PART I. PRINCIPLES OF THE THEORY OF DEMAND FOR A PRODUCT

1. The Expenditure Function of a Perfectly Competitive Purchaser of Products 13

Total Expenditure Function, 13. Marginal Expenditure Function, 16. Law of Constant Marginal Expenditure, 17. Average Expenditure Function, 18. Supply Curve of a Product Facing a Purchaser, 19. Iso-expenditure Function, 20. Summary, 23.

2. Utility Function 27

Total Utility Function, 27. Marginal Utility Function, 30. Law of Decreasing Marginal Utility, 31. Iso-utility Function, 32. Substitutes and Complements in Consumption and the Iso-utility Curve, 34. Substitutes in Consumption, 34. Complements in Consumption, 36. Marginal Rate of Substitution Function of a Product for Money, 37. Summary, 38.
APPENDIX: Preference Ordering Theory, 39.
Cardinal Versus Ordinal Ranking of Combinations, 40. Indifference Relation, 40. Preference Relation, 41. Indifference Map, 41. Summary, 42.

3. **Equilibrium of a Perfectly Competitive Purchaser of Products**   **44**

Ratio of Marginal Utilities Equals Ratio of Prices, 44. Marginal Rate of Substitution of a Product for Money Equals the Price of the Product, 46. Marginal Utility of a Product Equals Marginal Utility of Money Expended, 47. Equality of the Ratio of Marginal Utility to Price of Every Product, 48. Equimarginal Principle of Equilibrium of a Purchaser of Products, 49. Summary, 50.

4. **The Demand Function for a Product of a Perfectly Competitive Purchaser**   **53**

Demand Curve for a Product of a Purchaser, 53. Substitution and Income Effects, 55. Normal, Inferior, and Giffin Products, 56. Marginal Rate of Substitution Curve of a Product for a Product, 57. Marginal Rate of Substitution Curve of a Product for Money, 60. Law of Demand for a Product of a Purchaser, 61. Price of a Substitute, 62. Price of a Complement, 62. Purchaser's Money Income, 63. Summary, 65.

5. **The Market Demand Function for a Product**   **68**

Law of Market Demand for a Product, 68. Change in Demand and Change in Quantity Demanded, 69. Demand for a Product as a Function of the Price of a Substitute, 70. Demand for a Product as a Function of the Price of a Complement, 71. Demand for a Product as a Function of Aggregate Money Income of Purchasers, 73. Elasticity of Market Demand for a Product, 74. Price Elasticity and Aggregate Expenditure on a Product, 75. Geometry of Price Elasticity of Market Demand, 76. Price Elasticity Cases, 78. Price Cross Elasticity of Market Demand for a Product, 82. Income Elasticity of Market Demand for a Product, 82. Summary, 83.
APPENDIX: Price Elasticity of Demand and the Price-Consumption Curve, 85.

PART II. PRINCIPLES OF THE THEORY OF SUPPLY OF A PRODUCT

6. **Revenue Functions**   **92**

Perfectly Competitive Seller of a Product, 92. Total Revenue Curve of a Product of a Perfectly Competitive Seller, 93. Marginal Revenue Curve of a Product of a Perfectly Competitive Seller, 94. Average Revenue Curve of a Product of a Perfectly Competitive Seller, 95. Demand Curve for a Product Facing a Perfectly Competitive Seller, 96. Iso-Revenue Curve of a Perfectly Competitive Seller, 96. Imperfectly Competitive Seller of a Product, 99. Total Revenue Curve of a Product of a Monopolist, 99. Marginal Revenue Curve of a Product of a Monopolist, 101. Average Revenue Curve of a Product of a Monopolist, 101. Demand Curve for a Product Facing a Monopolist, 102.

Relationship Between Total, Marginal, and Average Revenue Curves of a Monopolist, 102. Relationship Between Marginal and Average Revenue Curves, 103. Price Elasticity of Market Demand and Total Revenue, 104. Iso-Revenue Curve of a Monopolist, 105. Summary, 106.

APPENDIX: Revenue Function of a First-Degree Price-Discriminating Monopolist, 108.

7. The Production Function — 111

Total Product Curve of a Factor of Production, 111. Marginal Product Curve of a Factor of Production, 114. Basis of Decreasing Marginal Product of a Factor of Production, 116. Average Product Curve of a Factor of Production, 116. Iso-Product Curve of Two Factors Not Related in Production, 117. Iso-Product Curve of Two Substitutes in Production, 119. Iso-Product Curve of Two Complements in Production, 121. Economic Region of Production, 123. Variable Proportions and Marginal Returns to Variable Input, 124. Fixed Proportions and Returns to Scale, 126. Basis of Returns to Scale, 127. Technological Progress, 127. Summary, 129.

APPENDIX: Symmetry of the Stages of Production, 132.

Stages of Production, 132. Product Curves of Labor, 133. Product Curves of Capital, 134. Total Product of Capital and Average Product of Labor, 135. Total Product of Labor and Average Product of Capital, 135. Basis of Symmetry, 135. Importance of Symmetry, 136.

8. Factor Cost Functions — 139

Perfectly Competitive Purchaser of a Factor of Production, 139. Total Factor Cost Curve of a Factor of Production of a Perfectly Competitive Purchaser, 140. Marginal Factor Cost Curve of a Factor of Production of a Perfectly Competitive Purchaser, 141. Average Factor Cost Curve of a Factor of Production of a Perfectly Competitive Purchaser, 142. Supply Curve of a Factor of Production Facing a Perfectly Competitive Purchaser, 143. Iso-Factor Cost Curve of a Perfectly Competitive Purchaser, 143. Imperfectly Competitive Purchaser of a Factor of Production, 145. Total Factor Cost Curve of a Factor of Production of a Monopsonist, 146. Marginal Factor Cost Curve of a Factor of Production of a Monopsonist, 147. Average Factor Cost Curve of a Factor of Production of a Monopsonist, 148. Supply Curve of a Factor of Production Facing a Monopsonist, 148. Relationship Between Total, Marginal, and Average Factor Cost Curves of a Monopsonist, 148. Iso-Factor Cost Curve of a Monopsonist, 149. Summary, 150.

APPENDIX: Factor Cost Curves of a First-Degree Price-Discriminating Monopsonist, 152.

9. Cost Functions — 155

Short-Run Total Cost Curve of a Product of a Perfectly Competitive Purchaser of a Variable Factor of Production, 155. Short-Run Marginal Cost Curve of a Product of a Perfectly Competitive Purchaser of a Variable Factor of Production,

159. Short-Run Average Cost Curve of a Product of a Perfectly Competitive Purchaser of a Variable Factor of Production, 161. Short-Run Cost Curves of a Product of an Imperfectly Competitive Purchaser of a Variable Factor of Production, 163. Long-Run Cost Curves of a Product, 166. Relationship Between Short-Run and Long-Run Average Cost Curves, 167. Relationship Between Short-Run and Long-Run Marginal Cost Curves, 169. Monetary and Real Costs, 169. Iso-Input Curve of Two Factors Not Related in Production, 170. Iso-Input Curve of Two Substitutes in Production, 172. Iso-Input Curve of Two Complements in Production, 173. Summary, 175.

10. Equilibrium of a Perfectly Competitive Seller of Products — 180

Price Equals Marginal Costs, 180. Equality of the Ratio of Price to Marginal Cost of Every Product, 181. Equimarginal Principle of Equilibrium of a Perfectly Competitive Seller of Products, 182. Ratio of Prices Equals Ratio of Marginal Costs, 183. Marginal Revenue-Product Equals Price of Input, 184. Ratio of Prices Equals Ratio of Marginal Inputs, 184. Output Expansion Path, 186. Summary, 188.

11. The Supply Function of a Product of a Perfectly Competitive Seller — 191

Supply Curve of a Product of a Seller, 191. Law of Supply of a Product of a Seller, 192. Price of a Substitute, 193. Supply Curve of a Substitute in Production, 193. Price of a Complement, 194. Supply Curve of a Complement in Production, 195. Summary, 196.

12. The Market Supply Function of a Product — 198

Law of Market Supply of a Product, 198. Change in Supply and Change in Quantity Supplied, 199. Supply of a Product as a Function of Price of a Substitute, 200. Supply of a Product as a Function of Price of a Complement, 201. Elasticity of Market Supply of a Product, 201. Summary, 204.

PART III. THEORY OF DETERMINATION OF PRICE AND QUANTITY IN A PRODUCT MARKET

13. Equilibrium and Disequilibrium in a Competitive Product Market — 209

Walrasian Market Demand and Supply, 210. Walrasian Equilibrium and Disequilibrium Market Price, 210. Walrasian Stable and Unstable Equilibrium, 211. Marshallian Market Demand and Supply, 213. Marshallian Equilibrium and Disequilibrium Market Quantity, 214. Marshallian Stable and Unstable Equilibrium, 214. Parameter Shifts in Market Demand Curve, 216. Parameter Shifts in Market Supply Curve, 217. Identification of Market Supply and Demand Curves, 219. Identification When Market Supply Increases, 220.

CONTENTS   xi

Identification When Market Supply Decreases, 221. Identification When Market Demand Increases, 222. Identification When Market Demand Decreases, 224. Cobweb Theorum, 224. Summary, 227.

14. Period Equilibrium of Competitive and Monopolistic Product Sellers   234

Short-Run Market Period, 234. Short-Run Supply Curve of a Perfectly Competitive Seller, 235. Short-Run "Supply Curve" of a Monopolist, 238. Short-Run Equilibrium of a Multi-Plant Monopolist, 241. Equilibrium of a Multi-Market Monopolist, 242. Very Short-Run Market Period, 244. Very Short-Run Market Model, 245. Very Short-Run Supply Curve of a Perfectly Competitive Seller, 246. Very Short-Run Supply Curve of a Monopolist, 247. Long-Run Market Period, 248. Long-Run Supply Curve of a Perfectly Competitive Seller, 248. Long-Run Supply Curve of a Perfectly Competitive Industry, 250. Constant-Cost Industry, 251. Increasing-Cost Industry, 252. Decreasing-Cost Industry, 253. Long-Run "Supply Curve" of a Monopolist, 254. Long-Run Equilibrium of a Multi-Plant Monopolist, 255. Summary, 256.
APPENDIX: Purchasers' and Sellers' Surplus and Net Welfare Loss, 259. Purchasers' Surplus, 259. Sellers' Surplus, 260. Net Welfare Loss, 260. Summary, 261.

15. Equilibrium of Monopolistic-Competitive and Oligopolistic Product Sellers   263

Monopolistic-Competitive Seller of a Product, 263. Demand Curve Facing a Monopolistic-Competitive Seller, 263. Short-Run Equilibrium, 264. Long-Run Equilibrium, 264. Interdependence of Demand Curves Model, 265. Oligopolistic Seller of a Product, 266. Classical Incapable-of-Learning Duopoly Models, 267. Cournot's Model, 267. Bertrand's Model, 269. Edgeworth's Model, 270. Chamberlin's Mutual Dependence Recognized Model, 271. Sweezy's Kinked Demand Curve Model, 272. Monopoly-Cartel Model, 273. Equal-Shares Price-Leadership Model, 275. Dominant-Seller Price-Leadership Model, 276. Baumol's Sales-Maximization Model, 277. Summary, 279.

PART IV. PRINCIPLES OF THE THEORY OF DEMAND FOR A FACTOR OF PRODUCTION

16. Revenue-Product Functions   284

Total Revenue-Product Curve of a Factor of a Perfectly Competitive Seller of a Product, 284. Marginal Revenue-Product Curve of a Factor of a Perfectly Competitive Seller of a Product, 287. Average Revenue-Product Curve of a Factor of a Perfectly Competitive Seller of a Product, 289. Revenue-Product Curves of a Factor of an Imperfectly Competitive Seller of a Product, 291. Summary, 292.

17. Equilibrium of a Perfectly Competitive Purchaser of Factors of Production 295

Marginal Revenue-Product Equals Price, 295. Equality of the Ratio of Marginal Revenue-Product to Price of Every Factor, 296. Equimarginal Principle of Equilibrium of a Perfectly Competitive Purchaser of Factors, 297. Ratio of Marginal Revenue-Products Equals Ratio of Prices, 298. Price of Output Equals Marginal Cost, 299. Ratio of Marginal Products Equals Ratio of Prices, 299. Input Expansion Path, 301. Summary, 303.

18. The Demand Function for a Factor of Production of a Perfectly Competitive Purchaser 306

Demand Curve for a Factor of a Purchaser, 306. Law of Demand for a Factor of a Purchaser, 308. Price of a Technical Substitute in Production, 308. Demand Curve for a Technical Substitute in Production, 309. Price of a Technical Complement in Production, 210. Demand Curve for a Technical Complement in Production, 310. Summary, 311.

19. The Market Demand Function for a Factor of Production 313

Rationale of the Law of Market Demand for a Factor, 313. Change in Demand and Change in Quantity Demanded, 314. Demand for a Factor as a Function of Price of a Technical Substitute in Production, 315. Demand for a Factor as a Function of Price of a Technical Complement in Production, 316. Summary, 316.
APPENDIX: Marginal Physical Productivity Theory of Income Distribution, 318. Input-Quantity Ratio as a Function of Input-Price Ratio, 318. Elasticity of Substitution, 318. Distribution of National Income, 319. Technological Progress, 320.

PART V. PRINCIPLES OF THE THEORY OF SUPPLY OF A FACTOR OF PRODUCTION

20. Income Function of a Perfectly Competitive Seller of Labor 323

Total Income Curve of Labor, 323. Marginal Income Curve of Labor, 324. Average Income Curve of Labor, 325. Demand Curve for Labor Facing a Seller, 326. Iso-Wage Curve, 326. Iso-Real-Wage Curve, 327. Summary, 328.

21. Equilibrium of a Perfectly Competitive Seller of Labor 331

Marginal Rate of Substitution of Leisure for Income Equals the Price of Leisure, 331. Marginal Utility of Leisure Equals Marginal Utility of Labor, 333. Equimarginal Principle of Equilibrium of a Seller of Labor, 334. Marginal Utility Per Dollar of Leisure Equals Marginal Utility of Income, 335. Ratio of Marginal Utilities Equals Ratio of Prices, 336. Summary, 336.

22. The Supply Function of Labor of a Perfectly Competitive Seller — 338

Law of Demand for Leisure of a Purchaser (Consumer), 338. Law of Supply of a Seller of Labor, 340. Substitution and Income Effects, 342. Quantity Sold of Labor as a Function of the Price of Products, 346. Summary, 348.

PART VI. THEORY OF DETERMINATION OF PRICE AND QUANTITY IN A FACTOR MARKET

23. Structural Equilibrium of a Factor Purchaser — 352

Perfect Competition in Product and Factor Markets, 352. Monopoly in Product Market—Perfect Competition in Factor Market, 354. Monopolistic Exploitation, 355. Perfect Competition in Product Market—Monopsony in Factor Market, 355. Monopsonistic Exploitation, 357. Monopoly in Product Market—Monopsony in Factor Market, 358. Bilateral Monopoly, 358. Preferred Equilibrium of Monopsonist (Business Firm), 359. Preferred Equilibrium of Monopolist (Labor Union), 359. Indeterminacy of Market Equilibrium, 360. Summary, 361.

PART VII. PARTIAL AND GENERAL EQUILIBRIUM THEORY

24. General Equilibrium Theory — 366

General Equilibrium of Households, 366. Optimum Allocation of Products, 368. General Equilibrium of Business Firms, 371. Optimum Allocation of Factors of Production, 374. General Equilibrium of Markets in an Exchange Economy, 376. General Equilibrium of Markets in a Production and Exchange Economy, 377. Summary, 378.

Index — 381

Introduction

> ... *courses should strive to develop the abilities . . . to understand the principles of logic and inquiry—in short, to learn the way in which a discipline is organized and carried out.*
>
> (Joseph Schwab, *College Curriculum and Student Protest*)

The subject matter of economic theory may be introduced via the circular flow of income diagram. This diagram separates an economic system into two parts, each of which is denoted by a rectangle. The right-side rectangle denotes purchasers of products and sellers of factors of production. The left-side rectangle denotes sellers of products and purchasers of factors of production. Products may be classified as goods (other than capital goods) or services. Factors of production may be classified as labor, capital, or land.[1] Thus resources may be classified as products or factors of production. The

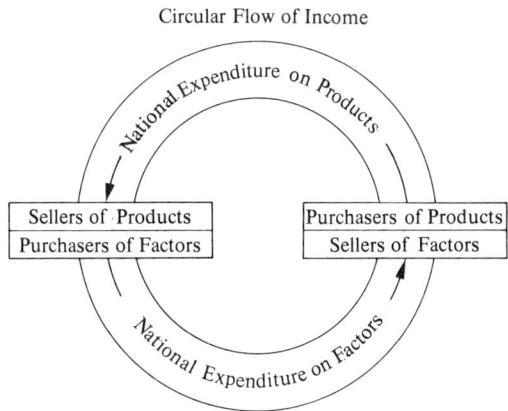

Circular Flow of Income

rectangles are connected by two loops. The upper loop denotes the national expenditure on products. The lower loop denotes the national expenditure on factors of production. The national expenditure on products (y_1) is identically equal to the sum of the expenditures on all products in an economic system in a year. The expenditure on a given product is identically equal to its quantity sold during the year (q) times its price (p). Thus,

$$y_1 \equiv p_1 q_1 + p_2 q_2 + \cdots + p_n q_n.$$

This expenditure is income to sellers and cost to purchasers of products. Similarly, the national expenditure on factors of production (y_2) is identically equal to the sum of the expenditures on all factors in an economic system in a year. The expenditure on a given factor of production is identically equal to its quantity sold during the year (f) times its price (w). Thus,

$$y_2 \equiv w_1 f_1 + w_2 f_2 + \cdots + w_n f_n.$$

This expenditure is income to sellers and cost to purchasers of factors of production.

Model of an Economic System

An economic system is a set of economic units; an economic unit is a seller or purchaser of products or factors of production. The economic units which make up an economic system may be classified as households, business firms, governments, and foreign economic units. In a simpler model of human behavior, however, an economic system consists of households and business firms; and the only factor of production exchanged in the market place is labor. In this model, households are the purchasers of products and the sellers of factors of production (labor), and business firms are the sellers of products and the purchasers of factors of production (labor). Thus, in this context, households are the source of the national expenditure on products and the receivers of the national expenditure on factors of production, and business firms are the source of the national expenditure on factors of production and the receivers of the national expenditure on products. According to this model, income flows from purchasers of products (= households) to sellers of products (= business firms); then, to complete the flow, income flows from purchasers of factors (= business firms) to sellers of factors (= households). The national expenditure on products in this model, therefore, is the income of business firms and the cost of living of households; and the national expenditure on factors of production is the income of households and the cost of production of business firms.

Microeconomic Theory

Microeconomic theory is the name of the principles of economics which are used to explain the size, composition, and allocation of the national expenditures on products and factors of production. The word "micro" refers to the relatively small degree of aggregation of the economic units which determine the size, composition, and allocation of the national expenditures on products and factors of production as they compete for relatively scarce resources to attain preferred positions. (Resources are scarce relative to wants.) The word "micro" refers also to the relatively small degree of aggregation of the economic variables which are used to express the composition of the national expenditures. The composition of the national expenditure on products is expressed by the prices and quantities of products—that is, by the sets of p and q variables. Similarly, the composition of the national expenditure on factors of production is expressed by the prices and quantities of factors—that is, by the sets of w and f variables.

Value Theory

An economic system performs the function of determining the size, composition, and allocation of the national expenditure on products. More succinctly, in competing for relatively scarce resources, purchasers and sellers of products determine the answer to the resource allocation question: what products (income) will be produced? To elaborate, what will be the allocation of resources between the production of public and private goods, between production for war and for the renovation of cities, between vacations for the rich and "commodities" for the poor? In short, what determines the prices and quantities of products? In a market economy, the answers of purchasers and sellers are expressed in the market place via their demands and supplies of products as they compete for relatively scarce resources to attain preferred positions. In other words, the price and quantity sold of a product (expenditure on a product) are determined in a market by the demand of purchasers and the supply of sellers. Value theory is the name of the demand, supply, and market principles used to explain how purchasers and sellers determine the expenditure on each product and thereby the size, composition, and allocation of the national expenditure on products. Value theory consists of the theory of demand for a product (Part I), the theory of supply of a product (Part II), and the theory of determination of price and quantity in a product market—that is, market theory (Part III).

Distribution Theory

An economic system also performs the function of determining the size, composition, and allocation of the national expenditure on factors of production. More succinctly, in competing for relatively scarce resources, purchasers and sellers of factors of production determine the answer to the resource allocation question: how will products (income) be distributed? To elaborate, how will income be distributed between the rich and the poor, between individuals, corporations, and governments, between the present (consumption) and the future (saving)? In short, what determines the prices and quantities of factors? In a market economy, the answers of purchasers and sellers are expressed in the market place via their demands and supplies of factors of production as they compete for relatively scarce resources to attain preferred positions. In other words, the price and quantity sold of a factor of production (expenditure on a factor) are determined in a market by the demand of purchasers and the supply of sellers. Distribution theory is the name of the demand, supply, and market principles used to explain how purchasers and sellers determine the expenditure on each factor and thereby the size, composition, and allocation of the national expenditure on factors. Distribution theory consists of the theory of demand for a factor (Part IV), the theory of supply of a factor (Part V), and the theory of determination of price and quantity in a factor market—that is, market theory (Part VI).

Theory of the Household and Theory of the Business Firm

In the United States, households and business firms play important roles in the determination of the size, composition, and allocation of the national expenditures on products and factors of production as they compete for relatively scarce resources to attain preferred positions. For this reason, microeconomic theory is based on a theory of the household and a theory of the business firm. These theories consist of principles of the optimum allocation via prices of relatively scarce resources to the satisfaction of competing wants of people seeking to attain preferred positions. An economic system that relies upon prices to allocate its relatively scarce resources in such a manner that people attain preferred positions is called a price system; and the economic theory of the operation of a price system is called price theory.

The basic theory of the household is presented in Parts I and V, and Chapter 13. The two most important principles of this theory are the principles of equilibrium of a purchaser (consumer) of products (Chapter 3) and of a seller of labor (Chapter 23). The principle of equilibrium of a purchaser of products is a rationale of the optimum allocation of a purchaser's income between various products. This principle provides the demand part of the answer to the question: what will be produced? The principle of equilibrium of a seller of labor is a rationale of the optimum allocation of a seller's time between leisure and work. This principle provides the supply part (with respect to labor) of the answer to the question: how will income be distributed? A purchaser of products and seller of labor is in a preferred position vis-a-vis products, leisure and work when he is in equilibrium. When the "workers" are in equilibrium, an economic system has solved the resource allocation problem of determining the role and degree of freedom of households. That is, it has determined the legal and institutional framework within which households purchase products and sell labor. More succinctly, it has determined the answer to the question: how will income and time be spent?

The basic theory of the business firm is presented in Parts II, III, IV, and VI. The two most important principles of this theory are the principles of equilibrium of a seller of products (Chapters 10, 13–17) and of a purchaser (user) of factors of production (Chapters 20 and 26). The principle of equilibrium of a seller of products is a rationale of the optimum output of a business firm, the optimum allocation of input between various products, and the optimum allocation of output between plants and markets. This principle provides the supply part of the answer to the question: what will be produced? The principle of equilibrium of a purchaser of factors of production is a rationale of the optimum input of a business firm and the optimum allocation of output between various factors of production. This principle provides the demand part of the answer to the question: how will income be distributed? A seller of products and purchaser of factors is in a preferred position vis-a-vis products and factors when he is in equilibrium. When the "capitalists" are in equilibrium, an economic system has solved the resource allocation problem of determining the role and degree of freedom of business firms or, in a broader sense, managers. That is, it has determined the legal and institutional framework within which business firms sell products and purchase factors of production. More succinctly, it has determined the answer to the question: how will products (income) be produced?

Partial and General Equilibrium Theory

Consider an economic system of households and business firms interacting in product and factor markets. A product market is in equilibrium when quantity supplied of the product equals quantity demanded. A factor market is in equilibrium when quantity supplied of the factor equals quantity demanded. A household is in general equilibrium when it is in equilibrium with respect to its purchases of products and sales of labor. A business firm is in general equilibrium when it is in equilibrium with respect to its sales of goods (including capital goods) and services and purchases of factors of production. Each product and factor market is in equilibrium when each household and business firm is in general equilibrium. The economic system is in general equilibrium when each of its product and factor markets is in equilibrium. It is in partial equilibrium when a market that, for analytical purposes, is considered in isolation from other markets is defined to be in equilibrium. Partial equilibrium theory is presented in Parts I–VI. General equilibrium theory is presented in Part VII.

General equilibrium theory consists of three interrelated sets of principles of economics. The first set consists of principles regarding the optimum allocation of a given amount of products (resources) among households as they compete to attain preferred positions. The second set consists of principles regarding the optimum allocation of a given amount of factors (resources) to the production of various products—that is, among business firms as they compete to attain preferred positions. The third set consists of principles regarding general equilibrium of all markets, in which case each person has attained a position that is preferred—given his command over resources and the prices of resources.

National Product Identity

The national expenditure on final (as distinguished from intermediate) goods and services, including capital goods, produced domestically in a year is called the gross national product (GNP). In this context, according to the national product (or income spent) identity, the GNP (Y) is identically equal to the expenditure of households on products, called consumption (C); plus the gross capital expenditure of business firms on buildings (including residential housing) and equipment, and for additions to inventory, called investment (I); plus the expenditure of government (G); plus the expenditure of foreign economic units on domestic goods and services, called exports (X); minus the expenditure of domestic economic units on foreign goods and services, called imports (Z). Thus, $Y \equiv C + I + G + X - Z$, where Y may be called national income spent.

National Income Identity

The gross national product may also be defined as the receipt of spending on final goods and services, including capital goods, produced domestically in a year. In this context, according to the national income (or income received) identity, the GNP (Y) is identically equal to the income received by households, which is used for consumption purposes (C) or is saved (S_h); plus the income received by business firms and not distributed to other economic units, called business saving (S_b); plus the tax revenue (income) of government (T_x), minus government transfer payments (T_r). Thus, by letting $S \equiv S_h + S_b$, $Y \equiv C + S + T_x - T_r$, where Y may be called national income received.

Aggregate Supply and Demand Functions for Output

By definition, the money GNP (Y) is identically equal to the index of the general price level of goods and services (P) times the index of the aggregate output of goods and services (y), which is the real GNP: $Y \equiv Py$. Also, by definition, the money GNP (Y) is identically equal to the money stock (M) times the velocity of the money stock (V), which is the average number of times per year that M is used in making expenditures on goods and services: $Y \equiv MV$. In this context, according to the equation of exchange, $MV \equiv Py$. Thus, by defining y as the aggregate output of goods and services which purchasers are willing to purchase per year (y_d), and by treating M and V as parameters, $y_d = D(P) = MV/P$, where $\Delta y_d/\Delta P < 0$. The values of M and V are explained via the aggregate supply and demand functions for money, $M_d = M_d(r)$ and $M_s = M_s(r)$, where r is the index of interest rates. At each point on $y_d = D(P)$, national income spent ($C + I + G + X - Z$) equals national income received ($C + S + T_x - T_r$), and the quantity demanded of money (M_d) equals the quantity supplied of money (M_s). The aggregate output of goods and services which sellers are willing to sell per year (y_s) is explained via the aggregate supply function of output, $y_s = S(P)$, where $\Delta y_s/\Delta P \gtreqless 0$. This function is a synthesis of the aggregate production function, $y = y(N)$, and the aggregate supply and demand functions for labor, $N_d = N_d(W/P)$ and $N_s = N_s(W/P)$, where W is an index of money wage rates. At each point on $y_s = S(P)$, actual output (y) has been determined by actual employment (N); and N is equal to the quantity demanded of labor (N_d) and/or the quantity supplied of labor (N_s).

Macroeconomic Theory

Macroeconomic theory is the name of the principles of economics which are used to explain the size and composition, the cyclical fluctuation, and the growth of Y, P, y, r, M, W, and N. The word "macro" refers to the relatively large degree of aggregation of the economic units (households, business firms, government, and foreign) which determine the size, composition, and movements of Y, etc. The word "macro" also refers to the relatively large degree of aggregation of the economic variables (Y, etc.) that are the subject matter of macroeconomic theory. Thus macroeconomic theory is also called aggregate economic analysis. It is also called national income theory, for "national income" may be used as a loose name for the precise term "gross national product." It is also called Keynesian economics, for the foremost exponent of this theory was John Maynard Keynes (1883–1946). Lastly, macroeconomic theory is also called the new economics, for Keynes' monumental work, *The General Theory of Employment, Interest, and Money*, was published in 1936 as a supplement to the older microeconomics.

SUMMARY

Microeconomic theory is the name of the principles of economics which are used to explain the size, composition, and allocation of the national expenditures on products and factors of production. The national expenditure on products is identically equal to the sum of the expenditures on all products in an economic system in a year. Value theory is the name of the demand, supply, and market principles used to explain how purchasers and sellers determine the expenditure on each product and thereby the size, composition, and allocation of the national expenditure on products. Value theory consists of the theory of demand for a product, the theory of supply of a product, and the theory of determination of price and quantity in a product market. The national expenditure on factors of production is identically equal to the sum of the expenditures on all factors of production in an economic system in a year. Distribution theory is the name of the demand, supply, and market principles used to explain how purchasers and sellers determine the expenditure on each factor and thereby the size, composition, and allocation of the national expenditure on factors. Distribution theory consists of the theory of demand for a factor, the theory of supply of a factor, and the theory of determination of price and quantity in a factor market.

Microeconomic theory is based on a theory of the household and a theory of the business firm. The two most important principles of the theory of the household are the principles of equilibrium of a purchaser of products and of a seller of labor. The two most important principles of the theory of the business firm are the principles of equilibrium of a seller of products and of a purchaser of factors of production. Each product and factor market is in equilibrium when each household and business firm is in equilibrium. An economic system is in general equilibrium when each product and factor market is in equilibrium. It is in partial equilibrium when a market that, for analytical purposes, is considered in isolation from other markets is defined to be in equilibrium. When an economic system is in general equilibrium, it has solved the four resource allocation problems of determining (1) what income will be produced, (2) how income will be produced, (3) how income will be distributed, and (4) how income and time will be spent.

Macroeconomic theory is the name of the principles of economics which are used to explain the size and composition, the cyclical fluctuation, and the growth of Y, P, y, r, M, W, and N. Macroeconomic theory consists of the theory of aggregate demand for output, the theory of aggregate supply of output, and the theory of determination of the general price level of goods and services (P) and the aggregate output of goods and services (y) in the aggregate output market. At each point on the aggregate demand curve for output, $y_d = D(P)$, national income spent ($C + I + G + X - Z$) equals national income received ($C + S + T_x - T_r$), and the quantity demanded of money (M_d) equals the quantity supplied of money (M_s) at the prevailing level of the interest rate (r) and the stock of money (M). At each point on the aggregate supply curve of output, $y_s = S(P)$, actual output (y) has been determined by the level of actual employment of labor (N); and N is equal to the quantity demanded of labor (N_d) and/or the quantity supplied of labor (N_s) at the prevailing level of the money wage rate (W). Thus, when $y_d = y_s$, the economic system of output, money, and labor markets is in general equilibrium. Macroeconomic theory is also called aggregate economic analysis, national income theory, Keynesian economics, or the new economics.

Questions

1. How would you describe an economic system?

2. What is microeconomic theory? Into what sets would you classify the principles of microeconomic theory?

3. What is value theory? Into what sets would you classify the principles of value theory?

4. What is distribution theory? Into what sets would you classify the principles of distribution theory?

5. What are the two most important principles of the basic theory of the household? How do these principles relate to value and distribution theory?

6. What are the two most important principles of the basic theory of the business firm? How do these principles relate to value and distribution theory?

7. What are the four resource allocation problems which every economic system must solve? How do these problems relate to value and distribution theory, and to the theory of the household and the theory of the business firm?

8. Can you distinguish between partial and general equilibrium theory? Into what sets would you classify the principles of general equilibrium theory?

9. What are the national product and national income identities?

10. What are the aggregate supply and demand functions for output?

11. What is macroeconomic theory? Into what sets would you classify the principles of macroeconomic theory? What distinguishes macro- and micro-economic theory?

12. Do you agree that the most important questions of this set are the questions of number 7? Why?

SELECTED READINGS

Lange, Oscar. "The Scope and Method of Economics," *The Review of Economic Studies*, XIII (1945-1946), pp. 19-32. Reprinted in Kamerschen, D. R. (editor). *Readings in Microeconomics*. Cleveland, Ohio: The World Publishing Company, 1967, pp. 3-22.

Klappholz, Kurt and J. Agassi. "Methodological Prescriptions in Economics," *Economica*. New Series; 26 (February 1959), pp. 60-74. Reprinted in Kamerschen, *ibid.*, pp. 23-39.

Schumpeter, Joseph A. "The Nature and Necessity of a Price System," *Economic Reconstruction*. New York: Columbia University Press, 1934, pp. 170-176. Reprinted in Kamerschen, *ibid.*, pp. 52-56.

Wicksteed, Philip H. "The Scope and Method of Political Economy," *The Economic Journal*, XXIV (1914), pp. 1-23. Reprinted in The American Economic Association. *Readings in Price Theory*. Edited by George J. Stigler and Kenneth E. Boulding. Homewood, Illinois: Richard D. Irwin, Inc., 1952, pp. 3-26.

NOTES

[1] Plant, equipment, and inventory are capital goods, but capital goods are not classified as products in this classificatory scheme to avoid double counting.

PART I

PRINCIPLES OF THE THEORY OF DEMAND FOR A PRODUCT

> ... the entire work of the understanding must be begun afresh, and the mind itself be, from the start, not left to take its own course, but be guided step by step.
>
> (Francis Bacon, *Novum organum*)

Six principles of the economic theory of demand for a product are of primary importance. They are the laws of constant marginal expenditure on a product to a perfectly competitive purchaser of products, decreasing marginal utility and decreasing marginal rate of substitution of a product for money to a purchaser (consumer) who is subject to diminishing marginal returns, equilibrium of a purchaser, demand for a product of a purchaser, and market demand for a product. Each of these principles of economics is a verbalization of an economic function (curve) or an inference drawn from an operation on a set of economic functions (curves). The law of constant marginal expenditure on a product is a verbalization of a marginal expenditure curve of a perfectly competitive purchaser—defined as a purchaser who can purchase all he wishes per unit of time at the prevailing market price ceteris paribus (see Chapter 1). The law of decreasing marginal utility of a product is a verbalization of a marginal utility curve of a consumer (see Chapter 2). The law of decreasing marginal rate of substitution of a product for money is a verbalization of a marginal rate of substitution of a product for money curve of a consumer (see Chapter 2). The principle of equilibrium of a purchaser is an inference drawn from an operation on the marginal expenditure and marginal rate of substitution of a product for money curves of a purchaser (see Chapter 3). The law of demand for a product of a purchaser is a verbalization of a demand curve of a purchaser (see Chapter 4). And the law of market demand for a product is a verbalization of a market demand curve (see Chapter 5).

SELECTED READINGS

Spencer, M. H. "Demand Analysis: Indifference Curves," *Basic Economics: A Book of Readings.* Edited by A. D. Gayers, C. L. Hariss, and M. H. Spencer. Englewood

Cliffs, N. J.: Prentice-Hall, Inc., 1951, pp. 91–104. Reprinted in Kamerschen, D. R. (editor). *Readings in Microeconomics*. Cleveland, Ohio: The World Publishing Company, 1967, pp. 59–72.

Levenson, A. M. and B. S. Solon. "Consumer Equilibrium," *Outline of Price Theory*. New York: Holt, Rinehart and Winston, Inc., 1964. Appendix 4A, pp. 74–75 and Appendix 5, p. 107. Reprinted in Kamerschen, *ibid.*, pp. 73–76.

Kuhlman, J. M. and R. G. Thompson. "Substitution and Values of Elasticities," *American Economic Review*, LVI:3 (June 1965), pp. 506–510. Reprinted in Kamerschen, *ibid.*, pp. 77–81.

Mishan, E. J. "Theories of Consumers' Behavior: A Cynical View," *Economica*. New Series; 28 (February 1961), pp. 1–11. Reprinted in Kamerschen, *ibid.*, pp. 82–94.

Leibenstein, H. "Bandwagon, Snob, and Veblen Effects in the Theory of Consumers' Demand," *The Quarterly Journal of Economics*, LXIV (May 1950), pp. 183–207. Reprinted in Kamerschen, *ibid.*, pp. 95–119.

Friedman, M. "The Marshallian Demand Curve," *Journal of Political Economy*, LVII (December 1949), pp. 463–495. Reprinted in Kamerschen, *ibid.*, pp. 120–168.

Bailey, M. J. "The Marshallian Demand Curve," *Journal of Political Economy*, LXII (June 1954), pp. 255–266. Reprinted in Kamerschen, *ibid.*, 169–179.

Strotz, R. H. "Cardinal Utility," *The American Economic Review*, XLII (May 1953), pp. 384–397. Reprinted in Kamerschen, *ibid.*, pp. 169–179.

Slutsky, E. E. "On the Theory of the Budget of the Consumer," *Giornale degli Economisti*, LI (1915), pp. 1–26. Reprinted in The American Economic Association. *Readings in Price Theory*. Edited by George J. Stigler and Kenneth E. Boulding. Homewood, Illinois: Richard D. Irwin, Inc., 1952, pp. 27–56.

Friedman, M. and L. J. Savage. "The Utility Analysis of Choices Involving Risk," *The Journal of Political Economy*, LVI (1948), pp. 279–304. Reprinted in The American Economic Association. *Readings in Price Theory*, *ibid.*, pp. 57–96.

Alchian, A. A. "The Meaning of Utility Measurement," *American Economic Review*, LXIII (March 1953), pp. 26–50.

Ellsberg, D. "Classic and Current Notions of 'Measurable Utility'," *Economic Journal*, LXIV (September 1954), pp. 528–556.

chapter 1

The Expenditure Function of a Perfectly Competitive Purchaser of Products

The method of scientific investigation is nothing but the expression of the necessary mode of working of the human mind ... at which all phenomena are reasoned about, rendered precise and exact.

(Thomas Henry Huxley, *The Scientific Mind*)

Expenditure is the money expended to purchase a quantity of products. "The expenditure function of a perfectly competitive purchaser of products" is the name of the relation between the expenditure of a purchaser who can purchase all he wishes at prevailing prices and the quantities purchased of products per unit of time. The general relation between a set of expenditure (E) numbers and two sets of quantity purchased (Q_1 and Q_2) numbers is denoted by $E = E_1(Q_1) + E_2(Q_2)$, which is read "E equals E_1 of Q_1 plus E_2 of Q_2." The symbols E_1 and E_2 denote the rules of transformation or mapping by which a number in each of the Q_1 and Q_2 sets of numbers is transformed or mapped into a number in the E set of numbers. According to the rule of transformation or mapping, each ordered pair of quantity purchased numbers is associated with one expenditure number. Thus this function is a set of ordered triples of numbers that satisfies the E_1 and E_2 rules of transformation or mapping that corresponding to each ordered pair of numbers from the Q_1 and Q_2 number sets is one number in the E set of numbers. The (linear) rule of transformation by which an ordered pair of quantity purchased numbers is transformed into an expenditure number is denoted by $E = P_{1_0}Q_1 + P_{2_0}Q_2$. In this equation, the prices of products one and two are denoted by P_1 and P_2. And the assumption that a purchaser can purchase all he wishes at prevailing prices is denoted by the zero subscript in P_{1_0} and P_{2_0}.

Total Expenditure Function

Total expenditure is the money expended to purchase a quantity of a product. The "total expenditure function" is the name of the relation between total

expenditure and quantity purchased of the product per unit of time. The general relation between a set of total expenditure (E_1, E_2, or to drop the subscript, E) numbers and a set of quantity purchased (Q) numbers is denoted by $E = E(Q)$, which is read "E equals E of Q" and is used in lieu of $E_1 = E_1(Q_1)$ or $E_2 = E_2(Q_2)$. The symbol E on the right side denotes the rule by which a number from the Q set of numbers is transformed or mapped into a number in the E set of numbers. According to the E rule of transformation or mapping each quantity purchased number is associated with one total expenditure number. Thus this function is a set of ordered pairs of quantity purchased and total expenditure numbers that satisfies the E rule of transformation or mapping that corresponding to each number in the Q set of numbers is one number in the E set of numbers.

The (linear) rule of transformation by which a quantity purchased number is transformed into a total expenditure number is denoted by $E = P_0 Q$. According to this rule, a total expenditure number is equal to the product of the price number and a quantity purchased number. Corresponding to each quantity purchased thus is a different total expenditure. Underlying this rule is the assumption that all things other than quantity purchased that determine total expenditure are being held constant—the so-called *ceteris paribus* ("other things being equal") assumption. These "other things" are called parameters of the function. The parameter of a total expenditure function of a perfectly competitive purchaser is the price of the product, as denoted by the zero subscript in P_0.

Selected numbers from the Q and E number sets are derived by assuming

TABLE 1.1: Hypothetical expenditure on a product of a perfectly competitive purchaser

$AE = E/Q = P_0$	Q	$E = P_0 Q$	$ME_d = \Delta E/\Delta Q$	$ME_c = dE/dQ$
$2	0	$0		$2
			$2	
2	1	2		2
			2	
2	2	4		2
			2	
2	3	6		2
			2	
2	4	8		2
			2	
2	5	10		2
			2	
2	6	12		2
			2	
2	7	14		2
			2	
2	8	16		2
			2	
2	9	18		2
			2	
2	10	20		2

that $P_0 = \$2$ (hence $E = 2Q$) and are presented in Table 1.1. The nonnegative set of quantity purchased numbers is plotted on the horizontal axis and the nonnegative set of total expenditure numbers is plotted on the vertical axis of Figure 1.1. In this figure, the nonnegative set of ordered pairs of quantity

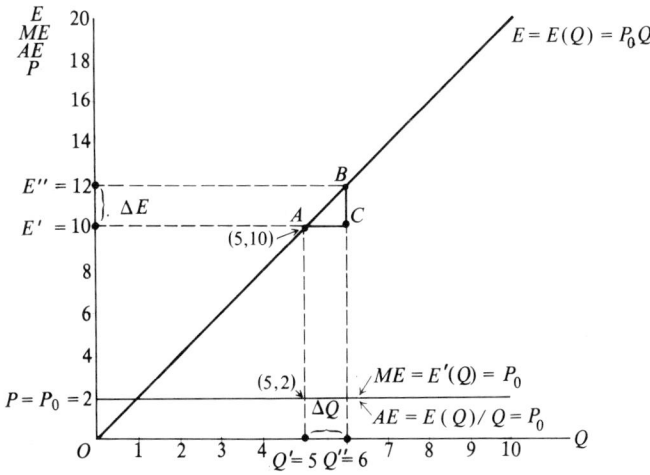

FIG. 1.1. Hypothetical expenditure curves of a product of a perfectly competitive purchaser

purchased and total expenditure numbers is depicted by the curve labeled $E = E(Q) = P_0 Q$, which is called the total expenditure curve. This curve depicts the E rule of mapping by which a quantity purchased number is mapped into a total expenditure number. A quantity purchased number is mapped into a total expenditure number by drawing a line from the point on the horizontal axis that denotes that quantity number (for example, 5) to the point on the total expenditure curve that denotes the ordered pair of quantity purchased and total expenditure numbers (5, 10) and then drawing a line to the point on the vertical axis that denotes the corresponding total expenditure number (10). Thus this curve shows the total expenditure corresponding to a quantity purchased and hence how total expenditure varies with quantity purchased per unit of time.

As seen in Figure 1.1, in the case of a perfectly competitive purchaser, the total expenditure curve is a ray, which is a linear curve that has a zero total expenditure intercept. The curve has a zero total expenditure intercept because total expenditure is zero when quantity purchased is zero: $E = P_0 \cdot 0 = 0$. It is linear because each successive unit is purchased at the same price of P_0 (= \$2); and hence each successive unit purchased adds the same amount, P_0, to total expenditure. The slope of $E = E(Q)$, therefore, remains constant as quantity purchased increases.

Marginal Expenditure Function

When quantity purchased varies by discrete amounts, the Q set of numbers contains integers but not fractions. Discrete marginal expenditure (ME_d) thus is the change in total expenditure (ΔE) associated with a change of one unit in quantity purchased of the product ($\Delta Q = 1$): $ME_d = \Delta E/\Delta Q$, where $\Delta Q = 1$. In this context, marginal expenditure is equal to the difference quotient ($\Delta E/\Delta Q$) of the straight line between two points which are one quantity unit apart on the total expenditure curve. In Figure 1.1, between points A and B on $E = E(Q)$,

$$ME_d = \lim_{\Delta Q \to 1} \frac{\Delta E}{\Delta Q} = \frac{E'' - E'}{Q'' - Q'} = \frac{CB}{AC} = \text{slope of line AB} = 2$$

Since a total expenditure curve of a perfectly competitive purchaser is linear, the difference quotient is the same for all changes in quantity purchased, and hence discrete marginal expenditure equals continuous marginal expenditure.[1]

The "marginal expenditure function" is the name of the relation between (continuous) marginal expenditure and quantity purchased of the product per unit of time. The general relation between a set of marginal expenditure (ME) numbers and a set of quantity purchased (Q) numbers is denoted by $ME = E'(Q)$, which is read "ME equals E prime of Q." The symbol E' denotes the rule of transformation or mapping by which a number in the Q set of numbers is transformed or mapped into a number in the ME set of numbers; the E' rule is derived from the E rule of $E = E(Q)$. According to the E' rule of transformation or mapping, each quantity purchased number is associated with one marginal expenditure number. Thus this function is a set of ordered pairs of quantity purchased and marginal expenditure numbers that satisfies the E' rule of transformation or mapping that corresponding to each number in the Q set of numbers is one number in the ME set of numbers.

Since $E = P_0 Q$, when quantity purchased increases from a given quantity (Q) to a larger quantity ($Q + \Delta Q$), the corresponding increase in total expenditure is denoted by

$$E + \Delta E = P_0(Q + \Delta Q)$$
$$= P_0 Q + P_0 \Delta Q$$

from which $E = P_0 Q$ may be subtracted to yield

$$\Delta E = P_0 \Delta Q$$

which is the change in total expenditure induced by the change in quantity purchased. By dividing both sides by ΔQ,

$$\frac{\Delta E}{\Delta Q} = P_0$$

which is the E' rule of transformation by which a quantity purchased number is transformed into a marginal expenditure ($\Delta E/\Delta Q$) number. According to this rule, a marginal expenditure number is equal to the price number (P_0) plus the product of zero and a quantity purchased number ($0 \cdot Q$). Corresponding to each quantity purchased thus is the same price—namely P_0. The parameters of a marginal expenditure function of a perfectly competitive purchaser are the parameters of the market demand and supply functions which determine P_0.

Selected numbers from the Q and ME number sets are derived by assuming that $P_0 = \$2$ (hence $\Delta E/\Delta Q = 2$) and are presented in Table 1.1. The nonnegative set of quantity purchased numbers is plotted on the horizontal axis and the nonnegative set of marginal expenditure numbers is plotted on the vertical axis of Figure 1.1. In this figure, the nonnegative set of ordered pairs of quantity purchased and marginal expenditure numbers is depicted by the curve labeled $ME = E'(Q) = P_0$, which is called the marginal expenditure curve. This curve depicts the E' rule of mapping by which a quantity purchased number is mapped into a marginal expenditure number. A quantity purchased number is mapped into a marginal expenditure number by drawing a line from the point on the horizontal axis that denotes that quantity number (for example, 5) to the point on the marginal expenditure curve that denotes the ordered pair of quantity purchased and marginal expenditure numbers (5, 2) and then drawing a line to the point on the vertical axis that denotes the corresponding marginal expenditure number (2). Thus this curve depicts the marginal expenditure corresponding to a quantity purchased and hence how marginal expenditure varies with quantity purchased per unit of time.

As seen in Figure 1.1, in the case of a perfectly competitive purchaser, the marginal expenditure curve is a line that is drawn parallel to the quantity axis to depict constant marginal expenditure. Each successive unit is purchased at the same price of P_0 ($= \$2$); and hence each successive unit purchased adds the same amount, P_0, to total expenditure. Marginal expenditure, therefore, remains constant as quantity purchased increases, as depicted by the parallel line.

Law of Constant Marginal Expenditure

According to the law of constant marginal expenditure on a product to a perfectly competitive purchaser, the expenditure associated with purchasing an additional unit of a product does not vary with quantity purchased per unit of time. Each additional unit purchased of a product per unit of time adds the same amount to total expenditure. Total expenditure on a product increases at a constant rate as quantity purchased of the product per unit of time increases. Marginal expenditure on a product is a constant function of quantity purchased of the product per unit of time.

As seen in Figure 1.1, according to the $ME = E'(Q) = P_0$ curve, marginal expenditure (ME) is a constant function of quantity purchased (Q) when total expenditure (E) increases at the constant rate P_0 as quantity increases. Thus the law of constant marginal expenditure is a verbalization of a marginal expenditure curve of a perfectly competitive purchaser. Since total expenditure increases at a constant rate, and since the phrase "increases at a constant rate" is another way of saying "constant marginal expenditure," a total expenditure curve of a perfectly competitive purchaser also depicts the law of constant marginal expenditure.

Average Expenditure Function

Average expenditure (AE) is the ratio of total expenditure (E) to quantity purchased of the product (Q): $AE = E/Q$. Average expenditure thus is equal to the difference quotient ($\Delta E/\Delta Q$) of the ray at a point on the total expenditure curve. In Figure 1.1, at point A on $E = E(Q)$,

$$AE = \frac{Q'A}{OQ'} = \text{slope of line OA} = 2$$

Since a total expenditure curve of a perfectly competitive purchaser is a ray, the difference quotient is the same at each point on the curve.

The "average expenditure function" is the name of the relation between average expenditure and quantity purchased of the product per unit of time. The general relation between a set of average expenditure (AE) numbers and a set of quantity purchased (Q) numbers is denoted by $AE = E(Q)/Q$, which is read "AE equals E of Q divided by Q." According to the rule of transformation or mapping, each quantity purchased number is associated with one average expenditure number. Thus this function is a set of ordered pairs of quantity purchased and average expenditure numbers that satisfies the rule of transformation or mapping that corresponding to each number in the Q set of numbers is one number in the AE set of numbers.

By dividing both sides of

$$E = P_0 Q$$

by Q,

$$\frac{E}{Q} = \frac{P_0 Q}{Q}$$

since $P_0 Q/Q = P_0$,

$$\frac{E}{Q} = P_0$$

THE EXPENDITURE FUNCTION OF A PURCHASER OF PRODUCTS

which is the rule of transformation by which a quantity purchased number is transformed into an average expenditure (E/Q) number. According to this rule, an average expenditure number is equal to the price number (P_0) plus the product of zero and a quantity purchased number ($0 \cdot Q$). Corresponding to each quantity purchased thus is the same price—namely P_0. The parameters of an average expenditure function of a perfectly competitive purchaser are the parameters of the market demand and supply functions which determine P_0.

Selected numbers from the Q and AE number sets are derived by assuming that $P_0 = \$2$ (hence $E/Q = 2$) and are presented in Table 1.1. The nonnegative set of quantity purchased numbers is plotted on the horizontal axis and the nonnegative set of average expenditure numbers is plotted on the vertical axis of Figure 1.1. In this figure, the nonnegative set of ordered pairs of quantity purchased and average expenditure numbers is depicted by the curve labeled $AE = E(Q)/Q = P_0$, which is called the average expenditure curve. This curve depicts the rule of mapping by which a quantity purchased number is mapped into an average expenditure number. A quantity purchased number is mapped into an average expenditure number by drawing a line from the point on the horizontal axis that denotes that quantity number (for example, 5) to the point on the average expenditure curve that denotes the ordered pair of quantity purchased and average expenditure numbers (5, 2) and then drawing a line to the point on the vertical axis that denotes the corresponding average expenditure number (2). Thus this curve shows the average expenditure corresponding to a quantity purchased and hence how average expenditure varies with quantity purchased per unit of time.

As seen in Figure 1.1, in the case of a perfectly competitive purchaser, the average expenditure curve is a line that is drawn parallel to the quantity axis to depict constant average expenditure. Each quantity is purchased at the same price of P_0 ($= \$2$); and hence each quantity purchased has the same average expenditure (P_0). Average expenditure, therefore, remains constant as quantity purchased increases, as depicted by the parallel line.

Supply Curve of a Product Facing a Purchaser

The supply curve of a product facing a purchaser depicts the price at which each quantity can be purchased. A perfectly competitive purchaser can purchase all he wishes per unit of time at the prevailing price ceteris paribus. Thus the supply curve of a product facing him is a line that is drawn parallel to the quantity axis to depict the given price. Moreover, at each quantity purchased, average expenditure equals marginal expenditure equals price: $AE = ME = P = P(Q)$. Consequently, the supply curve facing a perfectly competitive purchaser is his average expenditure curve, which is the same as his marginal expenditure curve. To conclude, average expenditure and marginal expenditure are equal and are constant functions of quantity purchased when the supply curve facing the purchaser is parallel to the quantity axis.

Iso-expenditure Function

Iso-expenditure is equal or constant expenditure. The "iso-expenditure function" is the name of the relation between quantities purchased of two products when expenditure is held constant. The general relation between the Q_2 set of quantity purchased numbers and the Q_1 set of quantity purchased numbers when expenditure is held constant is denoted by $Q_2 = E_0(Q_1)$, which is read "Q_2 equals E naught of Q_1." The symbol E_0 denotes the rule by which a number in the Q_1 set of numbers is transformed or mapped into a number in the Q_2 set of numbers when expenditure is held constant. According to the E_0 rule of transformation or mapping, each number in the Q_1 set is associated with one number in the Q_2 set when expenditure is held constant. Thus this function is a set of ordered pairs of quantities purchased of two products that satisfies the E_0 rule of transformation or mapping that corresponding to each number in the Q_1 set of numbers is one number in the Q_2 set of numbers and each pair of numbers is associated with the same expenditure.

By setting E equal to E_0 to denote constant expenditure, the two-product expenditure equation,

$$E = P_{1_0}Q_1 + P_{2_0}Q_2$$

becomes

$$E_0 = P_{1_0}Q_1 + P_{2_0}Q_2$$

from which E_0 and $P_{2_0}Q_2$ may be subtracted to yield

$$-P_{2_0}Q_2 = -E_0 + P_{1_0}Q_1$$

By multiplying both sides by -1 and dividing both sides by P_{2_0}

$$Q_2 = \frac{E_0}{P_{2_0}} - \frac{P_{1_0}}{P_{2_0}}Q_1$$

which is the E_0 rule of transformation by which a quantity purchased number in the Q_1 set is transformed into a quantity purchased number in the Q_2 set when expenditure is held constant. The parameters of an iso-expenditure function are the income of the purchaser (which determines his expenditure, E_0) and the prices of the products (P_{1_0} and P_{2_0}).

Selected numbers from the Q_1 and Q_2 number sets are derived by assuming that $E_0 = \$30$, $P_{1_0} = \$3$, and $P_{2_0} = \$2$ (hence $Q_2 = 15 - \frac{3}{2}Q_1$) and are presented in Table 1.2. The nonnegative Q_1 set of numbers is plotted on the

THE EXPENDITURE FUNCTION OF A PURCHASER OF PRODUCTS

TABLE 1.2: Hypothetical iso-expenditure on two products of a perfectly competitive purchaser

$E_0 = P_{1_0}Q_1 + P_{2_0}Q_2$ $30 = 3Q_1 + 2Q_2$	Q_1	$Q_2 = E_0/P_{2_0} - (P_{1_0}/P_{2_0})Q_1$ $Q_2 = 30/2 - 3/2Q_1$	$\Delta Q_2/\Delta Q_1$	dQ_2/dQ_1
$30	0	15.0		-1.5
			-1.5	
30	1	13.5		-1.5
			-1.5	
30	2	12.0		-1.5
			-1.5	
30	3	10.5		-1.5
			-1.5	
30	4	9.0		-1.5
			-1.5	
30	5	7.5		-1.5
			-1.5	
30	6	6.0		-1.5
			-1.5	
30	7	4.5		-1.5
			-1.5	
30	8	3.0		-1.5
			-1.5	
30	9	1.5		-1.5
			-1.5	
30	10	0.0		-1.5

horizontal axis and the nonnegative Q_2 set of numbers is plotted on the vertical axis of Figure 1.2. In this figure, the nonnegative set of ordered pairs of Q_1 and Q_2 numbers is depicted by the curve labeled $Q_2 = E_0(Q_1)$, which is called the iso-expenditure curve. This curve depicts the E_0 rule of mapping by which a quantity purchased in the Q_1 number set is mapped into a quantity

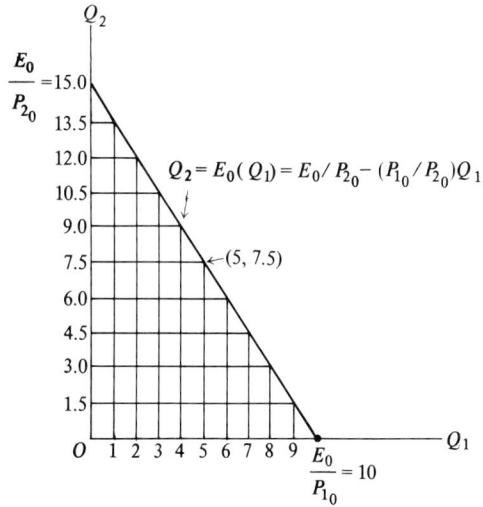

FIG. 1.2. Hypothetical iso-expenditure curve of a perfectly competitive purchaser

purchased in the Q_2 number set when expenditure is held constant. A Q_1 number is mapped into a Q_2 number by drawing a line from the point on the horizontal axis that denotes that Q_1 number (for example, 5) to the point on the iso-expenditure curve that denotes the ordered pair of Q_1 and Q_2 numbers (5, 7.5) and then drawing a line to the point on the vertical axis that denotes the corresponding Q_2 number (7.5). Thus this curve shows the Q_2 number corresponding to a Q_1 number and hence how Q_2 varies with Q_1 per unit of time, holding expenditure constant. In other words, an iso-expenditure curve depicts all combinations of quantities of two products that may be purchased by a purchaser with a given expenditure.

As seen in Figure 1.2, in the case of a perfectly competitive purchaser, the iso-expenditure curve is a negatively-sloped straight line.[2] It is negatively sloped because Q_1 and Q_2 are rivals for the dollars of a purchaser's expenditure (E_0); he may use his fixed number of dollars to increase Q_1 only by decreasing Q_2 (and vice versa). Thus, Q_2 is a decreasing function of Q_1: $\Delta Q_2/\Delta Q_1 < 0$. It is a straight line because its slope does not vary with Q_1 (or Q_2).

The slope of an iso-expenditure curve is denoted by dQ_2/dQ_1 and is equal to the negative of the ratio $ME_1/ME_2 (= P_1/P_2)$, where ME_1 is the marginal expenditure on product one and ME_2 is the marginal expenditure on product two: $dQ_2/dQ_1 = -ME_1/ME_2$.[3] By multiplying both sides by -1, $-dQ_2/dQ_1 = ME_1/ME_2$. The $-dQ_2/dQ_1$ notation and the ME_1/ME_2 notation denote numerical values and are verbalized in discrete terms as the amount of Q_2 that a purchaser has to give up ($-\Delta Q_2$) to purchase an additional unit of Q_1 (ΔQ_1) while holding expenditure constant.[4] If $ME_1 = P_{1_0} = \$3$ and $ME_2 = P_{2_0} = \$2$, the purchaser has to give up 1.5 units of Q_2 to purchase an additional unit of Q_1.

The slope of an iso-expenditure curve (dQ_2/dQ_1) is thus seen to change as more Q_1 and less Q_2 are purchased according to the change in ME_1 relative to the change in ME_2. In the case of a perfectly competitive purchaser, marginal expenditure is a constant function of quantity purchased, and is equal to price. Thus each successive unit increase in Q_1 increases expenditure by a constant amount equal to P_{1_0}, and each successive unit decrease in Q_2 decreases expenditure by a constant amount equal to P_{2_0}. Therefore, with each unit increase in Q_1 (ΔQ_1), the purchaser gives up a constant amount of Q_2 ($-\Delta Q_2$) to keep expenditure constant. Since the ratio $\Delta Q_2/\Delta Q_1$ remains constant as more Q_1 and less Q_2 are purchased, an iso-expenditure curve of a perfectly competitive purchaser is a straight line; that is, its slope does not vary with Q_1 (or Q_2).

An iso-expenditure curve is also called a budget-constraint curve, or curve of attainable combinations, since all combinations along and below it are attainable from a given budget or income. Thus an iso-expenditure curve may be drawn in Figure 1.2 for each level of income (= expenditure) of the purchaser. The higher the level of income, the larger the quantities of both products that may be purchased, and hence the farther away is the curve from the point of origin. Since two curves depict two different levels of income or expenditure, they cannot intersect. If the two curves did intersect, the same combination of quantities of the two products would be associated with two different levels of expenditure, which is inconsistent with the expenditure function $E = E_1(Q_1) + E_2(Q_2)$. According to this function, a combination of quantities of the two products is associated with only one level of expenditure.

SUMMARY

Dropping the zero subscript and thinking in terms of a perfectly competitive purchaser of *one* product, total expenditure on the product (E) is equal to price (P) times quantity purchased (Q): $E = PQ$. The curve expressing the relation between E and Q is called the total expenditure curve. The price of the product to the purchaser (P) is equal to average expenditure on the product (AE), since each is the ratio of total expenditure (E) to quantity purchased (Q): $AE = E/Q = P$. The curve expressing the relation between $AE (=P)$ and Q is called the average expenditure curve. Lastly, marginal expenditure on the product may be defined as the infinitesimally small change in E (dE) associated with an infinitesimally small change in Q (dQ), or as the addition to total expenditure (ΔE) of one additional unit of the product ($\Delta Q = 1$): $ME_c = dE/dQ$ and $ME_d = \Delta E/\Delta Q$, where $\Delta Q = 1$. The curve expressing the relation between dE/dQ and Q is called the marginal expenditure curve.

Average expenditure (= price) is the same as marginal expenditure in the case of perfect competition from the purchaser's side in the product market. In this case, the purchaser can purchase all he wishes per unit of time at the prevailing price ceteris paribus; hence each additional unit purchased per unit of time adds the same amount (= price) to total expenditure. Total expenditure (E), therefore, increases at the constant rate (P) as quantity purchased of the product (Q) increases per unit of time. Consequently, marginal expenditure on the product ($ME = P$) is a constant function of quantity purchased (Q) per unit of time. To generalize, according to the law of constant marginal expenditure on a product to a perfectly competitive purchaser, the expenditure associated with purchasing an additional unit of a product does not vary with quantity purchased per unit of time.

With price on the vertical axis, the supply curve of a product facing a perfectly competitive purchaser is a horizontal straight line that depicts the given price. This curve is his average (= marginal) expenditure curve. His total expenditure curve is derived from his average expenditure curve by multiplying each quantity purchased by price.

An iso-expenditure curve depicts all combinations of quantities of two products (Q_1 and Q_2) that may be purchased with a given expenditure (E), given the parameters P_1 and P_2. An iso-expenditure curve may be drawn for each level of E, given P_1 and P_2. The greater the value of E, the higher the curve lies in the OQ_1Q_2 plane. No two curves intersect, given P_1 and P_2. An iso-expenditure curve is a negatively-sloped straight line: its slope (dQ_2/dQ_1) is equal to $-P_1/P_2$, its Q_2 intercept is equal to E/P_2, and its Q_1 intercept is equal to E/P_1. The numerical value of the slope is denoted by $-dQ_2/dQ_1$ or ME_1/ME_2 $(= P_1/P_2)$ and is verbalized as the amount of Q_2 that a purchaser has to give up $(-\Delta Q_2)$ to purchase an additional unit of Q_1 (ΔQ_1) while keeping expenditure constant.

Questions

1. List the principles of the theory of demand for a product that are of primary importance. How do you account for the position of the law of constant marginal expenditure in this list? State in words this principle of economics.

2. Define total expenditure on a product. What is a total expenditure curve? Draw a total expenditure curve and describe its properties.

3. Define marginal expenditure on a product. What is a marginal expenditure curve? Draw a marginal expenditure curve and describe its properties. Relate the properties of the total and marginal expenditure curves.

4. Define average expenditure on a product. What is an average expenditure curve? Draw an average expenditure curve and describe its properties. Relate the properties of the total and average expenditure curves and the marginal and average expenditure curves.

5. What is the supply curve of a product facing a perfectly competitive purchaser? Relate this curve to the expenditure curves.

6. Define iso-expenditure. What is an iso-expenditure curve? Draw an iso-expenditure curve and describe its properties. Relate marginal expenditure and the slope of an iso-expenditure curve. Verbalize the numerical value of the slope of an iso-expenditure curve.

7. What would the total, marginal, average, and iso-expenditure curves of an imperfectly competitive purchaser look like? (Hint: see Chapter 8.)

NOTES

[1] When quantity purchased varies by continuous amounts, the Q set of numbers contains integers and fractions. Continuous marginal expenditure (ME_c) thus is the instantaneous rate of change of total expenditure as quantity purchased increases or decreases. With respect to $E = E(Q)$, the instantaneous rate of change is the infinitesimally small change in total expenditure (dE) associated with an infinitesimally small change in quantity purchased (dQ): $ME_c = dE/dQ$. In this context, marginal expenditure is the slope of the total expenditure curve. The slope of the total expenditure curve is equal to the difference quotient $(\Delta E/\Delta Q)$ of the tangent line at a point on the curve. In Figure 1.1, at point A on $E = E(Q)$,

$$ME_c = \frac{dE}{dQ} = \lim_{\Delta Q \to 0} \frac{\Delta E}{\Delta Q} = \frac{E'' - E'}{Q'' - Q'} = \frac{CB}{AC} = \text{slope of line AB} = 2$$

[2] With Q_2 on the vertical axis, the slope of an iso-expenditure curve of a perfectly competitive purchaser is equal to $-P_{1_0}/P_{2_0}$, its Q_2 intercept is E_0/P_{2_0}, and its Q_1 intercept is E_0/P_{1_0}:

$$E_0 = P_{1_0}Q_1 + P_{2_0}Q_2$$

$$Q_2 = \frac{E_0}{P_{2_0}} - \frac{P_{1_0}}{P_{2_0}}Q_1 \quad \text{and} \quad Q_1 = \frac{E_0}{P_{1_0}} - \frac{P_{2_0}}{P_{1_0}}Q_2$$

$$\frac{dQ_2}{dQ_1} = -\frac{P_{1_0}}{P_{2_0}} \quad \text{and} \quad \frac{dQ_1}{dQ_2} = -\frac{P_{2_0}}{P_{1_0}}$$

$$Q_2 = \frac{E_0}{P_{2_0}} \text{ when } Q_1 = 0 \quad \text{and} \quad Q_1 = \frac{E_0}{P_{1_0}} \text{ when } Q_2 = 0$$

[3] With respect to $E = E_1(Q_1) + E_2(Q_2)$, when Q_1 and Q_2 vary by discrete amounts, the increase in E because an additional unit of Q_1 is purchased is the unit gained of Q_1 times the marginal expenditure on that unit:

$$\Delta E_1 = \Delta Q_1 \frac{\Delta E_1}{\Delta Q_1}$$

The decrease in E because less Q_2 is purchased is the quantity given up of Q_2 times the marginal expenditure on that quantity:

$$\Delta E_2 = \Delta Q_2 \frac{\Delta E_2}{\Delta Q_2}$$

The total change in E is ΔE, and

$$\Delta E = \frac{\Delta E_1}{\Delta Q_1} \Delta Q_1 + \frac{\Delta E_2}{\Delta Q_2} \Delta Q_2$$

Since the total change in E is zero because E is a constant amount E_0, the decrease in E because less Q_2 is purchased must be offset exactly by the increase in E because more Q_1 is purchased. Therefore,

$$\Delta E = \frac{\Delta E_1}{\Delta Q_1} \Delta Q_1 + \frac{\Delta E_2}{\Delta Q_2} \Delta Q_2 = 0$$

$$\frac{\Delta E_2}{\Delta Q_2} \Delta Q_2 = -\frac{\Delta E_1}{\Delta Q_1} \Delta Q_1$$

$$\frac{\Delta Q_2}{\Delta Q_1} = -\frac{\Delta E_1/\Delta Q_1}{\Delta E_2/\Delta Q_2} = -\frac{ME_1}{ME_2}$$

When Q_1 and Q_2 vary by continuous amounts, the instantaneous rate of change of E with respect to Q_1 is the infinitesimally small change in E associated with an infinitesimally small change in Q_1: $ME_1 = \partial E/\partial Q_1$. The total infinitesimally small change in Q_1 is dQ_1. Thus, in terms of infinitesimally small changes, the change in E associated with a total change in Q_1 is

$$\frac{\partial E}{\partial Q_1} dQ_1$$

Similarly, the instantaneous rate of change of E with respect to Q_2 is the infinitesimally small change in E associated with an infinitesimally small change in Q_2: $ME_2 = \partial E/\partial Q_2$. The total infinitesimally small change in Q_2 is dQ_2. In terms of infinitesimally small changes, the change in E associated with a total change in Q_2 is

$$\frac{\partial E}{\partial Q_2} dQ_2$$

Therefore, in terms of infinitesimally small changes, the total change in E is dE, and

$$dE = \frac{\partial E}{\partial Q_1} dQ_1 + \frac{\partial E}{\partial Q_2} dQ_2$$

Since the total change in E along an iso-expenditure curve is zero,

$$dE = \frac{\partial E}{\partial Q_1} dQ_1 + \frac{\partial E}{\partial Q_2} dQ_2 = 0$$

$$\frac{\partial E}{\partial Q_2} dQ_2 = -\frac{\partial E}{\partial Q_1} dQ_1$$

$$\frac{dQ_2}{dQ_1} = -\frac{\partial E/\partial Q_1}{\partial E/\partial Q_2} = -\frac{ME_1}{ME_2}$$

[4] With respect to dQ_2/dQ_1, when Q_1 increases and Q_2 decreases, dQ_2 is a set of negative numbers and dQ_1 is a set of positive numbers. Thus dQ_2/dQ_1 is a set of negative numbers. Since the numerical (absolute) value of a negative number is that number multiplied by -1, and since $dQ_2/dQ_1 = -ME_1/ME_2$, $-dQ_2/dQ_1$ and $-(-ME_1/ME_2)$ or ME_1/ME_2 denote the numerical value of dQ_2/dQ_1. And $-dQ_2/dQ_1$ (or ME_1/ME_2) is a set of positive numbers.

chapter 2

Utility Function

Utility may be said to be the satisfaction associated with consuming a quantity of products. The "utility function" is the name of the relation between the utility of a consumer and the quantities consumed of products per unit of time. The general relation between a set of utility (U) numbers and two sets of quantity consumed (Q_1 and Q_2) numbers is denoted by $U = u(Q_1, Q_2)$, which is read "U equals u of Q_1 and Q_2." The symbol u denotes the rule of transformation or mapping by which a number in each of the Q_1 and Q_2 sets of numbers is transformed or mapped into a number in the U set of numbers. According to the u rule of transformation or mapping, each ordered pair of quantity consumed numbers is associated with one utility number.[1] Thus this function is a set of ordered triples of numbers that satisfies the u rule of transformation or mapping that corresponding to each ordered pair of numbers from the Q_1 and Q_2 number sets is one number in the U set of numbers.

Total Utility Function

Total utility may be said to be the satisfaction associated with consuming a quantity of a product. The "total utility function" is the name of the relation between total utility and quantity consumed of the product per unit of time. The general relation between a set of total utility (U) numbers and a set of quantity consumed (Q_1, Q_2, or to drop the subscript, Q) numbers is denoted by $U = U(Q)$, which is read "U equals U of Q" and is used in lieu of $U = U_1(Q_1)$ or $U = U_2(Q_2)$. The symbol U on the right side denotes the rule by which a number from the Q set of numbers is transformed or mapped into a number in the U set of numbers. According to the U rule of transformation or mapping each quantity consumed number is associated with one total utility number. Thus this function is a set of ordered pairs of quantity consumed and total utility numbers that satisfies the U rule of

28 PRINCIPLES OF THE THEORY OF DEMAND FOR A PRODUCT

transformation or mapping that corresponding to each number in the Q set of numbers is one number in the U set of numbers. The parameters of this function are the quantities of the products related in consumption to the given product and the consumer's taste for products.

Selected numbers from hypothetical Q and U number sets are presented in Table 2.1. The nonnegative set of quantity consumed numbers is plotted

TABLE 2.1: Hypothetical utility of a product

Q	U	$MU_d = \Delta U/\Delta Q$	$MU_c = dU/dQ$
0	0		20
		19	
1	19		18
		17	
2	36		16
		15	
3	51		14
		13	
4	64		12
		11	
5	75		10
		9	
6	84		8
		7	
7	91		6
		5	
8	96		4
		3	
9	99		2
		1	
10	100		0

on the horizontal axis and the nonnegative set of total utility (index) numbers is plotted on the vertical axis of Figure 2.1a. In this figure, the nonnegative set of ordered pairs of quantity consumed and total utility numbers is depicted by the curve labeled $U = U(Q)$, which is called the total utility curve. This curve depicts the U rule of mapping by which a quantity consumed number is mapped into a total utility number. A quantity consumed number is mapped into a total utility number by drawing a line from the point on the horizontal axis that denotes that quantity number (for example, 5) to the point on the total utility curve that denotes the ordered pair of quantity consumed and total utility numbers (5, 75) and then drawing a line to the point on the vertical axis that denotes the corresponding total utility number (75). Thus this curve shows the total utility corresponding to a quantity consumed and hence how total utility varies with quantity consumed per unit of time.

With reference to Figure 2.1a, let the product under consideration be coffee and let the total utility of coffee be expressed via a set of index numbers. If a consumer decides to stop drinking coffee, he may still have an amount

FIG. 2.1a. Hypothetical total utility curve of a product

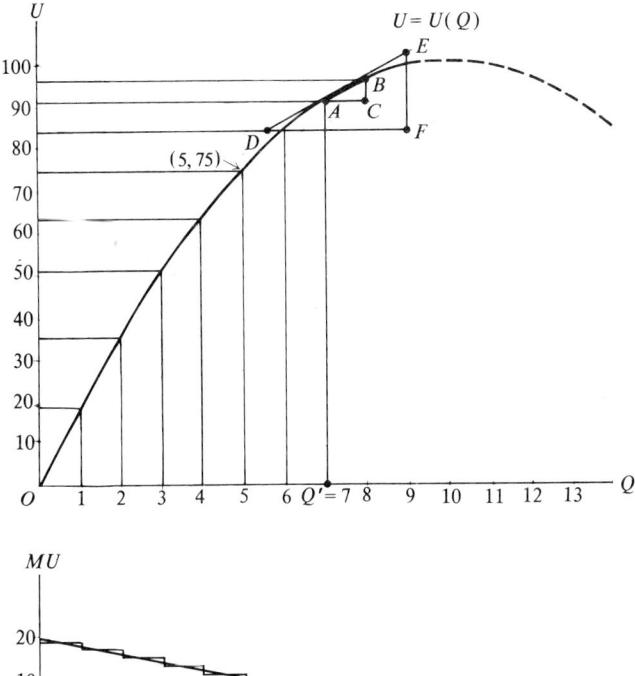

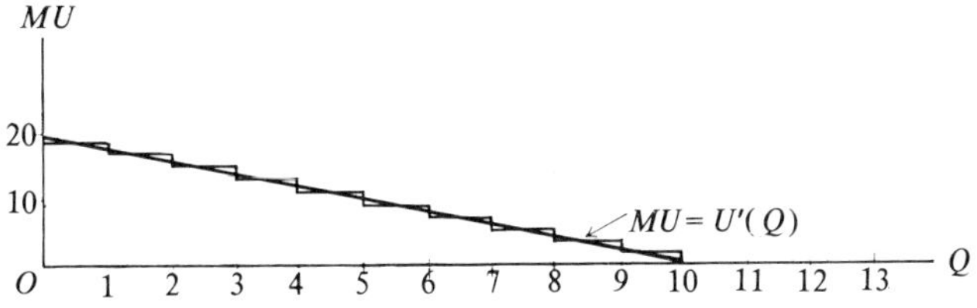

FIG. 2.1b. Hypothetical marginal utility curve of a product

of utility derived from other products he is still consuming. Thus his total utility curve of coffee may intersect the total utility axis at some hypothetical positive value. This value would denote his utility from other products when he is no longer drinking coffee. For present purposes, however, let the total utility intercept of coffee be zero, as seen in Figure 2.1a.

Assume that a consumer drinks 1, 2, 3, ..., n cups of coffee per day. Each cup is denoted on the horizontal axis of Figure 2.1a by vertical lines which are an equal distance apart. The total utility associated with the first cup is denoted by a horizontal line that intersects the vertical axis at an arbitrary distance above the total utility intercept. The second cup may add more or less than the first cup, or each may add the same amount, to his total utility. For purposes of analysis, assume that the second cup adds less than the first cup to his total utility. A horizontal line intersects the vertical axis at a distance above the first such line to denote the smaller contribution of the second cup. The numerical value of this distance need not be known, for by assumption it is less than the distance denoting the utility associated with the first cup. The total utility associated with each quantity of coffee is plotted on the diagram as points in the OQU plane. These points are connected by a curve which is extended to the total utility intercept. The segment of the curve depicting the contribution to total utility of the second cup slants downward to the right more than the segment depicting the contribution of the first cup. Thus, in this context, the total utility curve is concave downward; that is, it is concave from below a tangent line. Its slope becomes smaller as quantity consumed of the product increases. Total utility is increasing at a decreasing rate as quantity consumed of the product increases.

After a certain number of units of a product have been consumed per unit of time, an additional unit may add nothing to total utility. At this point on the total utility curve, its slope is zero; total utility is at its maximum value. Thereafter, total utility may decrease if additional units of the product are consumed. Thus, eventually an inverse relation may exist between total utility and quantity consumed of a product. Eventually, total utility may reach zero and then become negative as additional units are consumed per unit of time.

Marginal Utility Function

When quantity consumed varies by discrete amounts, the Q set of numbers contains integers but not fractions. Discrete marginal utility (MU_d) thus is the change in total utility (ΔU) associated with a change of one unit in quantity consumed of the product ($\Delta Q = 1$): $MU_d = \Delta U/\Delta Q$, where $\Delta Q = 1$. In this context, marginal utility is equal to the difference quotient ($\Delta U/\Delta Q$) of the straight line between two points one quantity unit apart on the total utility curve. In Figure 2.1a, between points A and B on $U = U(Q)$,

$$MU_d = \lim_{\Delta Q \to 1} \frac{\Delta U}{\Delta Q} = \frac{CB}{AC} = \text{slope of line AB} = 5$$

Since this total utility curve is non-linear, the difference quotient is not the same for all changes in quantity consumed, and hence discrete marginal utility is not the same as continuous marginal utility.[2]

The "marginal utility function" is the name of the relation between (continuous) marginal utility and quantity consumed of the product per unit of time. The general relation between a set of marginal utility (MU) numbers and a set of quantity consumed (Q) numbers is denoted by $MU = U'(Q)$, which is read "MU equals U prime of Q." The symbol U' denotes the rule of transformation or mapping by which a number in the Q set of numbers is transformed or mapped into a number in the MU set of numbers; the U' rule is derived from the U rule of $U = U(Q)$. According to the U' rule of transformation or mapping, each quantity consumed number is associated with one marginal utility number. Thus this function is a set of ordered pairs of quantity consumed and marginal utility numbers that satisfies the U' rule of transformation or mapping that corresponding to each number in the Q set of numbers is one number in the MU set of numbers. The parameters of a marginal utility curve are the parameters of the corresponding total utility curve that determine the slope of the total curve.

Selected numbers from hypothetical Q and MU number sets are presented in Table 2.1. The nonnegative set of quantity consumed numbers is plotted on the horizontal axis and the nonnegative set of marginal utility numbers is plotted on the vertical axis of Figure 2.1b. In this figure, the nonnegative set of ordered pairs of quantity consumed and marginal utility numbers is depicted by the curve labeled $MU = U'(Q)$, which is called the marginal utility curve. This curve depicts the U' rule of mapping by which a quantity consumed number is mapped into a marginal utility number. A quantity consumed number is mapped into a marginal utility number by drawing a line from the point on the horizontal axis that denotes that quantity number (for example, 5) to the point on the marginal utility curve that denotes the ordered pair of quantity consumed and marginal utility numbers (5, 10) and then drawing a line to the point on the vertical axis that denotes the corresponding marginal utility number (10). Thus this curve depicts the marginal utility corresponding to a quantity consumed and hence how marginal utility varies with quantity consumed per unit of time.

As seen in Figure 2.1b, in the case of a consumer who is subject to diminishing marginal returns, the marginal utility curve is drawn as a negatively-sloped curve to depict decreasing marginal utility. Each successive unit consumed adds a smaller amount to total utility. Marginal utility, therefore, decreases as quantity consumed increases, as depicted by the negatively-sloped curve.

Law of Decreasing Marginal Utility

According to the law of decreasing marginal utility of a product to a consumer who is subject to diminishing marginal returns, the utility associated with consuming an additional unit of a product varies inversely with quantity consumed per unit of time. Each additional unit consumed of a product per unit of time adds a smaller amount to total utility. Total utility of a product increases at a decreasing rate as quantity consumed of the product per unit of time increases. Marginal utility of a product is a decreasing function of quantity consumed of the product per unit of time.

As seen in Figure 2.1b, according to the $MU = U'(Q)$ curve, marginal utility (MU) is a decreasing function of quantity consumed (Q) when total utility (U) increases at a decreasing rate (dU/dQ) as quantity increases. Thus the law of decreasing marginal utility is a verbalization of a marginal utility curve of a consumer who is subject to diminishing marginal returns. Since total utility increases at a decreasing rate, and since the phrase "increases at a decreasing rate" is another way of saying "decreasing marginal utility," a total utility curve of a consumer who is subject to diminishing marginal returns also depicts the law of decreasing marginal utility.

Iso-utility Function

Iso-utility is equal or constant utility. The "iso-utility function" is the name of the relation between quantities consumed of two products when utility is held constant. The general relation between the Q_2 set of quantity consumed numbers and the Q_1 set of quantity consumed numbers when utility is held constant is denoted by $Q_2 = U_0(Q_1)$, which is read "Q_2 equals U naught of Q_1." The symbol U_0 denotes the rule by which a number in the Q_1 set of numbers is transformed or mapped into a number in the Q_2 set of numbers when utility is held constant. According to the U_0 rule of transformation or mapping each number in the Q_1 set is associated with one number in the Q_2 set when utility is held constant. Thus this function is a set of ordered pairs of quantities consumed of two products that satisfies the U_0 rule of transformation or mapping that corresponding to each number in the Q_1 set of numbers is one number in the Q_2 set of numbers and each pair of numbers is associated with the same utility. The parameters of this function are the quantities of the products related in consumption to the two given products and the consumer's taste for products.

The nonnegative Q_1 set of numbers is plotted on the horizontal axis and the nonnegative Q_2 set of numbers is plotted on the vertical axis of Figure 2.2a. In this figure, the nonnegative set of ordered pairs of Q_1 and Q_2 numbers is depicted by the curve labeled $Q_2 = U_0(Q_1)$, which is called the iso-utility curve. This curve depicts the U_0 rule of mapping by which a quantity consumed in the Q_1 number set is mapped into a quantity consumed in the Q_2 number set when utility is held constant. Thus this curve shows the Q_2 number corresponding to a Q_1 number and hence how Q_2 varies with Q_1 per unit of time, holding utility constant. In other words, an iso-utility curve depicts all combinations of quantities consumed of two products that yield the same level of utility to a consumer.

As seen in Figure 2.2a, in the case of a consumer who is subject to diminishing marginal returns, an iso-utility curve *in general* is a negatively-sloped curve that is concave from above a tangent line (that is, convex to the origin). It is negatively sloped because in general Q_1 and Q_2 are rivals in providing a given level of utility (U_0); a consumer may maintain a given level of utility by consuming more of Q_1 and less of Q_2 (and vice versa). Thus Q_2 is a decreasing function of Q_1: $\Delta Q_2/\Delta Q_1 < 0$. It is concave from above a tangent line because in general the numerical value of its slope varies inversely with Q_1.

The slope of an iso-utility curve is denoted by dQ_2/dQ_1 and is equal to the

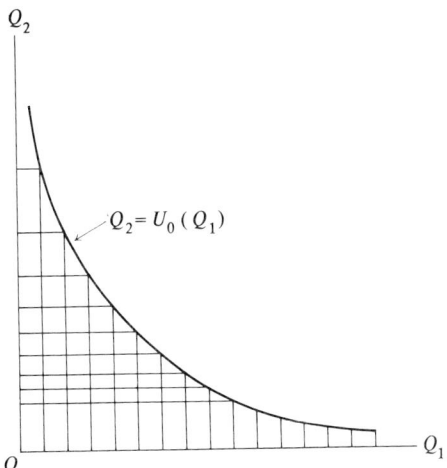

FIG. 2.2a. Hypothetical iso-utility curve of two products not related in consumption

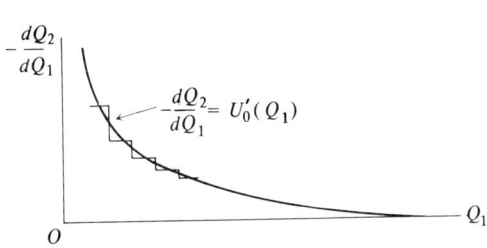

FIG. 2.2b. Marginal rate of substitution curve of two products not related in consumption. (The $-dQ_2/dQ_1$ scale is one half the Q_2 scale)

negative of the ratio MU_1/MU_2, where MU_1 is the marginal utility of product one and MU_2 is the marginal utility of product two: $dQ_2/dQ_1 = -MU_1/MU_2$.[3] By multiplying both sides by -1, $-dQ_2/dQ_1 = MU_1/MU_2$. The $-dQ_2/dQ_1$ notation and the MU_1/MU_2 notation denote numerical values and are called the marginal rate of substitution of Q_1 for Q_2, which is verbalized in discrete terms as the amount of Q_2 that a consumer is willing to give up ($-\Delta Q_2$) to consume an additional unit of Q_1 (ΔQ_1) while keeping utility constant.[4] If $MU_1 = 2$ and $MU_2 = 1$, the consumer is willing to give up 2 units of Q_2 to consume an additional unit of Q_1.

The slope of an iso-utility curve (dQ_2/dQ_1) is thus seen to change as more Q_1 and less Q_2 are consumed according to the change in MU_1 relative to the change in MU_2. In the case of a consumer who is subject to diminishing marginal returns, marginal utility is a decreasing function of quantity consumed of the product. Thus each successive unit increase in Q_1 increases utility by a decreasing amount; and each successive unit decrease in Q_2 decreases utility by an increasing amount. Therefore, with each unit increase in Q_1 (ΔQ_1), the consumer gives up a decreasing amount of Q_2 ($-\Delta Q_2$) to keep utility constant. Since the ratio $\Delta Q_2/\Delta Q_1$ decreases numerically as more Q_1 and less Q_2 are consumed, an iso-utility curve of a consumer who is subject to diminishing marginal returns is concave from above a tangent line—that is, it is convex to the origin.[5] In other words, as shown in Figure 2.2b, the marginal rate of substitution of Q_1 for Q_2 varies inversely with Q_1.

An iso-utility curve may be drawn in Figure 2.2a for each level of utility of the consumer. The larger the quantities consumed of both products, the higher the level of utility and hence the farther away is the curve from the point of origin. Since two curves depict two different levels of utility, they cannot intersect. If two curves did intersect, the same combination of quantities of the two products would be associated with two different levels of utility, which is inconsistent with the utility function $U = u(Q_1, Q_2)$. According to this function, a combination of quantities of the two products is associated with only one level of utility.

Substitutes and Complements in Consumption and the Iso-utility Curve

Two products are not related in consumption when the marginal utility of one product is a constant function of the quantity consumed of the other product—when $\Delta MU_1/\Delta Q_2 = 0$ and $\Delta MU_2/\Delta Q_1 = 0$. In this context, the numerical value of the slope of an iso-utility curve ($-dQ_2/dQ_1 = MU_1/MU_2$) varies inversely with Q_1 only because of the law of decreasing marginal utility of a product. Two products are related in consumption when the marginal utility of one product is an increasing or decreasing function of the quantity consumed of the other product—when $\Delta MU_1/\Delta Q_2 \gtreqless 0$ and $\Delta MU_2/\Delta Q_1 \gtreqless 0$. In this context $-dQ_2/dQ_1$ may or may not vary with Q_1.

Substitutes in Consumption

Two products are substitutes in consumption when the marginal utility of one product is a decreasing function of the quantity consumed of the other product—when $\Delta MU_1/\Delta Q_2 < 0$ and $\Delta MU_2/\Delta Q_1 < 0$. Thus, assuming decreasing marginal utility of a product, each successive unit increase in Q_1 decreases MU_1 (which tends to decrease MU_1/MU_2) and decreases MU_2 (which tends to increase MU_1/MU_2). Similarly, each successive unit decrease in Q_2 increases MU_2 (which tends to decrease MU_1/MU_2) and increases MU_1 (which tends to increase MU_1/MU_2). If Q_1 and Q_2 are imperfect substitutes in consumption, the tendency for MU_1/MU_2 to decrease because of decreasing marginal utility of a product more than offsets the tendency for MU_1/MU_2 to increase because of the substitute relationship between them; hence $-dQ_2/dQ_1$ decreases as more Q_1 and less Q_2 are consumed. In other words, as seen in Figure 2.3a, the iso-utility curve of two imperfect substitutes in consumption is concave from above a tangent line; and, as

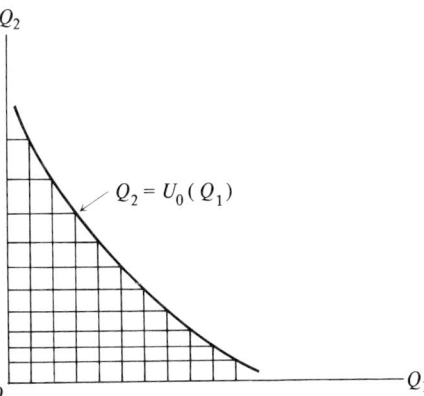

FIG. 2.3a. Hypothetical iso-utility curve of two imperfect substitutes in consumption

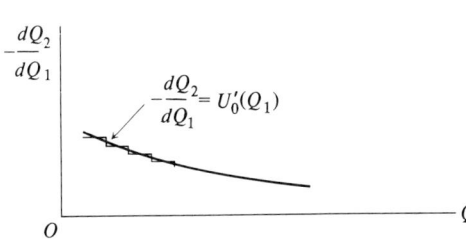

FIG. 2.3b. Marginal rate of substitution curve of two imperfect substitutes in consumption. (The $-dQ_2/dQ_1$ scale is one half the Q_2 scale)

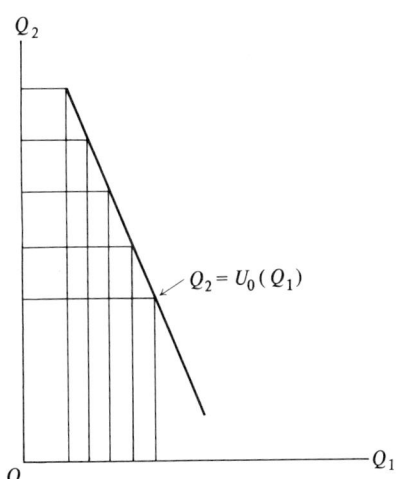

FIG. 2.4a. Hypothetical iso-utility curve of two perfect substitutes in consumption

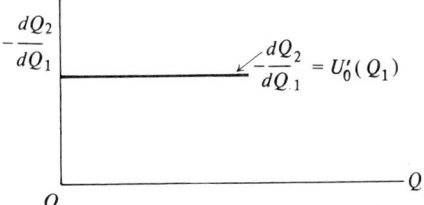

Fig. 2.4b. Marginal rate of substitution curve of two perfect substitutes in consumption. (The $-dQ_2/dQ_1$ scale is one half the Q_2 scale)

seen in Figure 2.3b, the marginal rate of substitution of Q_1 for Q_2 varies inversely with Q_1.

But if Q_1 and Q_2 are perfect substitutes in consumption, the tendency for MU_1/MU_2 to decrease because of decreasing marginal utility of a product is offset exactly by the tendency for MU_1/MU_2 to increase because of the substitute relationship between them; hence $-dQ_2/dQ_1$ remains constant as more Q_1 and less Q_2 are consumed. In other words, as seen in Figure 2.4a, the iso-utility curve of two perfect substitutes in consumption is a negatively-sloped straight line; and, as seen in Figure 2.4b, the marginal rate of substitution of Q_1 for Q_2 does not vary with Q_1.

Complements in Consumption

Two products are complements in consumption when the marginal utility of one product is an increasing function of the quantity consumed of the other product—when $\Delta MU_1/\Delta Q_2 > 0$ and $\Delta MU_2/\Delta Q_1 > 0$. Thus, assuming decreasing marginal utility of a product, each successive unit increase in Q_1 decreases MU_1 and increases MU_2, thereby tending to decrease MU_1/MU_2; and each successive unit decrease in Q_2 increases MU_2 and decreases MU_1, thereby tending to decrease MU_1/MU_2. Conversely, each successive unit

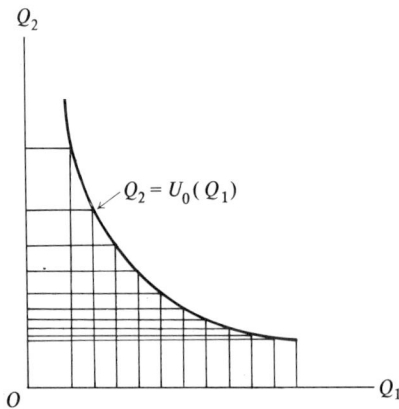

FIG. 2.5a. Hypothetical iso-utility curve of two imperfect complements in consumption

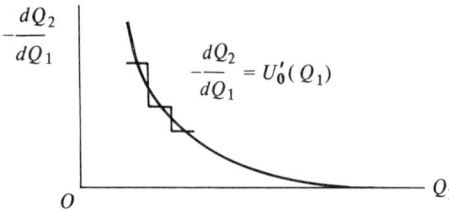

FIG. 2.5b. Marginal rate of substitution curve of two imperfect complements in consumption. (The $-dQ_2/dQ_1$ scale is one half the Q_2 scale)

increase in Q_2 decreases MU_2 and increases MU_1, thereby tending to increase MU_1/MU_2; and each successive unit decrease in Q_1 increases MU_1 and decreases MU_2, thereby tending to increase MU_1/MU_2. Therefore, as seen in Figure 2.5a, the iso-utility curve of two imperfect complements in consumption is concave from above a tangent line; and, as seen in Figure 2.5b, the marginal rate of substitution of Q_1 for Q_2 varies inversely with Q_1 and directly with Q_2.

But if Q_1 and Q_2 are perfect complements in consumption, MU_1/MU_2 is zero as Q_1 increases and is approaching infinity as Q_2 increases. Thus, as Q_1 increases, the iso-utility curve is a horizontal straight line (see the horizontal portion of the curve in Figure 2.6); and, as Q_2 increases, the iso-utility

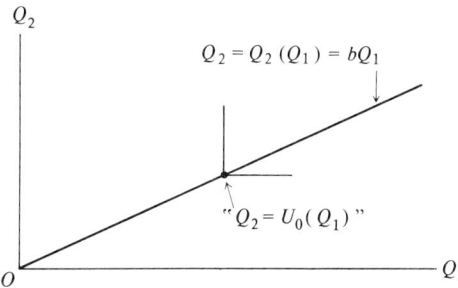

FIG. 2.6. Hypothetical iso-utility curve of two perfect complements in consumption

curve is a vertical straight line (see the vertical portion of the curve in Figure 2.6). In short, Q_1 and Q_2 are purchased in fixed proportion; and therefore the iso-utility "curve" is a point in the OQ_1Q_2 plane representing the constant ratio of Q_2 to Q_1. A set of constant Q_2/Q_1 ratios is represented by a ray, as in Figure 2.6.

Marginal Rate of Substitution Function of a Product for Money

Let Q denote the quantity consumed of a product; let MU denote the marginal utility of the product, $\Delta U/\Delta Q$; let M denote money; and let λ (lambda) denote the marginal utility of money, $\Delta U/\Delta M$. Then, if $MU = 2$ and $\lambda = 1$, the consumer is willing to give up 2 units of money ($-\Delta M = 2$) to consume an additional unit of the product ($\Delta Q = 1$)—that is,

$$-\frac{\Delta M}{\Delta Q} = \frac{MU}{\lambda} = \frac{\Delta U/\Delta Q}{\Delta U/\Delta M} = \frac{\Delta U}{\Delta Q} \cdot \frac{\Delta M}{\Delta U}$$

The $-\Delta M/\Delta Q$ and MU/λ notation connote the numerical value of the slope ($-dM/dQ$) of iso-utility curves relating M to Q and are called the marginal rate of substitution of a product for money. In discrete terms, the marginal rate of substitution of a product for money is verbalized as the amount of money a consumer is willing to give up ($-\Delta M$) to consume an additional unit of the product ($\Delta Q = 1$). According to the law of decreasing marginal rate of substitution of a product for money, MU/λ varies inversely with quantity consumed of the product (Q) per unit of time. Thus $MU/\lambda = \lambda(Q)$, where $\Delta(MU\lambda)/\Delta Q < 0$. MU/λ decreases along an iso-utility curve as Q increases (thereby decreasing MU) and M decreases (thereby increasing λ).

SUMMARY

A total utility curve shows how total utility (U) varies with quantity consumed of the product (Q) per unit of time. A marginal utility curve shows how the slope of the total utility curve (dU/dQ) varies with quantity consumed of the product (Q) per unit of time. In the case of a consumer who is subject to diminishing marginal returns, each additional unit consumed of a product per unit of time adds a smaller amount to total utility. Total utility (U), therefore, increases at a decreasing rate (dU/dQ) as quantity consumed (Q) increases. Consequently, marginal utility ($MU = dU/dQ$) is a decreasing function of quantity consumed (Q) per unit of time. To generalize, according to the law of decreasing marginal utility of a product to a consumer who is subject to diminishing marginal returns, the utility associated with consuming an additional unit of a product varies inversely with quantity consumed per unit of time.

An iso-utility curve depicts all combinations of quantities of two products (Q_1 and Q_2) that yield the same level of utility (U). An iso-utility curve may be drawn for each level of utility. The greater the value of U, the higher the curve lies in the OQ_1Q_2 plane. No two curves intersect. In general, an iso-utility curve is a negatively-sloped curve that is concave from above a tangent line. The numerical value of the slope is denoted by $-dQ_2/dQ_1$ or MU_1/MU_2 and is called the marginal rate of substitution of Q_1 for Q_2, which is verbalized in discrete terms as the amount of Q_2 that a consumer is willing to give up ($-\Delta Q_2$) to consume an additional unit of Q_1 (ΔQ_1) while keeping utility constant.

When Q_1 and Q_2 are not related in consumption, the marginal utility of one product is a constant function of the quantity consumed of the other product, and the value of $-dQ_2/dQ_1$ varies inversely with Q_1 because of decreasing marginal utility of a product. When Q_1 and Q_2 are imperfect substitutes in consumption, the marginal utility of one product is a decreasing function of the quantity consumed of the other product; and as Q_1 increases, the tendency for $-dQ_2/dQ_1$ to decrease because of decreasing marginal utility of a product more than offsets the tendency for $-dQ_2/dQ_1$ to increase because of the substitute relationship between them. When Q_1 and Q_2 are imperfect complements in consumption, the marginal utility of one product is an increasing function of the quantity consumed of the other product; and as Q_1 increases, the tendency for $-dQ_2/dQ_1$ to decrease because of decreasing marginal utility of a product is reinforced by the tendency for $-dQ_2/dQ_1$ to decrease because of the complementary relationship between them. Thus the greater the degree of complementarity, the greater the degree of concavity of the iso-utility curve. Conversely, the greater the degree of substitutability, the less the degree of concavity of the iso-utility curve. The iso-utility curve is a negatively-sloped straight line in the case of two perfect substitutes. But the iso-utility "curve" is a point in the OQ_1Q_2 plane in the case of two perfect complements in consumption, and dQ_2/dQ_1 cannot be calculated.

The marginal rate of substitution of a product for money $(-dM/dQ)$ is the amount of money a consumer is willing to give up to consume an additional unit of the product. According to the law of decreasing marginal rate of substitution of a product for money, $-dM/dQ \, (= MU/\lambda)$ varies inversely with Q as depicted by $-dM/dQ = \lambda(Q)$.

Questions

1. List the principles of the theory of demand for a product that are of primary importance. How do you account for the position of the law of decreasing marginal utility in this list? State in words this principle of economics.

2. Define total utility of a product. What is a total utility curve? Draw a total utility curve and describe its properties.

3. Define marginal utility of a product. What is a marginal utility curve? Draw a marginal utility curve and describe its properties. Relate the properties of the total and marginal utility curves.

4. Define iso-utility. What is an iso-utility curve? Draw an iso-utility curve and describe its properties. Relate marginal utility and the slope of an iso-utility curve. State in words the numerical value of the slope of an iso-utility curve.

5. Classify products in consumption via the marginal utility concept. Relate the classification to the slope of an iso-utility curve.

6. What is redundant about the phrase "marginal rate of substitution"?

7. How do you account for the position of the law of decreasing marginal rate of substitution of a product for money in the list of the principles of the theory of demand for a product? State in words this principle of economics. What is a marginal rate of substitution curve of a product for money? Relate the properties of the marginal utility curve of a product and the marginal rate of substitution curve of a product for money.

APPENDIX: Preference Ordering Theory

It has ever been the task of one race of philosophers to demolish the work of their predecessors, and elevate more splendid fantasies in their stead, which in turn are demolished and replaced by the air-castles of a succeeding generation.

(Washington Irving, *A History of New York*)

An iso-utility curve is also called an indifference curve, for the consumer is indifferent to all the combinations along the curve since all of them yield him the same utility. However, an indifference curve may be defined without reference to utility. Specifically, an indifference curve may be said to depict all combinations of quantities of two products (Q_1 and Q_2) that yield the same level of preference and hence to which the consumer is indifferent. Moreover, indifference curves may be rationalized without reference to cardinal numbers. Specifically, indifference curves may be rationalized via preference ordering theory, which is based on ordinal numbers.

Cardinal Versus Ordinal Ranking of Combinations

To distinguish between cardinal and ordinal numbers, imagine three combinations of Q_1 and Q_2, denoted by A, B, and C. If the three combinations are ranked according to cardinal utility numbers, each number describes *how many units of utility* are associated with each combination by using numbers such as 1, 2, 3, 4, ... If the three combinations are ranked according to ordinal numbers, each number describes only the *order of preference* of each combination by using numbers such as 1st, 2nd, 3rd, 4th, ... (which numbers cannot be added and subtracted, multiplied and divided). For example, in terms of order of preference, let $A = $ 1st, $B = $ 2nd, $C = $ 3rd, ... Thus, utility is a set of cardinal numbers describing a ranking of combinations $A, B, C, D, \ldots$, and preference is a set of ordinal numbers describing a ranking of combinations $A, B, C, D, \ldots$. Supposedly, most consumers rank combinations ordinally, for then only the order of preference, and not the numerical value, of each combination need be known; and the order may be established with or without reference to the concept of utility.

Indifference Relation

Preference ordering theory requires the consumer to compare various combinations of Q_1 and Q_2, and to establish completely his rank ordering of them, using ordinal numbers to describe the ranking. He does this by grouping into a set combinations of Q_1 and Q_2 that he is indifferent to, and then ranking each indifference set according to his preference (see Figure 2.7).

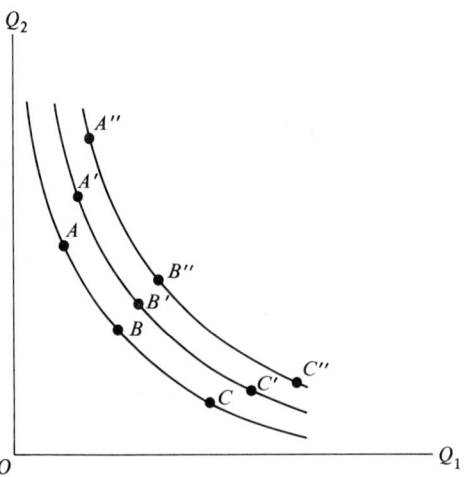

FIG. 2.7. Hypothetical indifference curves

A set of (Q_1, Q_2) values is an indifference set (curve) if it satisfies the indifference relation (I). In terms of modern algebra, the indifference relation is satisfied if, from the viewpoint of the consumer, any three combinations along the curve are reflexive, symmetric, and transitive. The combinations A, B, C along a curve are reflexive if the consumer is indifferent between A and A (AIA), between B and B (BIB), and between C and C (CIC). The same combinations are symmetric if, when he is indifferent between A and B, he is also indifferent between B and A (if AIB, then BIA). The same combinations are transitive if, when he is indifferent between A and B and between B and C, he is also indifferent between A and C (if AIB and BIC, then AIC). In terms of economic theory, when the indifference relation is satisfied, the consumer is indifferent to any combination (bundle or budget) of quantities of Q_1 and Q_2 along an indifference curve.

Preference Relation

In terms of modern algebra, indifference sets have been ranked by order of preference when the preference relation (P) is antisymmetric and transitive. The preference relation is antisymmetric when the consumer prefers A'' to A' and A' is not preferred to A'' ($A''PA'$ implies A' not PA''). The preference relation is transitive when he prefers A'' to A', A' to A, and A'' to A ($A''PA'$ and $A'PA$ implies $A''PA$). In terms of economic theory, when the preference relation is satisfied, the consumer prefers any combination along a higher indifference curve to any combination along a lower indifference curve; that is, he prefers to be on a higher indifference curve than on a lower one, and hence prefers always to move in one direction—to a higher indifference curve. By assumption, he never reaches a state of satiation, at which his satisfaction (utility or preference) is at a maximum, as he takes more of both Q_1 and Q_2.[6] In other words, a greater quantity of (say) Q_1, given the same or a larger quantity of Q_2, is always preferred to a smaller quantity of Q_1: a larger bundle is preferred to a smaller bundle.

Indifference Map

A set of curves that satisfies the indifference and preference relations is called an indifference map. The plane (two-dimensional diagram) on which an indifference map is drawn is called commodity space. An indifference map has five characteristics. (1) Since products are substituted for one another to provide a given level of preference, each indifference curve is negatively sloped. (2) For a consumer to be in equilibrium, each indifference curve must be concave from above a tangent line. (3) Since product quantities are described by sets of rational numbers, an indifference curve must pass through each of the points in a commodity space, and hence the indifference map is "everywhere dense" with indifference curves. (4) Since each higher indifference curve contains a larger quantity of both products when they are combined in a fixed proportion, each higher indifference curve represents a higher level of preference. Thus each indifference curve may be ranked ordinally according to the level of preference depicted by the curve as 1st, 2nd, 3rd, etc. (5) Given three combinations A, B, and C, if A and B are on the 1st curve and A and C are on the 2nd curve, then the 1st curve intersects the 2nd curve at A. Since the consumer is supposedly indifferent between A and B and between A and C, he is supposedly indifferent between B and C. But this cannot be true if C is preferred to B, because C lies on a higher indifference curve. Thus, if the indifference and preference relations are satisfied, no two indifference curves will intersect.

SUMMARY

An indifference curve may be said to depict all combinations of quantities of two products that yield the same level of preference. Thus an indifference curve may be rationalized via preference ordering theory. According to this theory, the consumer must rank combinations ordinally according to his indifference relation and his preference relation. When he has ranked combinations into indifference curves according to his indifference relation, he is indifferent to any combination along a curve. Each curve is negatively sloped and concave from above. When he has ranked indifference curves according to his preference relation, he prefers any combination along a higher curve to any combination along a lower curve. A curve passes through each point in commodity space; each higher curve represents a higher relative level of preference; and no two curves intersect.[7]

NOTES

[1] Thus "utility" is simply the name given a number associated with an ordered set of quantity consumed numbers.

[2] When quantity consumed varies by continuous amounts, the Q set of numbers contains integers and fractions. Continuous marginal utility (MU_c) thus is the instantaneous rate of change of total utility as quantity consumed increases or decreases. With respect to $U = U(Q)$, the instantaneous rate of change is the infinitesimally small change in total utility (dU) associated with an infinitesimally small change in quantity consumed (dQ): $MU_c = dU/dQ$. In this context, marginal utility is the slope of the total utility curve. The slope of the total utility curve is equal to the difference quotient ($\Delta U/\Delta Q$) of the tangent line at a point on the curve. In Figure 2.1a, at point A on $U = U(Q)$,

$$MU_c = \frac{dU}{dQ} = \lim_{\Delta Q \to 0} \frac{\Delta U}{\Delta Q} = \frac{FE}{DF} = \text{slope of line DE} = 6$$

[3] With reference to $U = u(Q_1, Q_2)$, when Q_1 and Q_2 vary by discrete amounts, the increase in U because an additional unit of Q_1 is consumed is the unit gained of Q_1 times the marginal utility of that unit:

$$\Delta U_1 = \Delta Q_1 \frac{\Delta U_1}{\Delta Q_1}$$

The decrease in U because less Q_2 is consumed is the quantity given up of Q_2 times the marginal utility of that quantity:

$$\Delta U_2 = \Delta Q_2 \frac{\Delta U_2}{\Delta Q_2}$$

The total change in U is ΔU, and

$$\Delta U = \frac{\Delta U_1}{\Delta Q_1} \Delta Q_1 + \frac{\Delta U_2}{\Delta Q_2} \Delta Q_2$$

Since the total change in U is zero because U is a constant amount U_0, the decrease in U because less Q_2 is consumed must be offset exactly by the increase in U because more Q_1 is consumed. Therefore

$$\Delta U = \frac{\Delta U_1}{\Delta Q_1}\Delta Q_1 + \frac{\Delta U_2}{\Delta Q_2}\Delta Q_2 = 0$$

$$\frac{\Delta U_2}{\Delta Q_2}\Delta Q_2 = -\frac{\Delta U_1}{\Delta Q_1}\Delta Q_1$$

$$\frac{\Delta Q_2}{\Delta Q_1} = -\frac{\Delta U_1/\Delta Q_1}{\Delta U_2/\Delta Q_2} = -\frac{MU_1}{MU_2}$$

When Q_1 and Q_2 vary by continuous amounts, the instantaneous rate of change of U with respect to Q_1 is the infinitesimally small change in U associated with an infinitesimally small change in Q_1: $MU_1 = \partial U/\partial Q_1$. The total infinitesimally small change in Q_1 is dQ_1. Thus, in terms of infinitesimally small changes, the change in U associated with a total change in Q_1 is

$$\frac{\partial U}{\partial Q_1}dQ_1$$

Similarly, the instantaneous rate of change of U with respect to Q_2 is the infinitesimally small change in U associated with an infinitesimally small change in Q_2: $MU_2 = \partial U/\partial Q_2$. The total infinitesimally small change in Q_2 is dQ_2. And in terms of infinitesimally small changes, the change in U associated with a total change in Q_2 is

$$\frac{\partial U}{\partial Q_2}dQ_2$$

Therefore, in terms of infinitesimally small changes, the total change in U is dU, and

$$dU = \frac{\partial U}{\partial Q_1}dQ_1 + \frac{\partial U}{\partial Q_2}dQ_2$$

Since the total change in U along an iso-utility curve is zero,

$$dU = \frac{\partial U}{\partial Q_1}dQ_1 + \frac{\partial U}{\partial Q_2}dQ_2 = 0$$

$$\frac{\partial U}{\partial Q_2}dQ_2 = -\frac{\partial U}{\partial Q_1}dQ_1$$

$$\frac{dQ_2}{dQ_1} = -\frac{\partial U/\partial Q_1}{\partial U/\partial Q_2} = -\frac{MU_1}{MU_2}$$

[4] With respect to dQ_2/dQ_1, when Q_1 increases and Q_2 decreases, dQ_2 is a set of negative numbers and dQ_1 is a set of positive numbers. Thus dQ_2/dQ_1 is a set of negative numbers. Since the numerical (absolute) value of a negative number is that number multiplied by -1, and since $dQ_2/dQ_1 = -MU_1/MU_2$, $-dQ_2/dQ_1$ and $-(-MU_1/MU_2)$ or MU_1/MU_2 denote the numerical value of dQ_2/dQ_1. And $-dQ_2/dQ_1$ (or MU_1/MU_2) is a set of positive numbers.

[5] Each successive unit increase in Q_2 increases utility by a decreasing amount; and each successive unit decrease in Q_1 decreases utility by an increasing amount. Therefore, with each unit increase in Q_2 (ΔQ_2), the consumer gives up a decreasing amount of Q_1 (ΔQ_1) to keep utility constant. Since the ratio $\Delta Q_2/\Delta Q_1$ increases numerically as more Q_2 and less Q_1 are consumed, an iso-utility curve is concave from above a tangent line.

[6] For a discussion of indifference curves that recognizes satiety, see Kenneth E. Boulding, *Economic Analysis*, 4th ed., Volume I, *Microeconomics* (New York: Harper & Row, 1966), Chapter 27.

[7] For a detailed presentation of preference ordering theory, see Cliff Lloyd, *Microeconomic Analysis* (Homewood, Illinois: Richard D. Irwin, Inc., 1967), Chapter 1. For a discussion of the related theory of revealed preference, see J. M. Henderson and R. E. Quandt, *Microeconomic Theory: A Mathematical Approach* (New York: McGraw-Hill Book Company, 1958), pp. 32–33, and Richard A. Bilas, *Microeconomic Theory: A Graphical Analysis* (New York: McGraw-Hill Book Company, 1967), pp. 83–87.

chapter **3**

Equilibrium of a Perfectly Competitive Purchaser of Products

The economist ... must concern himself with the ultimate aims of man.
(Alfred Marshall, *Principle of Economics*)

One of the ultimate aims of a consumer and purchaser of products is to maximize his utility subject to his constrained expenditure. His utility varies directly with his consumption of products. And his consumption varies directly with his expenditure on products. A budget constraint or limitation is imposed upon his expenditure by his money income. Thus he is faced with the problem of allocating his income so as to consume quantities that will maximize his utility. He is said to be in equilibrium when he has chosen the quantities that maximize his utility subject to his constrained expenditure. The concern of the economist with this ultimate aim of man is embodied in the so-called "principle of equilibrium of a perfectly competitive purchaser of products," which may be presented in several different ways.

Ratio of Marginal Utilities Equals Ratio of Prices

An iso-utility curve depicts all combinations of quantities of two products (Q_1 and Q_2) that yield the same level of utility to a purchaser, given his taste for the products. Similarly, an iso-expenditure curve depicts all combinations of quantities of two products (Q_1 and Q_2) attainable from a given level of expenditure (= money income) of the purchaser, given the prices of the products (P_1 and P_2). The conclusion follows that, when a purchaser is in equilibrium, he has chosen that combination of Q_1 and Q_2 at which the slope of the highest attainable iso-utility curve ($-MU_1/MU_2$) is the same as the slope of the iso-expenditure curve ($-P_1/P_2$) denoting his given expenditure: $-MU_1/MU_2 = -P_1/P_2$.

To see this, consider Figure 3.1. Combinations of Q_1 and Q_2 beyond iso-expenditure curve 1 are not attainable from a given expenditure (= money

EQUILIBRIUM OF A PERFECTLY COMPETITIVE PURCHASER OF PRODUCTS 45

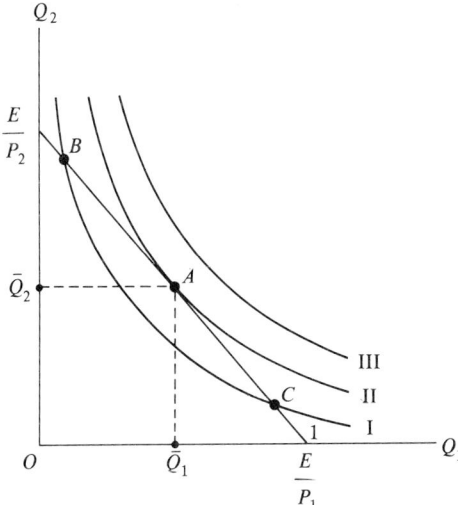

FIG. 3.1. Equilibrium of a perfectly competitive purchaser of products: ratio of marginal utilities equals ratio of prices

income). Combinations of Q_1 and Q_2 on and below iso-expenditure curve 1 are attainable from a given expenditure. The highest attainable combination of Q_1 and Q_2 ($\bar{Q}_1, \bar{Q}_2$) is on an iso-utility curve (curve II) that is tangent to iso-expenditure curve 1 at one unique point. At this point of tangency (point A), the slope of iso-utility curve II ($-MU_1/MU_2$) is the same as the slope of iso-expenditure curve 1 ($-P_1/P_2$). Therefore, by multiplying both slopes by -1, when he is in equilibrium, in effect he is choosing a combination of Q_1 and Q_2 such that

$$\frac{MU_1}{MU_2} = \frac{P_1}{P_2}$$

In other words, the marginal rate of substitution of Q_1 for Q_2 (MU_1/MU_2) on the highest attainable iso-utility curve (curve II) is equal to the numerical value of the slope of iso-expenditure curve 1 (P_1/P_2): $MU_1/MU_2 = P_1/P_2$. To generalize, when a perfectly competitive purchaser has determined the equilibrium set of product quantities, in effect he is allocating his money income in such a way that the marginal rate of substitution of any two products is equal to the ratio of their prices, or the ratio of their marginal utilities equals the ratio of their prices.

Point B on iso-expenditure curve 1 and iso-utility curve I in Figure 3.1 is attainable but not preferred to A; by purchasing more Q_1 and less Q_2, the purchaser can attain a higher level of satisfaction, that is, move onto the higher iso-utility curve II. He is in disequilibrium at B, since

$$\frac{MU_1}{MU_2} > \frac{P_1}{P_2}$$

and in equilibrium at A, since

$$\frac{MU_1}{MU_2} = \frac{P_1}{P_2}$$

From B to A, the ratio MU_1/MU_2 decreases as more Q_1 and less Q_2 are purchased per unit of time.

Similarly, point C on iso-expenditure curve 1 and iso-utility curve I in Figure 3.1 is attainable but not preferred to A; by purchasing more Q_2 and less Q_1, the purchaser can attain a higher level of satisfaction, that is, move onto the higher iso-utility curve II. He is in disequilibrium at C, since

$$\frac{MU_1}{MU_2} < \frac{P_1}{P_2}$$

and in equilibrium at A, since

$$\frac{MU_1}{MU_2} = \frac{P_1}{P_2}$$

From C to A, the ratio MU_1/MU_2 increases as more Q_2 and less Q_1 are purchased per unit of time.

Marginal Rate of Substitution of a Product for Money Equals the Price of the Product

The iso-utility curve drawn in Figure 3.2 (curve I) depicts all combinations of quantities of a product (Q) and of money (M) that yield the same level of

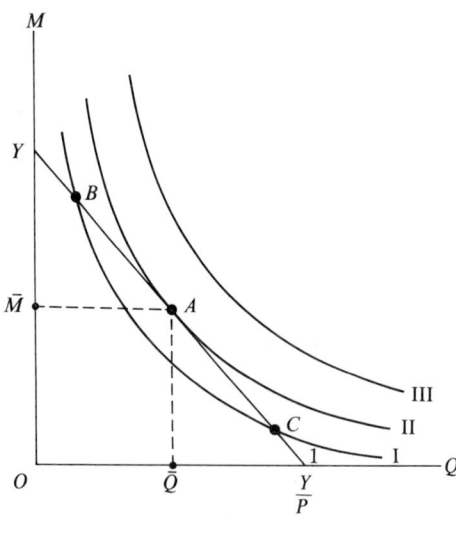

FIG. 3.2. Equilibrium of a perfectly competitive purchaser of products: marginal rate of substitution of a product for money equals price

EQUILIBRIUM OF A PERFECTLY COMPETITIVE PURCHASER OF PRODUCTS 47

utility or preference to a purchaser, given his taste for the product and money. The slope of this indifference curve (dM/dQ) is equal to the negative of the ratio MU/λ, where MU is the marginal utility of the product and λ is the marginal utility of money: $dM/dQ = -MU/\lambda$ (λ = lambda). The numerical ratio MU/λ is called the marginal rate of substitution of a product for money.[1]

The line of attainable combinations drawn in Figure 3.2 (curve 1) depicts all combinations of quantities of a product (Q) and of money (M) attainable from a given level of money income (Y) of the purchaser, given the price of the product (P). The slope of the line of attainable combinations (dM/dQ) is equal to the negative of the price of the product $(-P)$. Its M intercept is Y, and its Q intercept is Y/P:

$$Y = M + PQ$$

$$M = Y - PQ \quad \text{and} \quad Q = \frac{Y}{P} - \frac{1}{P}M$$

$$\frac{dM}{dQ} = -P \quad \text{and} \quad \frac{dQ}{dM} = -\frac{1}{P}$$

$$M = Y \text{ when } Q = 0 \quad \text{and} \quad Q = \frac{Y}{P} \text{ when } M = 0.$$

As seen in Figure 3.2, when a purchaser is in equilibrium, he has chosen that combination of M and Q ($\overline{Q}, \overline{M}$) at which the slope of the highest attainable iso-utility curve $(-MU/\lambda)$ is the same as the slope of the line of attainable combinations $(-P)$ denoting his given money income. By multiplying both slopes by -1, when he is in equilibrium, in effect he is choosing a combination of M and Q such that

$$\frac{MU}{\lambda} = P.$$

To generalize, when a perfectly competitive purchaser has determined the equilibrium set of product quantities, in effect he is allocating his money income in such a way that the marginal rate of substitution of each product for money equals the price of the product.

Marginal Utility of a Product Equals Marginal Utility of Money Expended

By multiplying each $MU/\lambda = P$ by λ, when a perfectly competitive purchaser has determined the equilibrium set of product quantities, in effect he is allocating his money income in such a way that the marginal utility of each product (MU) equals its price (P) times the marginal utility of money (λ):

$$MU = P\lambda$$

Lambda (λ) is thus seen to be the factor of proportionality that makes the two sides of each equation equal. For example, if the last unit purchased of a product yields 100 units of utility ($MU = 100$) and if it costs \$5 ($P = 5$), then the marginal utility of money is 20 units of utility ($\lambda = 20$) and the marginal utility of money expended is 100 units of utility ($P\lambda = 100$), when the purchaser is in equilibrium: $100 = 5(20)$. To generalize, when he is in equilibrium, the marginal utility of each product (MU) equals the marginal utility of money expended on each product ($P\lambda$).

By letting the marginal utility of money be one unit ($\lambda = 1$), when the purchaser is in equilibrium, the marginal utility of each product (MU) equals its price (P):

$$MU = P \text{ or } \frac{\Delta U}{\Delta Q} = \frac{\Delta E}{\Delta Q}$$

In this context, the last unit purchased of each product (ΔQ) adds as much to his total utility (ΔU) as it does to his total expenditure (ΔE), when he is in equilibrium. The "pain" of an additional unit (ΔE) is offset exactly by its "pleasure" (ΔU): $\Delta U = \Delta E$.

Equality of the Ratio of Marginal Utility to Price of Every Product

By dividing each $MU = P\lambda$ by P, when a perfectly competitive purchaser has determined the equilibrium set of product quantities, in effect he is allocating his money income in such a way that the marginal utility of each product (MU) divided by its price (P) equals the marginal utility of money (λ):[2]

$$\frac{MU}{P} = \lambda$$

By letting the last unit of each product cost \$1 when he is in equilibrium the utility of each unit received ($\Delta U/\Delta Q = \Delta U$) equals the utility of the last dollar given up ($\Delta U/\Delta M = \Delta U$).

In the two-product case, when he is in equilibrium,

(1) $\quad \dfrac{MU_1}{P_1} = \lambda$

(2) $\quad \dfrac{MU_2}{P_2} = \lambda$

By setting (1) equal to (2), when he is in equilibrium,

(3) $\quad \dfrac{MU_1}{P_1} = \dfrac{MU_2}{P_2} (= \lambda)$

which is equivalent to

$$\dfrac{MU_1}{MU_2} = \dfrac{P_1}{P_2}$$

With respect to products $Q_1, Q_2, Q_3, \ldots, Q_n$,

(3') $\quad \dfrac{MU_1}{P_1} = \dfrac{MU_2}{P_2} = \dfrac{MU_3}{P_3} = \ldots = \dfrac{MU_n}{P_n} (= \lambda)$

Thus, when a purchaser is in equilibrium, he is allocating his money income in such a way that the last dollar spent on Q_1 (P_1) yields the same amount of utility (MU_1) as the last dollar spent on $Q_2, Q_3, \ldots, Q_n$—the equimarginal principle of equilibrium of a purchaser of products.

Equimarginal Principle of Equilibrium of a Purchaser of Products

The equimarginal principle of equilibrium of a purchaser of products may be analyzed via the two-product case according to the two-faced (Janus) diagram in Figure 3.3. The expenditure on product Q_1 begins with zero at the origin and increases to the left on the horizontal axis. Conversely, the expenditure on product Q_2 begins with zero at the origin and increases to the right on the horizontal axis. Thus, all values on the horizontal axis are

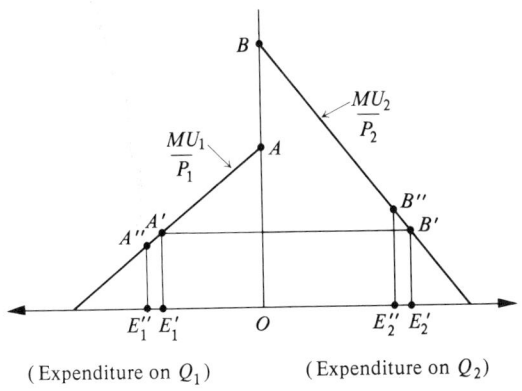

FIG. 3.3. Equimarginal principle of equilibrium of a perfectly competitive purchaser of products

50   PRINCIPLES OF THE THEORY OF DEMAND FOR A PRODUCT

either zero or positive (that is, nonnegative). The marginal utility per dollar of expenditure on a product begins with zero at the origin and increases up the vertical axis. When the expenditure on Q_1 increases, the quantity of Q_1 increases, since the price of Q_1 (P_1) is a parameter; and as the quantity of Q_1 increases, the marginal utility of Q_1 decreases according to the law of decreasing marginal utility of a product. Thus, given P_1, the marginal utility per dollar of expenditure on Q_1 (MU_1/P_1) decreases as the expenditure on Q_1 increases, as depicted by the curve labeled MU_1/P_1. Similarly, the curve labeled MU_2/P_2 depicts the inverse relation between MU_2/P_2 and the expenditure on Q_2.

The purchaser has $E_1'E_2'$ dollars to allocate between Q_1 and Q_2. The marginal utility per dollar of expenditure OE_1' is $E_1'A'$; therefore, the total utility of expenditure OE_1', which is the area under the MU_1/P_1 curve at OE_1', is area $E_1'A'AO$. Similarly, the marginal utility per dollar of expenditure OE_2' is $E_2'B'$; and the total utility of expenditure OE_2' is area $E_2'B'BO$. Since $E_1'A' = E_2'B'$, with this allocation the ratio of marginal utility to price is the same for both products: $MU_1/P_1 = MU_2/P_2$.

The magnitude $E_1'E_2'$ is the same as the magnitude $E_1''E_2''$. Thus, the purchaser has $E_1''E_2''$ dollars to allocate between Q_1 and Q_2. The marginal utility per dollar of expenditure OE_1'' is $E_1''A''$; and the total utility of expenditure OE_1'' is area $E_1''A''AO$. Similarly, the marginal utility per dollar of expenditure OE_2'' is $E_2''B''$; and the total utility of expenditure OE_2'' is area $E_2''B''BO$. Since $E_1''A'' < E_2''B''$, with this allocation the ratio of marginal utility to price is not the same for both products: $MU_1/P_1 < MU_2/P_2$.

The combined area when $MU_1/P_1 = MU_2/P_2$ ($E_1'A'AO + E_2'B'BO$) is larger than the combined area when $MU_1/P_1 < MU_2/P_2$ ($E_1''A''AO + E_2''B''BO$). To see this, increase the expenditure on Q_1 from OE_1' to OE_1'' ($= E_1'' - E_1'$), thereby increasing total utility by the area $E_1'A'A''E_1''$. Because of the budget restriction, the expenditure on Q_2 is decreased from OE_2' to OE_2'' ($= E_2' - E_2''$), thereby decreasing total utility by the area $E_2''B'B''E_2'$. The loss in utility ($E_2''B'B''E_2'$) is greater than the gain in utility ($E_1'A'A''E_1''$). Therefore, when $MU_1/P_1 < MU_2/P_2$, utility is increased by purchasing more Q_2 and less Q_1 until $MU_1/P_1 = MU_2/P_2$. As less Q_1 is purchased MU_1/P_1 increases, and as more Q_2 is purchased MU_2/P_2 decreases, until eventually $MU_1/P_1 = MU_2/P_2$.

SUMMARY

One of the ultimate aims of a consumer and purchaser of products is to maximize his utility subject to his expenditure, which is constrained (limited) by his money income. When he is maximizing his utility subject to his constrained expenditure, he is said to be in equilibrium: he cannot increase his utility by changing the quantities he purchases and consumes per unit of time with his money income, given the parameters of his expenditure and utility functions. When a perfectly competitive purchaser has determined the equilibrium set of product quantities, in effect he is allocating his money income in such a way that (1) the marginal rate of substitution of each product for money equals the price of the product. (2) The marginal utility of each product equals the marginal utility of money expended. (3) The ratio of marginal utility to price is the same for every product—the equimarginal principle of equilibrium of a perfectly competitive purchaser of products, which is analyzed via a Janus diagram. (4) The ratio of the marginal utilities of any two products equals the ratio of their prices—which is equivalent to saying that the marginal rate of substitution of one product for another product equals the ratio of the prices.

Questions

1. List the principles of the theory of demand for a product that are of primary importance. How do you account for the position of the principle of equilibrium of a purchaser of products in this list.

2. Use iso-expenditure and iso-utility curves to derive, analyze, and verbalize the equilibrium principle $MU_1/MU_2 = P_1/P_2$. (Note: an analysis of equilibrium includes an analysis of disequilibrium.) How would the equilibrium principle be stated if you did not accept the concepts of utility and marginal utility?

3. Derive and verbalize the equilibrium principle $MU/\lambda = P$.

4. Derive and verbalize the equilibrium principle $MU = P$.

5. Derive and verbalize the equimarginal principle of equilibrium of a purchaser of products for the two-products case and the n-products case.

6. Analyze this principle in the two-products case via a Janus diagram.

NOTES

[1] For a detailed discussion, see Kenneth E. Boulding, *Economic Analysis*, 4th ed., Volume I, *Microeconomics* (New York: Harper & Row, 1966), pp. 524–530.

[2] Alternatively, when he is in equilibrium, the marginal utility per dollar of each product equals the marginal utility per dollar of money ($\lambda/1$). Why is the price of money $1? In a barter economy, the price of a given product is the quantity of another product, called the *numeraire*, that must be given up to obtain a unit of the given product. Thus price is the rate of exchange, or substitution, of the product chosen as *numeraire* for the given product. That is, the *numeraire* is the unit of account, or measuring rod, of the purchasing power of other products.

For example, let a pound of rice be the *numeraire*, and let the price of a pound of corn be two pounds of rice. Then the rate of exchange of rice for corn is two pounds of rice per pound of corn. The purchasing power of a pound of corn is two pounds of rice. Conversely, the purchasing power of a pound of rice is half a pound of corn. The rate of exchange of the *numeraire* for the *numeraire* is a pound: a pound of rice exchanges for a pound of rice. Thus the price of the *numeraire* is a pound.

Similarly, in a money economy, the price of a given product is the quantity of money, the *numeraire*, that must be given up to obtain a unit of the given product. Thus price is the rate of exchange of money for the given product. That is, money is the unit of account, or measuring rod, of the purchasing power of a given product. The rate of exchange of money for money is $1: a dollar exchanges for a dollar. Thus the price of money considered as the *numeraire* is $1.

chapter 4

The Demand Function for a Product of a Perfectly Competitive Purchaser

"The demand function for a product of a perfectly competitive purchaser" is the name of the relation between the quantity of a product a purchaser is willing to purchase per unit of time (the dependent variable) and the price of the product, the price of a substitute product, the price of a complementary product, and the money income of the purchaser (the independent variables), given the parameter of his taste for products. The relation between the dependent variable and each of the independent variables is analyzed via the principle of equilibrium of a perfectly competitive purchaser of products. The analysis consists of changing the value of one independent variable, while holding constant the values of the remaining independent variables, and ascertaining the new equilibrium value of the dependent variable. The primary objective of the analysis is to ascertain the sign of each of the difference quotients denoting the change in the dependent variable associated with a change in an independent variable, given the ceteris paribus assumption that in each case "other things are equal" (or are unchanging). When the value of an independent variable is held constant via the ceteris paribus assumption, the variable is called a parameter of the relation being analyzed. Thus the price of a substitute product, the price of a complementary product, the money income of the purchaser, and his taste for products are parameters of the relation between the quantity of a product a purchaser is willing to purchase per unit of time and the price of the product.

Demand Curve for a Product of a Purchaser

The "demand curve for a product of a purchaser" depicts the relation between the quantity of a product a purchaser is willing to purchase (Q) per unit of time and the price of the product (P). The relation is denoted by $Q = d(P)$. The purchaser is in equilibrium with respect to each ordered pair of P and Q numbers on his demand curve. When a perfectly competitive purchaser is in equilibrium, in effect he is allocating his money income in such a way that the ratio of the marginal utilities of any two products equals the ratio of their prices. Thus, in Figure 4.1a, the purchaser is in equilibrium at A' and A'', for at both points the condition that MU_1/MU_2 must equal

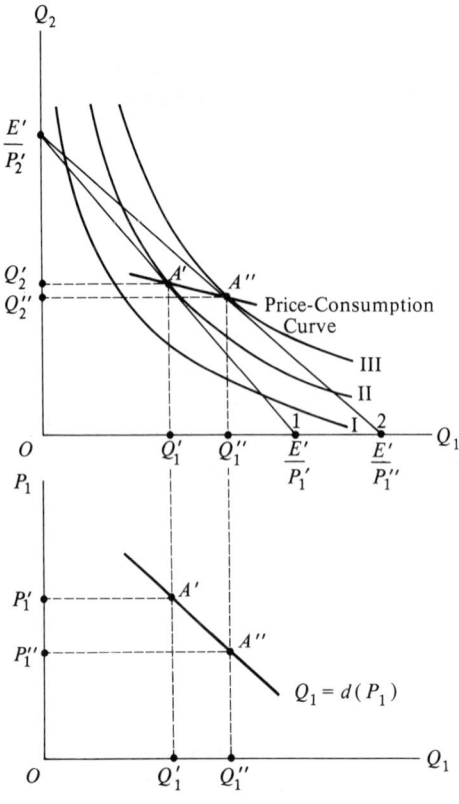

FIG. 4.1a. Equilibrium of a perfectly competitive purchaser of products: ratio of marginal utilities equals ratio of prices

FIG. 4.1b. Hypothetical demand curve for a product of a perfectly competitive purchaser

P_1/P_2 is satisfied. Points A' and A'' therefore represent equilibrium pairs of P_1 and Q_1 numbers. The (P_1, Q_1) equilibrium pairs of values appear in Figure 4.1b as points A' and A'' on the purchaser's demand curve for Q_1. Point A' denotes the equilibrium pair (P_1', Q_1'), and point A'' denotes the equilibrium pair (P_1'', Q_1''). The equilibrium pair (P_1'', Q_1'') is obtained by decreasing P_1 from P_1' to P_1'' and ascertaining the new equilibrium value of Q_1 (Q_1''). The decrease in P_1 effects a shift of iso-expenditure curve 1 until it is tangent to a higher iso-utility curve (curve III); that is, curve 1 becomes curve 2. With the decrease in P_1, the ratio of P_1 to P_2 (P_1/P_2) has decreased and the ratio E/P_1 has increased, while the ratio E/P_2 has not changed. At the new point of equilibrium (A''), the slope of iso-utility curve III equals the slope of iso-expenditure curve 2. In this case, the decrease in P_1 to P_1''

induces an increase in Q_1 to Q_1''—the law of demand for a product of a purchaser of products. Other equilibrium pairs of (P_1, Q_1) values along the Q_1 demand curve in Figure 4.1b may be rationalized in the same way. The corresponding equilibrium pairs of (Q_1, Q_2) numbers in Figure 4.1a are connected by a curve called the price–consumption curve.

Substitution and Income Effects

The total effect on Q_1 of a change in P_1 is the substitution effect plus the income effect, which analytically is distinct from the substitution effect. The substitution effect on Q_1 of a change in P_1 is the result of the corresponding change in relative product prices (that is, the change in the ratio P_1/P_2 of the iso-expenditure curve). The income effect on Q_1 of a change in P_1 is the result of the corresponding change in absolute product prices (that is, the change in the ratio E/P_1 of the iso-expenditure curve), which changes the purchaser's real income (that is, changes the purchasing power of his money income). In terms of iso-utility curve analysis, according to the substitution effect principle, as the price of Q_1 decreases relative to the price of Q_2, more Q_1 and less Q_2 are purchased, while the overall level of utility associated with both products remains constant. Thus, the substitution effect on Q_1 of a decrease in P_1 is depicted by a movement down a given iso-utility curve. According to the income effect principle, the purchaser's real income increases when P_1 decreases, and hence he can purchase more Q_1 and Q_2 to increase his utility or preference. Therefore, the income effect on Q_1 of a decrease in P_1 is a movement to a higher iso-utility curve.

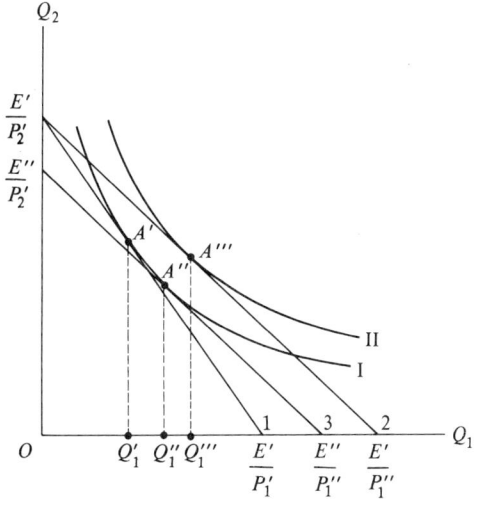

FIG. 4.2. Substitution and income effects (normal product case)

To see this, consider Figure 4.2. In this figure, the purchaser is initially in equilibrium at A', where iso-expenditure curve 1 is tangent to iso-utility curve I. Then P_1 decreases, and he is in equilibrium at A''', where iso-expenditure curve 2 is tangent to iso-utility curve II. The resulting increase in his real income may be eliminated for analytical purposes by reducing his money income, thereby decreasing E/P_1 to its initial value. Iso-expenditure curve 3 represents the various attainable combinations of Q_1 and Q_2 after his income has been adjusted so as to eliminate the income effect. It is parallel to iso-expenditure curve 2, since Q_1 and Q_2 are exchanged at the new price ratio; and it is tangent to iso-utility curve I, since his adjusted income is just sufficient for him to be on curve I. The total increase in Q_1 due to the decrease in P_1 is $Q_1''' - Q_1'$. The substitution effect is $Q_1'' - Q_1'$, and, in this case, the income effect is $Q_1''' - Q_1''$.

Normal, Inferior, and Giffen Products

The substitution effect on Q_1 of a change in P_1 is always negative: a decrease in P_1/P_2 due to a decrease in P_1 induces an increase in Q_1 by inducing a decrease in Q_2 and hence $\Delta Q_1/\Delta(P_1/P_2) < 0$. By definition, the income effect on Q_1 of a change in P_1 is positive in the case of a normal product: an increase in E/P_1 due to a decrease in P_1 induces an increase in Q_1 and hence $\Delta Q_1/\Delta(E/P_1) > 0$.[1] Thus, in the case of a normal product, the positive income effect strengthens the negative substitution effect (see Figure 4.2). But, by definition, the income effect is negative in the case of an inferior product: an increase in E/P_1 due to a decrease in P_1 induces a decrease in Q_1 and hence $\Delta Q_2/\Delta(E/P_1) < 0$. Thus, in the case of an inferior product, the negative income effect weakens the negative substitution effect (see Figure 4.3).

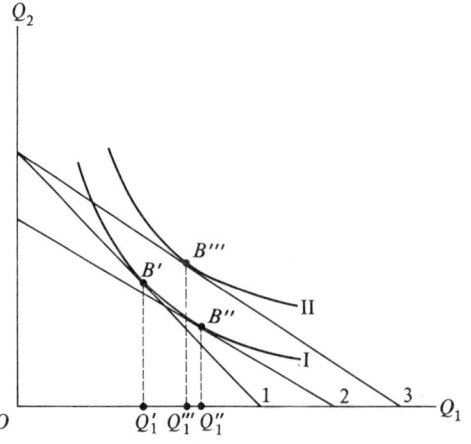

FIG. 4.3. Substitution and income effects (inferior product case)

The greater the percentage of a given income allocated to a given product, the greater the income effect of a change in price of the product. Conceivably, in the case of an inferior product that accounts for a very large percentage of the purchaser's income, the negative income effect may be more important than the negative substitution effect, and hence Q_1 may vary directly with P_1. This supposed exception to the law of demand for a product of a purchaser is called Giffen's paradox, and the relatively few products subject to this paradox are called Giffen products. To see the distinction between inferior and Giffen products, consider Figures 4.3 and 4.4.

In Figure 4.3, the total increase in Q_1 due to the decrease in P_1 is $Q_1''' - Q_1'$. The negative substitution effect is $Q_1'' - Q_1'$, and, in this case, the negative income effect is $Q_1'' - Q_1'''$. The product is inferior, but it is not a Giffen product. The law of demand for a product of a purchaser is not violated, for the negative substitution effect more than offsets the negative income effect. But in Figure 4.4, the total decrease in Q_1 due to the decrease in P_1 is $Q_1' - Q_1'''$.

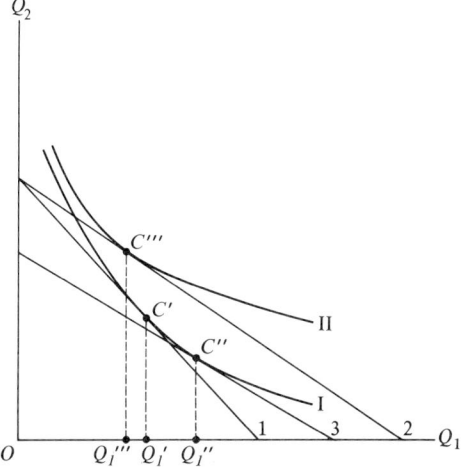

FIG. 4.4. Substitution and income effects (Giffen product case)

The negative substitution effect is $Q_1'' - Q_1'$, and, in this case, the negative income effect is $Q_1'' - Q_1'''$. The product is inferior, and it is also a Giffen product. The law of demand for a product of a purchaser is violated, for the negative substitution effect less than offsets the negative income effect. In short, a Giffen product is always an inferior product, but all inferior products are not Giffen products.

Marginal Rate of Substitution Curve of a Product for a Product

In general, an iso-utility curve is a negatively sloped curve that is concave from above a tangent line. The numerical value of the slope of an iso-utility curve $(-dQ_2/dQ_1)$ is called the marginal rate of substitution of a product for a product and is equal to the ratio MU_1/MU_2. The relation between MU_1/MU_2 or $-dQ_2/dQ_1$ and the quantity of Q_1 along a given iso-utility curve is denoted by $MU_1/MU_2 = U_0'(Q_1)$ or $-dQ_2/dQ_1 = U_0'(Q_1)$ and is called the marginal rate of substitution function of a product for a product. This function is a set of ordered pairs of Q_1 and MU_1/MU_2 numbers derived by calculating the slope at each value of Q_1 along the given iso-utility curve. Thus it contains a MU_1/MU_2 number for each point along the given iso-utility curve. By restricting the purchaser to a given real income, the substitution effect on Q_1 of a decrease in P_1 is depicted by a movement down a given iso-utility curve; and at each point of tangency of the income-adjusted iso-expenditure curve with the given iso-utility curve, $MU_1/MU_2 = P_1/P_2$. Thus the marginal rate of substitution curve of a product for a product depicts the substitution effect on Q_1 of a change in P_1.

The greater the degree of complementarity in consumption of Q_1 and Q_2, the greater the degree of concavity of the iso-utility curve, and hence the steeper the curve of $MU_1/MU_2 = U_0'(Q_1)$. Conversely, the greater the degree of substitutability in consumption of Q_1 and Q_2, the less the degree of concavity of the iso-utility curve, and hence the flatter the curve of $MU_1/MU_2 = U_0'(Q_1)$. Thus, since a given $MU_1/MU_2 = U_0'(Q_1)$ curve depicts the substitution effect, the numerical size of the substitution effect, and hence the numerical value of the slope of the purchaser's demand curve for Q_1, depends upon the relationship in consumption of Q_1 and Q_2.

To see this, consider the three marginal rate of substitution curves drawn in Figure 4.5. With respect to each of these curves, when the purchaser is in equilibrium $MU_1/MU_2 = P_1/P_2$. Thus, when P_1 decreases, the purchaser is in disequilibrium at the initial value of Q_1: $MU_1/MU_2 > P_1/P_2$. By holding his real income constant, he substitutes Q_1 for Q_2 according to an iso-utility curve until he is back in equilibrium. As he moves down the iso-utility curve, MU_1/MU_2 decreases according to the marginal rate of substitution curve derived from the given iso-utility curve.

Curve I in Figure 4.5 is a hypothetical marginal rate of substitution curve of two products (Q_1 and Q_2) not related in consumption. When two products are not related in consumption, the marginal utility of one product is a constant function of the quantity consumed of the other product; hence MU_1/MU_2 varies inversely with Q_1 solely because of decreasing marginal utility of a product. Specifically, when the purchaser substitutes Q_1 for Q_2 because P_1/P_2 has decreased, each additional unit of Q_1 induces a decrease in marginal utility of Q_1; and each successive unit decrease in Q_2 induces an increase in marginal utility of Q_2. Eventually, therefore, equilibrium is restored via these changes in Q_1 and Q_2; that is, once again $MU_1/MU_2 = P_1/P_2$. But now he is purchasing more units of Q_1 than before the decrease in its price. The increase in Q_1 required to restore equilibrium is $Q_1^{(4)} - Q_1'''$.

Curve II in Figure 4.5 is a hypothetical marginal rate of substitution curve

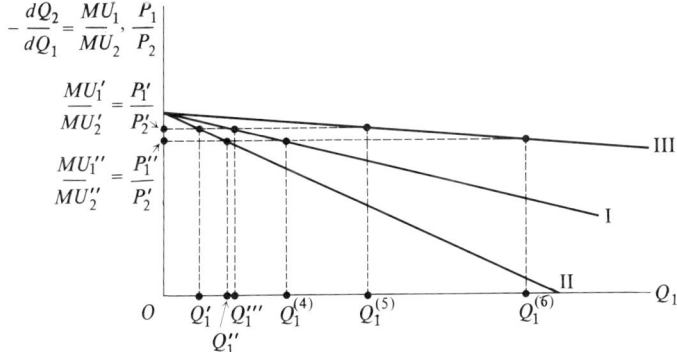

FIG. 4.5. Hypothetical marginal rate of substitution curves

of a product for an imperfect complement in consumption. When two products are imperfect complements in consumption, the marginal utility of one product is an increasing function of the quantity consumed of the other product; hence as Q_1 increases, the tendency for MU_1/MU_2 to decrease because of decreasing marginal utility of a product is reinforced by the tendency for MU_1/MU_2 to decrease because of the complementary relationship between them. Specifically, when the purchaser substitutes Q_1 for Q_2 because P_1/P_2 has decreased, each additional unit of Q_1 induces a decrease in marginal utility of Q_1 and an increase in marginal utility of Q_2. Similarly, each successive unit decrease in Q_2 induces an increase in marginal utility of Q_2 and a decrease in marginal utility of Q_1. Eventually, therefore, equilibrium is restored via these changes in Q_1 and Q_2. But now the increase in Q_1 required to restore equilibrium is $Q_1'' - Q_1'$, which is less than $Q_1^{(4)} - Q_1'''$. Thus, given the same decrease in P_1/P_2, the increase in Q_1 required to restore equilibrium by decreasing MU_1/MU_2 is less when Q_1 and Q_2 are complements in consumption than when they are not related in consumption. With Q_1 on the vertical axis, the numerical value of the slope of the purchaser's demand curve for Q_1 ($-dQ_1/dP_1$) varies inversely with the degree of complementarity of Q_1 and Q_2. With P_1 on the vertical axis, the greater the degree of complementarity, the steeper is the purchaser's demand curve for Q_1.

Curve III in Figure 4.5 is a hypothetical marginal rate of substitution curve of a product for an imperfect substitute in consumption. When two products are imperfect substitutes in consumption, the marginal utility of one product is a decreasing function of the quantity consumed of the other product; hence as Q_1 increases, the tendency for MU_1/MU_2 to decrease because of decreasing marginal utility of a product is partially offset by the tendency for MU_1/MU_2 to increase because of the substitute relationship between them. Specifically, when the purchaser substitutes Q_1 for Q_2 because P_1/P_2 has decreased, each additional unit of Q_1 induces a decrease in marginal utility of Q_1 and a decrease in marginal utility of Q_2. Similarly, each successive unit decrease in Q_2

induces an increase in marginal utility of Q_2 and an increase in marginal utility of Q_1. Eventually, as MU_1/MU_2 decreases as Q_1 increases, equilibrium is restored via these changes in Q_1 and Q_2. But now the increase in Q_1 required to restore equilibrium is $Q_1^{(6)} - Q_1^{(5)}$, which is greater than $Q_1^{(4)} - Q_1'''$. Thus, given the same decrease in P_1/P_2, the increase in Q_1 required to restore equilibrium by decreasing MU_1/MU_2 is greater when Q_1 and Q_2 are substitutes in consumption than when they are not related in consumption or are complements in consumption. With Q_1 on the vertical axis, the numerical value of the slope of the purchaser's demand curve for Q_1 ($-dQ_1/dP_1$) varies directly with the degree of substitutability of Q_1 and Q_2. With P_1 on the vertical axis, the greater the degree of substitutability, the flatter is the purchaser's demand curve for Q_1.

Marginal Rate of Substitution Curve of a Product for Money

When a perfectly competitive purchaser is in equilibrium, in effect he is allocating his money income in such a way that the marginal rate of substitution of a product for money (MU/λ) equals its price (P). That is, $MU/\lambda = P$ at each point of tangency of an iso-utility curve (depicting all combinations of quantities of a product (Q) and of money (M) that yield the same level of utility) with a line of attainable combinations (depicting all combinations of quantities of the product and of money attainable from a given level of money income). A marginal rate of substitution curve of a product for money depicts the relation between the marginal rate of substitution of a product for money and the quantity consumed of the product: $MU/\lambda = \lambda(Q)$. Thus, since $MU/\lambda = P$ at each value of Q, a perfectly competitive purchaser's marginal rate of substitution curve of a product for money, $MU/\lambda = \lambda(Q)$, is his demand curve for the product, $Q = d(P)$. And since $MU/\lambda = \lambda(Q)$ incorporates both the substitution and income effects, its slope is positive in the unusual case of a Giffen product.

A marginal rate of substitution curve of a product for money and the supply curve of the product facing a perfectly competitive purchaser are depicted in Figure 4.6. To analyze the equilibrium principle via this figure, given price P', the purchaser's utility is maximized at that quantity consumed of the product (Q') at which the marginal rate of substitution of the product for money (MU'/λ') is equal to the price of the product P'. For given P', the utility of the Q' unit is equal to the utility of the money required to purchase that unit (that is, $MU' = P'\lambda'$). The Q' unit therefore maximizes his utility. Thus (P', Q') is one point on the demand curve of the purchaser. Since $MU'/\lambda' = P'$ at Q', this point is on his marginal rate of substitution curve of the product for money. The same is true of other points, such as (P'', Q'')

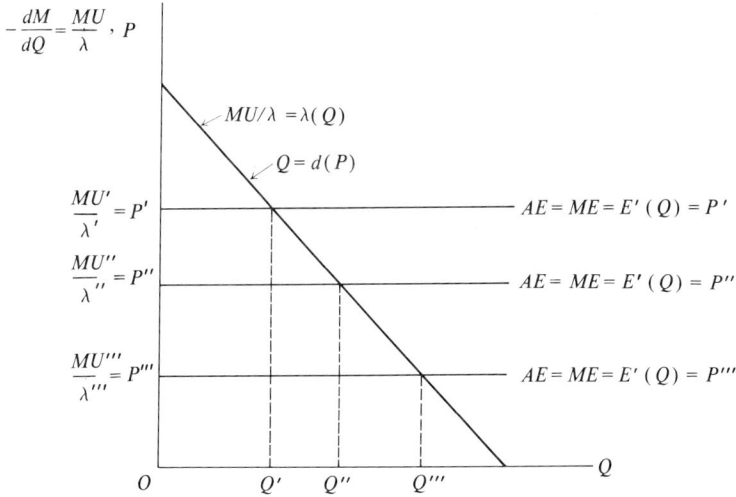

FIG. 4.6. Hypothetical marginal rate of substitution curve of a product for money

and (P''', Q'''), which are rationalized in the same way by shifting the supply curve facing the purchaser downward. Consequently, the purchaser's marginal rate of substitution curve of a product for money is his demand curve.

Law of Demand for a Product of a Purchaser

According to the law of demand for a product of a purchaser, the quantity of a product a purchaser is willing to purchase (Q) per unit of time is a decreasing function of the price of the product (P): quantity varies inversely with price—$\Delta Q/\Delta P < 0$. According to the law of decreasing marginal rate of substitution of a product for money, the marginal rate of substitution of a product for money is a decreasing function of quantity consumed: marginal rate of substitution of a product for money varies inversely with quantity—$\Delta(MU/\lambda)/\Delta Q < 0$. According to the principle of equilibrium of a perfectly competitive purchaser, when a purchaser is in equilibrium, in effect he is allocating his money income in such a way that the marginal rate of substitution of each product for money equals the price of the product: $MU/\lambda = P$. Thus the rationale of the law of demand is the law of decreasing marginal rate of substitution of a product for money and the principle of equilibrium of a perfectly competitive purchaser: a demand curve has a negative slope because the corresponding marginal rate of substitution curve of the product for money has a negative slope and the consumer-purchaser is assumed to maximize his utility.

Price of a Substitute

The quantity of a product a purchaser is willing to purchase (Q) per unit of time is a function of the price of the product (P): $Q = d(P)$. However, Q is also a function of the price of a substitute product in consumption (P_s). Thus the price of a substitute is a parameter of $Q = d(P)$.

To ascertain the sign of the difference quotient $\Delta Q/\Delta P_s$, consider the equilibrium principle

$$\frac{MU_1}{\lambda} = P_1 \quad \text{and} \quad \frac{MU_2}{\lambda} = P_2$$

The purchaser is in disequilibrium when

$$\frac{MU_1}{\lambda} = P_1 \quad \text{and} \quad \frac{MU_2}{\lambda} > P_2$$

because of a decrease in P_2. To regain equilibrium, he substitutes Q_2 for money—that is, he gives up money to consume more of Q_2. Aside from the effect of this substitution on MU_2 and λ, each additional unit of Q_2 induces a decrease in MU_1 because of the substitute relationship between Q_1 and Q_2, and hence

$$\frac{MU_1}{\lambda} < P_1$$

To be in equilibrium at the given value of P_1, he must increase MU_1/λ. According to the law of decreasing marginal rate of substitution of a product for money, MU_1/λ varies inversely with Q_1. Thus, to regain equilibrium, he consumes less of Q_1. Therefore, when Q_1 and Q_2 are substitutes in consumption, less of Q_1 is consumed when more of Q_2 is consumed as P_2 decreases. By letting Q_1 be Q and P_2 be P_s, the conclusion follows that $\Delta Q/\Delta P_s > 0$.[2]

Price of a Complement

The quantity of a product a purchaser is willing to purchase (Q) per unit of time is also a function of the price of a complementary product in consumption (P_c). Thus the price of a complement is a parameter of $Q = d(P)$.

To ascertain the sign of the difference quotient $\Delta Q/\Delta P_c$, consider the equilibrium principle

$$\frac{MU_1}{\lambda} = P_1 \quad \text{and} \quad \frac{MU_2}{\lambda} = P_2$$

THE DEMAND FUNCTION FOR A PRODUCT OF A PURCHASER

The purchaser is in disequilibrium when

$$\frac{MU_1}{\lambda} = P_1 \quad \text{and} \quad \frac{MU_2}{\lambda} > P_2$$

because of a decrease in P_2. To regain equilibrium, he substitutes Q_2 for money—that is, he gives up money to consume more of Q_2. Aside from the effect of this substitution on MU_2 and λ, each additional unit of Q_2 induces an increase in MU_1 because of the complementary relationship between Q_1 and Q_2, and hence

$$\frac{MU_1}{\lambda} > P_1$$

To be in equilibrium at the given value of P_1, he must decrease MU_1/λ. According to the law of decreasing marginal rate of substitution of a product for money, MU_1/λ varies inversely with Q_1. Thus, to regain equilibrium, he consumes more of Q_1. Therefore, when Q_1 and Q_2 are complements in consumption, more of Q_1 is consumed when more of Q_2 is consumed as P_2 decreases. By letting Q_1 be Q and P_2 be P_c, the conclusion follows that $\Delta Q/\Delta P_c < 0$.[3]

Purchaser's Money Income

The quantity of a product a purchaser is willing to purchase (Q) per unit of time is also a function of his money income (Y); thus Y is a parameter of $Q = d(P)$. The relation between Q and Y may be analyzed via the equilibrium principle $MU/\lambda = P$. In the first case, assume that Q and M (money) are not related in consumption—that MU is a constant function of M and λ is a constant function of Q. Then, when the purchaser's money income (Y) increases, λ decreases since M has increased, so that $MU/\lambda > P$. To regain equilibrium, he gives up money for the product; that is, he substitutes Q for M. Each successive unit increase in Q decreases MU, and each successive unit decrease in M increases λ, until eventually $MU/\lambda = P$. Since he is now purchasing more of the product than before the increase in Y that initially increased M, Q is an increasing (positive) function of Y—$\Delta Q/\Delta Y > 0$.

In the second case, assume that Q and M are complements in consumption—that MU is an increasing function of M and λ is an increasing function of Q. Then, when Y increases, λ decreases and MU increases since M has increased, so that $MU/\lambda > P$. To regain equilibrium, he substitutes Q for M. Each successive unit increase in Q decreases MU and increases λ, and each successive unit decrease in M increases λ and decreases MU, until eventually $MU/\lambda = P$. Since he is now purchasing more of the product than before the increase in Y that initially increased M, Q again is an increasing (positive) function of Y—$\Delta Q/\Delta Y > 0$. A product is called a normal product when the quantity purchased of the product increases as the purchaser's income increases.

In the third case, assume that Q and M are substitutes in consumption— that MU is a decreasing function of M and λ is a decreasing function of Q. Then, when Y increases, λ decreases and MU decreases since M has increased, so that $MU/\lambda \gtreqless P$. If the decrease in MU equals the decrease in λ, $MU/\lambda = P$; the purchaser buys the same quantity of the product as before the increase in Y, and hence $\Delta Q/\Delta Y = 0$. If the decrease in MU is less than the decrease in λ, $MU/\lambda > P$; the purchaser buys a larger quantity of the product than before the increase in Y, and hence $\Delta Q/\Delta Y > 0$. If the decrease in MU is greater than the decrease in λ, $MU/\lambda < P$; the purchaser buys a smaller quantity of the product than before the increase in Y, and hence $\Delta Q/\Delta Y < 0$. A product is called an inferior product when the quantity purchased of the product decreases as the purchaser's income increases.

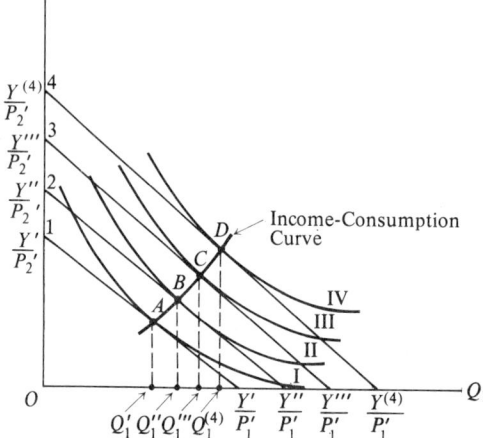

FIG. 4.7. Quantity purchased of a product as an increasing function of a purchaser's money income (normal product case)

The relation between Q and Y may also be analyzed via iso-utility curves by restricting the purchaser to two products (Q_1 and Q_2) and by using the budget constraint that expenditure (E) equals income (Y). The purchaser initially is in equilibrium at point A in Figure 4.7. Now, let his money income (and hence his expenditure) increase from Y' to Y'', while holding the prices of the products constant at P'_1 and P'_2. Then the iso-expenditure curve of Figure 4.7 shifts parallel to itself to the right, for with the larger income and the same prices, the purchaser can take more of Q_1 and Q_2. The new equilibrium point is B; other points such as C and D are derived in the same way. The curve connecting the equilibrium points is called the income–consumption curve. In Figure 4.7, the income–consumption curve has a positive slope throughout its designated length: as Y increases, Q_1 increases, and hence

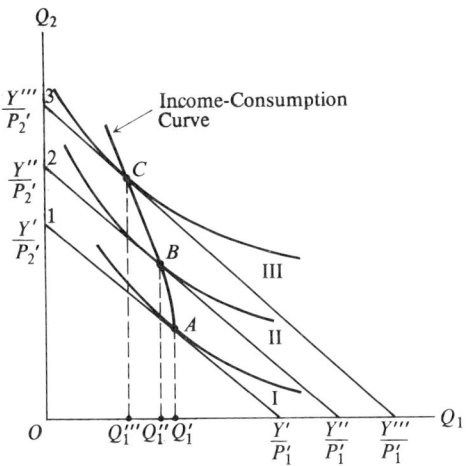

FIG. 4.8. Quantity purchased of a product as a decreasing function of a purchaser's money income (inferior product case)

$\Delta Q_1/\Delta Y > 0$. Thus this product is a normal product. But in Figure 4.8, the income–consumption curve has a negative slope: as Y increases, Q_1 decreases, and hence $\Delta Q/\Delta Y < 0$. Thus this product is an inferior product.

SUMMARY

The quantity of a product a perfectly competitive purchaser is willing to purchase (Q) per unit of time is a function of the price of the product (P), the price of a substitute product (P_s), the price of a complementary product (P_c), and his money income (Y), given the parameter of his taste for products.[4]

In general, given the parameters P_s, P_c, and Y (and taste), Q varies inversely with its price (P) in accordance with the law of demand for a product of a purchaser: $\Delta Q/\Delta P < 0$. The total effect on Q of a change in P is the substitution effect plus the income effect. The substitution effect on Q of a change in P is always consistent with the law of demand for a product of a purchaser. The income effect on Q of a change in P is consistent with this law in the case of a normal product, and inconsistent with it in the cases of inferior and Giffen products; but only Giffen products are exceptions to this law. The substitution effect is depicted by the marginal rate of substitution curve of a product for a product, which is derived from a given iso-utility curve. The greater the degree that two products are substitutes in consumption, the flatter is the curve and hence the greater is the substitution effect. The income effect is depicted by a movement to a higher iso-utility curve. The geometrical presentation of the income effect is usually grossly overstated, for the importance of the income effect varies directly with the percentage of a purchaser's income currently expended on the product, and in most cases this is relatively small. The total effect is depicted by the marginal rate of substitution curve of the product for money, which is the purchaser's demand curve for the product.

In general, given the parameters P, P_c, and Y (and taste), the quantity purchased of a product a purchaser is willing to purchase (Q) per unit of time varies directly with the price of a substitute product (P_s): $\Delta Q/\Delta P_s > 0$. Similarly, in general, given P, P_s, and Y (and taste), Q varies inversely with P_c: $\Delta Q/\Delta P_c < 0$. Lastly, given the parameters P, P_s, P_c and (taste) Q varies directly with Y if Q and Y are complements in consumption: $\Delta Q/\Delta Y > 0$. But $\Delta Q/\Delta Y \gtreqless 0$ if Q and Y are substitutes in consumption. The purchaser's income–consumption curve has a positive slope in the case of a normal product (that is, when $\Delta Q/\Delta Y > 0$) and a negative slope in the case of an inferior product (that is, when $\Delta Q/\Delta Y < 0$).

To conclude, from now on the quantity of a product a purchaser is willing to purchase (Q) per unit of time is said to be a decreasing function of its price (P) and the price of a complement (P_c), and an increasing function of the price of a substitute (P_s), given his money income (Y) and his taste for products.[5] This conclusion is consistent with the substitution effect; when it is inconsistent with the income effect, the substitution effect in general will dominate the income effect. Moreover, in those rare cases in which this conclusion is not acceptable with respect to an individual purchaser, it may very well be acceptable with respect to all purchasers, for what is true of one individual may not be true in the aggregate for all individuals. Thus, in the aggregate, $\Delta Q/\Delta P < 0$, $\Delta Q/\Delta P_s > 0$, and $\Delta Q/\Delta P_c < 0$.

Questions

1. List the principles of the theory of demand for a product that are of primary importance. How do you account for the position of the law of demand for a product of a purchaser in this list? Verbalize this principle of economics. It is based upon what other principles of economics?

2. Use iso-expenditure and iso-utility curves to analyze the law of demand for (a) a normal product, (b) an inferior product, and (c) a Giffen product. In each analysis, derive the price–consumption and demand curves, and identify the substitution, income, and total effects on the quantity purchased of the product of a change in its price.

3. Analyze the substitution effect via marginal rate of substitution curves of a product for a product.

4. Use the equilibrium principle $MU/\lambda = P$ and the law of decreasing marginal rate of substitution of a product for money to analyze the difference quotients $\Delta Q/\Delta P < 0$, $\Delta Q/\Delta P_s > 0$, $\Delta Q/\Delta P_c < 0$, and $\Delta Q/\Delta Y \gtreqless 0$.

5. Analyze the principle that $\Delta Q/\Delta Y \gtreqless 0$ via (a) the equilibrium principle that $MU/\lambda = P$ and (b) income–consumption curves. Include a discussion of products related in consumption in your analysis.

NOTES

[1] This notation is symbolic of the substitution and income effects, and is not to be considered in any way as a mathematical presentation of the two effects. For a mathematical presentation, see A. C. Chiang, *Fundamental Methods of Mathematical Economics* (New York: McGraw-Hill Book Company, 1967), pp. 361–369.

[2] Professor Hicks defines substitutes and complements in terms of the substitution effect, rather than the total effect. (See J. R. Hicks, *Value and Capital*, 2nd ed. (London: Oxford University Press, 1946), Chapter III.) Specifically, Q_1 and Q_2 are substitutes if (a) the marginal rate of substitution of Q_1 for money ($-\Delta M/\Delta Q_1 = MU_1/\lambda$) decreases when (b) Q_2 is substituted for money in (c) such a way as to leave the purchaser at the same level of utility as before the decrease in price of Q_2. By restricting the purchaser to the same level of utility, part (c) of this definition eliminates the income effect, for the income effect is a change in the level of utility. Therefore, between two substitutes, $\Delta Q_1/\Delta P_2 > 0$. Part (b) says that the purchaser gives up money to obtain Q_2 when the price of Q_2 decreases. Part (a) *may be interpreted to say* that, when more Q_2 is purchased as P_2 decreases, MU_1 decreases autonomously of Q_1, thereby decreasing the ratio MU_1/λ and hence decreasing the ratio $-\Delta M/\Delta Q_1$. Given this interpretation, MU_1 is a decreasing function of Q_2 when Q_1 and Q_2 are substitutes in consumption—a definition of substitutes introduced in Chapter 2. Since in this context MU_1/λ decreases when Q_2 increases, and since $MU_1/\lambda = P_1$ when the purchaser is in equilibrium, to remain in equilibrium at the given value of P_1 he must increase MU_1/λ by decreasing Q_1. Thus, in this context, the quantity purchased of Q_1 decreases when the quantity purchased of Q_2 increases. Consequently, in the same context, Q_1 and Q_2 are substitutes if, when more Q_2 is purchased, less Q_1 is purchased.

[3] In the definition of substitutes and complements given by Hicks (*ibid.*), money (M) is a proxy variable for a third product, Q_3. Specifically, Q_1 and Q_2 are complements if (a) the marginal rate of substitution of Q_1 for money ($-\Delta M/\Delta Q_1 = MU_1/\lambda$) increases when (b) Q_2 is substituted for money in (c) such a way as to leave the purchaser at the same level of utility as before the decrease in price of Q_2. By restricting the purchaser to the same level of utility, part (c) of this definition eliminates the income effect, for the income effect is a change in the level of utility. Therefore, between two complements, $\Delta Q_1/\Delta P_2 < 0$. Part (b) says that the purchaser gives up money to obtain Q_2 when the price of Q_2 decreases. Part (a) *may be interpreted to say* that, when more Q_2 is purchased as P_2 decreases, MU_1 increases autonomously of Q_1, thereby increasing the ratio MU_1/λ and hence increasing the ratio $-\Delta M/\Delta Q_1$. Given this interpretation, MU_1 is an increasing function of Q_2 when Q_1 and Q_2 are complements in consumption—a definition of complements introduced in Chapter 2. Since in this context MU_1/λ increases when Q_2 increases, and since $MU_1/\lambda = P_1$ when the purchaser is in equilibrium, to remain in equilibrium at the given value of P_1 he must decrease MU_1/λ by increasing Q_1. Thus, in this context, the quantity purchased of Q_1 increases when the quantity purchased of Q_2 increases. Consequently, Q_1 and Q_2 are complements if, when more Q_2 is purchased, more Q_1 is purchased—a conclusion that is true only in the context of an equilibrium model of three or more products.

[4] By definition, Q increases with an increase in the purchaser's taste for the product; Q may also vary with expected changes in prices and his income (see J. R. Hicks, *Value and Capital*, *op. cit.*, pp. 203–206).

chapter 5

The Market Demand Function for a Product

"The market demand function for a product" is the name of the relation between the aggregate quantity of a product purchasers are willing to purchase (Q_d) per unit of time and the price of the product (P), the price of a substitute product (P_s), the price of a complementary product (P_c), and the aggregate money income of purchasers (Y_d). The parameters of this function are the size of a given population and the aggregate taste for the product of the population, which is related to the age, sex, race, religion, and nationality composition of the population. By treating P_s, P_c, and Y_d as parameters, this function is reduced to a relation between Q_d and P, which is depicted by the market demand curve for the product. The market demand curve for a product thus shows how the aggregate quantity of the product purchasers are willing to purchase (Q_d) per unit of time varies with the price of the product (P) ceteris paribus: $Q_d = D(P)$.

Law of Market Demand for a Product

The market demand curve for a product depicts the law of market demand for a product. According to this law, Q_d varies inversely with P: $\Delta Q_d/\Delta P < 0$. In part, the rationale of the law of market demand for a product ($\Delta Q_d/\Delta P < 0$) is the law of demand for a product of a purchaser ($\Delta Q/\Delta P < 0$). As seen in Figure 5.1, which depicts hypothetical data presented in Table 5.1, demand curves of individual purchasers may be aggregated into the market demand curve by summing the quantity each purchaser is willing to purchase at each given price of the product, holding P_s, P_c, and Y_d constant. In addition to this rationale, however, aggregate quantity varies inversely with price if for any reason the *number* of purchasers from a given population increases as price decreases. In particular, price decreases may attract new purchasers from the lower income classes who previously had not purchased any of the product. Also, because of their relatively low taste for the product, purchasers of all income classes may not have a demand for the product until its price decreases. In other words, as seen in Figure 5.1, the quantity each purchaser *currently* in the market is willing to purchase increases as the price decreases;

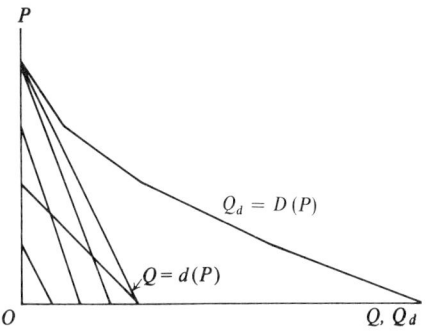

FIG. 5.1. Hypothetical market demand curve for a product

and the price and quantity intercepts of the demand curves of purchasers may differ because of differences in taste and income in such a way that the *number* of purchasers increases as the price decreases.

TABLE 5.1: Hypothetical market demand curve for a product

P	Q	Q	Q	Q	Q	Q_d
0	8	4.00	8	2	6.00	28.00
1	7	3.33	6	1	5.25	22.58
2	6	2.67	4	0	4.50	17.17
3	5	2.00	2	0	3.75	12.75
4	4	1.33	0	0	3.00	8.33
5	3	0.67	0	0	2.25	5.92
6	2	0	0	0	1.50	3.50
7	1	0	0	0	0.75	1.75
8	0	0	0	0	0	0

Change in Demand and Change in Quantity Demanded

The aggregate quantity of a product purchasers are willing to purchase (Q_d) per unit of time at various prices of the product (P) is called the market demand for the product. A given market demand curve, $Q_d = D(P)$, depicts the aggregate quantity of a product purchasers are willing to purchase (Q_d) per unit of time at various prices of the product (P). Thus $Q_d = D(P)$ represents a given market demand. For this reason, (1) a change in price of the product (P) does not effect a change in (market) demand for the product, $Q_d = D(P)$. Instead, a change in price of the product (P) is said to effect a change in (market) quantity demanded of the product. Changes in quantity demanded of the product, therefore, are depicted by movements along a given demand curve as price of the product (P) changes. (2) A change in P_s, P_c, or Y_d does effect a change in demand for the product, $Q_d = D(P)$; for at any given value of P, a change in P_s, P_c, or Y_d effects a change in Q_d and hence $Q_d = D(P)$. Changes in demand for the product, therefore, are depicted by shifts in the market demand curve, $Q_d = D(P)$, as P_s, P_c, or Y_d change.

The conclusion follows from this analysis that Q_d may be called three different things. (1) Q_d is the aggregate quantity of a product purchasers are willing to purchase. (2) When Q_d changes because of a change in P (holding P_s, P_c, and Y_d constant), Q_d may be called quantity demanded of the product, for quantity demanded is a function of P. (3) When Q_d changes because of a change in P_s, P_c, or Y_d (holding P constant), Q_d may be called demand for the product, for demand is a function of P_s, P_c, and Y_d.

Demand for a Product as a Function of the Price of a Substitute

As seen in Figure 5.2a, the quantity demanded of a product (for example, coffee) per unit of time is a decreasing function of the price of the product ceteris paribus: $\Delta Q_d/\Delta P < 0$. And as seen in Figure 5.2b, the demand for coffee (Q_d) per unit of time is an increasing function of the price of a substitute product (for example, tea) ceteris paribus: $\Delta Q_d/\Delta P_s > 0$. As may be seen by an analysis of these two functions, corresponding to each price of tea is a different demand curve for coffee. Since Q_d is plotted on the horizontal axis in Figures 5.2a and 5.2b, the relation between the price of tea and the demand curve for coffee may be analyzed by mapping upward from Figure 5.2b into Figure 5.2a. In Figure 5.2b, an increase in the price of tea from P'_s to P''_s induces an increase in demand for coffee from Q'_d to Q''_d, as depicted by a movement upward along the $Q_d = a(P|P')$ curve. In Figure 5.2a, Q'_d and Q''_d are associated with the same price of coffee (P'). Thus, as depicted by the $Q_d = D(P|P'_s)$ and $Q_d = D(P|P''_s)$ curves, with the increase in P_s from P'_s to P''_s, the demand curve for coffee shifts parallel to itself to the right to portray the increase in Q_d from Q'_d to Q''_d. To generalize, market demand for a product increases as the price of a substitute product increases and decreases as the price of a substitute product decreases ceteris paribus. The negatively-sloped market demand curve for a product thus shifts to the right as price of a substitute product increases and to the left as the price of a substitute decreases.

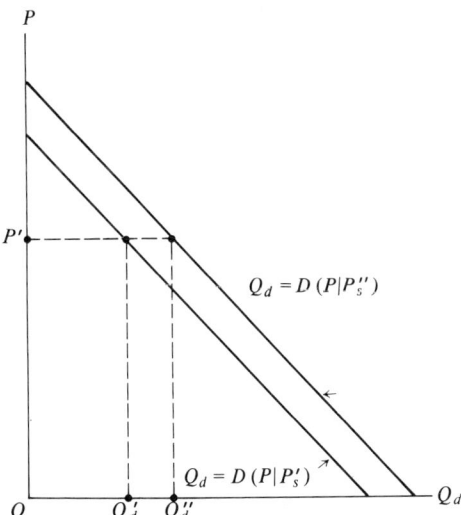

FIG. 5.2a. Quantity demanded of a product varies inversely with price of the product

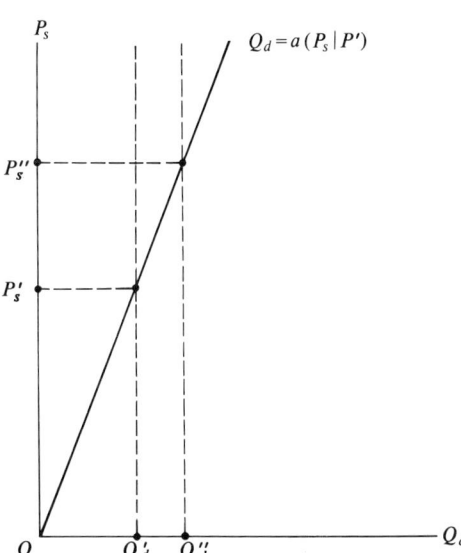

FIG. 5.2b. Demand for a product varies directly with price of a substitute

Demand for a Product as a Function of the Price of a Complement

As seen in Figure 5.3a, the quantity demanded of coffee per unit of time is a decreasing function of the price of coffee. And as seen in Figure 5.3b, the demand for coffee (Q_d) per unit of time is a decreasing function of price of a

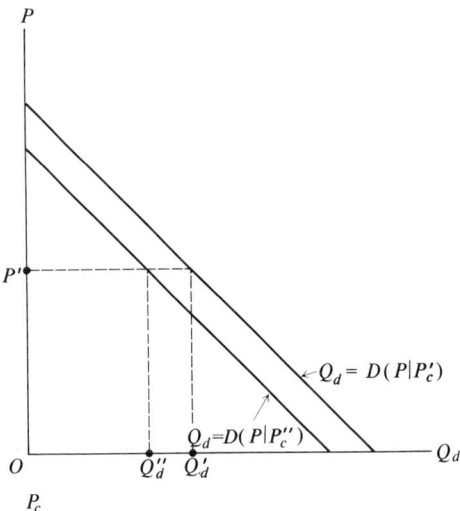

FIG. 5.3a. Quantity demanded of a product varies inversely with price of the product

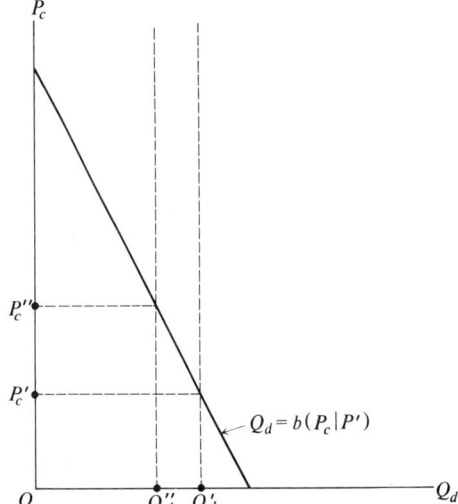

FIG. 5.3b. Demand for a product varies inversely with price of a complement

complementary product (for example, cream) ceteris paribus: $\Delta Q_d/\Delta P_c < 0$. In this diagram, the price of cream (P_c) is measured on the vertical axis, and the market demand for coffee (Q_d) is measured on the horizontal axis. In Figure 5.3b, an increase in the price of cream from P'_c to P''_c induces a decrease in the market demand for coffee from Q'_d to Q''_d. In Figure 5.3a, Q'_d and Q''_d are associated with the same price of coffee (P'). Thus, with the increase in P_c from P'_c to P''_c, the demand curve for coffee has shifted to the left to portray the decrease in Q_d from Q'_d to Q''_d. To generalize, the market demand for a product decreases as price of a complementary product increases and increases as price of a complement decreases ceteris paribus. The

Demand for a Product as a Function of Aggregate Money Income of Purchasers

To repeat, the market quantity demanded of a product per unit of time is a decreasing function of the price of the product, as depicted also in Figures 5.4a and 5.5a: $\Delta Q/\Delta P < 0$. As seen in Figure 5.4b, in the case of a normal product, the market demand for the product is an increasing function of the aggregate money income of purchasers: $\Delta Q/\Delta Y_d > 0$. But in the case of an inferior product, as seen in Figure 5.5b, the market demand for the

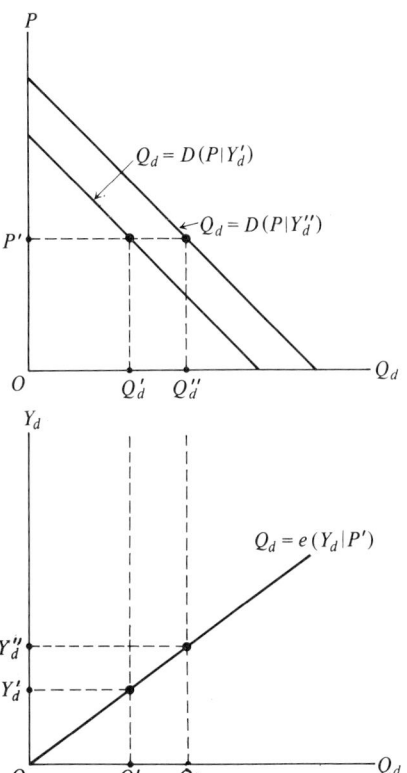

FIG. 5.4a. Quantity demanded of a product varies inversely with price of the product

FIG. 5.4b. Demand for a normal product varies directly with aggregate money income of purchasers

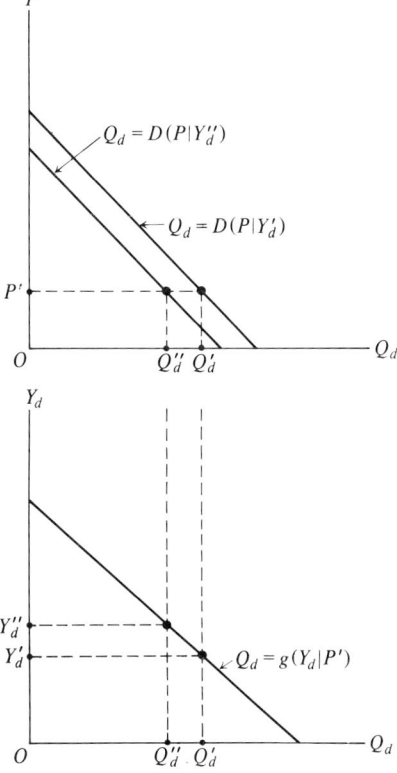

FIG. 5.5a. Quantity demanded of a product varies inversely with price of the product

FIG. 5.5b. Demand for an inferior product varies inversely with aggregate money income of purchasers

product is a decreasing function of the aggregate money income of purchasers: $\Delta Q/\Delta Y_d < 0$.

In Figure 5.4b, an increase in the aggregate money income of purchasers from Y'_d to Y''_d induces an increase in the market demand for the product from Q'_d to Q''_d. In Figure 5.4a, Q'_d and Q''_d are associated with the same price of the product (P'). Thus, with the increase in Y_d from Y'_d to Y''_d, the demand curve for the normal product has shifted to the right. To generalize, market demand for a normal product increases as aggregate money income of purchasers increases and decreases as aggregate money income of purchasers decreases. The negatively-sloped market demand curve of a normal product shifts to the right as aggregate money income of purchasers increases and to the left as aggregate money income of purchasers decreases.

In Figure 5.5b, an increase in Y_d from Y'_d to Y''_d induces a decrease in Q_d from Q'_d to Q''_d. In Figure 5.5a, Q'_d and Q''_d are associated with P'. Thus, with the increase in Y_d from Y'_d to Y''_d, the demand curve for the inferior product has shifted to the left. To generalize, market demand for an inferior product decreases as Y_d increases and increases as Y_d decreases. The negatively-sloped market demand curve of an inferior product shifts to the left as Y_d increases and to the right as Y_d decreases.

Elasticity of Market Demand for a Product

The slope of the market demand curve for a product (dQ_d/dP) is a measure of the responsiveness of quantity demanded (Q_d) to a change in price (P). The price elasticity of demand for a product, denoted by ε_d (ε = epsilon), which is the percentage change in the dependent variable (Q_d) divided by the percentage change in the independent variable (P), is a related measure of the responsiveness of quantity demanded to a change in price. The value of dQ_d/dP varies with the unit of measurement of Q_d and P; the value of ε_d does not vary with the unit of measurement, for a percentage change is a pure number and hence is not influenced by the unit of measurement. For this reason, the elasticity measure is often used in lieu of the slope measure. The elasticity measure is also used to explain the relationship between a set of total, marginal, and average curves.

When quantity demanded is varied by discrete amounts, the percentage change in quantity demanded is $\Delta Q_d/Q$; the percentage change in price is $\Delta P/P$; and ε_d is called arc elasticity, since it is calculated by using small finite changes in Q_d and P between two points on the curve. In this context, by dropping the d subscript of Q_d,

$$\varepsilon_d = \frac{\Delta Q/Q}{\Delta P/P} \quad \text{or} \quad \varepsilon_d = \frac{\Delta Q}{\Delta P} \cdot \frac{P}{Q} \quad \text{or} \quad \varepsilon_d = \frac{\Delta Q/\Delta P}{Q/P}$$

However, the percentage change in quantity demanded can be calculated by using as its base its initial value, its new value, or an average of both:

$$\frac{\Delta Q}{Q'}; \quad \frac{\Delta Q}{Q''}; \quad \frac{\Delta Q}{\frac{1}{2}(Q' + Q'')}$$

Therefore, arc elasticity may be calculated in various ways, each yielding a different measure of elasticity:

$$\varepsilon_d = \frac{\Delta Q/Q'}{\Delta P/P'}; \quad \varepsilon_d = \frac{\Delta Q/Q''}{\Delta P/P''}; \quad \varepsilon_d = \frac{\Delta Q/[\frac{1}{2}(Q' + Q'')]}{\Delta P/[\frac{1}{2}(P' + P'')]};$$

$$\varepsilon_d = \frac{\Delta Q/(Q' + Q'')}{\Delta P/(P' + Q'')}$$

When quantity demanded varies by continuous amounts, the percentage change in quantity demanded is dQ_d/Q; the percentage change in price is dP/P; and ε_d is called point elasticity, since it is calculated by using infinitesimally small changes in Q_d and P at a point on the curve. In this context, by dropping the d subscript of Q_d,

(1) $\quad \varepsilon_d = \dfrac{dQ/Q}{dP/P} \quad$ or

(2) $\quad \varepsilon_d = \dfrac{dQ}{dP} \cdot \dfrac{P}{Q} \quad$ or

(3) $\quad \varepsilon_d = \dfrac{dQ/dP}{Q/P}$

Price Elasticity and Aggregate Expenditure on a Product

With respect to formula (1), the market demand curve for a product is said to be perfectly elastic at the point(s) at which the numerical value of price elasticity of market demand approaches infinity, denoted by $|\varepsilon_d| \to \infty$. In this case, a percentage change in quantity demanded is related to a zero percentage change in price, since P does not change as Q_d changes:

$$|\varepsilon_d| \to \infty \quad \text{as} \quad \frac{dP}{P} \to 0$$

Market demand is said to be elastic at the point(s) at which the numerical value of elasticity is greater than one, denoted by $|\varepsilon_d| > 1$. In this case, a percentage increase in quantity demanded is greater numerically than a percentage decrease in price, and hence aggregate expenditure on the product (PQ) increases as its price decreases:

$$|\varepsilon_d| > 1 \quad \text{since} \quad \left|\frac{dQ}{Q}\right| > \left|\frac{dP}{P}\right|$$

Conversely, a percentage decrease in quantity demanded is greater numerically than a percentage increase in price, and hence aggregate expenditure on the product (PQ) decreases as its price increases.

Market demand is said to be unitary elastic at the point(s) at which the numerical value of elasticity is equal to one, denoted by $|\varepsilon_d| = 1$. In this case, a percentage increase (decrease) in quantity demanded is equal numerically to a percentage decrease (increase) in price, and hence aggregate expenditure on the product (PQ) does not change as its price changes:

$$|\varepsilon_d| = 1 \quad \text{since} \quad \left|\frac{dQ}{Q}\right| = \left|\frac{dP}{P}\right|$$

Market demand is said to be inelastic at the point(s) at which $|\varepsilon_d| < 1$. In this case, a percentage increase in quantity demanded is less numerically than a percentage decrease in price, and hence aggregate expenditure on the product (PQ) decreases as its price decreases:

$$|\varepsilon_d| < 1 \quad \text{since} \quad \left|\frac{dQ}{Q}\right| < \left|\frac{dP}{P}\right|$$

Conversely, a percentage decrease in quantity demanded is less numerically than a percentage increase in price, and hence aggregate expenditure on the product (PQ) increases as its price increases.

Lastly, the market demand curve for a product is said to be perfectly inelastic at the point(s) at which $|\varepsilon_d| = 0$. In this case, a percentage change in price is related to a zero percentage change in quantity demanded, since Q does not change as P changes:

$$|\varepsilon_d| = 0 \quad \text{since} \quad \left|\frac{dQ}{Q}\right| = 0$$

Geometry of Price Elasticity of Market Demand

With respect to formula (3), by dropping the d subscript of Q_d, the elasticity of Q with respect to P at a point on a $Q = D(P)$ curve is equal to the instantaneous rate of change at that point (dQ/dP) divided by the ratio of the dependent variable (Q) to the independent variable (P):

$$\varepsilon_d = \frac{dQ/dP}{Q/P}$$

Therefore, $|\varepsilon_d| \gtreqless 1$ according to whether $|dQ/dP| \gtreqless |Q/P|$. The value of dQ/dP at a point on a $Q = D(P)$ curve is equal to the difference quotient ($\Delta Q/\Delta P$) of the tangent line at that point. The value of Q/P at the same point on the $Q = D(P)$ curve is equal to the difference quotient ($\Delta Q/\Delta P$) of the ray at that point. Consequently, ε_d may be determined geometrically at various points along any demand curve by dividing these two difference quotients. To generalize, in the lingo of economics, the elasticity of a total function, $Q = D(P)$, is the ratio of the marginal function, $dQ/dP = D'(P)$, to the average function, $Q/P = D(P)/P$.

For example, in Figure 5.6, the value of dQ/dP at point B on the demand

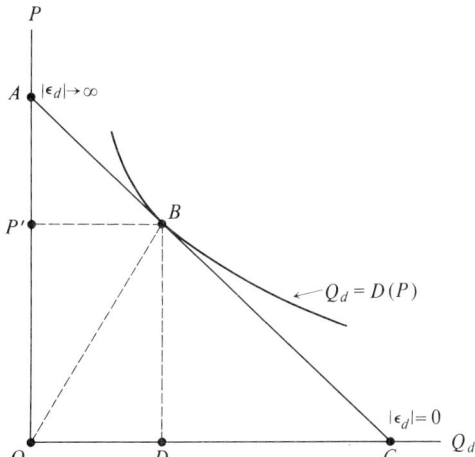

FIG. 5.6. Geometry of price elasticity of market demand

curve is equal to the difference quotient $(\Delta Q/\Delta P)$ of the tangent line AC at B:

$$\frac{dQ}{dP} = \frac{OC}{OA} = \frac{DC}{DB}$$

Similarly, the value of Q/P at point B on the demand curve is equal to the difference quotient $(\Delta Q/\Delta P)$ of the ray OB at B:

$$\frac{Q}{P} = \frac{OD}{DB}$$

Therefore, the value of ε_d at point B is the ratio DC/OD:

$$\frac{DC}{DB} \div \frac{OD}{DB} = \frac{DC}{DB} \cdot \frac{DB}{OD} = \frac{DC}{OD}$$

When $DC = OD$, $|\varepsilon_d| = 1$, for $|dQ/dP| = |Q/P|$: area BDC equals area BOD. In this case, B would be at the midpoint of the tangent line AC; thus, when $|\varepsilon_d| = 1$, $BC = BA$. When $DC > OD$, $|\varepsilon_d| > 1$, for $|dQ/dP| > |Q/P|$: area BDC is greater than area BOD. In this case, B would be above the midpoint of the tangent line AC, as it is in Figure 5.6; thus, when $|\varepsilon_d| > 1$, $BC > BA$. When $DC < OD$, $|\varepsilon_d| < 1$, for $|dQ/dP| < |Q/P|$: area BDC is

78   PRINCIPLES OF THE THEORY OF DEMAND FOR A PRODUCT

less than area *BOD*. In this case, *B* would be below the midpoint of the tangent line *AC*; thus, when $|\varepsilon_d| < 1$, $BC < BA$. In short,

$$|\varepsilon_d| = \frac{BC}{BA} \gtreqless 1$$

Price Elasticity Cases

With respect to formula (2), by dropping the *d* subscript of Q_d, the elasticity of *Q* with respect to *P* at a given point on the $Q = D(P)$ curve is equal to the instantaneous rate of change at that point (dQ/dP) multiplied by the ratio of the independent variable (*P*) to the dependent variable (*Q*):

$$\varepsilon_d = \frac{dQ}{dP} \cdot \frac{P}{Q}$$

If *Q* is a linear decreasing function of *P*, $Q = a - bP$ and $dQ/dP = -b$; hence

$$\varepsilon_d = \frac{-bP}{-bP + a}$$

In this case, the sign and value of ε_d depend upon the sign and value of the *a* and *b* parameter coefficients and the value of the independent variable (*P*). (In all cases $a \geqslant bP$.)

Consider the linear demand curve of Figure 5.7. At that value of *Q* at which the curve intersects the *Q* axis, demand is perfectly inelastic, for at that point $P = 0$; hence

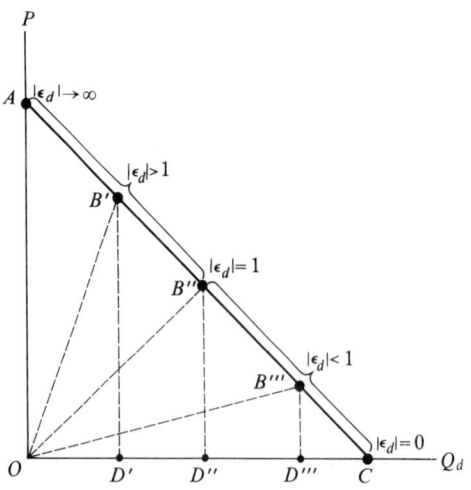

FIG. 5.7. Elasticity varies directly with price of the product

$$|\varepsilon_d| = \left|\frac{-b \cdot 0}{-b \cdot 0 + a}\right| = \frac{0}{a} = 0$$

At point B''', demand is inelastic, for at that point $D'''C < OD'''$ or $B'''C < B'''A$. Unitary elasticity occurs at a point (B'') halfway down the curve, for at the midpoint $D''C = OD''$ or $B''C = B''A$. At point B', demand is elastic, for at that point $D'C > OD'$ or $B'C > B'A$. At that value of P at which the curve intersects the P axis, demand is perfectly elastic, for at that point $Q = 0$; hence

$$|\varepsilon_d| = \frac{-bP}{0}$$

which is undefined. But $|\varepsilon_d|$ approaches infinity as Q approaches zero. To generalize, as P increases from zero, demand becomes more elastic (less inelastic) as it passes through the area of inelasticity on its way to unitary elasticity. As P continues to increase, demand enters the area of elasticity; finally, when P has increased to the extent that Q is zero, demand is perfectly elastic. To conclude, the numerical value of elasticity varies directly with the price of the product:

$$|\varepsilon_d| = \left|\frac{-bP}{-bP + a}\right| \quad \text{increases as } P \text{ increases}$$

Consider now the two linear demand curves of Figure 5.8. Both curves have the same Q intercept. Therefore, both curves have the same a para-

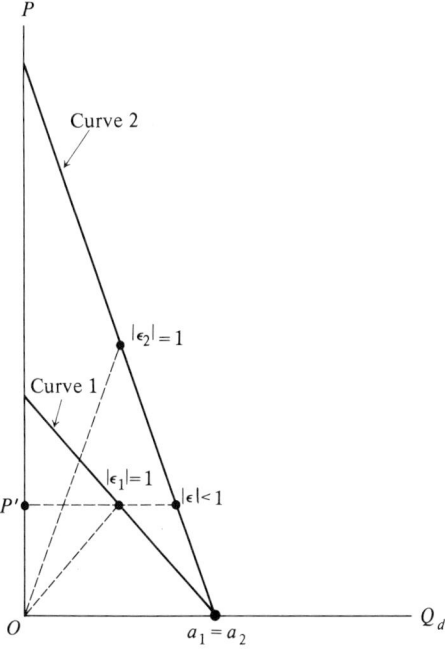

FIG. 5.8. Elasticity varies inversely with numerical value of dP/dQ and directly with numerical value of dQ/dP:

$$\left|\frac{dP_1}{dQ_1}\right| < \left|\frac{dP_2}{dQ_2}\right|; \left|\frac{dQ_1}{dP_1}\right| > \left|\frac{dQ_2}{dP_2}\right|; |\varepsilon_1| > |\varepsilon_2|$$

meter coefficient: $a_1 = a_2$. As the numerical value of dP_1/dQ_1 is less than the numerical value of dP_2/dQ_2, the numerical value of dQ_1/dP_1 is greater than the numerical value of dQ_2/dP_2. Therefore, the b parameter coefficient of curve 1 is greater than the b parameter coefficient of curve 2: $b_1 > b_2$. As seen in Figure 5.8, at any P value P', $|\varepsilon_1| > |\varepsilon_2|$:

$$\left|\frac{-b_1 P'}{-b_1 P' + a}\right| > \left|\frac{-b_2 P'}{-b_2 P' + a}\right| \quad \text{since} \quad b_1 > b_2$$

To conclude, the numerical value of elasticity varies inversely with the numerical value of dP/dQ, and directly with the numerical value of dQ/dP, of the demand curve. That is, with P on the vertical and Q on the horizontal if two curves have the same Q intercept, the steepest curve has the smallest numerical elasticity at any given price.

Consider now the two linear demand curves of Figure 5.9. Both curves

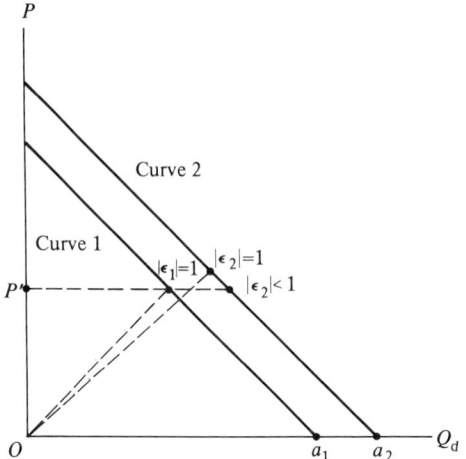

FIG. 5.9. Elasticity varies inversely with Q_d intercept of the demand curve

have the same slope. Therefore, both curves have the same b parameter coefficient: $b_1 = b_2$. The Q intercept of curve 1 is less that the Q intercept of curve 2. Therefore, the a parameter coefficient of curve 1 is less than the a parameter coefficient of curve 2: $a_1 < a_2$. As seen in Figure 5.9, at any P value P', $|\varepsilon_1| > |\varepsilon_2|$:

$$\left|\frac{-b_1 P'}{-b_1 P' + a_1}\right| > \left|\frac{-b_2 P'}{-b_2 P' + a_2}\right| \quad \text{since} \quad a_1 < a_2$$

To conclude, elasticity varies inversely with the Q intercept of the demand curve. That is, if two curves have the same slope, the curve lying closest to the point of origin has the greatest numerical elasticity at any given price.

Lastly, consider the three demand curves of Figure 5.10. According to

THE MARKET DEMAND FUNCTION FOR A PRODUCT

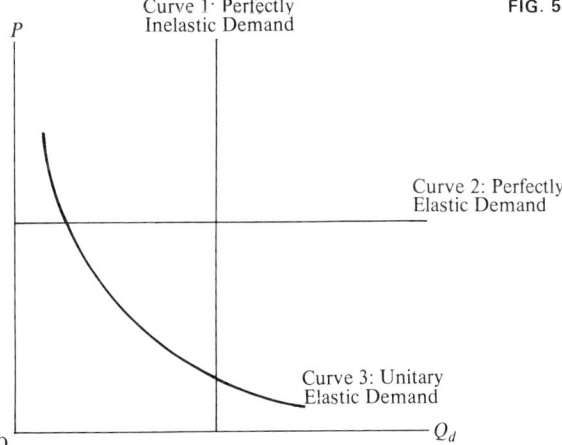

FIG. 5.10. Three other elasticity cases

curve 1, Q is a constant function of P. In this case, a percentage change in P is related to a zero percentage change in Q. Since Q does not vary with P, $\Delta Q = 0$, and hence demand is perfectly inelastic:

$$|\varepsilon_d| = \left|\frac{\Delta Q}{Q}\right| \div \left|\frac{\Delta P}{P}\right| = 0 \quad \text{since} \quad \Delta Q = 0$$

According to curve 2, P is a constant function of Q. In this case, a percentage change in Q is related to a zero percentage change in P. Since P does not vary with Q, $\Delta P = 0$, and hence $|\varepsilon_d|$ is undefined:

$$|\varepsilon_d| = \left|\frac{\Delta Q}{Q}\right| \div \left|\frac{\Delta P}{P}\right| \quad \text{is undefined when} \quad \Delta P = 0$$

However, by letting ΔP approach zero, rather than being zero, demand is perfectly (or infinitely) elastic:

$$|\varepsilon_d| = \left|\frac{\Delta Q}{Q}\right| \div \left|\frac{\Delta P}{P}\right| \to \infty \quad \text{as} \quad \Delta P \to 0$$

The demand curve depicted by curve 3 is a member of the set of curves having constant elasticity at every point. Curve 3 is a rectangular hyperbola. In this case, a percentage change in Q is always equal to a percentage change in P, and hence demand is unitary elastic at every point on the curve:

$$|\varepsilon_d| = \left|\frac{\Delta Q}{Q}\right| \div \left|\frac{\Delta P}{P}\right| = 1 \quad \text{since} \quad \left|\frac{\Delta Q}{Q}\right| = \left|\frac{\Delta P}{P}\right|$$

Price Cross Elasticity of Market Demand for a Product

In statistical studies and antitrust court cases, two products (Q_1 and Q_2) are classified as substitutes or complements according to the sign of their price cross elasticity of demand. Price cross elasticity is defined as the percentage change in demand for Q_1 divided by the related percentage change in price of Q_2:

$$\varepsilon_{12} = \frac{\Delta Q_1/Q_1}{\Delta P_2/P_2} \quad \text{or} \quad \varepsilon_{12} = \frac{\Delta Q_1}{\Delta P_2} \cdot \frac{P_2}{Q_1} \quad \text{or} \quad \varepsilon_{12} = \frac{\Delta Q_1/\Delta P_2}{Q_1/P_2}.$$

Since P_2/Q_1 is positive, $\varepsilon_{12} \gtreqless 0$ according to whether $\Delta Q_1/\Delta P_2 \gtreqless 0$. In the case of two substitutes in consumption, the demand for Q_1 per unit of time is an increasing (positive) function of the price of Q_2 ceteris paribus: $\Delta Q_1/\Delta P_2 > 0$. In the case of two complements in consumption, the demand for Q_1 per unit of time is a decreasing (negative) function of the price of Q_2 ceteris paribus: $\Delta Q_1/\Delta P_2 < 0$. Thus, products are classified as substitutes when their price cross elasticity is positive and as complements when their price cross elasticity is negative.

Income Elasticity of Market Demand for a Product

The curve expressing the relation between the demand for a product (Q_d) per unit of time and the aggregate money income of purchasers (Y_d) is sometimes called the income–demand curve. Such curves may be classified according to the concept of income elasticity of market demand for a product (ε_y). By dropping the d subscript of Q_d and Y_d,

$$\varepsilon_y = \frac{\Delta Q/Q}{\Delta Y/Y} \quad \text{or} \quad \varepsilon_y = \frac{\Delta Q}{\Delta Y} \cdot \frac{Y}{Q} \quad \text{or} \quad \varepsilon_y = \frac{\Delta Q/\Delta Y}{Q/Y}$$

If Q is a linear function of Y, $Q = \pm a \pm bY$ and $\Delta Q/\Delta Y = \pm b$; hence

$$\varepsilon_y = \frac{\pm bY}{\pm bY \pm a}$$

In this case, the sign and value of ε_y depend upon the sign and value of the a and b parameter coefficients and the value of the independent variable (Y).

In Figure 5.11, income elasticity is greater than unity along the relatively flat income–demand curve 1, the equation of which is $Q = -a + bY$ (where $a < bP$):

$$\varepsilon_y = \frac{bY}{bY - a} > 1 \quad \text{since} \quad bY > bY - a$$

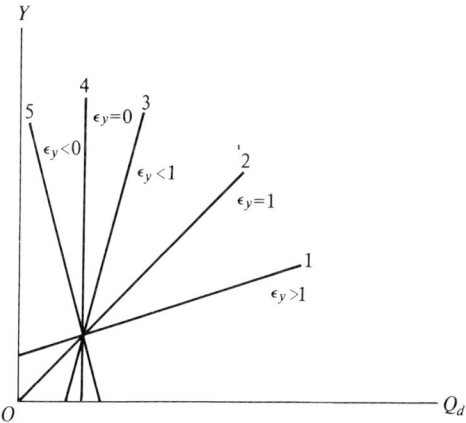

FIG. 5.11. Income–demand curves and income elasticity

In this case, income elasticity is said to be high, and the product is said to be a luxury. Income elasticity is equal to unity along the income–demand curve 2, which is a ray, the equation of which is $Q = bY$:

$$\varepsilon_y = \frac{bY}{bY} = 1 \quad \text{since} \quad a = 0$$

Income elasticity is less than unity along the relatively steep income–demand curve 3, the equation of which is $Q = a + bY$:

$$\varepsilon_y = \frac{bY}{bY + a} < 1 \quad \text{since} \quad bY < bY + a$$

In this case, income elasticity is said to be low, and the product is said to be a necessity. Income elasticity is zero along the vertical income–demand curve 4, the equation of which is $Q = a$:

$$\varepsilon_y = \frac{0}{a} = 0 \quad \text{since} \quad b = 0$$

Lastly, income elasticity is negative along the negatively-sloped income–demand curve 5, the equation of which is $Q = a - bY$ (where $a > bY$):

$$\varepsilon_y = \frac{-bY}{Q} < 0$$

SUMMARY

According to the law of market demand for a product, the aggregate quantity of a product purchasers are willing to purchase (Q_d) per unit of time is a decreasing function of price of the product (P) ceteris paribus. As P decreases, other things being equal, the quantity each purchaser *currently* in the market is willing to purchase per unit of time increases and the *number of purchasers* increases. The relation between Q_d and P is depicted by the market demand curve. Quantity demanded of the product (Q_d) varies inversely with its price (P). Demand for the product (Q_d) varies directly with price of a substitute (P_s) and inversely with the price of a complement (P_c). Demand for a normal product (Q_d) varies directly with the aggregate money income of purchasers (Y_d); but demand for an inferior product varies inversely with Y_d. In short, $\Delta Q_d/\Delta P < 0$; $\Delta Q_d/\Delta P_s > 0$; $\Delta Q_d/\Delta P_c < 0$; and $\Delta Q_d/\Delta Y_d \geq 0$.

The elasticity of Q_d with respect to P (ε_d) is

$$\frac{\Delta Q_d}{\Delta P} \cdot \frac{P}{Q_d}$$

Demand for a product may be perfectly elastic, elastic, unitary elastic, inelastic, or perfectly inelastic. The relationship between aggregate expenditure on the product (PQ) and its price (P) depends upon ε_d. If $|\varepsilon_d| = 1$, PQ is a constant function of P; if $|\varepsilon_d| > 1$, PQ is a decreasing function of P; if $|\varepsilon_d| < 1$, PQ is an increasing function of P. The value of ε_d at any point on a demand curve is equal to the difference quotient of the tangent line at that point divided by the difference quotient of the ray at the same point. The value of $|\varepsilon_d|$ varies directly with the price of the product along a linear demand curve. If two curves have the same Q_d intercept, the steepest curve has the smallest $|\varepsilon_d|$ at any given price of the product. If two curves have the same slope, the curve lying closest to the point of origin has the largest $|\varepsilon_d|$ at any given price of the product. Demand is perfectly elastic when the demand curve is a horizontal straight line, perfectly inelastic when the demand curve is a vertical straight line, and unitary elastic when the demand curve is a rectangular hyperbola.

The elasticity of Q_d with respect to P_s and P_c (ε_{12}) is called price cross elasticity of market demand for a product. In the case of two substitutes,

$$\varepsilon_{12} = \frac{\Delta Q_1}{\Delta P_2} \cdot \frac{P_2}{Q_1} > 0 \quad \text{or} \quad \varepsilon_{12} = \frac{\Delta Q_d}{\Delta P_s} \cdot \frac{P_s}{Q_d} > 0$$

In the case of two complements,

$$\varepsilon_{12} = \frac{\Delta Q_1}{\Delta P_2} \cdot \frac{P_2}{Q_1} < 0 \quad \text{or} \quad \varepsilon_{12} = \frac{\Delta Q_d}{\Delta P_c} \cdot \frac{P_c}{Q_d} < 0$$

The elasticity of Q_d with respect to Y_d (ε_y) is called income elasticity of market demand for a product. In the case of a normal product,

$$\varepsilon_y = \frac{\Delta Q_d}{\Delta Y_d} \cdot \frac{Y_d}{Q_d} > 0$$

THE MARKET DEMAND FUNCTION FOR A PRODUCT

In the case of an inferior product,

$$\varepsilon_y = \frac{\Delta Q_d}{\Delta Y_d} \cdot \frac{Y_d}{Q_d} < 0$$

If Q_d is a linear function of Y_d, the value of ε_y depends upon the sign and value of the parameter coefficients of the equation and the value of Y_d. A normal product with a high income elasticity (that is, $\varepsilon_y > 1$) is said to be a luxury. A normal product with a low income elasticity (that is, $\varepsilon_y < 1$) is said to be a necessity.

Questions

1. List the principles of the theory of demand for a product that are of primary importance. How do you account for the position of the law of market demand for a product in this list? Verbalize this principle of economics.

2. What is the rationale of the law of market demand for a product?

3. Distinguish between a change in demand and a change in quantity demanded.

4. Use diagrams to analyze shifts in a market demand curve due to changes in the price of a substitute.

5. Use diagrams to analyze shifts in a market demand curve due to changes in the price of a complement.

6. Use diagrams to analyze shifts in a market demand curve due to changes in aggregate money income of purchasers.

7. Define elasticity in general. Why is this concept used in economics? Define price elasticity of market demand for a product. Distinguish between arc and point price elasticity.

8. Relate price elasticity to aggregate expenditure on a product.

9. Relate price elasticity of any total function to the corresponding marginal and average functions. Apply this analysis to $Q_d = D(P)$ and show how elasticity may be ascertained at each point on this curve.

10. With reference to $Q_d = a - bP$, show that $|\varepsilon_d|$ is a function of a, b, and P. Discuss also the cases of perfect elasticity, perfect inelasticity, and unitary elasticity throughout the length of a market demand curve. With reference to $Q_d = a - bP$, state what is wrong with the statement, "the demand for the good is elastic."

11. Define price cross elasticity of market demand for a product and analyze the two cases of ε_{12}.

12. Define income elasticity of market demand for a product. With reference to $Q_d = \pm a \pm bY$, show that ε_y is a function of a, b, and Y, and analyze the various cases.

APPENDIX: Price Elasticity of Demand and the Price-Consumption Curve

The relation between the price elasticity of demand for a product of a purchaser, defined as $\varepsilon = (\Delta Q/\Delta P) \cdot (P/Q)$, and his expenditure on the product (PQ) as its price (P)

decreases and his quantity demanded (Q) increases may be analyzed via the price–consumption curves depicted in Figures 5.12, 5.13, and 5.14. For a description of this type of diagram, see the analysis of Figure 3.2, pages 46–47. In these diagrams, each point on a price–consumption curve denotes an equilibrium pair of values of quantities of a product (Q) and of money (M) corresponding to a price of the product (P). When a purchaser is in equilibrium, the distance from the horizontal line denoting his money income (Y) to the point of tangency of the iso-utility curve and the line of attainable combinations is the amount of his expenditure on the product.

As seen in Figure 5.12, as P decreases, the equilibrium value of Q increases from Q' to Q'', but the purchaser's expenditure on the product remains constant at $Y - M'$. Consequently, his demand for the product is unitary elastic: the percentage increase in quantity purchased equals numerically the percentage decrease in price, and hence his expenditure on the product (PQ) is constant. To conclude, his price–consumption curve has a zero slope when his demand is unitary elastic.

As seen in Figure 5.13, as P decreases, the equilibrium value of Q increases from Q' to Q'', and his expenditure on the product increases by the amount $M' - M''$. Consequently, his demand for the product is elastic: the percentage increase in quantity purchased is greater than the percentage decrease in price, and hence his expenditure on the product (PQ) increases. To conclude, his price–consumption curve has a negative slope when his demand is elastic.

As seen in Figure 5.14, as P decreases, the equilibrium value of Q increases from Q' to Q'', but his expenditure on the product decreases by the amount $M'' - M'$. Consequently, his demand for the product is inelastic: the percentage increase in quantity purchased is less numerically than the percentage decrease in price, and hence his expenditure on the product (PQ) decreases. To conclude, his price–consumption curve has a positive slope when his demand is inelastic.

THE MARKET DEMAND FUNCTION FOR A PRODUCT

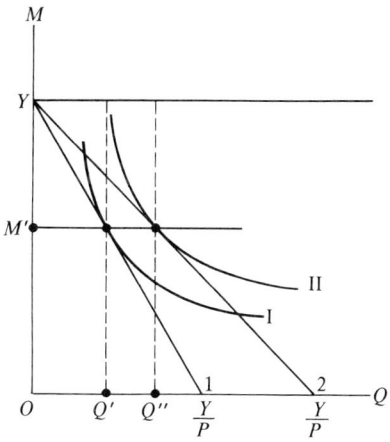

FIG. 5.12. Unitary elastic demand and the price–consumption curve

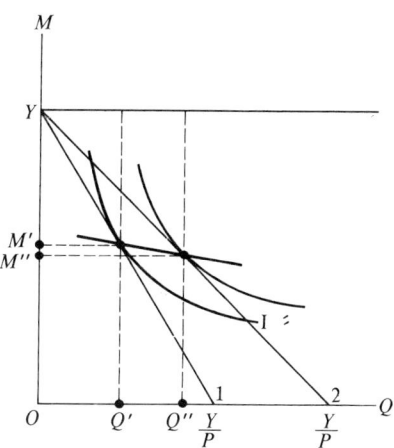

FIG. 5.13. Elastic demand and the price–consumption curve

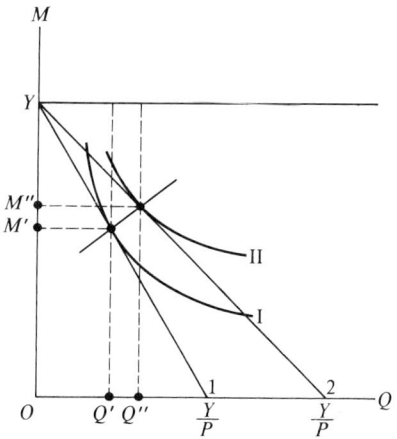

FIG. 5.14. Inelastic demand and the price–consumption curve

PART II

PRINCIPLES OF THE THEORY OF SUPPLY OF A PRODUCT

> *The long chains of simple and easy reasonings by means of which geometers are accustomed to reach the conclusions of their most difficult demonstrations had led me to imagine that all things to the knowledge of which men are capable are mutually connected in the same way*
>
> (René Descartes, *Discourse on Method*)

Seven principles of the economic theory of supply of a product are of primary importance. They are the laws of constant marginal revenue of a product to a perfectly competitive seller (producer) of products, decreasing marginal (physical) product of a factor of production to a user of factors who is subject to diminishing marginal returns, constant marginal factor cost of a factor of production to a perfectly competitive purchaser of factors, increasing marginal cost of a product to a producer of products who is subject to diminishing marginal returns, equilibrium of a seller, supply of a product of a seller, and market supply of a product.

Each of these principles of economics is a verbalization of an economic function (curve) or an inference drawn from an operation on a set of economic functions (curves). The law of constant marginal revenue of a product is a verbalization of a marginal revenue curve of a perfectly competitive seller—defined as a seller who can sell all he wishes per unit of time at the prevailing price ceteris paribus (see Chapter 6). The law of decreasing marginal product of a factor of production is a verbalization of a marginal product curve of a user of factors (see Chapter 7). The law of constant marginal factor cost of a factor of production is a verbalization of a marginal factor cost curve of a perfectly competitive purchaser—defined as a purchaser who can purchase all he wishes per unit of time at the prevailing price ceteris paribus (see Chapter 8). The law of increasing marginal cost of a product is a verbalization of a marginal cost curve of a producer (see Chapter 9). The principle of equilibrium of a seller is an inference drawn from an operation on the marginal cost and marginal revenue curves of a seller (see Chapter 10). The law of supply of a product of a seller is a verbalization of a supply curve of a seller (see Chapter 11). Finally, the law of market supply of a product is a verbalization of a market supply curve (see Chapter 12).

SELECTED READINGS

Viner, Jacob. "Cost Curves and Supply Curves," *Zeithschrift für Nationalökonomie*, III (September 1931), pp. 23–46. Reprinted in Kamerschen, D. R. (editor). *Readings in Microeconomics*. Cleveland, Ohio: The World Publishing Company, 1967, pp. 197–228.

Brumberg, R. E. "*Ceteris Paribus* for Supply Curves," *The Economic Journal*, LXIII (June 1953), pp. 462–467. Reprinted in Kamerschen, *ibid.*, pp. 229–234.

Leibenstein, Harvey. "The Proportionality Controversy and the Theory of Production," *The Quarterly Journal of Economics*, LXIX (November 1955), pp. 619–625. Reprinted in Kamerschen, *ibid.*, pp. 235–241.

Tangri, O. P. "Omissions in the Treatment of the Law of Variable Proportions," *American Economic Review*, LVI: 3 (June 1966), pp. 484–493. Reprinted in Kamerschen, *ibid.*, pp. 242–252.

Levenson, A. M. and B. S. Solon. "Returns to Scale and the Spacing of Isoquants," *American Economic Review*, LVI: 3 (June 1966), pp. 501–505. Reprinted in Kamerschen, *ibid.*, pp. 253–257.

Apel, Hans. "Marginal Cost Constancy and Its Implications," *The American Economic Review*. (December 1948), pp. 870–885. Reprinted in Kamerschen, *ibid.*, pp. 258–274.

Stigler, G. J. "What do Entrepreneurs Seek?" *Theory of Price*. New York: The Macmillan Company, 1952, pp. 148–150. Reprinted in Kamerschen, *ibid.*, pp. 275–277.

Nordquist, G. L. "The Breakup of the Maximization Principle," *Quarterly Review of Economics and Business*, V (Fall 1965), pp. 33–46. Reprinted in Kamerschen, *ibid.*, pp. 278–295.

Robinson, Joan. "Rising Supply Price," *Economica*, New Series; VIII (1941), pp. 1–8. Reprinted in The American Economic Association. *Readings in Price Theory*. Edited by George J. Stigler and Kenneth E. Boulding. Homewood, Illinois: Richard D. Irwin, Inc., 1952, pp. 233–241.

Ellis, H. S. and William Fellner. "External Economies and Diseconomies," *The American Economic Review*, XXXIII (1943), pp. 493–511. Reprinted in the American Economic Association. *Readings in Price Theory, ibid.*, pp. 242–263.

Staehle, Hans. "The Measurement of Statistical Cost Functions: An Appraisal of Some Recent Contributions," *The American Economic Review*, XXXII (1942), pp. 321–333. Reprinted in The American Economic Association. *Readings in Price Theory, ibid.*, pp. 264–279.

Cassells, J. M. "On the Law of Variable Proportions," *Explorations in Economics*. New York: McGraw-Hill Book Co., 1936, pp. 223–236. Reprinted in The American Economic Association. *Readings in the Theory of Income Distribution*. Edited by William Fellner and Bernard F. Haley. Homewood, Illinois: Richard D. Irwin, Inc., pp. 103–118.

Machlup, Fritz. "On the Meaning of the Marginal Product," *Explorations in Economics*. New York: McGraw-Hill Book Co., 1936, pp. 250–263. Reprinted in The American

Economic Association. *Readings in the Theory of Income Distribution*, ibid., pp. 158–174.

Robinson, Joan. "The Classification of Inventions," *Review of Economic Studies*, V (1937–1938), pp. 139–142. Reprinted in The American Economic Association. *Readings in the Theory of Income Distribution*, ibid., pp. 175–180.

Lange, Oscar, "A Note on Innovations," *Review of Economic Statistics*, XXV (1943), pp. 19–25. Reprinted in The American Economic Association. *Readings in the Theory of Income Distribution*, ibid., pp. 181–196.

chapter **6**

Revenue Functions

According to the law of constant marginal revenue of a product to a perfectly competitive seller, the revenue associated with selling an additional unit of a product does not vary with quantity sold per unit of time. Each additional unit sold of a product per unit of time adds the same amount to total revenue. Total revenue of a product increases at a constant rate as quantity sold of the product per unit of time increases. Marginal revenue of a product is a constant function of quantity sold of the product per unit of time.

Consider now the law of decreasing marginal revenue of a product to an imperfectly competitive seller—defined as a seller who has to accept a lower price to sell a larger quantity of a product per unit of time ceteris paribus. According to this law, the revenue associated with selling an additional unit of a product varies inversely with quantity sold per unit of time. Each additional unit sold of a product per unit of time adds a smaller amount to total revenue. Total revenue of a product increases at a decreasing rate as quantity sold of the product per unit of time increases. Marginal revenue of a product is a decreasing function of quantity sold of the product per unit of time.

Perfectly Competitive Seller of a Product

A product market may be classified as perfectly competitive or imperfectly competitive from the seller's side of the market. A perfectly competitive product market is defined as a market in which the number of sellers of homogeneous products is so large that no seller can influence the price of his product.[1] Moreover, purchasers and sellers have perfect (that is, full) information on price and characteristics of products, and products are perfectly mobile in that they are shipped from one geographical area to another in response to price differentials. Similarly, factors of production are mobile geographically and occupationally in response to price differentials. Sellers market their products on exchanges and at auctions, and they are free to enter and leave markets.

Perfect competition is approximated in a few well-organized stock, bond, and agricultural markets. However, the significance of perfect competition as a model in which market supply and demand determine market quantity and price is much greater than is implied by the number of markets that may be classified as perfectly competitive; for as a market model of price and quantity determination, it provides conclusions (such as those of Chapter 13) that are applicable to many imperfectly competitive markets. Moreover, it provides norms of resource allocation and pricing (such as those in Chapters 14 and 24) by which the performance of imperfectly competitive markets may be evaluated. Thus it is the most often used market model of price and quantity determination.

Since no seller can influence the price of his product, each seller is a price-taker, rather than a price-maker. Since price is a parameter to each seller, a perfectly competitive seller is defined as a seller who can sell all he wishes per unit of time at the prevailing price ceteris paribus. In other words, the demand curve for a product facing a perfectly competitive seller is perfectly elastic at the prevailing price. In this context, the market is impersonal to a perfectly competitive seller; he is not in direct competition with sellers of products that are substitutes for his product, and hence sellers are not rivals in the ordinary meaning of the word. In short, since price is a parameter, the revenue function of one seller is independent of the revenue functions of other sellers.

Total Revenue Curve of a Product of a Perfectly Competitive Seller

Total revenue is the money received from selling a quantity of a product. The total revenue curve of a product is a set of ordered pairs of quantity sold (Q) and revenue (R) having the property that corresponding to each number in the Q set of numbers is one number in the R set of numbers: $R = R(Q)$. Thus, the total revenue curve shows the R value corresponding to each Q value, and hence how R varies with Q per unit of time. The parameter of a total revenue curve of a perfectly competitive seller is the price of the product (P): $P = P_0$.

As seen in Figure 6.1, which depicts hypothetical data presented in Table 6.1, a total revenue curve of a perfectly competitive seller is a ray, the equation of which is $R = R(Q) = P_0 Q$. The curve has a zero total revenue intercept because total revenue of the product is zero when quantity sold is zero: $R = P_0 \cdot 0 = 0$. It is linear because each successive unit is sold at the same price ($P_0 = 2$); hence each successive unit sold adds the same amount ($2)

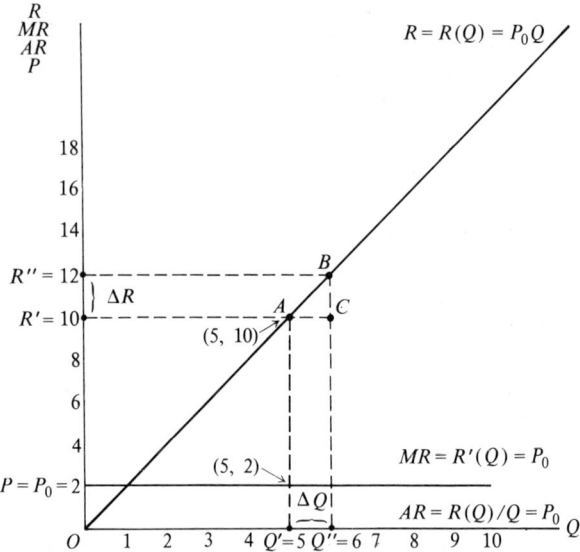

FIG. 6.1. Hypothetical revenue curves of a product of a perfectly competitive seller

TABLE 6.1: Hypothetical revenue of a product to a perfectly competitive seller

$AR = R/Q = P_0$	Q	$R = P_0 Q$	$MR_d = \Delta R/\Delta Q$	$MR_c = dR/dQ$
2	0	0		2
			2	
2	1	2		2
			2	
2	2	4		2
			2	
2	3	6		2
			2	
2	4	8		2
			2	
2	5	10		2
			2	
2	6	12		2
			2	
2	7	14		2
			2	
2	8	16		2
			2	
2	9	18		2
			2	
2	10	20		2

to total revenue. The slope of $R = R(Q)$, therefore, remains constant as the quantity sold increases.

Marginal Revenue Curve of a Product of a Perfectly Competitive Seller

When quantity sold varies by discrete amounts, discrete marginal revenue (MR_d) is the change in total revenue (ΔR) associated with a change of one unit in quantity sold of the product ($\Delta Q = 1$): $MR_d = \Delta R/\Delta Q$, where

$\Delta Q = 1$. In this context, marginal revenue is equal to the difference quotient ($\Delta R/\Delta Q$) of the straight line between two points one Q unit apart on the curve. In Figure 6.1, between points A and B on $R = R(Q)$,

$$MR_d = \lim_{\Delta Q \to 1} \frac{\Delta R}{\Delta Q} = \frac{R'' - R'}{Q'' - Q'} = \frac{CB}{AC} = \text{slope of line } AB = 2$$

Since a total revenue curve of a perfectly competitive seller is linear, the difference quotient is the same for all changes in quantity sold, and hence discrete marginal revenue equals continuous marginal revenue.[2]

The marginal revenue curve of a product is a set of ordered pairs of quantity sold (Q) and (continuous) marginal revenue (MR) having the property that corresponding to each number in the Q set of numbers is one number in the MR set of numbers: $MR = R'(Q)$. Thus, the marginal revenue curve shows the MR value corresponding to each Q value, and hence how MR varies with Q per unit of time. The parameters of a marginal revenue curve of a perfectly competitive seller are the parameters of the market demand (see Chapter 5) and supply curves (see Chapter 12).

As seen in Figure 6.1, which depicts hypothetical data presented in Table 6.1, a marginal revenue curve of a perfectly competitive seller is a zero-sloped (horizontal) straight line ($\Delta MR/\Delta Q = 0$), the equation of which is $MR = R'(Q) = P_0$. The curve is a horizontal straight line because each successive unit is sold at the same price ($P_0 = \$2$); hence each successive unit sold adds the same amount (\$2) to total revenue. Marginal revenue, therefore, remains constant as quantity sold increases.

To conclude, marginal revenue (MR) is a constant function of quantity sold (Q) when total revenue (R) increases at the constant rate (P_0) as quantity increases. Thus, the law of constant marginal revenue is a verbalization of a marginal revenue curve of a perfectly competitive seller. Since total revenue increases at a constant rate, and since the phrase "increases at a constant rate" is another way of saying "constant marginal revenue," a total revenue curve of a perfectly competitive seller also depicts the law of constant marginal revenue.

Average Revenue Curve of a Product of a Perfectly Competitive Seller

Average revenue (AR) is the ratio of total revenue (R) to quantity sold of the product (Q): $AR = R/Q$. Average revenue is equal to the difference quotient ($\Delta R/\Delta Q$) of the ray at a point on the total revenue curve. In Figure 6.1, at point A on $R = R(Q)$,

$$AR = \frac{Q'A}{OQ'} = \text{slope of line } OA = 2$$

Since a total revenue curve of a perfectly competitive seller is a ray, the difference quotient is the same at each point on the curve.

The average revenue curve of a product is a set of ordered pairs of quantity sold (Q) and average revenue (AR) having the property that corresponding to each number in the Q set of numbers is one number in the AR set of numbers: $AR = R(Q)/Q$. Thus, the average revenue curve shows the AR value corresponding to each Q value, and hence how AR varies with Q per unit of time. The parameters of an average revenue curve of a perfectly competitive seller are the parameters of the market demand (see Chapter 5) and supply curves (see Chapter 12).

As seen in Figure 6.1, which depicts hypothetical data presented in Table 6.1, an average revenue curve of a perfectly competitive seller is a zero-sloped (horizontal) straight line ($\Delta AR/\Delta Q = 0$), the equation of which is $AR = R(Q)/Q = P_0$. The curve is a horizontal straight line because each quantity is sold at the same price ($P_0 = \$2$); hence each quantity sold has the same average revenue (\$2). Average revenue, therefore, remains constant as the quantity sold increases.

Demand Curve for a Product Facing a Perfectly Competitive Seller

The demand curve for a product facing a seller shows the price at which each quantity can be sold. A perfectly competitive seller can sell all he wishes per unit of time at the prevailing price ceteris paribus. Thus, the demand curve for a product facing him is a line that is drawn parallel to the quantity axis to depict the given price. Moreover, at each quantity sold average revenue equals marginal revenue equals price: $AR = MR = P = P(Q)$. Consequently, the demand curve facing a perfectly competitive seller is his average revenue curve, which is the same as his marginal revenue curve. To conclude, average and marginal revenue are constant functions of quantity sold when the demand curve facing the seller is parallel to the quantity axis.

Iso-Revenue Curve of a Perfectly Competitive Seller

Iso-revenue of two products is the constant (equal) amount of money received from selling various combinations of quantities of the products. An iso-revenue curve of two products is a set of ordered pairs of quantities sold of the two products (Q_1 and Q_2) having the properties that (1) corresponding to each number in the Q_1 set of numbers is one number in the Q_2 set of numbers and (2) each pair of numbers of the function is associated with the same revenue: $Q_2 = R_0(Q_1)$. Thus, an iso-revenue curve shows the Q_2 value corresponding to each Q_1 value and hence how Q_2 varies with Q_1 per unit of time, holding revenue constant. In other words, *an iso-revenue curve depicts all combinations of quantities sold of two products that yield the same level of revenue to a seller.* The parameters of an iso-revenue curve are the parameters of the seller's two-product revenue function. The parameters of the two-product revenue function of a perfectly competitive seller are the prices of the products (P_1 and P_2): $P_1 = P_{1_0}$ and $P_2 = P_{2_0}$.

As seen in Figure 6.2, an iso-revenue curve of a perfectly competitive

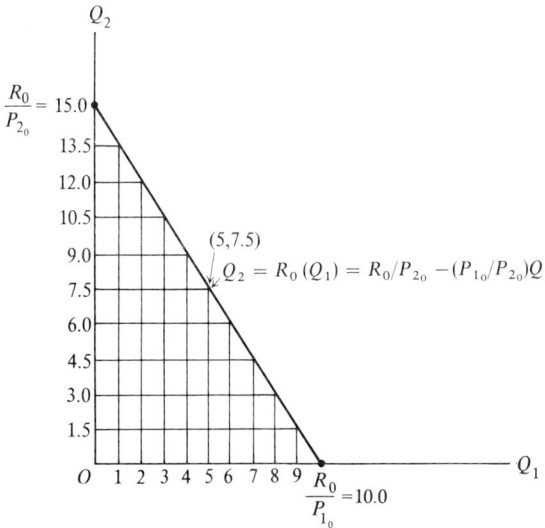

FIG. 6.2. Hypothetical iso-revenue curve of a perfectly competitive seller

seller is a negatively-sloped straight line, the equation of which is $Q_2 = R_0(Q_1) = R_0/P_{2_0} - (P_{1_0}/P_{2_0})Q_1$, where the second R_0 stands for a given amount of revenue.[3] It is negatively sloped because products Q_1 and Q_2 are rivals in providing a given level of revenue (R_0); a seller may maintain a given level of revenue by selling more of Q_1 and less of Q_2 (and vice versa). Thus, product Q_2 is a decreasing function of product Q_1: $\Delta Q_2/\Delta Q_1 < 0$. It is a straight line because its slope does not vary with Q_1 (or Q_2).

The slope of an iso-revenue curve is denoted by dQ_2/dQ_1 and is equal to the negative of the ratio MR_1/MR_2, where MR_1 is the marginal revenue of product one and MR_2 is the marginal revenue of product two: $dQ_2/dQ_1 = -MR_1/MR_2$. By multiplying both sides by -1, $-dQ_2/dQ_1 = MR_1/MR_2$. The $-dQ_2/dQ_1$ notation and the MR_1/MR_2 notation denote numerical values and are verbalized in discrete terms as the amount of Q_2 that a seller is willing to give up ($-\Delta Q_2$) to sell an additional unit of Q_1 (ΔQ_1) while keeping revenue constant. If $MR_1 = P_{1_0} = 3$ and $MR_2 = P_{2_0} = \$2$, the seller is willing to give up 1.5 units of Q_2 to sell an additional unit of Q_1.

When Q_1 and Q_2 vary by discrete amounts,[4] the increase in R because an additional unit of Q_1 is sold is the unit sold of Q_1 times the marginal revenue of that unit:

$$\Delta R_1 = \Delta Q_1 \frac{\Delta R_1}{\Delta Q_1}$$

The decrease in R because less Q_2 is sold is the quantity given up of Q_2 times the marginal revenue of that quantity:

$$\Delta R_2 = \Delta Q_2 \frac{\Delta R_2}{\Delta Q_2}$$

The total change in R is ΔR, and

$$\Delta R = \frac{\Delta R_1}{\Delta Q_1} \Delta Q_1 + \frac{\Delta R_2}{\Delta Q_2} \Delta Q_2$$

Since the total change in R is zero, because R is a given amount (R_0), the decrease in R because less Q_2 is sold must be offset exactly by the increase in R because more Q_1 is sold. Therefore,

$$\Delta R = \frac{\Delta R_1}{\Delta Q_1} \Delta Q_1 + \frac{\Delta R_2}{\Delta Q_2} \Delta Q_2 = 0$$

$$\frac{\Delta R_2}{\Delta Q_2} \Delta Q_2 = - \frac{\Delta R_1}{\Delta Q_1} \Delta Q_1$$

$$\frac{\Delta Q_2}{\Delta Q_1} = - \frac{\Delta R_1/\Delta Q_1}{\Delta R_2/\Delta Q_2} = - \frac{MR_1}{MR_2}$$

The slope of an iso-revenue curve (dQ_2/dQ_1) is thus seen to change as more Q_1 and less Q_2 are sold according to the change in MR_1 relative to the change in MR_2. In the case of a perfectly competitive seller, marginal revenue is a constant function of quantity sold and is equal to price. Thus, each successive unit increase in Q_1 increases revenue by a constant amount equal to P_{1_0}, and each successive unit decrease in Q_2 decreases revenue by a constant amount equal to P_{2_0}. Therefore, with each unit increase in Q_1 (ΔQ_1), the seller gives up a constant amount of Q_2 ($-\Delta Q_2$) to keep revenue constant. Since the ratio $\Delta Q_2/\Delta Q_1$ remains constant as more Q_1 and less Q_2 are sold, an iso-revenue curve of a perfectly competitive seller is a straight line; that is, its slope does not vary with Q_1 (or Q_2).

An iso-revenue curve may be drawn in Figure 6.2 for each level of revenue of the seller. The larger the quantities sold of both products, the higher the level of revenue and hence the farther away from the point of origin lies the curve. Two curves which depict two different levels of revenue cannot intersect; for if the two curves intersected, the same combination of quantities of the two products would be associated with two different levels of revenue, which is inconsistent with the revenue function $R = R_1(Q_1) + R_2(Q_2)$. According to this function, a combination of quantities of two products is associated with one level of revenue.

Imperfectly Competitive Seller of a Product

To repeat, a product market may be classified as perfectly competitive or imperfectly competitive from the seller's side of the market. An imperfectly competitive product market is defined as a market in which the number of sellers is so small that a seller may be able to influence the price of his product. If a seller can influence price, he is a price-maker, rather than a price-taker. In this case, since price is a variable rather than a parameter, an imperfectly competitive seller is defined as a seller who cannot sell all he wishes per unit of time at the prevailing price ceteris paribus. Specifically, he has to decrease his price to sell a larger quantity per unit of time ceteris paribus. In other words, the demand curve for a product facing an imperfectly competitive seller has a negative slope.

Imperfectly competitive product markets may be classified as monopolistic-competitive, oligopolistic, or monopolistic markets. The revenue function of a monopolistic-competitive seller of a product is analyzed in Chapter 15. The revenue function of an oligopolistic seller of a product is also analyzed in Chapter 15. The revenue function of a monopolistic seller of a product is analyzed in the present chapter. The present analysis is applicable to all imperfectly competitive sellers to the extent that they have one characteristic in common – namely, a negatively-sloped demand curve facing the seller.

A monopolistic product market is defined as a market in which the sole seller (the monopolist) of a product that has no close substitutes (for example, water) can determine price. Since he is the sole seller of the product, the demand curve for the product facing the monopolist is the market demand curve. Since his product has no close substitutes, the cross elasticity of his product with substitutes is low. Since he can determine the market price, the monopolist is a price-maker, rather than a price-taker.[5] In this context, the market is impersonal to the monopolist; he is not in direct competition with sellers of products that are weak substitutes for his product. He makes his decisions on price without regard to their pricing policies. In short, the revenue function of a monopolist is independent of the revenue functions of other sellers. The significance of monopoly is that, as a model of price and quantity determination, it provides an introduction to the models of monopolistic-competition and oligopoly; and it provides conclusions about resource allocation and pricing that may be compared to the conclusions drawn from the perfect competition model.

Total Revenue Curve of a Product of a Monopolist

To repeat, the total revenue curve of a product shows how total revenue (R) varies with quantity sold of the product (Q) per unit of time ceteris paribus: $R = R(Q)$. But price of the product (P) is not a parameter of the monopolist's

100   PRINCIPLES OF THE THEORY OF SUPPLY OF A PRODUCT

total revenue curve, for now price varies inversely with quantity sold (Q), and hence is a variable: $P = P(Q)$, where $\Delta P/\Delta Q < 0$. Thus $R = R(Q) = PQ$, where $P = P(Q)$, or $R = R(Q) = P(Q) \cdot Q$. The parameters of a total revenue curve of a monopolist are the parameters of the market demand curve (see Chapter 5).

FIG. 6.3a. Hypothetical total revenue curve of a product of a monopolist

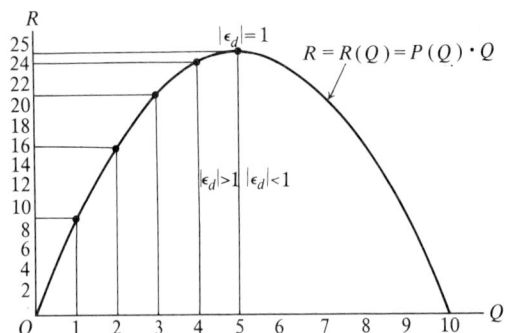

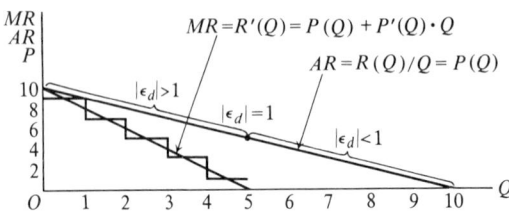

FIG. 6.3b. Hypothetical marginal and average revenue curves of a product of a monopolist

TABLE 6.2: Hypothetical revenue of a product to a monopolist

$AR = R/Q = P$	Q	$R = PQ$	$MR_d = \Delta R/\Delta Q$	$MR_c = dR/dQ$	$\varepsilon_d = \dfrac{dQ/Q}{dP/P}$
10	0	0		10	
			9		
9	1	9		8	$|e| > 1$
			7		
8	2	16		6	$|e| > 1$
			5		
7	3	21		4	$|e| > 1$
			3		
6	4	24		2	$|e| > 1$
			1		
5	5	25		0	$|e| = 1$
			-1		
4	6	24		-2	$|e| < 1$
			-3		
3	7	21		-4	$|e| < 1$
			-5		
2	8	16		-6	$|e| < 1$
			-7		
1	9	9		-8	$|e| < 1$
			-9		
0	10	0		-10	

As seen in Figure 6.3a, which depicts hypothetical data presented in Table 6.2, a total revenue curve of a monopolist has a zero total revenue intercept and is concave from below a tangent line. The curve has a zero total revenue intercept because total revenue of the product is zero when quantity sold is zero: $R = P(Q) \cdot 0 = 0$. It is concave from below because each successive quantity is sold at a lower price; hence, as quantity increases by a unit, each successive unit sold adds a smaller amount (less than P) to total revenue.[6] The slope of $R = P(Q) \cdot Q$ therefore decreases as quantity sold increases.

Marginal Revenue Curve of a Product of a Monopolist

The marginal revenue curve of a product shows how continuous marginal revenue (MR_c) varies with quantity sold of the product (Q) per unit of time, given the parameters of the curve. With respect to $R = R(Q) = P(Q) \cdot Q$, $MR = R'(Q) = P(Q) + P'(Q) \cdot Q$.[7] The parameters of a marginal revenue curve of a monopolist are the parameters of the market demand curve (see Chapter 5).

As seen in Figure 6.3b, a marginal revenue curve of a monopolist is a negatively-sloped curve ($\Delta MR/\Delta Q < 0$). The curve is negatively sloped because each successive quantity is sold at a lower price; hence, as quantity increases by a unit, each successive unit sold adds a smaller amount (less than P) to total revenue. Marginal revenue therefore decreases as quantity sold increases.

To conclude, marginal revenue (MR) is a decreasing function of quantity sold (Q) when total revenue (R) increases at a decreasing rate as quantity increases. Thus, the law of decreasing marginal revenue is a verbalization of a marginal revenue curve of an imperfectly competitive seller, as exemplified by a monopolist. Since total revenue increases at a decreasing rate, and since the phrase "increases at a decreasing rate" is another way of saying "decreasing marginal revenue," a total revenue curve of a monopolist also depicts the law of decreasing marginal revenue.

Average Revenue Curve of a Product of a Monopolist

The average revenue curve of a product shows how average revenue (AR) varies with quantity sold of the product (Q) per unit of time, given the parameters of the curve. With respect to $R = R(Q) = P(Q) \cdot Q$, $AR = R(Q)/Q = P(Q)$. The parameters of an average revenue curve of a monopolist are the parameters of the market demand curve (see Chapter 5).

As seen in Figure 6.3b, an average revenue curve of a monopolist is a negatively-sloped curve ($\Delta AR/\Delta Q < 0$). The curve is negatively sloped because each successive quantity is sold at a lower price; hence each suc-

Demand Curve for a Product Facing a Monopolist

To repeat, the demand curve for a product facing a seller shows the price at which each quantity can be sold. A monopolist has to accept a lower price to sell a larger quantity per unit of time ceteris paribus. Thus, the demand curve for a product facing him is a negatively-sloped curve. Moreover, in the present case, at each Q value average revenue equals price: $AR = R/Q = P = P(Q)$. Consequently, the demand curve facing a monopolist is his average revenue curve.[8] However, his average revenue curve is not the same as his marginal revenue curve, for at any given quantity marginal revenue is less than average revenue by the numerical value of $P'(Q) \cdot Q$, as seen below. To conclude, average revenue and marginal revenue are decreasing functions of quantity sold when the demand curve facing the seller is a negatively-sloped curve.

Relationship Between Total, Marginal, and Average Revenue Curves of a Monopolist

Consider Figures 6.3a and 6.3b in detail. The total revenue curve is subdivided into two halves. The first half is the area under the curve in which total revenue is an increasing function of quantity sold; that is, marginal revenue is positive. The second half is the area under the curve in which total revenue is a decreasing function of quantity sold; that is, marginal revenue is negative. These two areas are equal to one another. Thus, in this case, the revenue function of a monopolist is said to be symmetrical. The boundary between these two halves is that value of Q (five units) at which total revenue is maximum. Marginal revenue is zero when total revenue is maximum since the slope ($= MR$) of the total revenue curve is zero. Average revenue is zero when total revenue is zero at a positive value of Q (ten units). The value of Q at which marginal revenue is zero is one-half the value of Q at which average revenue is zero. The value of Q at which marginal revenue is zero denotes the midpoint of the average revenue curve. Total, (discrete) marginal, and average revenue of the first unit is the same value ($9).[9] The linear marginal revenue curve bisects a straight line drawn from the vertical axis to the linear average revenue curve. The slope of the average revenue curve is one-half the slope of the marginal revenue curve. The rate of decrease of marginal revenue is twice the rate of decrease of average revenue as quantity sold increases.

Relationship Between Marginal and Average Revenue Curves

At any quantity sold, according to $MR = P(Q) + P'(Q) \cdot Q$, marginal revenue equals average revenue (or price) plus the product of quantity purchased and the slope of the average revenue curve. Alternatively, since $P'(Q)$ is negative, marginal revenue equals average revenue minus the product of quantity purchased and the numerical value of the slope of the average revenue curve. Thus the marginal revenue curve can be derived geometrically from the average revenue curve.

In Figure 6.4 the Q value corresponding to point B on the nonlinear average revenue curve is

$$OQ' = P'B$$

The $P'(Q)$ or dP/dQ value at point B is equal to the slope of the tangent line AC, as measured by the ratio

$$\frac{OA}{OC} = \frac{P'A}{P'B}$$

Thus the numerical value of $P'(Q) \cdot Q$ at point B is

$$\frac{P'A}{P'B} P'B = P'A$$

The distance $P'A$ is the same as the distance DB. Since Marginal revenue is less than average revenue by the numerical value of $P'(Q) \cdot Q \, (=DB)$, point D is on the marginal revenue curve corresponding to the given average revenue

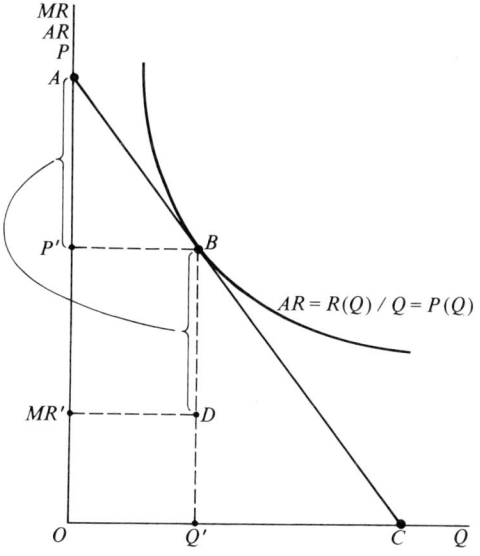

FIG. 6.4. Relationship between marginal and average revenue curves

curve. Other points on the marginal revenue curve may be determined in the same way.

To summarize, draw a line tangent to the average revenue curve at a given point B. Extend the tangent line to the vertical (price) axis to determine point A. Draw a horizontal line from point B to the vertical axis to determine point P'. Beneath point B mark a distance $DB = P'A$ to determine point D on the marginal revenue curve. Continue this procedure until the corresponding marginal revenue curve has been derived. As seen in Figure 6.3b, when this procedure is applied to a linear average revenue curve, the linear marginal revenue curve bisects a straight line drawn from the vertical axis to the linear average revenue curve.

Price Elasticity of Market Demand and Total Revenue

Consider again Figures 6.3a and 6.3b. The average revenue curve is the market demand curve in Figure 6.3b. From the seller's viewpoint, the price elasticity of market demand (ε_d) is the percentage change in quantity sold ($\Delta Q/Q$) divided by the percentage change in price ($\Delta P/P$):

$$\varepsilon_d = \frac{\Delta Q/Q}{\Delta P/P}$$

At any given quantity sold, marginal revenue equals average revenue (=price) plus the ratio of average revenue to the price elasticity of market demand: $MR = P + P/\varepsilon_d$.[10] Alternatively, since ε_d is a negative number, marginal revenue equals average revenue minus the ratio of average revenue to the numerical value of the price elasticity of market demand: $MR = P - P/|\varepsilon_d|$. The relation between MR, AR (=P), and $|\varepsilon_d|$ may be used to determine the effect on total revenue of a change in price.

When $|\varepsilon_d| = 1$, $MR = P - P/1 = P - P = 0$, and demand is said to be unitary elastic. Since total revenue is a maximum when $MR = 0$, demand is unitary elastic at the boundary between the two halves of the total revenue curve of Figure 6.3a, that is, at the midpoint on the demand curve. An infinitesimally small percentage change in price is exactly offset numerically by an infinitesimally small percentage change in quantity sold, and hence total revenue remains at its maximum value. To conclude, marginal revenue is zero when demand is unitary elastic, and total revenue does not vary with price.

When $|\varepsilon_d| > 1$, $MR > 0$ since $P > P/|\varepsilon_d|$, and demand is said to be elastic. Since total revenue is an increasing function of quantity sold when $MR > 0$, demand is elastic within the first half of the total revenue curve of Figure 6.3a, that is, within the upper portion of the demand curve. A percentage decrease in price is more than offset numerically by a percentage increase in quantity sold, and hence total revenue increases. Conversely, a percentage increase in price is more than offset numerically by a percentage decrease in quantity sold, and hence total revenue decreases. To conclude, marginal revenue is positive when demand is elastic, and total revenue varies inversely with price.

When $|\varepsilon_d| < 1$, $MR < 0$ since $P < P/|\varepsilon_d|$, and demand is said to be inelastic. Since total revenue is a decreasing function of quantity sold when $MR < 0$, demand is inelastic within the second half of the total revenue curve of Figure 6.3a, that is, within the lower portion of the demand curve. A percentage decrease in price is less than offset numerically by a percentage increase in quantity sold, and hence total revenue decreases. Conversely, a percentage increase in price is less than offset numerically by a percentage decrease in quantity sold, and hence total revenue increases. To conclude, marginal revenue is negative when demand is inelastic, and total revenue varies directly with price.

Iso-Revenue Curve of a Monopolist

To repeat, an iso-revenue curve depicts all combinations of quantities sold of two products that yield the same level of revenue: $Q_2 = R_0(Q_1)$. The slope of an iso-revenue curve (dQ_2/dQ_1) changes as more Q_1 and less Q_2 are sold according to the change in MR_1 relative to the change in MR_2, since $dQ_2/dQ_1 = -MR_1/MR_2$. In the case of an imperfectly competitive seller, as exemplified by a monopolist, marginal revenue is a decreasing function of quantity sold. Thus, each successive unit increase in Q_1 increases revenue by a decreasing amount, and each successive unit decrease in Q_2 decreases revenue by an increasing amount. Therefore, as seen in Figure 6.5, with each unit increase in Q_1 (ΔQ_1), the seller gives up a decreasing amount of Q_2

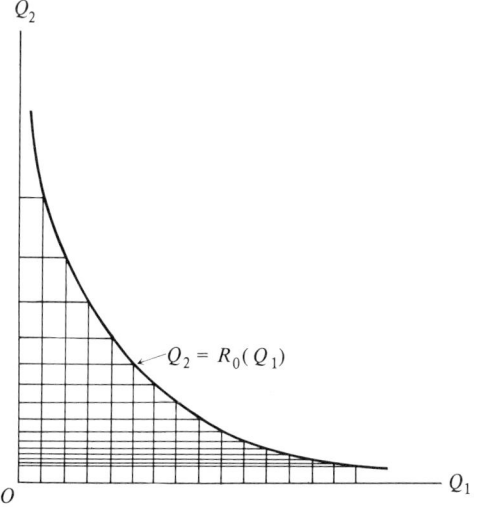

FIG. 6.5. Hypothetical iso-revenue curve of a monopolist

($-\Delta Q_2$) to keep revenue constant. Since the ratio $\Delta Q_2/\Delta Q_1$ decreases numerically as more Q_1 and less Q_2 are sold, an iso-revenue curve of an imperfectly competitive seller is concave from above a tangent line—that is, convex to the origin.

SUMMARY

Dropping the zero subscript and remembering that P may be a parameter or a variable, total revenue of a product of a seller (R) is equal to its price (P) times its quantity sold (Q): $R = PQ$. The curve expressing the relation between R and Q is called the total revenue curve. Price of a product of a seller (P) is equal to his average revenue from the product (AR), since each is the ratio of his total revenue (R) to his quantity sold (Q): $AR = R/Q = P$. The curve expressing the relation between AR ($=P$) and Q is called the average revenue curve. Lastly, marginal revenue of a product may be defined as the infinitesimally small change in R (dR) associated with an infinitesimally small change in Q (dQ), or as the addition to total revenue (ΔR) of one additional unit of the product ($\Delta Q = 1$): $MR_c = dR/dQ$ and $MR_d = \Delta R/\Delta Q$, where $\Delta Q = 1$. The curve expressing the relation between dR/dQ and Q is called the marginal revenue curve.

Average revenue (=price) is the same as marginal revenue in the case of perfect competition from the seller's side in the product market, for in this case the seller can sell all he wishes per unit of time at the prevailing price ceteris paribus; hence each additional unit sold per unit of time adds the same amount (equal to price) to total revenue. Total revenue (R) therefore increases at the constant rate P as quantity sold of the product (Q) per unit of time increases. Consequently, marginal revenue of the product ($MR = P$) is a constant function of quantity sold (Q) per unit of time. To generalize, according to the law of constant marginal revenue of a product to a perfectly competitive seller, the revenue associated with selling an additional unit of a product does not vary with quantity sold per unit of time.

In the case of an imperfectly competitive seller of products, as exemplified by a monopolist, the seller by definition has to accept a lower price to sell a larger quantity of a product per unit of time ceteris paribus. Thus, each additional unit sold per unit of time adds a smaller amount (less than price) to total revenue. Total revenue (R) therefore increases at a decreasing rate as quantity sold of the product (Q) increases. Consequently, marginal revenue of the product ($MR < P$) is a decreasing function of quantity sold (Q) per unit of time. To generalize, according to the law of decreasing marginal revenue of a product to an imperfectly competitive seller of products, the revenue associated with selling an additional unit of a product varies inversely with quantity sold per unit of time.

The demand curve for a product facing a perfectly competitive seller is a horizontal straight line that depicts the given price. This curve is his average

(= marginal) revenue curve. His total revenue curve is derived from his average revenue curve by multiplying each quantity sold by price. Similarly, the total revenue curve of a monopolist is derived from his average revenue curve by multiplying each quantity sold by price. However, the demand curve for a product facing a monopolist is a negatively-sloped curve that is the market demand curve; although this curve is his average revenue curve, it is not his marginal revenue curve. The marginal revenue curve of a monopolist may be derived from his average revenue curve via the equation $MR = P(Q) + P'(Q) \cdot Q$. The relation between the total, marginal, and average revenue of a product of a monopolist may be analyzed via the formula $MR = P - P/|\varepsilon_d|$.

An iso-revenue curve depicts all combinations of quantities of two products (Q_1 and Q_2) that yield the same level of revenue (R). An iso-revenue curve may be drawn for each level of R. The greater the value of R, the higher the curve lies in the OQ_1Q_2 plane. No two curves intersect ceteris paribus. An iso-revenue curve of a perfectly competitive seller is a negatively-sloped straight line. An iso-revenue curve of a monopolist is a negatively-sloped curve that is concave from above a tangent line.

Questions

1. List the principles of the theory of supply of a product that are of primary importance. How do you account for the position of the law of constant marginal revenue in this list? Verbalize this principle of economics. Verbalize also the law of decreasing marginal revenue.

2. Define total revenue of a product. What is a total revenue curve? Draw a total revenue curve of a perfectly competitive seller and describe its properties. Draw also a total revenue curve of a monopolist and describe its properties.

3. Define marginal revenue of a product. What is a marginal revenue curve? Draw a marginal revenue curve of a perfectly competitive seller, describe its properties, and relate the properties of the total and marginal revenue curves. Do the same analysis for a monopolist.

4. Define average revenue of a product. What is an average revenue curve? Draw an average revenue curve of a perfectly competitive seller, describe its properties, and then relate the properties of the total and average revenue curves and the marginal and average revenue curves. Do the same analysis for a monopolist.

5. What is the demand curve for a product facing a perfectly competitive seller? What is the demand curve for a product facing a monopolist? In each case, relate this curve to the corresponding revenue curves.

6. Define iso-revenue of two products. What is an iso-revenue curve? Draw an iso-revenue curve of a perfectly competitive seller, describe its properties, and relate marginal revenue and the slope of an iso-revenue curve. Do the same analysis for a monopolist. Verbalize the numerical value of the slope of an iso-revenue curve.

7. Derive the marginal revenue curve of a monopolist from his nonlinear average revenue curve.

8. Relate price elasticity to the total revenue curve of a monopolist.

APPENDIX: Revenue Function of a First-Degree Price-Discriminating Monopolist

A monopolist who charges a lower price for each successive *quantity* of a product, but charges the same price for each unit of a given quantity, is called a non-price-discriminating monopolist. By contrast, a first-degree price-discriminating monopolist is defined as a monopolist who charges a lower price for each successive *unit* of a product. As seen in Figure 6.6, which depicts hypothetical data presented in Table 6.3, the total revenue curve of a first-degree price-discriminating monopolist is concave from below a tangent line. Since each successive unit is sold at a lower price, each successive unit sold adds a smaller amount (equal to price) to total revenue. Total revenue therefore increases at a decreasing rate as quantity sold increases. Marginal and average revenue vary inversely with quantity sold.

FIG. 6.6. Hypothetical revenue curves of a product of a first-degree price-discriminatory monopolist

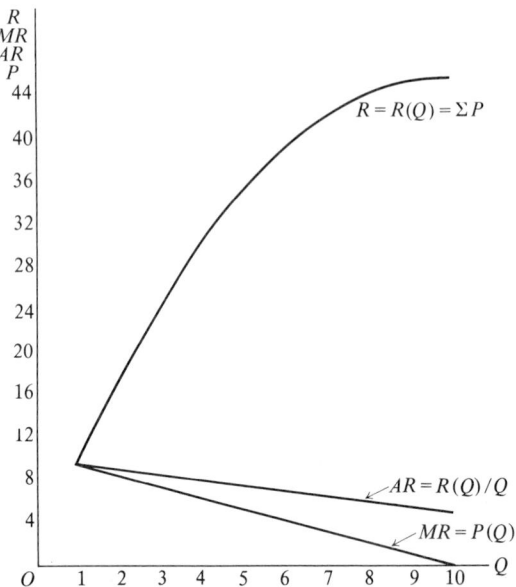

The demand curve facing a seller shows the price at which each unit can be sold. His marginal revenue curve denotes the marginal revenue of each unit sold. In the present case, the price of each unit is its marginal revenue, since each unit adds to total revenue its price: $MR = \Delta R/\Delta Q = P$. Therefore, the demand curve facing a first-degree price-discriminating monopolist is his marginal revenue curve. As seen in Table 6.3, his total revenue curve is derived from his marginal revenue curve by summing the price of each successive unit; and his average revenue curve is derived from his total revenue curve by dividing the total revenue of each quantity by that quantity.

TABLE 6.3: Hypothetical revenue of a product to a first-degree price-discriminating monopolist

$MR = \Delta R/\Delta Q = P$	Q	$R = \Sigma P$	$AR = R/Q$
9	1	9	9.00
8	2	17	8.50
7	3	24	8.00
6	4	30	7.50
5	5	35	7.00
4	6	39	6.50
3	7	42	6.00
2	8	44	5.50
1	9	45	5.00
0	10	45	4.50

NOTES

[1] Some economists would say that this sentence is a definition of pure competition and that it and the remainder of the paragraph define perfect competition.

[2] When quantity is varied continuously, continuous marginal revenue of a product (MR_c) is the instantaneous rate of change of total revenue as quantity sold of the product increases or decreases. With respect to the one-product revenue function $R = R(Q)$, the instantaneous rate of change is the infinitesimally small change in R (dR) associated with an infinitesimally small change in Q (dQ): $MR_c = dR/dQ$. In this context, marginal revenue is the slope of the total revenue curve of the product. The slope of the total revenue curve is equal to the difference quotient ($\Delta R/\Delta Q$) of the tangent line at a point on the curve. In Figure 6.1, at point A on $R = R(Q)$,

$$MR_c = \frac{dR}{dQ} = \lim_{\Delta Q \to 0} \frac{\Delta R}{\Delta Q} = \frac{R'' - R'}{Q'' - Q'} = \frac{CB}{AC} = \text{slope of line } AB = 2$$

[3] The slope of an iso-revenue curve of a perfectly competitive seller is $-P_{1_0}/P_{2_0}$; its Q_2 intercept is R_0/P_{2_0}; and its Q_1 intercept is R_0/P_{1_0}.

$$R_0 = P_{1_0} Q_1 + P_{2_0} Q_2$$

$$Q_2 = \frac{R_0}{P_{2_0}} - \frac{P_{1_0}}{P_{2_0}} Q_1 \quad \text{and} \quad Q_1 = \frac{R_0}{P_{1_0}} - \frac{P_{2_0}}{P_{1_0}} Q_2$$

$$\frac{dQ_2}{dQ_1} = -\frac{P_{1_0}}{P_{2_0}} \quad \text{and} \quad \frac{dQ_1}{dQ_2} = -\frac{P_{2_0}}{P_{1_0}}$$

$$Q_2 = \frac{R_0}{P_{2_0}} \quad \text{when} \quad Q_1 = 0 \quad \text{and} \quad Q_1 = \frac{R_0}{P_{1_0}} \quad \text{when} \quad Q_2 = 0$$

[4] With respect to a two-product revenue function, the instantaneous rate of change of R with respect to Q_1 is the infinitesimally small change in R associated with an infinitesimally small change in Q_1: $MR_1 = \partial R/\partial Q_1$. The total infinitesimally small change in Q_1 is dQ_1. Thus, in terms of infinitesimally small changes, the change in R associated with a total change in Q_1 is

$$\frac{\partial R}{\partial Q_1} dQ_1$$

Similarly, the instantaneous rate of change of R with respect to Q_2 is the infinitesimally small change in R associated with an infinitesimally small change in Q_2: $MR_2 = \partial R/\partial Q_2$. The total infinitesimally small change in Q_2 is dQ_2. In terms of infinitesimally small changes, the change in R associated with a total change in Q_2 is

$$\frac{\partial R}{\partial Q_2} dQ_2$$

Therefore, in terms of infinitesimally small changes, the total change in R is dR, and

$$dR = \frac{\partial R}{\partial Q_1} dQ_1 + \frac{\partial R}{\partial Q_2} dQ_2$$

Since the total change in R along an iso-revenue curve is zero,

$$dR = \frac{\partial R}{\partial Q_1} dQ_1 + \frac{\partial R}{\partial Q_2} dQ_2 = 0$$

$$\frac{\partial R}{\partial Q_2} dQ_2 = -\frac{\partial R}{\partial Q_1} dQ_1$$

$$\frac{dQ_2}{dQ_1} = -\frac{\partial R/\partial Q_1}{\partial R/\partial Q_2} = -\frac{MR_1}{MR_2}$$

[5] However, his freedom to determine price may be limited by government, and if he sets the price his customers determine the quantity they will purchase and vice versa.

[6] A monopolist who charges a lower price for each successive *quantity* of a product, but charges the same price for each unit of a given quantity (which is the case being analyzed), is called a non-price-discriminating monopolist. By contrast, a first-degree price-discriminating monopolist is defined as a monopolist who charges a lower price for each successive *unit* of a product. This case is analyzed in the appendix to this chapter.

[7] Let $P = P(Q) = a - bQ$. Then $R = P(Q) \cdot Q = (a - bQ)Q = aQ - bQ^2$. And

$$MR = \frac{dR}{dQ} = \lim_{\Delta Q \to 0} \frac{\Delta R}{\Delta Q} = \frac{[a(Q + \Delta Q) - b(Q + \Delta Q)^2] - (aQ - bQ^2)}{\Delta Q}$$

$$= \frac{aQ + a\Delta Q - b(Q^2 + 2Q\Delta Q + \Delta Q^2) - aQ + bQ^2}{\Delta Q}$$

$$= \frac{aQ + a\Delta Q - bQ^2 - 2bQ\Delta Q - b\Delta Q^2 - aQ + bQ^2}{\Delta Q}$$

$$= \frac{\Delta Q(a - 2bQ - b\Delta Q)}{\Delta Q} = a - 2bQ - b\Delta Q$$

$$= a - 2bQ = a - bQ - bQ = P - bQ$$

In general notation, $AR = P = P(Q)$ and $-b = P'(Q) = dP/dQ$. Thus

$$MR = P(Q) + P'(Q) \cdot Q \quad \text{or} \quad MR = AR + \frac{dP}{dQ} Q \quad \text{or} \quad MR = P + \frac{dP}{dQ} Q$$

[8] This statement is true only if he is a non-price discriminating monopolist (see the appendix to this chapter).

[9] $MR_c = 8; MR_d = 9$.

[10] In continuous terms,

$$\varepsilon_d = \frac{dQ}{dP} \cdot \frac{P}{Q}$$

To continue from footnote 7,

$$MR = P + \frac{dP}{dQ} Q = P(1 + \frac{Q}{P} \frac{dP}{dQ}) = P(1 + \frac{1}{\varepsilon_d}) = P + \frac{P}{\varepsilon_d}$$

chapter 7

The Production Function

According to the law of decreasing marginal product of a factor of production to a purchaser (user) of factors who is subject to diminishing marginal returns, the product associated with purchasing and/or using an additional unit of a factor varies inversely with quantity purchased and/or used per unit of time. Each additional unit used of a factor per unit of time adds a smaller amount to total product. Total product of a factor increases at a decreasing rate as quantity used of the factor per unit of time increases. Marginal product of a factor is a decreasing function of quantity used of the factor per unit of time.

Total Product Curve of a Factor of Production

The total product of a factor of production is the quantity produced (output) of a product associated with a quantity used (input) of the factor. Factors which are man-made are called capital. The accumulation of man-made resources over time is called the capital stock—an example of a stock variable. The rate of change of the capital stock with respect to time is called investment—an example of a flow variable. If the unit of time is a year, then investment is the change in the capital stock during the year. Similarly, the accumulation over time of output not sold is called inventory, a stock variable; but the rate of addition to inventory is a flow variable. Factors which are provided by nature are called land. Factors of all types of labor skills are called labor. Income received by owners of capital and land is called property income. Thus, capital and land factors may be referred to jointly as capital by defining capital as the source of property income. Income received by all remaining types of factors may then be called labor income.

The total product curve of a factor of production is a set of ordered pairs of input of the factor (F) and output of the product (Q) having the property that corresponding to each number in the F set of numbers is one number in

112 PRINCIPLES OF THE THEORY OF SUPPLY OF A PRODUCT

the Q set of numbers: $Q = Q(F)$. Thus the total product curve shows the Q value corresponding to each F value, and hence how Q varies with F per unit of time. The parameters of a total product curve of a user are the quantities of the factors related to the given factor in production and the techniques for transforming input into output. In the two-factor (F_1 and F_2) case, $Q = Q(F_1)$, where $F_2 = F_{2_0}$; or $Q = q(F_2)$, where $F_1 = F_{1_0}$. With respect to $Q = Q(F_1)$,

FIG. 7.1a. Hypothetical total product curve of a factor of production

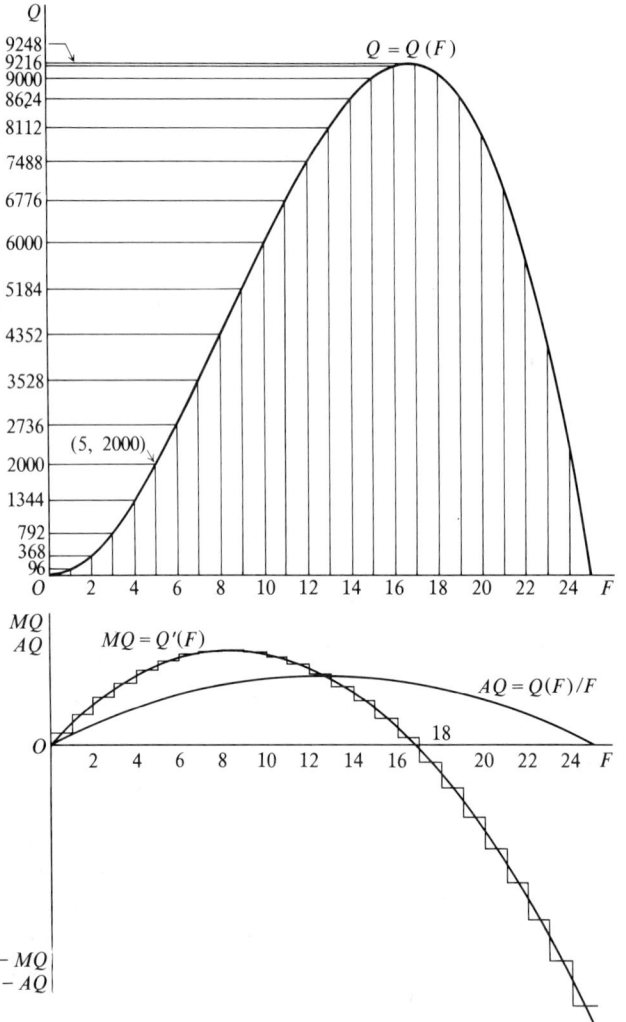

FIG. 7.1b. Hypothetical marginal and average product curves of a factor of production

THE PRODUCTION FUNCTION

F_1 is called the variable factor and F_2 is called the fixed factor. Conversely, with respect to $Q = q(F_2)$, F_2 is called the variable factor and F_1 is called the fixed factor.

Let the variable factor under consideration be ditch-digging labor. If a firm decides to stop using this type of labor, its total product may still be positive. Thus the total product curve of a variable factor may intersect the total product axis at some hypothetical positive value. This value would denote the output from fixed factors when zero units of the variable factor are used per unit of time. However, a minimum amount of ditch-digging labor may be required before production can begin. In this case, the input intercept is positive, and hence the output intercept is negative (if it exists). For present purposes, let the output intercept of ditch-digging labor be zero, as in Figure 7.1a, which depicts hypothetical data presented in Table 7.1.

Assume that a business firm uses 1, 2, 3, ..., n man-hours of ditch-digging labor per day. Each man-hour is denoted on the horizontal axis of Figure 7.1a by vertical lines equal distance apart. The total product associated with the first man-hour is denoted by a horizontal line that intersects the vertical axis

TABLE 7.1: Hypothetical product of a factor of production

F	Q	$MQ_d = \Delta Q/\Delta F$	$MQ_c = dQ/dF$	$AQ = Q/F$
0	0		0	0
		96		
1	96		188	96
		272		
2	368		352	184
		424		
3	792		492	264
		552		
4	1344		608	336
		656		
5	2000		700	400
		736		
6	2736		768	456
		792		
7	3528		812	504
		824		
8	4352		832	544
		832		
9	5184		828	576
		816		
10	6000		800	600
		776		
11	6776		748	616
		712		
12	7488		672	624
		624		
13	8112		572	624
		512		
14	8624		448	616
		376		
15	9000		250	600
		216		
16	9216		128	576
		32		
17	9248		−68	544
		−176		
18	9072		−288	504
		−408		
19	8664		−504	456
		−664		
20	8000		−800	400
		−946		
21	7056		−1092	336
		−1248		
22	5808		−1408	264
		−1576		
23	4232		−1748	184
		−1928		
24	2304		−2112	96
		−2304		
25	0		−2500	0

at an arbitrary distance above the total product intercept. The second man-hour may add more than or less than the first man-hour, or each man-hour may add the same amount, to the total product. For purposes of analysis, assume that the second man-hour adds more than the first man-hour to the total product. A horizontal line intersects the vertical axis at a distance above the first such line to denote the larger contribution of the second man-hour. The numerical value of this distance need not be known, for by assumption it is greater than the distance denoting the product of the first man-hour. The product associated with each quantity is plotted on the diagram as points in the OFQ plane. These points are connected by a curve, which is extended to the product intercept. The segment of the curve depicting the contribution to total product of the second man-hour slants upward more than the segment denoting the contribution of the first man-hour. Thus, in this context, the total product curve is concave upward; that is, it is concave from above a tangent line. Its slope becomes larger as quantity of the factor increases. Total product is increasing at an increasing rate as quantity of the factor increases.

However, given the unit of time, eventually an additional unit of a factor adds less to total product than does the previous unit. Assume that this happens with the tenth man-hour. Then the distance marked off on the vertical axis to denote the contribution to total product of the tenth man-hour is less than the distance marked off to denote the contribution of the ninth man-hour. Total product is now increasing at a decreasing rate as quantity of the factor increases. The slope of the total product curve is decreasing to zero as more man-hours are used. The curve is concave downward; that is, it is concave from below a tangent line.

After a certain number of units of a factor have been used per unit of time, an additional unit may add nothing to total product. At this point on the total product curve, its slope is zero; total product is at its maximum value. Thereafter, total product may decrease if additional units of a factor are used. Thus an inverse relation may exist between total product and quantity of a factor. Eventually, total product may reach zero and then become negative as additional units are used per unit of time.

Marginal Product Curve of a Factor of Production

When quantity is varied by discrete amounts, discrete marginal product of a factor (MQ_d) is the change in Q (ΔQ) associated with a change of one unit in F $(\Delta F = 1)$: $MQ_d = \Delta Q/\Delta F$, where $\Delta F = 1$. In this context, marginal product is equal to the difference quotient $\Delta Q/\Delta F$ of the straight line between two points one F unit apart on the curve. In Table 7.1, the MQ_d of the tenth unit equals

$$\lim_{\Delta Q \to 1} \frac{\Delta Q}{\Delta F} = 816$$

Since the total product curve of Figure 7.1a is nonlinear, the difference quotient is not the same for all changes in quantity, and hence discrete marginal product is not the same as continuous marginal product.[1]

The marginal product curve of a factor is a set of ordered pairs of input (F) and (continuous) marginal product (MQ) having the property that corresponding to each number in the F set of numbers is one number in the MQ set of numbers: $MQ = Q'(F)$. Thus the marginal product curve shows the MQ value corresponding to each F value, and hence how MQ varies with F per unit of time. The parameters of a marginal product curve are the parameters of the corresponding total product curve that determine the slope of the total curve.

As seen in Figure 7.1a, which depicts hypothetical data presented in Table 7.1, the slope of the total product curve is larger when two units are used than when one unit is used; the second unit adds more to output than the first unit. Likewise, depending on the total product curve, each subsequent unit used, until a given unit is used, may add more to output than does the previous unit. In this context, as seen in Figure 7.1b, a direct relation exists between MQ and F; the marginal product curve of a factor has a positive slope. Marginal product (MQ) is an increasing function of quantity of the factor (F) when total product (Q) increases at an increasing rate (dQ/dF) as quantity of the factor increases.

Eventually, however, as seen in Figure 7.1b, the slope of the total product curve of a factor attains its highest value. This point on the total product curve is the inflection point dividing increasing marginal product from decreasing marginal product. At this point, the marginal product curve is at its peak; its slope is zero. Thereafter, the slope of the total product curve, while still positive, decreases to zero. Decreasing marginal returns have set in. Marginal product is approaching zero and becomes zero when the slope of the total product curve is zero. The marginal product curve, which now has a negative slope, intersects the horizontal axis at that quantity of the factor at which output is at a maximum. As output decreases absolutely, marginal product is negative.

As seen in Figure 7.1b, a marginal product curve of a firm that is subject to diminishing marginal returns is a negatively-sloped curve ($\Delta MQ/\Delta F < 0$). Marginal product (MQ) is a decreasing function of quantity (F) when total product (Q) increases at a decreasing rate (dQ/dF) as quantity of the factor increases. Thus, the law of decreasing marginal product is a verbalization of a marginal product curve of a firm that is subject to diminishing marginal returns. Since total product increases at a decreasing rate, and since the phrase "increases at a decreasing rate" is another way of saying "decreasing marginal product," a total product curve of a firm that is subject to diminishing marginal returns also depicts the law of decreasing marginal product.

Basis of Decreasing Marginal Product of a Factor of Production

Consider a set of factors purchased and used in a year by a business firm. Factors of the set are not divisible into the same unit of physical measurement, and they are not purchased and used per the same unit of time within the year. Some are purchased and used on an irregular basis per unit of time. Others are purchased on an irregular basis and used on a regular basis per unit of time. Consequently, as an empirical fact, factors of the set are purchased and used in varying proportions per unit of time. Decreasing marginal product of a variable factor supposedly sets in eventually as the ratio (proportion) of it to fixed factors increases; for as the variable factor is used intensively relative to fixed factors per unit of time, each additional unit of the variable factor adds less to the firm's product per the same unit of time. Thus, a limit is placed by fixed factors on the upward movement of total product associated with units of the variable factor. Because of this limit, the total product curve of a variable factor eventually is concave from below a tangent line—a graphical representation of decreasing marginal product. Hence this law may also be called the law of variable proportions.

Average Product Curve of a Factor of Production

Average product of a factor of production (AQ) is the ratio of total product (Q) to quantity used (F): $AQ = Q/F$. Average product is equal to the difference quotient ($\Delta Q/\Delta F$) of the ray at a point on the total product curve. In Table 7.1, the AQ of the tenth unit equals $6000/10 = 600$. Since a total product curve of a factor is not a ray when the firm is subject to diminishing marginal returns, the difference quotient varies with F.

An average product curve of a factor is a set of ordered pairs of input (F) and average product (AQ) having the property that corresponding to each number in the F set of numbers is one number in the AQ set of numbers: $AQ = Q(F)/F$. Thus the average product curve shows the AQ value corresponding to each F value, and hence how AQ varies with F per unit of time. The parameters of an average product curve are the parameters of the corresponding total product curve that determine the intercept or the slope of the total curve.

The total product curve of Figure 7.1a shows that (by assumption) total product first increases at an increasing rate and then at a decreasing rate as quantity of the factor increases. Therefore, average product first increases and then decreases with quantity of the factor. The peak of the average product curve occurs at a quantity of the factor that is greater than the quantity at which the marginal product curve peaks. The average product curve is intersected at its peak from above by the marginal product curve; then the rate of decrease of average product is less (numerically) than the rate of decrease of marginal product. Average product is zero when total product is zero. In short, the average is determined by all units of a given quantity; the marginal is determined by the last unit. Thus, the only way for an average to stop increasing, reach its maximum value, and then decrease is for the marginal to stop increasing first, reach its maximum value first, and then decrease at a (numerical) rate that is faster than the rate of decrease of the average.

Iso-Product Curve of Two Factors Not Related in Production

The iso-product of two factors is the constant (equal) amount of product (output) associated with various combinations of quantities (inputs) of the factors. An iso-product curve of two factors is a set of ordered pairs of quantities of the two factors (F_1 and F_2) having the properties that (1) corresponding to each number in the F_1 set of numbers is one number in the F_2 set of numbers and (2) each pair of numbers of the function is associated with the same output: $F_2 = Q_0(F_1)$. Thus an iso-product curve shows the F_2 value corresponding to each F_1 value, and hence how F_2 varies with F_1 per unit of time, holding output constant. In other words, *an iso-product (or iso-quant) curve depicts all combinations of quantities of two variable factors of production that yield the same level of product to a user.* The parameters of an iso-product curve are the quantities of the factors related to F_1 and F_2 in production and the firm's state of technology.

As seen in Figure 7.2a, within the economic region of production (discussed below), an iso-product curve of a user who is subject to diminishing marginal returns in general is a negatively-sloped curve that is concave from above a tangent line—that is, convex to the origin. It is negatively sloped because factors F_1 and F_2 are rivals in providing a given level of output; a user may maintain a given level of output by increasing the input of F_1 and decreasing the input of F_2 (and vice versa). Thus, factor F_2 is a decreasing function of factor F_1: $\Delta F_2/\Delta F_1 < 0$. It is concave from above a tangent line because the numerical value of its slope varies inversely with F_1.

The slope of an iso-product curve (dF_2/dF_1) is equal to the negative of the ratio MQ_1/MQ_2, where MQ_1 is the marginal product of factor F_1 and MQ_2 is the marginal product of factor F_2: $dF_2/dF_1 = -MQ_1/MQ_2$. By multiplying both sides by -1, $-dF_2/dF_1 = MQ_1/MQ_2$. The $-dF_2/dF_1$ notation

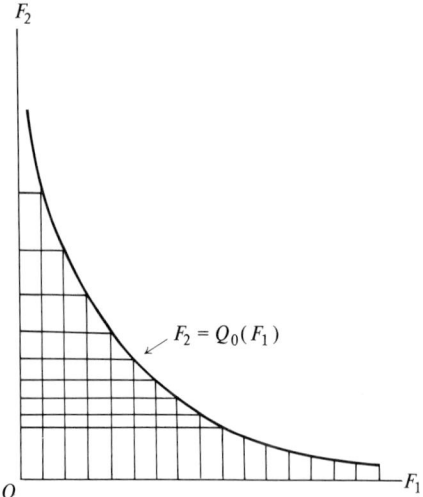

FIG. 7.2a. Hypothetical iso-product curve of two factors not related in production

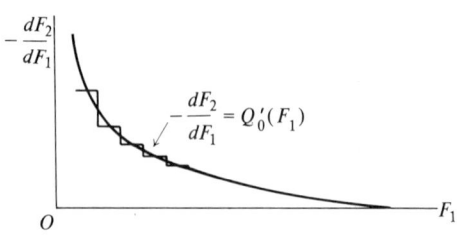

FIG. 7.2b. Marginal rate of technical substitution curve of two factors not related in production. (The $-dF_2/dF_1$ scale is one half the F_2 scale.)

and the MQ_1/MQ_2 notation denote numerical values and are called the marginal rate of technical substitution of F_1 for F_2, which is verbalized in discrete terms as the amount of F_2 that a user is willing to give up ($-\Delta F_2$) to use an additional unit of F_1 (ΔF_1) while keeping output constant. If $MQ_1 = 2$ and $MQ_2 = 1$, the user is willing to give up two units of F_2 to use an additional unit of F_1.

When F_1 and F_2 are varied by discrete amounts,[2] the increase in Q because an additional unit of F_1 is used is the unit gained of F_1 times the marginal product of that unit:

$$\Delta Q_1 = \Delta F_1 \frac{\Delta Q_1}{\Delta F_1}$$

The decrease in Q because less F_2 is used is the quantity given up of F_2 times the marginal product of that quantity:

$$\Delta Q_2 = \Delta F_2 \frac{\Delta Q_2}{\Delta F_2}$$

The total change in Q is ΔQ, and

$$\Delta Q = \frac{\Delta Q_1}{\Delta F_1} \Delta F_1 + \frac{\Delta Q_2}{\Delta F_2} \Delta F_2$$

Since the total change in Q is zero because Q is a given amount (Q_0), the decrease in Q because less F_2 is used must be offset exactly by the increase in Q because more F_1 is used. Therefore,

$$\Delta Q = \frac{\Delta Q_1}{\Delta F_1} \Delta F_1 + \frac{\Delta Q_2}{\Delta F_2} \Delta F_2 = 0$$

$$\frac{\Delta Q_2}{\Delta F_2} \Delta F_2 = -\frac{\Delta Q_1}{\Delta F_1} \Delta F_1$$

$$\frac{\Delta F_2}{\Delta F_1} = -\frac{\Delta Q_1/\Delta F_1}{\Delta Q_2/\Delta F_2} = -\frac{MQ_1}{MQ_2}$$

$$\frac{dF_2}{dF_1} = \lim_{\Delta F_1 \to 0} \frac{\Delta F_2}{\Delta F_1}$$

The slope of an iso-product curve (dF_2/dF_1) is thus seen to change as more F_1 and less F_2 are used according to the change in MQ_1 relative to the change in MQ_2. In the case of two factors that are not related in production, the marginal product of one factor is a constant function of the quantity used of the other factor: $\Delta MQ_1/\Delta F_2 = 0$ and $\Delta MQ_2/\Delta Q_1 = 0$. However, assuming decreasing marginal product of a factor of production, the marginal product of a factor is a decreasing function of the quantity of the factor: $\Delta MQ_1/\Delta F_1 < 0$ and $\Delta MQ_2/\Delta Q_2 < 0$. Thus, each successive unit increase in F_1 increases output by a decreasing amount, and each successive unit decrease in F_2 decreases output by an increasing amount. Therefore, as seen in Figures 7.2a and 7.2b, with each unit increase in F_1 (ΔF_1), the user gives up a decreasing amount of F_2 ($-\Delta F_2$) to keep output constant. Since the ratio $\Delta F_2/\Delta F_1$ decreases numerically as more F_1 and less F_2 are used, an iso-product curve of a user that is subject to diminishing marginal returns is concave from above a tangent line—that is, convex to the origin (see Figure 7.2a).[3] In other words, as seen in Figure 7.2b, the marginal rate of technical substitution of F_1 for F_2 varies inversely with F_1.

An iso-product curve may be drawn in Figure 7.2a for each level of output. The larger the input of both factors, the higher the level of output and hence the farther away from the point of origin lies the curve. Two curves which depict two different levels of output cannot intersect; for if the two curves intersected, the same input of the two factors would be associated with two different levels of output, which is inconsistent with the production function $Q = Q(F_1, F_2)$. According to this function, an input of the two factors is associated with one level of output.

Iso-Product Curve of Two Substitutes in Production

Two factors are substitutes in production when the marginal product of one factor is a decreasing function of the quantity used of the other factor, when $\Delta MQ_1/\Delta F_2 < 0$ and $\Delta MQ_2/\Delta F_1 < 0$. Thus, assuming decreasing marginal product of a factor of production, each successive unit increase in F_1 decreases MQ_1 (which tends to decrease MQ_1/MQ_2 and hence $-\Delta F_2/\Delta F_1$) and decreases MQ_2 (which tends to increase MQ_1/MQ_2 and hence $-\Delta F_2/\Delta F_1$). Similarly, each successive unit decrease in Q_2 increases MQ_2 (which tends to decrease MQ_1/MQ_2 and hence $-\Delta F_2/\Delta F_1$) and increases MQ_1 (which tends to increase MQ_1/MQ_2 and hence $-\Delta F_2/\Delta F_1$). If F_1 and F_2 are imperfect substitutes in production, the tendency for MQ_1/MQ_2 to decrease because of decreasing marginal product of a factor more than offsets the tendency for MQ_1/MQ_2 to increase because of the substitute relationship between them; hence the ratio $\Delta F_2/\Delta F_1$ decreases numerically as more F_1 and less F_2 are used. In other words, as seen in Figure 7.3a, the iso-product curve of two imperfect substitutes in production is concave from above a tangent line; as seen in Figure 7.3b, the marginal rate of technical substitution of F_1 for F_2 varies inversely with F_1.

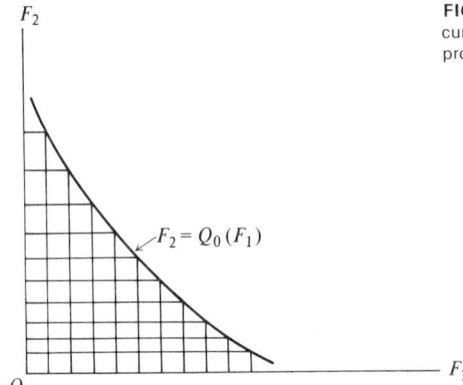

FIG. 7.3a. Hypothetical iso-product curve of two imperfect substitutes in production

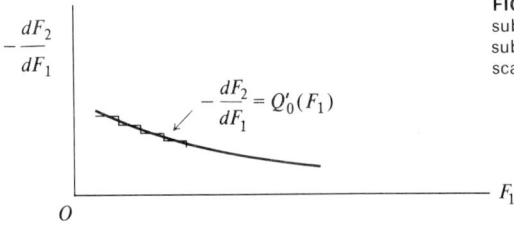

FIG. 7.3b. Marginal rate of technical substitution curve of two imperfect substitutes in production. (The $-dF_2/dF_1$ scale is one half the F_2 scale.)

But if F_1 and F_2 are perfect substitutes in production, the tendency for MQ_1/MQ_2 to decrease because of decreasing marginal product of a factor is offset exactly by the tendency for MQ_1/MQ_2 to increase because of the substitute relationship between them; hence the ratio $\Delta F_2/\Delta F_1$ remains constant as more F_1 and less F_2 are used. In other words, as seen in Figure 7.4a, the iso-product curve of two perfect substitutes in production is a negatively-sloped straight line; as seen in Figure 7.4b, the marginal rate of technical substitution of F_1 for F_2 does not vary with F_1.

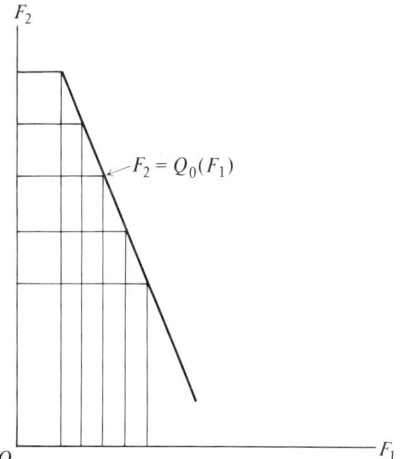

FIG. 7.4a. Hypothetical iso-product curve of two perfect substitutes in production

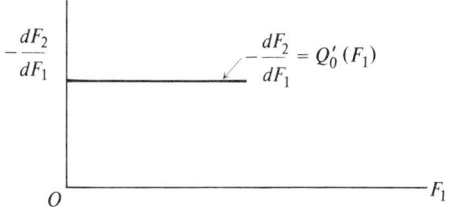

FIG. 7.4b. Marginal rate of technical substitution curve of two perfect substitutes in production. (The $-dF_2/dF_1$ scale is one half the F_2 scale.)

Iso-Product Curve of Two Complements in Production

Two factors are complements in production when the marginal product of one factor is an increasing function of the quantity used of the other factor, when $\Delta MQ_1/\Delta Q_2 > 0$ and $\Delta MQ_2/\Delta Q_1 > 0$. Thus, assuming decreasing marginal product of a factor of production, each successive unit increase in F_1 decreases MQ_1 and increases MQ_2, thereby tending to decrease MQ_1/MQ_2 and hence $-\Delta F_2/\Delta F_1$; and each successive unit decrease in F_2 increases MQ_2 and decreases MQ_1, thereby tending to decrease MQ_1/MQ_2 and hence $-\Delta F_2/\Delta F_1$. Conversely, each successive unit increase in F_2 decreases MQ_2 and increases MQ_1, thereby tending to increase MQ_1/MQ_2 and hence $-\Delta F_2/\Delta F_1$; and each successive unit decrease in F_1 increases MQ_1 and decreases MQ_2, thereby tending to increase MQ_1/MQ_2 and hence $-\Delta F_2/\Delta F_1$. Therefore, as seen in Figure 7.5a, the iso-product curve of two imperfect complements in production is concave from above a tangent line; the

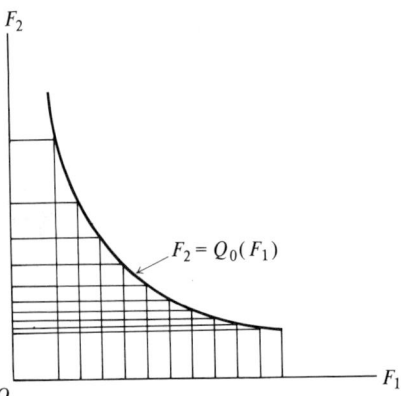

FIG. 7.5a. Hypothetical iso-product curve of two imperfect complements in production

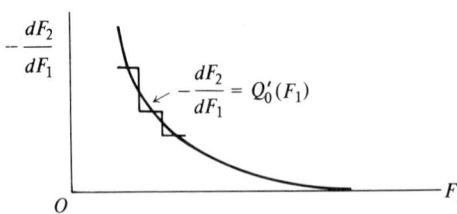

FIG. 7.5b. Marginal rate of technical substitution curve of two imperfect complements in production. (The $-dF_2/dF_1$ scale is one half the F_2 scale.)

marginal rate of technical substitution of F_1 for F_2 varies inversely with F_1 (as seen in Figure 7.5b) and directly with F_2.

But if F_1 and F_2 are perfect complements in production, MQ_1/MQ_2 is zero as F_1 increases and is approaching infinity as F_2 increases. Thus, as F_1 increases, the iso-product curve is a horizontal straight line (see the horizontal portion of the curve in Figure 7.6); and, as F_2 increases, the iso-product curve is a vertical straight line (see the vertical portion of the curve in Figure 7.6). In short, F_1 and F_2 are purchased in fixed proportion; therefore, the iso-product "curve" is a point in the OF_1F_2 plane representing the constant ratio of F_2 to F_1. A set of constant F_2/F_1 ratios is represented by a ray, as seen in Figure 7.6.

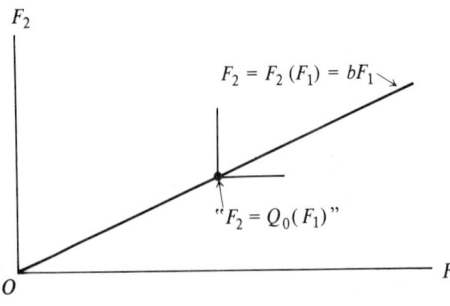

FIG. 7.6. Hypothetical iso-product curve of two perfect complements in production

Economic Region of Production

In production theory, a distinction is made between three stages of production of a variable factor of production. With respect to the two-factor production function $Q = Q(F_1, F_2)$, stage I of production of factor F_1 is the set of F_1 values over which the average product of F_1 (AQ_1) increases as F_1 increases. Its stage II of production is the set of F_1 values over which the average product of F_1 decreases and the marginal product of F_1 (MQ_1) is positive. Its stage III of production is the set of F_1 values over which the marginal product of F_1 is negative. Similarly, stage I of production of factor F_2 is the set of F_2 values over which the average product of F_2 (AQ_2) increases as F_2 increases. Its stage II of production is the set of F_2 values over which the average product of F_2 decreases and the marginal product of F_2 (MQ_2) is positive. Its stage III of production is the set of F_2 values over which the marginal product of F_2 is negative. As seen in the appendix to this chapter, factor F_1's stage I is the same as factor F_2's stage III; F_1's stage III is the same as F_2's stage I; and F_1's stage II is the same as F_2's stage II. The economic region of production is stage II of both factors, for the output of both factors is greater within stage II than it is outside stage II—a conclusion that may be analyzed via a set of iso-product curves, called an iso-product map.

In the context of continuous number sets, each point in an OF_1F_2 plane lies on an iso-product curve. But all points on a curve do not necessarily lie within the economic region of production, within stage II of F_1 and F_2. That is, a portion of an iso-product curve may lie outside the economic region. In Figure 7.7, all points within the OF_2 and OF_1 "ridge lines" are within the

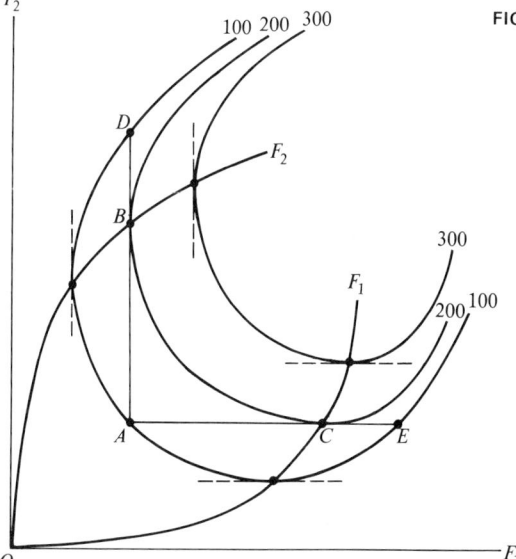

FIG. 7.7. Economic region of production

economic region; all points outside these lines are outside the economic region; and all points on these lines separate the economic and noneconomic regions.

Points on negatively-sloped portions of iso-product curves are within the economic region. To see this, let a user start at point A within the ridge lines and move toward point B by increasing F_2 while holding F_1 constant, or toward point C by increasing F_1 while holding F_2 constant. In either case, he moves to a higher iso-product curve when he uses more of one factor and a constant amount of the other factor. Thus, total product increases as more of the variable factor is used with the given amount of the fixed factor. Therefore, marginal product of the variable factor is positive within the ridge lines. Consequently, all points within the ridge lines are within stage II of F_2 and F_1.

Points on positively-sloped portions of iso-product curves are outside the economic region. To see this, let the user start at point B on the ridge line OF_2 and move toward point D by increasing F_2 while holding F_1 constant. Or let him start at point C on the ridge line OF_1 and move toward point E by increasing F_1 while holding F_2 constant. In either case, he moves to a lower iso-product curve when he uses more of one factor and a constant amount of the other factor. Thus, total product decreases as more of the variable factor is used with the given amount of the fixed factor. Therefore, marginal product of the variable factor is negative outside the ridge lines. Consequently, all points outside the ridge lines are either in stages I or III. All points outside the ridge line OF_2 are within stage III of F_2 and stage I of F_1, for relatively little F_1 is used with relatively much F_2; all points outside the ridge line OF_1 are within stage III of F_1 and stage I of F_2, for relatively little F_2 is used with relatively much F_1.

To repeat, marginal product of the variable factor is positive within the ridge lines and negative outside the ridge lines. Therefore, marginal product of the variable factor is zero on the ridge lines. The OF_2 ridge line represents zero MQ_2 at various values of F_1, and the OF, ridge line represents zero MQ_1 at various values of F_2. Consequently, all points on the ridge lines separate stage II from stages I and III. All points on the ridge line OF_2 separate stage II of F_2 from its stage III, and stage II of F_1 from its stage I; and all points on the ridge line OF_1 separate stage II of F_1 from its stage III, and stage II of F_2 from its stage I.

Variable Proportions and Marginal Returns to Variable Input

In production theory, a distinction is made between two production periods, the short run and the long run. In the short run total product varies with the input of variable factors of production, given the input of fixed factors and the state of technology. In this context, a user (business firm) hypothetically may be subject to increasing, constant, and decreasing marginal returns to the variable input. Decreasing marginal returns to the variable input is also called the law of variable proportions. The word "proportion" here means that total product is changing as the ratio (proportion) of the variable input to the fixed input changes. These three marginal-return cases may be analyzed via an iso-product map, in the context of the two-factor production function $Q = Q(F_1, F_2)$, given the state of technology.

In Figure 7.8, let a firm start at point A' and move toward point E' by

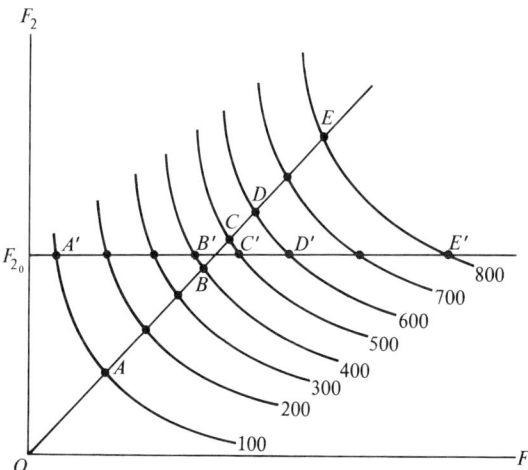

FIG. 7.8. Variable and fixed proportions of inputs

increasing F_1 (the variable input) according to the horizontal line $A'B'C'D'E'$, while holding F_2 (the fixed input) constant at F_{2_0}. Then $Q = Q(F_1)$, where $F_2 = F_{2_0}$. The intersection of the horizontal line with higher iso-product curves denotes the amount of total product associated with each level of input of F_1 and the given input F_{2_0}. According to this line, total product increases as the input of F_1 increases; thus all points along this line are within the economic region of production.

As F_1 increases from A' to B', the $A'B'$ segment of the horizontal line depicts increasing marginal returns to the variable input, for this segment intersects higher iso-product curves denoting multiples of 100 units of output at smaller intervals of F_1. Thus the iso-product curves are closer and closer together; each additional unit of F_1, utilized in the increasing ratio F_1/F_2, adds a larger amount to total product. Total product, therefore, is increasing at an increasing rate as F_1 increases—a way of saying increasing marginal product of F_1. As F_1 increases from B' to D', the $B'D'$ segment depicts constant marginal returns to scale, for this segment intersects higher iso-product curves at equal intervals of F_1. Thus the iso-product curves are an equal distance apart; each additional unit of F_1 adds the same amount to total product. Total product, therefore, is increasing at a constant rate as F_1 increases—a way of saying constant marginal product of F_1. Lastly, as F_1

increases from C' to E', the $C'E'$ segment depicts decreasing marginal returns to the variable input, for this segment intersects higher iso-product curves at larger intervals of F_1. Thus the iso-product curves are farther and farther apart; each additional unit of F_1 adds a smaller amount to total product. Total product, therefore, is increasing at a decreasing rate as F_1 increases—a way of saying decreasing marginal product of F_1.

Fixed Proportions and Returns to Scale

In the long run, all factors of production may be defined to be variable; thus total product may be said to vary with the input of all factors of production, given the state of technology. In this context, a firm hypothetically may be subject to increasing, constant, and decreasing returns to scale. The word "scale" here means that total product is changing as the overall size (scale) of the firm changes. These three returns-to-scale cases may be analyzed via an iso-product map, in the context of the two-factor production function $Q = Q(F_1, F_2)$.

With respect to a given iso-product curve, $F_2 = Q_0(F_1)$, both F_1 and F_2 are variable factors and are used in varying proportions; that is, the ratio F_1/F_2 increases as more F_1 and less F_2 are used (and vice versa). With respect to a given ray, $F_2 = bF_1$ (where $b = F_2/F_1$), that intersects each of the iso-product curves of a map, both F_1 and F_2 are variable factors and are used in fixed proportion; that is, the ratio F_2/F_1 (or F_1/F_2) remains constant as more F_1 and more F_2 are used. For example, if the first unit of (variable) input contains five units of labor (for example, five ditch-digging laborers) and five units of capital (for example, five shovels), then its second unit contains ten units of labor and ten units of capital, and its third unit contains fifteen units of labor and fifteen units of capital, etc.

In Figure 7.8, let a firm start at point A and move toward point E by increasing F_1 and F_2 according to the ray $ABCDE$. Then $Q = (F_1, F_2)$, where $F_2/F_1 = b$. The intersection of the ray with iso-product curves denotes the amount of total product associated with each level of input of F_1 and F_2. As input increases from A to B, the AB segment of the ray depicts increasing returns to scale, for this segment intersects higher iso-product curves denoting multiples of 100 units of product at smaller intervals of F_1 and F_2. Thus the iso-product curves are closer and closer together; a doubling of the inputs (F_1 and F_2) more than doubles output. Long-run total product increases at an increasing rate as input increases from A to B. As input increases from B to D, the BD segment depicts constant returns to scale, for this segment intersects higher iso-product curves at equal intervals of F_1 and F_2. Thus the iso-product curves are an equal distance apart; a doubling of the inputs doubles output. Long-run total product increases at a constant rate as input increases from B to D. Lastly, as input increases from C to E, the CE segment depicts decreasing returns to scale, for this segment intersects higher iso-product curves at larger intervals of F_1 and F_2. Thus the iso-product curves are farther and farther apart; a doubling of the inputs less than doubles output. Long-run total product increases at a decreasing rate as input increases from C to E.

Basis of Returns to Scale

Think in terms of management planning to increase output by increasing labor and capital, not necessarily in fixed proportion, given today's known technology. As it plans for the future, management may impute increasing returns to scale to division and specialization of labor and to technological factors. The results of division and specialization of labor are greater concentration of effort by a worker, simplification of his job, and reduction in number of time-consuming interchanges of tools and locations. But these advantages may be available only if the work force is increased.

Similarly, technological factors which result in increasing returns to scale may be attainable only if more capital is used. Because of their indivisibility, a larger capacity machine of greater output per unit of input may not be purchased to replace a smaller capacity machine until a certain output level has been attained. Moreover, because of their indivisibility, two machines currently being used may require a higher output level if they are to be used more economically together. For example, if a firm uses five machines of type A, each producing 10,000 units a day, and two machines of type B, each producing 25,000 units a day, output will have to be 50,000 units a day if the capacity of the firm is to be fully utilized. Lastly, up to a point, larger units of capital have dimensional efficiency; for example, the flow through a pipe may more than double when its diameter is doubled.

Constant returns to scale supposedly are an empirical fact in some industries over a range of output. The best known empirical study in production theory is the study of Cobb and Douglas, who assumed constant returns to scale.[4] For lack of a better a priori rationale, constant returns to scale may be attributed to a stalemate between the forces of increasing returns to scale and decreasing returns to scale.

The a priori basis of decreasing returns to scale may be said to be management. Management supposedly is not a factor of production that can continually increase in size and retain its efficiency. It is supposed to be subject to communication and coordination difficulties as scale passes a certain size.[5]

Technological Progress

With each improvement in technology, the same level of input now yields more output. Thus a given iso-product curve may now be said to denote a higher level of output. Conversely, the same level of output now requires less input. Thus a given iso-product curve may now be said to denote the same level of output, but has shifted toward the origin. In effect, as seen in Figures 7.9, 7.10, and 7.11, curve I' becomes curve I'' with the first improve-

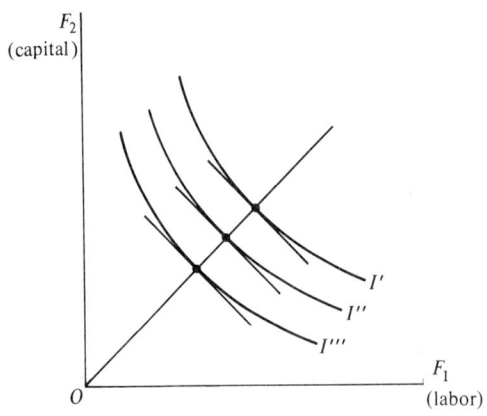

FIG. 7.9. Neutral technological progress

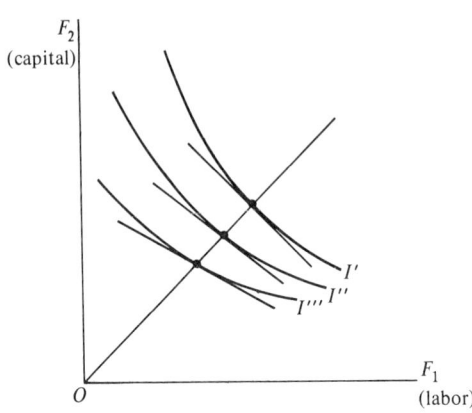

FIG. 7.10. Capital using technological progress

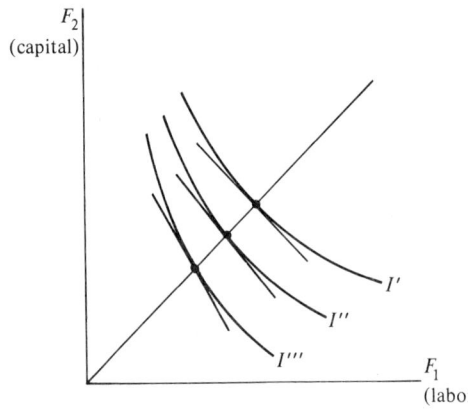

FIG. 7.11. Labor using technological progress

ment; and curve I'' becomes curve I''' with the next improvement, etc. In other words, I', I'', and I''' represent the same output (I), but I''' requires less input of both factors than I'', and I'' requires less input of both factors than I'.

The ray in Figures 7.9, 7.10, and 7.11 represents the originally prevailing ratio of capital (F_2) to labor (F_1). This ray intersects the given iso-product curve as it shifts toward the origin to represent improvements in technology. At each intersection of the ray, the tangent line to the curve depicts the marginal rate of technical substitution of labor for capital ($-dF_2/dF_1$). Professor Hicks classifies technological progress according to its effect on the marginal rate of technical substitution along the originally prevailing ray.[6]

Technological progress is *neutral* if the marginal rate of technical substitution remains unchanged as technology improves (see Figure 7.9). In this case, the increase in marginal product of labor equals the increase in marginal product of capital. Graphically, the steepness of the tangent to I' is the same as the steepness of the tangent to I'' and to I'''. The firm has no incentive to change its use of capital relative to labor, for the marginal product of capital has not changed relative to the marginal product of labor.

Technological progress is *capital using* if the marginal rate of technical substitution decreases as technology improves (see Figure 7.10). In this case, the increase in marginal product of labor is less than the increase in marginal product of capital. Graphically, the tangent to I' is steeper than the tangent to I'', which is steeper than the tangent to I'''. The firm has an incentive to use more capital relative to labor, for the marginal product of capital has increased relative to the marginal product of labor.

Technological progress is *labor using* if the marginal rate of technical substitution increases as technology improves (see Figure 7.11). In this case, the increase in marginal product of labor is greater than the increase in marginal product of capital. Graphically, the tangent to I' is flatter than the tangent to I'', which is flatter than the tangent to I'''. The firm has an incentive to use more labor relative to capital, for the marginal product of labor has increased relative to the marginal product of capital.

SUMMARY

The total product curve of a factor of production shows how total product (Q) varies with quantity purchased (and/or used) of the factor (F) per unit of time. The marginal product curve of a factor shows how the slope of the total product curve (dQ/dF) varies with quantity purchased of the factor (F) per unit of time. The average product curve of a factor shows how the ratio of total product to input (Q/F) varies with quantity purchased of the factor (F) per unit of time. In the case of a user who is subject to diminishing marginal returns, each additional unit purchased of a factor per unit of time adds a smaller amount to total product. Total product (Q) therefore increases at a decreasing rate (dQ/dF) as quantity used (F) increases. Consequently, marginal product of the factor $(MQ = dQ/dF)$ is a decreasing function of quantity used (F) per unit of time. To generalize, according to the law of decreasing marginal product of a factor to a user who is subject to diminishing marginal returns, the product associated with using an additional unit of a factor varies inversely with quantity used per unit of time. Average product of the factor $(AQ = Q/F)$ is a decreasing function of quantity used (F) when marginal product is a continuously decreasing function of quantity.

With respect to Figures 7.1a and 7.1b, marginal and average products of a factor of production are increasing when output is increasing at an increasing rate with respect to the factor, and the marginal product curve lies above the average product curve. The marginal product curve is at its maximum value, but average product continues to increase, at that quantity of the factor at which output begins to increase at a decreasing rate. Eventually, as more units of the factor are used, marginal product decreases sufficiently to make average product reach its maximum value. When this happens, the marginal product curve is intersecting the average product curve from above. Thereafter, average product also decreases, and the marginal product curve lies below the average product curve. Thus the law of decreasing marginal product applies to the negatively-sloped portion of the marginal product curve and to that portion of the total product curve denoting that total product is increasing at a decreasing rate. When output reaches its maximum value, marginal product is zero, but average product is some positive value. When output decreases, marginal product is negative. Average product continues to decrease toward zero, and becomes zero when output is zero.

An iso-product curve depicts all combinations of quantities of two variable factors $(F_1$ and $F_2)$ that yield the same level of product (Q), given the parameter of technology. An iso-product curve may be drawn for each level of Q. The greater the value of Q, the higher the curve lies in the OF_1F_2 plane. No two curves intersect. In general, an iso-product curve is a negatively-sloped curve that is concave from above a tangent line. The numerical value of its slope $(-dF_2/dF_1)$ is called the marginal rate of technical substitution of factor F_1 for factor F_2. The relation between the numerical value of dF_2/dF_1 and the quantity of F_1 is depicted by the marginal rate of technical substitution curve of factor F_1.

When F_1 and F_2 are not related in production, the marginal product of one factor is a constant function of the quantity of the other factor; and the numerical value of dF_2/dF_1 varies inversely with F_1 because of decreasing marginal product of a factor. When F_1 and F_2 are imperfect substitutes in production, the marginal product of one factor is a decreasing function of the quantity of the other factor; as F_1 increases the tendency for $-dF_2/dF_1$ to decrease because of decreasing marginal product of a factor more than offsets the tendency for $-dF_2/dF_1$ to increase because of the substitute relationship between them. When F_1 and F_2 are imperfect complements in production, the marginal product of one factor is an increasing function of the quantity of the other factor; as F_1 increases, the tendency for $-dF_2/dF_1$ to decrease because of decreasing marginal product of a factor is reinforced by the tendency for $-dF_2/dF_1$ to decrease because of the complementary relationship between them. Thus, the greater the degree of complementarity, the greater the degree of concavity of the iso-product curve, and the steeper the marginal rate of technical substitution curve. Conversely, the greater the degree of substitutability, the less the degree of concavity of the iso-product curve, and the flatter the marginal rate of technical substitution curve. The iso-product curve is a negatively-sloped straight line in the case of two perfect substitutes, and the marginal rate of technical substitution curve is a horizontal straight line. But the iso-product curve is a point in the OF_1F_2 plane in the case of two perfect complements in production, and dF_2/dF_1 cannot be calculated.

The economic region of production is the region in which the marginal product of each factor of production is positive, for then total product is larger than it would otherwise be. All points within the ridge lines of an iso-product map are within the economic region. All points outside the ridge lines are outside the economic region. Within the ridge line, each factor is in its stage II. Outside the ridge lines, a factor is in its stage III if it is being used in large amounts relative to other factors; and it is in its stage I if it is being used in small amounts relative to other factors. In the context of the short run, a horizontal line drawn through an iso-product map depicts increasing marginal returns to variable input when it intersects higher iso-product curves at smaller intervals of the input, constant marginal returns when it intersects curves at equal intervals, and decreasing marginal returns when it intersects curves at larger intervals. In the context of the long run, a ray drawn through an iso-product map depicts increasing returns to scale when it intersects higher iso-product curves at smaller intervals of all input, constant returns to scale when it intersects curves at equal intervals, and decreasing returns to scale when it intersects curves at larger intervals. Measuring labor on the horizontal axis and capital on the vertical axis of an iso-product diagram, technological progress is neutral if the marginal rate of technical substitution of labor for capital remains unchanged as technology improves; it is capital using if the marginal rate of technical substitution decreases as technology improves; and it is labor using if the marginal rate of technical substitution increases as technology improves.

Questions

1. List the principles of the theory of supply of a product that are of primary importance. How do you account for the position of the law of decreasing marginal product in this list? Verbalize this principle of economics.

132   PRINCIPLES OF THE THEORY OF SUPPLY OF A PRODUCT

2. Define total product of a factor of production. What is a total product curve? Draw a total product curve and describe its properties.

3. Define marginal product of a factor of production. What is a marginal product curve? Draw a marginal product curve and describe its properties. Relate the properties of the total and marginal product curves.

4. Define average product of a factor of production. What is an average product curve? Draw an average product curve and describe its properties. Relate the properties of the total and average product curves, and the marginal and average product curves.

5. Define the iso-product of two factors of production. What is an iso-product curve? Draw an iso-product curve and describe its properties. Relate marginal product and the slope of an iso-product curve. Verbalize the numerical value of the slope of an iso-product curve.

6. Classify factors in production via the marginal product concept. Relate your classification to the slope of an iso-product curve.

7. Analyze the concept of the economic region of production via the concept of an iso-product map.

8. Analyze the law of variable proportions via an iso-product map.

9. Analyze the concept of returns to scale via an iso-product map.

10. Analyze technological progress via iso-product maps.

APPENDIX: Symmetry of the Stages of Production

To present the concept of symmetry of the stages of production, let total product (Q) be a function of two factors, labor and capital (N and K). Labor is measured on the horizontal axis of Figure 7.12a, and capital is measured on the horizontal axis of Figure 7.12b. The ratio N/K of Figure 7.12a increases as N increases while K remains constant. Thus, when N is the variable factor and K is the fixed factor, Figure 7.12a is read from left to right. But N/K is the reciprocal of K/N, the set of fractions representing capital. Thus, as N/K decreases from right to left in Figure 7.12a, K/N (that is, capital) increases from right to left in Figure 7.12b. Therefore, when K is the variable factor and N is the fixed factor, Figure 7.12b is read from right to left.

Stages of Production

By definition, as seen in Figure 7.12a, labor's stage I of production is the set of labor values over which the average product of labor (AQ_n) increases as N/K increases. Its stage II is the set of labor values over which the average product of labor decreases and the marginal product of labor (MQ_n) is positive. Its stage III is the set of labor values over which the marginal product of labor is negative. Similarly, as seen in Figure 7.12b, capital's stage I of production is the set of capital values over which the average product of capital (AQ_k) increases as K/N increases. Its stage II is the set of capital values over which the average product of capital decreases and the marginal product of capital (MQ_k) is positive. Its stage III is the set of capital values over which the

FIG. 7.12a. Symmetry of the stages of production

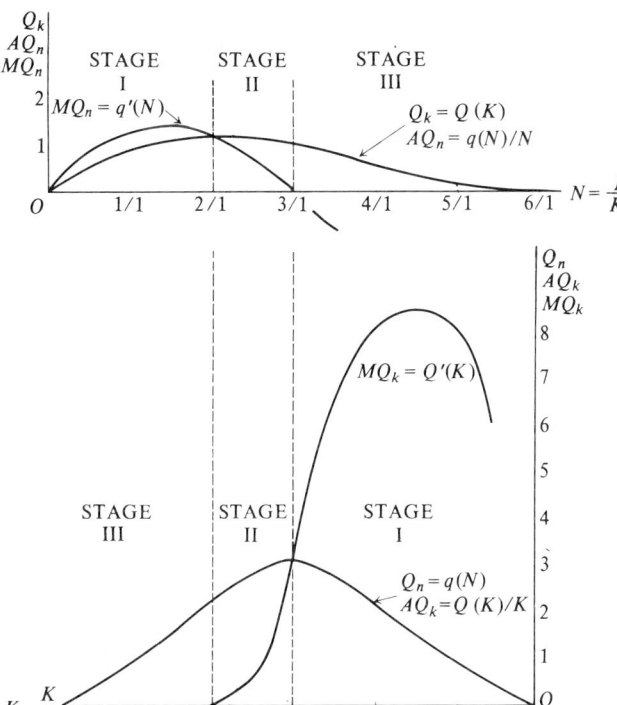

FIG. 7.12b. Symmetry of the stages of production

marginal product of capital is negative. By comparing Figures 7.12a and 7.12b, labor's stage I is seen to be the same as capital's stage III; labor's stage III is seen to be the same as capital's stage I; and labor's stage II is seen to be the same as capital's stage II.

Product Curves of Labor

Table 7.2 provides the hypothetical data depicted in Figures 7.12a and 7.12b. Given one unit of capital (column 1), the data of columns 2 and 5 are used to construct the data of the remaining columns in Table 7.2. The total product curve of labor, $Q_n = q(N)$, depicts the relation between the set of N numbers of column 2 and the set of Q_n numbers of column 5. This relation is the same as the relation between the set of N/K numbers of column 3 and the set of Q_n numbers of column 5, for by assumption K is one unit (column 1): $Q_n = q(N/K)$. The average product curve of labor, $AQ_n = q(N)/N$, depicts the relation between the set of N numbers of column 2 and the set of AQ_n numbers of column 6. It is derived by dividing each Q_n number of column 5 by the corresponding N number of column 2 and relating the resulting set of Q_n/N numbers (column 6) to the set of N numbers: $AQ_n = Q_n/N$. It may also be derived by dividing

PRINCIPLES OF THE THEORY OF SUPPLY OF A PRODUCT

TABLE 7.2: Symmetry of the stages of production

		Labor							Capital		
(1)	(2)	(3)	(4)	(5)	(6)	(7)	(8)	(9)	(10)	(11)	(12)
K	N	$\dfrac{N}{K}$	$\dfrac{K}{N}$	Q_n	AQ_n	MQ_n	K	N	Q_k	AQ_k	MQ_k
1	0	0		0.00	0.000						
1	1	1/1	1/1	1.00	1.000	1.00	1/1	1	1.000	1.00	−0.50
1	2	2/1	1/2	2.50	1.250	1.50	1/2	1	1.250	2.50	0.50
1	3	3/1	1/3	3.50	1.167	1.00	1/3	1	1.167	3.50	6.50
1	4	4/1	1/4	2.50	0.625	−1.00	1/4	1	0.625	2.50	8.50
1	5	5/1	1/5	1.00	0.200	−1.50	1/5	1	0.200	1.00	6.00
1	6	6/1	1/6	0.00	0.000	−1.00	1/6	1	0.000	0.00	

each Q_n number by the corresponding N/K ($= N$) number of column 3 and relating the resulting set of $Q_n \div N/K$ numbers (column 6) to the set of N/K numbers: $AQ_n = Q_n \div N/K$. The marginal product curve of labor, $MQ_n = q'(N)$, depicts the relation between the set of N numbers of column 2 and the set of MQ_n numbers of column 7. It is derived (approximately) by dividing each ΔQ_n number by the corresponding ΔN number and relating the resulting set of $\Delta Q_n/\Delta N$ numbers (column 7) to the set of N numbers: $MQ_n = \Delta Q_n/\Delta N$. It may also be derived (approximately) by dividing each ΔQ_n number by the corresponding $\Delta(N/K)$ number and relating the resulting set of $\Delta Q_n \div \Delta(N/K)$ numbers (column 7) to the set of N/K ($= N$) numbers (column 3): $MQ_n = \Delta Q_n \div \Delta(N/K)$.

Product Curves of Capital

The total product curve of capital, $Q_k = Q(K)$, depicts the relation between the set of K numbers of column 8 and the set of Q_k numbers of column 10. This relation is the same as the relation between the set of K/N numbers of column 4 and the set of Q_k numbers of column 10, for by assumption the set of K numbers is the set of K/N numbers, a set of fractions: $Q_k = Q(K/N)$. The average product curve of capital, $AQ_k = Q(K)/K$, depicts the relation between the set of K numbers of column 8 and the set of AQ_k numbers of column 11. It is derived by dividing each Q_k number of column 10 by the corresponding K number of column 8 and relating the resulting set of Q_k/K numbers (column 11) to the set of K numbers: $AQ_k = Q_k/K$. It may also be derived by dividing each Q_k number by the corresponding K/N ($= K$) number of column 4 and relating the resulting set of $Q_k \div K/N$ numbers (column 11) to the set of K/N numbers: $AQ_k = Q_k \div K/N$. The marginal product curve of capital, $MQ_k = Q'(K)$, depicts the relation between the set of K numbers of column 8 and the set of MQ_k numbers of column 12. It is derived (approximately) by dividing each ΔQ_k number by the corresponding ΔK number and relating the resulting set of $\Delta Q_k/\Delta K$ numbers (column 12) to the set of K numbers: $MQ_k = \Delta Q_k/\Delta K$. It may also be derived (approximately) by dividing each ΔQ_k number by the corresponding $\Delta(K/N)$ number and relating the resulting set of $\Delta Q_k \div \Delta(K/N)$

numbers (column 12) to the set of K/N ($= K$) numbers (column 4): $MQ_k = \Delta Q_k \div \Delta(K/N)$.

Total Product of Capital and Average Product of Labor

The total product curve of capital is derived from the total product curve of labor by assuming constant returns to scale. Given this assumption, when labor and capital are each divided by the same number, output also is divided by that number. Thus, given the data of columns 1, 2, and 5, if 1 unit of K and 2 units of N produce 2.50 units of Q_n, then (by dividing by 2) 1/2 of a unit of K ($= K/N$) and 1 unit of N produce 1.25 units of Q_k. Similarly, if 1 unit of K and 3 units of N produce 3.50 units of Q_n, then (by dividing by 3) 1/3 of a unit of K ($= K/N$) and 1 unit of N produce 1.167 units of Q_k, etc. The total product of capital at various values of K/N, therefore, is derived by dividing each Q_n number of column 5 by the corresponding N/K ($= N$) number of column 3: $Q_k = Q_n \div N/K$. But this is the same method used to calculate the average product of labor at various values of N/K, for $AQ_n = Q_n \div N/K$. Thus, with respect to each N/K (that is, K/N) ratio, the total product of capital (Q_k) is the same as the average product of labor (AQ_n). The total product curve of capital, therefore, is the converse of the average product curve of labor, for K/N decreases as N/K increases, as depicted in Figure 7.12a by the curve labeled $Q_k = Q(K)$ and $AQ_n = q(N)/N$.

Total Product of Labor and Average Product of Capital

The total product curve of labor may also be derived from the total product curve of capital by assuming constant returns to scale. Given this assumption, when labor and capital are each multiplied by the same number, output also is multiplied by that number. Thus, given the data of columns 8, 9, and 10, if 1/2 of a unit of K and 1 unit of N produce 1.25 units of Q_k, then (by multiplying by 2) 1 unit of K and 2 units of N ($= N/K$) produce 2.50 units of Q_n. Similarly, if 1/3 of a unit of K and 1 unit of N produce 1.167 units of Q_k, then (by multiplying by 3) 1 unit of K and 3 units of N ($= N/K$) produce 3.50 units of Q_n, etc. The total product of labor at various values of N/K, therefore, may be derived by multiplying each Q_k number of column 10 by the corresponding N/K ($= N$) number of column 3: $Q_n = Q_k \cdot N/K$. The same result may be obtained, however, by dividing each Q_k number by the corresponding K/N number of column 4: $Q_n = Q_k \div K/N$. But this is the same method used to calculate the average product of capital at various values of K/N, for $AQ_k = Q_k \div K/N$. Thus, with respect to each K/N (that is, N/K) ratio, the total product of labor (Q_n) is the same as the average product of capital (AQ_k). The total product curve of labor, therefore, is the converse of the average product curve of capital, for N/K increases as K/N decreases, as depicted in Figure 7.12b by the curve labeled $Q_n = q(N)$ and $AQ_k = Q(K)/K$.

Basis of Symmetry

The relation between the total product curve of one factor and the average product curve of the other factor is the basis of the symmetry of the stages of production. To see that stage I of labor is the same as stage III of capital, first read from right to left in

Figures 7.12a and 7.12b. When the total product of capital (= average product of labor) is a maximum (Figure 7.12a), the marginal product of capital is zero (Figure 7.12b). By definition, capital's stage II ends and its stage III begins at the peak of the total product curve of capital; that is, when the K/N ratio is so large (the N/K ratio so small) that the marginal product of capital is zero. Now, read from left to right. The reason why labor's stage I ends and its stage II begins at the peak of the average product curve of labor may now be stated: the marginal product of capital is zero at that N/K ratio, is negative at a lower N/K ratio, and is positive at a higher N/K ratio. To repeat, reading from left to right, the boundary between stages I and II of labor is the peak of the average product curve of labor. Reading from right to left, the boundary between stages II and III of capital is the peak of the total product curve of capital. To the left of this boundary, labor's stage I is the same as capital's stage III. To the right of this boundary, labor's stage II is the same as capital's stage II.

To see that stage I of capital is the same as stage III of labor, first read from left to right in Figures 7.12a and 7.12b. When the total product of labor (= average product of capital) is a maximum (Figure 7.12b), the marginal product of labor is zero (Figure 7.12a). By definition, labor's stage II ends and its stage III begins at the peak of the total product curve of labor; that is, when the N/K ratio is so large (the K/N ratio so small) that the marginal product of labor is zero. Now, read from right to left. The reason why capital's stage I ends and its stage II begins at the peak of the average product curve of capital may now be stated: the marginal product of labor is zero at that K/N ratio, is negative at a lower K/N ratio, and is positive at a higher K/N ratio. To repeat, reading from right to left, the boundary between stages I and II of capital is the peak of the average product curve of capital. Reading from left to right, the boundary between stages II and III of labor is the peak of the total product curve of labor. To the right of this boundary, capital's stage I is the same as labor's stage III. To the left of this boundary, capital's stage II is the same as labor's stage II.

Importance of Symmetry

The symmetry of the stages of production of labor and capital is important because of the inference that may be drawn from it concerning the maximization of output from a given input of labor and capital (that is, the minimization of input required to produce a given output). Given this objective, one may infer from Figures 7.12a and 7.12b that production does not occur in labor's stage I (= capital's stage III). Relatively little labor when used with relatively much capital yields positive marginal products of labor and negative marginal products of capital. Therefore, more labor and less capital is used if the objective is to maximize the output per a given input of both factors. Stage II is entered as labor is substituted for capital. Similarly, given the same objective, one may infer from Figures 7.12a and 7.12b that production does not occur in capital's stage I (= labor's stage III). Relatively little capital when used with relatively much labor yields positive marginal products of capital and negative marginal products of labor. Therefore, more capital and less labor is used if the objective is to maximize the output per a given input of both factors. Stage II is entered again as capital is substituted for labor.

To conclude, given the objective of maximizing output per a given input (or minimizing input per a given output), production occurs in stage II of labor and capital. Within this stage, the various combinations of labor and capital yield positive marginal products of both factors. Outside this stage, the various combinations of labor and capital yield negative marginal products of at least one of the factors. Therefore, the output per a given input of both factors is greater within stage II than it is outside stage II. In short, the economic region of production is stage II of labor and capital.

NOTES

[1] When quantity is varied continuously, continuous marginal product of a factor of production (MQ_c) is the instantaneous rate of change of total product as quantity used of the factor increases or decreases. With respect to the one-factor function $Q = Q(F)$, the instantaneous rate of change is the infinitesimally small change in Q (dQ) associated with an infinitesimally small change in F (dF): $MQ_c = dQ/dF$. In this context, marginal product is the slope of the total product curve of the factor. The slope of the total product curve is equal to the difference quotient ($\Delta Q/\Delta F$) of the tangent line at a point on the curve. In Table 7.1, the MQ_c of the tenth unit equals

$$\frac{dQ}{dF} = \lim_{\Delta F \to 0} \frac{\Delta Q}{\Delta F} = 800$$

[2] With respect to the two-factor production function $Q = Q(F_1, F_2)$, the rate of change of Q with respect to F_1 is the infinitesimally small change in Q associated with an infinitesimally small change in F_1: $MQ_1 = \partial Q/\partial F_1$. The total infinitesimally small change in F_1 is dF_1. Thus, in terms of infinitesimally small changes, the change in Q associated with a total change in F_1 is

$$\frac{\partial Q}{\partial F_1} dF_1$$

Similarly, the instantaneous rate of change of Q with respect to F_2 is the infinitesimally small change in Q associated with an infinitesimally small change in F_2: $MQ_2 = \partial Q/\partial F_2$. The total infinitesimally small change in F_2 is dF_2. In terms of infinitesimally small changes, the change in Q associated with a total change in F_2 is

$$\frac{\partial Q}{\partial F_2} dF_2$$

Therefore, in terms of infinitesimally small changes, the total change in Q is dQ, and

$$dQ = \frac{\partial Q}{\partial F_1} dF_1 + \frac{\partial Q}{\partial F_2} dF_2$$

Since the total change in Q along an iso-product curve is zero,

$$dQ = \frac{\partial Q}{\partial F_1} dF_1 + \frac{\partial Q}{\partial F_2} dF_2 = 0$$

$$\frac{\partial Q}{\partial F_2} dF_2 = -\frac{\partial Q}{\partial F_1} dF_1$$

$$\frac{dF_2}{dF_1} = -\frac{\partial Q/\partial F_1}{\partial Q/\partial F_2} = -\frac{MQ_1}{MQ_2}$$

[3] Each successive unit increase in F_2 increases output by a decreasing amount, and each successive unit decrease in F_1 decreases output by an increasing amount. Therefore, with each unit increase in F_2 (ΔF_2), the firm gives up a decreasing amount of F_1 ($-\Delta F_1$) to keep output constant. Since the ratio $\Delta F_2/\Delta F_1$ increases numerically as more F_2 and less F_1 are used, an iso-product curve is concave from above a tangent line.

[4] C. W. Cobb and P. H. Douglas, "A Theory of Production," *American Economic Review* (supplement), XVIII (1928), pp. 139–165; P. H. Douglas, "Are There Laws of Production," *American Economic Review*, XXXVIII (March 1948), pp. 1–41. The assumption of constant

returns to scale is consistent with the assumption of decreasing marginal product of a factor of production. For a discussion, see G. Warren Nutter, "Diminishing Returns and Linear Homogeneity," *American Economic Review*, LIII (December 1963), pp. 1084–1085; and the comments of H. H. Liebhafsky, Ryuzo Sato, John W. Rowe, Jr., Dieter Schneider, Patrick B. DeFontenay, and G. Warren Nutter in the *American Economic Review*, LIV (September 1964), pp. 739–753. A production function exhibiting constant returns to scale is linearly homogeneous or homogeneous of the first degree. For a concise verbal discussion of this concept, see Alpha C. Chiang, *Fundamental Methods of Mathematical Economics* (New York: McGraw-Hill Book Company, 1967), p. 371.

[5] See O. E. Williamson, "Hierarchical Control and Optimum Firm Size," *Journal of Political Economy*, LXXV:2 (April 1967), pp. 123–127.

[6] See J. R. Hicks, *The Theory of Wages*, 2nd ed. (London: Macmillan & Co. Ltd., 1963), Chapter VI.

chapter 8

Factor Cost Functions

According to the law of constant marginal factor cost of a factor of production to a perfectly competitive purchaser, the factor cost associated with purchasing an additional unit of a factor does not vary with quantity purchased per unit of time. Each additional unit purchased of a factor per unit of time adds the same amount to total factor cost. Total factor cost of a factor increases at a constant rate as quantity purchased of the factor per unit of time increases. Marginal factor cost of a factor is a constant function of quantity purchased of the factor per unit of time.

Consider now the law of increasing marginal factor cost of a factor of production to an imperfectly competitive purchaser—defined as a purchaser who has to pay a higher price to purchase a larger quantity of a factor per unit of time ceteris paribus. According to this law, the factor cost associated with purchasing an additional unit of a factor varies directly with quantity purchased per unit of time. Each additional unit purchased of a factor per unit of time adds a larger amount to total factor cost. Total factor cost of a factor increases at an increasing rate as quantity purchased of the factor per unit of time increases. Marginal factor cost of a factor is an increasing function of quantity purchased of the factor per unit of time.

Perfectly Competitive Purchaser of a Factor of Production

A factor market may be classified as perfectly competitive or imperfectly competitive from the purchaser's side of the market. A perfectly competitive factor market is defined as a market in which the number of purchasers of a factor is so large that no purchaser can influence the price of the factor. Since no purchaser can influence the price of a factor, each purchaser is a price-taker, rather than a price-maker. Since price is a parameter to each purchaser, a perfectly competitive purchaser is defined as a purchaser who can purchase all he wishes per unit of time at the prevailing price ceteris paribus. In other words, the supply curve of a factor facing a perfectly competitive purchaser is perfectly elastic at the prevailing price.

Total Factor Cost Curve of a Factor of Production of a Perfectly Competitive Purchaser

Total factor cost is the money expended to purchase a quantity of a factor of production. The total factor cost curve of a factor is a set of ordered pairs of quantity purchased (F) and factor cost (C) having the property that corresponding to each number in the F set of numbers is one number in the C set of numbers: $C = c(F)$. Thus, the total factor cost curve shows the C value corresponding to each F value, and hence how C varies with F per unit of time. The parameter of a total factor cost curve of a perfectly competitive purchaser is the price of the factor (W): $W = W_0$.

As seen in Figure 8.1, which depicts hypothetical data presented in Table 8.1, a total factor cost curve of a perfectly competitive purchaser is a ray,

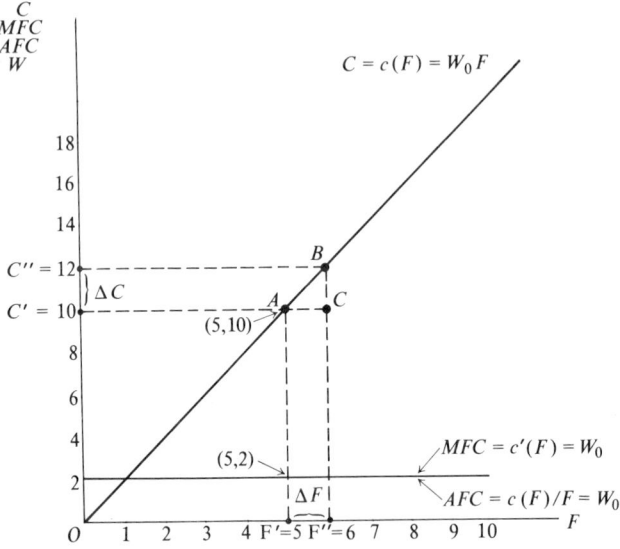

FIG. 8.1. Hypothetical factor cost curves of a factor of a perfectly competitive purchaser

the equation of which is $C = c(F) = W_0 F$. The curve has a zero total factor cost intercept because total factor cost of the factor is zero when quantity purchased is zero: $C = W_0 \cdot 0 = 0$. It is linear because each successive unit is purchased at the same price ($W_0 = 2$); hence each successive unit purchased adds the same amount ($\$2$) to total factor cost. The slope of $C = c(F)$ therefore remains constant as quantity purchased increases.

FACTOR COST FUNCTIONS

TABLE 8.1: Hypothetical factor cost of a factor to a perfectly competitive purchaser

$AFC = C/F = W_0$	F	$C = W_0 F$	$MFC_d = \Delta C/\Delta F$	$MFC_c = dC/dF$
2	0	0		2
2	1	2	2	2
2	2	4	2	2
2	3	6	2	2
2	4	8	2	2
2	5	10	2	2
2	6	12	2	2
2	7	14	2	2
2	8	16	2	2
2	9	18	2	2
2	10	20	2	2

Marginal Factor Cost Curve of a Factor of Production of a Perfectly Competitive Purchaser

When quantity purchased varies by discrete amounts, discrete marginal factor cost (MFC_d) is the change in C (ΔC) associated with a change of one unit in quantity purchased of the factor ($\Delta F = 1$): $MFC_d = \Delta C/\Delta F$, where $\Delta F = 1$. In this context, marginal factor cost is equal to the difference quotient ($\Delta C/\Delta F$) of the straight line between two points one F unit apart on the curve. In Figure 8.1, between points A and B on $C = c(F)$,

$$MFC_d = \lim_{\Delta F \to 1} \frac{\Delta C}{\Delta F} = \frac{C'' - C'}{F'' - F'} = \frac{CB}{AC} = \text{slope of line } AB = 2$$

Since a total factor cost curve of a perfectly competitive purchaser is linear, the difference quotient is the same for all changes in quantity purchased, and hence discrete marginal factor cost equals continuous marginal factor cost.[1]

The marginal factor cost curve of a factor is a set of ordered pairs of quantity purchased (F) and (continuous) marginal factor cost (MFC) having the property that corresponding to each number in the F set of numbers is one number in the MFC set of numbers: $MFC = c'(F)$. Thus, the marginal factor cost curve shows the MFC value corresponding to each F value and hence how MFC varies with F per unit of time. The parameters of a marginal factor cost curve of a perfectly competitive purchaser are the parameters of the market demand (see Chapters 5 and 19) and supply curves (see Chapters 12 and 22).

As seen in Figure 8.1, which depicts hypothetical data presented in Table 8.1, a marginal factor cost curve of a perfectly competitive purchaser is a zero-sloped (horizontal) straight line ($\Delta MFC/\Delta F = 0$), the equation of which is $MFC = c'(F) = W_0$. The curve is a horizontal straight line because each successive unit is purchased at the same price ($W_0 = \$2$); hence each successive unit purchased adds the same amount (\$2) to total factor cost. Marginal factor cost therefore remains constant as quantity purchased increases.

To conclude, marginal factor cost (MFC) is a constant function of quantity purchased (F) when total factor cost (C) increases at the constant rate W_0 as quantity increases. Thus, the law of constant marginal factor cost is a verbalization of a marginal factor cost curve of a perfectly competitive purchaser. Since total factor cost increases at a constant rate, and since the phrase "increases at a constant rate" is another way of saying "constant marginal factor cost," a total factor cost curve of a perfectly competitive purchaser also depicts the law of constant marginal factor cost.

Average Factor Cost Curve of a Factor of Production of a Perfectly Competitive Purchaser

Average factor cost (AFC) is the ratio of total factor cost (C) to quantity purchased of the factor (F): $AFC = C/F$. Average factor cost is equal to the difference quotient ($\Delta C/\Delta F$) of the ray at a point on the total factor cost curve. In Figure 8.1, at point A on $C = c(F)$,

$$AFC = \frac{F'A}{OF'} = \text{slope of line } OA = 2$$

Since a total factor cost curve of a perfectly competitive purchaser is a ray, the difference quotient is the same at each point on the curve.

The average factor cost curve of a factor is a set of ordered pairs of quantity purchased (F) and average factor cost (AFC) having the property that corresponding to each number in the F set of numbers is one number in the AFC set of numbers: $AFC = c(F)/F$. Thus, the average factor cost curve shows the AFC value corresponding to each F value and hence how AFC varies with F per unit of time. The parameters of an average factor cost curve of a perfectly competitive purchaser are the parameters of the market demand (see Chapters 5 and 19) and supply curves (see Chapters 12 and 22).

As seen in Figure 8.1, which depicts hypothetical data presented in Table 8.1, an average factor cost curve of a perfectly competitive purchaser is a zero-sloped (horizontal) straight line ($\Delta AFC/\Delta F = 0$), the equation of which is $AFC = c(F)/F = W_0$. The curve is a horizontal straight line because each quantity is purchased at the same price ($W_0 = \$2$); hence each quantity purchased has the same average factor cost (\$2). Average factor cost therefore remains constant as quantity sold increases.

Supply Curve of a Factor of Production Facing a Perfectly Competitive Purchaser

The supply curve of a factor facing a purchaser shows the price at which each quantity can be purchased. A perfectly competitive purchaser can purchase all he wishes per unit of time at the prevailing price ceteris paribus. Thus, the supply curve of a factor facing him is a line that is drawn parallel to the quantity axis to depict the given price. Moreover, at each quantity purchased, average factor cost equals marginal factor cost equals price: $AFC = MFC = W = W(F)$. Consequently, the supply curve facing a perfectly competitive purchaser is his average factor cost curve, which is the same as his marginal factor cost curve. To conclude, average and marginal factor cost are constant functions of quantity purchased when the supply curve facing the purchaser is parallel to the quantity axis.

Iso-Factor Cost Curve of a Perfectly Competitive Purchaser

The iso-factor cost of two factors is the constant (equal) amount of money expended to purchase various combinations of quantities of the factors. An iso-factor cost curve of two factors is a set of ordered pairs of quantities purchased of the two factors (F_1 and F_2) having the properties that (1) corresponding to each number in the F_1 set of numbers is one number in the F_2 set of numbers and (2) each pair of numbers of the function is associated with the same factor cost: $F_2 = c_0(F_1)$. Thus, an iso-factor cost curve shows the F_2 value corresponding to each F_1 value and hence how F_2 varies with F_1 per unit of time, holding factor cost constant. In other words, *an iso-factor cost curve depicts all combinations of quantities of two factors that may be purchased by a purchaser with a given expenditure.* The parameters of an iso-factor cost curve are the parameters of the purchaser's two-factor cost function. The parameters of the two-factor cost function of a perfectly competitive purchaser are the prices of the factors (W_1 and W_2): $W_1 = W_{1_0}$ and $W_2 = W_{2_0}$.

As seen in Figure 8.2, an iso-factor cost curve of a perfectly competitive purchaser is a negatively-sloped straight line, the equation of which is $F_2 = c_0(F_1) = C_0/W_{2_0} - (W_{1_0}/W_{2_0})F_1$, where the symbol C_0 stands for a given amount of factor cost.[2] It is negatively sloped because factors F_1 and F_2 are rivals for the dollars of a purchaser's factor cost (C_0); he may use his fixed number of dollars to purchase more of F_1 by decreasing the quantity purchased of F_2 (and vice versa). Thus, factor F_2 is a decreasing function of factor F_1: $\Delta F_2/\Delta F_1 < 0$. It is a straight line because its slope does not vary with F_1 (or F_2).

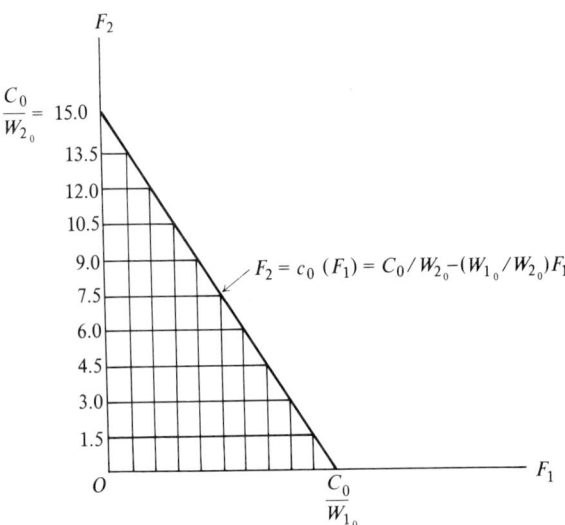

FIG. 8.2. Hypothetical iso-factor cost curve of a perfectly competitive purchaser

The slope of an iso-factor cost curve is denoted by dF_2/dF_1 and is equal to the negative of the ratio MFC_1/MFC_2, where MFC_1 is the marginal factor cost of factor one and MFC_2 is the marginal factor cost of factor two: $dF_2/dF_1 = -MFC_1/MFC_2$. By multiplying both sides by -1, $-dF_2/dF_1 = MFC_1/MFC_2$. The $-dF_2/dF_1$ notation and the MFC_1/MFC_2 notation denote numerical values and are verbalized in discrete terms as the amount of F_2 that a purchaser has to give up ($-\Delta F_2$) to purchase an additional unit of F_1 (ΔF_1) while holding factor cost constant. If $MFC_1 = W_{1_0} = \$3$ and $MFC_2 = W_{2_0} = \$2$, the purchaser has to give up 1.5 units of F_2 to purchase an additional unit of F_1.

When F_1 and F_2 vary by discrete amounts,[3] the increase in C because an additional unit of F_1 is purchased is the unit purchased of F_1 times the marginal factor cost of that unit:

$$\Delta C_1 = \Delta F_1 \frac{\Delta C_1}{\Delta F_1}$$

The decrease in C because less F_2 is purchased is the quantity given up of F_2 times the marginal factor cost of that quantity:

$$\Delta C_2 = \Delta F_2 \frac{\Delta C_2}{\Delta F_2}$$

The total change in C is ΔC, and

$$\Delta C = \frac{\Delta C_1}{\Delta F_1} \Delta F_1 + \frac{\Delta C_2}{\Delta F_2} \Delta F_2$$

Since the total change in C is zero because C is a given amount C_0, the decrease in C because less F_2 is purchased must be offset exactly by the increase in C because more F_1 is purchased. Therefore,

$$\Delta C = \frac{\Delta C_1}{\Delta F_1} \Delta F_1 + \frac{\Delta C_2}{\Delta F_2} \Delta F_2 = 0$$

$$\frac{\Delta C_2}{\Delta F_2} \Delta F_2 = -\frac{\Delta C_1}{\Delta F_1} \Delta F_1$$

$$\frac{\Delta F_2}{\Delta F_1} = -\frac{\Delta C_1/\Delta F_1}{\Delta C_2/\Delta F_2} = -\frac{MFC_1}{MFC_2}$$

The slope of an iso-factor cost curve (dF_2/dF_1) is thus seen to change as more F_1 and less F_2 are purchased according to the change in MFC_1 relative to the change in MFC_2. In the case of a perfectly competitive purchaser, marginal factor cost is a constant function of quantity purchased and is equal to price. Thus, each successive unit increase in F_1 increases factor cost by a constant amount equal to W_{1_0}; and each successive unit decrease in F_2 decreases factor cost by a constant amount equal to W_{2_0}. Therefore, with each unit increase in F_1 (ΔF_1), the purchaser gives up a constant amount of F_2 ($-\Delta F_2$) to keep factor cost constant. Since the ratio $\Delta F_2/\Delta F_1$ remains constant as more F_1 and less F_2 are purchased, an iso-factor cost curve of a perfectly competitive purchaser is a straight line.

An iso-factor cost curve can be drawn in Figure 8.2 for each level of factor cost of the purchaser. The higher the level of factor cost, the larger the quantities of both factors that can be purchased, and hence the farther away from the point of origin lies the curve. Two curves which depict two different levels of factor cost cannot intersect; for if the two curves intersected, the same combination of quantities of the two factors would be associated with two different levels of factor cost, which is inconsistent with the factor cost function $C = c_1(F_1) + c_2(F_2)$. According to this function, a combination of quantities of two factors is associated with one level of factor cost.

Imperfectly Competitive Purchaser of a Factor of Production

To repeat, a factor market may be classified as perfectly competitive or imperfectly competitive from the purchaser's side of the market. An imperfectly competitive factor market is defined as a market in which the number of purchasers is so small that a purchaser may be able to influence the price of the factor. If a purchaser can influence price, he is a price-maker, rather than a price-taker. In this case, since price is a variable rather than a parameter, an imperfectly competitive purchaser is defined as a purchaser who cannot purchase all he wishes per unit of time at the prevailing price ceteris paribus. Specifically, he has to increase price to purchase a larger

146 PRINCIPLES OF THE THEORY OF SUPPLY OF A PRODUCT

quantity per unit of time ceteris paribus. In other words, the supply curve of a factor facing an imperfectly competitive purchaser has a positive slope. For purposes of analysis, think in terms of a monopsonist, the sole purchaser of a factor. Since he is the sole purchaser, the supply curve of the factor facing the monopsonist is the market supply curve.

Total Factor Cost Curve of a Factor of Production of a Monopsonist

To repeat, the total factor cost curve of a factor of production shows how total factor cost (C) varies with quantity purchased of the factor (F) per unit of time ceteris paribus: $C = c(F)$. But price of the factor (W) is not a parameter of the monopsonist's total factor cost curve, for now price varies directly with quantity purchased (F) and hence is a variable: $W = W(F)$, where $\Delta W/\Delta F > 0$. Thus $C = c(F) = WF$, where $W = W(F)$, or $C = c(F) = W(F) \cdot F$. The parameters of a total factor cost curve of a monopsonist are the parameters of the market supply curve (see Chapters 12 and 22).

FIG. 8.3a. Hypothetical total factor cost curve of a factor of a monopsonist

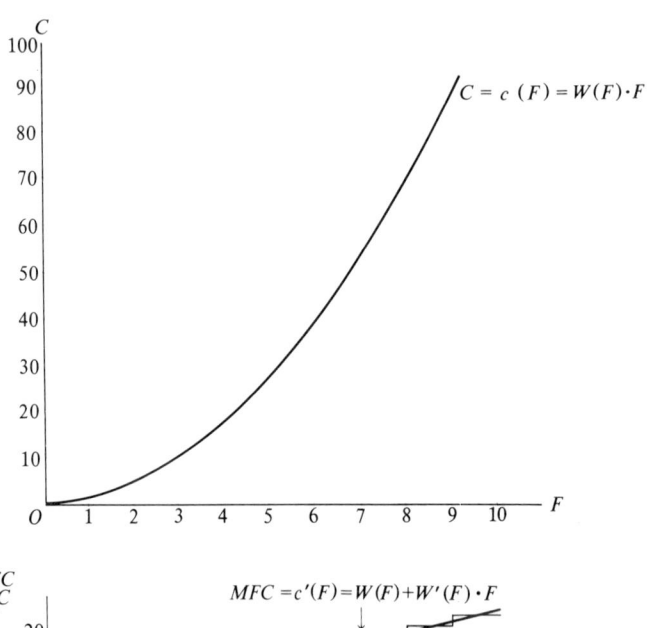

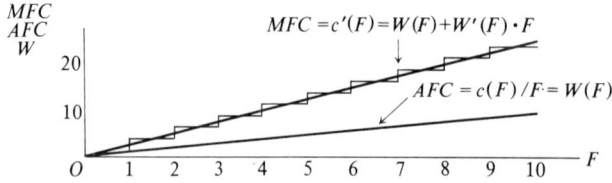

FIG. 8.3b. Hypothetical marginal and average factor cost curves of a factor of a monopsonist

TABLE 8.2: Hypothetical factor cost of a factor to a monopsonist

$AFC = C/F = W$	F	$C = WF$	$MFC_d = \Delta C/\Delta F$	$MFC_c = dC/dF$
0	0	0		0
			1	
1	1	1		2
			3	
2	2	4		4
			5	
3	3	9		6
			7	
4	4	16		8
			9	
5	5	25		10
			11	
6	6	36		12
			13	
7	7	49		14
			15	
8	8	64		16
			17	
9	9	81		18
			19	
10	10	100		20

As seen in Figure 8.3a, which depicts hypothetical data presented in Table 8.2, a total factor cost curve of a monopsonist has a zero total factor cost intercept and is concave from above a tangent line. The curve has a zero total factor cost intercept because total factor cost of the factor is zero when quantity purchased is zero: $C = W(F) \cdot 0 = 0$. It is concave from above because each successive quantity is purchased at a higher price; hence, as quantity increases by a unit, each successive unit purchased adds a larger amount (greater than W) to total factor cost.[4] The slope of $C = W(F) \cdot F$ therefore increases as quantity purchased increases.

Marginal Factor Cost Curve of a Factor of Production of a Monopsonist

The marginal factor cost curve of a factor of production shows how continuous marginal factor cost (MFC_c) varies with quantity purchased of the factor (F) per unit of time, given the parameters of the curve. With respect to $C = c(F) = W(F) \cdot F$, $MFC = c'(F) = W(F) + W'(F) \cdot F$.[5] The parameters of a marginal factor cost curve of a monopsonist are the parameters of the market supply curve (see Chapters 12 and 22).

As seen in Figure 8.3b, a marginal factor cost curve of a monopsonist is a positively-sloped curve ($\Delta MFC/\Delta F > 0$). The curve is positively sloped because each successive quantity is purchased at a higher price; hence, as quantity increases by a unit, each successive unit purchased adds a larger amount (greater than W) to total factor cost. Marginal factor cost therefore increases as quantity purchased increases.

To conclude, marginal factor cost (MFC) is an increasing function of quantity purchased (F) when total factor cost (C) increases at an increasing rate as quantity increases. Thus, the law of increasing marginal factor cost is a verbalization of a marginal factor cost curve of an imperfectly competitive purchaser, as exemplified by a monopsonist. Since total factor cost increases at an increasing rate, and since the phrase "increases at an increasing rate" is another way of saying "increasing marginal factor cost," a total factor cost curve of a monopsonist also depicts the law of increasing marginal factor cost.

Average Factor Cost Curve of a Factor of Production of a Monopsonist

The average factor cost curve of a factor of production shows how average factor cost (AFC) varies with quantity purchased of the factor (F) per unit of time, given the parameters of the curve. The parameters of an average factor cost curve of a monopsonist are the parameters of the market supply curve (see Chapters 12 and 22). With respect to $C = c(F) = W(F) \cdot F$, $AFC = c(F)/F = W(F)$.

As seen in Figure 8.3b, an average factor cost curve of a monopsonist is a positively-sloped curve ($\Delta AFC/\Delta F > 0$). The curve is positively sloped because each successive quantity is purchased at a higher price; hence each successive quantity purchased has a higher average factor cost. Average factor cost therefore increases as quantity purchased increases.

Supply Curve of a Factor of Production Facing a Monopsonist

To repeat, the supply curve of a factor facing a purchaser shows the price at which each quantity can be purchased. A monopsonist has to pay a higher price to purchase a larger quantity per unit of time ceteris paribus. Thus, the supply curve of a factor facing him is a positively-sloped curve. Moreover, in the present case, at each F value average factor cost equals price: $AFC = C/F = W = W(F)$. Consequently, the supply curve facing a monopsonist is his average factor cost curve.[6] But his average factor cost curve is not the same as his marginal factor cost curve, for at any given quantity marginal factor cost is greater than average factor cost by the amount $W'(F) \cdot F$, as seen below. To conclude, average and marginal factor cost are increasing functions of quantity purchased when the supply curve facing the purchaser is a positively-sloped curve.

Relationship Between Total, Marginal, and Average Factor Cost Curves of a Monopsonist

In Figure 8.3b, the slope of the average factor cost curve (b) is one-half the slope of the marginal factor cost curve ($2b$):

(1) $AFC = W(F) = a + bF$

(2) $\quad C = W(F) \cdot F = (a + bF)F = aF + bF^2$
(3) $\quad MFC = a + 2bF.$[7]

At any given quantity purchased, according to a form of equation (3), marginal factor cost is greater than average factor cost by the amount bF:

(3') $\quad MFC = a + 2bF = a + bF + bF$
$\qquad \qquad = AFC + bF \text{ (since } AFC = a + bF\text{)}$

In general notation, $AFC = W = W(F)$ and $b = W'(F) = dW/dF$; hence

$$MFC = W(F) + W'(F) \cdot F \quad \text{or} \quad MFC = AFC + \frac{dW}{dF}F$$
$$\text{or} \quad MFC = W + \frac{dW}{dF}F$$

In words, marginal factor cost equals average factor cost plus the product of the slope of the average factor cost curve and quantity purchased. Since the slope of the average factor cost curve is positive ($dW/dF > 0$), the slope of the marginal factor cost curve is positive ($dC/dF > 0$).

Iso-Factor Cost Curve of a Monopsonist

To repeat, an iso-factor cost curve depicts all combinations of quantities purchased of two factors that may be purchased with a given expenditure: $F_2 = c_0(F_1)$. The slope of an iso-factor cost curve (dF_2/dF_1) changes as more F_1 and less F_2 are purchased according to the change in MFC_1 relative to the change in MFC_2, since $dF_2/dF_1 = -MFC_1/MFC_2$. In the case of an imperfectly competitive purchaser, as exemplified by a monopsonist,

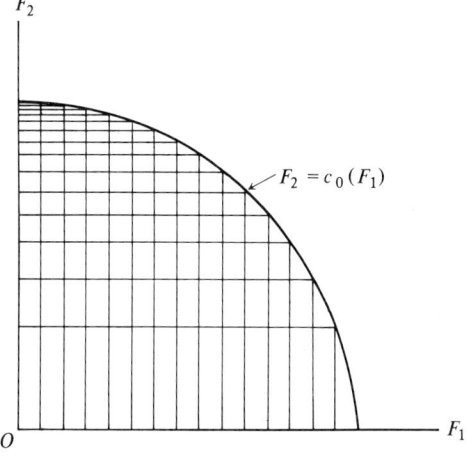

FIG. 8.4. Hypothetical iso-factor cost curve of a monopsonist

marginal factor cost is an increasing function of quantity purchased. Thus, each successive unit increase in F_1 increases factor cost by an increasing amount; and each successive unit decrease in F_2 decreases factor cost by a decreasing amount. Therefore, as seen in Figure 8.4, with each unit increase in $F_1 (\Delta F_1)$, the purchaser gives up an increasing amount of $F_2 (-\Delta F_2)$ to keep factor cost constant. Since the ratio $\Delta F_2/\Delta F_1$ increases numerically as more F_1 and less F_2 are purchased, an iso-factor cost curve of an imperfectly competitive purchaser is concave from below a tangent line.

SUMMARY

Dropping the zero subscript and remembering that W may be a parameter or a variable, total factor cost of a factor of production (C) is equal to its price (W) times its quantity purchased (F): $C = WF$. The curve expressing the relation between C and F is called the total factor cost curve of a factor of a purchaser. Price of a factor to a purchaser (W) is equal to the average factor cost of the factor (AFC), since each is the ratio of total factor cost (C) to quantity purchased (F): $AFC = C/F = W$. The curve expressing the relation between $AFC (=W)$ and F is called the average factor cost curve of a factor of a purchaser. Lastly, marginal factor cost of a factor of production may be defined as the infinitesimally small change in C (dC) associated with an infinitesimally small change in F (dF), or as the addition to total factor cost (ΔC) of one additional unit of the factor ($\Delta F = 1$): $MFC_c = dC/dF$ and $MFC_d = \Delta C/\Delta F$, where $\Delta F = 1$. The curve expressing the relation between dC/dF and F is called the marginal factor cost curve of a factor of a purchaser of factors.

Average factor cost ($=$ price) is the same as marginal factor cost in the case of perfect competition from the purchaser's side in the factor market. In this case, the purchaser can purchase all he wishes per unit of time at the prevailing price ceteris paribus; hence each additional unit purchased per unit of time adds the same amount (equal to price) to total factor cost. Total factor cost (C) therefore increases at the constant rate W as quantity purchased of the factor (F) per unit of time increases. Consequently, marginal factor cost of the factor ($MFC = W$) is a constant function of quantity purchased (F) per unit of time. To generalize, according to the law of constant marginal factor cost of a factor to a perfectly competitive purchaser, the factor cost associated with purchasing an additional unit of a factor does not vary with quantity purchased per unit of time.

In the case of an imperfectly competitive purchaser of factors of production, as exemplified by a monopsonist, the purchaser by definition has to pay a higher price to purchase a larger quantity of a factor per unit of time ceteris paribus. Thus, each additional unit purchased per unit of time adds a larger amount (greater than price) to total factor cost. Total factor cost (C) increases at an increasing rate as quantity purchased (F) per unit of time increases. To generalize, according to the law of increasing marginal factor cost of a factor to an imperfectly competitive purchaser of factors, the expenditure associated with purchasing an additional unit of a factor varies directly with quantity purchased per unit of time.

The supply curve of a factor facing a perfectly competitive purchaser is a horizontal straight line that depicts the given price. This curve is his average (= marginal) factor cost curve. His total factor cost curve is derived from his average factor cost curve by multiplying each quantity purchased by price. Similarly, the total factor cost curve of a monopsonist is derived from his average factor cost curve by multiplying each quantity purchased by price. But the supply curve of a factor facing a monopsonist is a positively-sloped curve that is the market supply curve; and although this curve is his average factor cost curve, it is not his marginal factor cost curve, for at any quantity purchased, $MFC = W(F) + W'(F) \cdot F$.

An iso-factor cost curve depicts all combinations of quantities of two factors (F_1 and F_2) that may be purchased with a given expenditure (C). An iso-factor cost curve may be drawn for each level of C. The greater the value of C, the higher the curve lies in the OF_1F_2 plane. No two curves intersect ceteris paribus. An iso-factor cost curve of a perfectly competitive purchaser is a negatively-sloped straight line. An iso-factor cost curve of a monopsonist is a negatively-sloped curve that is concave from below a tangent line.

Questions

1. List the principles of the theory of supply of a product that are of primary importance. How do you account for the position of the law of constant marginal factor cost in this list? Verbalize this principle of economics. Verbalize also the law of increasing marginal factor cost.

2. Define total factor cost of a factor. What is a total factor cost curve? Draw a total factor cost curve of a perfectly competitive purchaser and describe its properties. Draw also a total factor cost curve of a monopsonist and describe its properties.

3. Define marginal factor cost of a factor. What is a marginal factor cost curve? Draw a marginal factor cost curve of a perfectly competitive purchaser; describe its properties; and relate the properties of the total and marginal factor cost curves. Do the same analysis for a monopsonist.

4. Define average factor cost of a factor. What is an average factor cost curve? Draw an average factor cost curve of a perfectly competitive purchaser; describe its properties; and then relate the properties of the total and average factor cost curves, and the marginal and average factor cost curves. Do the same analysis for a monopsonist.

5. What is the supply curve of a factor facing a perfectly competitive purchaser? What is the supply curve of a factor facing a monopsonist? In each case, relate this curve to the corresponding factor cost curves.

6. Define the iso-factor cost of two factors. What is an iso-factor cost curve? Draw an iso-factor cost curve of a perfectly competitive purchaser; describe its properties; and relate marginal factor cost and the slope of an iso-factor cost curve. Do the same analysis for a monopsonist. Verbalize the numerical value of the slope of an iso-factor cost curve.

APPENDIX: Factor Cost Curves of a First-Degree Price-Discriminating Monopsonist

A monopsonist who pays a higher price for each successive *quantity* of a factor, but pays the same price for each unit of a given quantity, which is the case being analyzed, is called a non-price-discriminating monopsonist. In contrast, a first-degree price-discriminating monopsonist is defined as a monopsonist who pays a higher price for each successive *unit* of a factor. As seen in Figure 8.5, which depicts hypothetical data

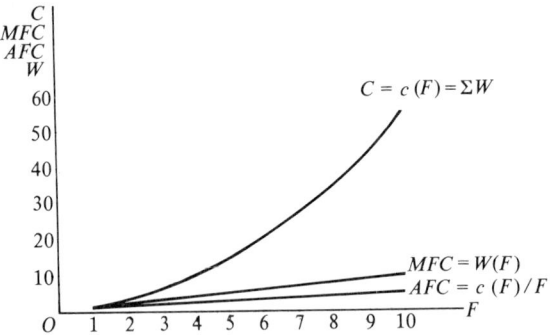

FIG. 8.5. Hypothetical factor cost curves of a factor of a first-degree price-discriminating monopsonist

presented in Table 8.3, the total factor cost curve of a first-degree price-discriminating monopsonist is concave from above a tangent line. Since each successive unit is purchased at a higher price, each successive unit purchased adds a larger amount (equal to price) to total factor cost. Total factor cost therefore increases at an increasing rate as quantity purchased increases. Marginal and average factor cost vary directly with quantity purchased.

TABLE 8.3: Hypothetical factor cost of a factor to a first-degree price-discriminating monopsonist

$MFC = \Delta C/\Delta F = W$	F	$C = \Sigma W$	$AFC = C/F$
0	0	0	
1	1	1	1.00
2	2	3	1.50
3	3	6	2.00
4	4	10	2.50
5	5	15	3.00
6	6	21	3.50
7	7	28	4.00
8	8	36	4.50
9	9	45	5.00
10	10	55	5.50

FACTOR COST FUNCTIONS 153

The supply curve facing a purchaser shows the price at which each unit can be purchased. His marginal factor cost curve denotes the marginal factor cost of each unit purchased. In the present case, the price of each unit is its marginal factor cost, since each unit adds its price to total factor cost: $MFC = \Delta C/\Delta F = W$. Therefore, the supply curve facing a first-degree price-discriminating monopsonist is his marginal factor cost curve. As seen in Table 8.3, his total factor cost curve is derived from his marginal factor cost curve by summing the price of each successive unit; and his average factor cost curve is derived from his total factor cost curve by dividing the total factor cost of each quantity by that quantity.

NOTES

[1] When quantity is varied continuously, continuous marginal factor cost of a factor (MFC_c) is the instantaneous rate of change of total factor cost as quantity purchased of the factor increases or decreases. With respect to the one-factor cost function $C = c(F)$, the instantaneous rate of change is the infinitesimally small change in C (dC) associated with an infinitesimally small change in F (dF): $MFC_c = dC/dF$. In this context, marginal factor cost is the slope of the total factor cost curve of the factor. The slope of the total factor cost curve is equal to the difference quotient ($\Delta C/\Delta F$) of the tangent line at a point on the curve. In Figure 8.1, at point A on $C = c(F)$,

$$MFC_c = \frac{dC}{dF} = \lim_{\Delta F \to 0} \frac{\Delta C}{\Delta F} = \frac{C'' - C'}{F'' - F'} = \frac{CB}{AC} = \text{slope of line } AB = 2$$

[2] The slope of an iso-factor cost curve of a perfectly competitive purchaser is $-W_{1_0}/W_{2_0}$; its F_2 intercept is C_0/W_{2_0}; and its F_1 intercept is C_0/W_{1_0}:

$$C_0 = W_{1_0}F_1 + W_{2_0}F_2$$

$$F_2 = \frac{C_0}{W_{2_0}} - \frac{W_{1_0}}{W_{2_0}}F_1 \quad \text{and} \quad F_1 = \frac{C_0}{W_{1_0}} - \frac{W_{2_0}}{W_{1_0}}F_2$$

$$\frac{dF_2}{dF_1} = -\frac{W_{1_0}}{W_{2_0}} \quad \text{and} \quad \frac{dF_1}{dF_2} = -\frac{W_{2_0}}{W_{1_0}}$$

$$F_2 = \frac{C_0}{W_{2_0}} \quad \text{when} \quad F_1 = 0 \quad \text{and} \quad F_1 = \frac{C_0}{W_{1_0}} \quad \text{when} \quad F_2 = 0$$

[3] With respect to a two-factor cost function, the instantaneous rate of change of C with respect to F_1 is the infinitesimally small change in C associated with an infinitesimally small change in F_1: $MFC_1 = \partial C/\partial F_1$. The total infinitesimally small change in F_1 is dF_1. Thus, in terms of infinitesimally small changes, the change in C associated with a total change in F_1 is

$$\frac{\partial C}{\partial F_1}dF_1$$

Similarly, the instantaneous rate of change of C with respect to F_2 is the infinitesimally small change in C associated with an infinitesimally small change in F_2: $MFC_2 = \partial C/\partial F_2$. The total infinitesimally small change in F_2 is dF_2. In terms of infinitesimally small changes, the change in C associated with a total change in F_2 is

$$\frac{\partial C}{\partial F_2}dF_2$$

Therefore, in terms of infinitesimally small changes, the total change in C is dC, and

$$dC = \frac{\partial C}{\partial F_1}dF_1 + \frac{\partial C}{\partial F_2}dF_2$$

Since the total change in C along an iso-factor cost curve is zero,

$$dC = \frac{\partial C}{\partial F_1}dF_1 + \frac{\partial C}{\partial F_2}dF_2 = 0$$

$$\frac{\partial C}{\partial F_2}dF_2 = -\frac{\partial C}{\partial F_1}dF_1$$

$$\frac{dF_2}{dF_1} = -\frac{\partial C/\partial F_1}{\partial C/\partial F_2} = -\frac{MFC_1}{MFC_2}$$

[4] A monopsonist who pays a higher price for each successive *quantity* of a factor, but pays the same price for each unit of a given quantity, which is the case being analyzed, is called a non-price-discriminating monopsonist. In contrast, a first-degree price-discriminating monopsonist is defined as a monopsonist who pays a higher price for each successive *unit* of a factor. This case is analyzed in the appendix to this chapter.

[5] To see that $MFC = c'(F) = W(F) + W'(F) \cdot F$, see page 149.

[6] This statement is true only if he is a non-price-discriminating monopsonist (see the appendix to this chapter).

[7]
$$MFC = \frac{dC}{dF} = \lim_{\Delta F \to 0} \frac{\Delta C}{\Delta F} = \frac{[a(F + \Delta F) + b(F + \Delta F)^2] - (aF + bF^2)}{\Delta F}$$

$$= \frac{aF + a\Delta F + b(F^2 + 2F\Delta F + \Delta F^2) - aF - bF^2}{\Delta F}$$

$$= \frac{aF + a\Delta F + bF^2 + 2bF\Delta F + b\Delta F^2 - aF - bF^2}{\Delta F}$$

$$= \frac{\Delta F(a + 2bF + b\Delta F)}{\Delta F} = a + 2bF + b\Delta F = a + 2bF$$

chapter 9

Cost Functions

According to the law of increasing marginal cost of a product to a seller of products (producer) who is subject to diminishing marginal returns, the cost associated with producing an additional unit of a product varies directly with quantity produced per unit of time. Each additional unit produced of a product per unit of time adds a larger amount to total cost. Total cost of a product increases at an increasing rate as quantity produced of the product per unit of time increases. Marginal cost of a product is an increasing function of quantity produced of the product per unit of time.

The cost function of a seller of products and purchaser of factors of production (business firm) is a transformation of his production function from physical input units into monetary cost units. To see this, think in terms of the input of one variable factor of production (F) and the output of one product (Q). Then, in functional notation form,

(1) $C = c(F)$ (total factor cost function of Chapter 8)
(2) $F = F(Q)$ (inverse of total product function $Q = Q(F)$ of Chapter 7)
(3) $C = c[F(Q)]$ or $C = C(Q)$ (total cost function of the present chapter)

The total cost of a product is thus the money expended on input to produce a quantity of the product. To generalize, the cost of output is the cost of input.

Short-Run Total Cost Curve of a Product of a Perfectly Competitive Purchaser of a Variable Factor of Production

The total cost curve of a product is a set of ordered pairs of quantity produced (output) of the product (Q) and cost of the product (C) having the property that corresponding to each number in the Q set of numbers is one number in the C set of numbers: $C = C(Q)$. Thus, the total cost curve shows the C value corresponding to each Q value, and hence how C varies with Q per unit of time. The parameters of a total cost curve of a producer are the parameters of the corresponding factor cost and production functions. As analyzed in Chapter 7, in the short run, total product may be said to vary with the input of a variable factor, given the input of fixed factors and the state of technology. As analyzed in Chapter 8, a perfectly competitive purchaser of a variable factor can purchase all he wishes per unit of time at the prevailing price ceteris paribus. Thus, the parameters of a short-run total cost curve of a product of a perfectly competitive purchaser of a variable factor of production are the price of the variable factor ($W = W_0$), the price of the fixed factor ($W_f = W_{f0}$), the quantity of the fixed factor ($F_f = F_{f0}$), and the state of technology.

Short-run total cost (C or STC) is equal to fixed cost (FC) plus variable cost (VC): $C = FC + VC$. The fixed cost of a product is the cost of the fixed factor used to produce a quantity of the product. It is equal to the quantity used (input) of the fixed factor times the price of the fixed factor: $FC = W_{f0} \cdot F_{f0}$; and is that portion of total cost not explained by quantity produced of the product. It must be paid in the short run when quantity produced is zero. The variable cost of a product is the cost of the variable factor used to produce a quantity of the product. It is equal to the quantity used of the variable factor times the price of the variable factor: $VC = W_0 \cdot F$; and is that portion of total cost explained by quantity produced of the product. It is not paid in the short run when quantity produced is zero.

As seen in Figure 9.1c, which depicts hypothetical data presented in Table 9.1, the properties of a short-run total cost curve of a product, $C = C(Q) = FC + VC$, are a composite of the properties of the fixed cost and variable cost curves. The fixed cost curve of a product, $FC = W_{f0} \cdot F_{f0}$, is a straight line that intersects the cost axis at the given value of fixed cost. The intercept of the fixed cost curve is the intercept of the short-run total cost curve, for total cost equals fixed cost when quantity produced of the product is zero. The variable cost curve of a product of a perfectly competitive purchaser of a variable factor, $VC = WF$, where $W = W_0$ and $F = F(Q)$, or $VC = W_0 \cdot F(Q)$, is parallel to the short-run total cost curve and intersects the cost axis at the point of origin. The total cost and variable cost curves are an equal vertical distance apart by the amount of fixed cost. The slope of the variable cost curve is the slope of the total cost curve; each additional unit of the product increases total cost and variable cost by the same amount.

The variable cost curve of Figure 9.1c is derived by transforming the physical input units of the total product curve of Figure 9.1b into monetary cost units. This transformation is effected at each quantity of the product (Q) by multiplying the corresponding quantity of the variable factor (F) by its price ($W = W_0$). The price at which a quantity of a variable factor can be purchased is denoted by the supply curve facing the purchaser, which in the case of a perfectly competitive purchaser is denoted by $W = W(F) = W_0$, as

COST FUNCTIONS 157

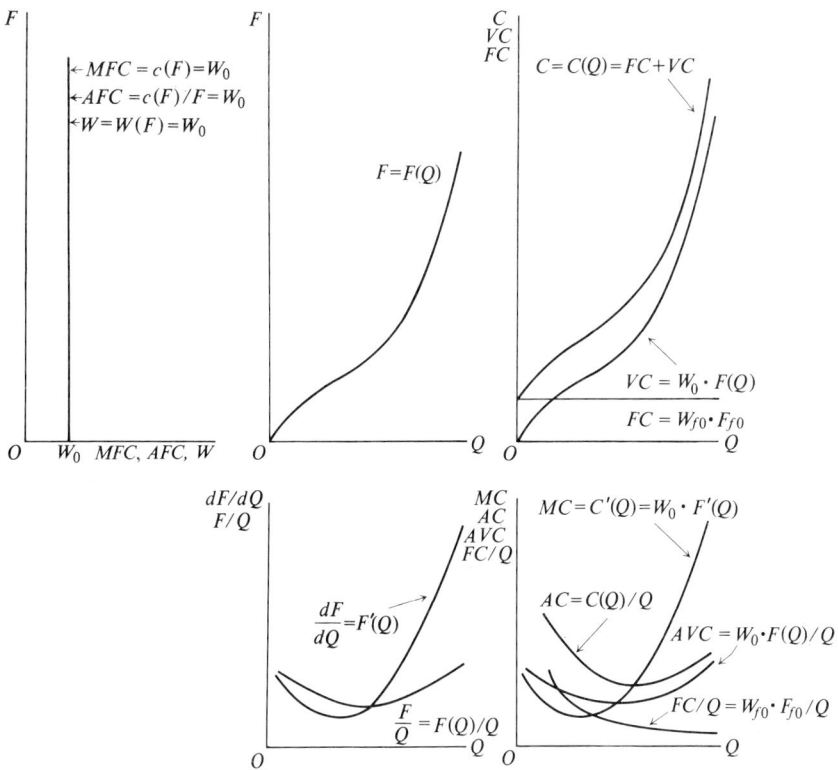

FIG. 9.1a. Hypothetical supply curve of a variable factor facing a perfectly competitive purchaser

FIG. 9.1b. Hypothetical total input curve of a product

FIG. 9.1c. Hypothetical total cost curve of a product of a perfectly competitive purchaser of a variable factor of production

FIG. 9.1d. Hypothetical marginal and average input curves of a product

FIG. 9.1e. Hypothetical marginal and average cost curves of a product

seen in Figure 9.1a. Thus, the $VC = W_0 \cdot F(Q)$ curve of Figure 9.1c is the mathematical product of the $W = W(F) = W_0$ curve of Figure 9.1a and the $F = F(Q)$ curve of Figure 9.1b. In short, at each value of Q, $VC = W_0 \cdot F$, where $F = F(Q)$.

With respect to Figure 9.1b, quantity produced of the product (Q) first increases at an increasing rate as input of the variable factor (F) increases; each additional unit of F adds a larger amount to Q. Therefore, input first increases at a decreasing rate as quantity produced increases; each additional unit of Q adds a smaller amount to F. With respect to Figure 9.1c, variable cost (VC) first increases at a decreasing rate as quantity produced of the product (Q) increases; each additional unit of Q adds a smaller amount to

158   PRINCIPLES OF THE THEORY OF SUPPLY OF A PRODUCT

VC if it uses a smaller amount of F, given $W = W_0$. To conclude, the slope of the variable cost curve decreases as quantity produced increases if the slope of the inverse of the total product curve decreases as quantity produced increases—if the slope of the total product curve increases as input increases.

TABLE 9.1: Hypothetical cost of a product to a perfectly competitive purchaser of a variable factor of production

(Figure 9.1a)		(Figure 9.1b)	
$MFC = AFC = W = W(F) = W_0$	F	$F = F(Q)$	Q
1	0	0	0
1	5	5	1
1	8	8	2
1	15	15	3
1	32	32	4

(Figure 9.1c)

$VC = W_0 \cdot F(Q)$	$FC = W_{f0} \cdot F_{f0}$	$C = C(Q) = FC + VC$	Q
0	4	4	0
5	4	9	1
8	4	12	2
15	4	19	3
32	4	36	4

(Figure 9.1d)

$dF/dQ = F'(Q)$	$F/Q = F(Q)/Q$	Q
8	8	0
3	5	1
4	4	2
11	5	3
24	8	4

(Figure 9.1e)

$AVC = W_0 \cdot F(Q)/Q$	$FC/Q = W_{f0} \cdot F_{f0}/Q$	$AC = C(Q)/Q$	$MC_c = C'(Q)$	$MC_d = \Delta C/\Delta Q$	Q
8			8	5	0
5	4.00	9.00	3	3	1
4	2.00	6.00	4	7	2
5	1.33	6.33	11	17	3
8	1.00	9.00	24		4

Again, with respect to Figure 9.1b, quantity produced (Q) eventually increases at a decreasing rate as input (F) increases; each additional unit of F now adds a smaller amount to Q. Therefore, input is now increasing at an increasing rate as quantity produced increases; each additional unit of Q now adds a larger amount to F. With respect to Figure 9.1c, variable cost (VC) now increases at an increasing rate as quantity produced (Q) increases; each additional unit of Q adds a larger amount to VC if it uses a larger amount of F. To conclude, the slope of the variable cost curve increases as quantity produced increases if the slope of the inverse of the total product curve increases as quantity produced increases—if the slope of the total product curve decreases as input increases.[1]

Short-Run Marginal Cost Curve of a Product of a Perfectly Competitive Purchaser of a Variable Factor of Production

When quantity is varied by discrete amounts, discrete marginal cost of a product (MC_d) is the change in C (ΔC) associated with a change of one unit in Q ($\Delta Q = 1$): $MC_d = \Delta C/\Delta Q$, where $\Delta Q = 1$. In this context, marginal cost is equal to the difference quotient $\Delta C/\Delta Q$ of the straight line between two points one Q unit apart on the curve. In Table 9.1, the MC_d of the third unit equals the

$$\lim_{\Delta Q \to 1} \frac{\Delta C}{\Delta Q} = 7$$

Since the total cost curve of Figure 9.1c is nonlinear, the difference quotient is not the same for all changes in quantity, and hence discrete marginal cost is not the same as continuous marginal cost.[2]

The marginal cost curve of a product is a set of ordered pairs of quantity produced (Q) and (continuous) marginal cost (MC) having the property that corresponding to each number in the Q set of numbers is one number in the MC set of numbers: $MC = C'(Q)$. Thus, the marginal cost curve shows the MC value corresponding to each Q value and hence how MC varies with Q per unit of time. The parameters of a marginal cost curve are the parameters of the corresponding total cost curve that determine the slope of the total curve.

As seen in Figure 9.1c, which depicts hypothetical data presented in Table 9.1, the slope of the total cost curve initially decreases as quantity produced of the product increases; initially, each subsequent unit produced adds less to total cost than the previous unit. In this context, as seen in Figure 9.1e, an inverse relation exists between MC and Q; the marginal cost curve has a negative slope. Marginal cost (MC) is a decreasing function of quantity produced (Q) when total cost (C) increases at a decreasing rate as quantity increases.

Eventually, however, as seen in Figure 9.1e, the slope of the total cost curve of a product attains its lowest value. This point on the total cost curve is the inflection point dividing decreasing marginal cost from increasing marginal cost. At this point, the marginal cost curve is at its trough; its slope is zero.

Thereafter, the slope of the total cost curve increases as quantity produced of the product increases; each subsequent unit produced now adds more to total cost than the previous unit. In this context, as seen in Figure 9.1e, a direct relation exists between MC and Q; the marginal cost curve has a positive slope. Marginal cost (MC) is an increasing function of quantity produced (Q) when total cost (C) increases at an increasing rate as quantity increases.

The marginal cost curve of Figure 9.1e may also be derived by transforming the physical slope values of the $dF/dQ = F'(Q)$ curve of Figure 9.1d into monetary slope values. This transformation is effected at each quantity produced of the product (Q) by multiplying the corresponding dF/dQ value by the marginal factor cost (dC/dF) of the corresponding quantity of the variable factor (F). The marginal factor cost at various quantities of the variable factor is denoted by the marginal factor cost curve, which, as in Figure 9.1a, is the same as the supply curve of the factor facing the perfectly competitive purchaser: $MFC = c'(F) = W_0$. Thus the $MC = C'(Q) = W_0 \cdot F'(Q)$ curve of Figure 9.1e is the mathematical product of the $MFC = c'(F) = W_0$ curve of Figure 9.1a and the $dF/dQ = F'(Q)$ curve of Figure 9.1d. In short, at each value of Q,

$$MC = \frac{dC}{dQ} = \frac{dC}{dF} \cdot \frac{dF}{dQ} \text{ or } MC = C'(Q) = c'(F) \cdot F'(Q) \text{ or } MC = \frac{W_0}{MQ}$$

In terms of discrete marginal cost, marginal cost of a product is the cost of the variable factor used to produce an additional unit of the product. In this context, discrete marginal cost ($MC = \Delta C/\Delta Q$) is equal to the discrete marginal factor cost of the variable factor ($MFC = \Delta C/\Delta F$) times the additional amount of the variable factor used to produce an additional unit of the product ($\Delta F/\Delta Q$). Thus, it is equal to discrete marginal factor cost times the reciprocal of discrete marginal product ($1/MQ = \Delta F/\Delta Q$). Assuming perfect competition in the market for the variable factor, marginal factor cost (MFC) is the same as price of the factor (W_0). Therefore, the cost of an additional unit of the product ($\Delta C/\Delta Q$) is the amount of the variable factor used to produce that unit ($\Delta F/\Delta Q$) times the price of the factor (W_0). In short,

$$MC = \frac{\Delta C}{\Delta Q} = \frac{\Delta C}{\Delta F} \cdot \frac{\Delta F}{\Delta Q} = W_0 \cdot \frac{\Delta F}{\Delta Q}$$

In other words, the addition to total cost (ΔC) of a unit of output (ΔQ) is the addition to input (ΔF) of that unit (ΔQ) times the price of input (W_0).[3]

With respect to Figure 9.1d, the $dF/dQ = F'(Q)$ curve first has a negative slope; each additional unit of Q adds a smaller amount to F. With respect to Figure 9.1e, the marginal cost curve first has a negative slope; each additional unit of Q adds a smaller amount to C if it uses a smaller amount of F, given $W = W_0$. To conclude, marginal cost decreases if dF/dQ decreases—if marginal product (dQ/dF) increases. However, as also seen in Figure 9.1d, the $dF/dQ = F'(Q)$ curve eventually has a positive slope; each additional unit of Q now adds a larger amount to F. Thus, as seen in Figure 9.1e, the marginal cost curve now has a positive slope; each additional unit of Q adds a larger amount to C if it uses a larger amount of F, given $W = W_0$. To conclude, marginal cost increases if dF/dQ increases—if marginal product (dQ/dF) decreases. In other words, marginal cost varies inversely with marginal product.

As seen in Figure 9.1e, a marginal cost curve of a seller of products and purchaser of factors of production who is subject to diminishing marginal returns—decreasing marginal product—is a positively-sloped curve ($\Delta MC/\Delta Q > 0$). Marginal cost (MC) is an increasing function of quantity produced (Q) when total cost (C) increases at an increasing rate (dC/dQ) as quantity produced of the product increases. Thus, the law of increasing marginal cost is a verbalization of a marginal cost curve of a producer who is subject to diminishing marginal returns. Since total cost increases at an increasing rate in this case, and since the phrase "increases at an increasing rate" is another way of saying "increasing marginal cost," a total cost curve of a producer who is subject to diminishing marginal returns also depicts the law of increasing marginal cost.

Short-Run Average Cost Curve of a Product of a Perfectly Competitive Purchaser of a Variable Factor of Production

Average cost of a product (AC) is the ratio of total cost (C) to quantity produced (Q): $AC = C/Q$. Average cost is equal to the difference quotient $\Delta C/\Delta Q$ of the ray at a point on the total cost curve. In Table 9.1, the AC of the third unit equals $19/3 = 6.33$. Since the total cost curve of a product is not a ray when the producer is subject to diminishing marginal returns, the difference quotient varies with Q.

The average cost curve of a product is a set of ordered pairs of quantity produced (Q) and average cost (AC) having the property that corresponding to each number in the Q set of numbers is one number in the AC set of numbers: $AC = C(Q)/Q$. Thus, the average cost curve shows the AC value corresponding to each Q value, and hence how AC varies with Q per unit of time. The parameters of an average cost curve are the parameters of the corresponding total cost curve that determine the intercept or the slope of the total curve.

The average cost of the first unit of a product is the same as its total cost:

$AC = C/Q = C/1 = C$. The total cost curve of Figure 9.1c, which depicts hypothetical data presented in Table 9.1, shows that (by assumption) total cost first increases at a decreasing rate and then at an increasing rate as quantity produced of the product increases. Therefore, average cost first decreases and then increases with quantity produced of the product. The trough of the average cost curve occurs at a quantity of the product that is greater than the quantity at which the marginal cost curve troughs. The average cost curve is intersected at its trough from below by the marginal cost curve; then the rate of increase of average cost is less than the rate of increase of marginal cost. The average is determined by all units of a given quantity; the marginal is determined by the last unit. Thus, the only way for an average to stop decreasing, reach its minimum value, and then increase is for the marginal to stop decreasing first, reach its minimum value first, and then increase at a rate that is greater than the rate of increase of the average.

Short-run average cost (AC or SAC) is equal to average fixed cost (FC/Q) plus average variable cost ($AVC = VC/Q$):

$$AC = \frac{FC}{Q} + \frac{VC}{Q}.$$

Thus, as seen in Figure 9.1e, the properties of a short-run average cost curve of a product are a composite of the properties of the average fixed cost and average variable cost curves. The average fixed cost curve of a product, $FC/Q = W_{f0} \cdot F_{f0}/Q$ is a rectangular hyperbola, for a given value (FC) when divided by increasing values (Q) becomes smaller and smaller, approaching but never quite reaching zero. The average variable cost curve, $AVC = W_0 \cdot F(Q)/Q$, has the same general shape as the average cost curve. But the average cost curve lies above the average variable cost curve by the amount of average fixed cost. Moreover, since decreasing average fixed cost continues to decrease average cost after average variable cost has begun to increase, the minimum point on the average cost curve is at a larger output than the minimum point on the average variable cost curve. Thus, the marginal cost curve intersects the average variable cost curve at a smaller output of the product than it does the average cost curve.

The average variable cost curve of Figure 9.1e may also be derived by transforming the physical ratio units of the $F/Q = F(Q)/Q$ curve of Figure 9.1d into monetary ratio units. This transformation is effected at each quantity produced of the product (Q) by multiplying the corresponding F/Q value by the average factor cost (C/F) of the corresponding quantity of the variable factor (F). The average factor cost at various quantities of the variable factor is denoted by the average factor cost curve, which, as seen in Figure 9.1a, is the same as the supply curve of the factor facing the perfectly competitive purchaser: $AFC = c(F)/F = W_0$. Thus, the $AVC = W_0 \cdot F(Q)/Q$ curve of Figure 9.1e is the mathematical product of the $AFC = c(F)/F = W_0$ curve of Figure 9.1a and the $F/Q = F(Q)/Q$ curve of Figure 9.1d. In short, at each value of Q,

$$AVC = \frac{VC}{Q} = \frac{C}{F} \cdot \frac{F}{Q} \text{ or } AVC = \frac{c(F)}{F} \cdot \frac{F(Q)}{Q} \text{ or } AVC$$

$$= W_0 \cdot \frac{F}{Q} \text{ or } AVC = \frac{W_0}{AQ}$$

Short-Run Cost Curves of a Product of an Imperfectly Competitive Purchaser of a Variable Factor of Production

As analyzed in Chapter 8, the price of a variable factor (W) is not a parameter of a total factor cost curve of an imperfectly competitive purchaser, as exemplified by a monopsonist, for now W varies directly with quantity purchased (F) and hence is a variable: $W = W(F)$, where $\Delta W/\Delta F > 0$. Thus W is a variable of the total cost curve of a product of an imperfectly competitive purchaser of a variable factor, as seen in Table 9.2 and Figure 9.2. The $VC = W(F) \cdot F(Q)$ curve of Figure 9.2c is the mathematical product of the $W = W(F)$ curve of Figure 9.2a and the $F = F(Q)$ curve of Figure 9.2b; the $MC = C'(Q) = c'(F) \cdot F'(Q)$ curve of Figure 9.2e is the mathematical product of the $MFC = c'(F)$ curve of Figure 9.1a and the $dF/dQ = F'(Q)$ curve of Figure 9.2d; and the $AVC = W(F) \cdot F(Q)/Q$ curve of Figure 9.2e is the mathematical product of the $AFC = c(F)/F$ curve of Figure 9.2a and the $F/Q = F(Q)/Q$ curve of Figure 9.2d. In other words, at each value of Q,

(1) $\quad VC = W \cdot F$, where $W = W(F)$ and $F = F(Q)$

(2) $\quad MC = \dfrac{dC}{dQ} = \dfrac{dC}{dF} \cdot \dfrac{dF}{dQ}$ or $MC = C'(Q) = c'(F) \cdot F'(Q)$ or $MC = \dfrac{MFC}{MQ}$

(3) $\quad AVC = \dfrac{VC}{Q} = \dfrac{C}{F} \cdot \dfrac{F}{Q}$ or $AVC = \dfrac{c(F)}{F} \cdot \dfrac{F(Q)}{Q}$ or AVC

$$= W \cdot \frac{F}{Q} \text{ or } AVC = \frac{W}{AQ}.$$

Let quantity produced (Q) first increase at an increasing rate as the input of a variable factor (F) increases; then each additional unit of F adds a larger amount to Q. Thus, each additional unit of Q adds a smaller amount to F and hence variable cost. But each additional unit of F adds a larger amount to total factor cost and hence variable cost. Therefore, given the same production function, the rate of increase of variable cost as Q increases is greater in the case of an imperfectly competitive purchaser than in the case of a perfectly competitive purchaser of a variable factor of production. The slope of the variable cost curve of Figure 9.2c is greater at any given Q value than the slope of the variable cost curve of Figure 9.1c.

Now, let Q increase at a decreasing rate as F increases. Then each additional unit of F adds a smaller amount to Q. Thus, each additional unit of Q adds a larger amount to F and hence variable cost. But each additional unit of F also adds a larger amount to total factor cost and hence variable cost. Therefore, given the same production function, the rate of increase of variable cost as Q increases is again greater in the case of an imperfectly competitive purchaser than in the case of a perfectly competitive purchaser of a variable factor of production. The variable cost curve of Figure 9.2c lies above the variable cost curve of Figure 9.1c.

Two separate reasons now exist for assuming increasing marginal cost

FIG. 9.2a. Hypothetical supply curve of a variable factor facing a monopsonist

FIG. 9.2b. Hypothetical total input curve of a product

FIG. 9.2c. Hypothetical total cost curve of a product of a monopsonist in a factor market

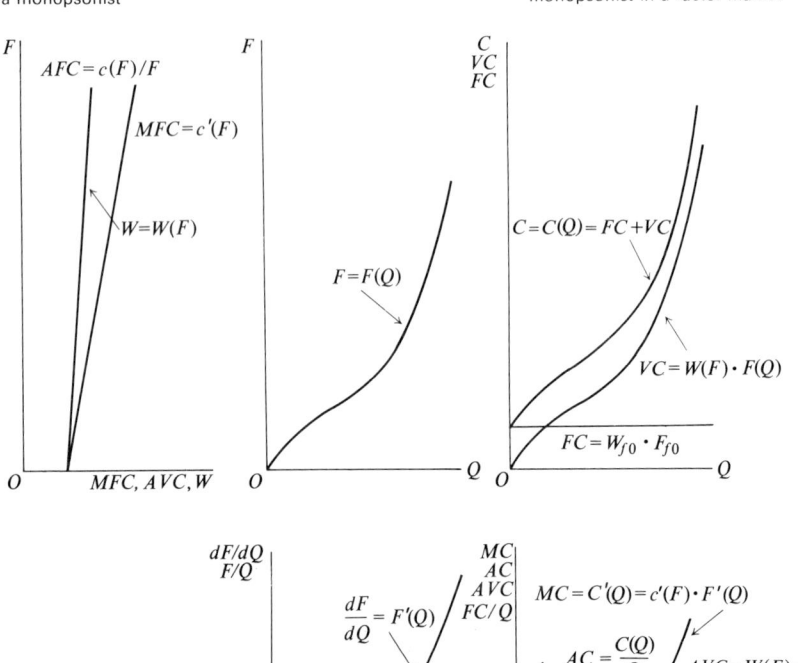

FIG. 9.2d. Hypothetical marginal and average input curve of a product

FIG. 9.2e. Hypothetical marginal and average cost curves of a product

COST FUNCTIONS 165

of a product. The first reason is decreasing marginal product of a variable factor of production. The second reason is increasing marginal factor cost of a variable factor of production. Consequently, the marginal cost curve of Figure 9.1e is closer to the horizontal axis than is the marginal cost curve of

TABLE 9.2: Hypothetical cost of a product to an imperfectly competitive purchaser of a variable factor of production

(Figure 9.2a)				(Figure 9.2b)	
$MFC = c'(F)$	$AFC = W = W(F)$	F		$F = F(Q)$	Q
1.00	1.000	0		0	0
1.25	1.125	5		5	1
1.40	1.200	8		8	2
1.75	1.375	15		15	3
2.60	1.800	32		32	4

(Figure 9.2c)

$VC = W(F) \cdot F(Q)$	$FC = W_{f0} \cdot F_{f0}$	$C = C(Q) = FC + VC$	Q
0.000	4	4.000	0
5.625	4	9.625	1
9.600	4	13.600	2
20.625	4	24.625	3
57.600	4	61.600	4

(Figure 9.2d)

$dF/dQ = F'(Q)$	$F/Q = F(Q)/Q$	Q
8	8	0
3	5	1
4	4	2
11	5	3
24	8	4

(Figure 9.2e)

$AVC = W(F) \cdot F(Q)/Q$	$FC/Q = W_{f0} \cdot F_{f0}/Q$	$AC = C(Q)/Q$	$MC_c = C'(Q)$	$MC_d = \Delta C/\Delta Q$	Q
8.000			8.00		0
5.625	4.00	9.625	3.75	5.625	1
4.800	2.00	6.800	5.60	3.975	2
6.875	1.33	8.205	19.25	11.025	3
14.400	1.00	15.400	62.60	36.975	4

Figure 9.2e. The value of MC at any given value of Q is greater when both dF/dQ and dC/dF increase than when only dF/dQ increases as Q increases. The positively-sloped portion of the marginal cost curve of Figure 9.2e lies to the left of the positively-sloped portion of the marginal cost curve of Figure 9.1e.

Long-Run Cost Curves of a Product

As analyzed in Chapter 7, in the long run, total product may be said to vary with the input of all factors of production, given the state of technology. Thus, as seen in Figure 9.3a, the long-run total cost of a product is zero when the quantity produced (output) is zero, since the input of all factors is then zero. As also analyzed in Chapter 7, in the long run, a firm may be subject to increasing, constant, and decreasing returns to scale, in that order. These three returns-to-scale cases help to explain the slope of the long-run total cost

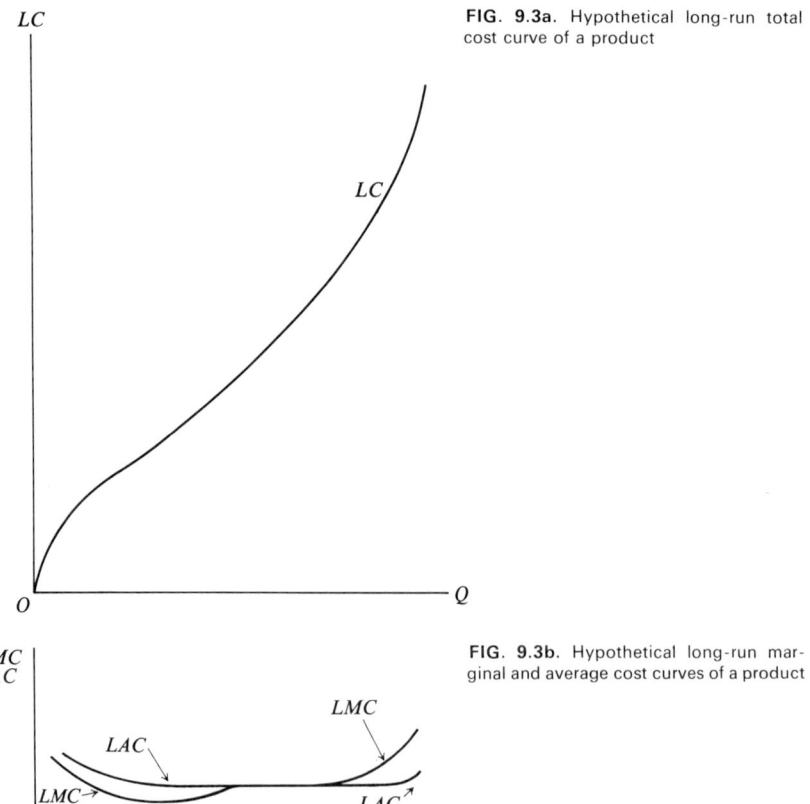

FIG. 9.3a. Hypothetical long-run total cost curve of a product

FIG. 9.3b. Hypothetical long-run marginal and average cost curves of a product curve drawn in Figure 9.3a. The corresponding long-run marginal and average cost curves are drawn in Figure 9.3b.

In the case of increasing returns to scale, long-run total product increases at an increasing rate as input increases. Therefore, input increases at a decreasing rate as output increases—the case of internal economies of scale. Thus, ceteris paribus, long-run total cost increases at a decreasing rate as output increases; each additional unit of output adds a smaller amount to total cost if it adds a smaller amount to input. In short, increasing returns to scale imply internal economies of scale.[4] In the case of constant returns to scale, long-run total product increases at a constant rate as input increases. Therefore, input increases at a constant rate as output increases. Thus, ceteris paribus, long-run total cost increases at a constant rate as output increases; each additional unit of output adds the same amount to total cost if it adds the same amount to input. Lastly, in the case of decreasing returns to scale, long-run total product increases at a decreasing rate as input increases. Therefore, input increases at an increasing rate as output increases —the case of internal diseconomies of scale. Thus, ceteris paribus, long-run total cost increases at an increasing rate as output increases; each additional unit of output adds a larger amount to total cost if it adds a larger amount to input. In short, decreasing returns to scale imply internal diseconomies of scale.

Relationship Between Short-Run and Long-Run Average Cost Curves

Each short-run average cost (SAC) curve in Figure 9.4 depicts how average cost varies with output as output varies with the input of variable factors, given the price of factors and the state of technology. By letting labor be the variable factor and capital the fixed factor, an SAC curve may be drawn for each input of capital, and each input of capital represents a plant size. Thus, each SAC curve represents a hypothetical plant size, and plant size varies directly with output. Each point on an SAC curve (for example, point A on SAC_1) represents the lowest average cost of producing the corresponding output from the given plant. A larger output along the same curve (points B and C) can be produced at the lowest average cost by increasing the input of labor—by using the same plant more intensively. Each plant is designed to produce a particular output at absolute minimum average cost for that plant size, as denoted by the minimum point on the plant's SAC curve (point B). Thus, hypothetically an SAC curve exists for each planned output. Only a few representative SAC curves are drawn in Figure 9.4. In Figure 9.4, absolute minimum average cost initially varies inversely with output, because of internal economies of scale, as larger size plants are built.

The long-run average cost (LAC) curve in Figure 9.4 depicts how average cost varies with output as output varies with the input of all factors of produc-

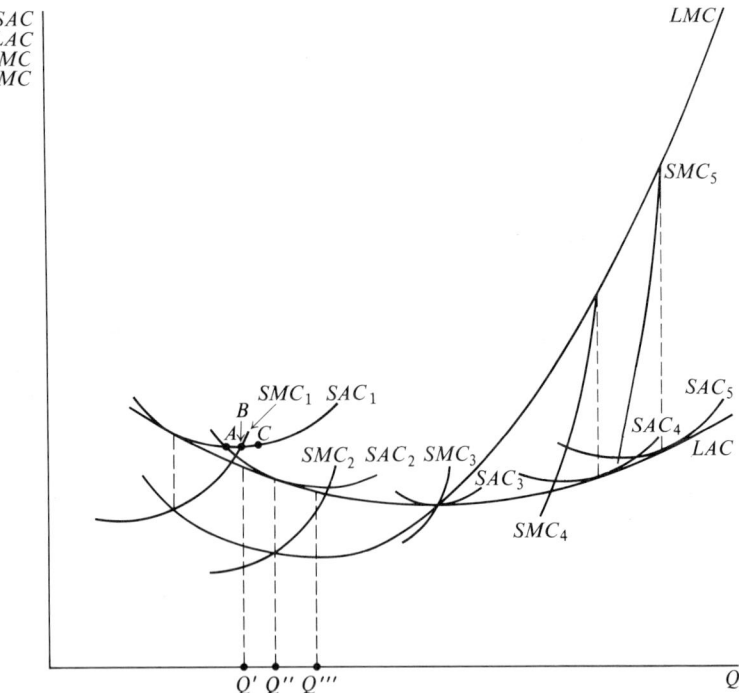

FIG. 9.4. Relationship between short-run and long-run marginal and average cost curves

tion, given the price of factors and the state of technology. It is also called the long-run planning curve, for each point on it denotes a plant size (SAC curve) which would result in the lowest average cost of producing the corresponding output. Thus, it shows how average cost varies with output when the seller has time to build any desired scale of plant. It is also called the envelope curve since it envelopes the short-run average cost curves. The lowest point on each SAC curve (absolute minimum average cost), however, may not be the point of tangency with the LAC curve. When LAC is decreasing, points of tangency of SAC curves with the LAC curve are on the negatively-sloped portions of the SAC curves; and when LAC is increasing, points of tangency are on the positively-sloped portions of the SAC curves. But when LAC is constant, points of tangency are on the zero-sloped portions of the SAC curves. Thus, the lowest point on an SAC curve is tangent to the LAC curve only at the lowest point(s) on the LAC curve.

When LAC is changing, any output can be produced at the same average cost by two different plant sizes (SAC_1 and SAC_2 at point A). When LAC is decreasing, the decision may be made to go to a larger plant before the smaller plant is used intensively enough to produce that output corresponding to its absolute minimum average cost (point B on SAC_1). The smaller plant (SAC_1) has a smaller capital stock, but output greater than A can be produced

Relationship Between Short-Run and Long-Run Marginal Cost Curves

Each short-run marginal cost (SMC) curve in Figure 9.4 depicts how marginal cost varies with output as output varies with the input of variable factors, given the price of factors and the state of technology. Each point on an SMC curve, therefore, represents how the seller adjusts the input of variable factors in association with a given plant to produce an additional unit of output. The long-run marginal cost (LMC) curve in Figure 9.4 depicts how marginal cost varies with output as output varies with the input of all factors, given the prices of factors and the state of technology. Each point on the LMC curve, therefore, represents how the seller adjusts the scale of plant to produce an additional unit of output.

The LMC curve is a locus (graph) of SMC values and particular output values. Each of these output values represents a tangency of an SAC curve with the LAC curve. Thus, each point on the LMC curve represents an SMC value at which the corresponding SAC curve is tangent to the LAC curve. Specifically, at Q'' in Figure 9.4, $SAC = LAC$. Therefore, short-run total cost equals long-run total cost at Q''. But at Q' short-run total cost is greater than long-run total cost since $SAC > LAC$. Thus, as output increases from Q' to Q'', the addition to long-run total cost (LMC) must be greater than the addition to short-run total cost (SMC): $LMC > SMC$. At Q''' short-run total cost again is greater than long-run total cost since $SAC > LAC$. Thus, as output decreases from Q''' to Q'', the decrease in short-run total cost (SMC) must be greater than the decrease in long-run total cost (LMC): $LMC < SMC$. Hence $LMC = SMC$ at Q'', since $LMC > SMC$ to the left of Q'' and $LMC < SMC$ to the right of Q''. Every other point on the LMC curve may be rationalized in the same way.

Monetary and Real Costs

By dividing both sides of $C = WF$ by W, the monetary cost of output (C or WF) is transformed into the real cost of output (C/W or F), which is the input required to produce output. Similarly, by dividing both sides of $\Delta C/\Delta Q = W(\Delta F/\Delta Q)$ by W, the monetary marginal cost of a product ($\Delta C/\Delta Q$) is transformed into the real marginal cost of the product ($\Delta F/\Delta Q$), which is the additional amount of input (ΔF) required to produce an additional unit of the product (ΔQ). The real marginal cost of a product ($\Delta F/\Delta Q$) is also called marginal input of the product.

Iso-Input Curve of Two Products Not Related in Production

The iso-input of two products is the constant (equal) amount of input used to produce various combinations of quantities of the products. An iso-input curve of two products is a set of ordered pairs of quantities produced of the two products (Q_1 and Q_2) having the properties that (1) corresponding to each number in the Q_1 set of numbers is one number in the Q_2 set of numbers and (2) each pair of numbers of the function is associated with the same input: $Q_2 = F_0(Q_1)$. Thus, an iso-input curve shows the Q_2 value corresponding to each Q_1 value, and hence how Q_2 varies with Q_1 per unit of time, holding input constant. In other words, *an iso-input curve depicts all combinations of quantities of two products that may be produced by a seller with a given input of factors of production.*

As seen in Figure 9.5, an iso-input curve of a producer who is subject to diminishing marginal returns in general is a negatively sloped curve that is concave from below a tangent line. It is negatively sloped because products Q_1 and Q_2 are rivals for a producer's input (F_0); he may use his fixed quantity of input to produce more of Q_1 by decreasing the quantity produced of Q_2 (and vice versa). Thus, product Q_2 is a decreasing function of product Q_1: $\Delta Q_2/\Delta Q_1 < 0$. It is concave from below a tangent line because the numerical value of its slope varies directly with Q_1.

The slope of an iso-input curve is denoted by dQ_2/dQ_1 and is equal to the negative of the ratio MF_1/MF_2, where MF_1 is the marginal input of product one and MF_2 is the marginal input of product two: $dQ_2/dQ_1 = -MF_1/MF_2$. By multiplying both sides by -1, $-dQ_2/dQ_1 = MF_1/MF_2$. The $-dQ_2/dQ_1$ notation and the MF_1/MF_2 notation denote numerical values and are called

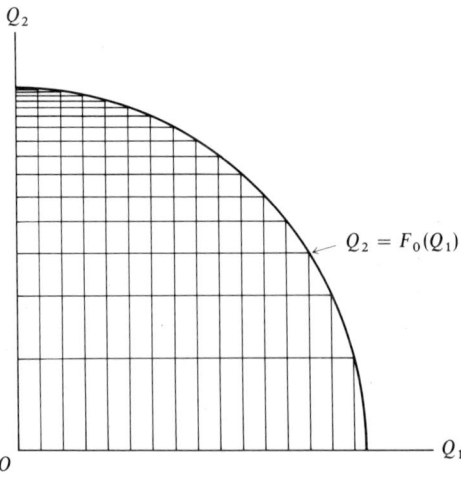

FIG. 9.5. Hypothetical iso-input curve of two products not related in production

the marginal rate of transformation of Q_2 into Q_1, which is verbalized in discrete terms as the amount of Q_2 that a producer has to give up $(-\Delta Q_2)$ to produce an additional unit of Q_1 (ΔQ_1) while keeping input constant. If $MF_1 = 2$ and $MF_2 = 1$, the producer has to give up two units of Q_2 to produce an additional unit of Q_1.

When Q_1 and Q_2 vary by discrete amounts,[5] the increase in F because an additional unit of Q_1 is produced is the unit gained of Q_1 times the marginal input of that unit:

$$\Delta F_1 = \Delta Q_1 \frac{\Delta F_1}{\Delta Q_1}.$$

The decrease in F because less Q_2 is produced is the quantity given up of Q_2 times the marginal input of that quantity:

$$\Delta F_2 = \Delta Q_2 \frac{\Delta F_2}{\Delta Q_2}$$

The total change in F is ΔF, and

$$\Delta F = \frac{\Delta F_1}{\Delta Q_1} \Delta Q_1 + \frac{\Delta F_2}{\Delta Q_2} \Delta Q_2$$

Since the total change in F is zero because F is a given amount (F_0), the decrease in F because less Q_2 is produced must be offset exactly by the increase in F because more Q_1 is produced. Therefore,

$$\Delta F = \frac{\Delta F_1}{\Delta Q_1} \Delta Q_1 + \frac{\Delta F_2}{\Delta Q_2} \Delta Q_2 = 0$$

$$\frac{\Delta F_2}{\Delta Q_2} \Delta Q_2 = -\frac{\Delta F_1}{\Delta Q_1} \Delta Q_1$$

$$\frac{\Delta Q_2}{\Delta Q_1} = -\frac{\Delta F_1/\Delta Q_1}{\Delta F_2/\Delta Q_2} = -\frac{MF_1}{MF_2}.[6]$$

The slope of an iso-input curve dQ_2/dQ_1 is thus seen to change as more Q_1 and less Q_2 are produced according to the change in MF_1 relative to the change in MF_2. In the case of two products that are not related in production, the marginal input of one product is a constant function of the quantity produced of the other product: $\Delta MF_1/\Delta Q_2 = 0$ and $\Delta MF_2/\Delta Q_1 = 0$. But assuming increasing marginal input of a product, the marginal input of a product is an increasing function of the quantity produced of the product: $\Delta MF_1/\Delta Q_1 > 0$ and $\Delta MF_2/\Delta Q_2 > 0$. Thus, each successive unit increase in Q_1 increases input by an increasing amount; and each successive unit decrease in Q_2 decreases input by a decreasing amount. Therefore, as seen in Figure 9.5, with each unit increase in Q_1 (ΔQ_1), the producer gives up an increasing amount of Q_2 (ΔQ_2) to keep input constant. Since the ratio $\Delta Q_2/\Delta Q_1$ increases numerically as more Q_1 and less Q_2 are produced, an iso-input curve of a producer who is subject to diminishing marginal returns is concave from below a tangent line.[7]

An iso-input curve is also called a production-possibilities or transformation curve, for it represents all possible combinations of Q_1 and Q_2 that may be produced at a given overall input by transforming input from the production of one product to the production of another product. It is also called a budget-constraint curve or curve of attainable combinations, since all combinations along and below it are attainable from a given budget, cost, or input. Lastly, it is also called the alternative cost, opportunity cost, social cost, or butter–guns curve, for it represents the alternative, opportunity, or social cost of producing more of one product (guns), which is the amount of the other product (butter) that must be given up to produce more guns.

An iso-input curve may be drawn in Figure 9.5 for each level of input of the seller. The higher the level of input, the larger the quantities of both products that may be produced, and hence the farther away from the point of origin lies the curve. Two curves which depict two different levels of input cannot intersect; for if the two curves intersected, the same output of the two products would be associated with two different levels of input, which is inconsistent with the input function $F = F(Q_1, Q_2)$. According to this function, an output of the two products is associated with one level of input.

Iso-Input Curve of Two Substitutes in Production

Two products are substitutes or rivals in production when the marginal input of one product is an increasing function of the quantity produced of the other product, when $\Delta MF_1/\Delta Q_2 > 0$ and $\Delta MF_2/\Delta Q_1 > 0$. Thus, assuming

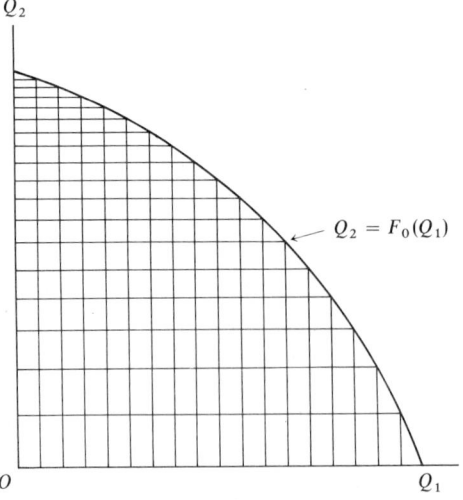

FIG. 9.6. Hypothetical iso-input curve of two imperfect substitutes in production

increasing marginal input of a product, each successive unit increase in Q_1 increases MF_1 (which tends to increase MF_1/MF_2 and hence $-\Delta Q_2/\Delta Q_1$) and increases MF_2 (which tends to decrease MF_1/MF_2 and hence $-\Delta Q_2/\Delta Q_1$). Similarly, each successive unit decrease in Q_2 decreases MF_2 (which tends to increase MF_1/MF_2 and hence $-\Delta Q_2/\Delta Q_1$) and decreases MF_1 (which tends to decrease MF_1/MF_2 and hence $-\Delta Q_2/\Delta Q_1$). If Q_1 and Q_2 are imperfect substitutes in production, the tendency for MF_1/MF_2 to increase because of increasing marginal input of a product more than offsets the tendency for MF_1/MF_2 to decrease because of the substitute relationship between them; hence the ratio $\Delta Q_2/\Delta Q_1$ increases numerically as more Q_1 and less Q_2 are produced. In other words, as seen in Figure 9.6, the iso-input curve of two imperfect substitutes in production is concave from below a tangent line.

If Q_1 and Q_2 are perfect substitutes in production, the tendency for MF_1/MF_2 to increase because of increasing marginal input of a product is offset exactly by the tendency for MF_1/MF_2 to decrease because of the substitute relationship between them; hence the ratio $\Delta Q_2/\Delta Q_1$ remains constant as more Q_1 and less Q_2 are produced. In other words, as seen in Figure 9.7, the iso-input curve of two perfect substitutes in production is a negatively-sloped straight line.

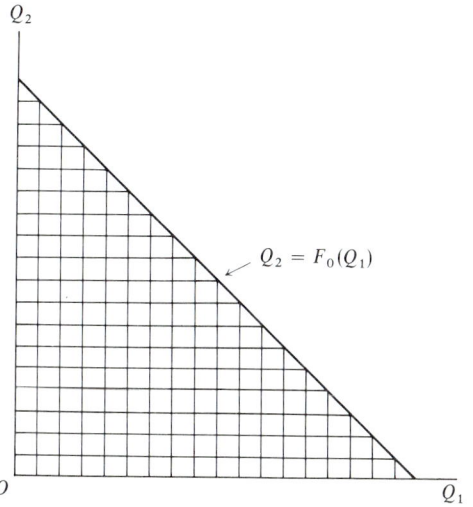

FIG. 9.7. Hypothetical iso-input curve of two perfect substitutes in production

Iso-Input Curve of Two Complements in Production

Two products are complements or joint products in production when the marginal input of one product is a decreasing function of the quantity produced of the other product, when $\Delta MF_1/\Delta Q_2 < 0$ and $\Delta MF_2/\Delta Q_1 > 0$. Thus, assuming increasing marginal input of a product, each successive unit increase in Q_1 increases MF_1 and decreases MF_2, thereby tending to increase MF_1/MF_2 and hence $-\Delta Q_2/\Delta Q_1$; and each successive unit decrease in Q_2 decreases MF_2 and increases MF_1, thereby tending to increase MF_1/MF_2 and hence $-\Delta Q_2/\Delta Q_1$. Conversely, each successive unit increase in Q_2 increases MF_2 and decreases MF_1, thereby tending to decrease MF_1/MF_2 and hence $-\Delta Q_2/\Delta Q_1$; and each successive unit decrease in Q_1 decreases MF_1 and increases MF_2, thereby tending to decrease MF_1/MF_2 and hence $-\Delta Q_2/\Delta Q_1$. Therefore, as seen in Figure 9.8, the iso-input curve of two imperfect complements in production is concave from below a tangent line.

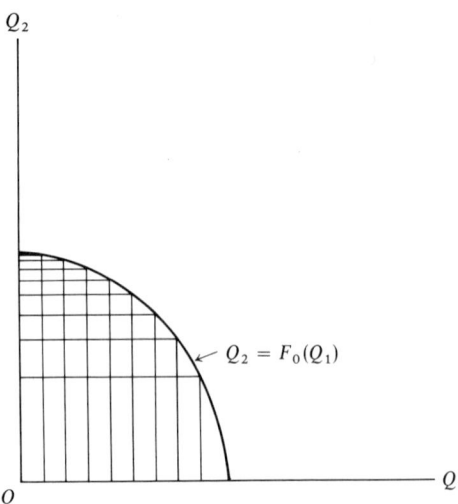

FIG. 9.8. Hypothetical iso-input curve of two imperfect complements in production

As the degree of complementary in production increases, MF_1/MF_2 approaches infinity as Q_1 increases and approaches zero as Q_2 increases. In the limiting case, as Q_1 increases by an infinitesimally small amount, the iso-input curve is a vertical straight line (see the vertical portion of the curve in Figure 9.9); and as Q_2 increases by an infinitesimally small amount, the iso-input curve is a horizontal straight line (see the horizontal portion of the

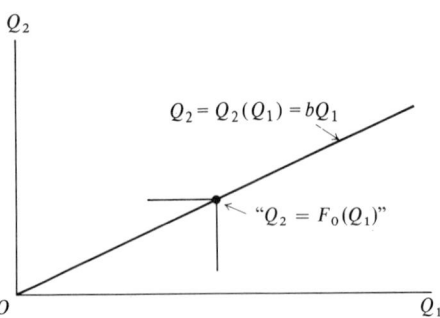

FIG. 9.9. Hypothetical iso-input curve of two perfect complements in production

curve in Figure 9.9). In this case, Q_1 and Q_2 are produced in a fixed proportion; therefore the iso-input "curve" is a point in the OQ_1Q_2 plane representing the constant ratio of Q_2 to Q_1. A set of constant or fixed Q_2/Q_1 ratios is represented by a ray $Q_2 = Q_2(Q_1) = bQ_1$, as in Figure 9.9.

SUMMARY

The total cost curve of a product shows how total cost (C) varies with quantity produced (output) of the product (Q) per unit of time. The marginal cost curve of a product shows how the slope of the total cost curve (dC/dQ) varies with quantity produced of the product (Q) per unit of time. The average cost curve of a product shows how the ratio of total cost to quantity produced (C/Q) varies with quantity produced of the product (Q) per unit of time. In the case of a producer or seller who is subject to diminishing marginal returns, each additional unit produced of a product per unit of time adds a larger amount to total cost. Total cost (C) therefore increases at an increasing rate (dC/dQ) as quantity produced (Q) increases. Consequently, marginal cost of the product ($MC = dC/dQ$) is an increasing function of quantity produced (Q) per unit of time. To generalize, according to the law of increasing marginal cost of a product to a producer who is subject to diminishing marginal returns, the cost associated with producing an additional unit of a product varies directly with quantity produced per unit of time.

Marginal and average cost of a product are decreasing when total cost is increasing at a decreasing rate as quantity produced of the product increases, and the marginal cost curve lies below the average cost curve. The marginal cost curve is at its minimum value, but average cost continues to decrease, at that quantity produced of the product at which total cost begins to increase at an increasing rate. Eventually, as more units of the product are produced, marginal cost increases sufficiently to make average cost reach its minimum value. When this happens, the marginal cost curve intersects the average cost curve from below. Thereafter, average cost also increases, and the marginal cost curve lies above the average cost curve. Thus, the law of increasing marginal cost applies to the positively-sloped portion of the marginal cost curve and to that portion of the total cost curve denoting that total cost is increasing at an increasing rate.

When W is an increasing function of F, marginal cost increases as Q increases for two different reasons, each reinforcing the other. First, MC increases as Q increases because of diminishing marginal returns. Second, MC increases as Q increases because of increasing marginal factor cost. Consequently, with respect to positively-sloped curves, the slope of the marginal cost curve of an imperfectly competitive purchaser of a variable factor of production is greater than the slope of the marginal cost curve of a perfectly competitive purchaser, given the same production function.

Long-run total cost increases at a decreasing rate as quantity produced increases, in the case of increasing economies of scale, and increases at an increasing rate, in the case of decreasing economies of scale. In between these two cases, long-run total cost may increase at a constant rate as quantity produced increases due to increases in the input of all factors of production, given the price of factors and the state of technology.

The long-run average cost (LAC) curve depicts how average cost varies with output as output varies with the input of all factors, given the prices of factors and the state of technology. An LAC curve envelopes a set of short-run average cost (SAC) curves. Each SAC curve depicts how average cost varies with output as output varies with the input of variable factors, given the input of fixed factors, the price of factors, and the state of technology. Each point on a long-run marginal cost (LMC) curve represents a short-run marginal cost (SMC) value at which the corresponding SAC curve is tangent to the LAC curve.

An iso-input curve depicts all combinations of quantities of two products (Q_1 and Q_2) that may be produced by a seller with a given input of factors of production (F), given the state of technology. An iso-input curve may be drawn for each level of F. The greater the value of F, the higher the curve lies in the OQ_1Q_2 plane. No two curves intersect. In general, an iso-input curve is a negatively-sloped curve that is concave from below a tangent line. The numerical value of its slope ($-dQ_2/dQ_1$) is called the marginal rate of transformation of product Q_2 into Q_1, and is equal to the ratio MF_1/MF_2.

When Q_1 and Q_2 are not related in production, the marginal input of one product is a constant function of the quantity produced of the other product; and the numerical value of dQ_2/dQ_1 varies directly with Q_1 because of increasing marginal input of a product. When Q_1 and Q_2 are imperfect substitutes in production or are rival products, the marginal input of one product is an increasing function of the quantity produced of the other product; and as Q_1 increases the tendency for $-dQ_2/dQ_1$ to increase because of increasing marginal input of a product more than offsets the tendency for $-dQ_2/dQ_1$ to decrease because of the substitute relationship between them. When Q_1 and Q_2 are imperfect complements in production or are joint products, the marginal input of one product is a decreasing function of the quantity produced of the other product; and as Q_1 increases, the tendency for $-dQ_2/dQ_1$ to increase because of increasing marginal input of a product is reinforced by the tendency for $-dQ_2/dQ_1$ to increase because of the complementary relationship between them. Thus, the greater the degree of complementarity, the greater the degree of concavity of the iso-input curve. Conversely, the greater the degree of substitutability, the less the degree of concavity of the iso-input curve. The iso-input curve is a negatively-sloped straight line in the case of two perfect substitutes, but it is a point in the OQ_1Q_2 plane in the case of two perfect complements in production.

Questions

1. List the principles of the theory of supply of a product that are of primary importance. How do you account for the position of the law of increasing marginal cost in this list? Verbalize this principle of economics.

2. Define total cost of a product. What is a total cost curve? Draw a set of total cost, variable cost, and fixed cost curves and describe their properties and relationships to one another. Derive a total variable cost curve of a perfectly competitive purchaser of a variable factor from his $F = F(Q)$ and $W = W(F) = W_0$ curves and describe their relationships. Do the same analysis for an imperfectly competitive purchaser of a variable factor. What conclusions do you draw from a comparison of the two total variable cost curves?

3. Define marginal cost of a product. What is a marginal cost curve? Draw a marginal cost curve and describe its properties. Relate the properties of the total and marginal cost curves. Derive a marginal cost curve of a perfectly competitive purchaser of a variable factor from his $dF/dQ = F'(Q)$ and $MFC = c'(F) = W_0$ curves and describe their relationships. Do the same analysis for an imperfectly competitive purchaser of a variable factor. What conclusions do you draw from a comparison of the two marginal cost curves?

4. Define average cost of a product. What is an average cost curve? Draw an average cost curve and describe its properties. Relate the properties of the total and the average cost curves, and the marginal and average cost curves. Derive an average cost curve of a perfectly competitive purchaser of a variable factor from his $F/Q = F(Q)/Q$ and $AFC = c(F)/F = W_0$ curves and describe their relationships. Do the same analysis for an imperfectly competitive purchaser of a variable factor. What conclusions do you draw from a comparison of the two average cost curves?

5. Relate the long-run total, marginal, and average cost curves of a product to the concepts of increasing, constant, and decreasing returns to scale.

6. What does an SAC curve depict? What does an LAC curve depict? What is the relationship between these two curves?

7. What does an SMC curve depict? What does an LMC curve depict? What is the relationship between these two curves?

8. Define the iso-input of two products. What is an iso-input curve? Draw an iso-input curve and describe its properties. Relate marginal input and the slope of an iso-input curve. Verbalize the numerical value of the slope of an iso-input curve.

9. Classify products in production via the marginal input concept. Relate your classification to the slope of an iso-input curve.

NOTES

[1] Figure 9.1b does not show that an additional unit of input may add nothing to output. But if the assumption is made, then the additional unit of input still adds its price to variable cost. Moreover, if an additional unit of input reduces output, it still adds its price to variable cost. Thus, output may reach a limit and then decrease, but variable cost continues to increase as more

input is purchased. This "backward bending" portion of the variable cost curve is not shown in Figure 9.1c, for if it were shown the curve would not be a function. (It would be a relation, however.)

[2] When quantity is varied continuously, continuous marginal cost of a product (MC_c) is the instantaneous rate of change of total cost as quantity produced of the product increases or decreases. With respect to the one-product cost function $C = C(Q)$, the instantaneous rate of change is the infinitesimally small change in C (dC) associated with an infinitesimally small change in Q (dQ): $MC_c = dC/dQ$. In this context, marginal cost is the slope of the total cost curve of the product. The slope of the total cost curve is equal to the difference quotient $\Delta C/\Delta Q$ of the tangent line at a point on the curve. In Table 9.1, the MC_c of the third unit equals

$$\frac{dC}{dQ} = \lim_{\Delta Q \to 0} \frac{\Delta C}{\Delta Q} = 11$$

[3] Let the wage be \$1 per unit of labor; and let an additional unit of labor add two units to output. Then $MC = W \cdot \Delta F/\Delta Q = \$1 \cdot 1/2 = \$0.50$. The additional unit of output cost 50 cents because it required 1/2 of a unit, at \$1 per unit, of labor.

[4] Internal economies of scale do not necessarily imply increasing returns to scale, for internal economies of scale may be attributable to things other than increasing returns to scale. In other words, the long-run total cost curve is not simply the transformation of the long-run total product curve from physical input units to monetary output units.

[5] The instantaneous rate of change of F with respect to Q_1 is the infinitesimally small change in F associated with an infinitesimally small change in Q_1: $MF_1 = \partial F/\partial Q_1$. The total infinitesimally small change in Q_1 is dQ_1. Thus, in terms of infinitesimally small changes, the change in F associated with a total change in Q_1 is

$$\frac{\partial F}{\partial Q_1} dQ_1$$

Similarly, the instantaneous rate of change of F with respect to Q_2 is the infinitesimally small change in F associated with an infinitesimally small change in Q_2: $MF_2 = \partial F/\partial Q_2$. The total infinitesimally small change in Q_2 is dQ_2. In terms of infinitesimally small changes, the change in F associated with a total change in Q_2 is

$$\frac{\partial F}{\partial Q_2} dQ_2$$

Therefore, in terms of infinitesimally small changes, the total change in F is dF, and

$$dF = \frac{\partial F}{\partial Q_1} dQ_1 + \frac{\partial F}{\partial Q_2} dQ_2$$

Since the total change in F along an iso-input curve is zero,

$$dF = \frac{\partial F}{\partial Q_1} dQ_1 + \frac{\partial F}{\partial Q_2} dQ_2 = 0$$

$$\frac{\partial F}{\partial Q_2} dQ_2 = -\frac{\partial F}{\partial Q_1} dQ_1$$

$$\frac{dQ_2}{dQ_1} = -\frac{\partial F/\partial Q_1}{\partial F/\partial Q_2} = -\frac{MF_1}{MF_2}.$$

[6] Verbalize $\partial Q_1/\partial F$ as the marginal product of F in the production of Q_1 and $\partial Q_2/\partial F$ as the marginal product of F in the production of Q_2. Then

$$\frac{dQ_2}{dQ_1} = -\frac{MF_1}{MF_2} = -\frac{\partial F/\partial Q_1}{\partial F/\partial Q_2} = -\frac{\partial Q_2/\partial F}{\partial Q_1/\partial F}$$

As input (F) is transferred from the production of Q_2 to the production of Q_1, $\partial Q_2/\partial F$ increases and $\partial Q_1/\partial F$ decreases according to the law of decreasing marginal physical productivity of a factor of production. Thus dQ_2/dQ_1 increases numerically as Q_1 increases and Q_2 decreases because of diminishing marginal returns. In other words, the iso-input curve is concave from below a tangent line because of diminishing marginal returns.

[7] Each successive unit increase in Q_2 increases input by an increasing amount, and each successive unit decrease in Q_1 decreases input by a decreasing amount. Therefore, with each unit increase in Q_2 (ΔQ_2), the producer gives up an increasing amount of Q_1 ($-\Delta Q_1$) to keep input constant. Since the ratio $\Delta Q_2/\Delta Q_1$ decreases numerically as more Q_2 and less Q_1 are produced, an iso-input curve is concave from below a tangent line.

chapter 10

Equilibrium of a Perfectly Competitive Seller of Products

If ... it usually costs twice the labor to kill a beaver which it costs to kill a deer, one beaver should naturally exchange for or be worth two deer.
(Adam Smith, *Wealth of Nations*)

One of the ultimate aims of a producer and seller of products is to maximize his profit. Profit equals revenue minus cost. Revenue varies with the quantities sold of products. Cost varies with the quantities produced of products. Thus, a producer-seller is faced with the problem of determining the profit-maximizing quantity to produce and sell of each of his products per unit of time. He is said to be in equilibrium when he has chosen the quantities that maximize his profit. The concern of the economist with this ultimate aim of man is embodied in the so-called "principle of equilibrium of a perfectly competitive seller of products," which may be presented in several different ways.[1]

Price Equals Marginal Cost

Profit $(R - C)$ is maximized at that quantity produced and sold of a product (Q) at which the profit curve, $R - C = R(Q) - C(Q)$, is at its peak. When the profit curve is at its peak, its slope, $R'(Q) - C'(Q)$, is zero. Thus profit is maximized at that quantity of the product (Q) at which marginal revenue, $R'(Q)$, equals marginal cost, $C'(Q)$. The profit-maximizing quantity of a product therefore may be determined by setting the marginal revenue function, $MR = R'(Q)$, equal to the marginal cost function, $MC = C'(Q)$, and solving for Q. The principle of equilibrium of a seller of products is thus an inference drawn from an operation on the marginal revenue and marginal cost functions of a seller. Assuming perfect competition in the product market, at each quantity sold, average revenue equals marginal revenue equals price: $AR = MR = P = P(Q)$. Consequently, when a perfectly competitive seller

EQUILIBRIUM OF A PERFECTLY COMPETITIVE SELLER OF PRODUCTS

is in equilibrium, he has determined the quantity to produce and sell of each product at which the price of a product (P) equals the marginal cost of the product (MC). To elucidate this principle, when a perfectly competitive seller is in equilibrium, the amount of money he is willing to accept to sell an additional unit of a product (P) is equal to the amount of money he has to give up to produce an additional unit of the product (MC):

$$P = MC \quad \text{or} \quad \frac{\Delta R}{\Delta Q} = \frac{\Delta C}{\Delta Q}$$

In other words, the last unit sold of each product (ΔQ) adds as much to his revenue (ΔR) as it adds to his cost (ΔC); the "pleasure" of an additional unit (ΔR) is offset exactly by its "pain" (ΔC).

In the two-products case,

(1) $\quad P_1 = MC_1 \quad \text{or} \quad MR_1 = MC_1 \quad \text{since} \quad P_1 = MR_1$

(2) $\quad P_2 = MC_2 \quad \text{or} \quad MR_2 = MC_2 \quad \text{since} \quad P_2 = MR_2$

When two products are not related in production, the marginal input and hence the marginal cost of one product do not vary with the quantity produced of the other product. And thus each equation is independent of the other equation: as Q_1 changes, MC_2 does not change; and as Q_2 changes, MC_1 does not change.[2] But when two products are related in production, the marginal input and hence the marginal cost of one product vary with the quantity produced of the other product. And thus each equation is dependent upon the other equation: as Q_1 changes, MC_2 changes; and as Q_2 changes, MC_1 changes.[3]

Equality of the Ratio of Price to Marginal Cost of Every Product

Cost varies with the quantities produced of products. Thus, when a producer has determined the profit-maximizing quantities to produce, he has also determined the profit-maximizing cost. By dividing both sides of equation (1) by MC_1 and both sides of equation (2) by MC_2,

(1') $\quad \dfrac{P_1}{MC_1} = 1$

(2') $\quad \dfrac{P_2}{MC_2} = 1$

By setting (1') equal to (2'),

(3) $\quad \dfrac{P_1}{MC_1} = \dfrac{P_2}{MC_2} (=1)$

With respect to products $Q_1, Q_2, Q_3, \ldots, Q_n$,

(3') $$\frac{P_1}{MC_1} = \frac{P_2}{MC_2} = \frac{P_3}{MC_3} = \cdots = \frac{P_n}{MC_n} (=1)$$

Therefore, when a perfectly competitive seller is in equilibrium, he is allocating his profit-maximizing cost in such a way that the last dollar spent on Q_1 (MC_1) yields the same amount of revenue (P_1) as the last dollar spent on $Q_2, Q_3, \ldots, Q_n$—the equimarginal principle of equilibrium of a perfectly competitive seller of products.

Equimarginal Principle of Equilibrium of a Perfectly Competitive Seller of Products

The equimarginal principle of equilibrium of a perfectly competitive seller of products may be analyzed via the two-products case according to the two-faced (Janus) diagram in Figure 10.1. In this analysis, "marginal revenue" is used in lieu of "price" and "dollar of outlay" is used in lieu of "marginal cost."

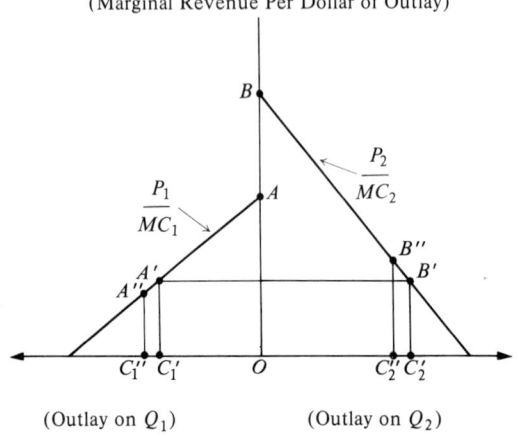

FIG. 10.1. Equimarginal principle of equilibrium of a seller of products

In Figure 10.1, the outlay on product Q_1 begins with zero at the origin and increases to the left on the horizontal axis. Conversely, the outlay on product Q_2 begins with zero at the origin and increases to the right on the horizontal axis. Thus, all values on the horizontal axis are either zero or positive (that is, nonnegative). The marginal revenue per dollar of outlay on a product begins with zero at the origin and increases up the vertical axis. When the outlay on Q_1 increases, the quantity produced of Q_1 increases; and as the

EQUILIBRIUM OF A PERFECTLY COMPETITIVE SELLER OF PRODUCTS 183

quantity produced of Q_1 increases, the marginal cost of Q_1 increases according to the law of increasing marginal cost of a product. Thus, given P_1, the marginal revenue per dollar of outlay on Q_1 (P_1/MC_1) decreases as the outlay on Q_1 increases, as depicted by the curve labeled P_1/MC_1. Similarly, the curve labeled P_2/MC_2 depicts the inverse relation between P_2/MC_2 and the outlay on Q_2.

The seller has $C_1'C_2'$ profit-maximizing dollars to allocate between Q_1 and Q_2. The marginal revenue per dollar of outlay OC_1' is $C_1'A'$; therefore, the total revenue of outlay OC_1', which is the area under the P_1/MC_1 curve at OC_1', is area $C_1'A'AO$. Similarly, the marginal revenue per dollar of outlay OC_2' is $C_2'B'$; and the total revenue of outlay OC_2' is area $C_2'B'BO$. Since $C_1'A' = C_2'B'$, with this allocation the ratio of price to marginal cost is the same for both products: $P_1/MC_1 = P_2/MC_2$.

The magnitude $C_1'C_2'$ is the same as the magnitude $C_1''C_2''$. Thus the seller has $C_1''C_2''$ profit-maximizing dollars to allocate between Q_1 and Q_2. The marginal revenue per dollar of outlay OC_1'' is $C_1''A''$; and the total revenue of outlay OC_1'' is area $C_1''A''AO$. Similarly, the marginal revenue per dollar of outlay OC_2'' is $C_2''B''$; and the total revenue of outlay OC_2'' is area $C_2''B''BO$. Since $C_1''A'' < C_2''B''$, with this allocation the ratio of price to marginal cost is not the same for both products: $P_1/MC_1 < P_2/MC_2$.

The combined area when $P_1/MC_1 = P_2/MC_2$ ($C_1'A'AO + C_2'B'BO$) is larger than the combined area when $P_1/MC_1 < P_2/MC_2$ ($C_1''A''AO + C_2''B''BO$). To see this, increase the outlay on Q_1 from OC_1' to OC_1'' ($= C_1'' - C_1'$), thereby increasing total revenue by the area $C_1'A'A''C_1''$. The outlay on Q_2 is decreased from OC_2' to OC_2'' ($= C_2' - C_2''$), thereby decreasing total revenue by the area $C_2'B'B''C_2''$. The loss in revenue ($C_2'B'B''C_2''$) is greater than the gain in revenue ($C_1'A'A''C_1''$). Therefore, when $P_1/MC_1 < P_2/MC_2$, revenue is increased by producing more Q_2 and less Q_1 until $P_1/MC_1 = P_2/MC_2$. As less Q_1 is produced, P_1/MC_1 increases; and as more Q_2 is produced, P_2/MC_2 decreases, until eventually $P_1/MC_1 = P_2/MC_2$.

Ratio of Prices Equals Ratio of Marginal Costs

By multiplying both sides of equation (3) by MC_1 and dividing both sides by P_2,

$$(4) \quad \frac{P_1}{P_2} = \frac{MC_1}{MC_2} \left(= \frac{MC_1}{P_2}\right)$$

Thus, when a perfectly competitive seller is in equilibrium, he is allocating his profit-maximizing cost in such a way that the ratio of the prices of any two products is equal to the ratio of their marginal costs.

Marginal Revenue-Product Equals Price of Input

Input varies with the quantities produced of products. Thus, when a producer has determined the profit-maximizing quantities to produce, he has also determined the profit-maximizing input. By setting MC_1 equal to $W(\Delta F/\Delta Q_1)$ and MC_2 equal to $W(\Delta F/\Delta Q_2)$, equations (1) and (2) are transformed into

$$P_1 = W(\Delta F/\Delta Q_1) \text{ and } P_2 = W(\Delta F/\Delta Q_2)$$

which are equivalent to

$$P_1(\Delta Q_1/\Delta F) = W \text{ and } P_2(\Delta Q_2/\Delta F) = W$$

and hence

(5) $\quad P_1(\Delta Q_1/\Delta F) = P_2(\Delta Q_2/\Delta F) = W$

or

$$\frac{\Delta R_1}{\Delta Q_1} \cdot \frac{\Delta Q_1}{\Delta F} = \frac{\Delta R_2}{\Delta Q_2} \cdot \frac{\Delta Q_2}{\Delta F} = \frac{\Delta C}{\Delta F}$$

or

$$\frac{\Delta R_1}{\Delta F} = \frac{\Delta R_2}{\Delta F} = \frac{\Delta C}{\Delta F}$$

Therefore, the profit-maximizing input is that input at which the marginal revenue-product of input in the production of each product[4] equals the price of input: the last unit of input allocated to each product adds as much to revenue as to cost. By dividing equation (5) through by W,

$$\frac{P_1(\Delta Q_1/\Delta F)}{W} = \frac{P_2(\Delta Q_2/\Delta F)}{W} (= 1)$$

which is an alternative form of the equimarginal principle of equilibrium of a perfectly competitive seller of products.

Ratio of Prices Equals Ratio of Marginal Inputs

By setting MC_1 equal to $W(\Delta F/\Delta Q_1)$ and MC_2 equal to $W(\Delta F/\Delta Q_2)$, equation (4) is transformed into

$$\frac{P_1}{P_2} = \frac{W(\Delta F/\Delta Q_1)}{W(\Delta F/\Delta Q_2)}$$

which is equivalent to

(6) $\quad \dfrac{P_1}{P_2} = \dfrac{\Delta F/\Delta Q_1}{\Delta F/\Delta Q_2} \text{ or } \dfrac{P_1}{P_2} = \dfrac{MF_1}{MF_2}$

Therefore, when a perfectly competitive seller is in equilibrium, he is using his profit-maximizing input in such a way that the ratio of the prices of any two products is equal to the ratio of their marginal inputs.

The ratio P_1/P_2 is a number that denotes the amount of Q_2 that a perfectly competitive seller is willing to give up to sell an additional unit of Q_1. Similarly, the ratio MF_1/MF_2 is a number that denotes the amount of Q_2 he has to give up to produce an additional unit of Q_1. Thus, when a perfectly competitive seller is in equilibrium, the amount of Q_2 he is willing to give up to sell an additional unit of Q_1 (P_1/P_2) is equal to the amount of Q_2 he has to give up to produce an additional unit of Q_1 (MF_1/MF_2).

The ratio P_1/P_2 is the numerical value of the slope of an iso-revenue curve. The ratio MF_1/MF_2 is called the marginal rate of transformation of Q_2 into Q_1. Thus, when a perfectly competitive seller is in equilibrium, the numerical value of the slope of an iso-revenue curve (P_1/P_2) is equal to the marginal rate of transformation of Q_2 into Q_1 (MF_1/MF_2). In other words, when a perfectly competitive seller is in equilibrium, he is using his profit-maximizing input in such a way that the ratio of the prices of any two products is equal to their marginal rate of transformation.

The ratio MF_1/MF_2 is the numerical value of the slope of an iso-input curve. An iso-input curve depicts all combinations of quantities of two products (Q_1 and Q_2) that may be produced by a producer with a given input. Thus, when a perfectly competitive seller is in equilibrium, he has chosen a combination of Q_1 and Q_2 at which the slope of an iso-revenue curve is equal to the slope of the iso-input curve that denotes his profit-maximizing input: that is, $-P_1/P_2 = MF_1/MF_2$. In Figure 10.2, assume that iso-input curve 1 represents the profit-maximizing input. The slope of iso-revenue curve II ($-P_1/P_2$) is equal to the slope of iso-input curve 1 ($-MF_1/MF_2$) at point A. By multiplying both slopes by -1, $P_1/P_2 = MF_1/MF_2$ at point A. Since at point B, $P_1/P_2 > MF_1/MF_2$, he is in disequilibrium at B. From B to A, the ratio MF_1/MF_2 increases as more Q_1 and less Q_2 are produced per unit of time until, at A, $P_1/P_2 = MF_1/MF_2$. Similarly, at point C, $P_1/P_2 < MF_1/MF_2$, and hence he is in disequilibrium. From C to A, the ratio MF_1/MF_2 decreases as more Q_2 and less Q_1 are produced per unit of time until, at A, $P_1/P_2 = MF_1/MF_2$.

An iso-revenue curve depicts all combinations of quantities of two products (Q_1 and Q_2) that yield the same level of revenue to a seller. And the higher an iso-revenue curve lies in the plane, the greater the level of revenue. Combination A on iso-input curve 1 and iso-revenue curve II therefore is preferred to all other combinations that lie on curve 1: it is the combination associated with the highest level of revenue per the profit-maximizing level of input. It lies on the highest attainable iso-revenue curve, which is curve II, and is the only attainable combination on this curve. Combination B on iso-input curve 1 and iso-revenue curve I is attainable but not preferred to A. For by selling more Q_1 and less Q_2, the seller can attain a higher level of

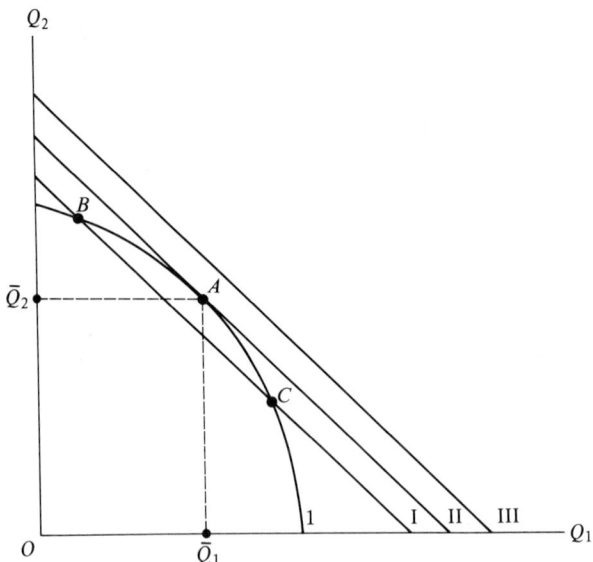

FIG. 10.2. Equilibrium of a perfectly competitive seller of products: ratio of prices equals ratio of marginal costs

revenue (and therefore profit) and hence a preferred position; that is, he can move onto the higher iso-revenue curve II. Similarly, combination C on iso-input curve 1 and iso-revenue curve I is attainable but not preferred to A. For by selling more Q_2 and less Q_1, the seller can attain a higher level of revenue (and therefore profit) and hence a preferred position; that is, he can move onto the higher iso-revenue curve II.

Output Expansion Path

Profit is maximized when the producer has chosen the combination of Q_1 and Q_2 that maximizes the surplus of revenue over cost. According to equation (5), when he has chosen the profit-maximizing combination,

(5) $\quad P_1(\Delta Q_1/\Delta F) = P_2(\Delta Q_2/\Delta F) = W$

In contrast, revenue is maximized when the producer has chosen the combination of Q_1 and Q_2 that maximizes the revenue attainable from a specified input, which may or may not be the profit-maximizing input. According to equation (6), when he has chosen the revenue-maximizing combination,

$$\frac{P_1}{P_2} = \frac{\Delta F/\Delta Q_1}{\Delta F/\Delta Q_2}$$

which is equivalent to

$$\frac{P_1}{P_2} = \frac{\Delta Q_2/\Delta F}{\Delta Q_1/\Delta F}$$

which is equivalent to

(6') $\quad P_1(\Delta Q_1/\Delta F) = P_2(\Delta Q_2/\Delta F)$

or

$$\frac{\Delta R_1}{\Delta Q_1} \cdot \frac{\Delta Q_1}{\Delta F} = \frac{\Delta R_2}{\Delta Q_2} \cdot \frac{\Delta Q_2}{\Delta F}$$

or

$$\frac{\Delta R_1}{\Delta F} = \frac{\Delta R_2}{\Delta F}$$

Therefore, the revenue-maximizing input is that input at which the marginal revenue-product of input in the production of Q_1 equals the marginal revenue-product of input in the production of Q_2: the last unit of input allocated to each product adds the same amount to revenue.

By comparing equation (5), in which W appears, to equation (6'), in which W does not appear, one may infer that a necessary but not sufficient condition for profit maximization is revenue maximization; and a sufficient condition for revenue maximization is profit maximization. Revenue is maximized when profit is maximized, for revenue is maximized per the profit-maximizing level of input. But profit may not be maximized when revenue is maximized, for revenue is maximized per any specified level of input.

A point on a total revenue-product curve (see pages 284–287) denotes the maximum revenue attainable from a specified input. Thus, with reference to each point on this curve, the producer must determine the combination of Q_1 and Q_2 that maximizes revenue per the specified input. When he has chosen the revenue-maximizing combination associated with a specified input, he is on the highest iso-revenue curve having a common point with the iso-input curve of the specified input, and hence $P_1/P_2 = MF_1/MF_2$. Corresponding to each tangency of an iso-revenue curve and a specified iso-input curve, therefore, is a point on a total revenue-product curve. Since in this frame of reference a specified input constrains revenue, this case is called constrained revenue maximization.

Conversely, a point on a total revenue-product curve denotes the minimum input required to yield a specified revenue. Thus, with reference to each point on this curve, the producer must determine the combination of Q_1 and Q_2 that minimizes the input required to yield a specified revenue. When he has chosen the input-minimizing combination associated with a specified revenue, he is on the lowest iso-input curve having a common point with the iso-revenue curve of the specified revenue, and hence $P_1/P_2 = MF_1/MF_2$. Corresponding to each tangency of an iso-input curve and a specified iso-revenue curve, therefore, is a point on a total revenue-product curve. Since in this frame of reference a specified revenue constrains input, this case is called constrained input minimization.

Constrained revenue maximization and constrained input minimization are depicted graphically in Figure 10.3 by each point of tangency of an iso-input curve and an iso-revenue curve: with reference to each point, $P_1/P_2 = MF_1/MF_2$. The locus (set) of tangencies is called the output expansion path.

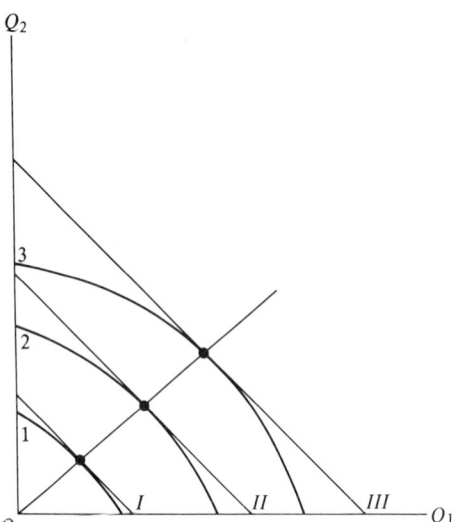

FIG. 10.3. Output expansion path

SUMMARY

One of the ultimate aims of a producer and seller of products is to maximize his profit. When he is maximizing his profit, he is said to be in equilibrium: he cannot increase his profit by changing the quantities he produces and sells per unit of time, given the parameters of his revenue and cost functions. When a perfectly competitive seller has determined the profit-maximizing set of product quantities, in effect he has determined his profit-maximizing cost and is allocating it in such a way that (1) the price of each product equals its marginal cost. (2) The ratio of price to marginal cost is the same for every product—the equimarginal principle of equilibrium of a perfectly competitive seller of products, which is analyzed via a Janus diagram. (3) The ratio of the prices of any two products equals the ratio of their marginal costs. (4) The marginal revenue-product of input in the production of each product equals the price of input. (5) The ratio of the prices of any two products equals the ratio of their marginal inputs—which is equivalent to saying that the ratio of the prices of any two products equals the marginal rate of transformation of one product into the other product. When a perfectly competitive seller has determined a revenue-maximizing set of product quantities, in effect he has determined a revenue-maximizing input and is allocating it in such a way that the marginal revenue-product of input in the production of one product equals the marginal revenue-product of input in the production of every other product. The producer is maximizing his revenue when he is maximizing his profit, but he may or may not be maximizing his profit when he is maximizing his revenue.

Questions

1. List the principles of the theory of supply of a product that are of primary importance. How do you account for the position of the principle of equilibrium of a seller of products in this list?

2. Derive and verbalize the equilibrium principle $P = MC$.

3. Derive and verbalize the equimarginal principle of equilibrium of a perfectly competitive seller of products for the two-products case and the n-products case.

4. Analyze this principle in the two-products case via a Janus diagram.

5. Derive and verbalize the equilibrium principle $P_1/P_2 = MC_1/MC_2$.

6. Derive and verbalize the equilibrium principle $P_1(\Delta Q_1/\Delta F) = P_2(\Delta Q_2/\Delta F) = W$.

7. Use iso-revenue and iso-input curves to derive, analyze, and verbalize the equilibrium principle $P_1/P_2 = MF_1/MF_2$. (Note: an analysis of equilibrium includes an analysis of disequilibrium.) How would the equilibrium principle be stated if you did not accept the concepts of input (that is, cost) and marginal input (that is, marginal cost)?

8. Prove via equations that revenue maximization is not necessarily profit maximization, but profit maximization is revenue maximization.

9. Analyze the concept of the output expansion path via the concepts of constrained revenue maximization and constrained input minimization.

NOTES

[1] The principle of equilibrium of a perfectly competitive seller of products is *introduced* in this chapter and is analyzed further in Chapter 14. By assumption, in the present chapter, a perfectly competitive seller produces and sells products that may or may not be related in production. The production period is the short run. Each product is produced in one plant and is sold in one market. The price of a product is equal to or greater than average variable cost of the product. The marginal cost curve intersects the marginal revenue curve from below; and the intersection occurs at one point only. The significance of these simplifying assumptions is demonstrated in Chapter 14. They enable the most general type of equilibrium analysis to be presented here. They are also applicable to Chapter 11.

[2] In this case, the total cost function of one product is independent of the total cost function of the other product, and hence the two total cost functions may be added to derive the producer's cost function. In the case of a perfectly competitive seller, the total revenue function of one

product is independent of the total revenue function of the other product, and hence the two total revenue functions may be added to derive the seller's revenue function. In maximizing his profit, the producer-seller is assumed not to be subject to a cost constraint. Given these three assumptions, equilibrium of a multi-product seller may be analyzed in exactly the same way as equilibrium of a single-product seller (see Chapter 14).

[3] In this case, the total cost function of one product is interdependent with the total cost function of the other product, and hence the two total cost functions may not be added to derive the producer's cost function. Equilibrium of a multi-product seller thus may not be analyzed in exactly the same way as equilibrium of a single-product seller.

[4] Verbalize $P_1(\Delta Q_1/\Delta F)$ as the marginal revenue-product of input in the production of Q_1 and $P_2(\Delta Q_2/\Delta F)$ as the marginal revenue-product of input in the production of Q_2.

chapter 11

The Supply Function of a Product of a Perfectly Competitive Seller

"The supply function of a product of a perfectly competitive seller" is the name of the relation between the quantity of a product a seller is willing to sell per unit of time (the dependent variable) and the price of the product, the price of a substitute or rival product, and the price of a complementary or joint product (the independent variables), given the parameters of the state of technology and (assuming perfect competition in factor markets) the price of input. The relation between the dependent variable and each of the independent variables is analyzed via the principle of equilibrium of a perfectly competitive seller of products. The analysis consists of changing the value of one independent variable, while holding constant the values of the remaining independent variables, and ascertaining the new equilibrium value of the dependent variable. The primary objective of the analysis is to ascertain the sign of each of the difference quotients denoting the change in the dependent variable associated with a change in an independent variable, given the ceteris paribus assumption that in each case "other things are equal" (or are unchanging). When the value of an independent variable is held constant via the ceteris paribus assumption, the variable is called a parameter of the relation being analyzed. Thus the price of a substitute product, the price of a complementary product, the state of technology, and the price of input are parameters of the relation between the quantity of a product a seller is willing to sell per unit of time and the price of the product.

Supply Curve of a Product of a seller

The "supply curve of a product of a seller" depicts the relation between the quantity of a product a seller is willing to sell (Q) per unit of time and the price of the product (P). The relation is denoted by $Q = s(P)$. The seller is in equilibrium with respect to each ordered pair of P and Q numbers on his supply curve. When he is in equilibrium, in effect he has determined his profit-maximizing cost and is allocating it in such a way that the price of each product equals its marginal cost: $P = MC$. A marginal cost curve depicts the relation between marginal cost and quantity produced of the product: $MC = C'(Q)$. Thus, since $P = MC$ at each value of Q, a perfectly competitive seller's marginal cost curve of a product, $MC = C'(Q)$, is his supply curve of the product, $Q = s(P)$—provided that in the case of a multi-product seller his products are not related in production.[1]

A marginal cost curve of a product and the demand curve for the product facing a perfectly competitive seller are depicted in Figure 11.1. To analyze

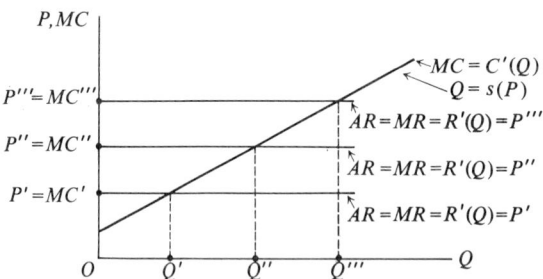

FIG. 11.1. Hypothetical marginal cost and supply curves of a product of a perfectly competitive seller of products not related in production

the equilibrium principle via this figure, given P', the seller's profit is maximized at that quantity produced of the product (Q') at which marginal cost (MC') is equal to price (P'). For given P', the revenue of the last unit before Q' is greater than the cost of that unit ($MR > MC$); hence that unit would increase his profit. Similarly, given P', the revenue of the first unit after Q' is less than the cost of that unit ($MR < MC$); hence that unit would decrease his profit. But, given P', the revenue of the last unit of Q' is equal to the cost of that unit ($MR = MC$); hence that unit maximizes his profit. Thus (P', Q') is one point on the supply curve of the seller; and since $P' = MC'$ at Q', this point is on his marginal cost curve. The same is true of other points such as (P'', Q'') and (P''', Q'''), which are rationalized in the same way by shifting the demand curve facing the seller upward. Consequently, subject to the assumptions already noted, the seller's marginal cost curve is his supply curve.

Law of Supply of a Product of a Seller

According to the law of supply of a product of a seller, the quantity of a product a seller is willing to sell (Q) per unit of time is an increasing function of the price of the product (P): quantity varies directly with price—

SUPPLY FUNCTION OF A PRODUCT OF A PERFECTLY COMPETITIVE SELLER

$\Delta Q/\Delta P > 0$. According to the law of increasing marginal cost of a product, marginal cost (MC) is an increasing function of quantity produced (Q): marginal cost varies directly with quantity — $\Delta MC/\Delta Q > 0$. According to the principle of equilibrium of a perfectly competitive seller, when a seller is in equilibrium, the price of each product equals its marginal cost: $P = MC$. Thus the rationale of the law of supply is the law of increasing marginal cost of a product and the principle of equilibrium of a perfectly competitive seller: a supply curve has a positive slope because the corresponding marginal cost curve has a positive slope and the producer-seller is assumed to maximize profit.

Price of a Substitute

The quantity of a product a seller is willing to sell (Q) per unit of time is a function of the price of the product (P): $Q = s(P)$. However, Q is also a function of the price of a substitute or rival product in production (P_r). Thus the price of a substitute is a parameter of $Q = s(P)$.

To ascertain the sign of the difference quotient $\Delta Q/\Delta P_r$, consider the equilibrium principle

$$P_1 = MC_1 \text{ and } P_2 = MC_2$$

The seller is in disequilibrium when

$$P_1 = MC_1 \text{ and } P_2 > MC_2$$

because of an increase in P_2. To regain equilibrium, he produces more of Q_2. Aside from the effect on MC_2, each additional unit of Q_2 induces an increase in MC_1 because of the substitute relationship between Q_1 and Q_2, and hence

$$P_1 < MC_1$$

To be in equilibrium at the given value of P_1, he must decrease MC_1. According to the law of increasing marginal cost of a product, MC_1 varies directly with Q_1. Thus, to regain equilibrium, he produces less of Q_1. Therefore, when Q_1 and Q_2 are substitutes in production, less of Q_1 is produced when more of Q_2 is produced as P_2 increases. By letting Q_1 be Q and P_2 be P_r, the conclusion follows that $\Delta Q/\Delta P_r < 0$.

Supply Curve of a Substitute in Production

When products are substitutes or rivals in production, a perfectly competitive seller's marginal cost curve of a product is not his supply curve of the product. Instead, his supply curve is the set of (P, Q) numbers determined by the intersection of his shifting marginal cost and marginal ($=$ average) revenue curves. Butter (Q_1) and milk (Q_2) are substitutes in production: the marginal cost of butter (MC_1) is an increasing function of the quantity produced of milk; and the marginal cost of milk (MC_2) is an increasing function of the quantity produced of butter. Thus, as Q_1 increases from Q'_1 to Q''_1 in Figure 11.2a because P_1 has increased from P'_1 to P''_1, MC_2 increases autonomously of Q'_2 in Figure 11.2b from MC'_2 to MC''_2, thereby

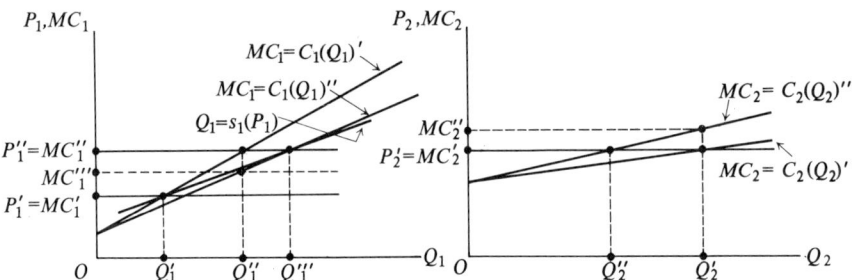

FIG. 11.2a. Hypothetical supply curve of a product of a perfectly competitive seller of substitutes in production

FIG. 11.2b. Quantity sold of a product is a decreasing function of price of a substitute or rival product

shifting the marginal cost curve of Q_2 upward from $MC_2 = C_2(Q_2)'$ to $MC_2 = C_2(Q_2)''$. Since P_2 by assumption has not changed from P'_2 in Figure 11.2b, Q_2 must decrease from Q'_2 to Q''_2 to decrease MC_2 from MC''_2 to the equilibrium level $MC'_2 = P'_2$. As Q_2 decreases from Q'_2 to Q''_2 in Figure 11.2b, MC_1 decreases autonomously of Q''_1 from MC''_1 to MC'''_1, thereby shifting the marginal cost curve of Q_1 downward from $MC_1 = C_1(Q_1)'$ to $MC_1 = C_1(Q_1)''$. Since P_1 by assumption has not changed from P''_1 in Figure 11.2a, Q_1 must increase from Q''_1 to Q'''_1 to increase MC_1 from MC'''_1 to the equilibrium level $MC''_1 = P''_1$. The seller thus equates P''_1 with MC''_1 on the lower marginal cost curve to determine equilibrium quantity Q'''_1. The curve labeled $Q_1 = s_1(P_1)$ connects the points (P'_1, Q'_1) and (P''_1, Q'''_1); therefore, it is the seller's supply curve of Q_1.

Price of a Complement

The quantity of a product a seller is willing to sell (Q) per unit of time is a function of the price of the product (P): $Q = s(P)$. However, Q is also a function of the price of a complementary or joint product in production (P_j). Thus the price of a complement is a parameter of $Q = s(P)$.

To ascertain the sign of the difference quotient $\Delta Q / \Delta P_j$, consider the equilibrium principle

$$P_1 = MC_1 \text{ and } P_2 = MC_2$$

SUPPLY FUNCTION OF A PRODUCT OF A PERFECTLY COMPETITIVE SELLER

The seller is in equilibrium when

$$P_1 = MC_1 \text{ and } P_2 > MC_2$$

because of an increase in P_2. To regain equilibrium, he produces more of Q_2. Aside from the effect on MC_2, each additional unit of Q_2 induces a decrease in MC_1 because of the complementary relationship between Q_1 and Q_2, and hence

$$P_1 > MC_1$$

To be in equilibrium at the given value of P_1, he must increase MC_1. According to the law of increasing marginal cost of a product, MC_1 varies directly with Q_1. Thus, to regain equilibrium, he produces more of Q_1. Therefore, when Q_1 and Q_2 are complements in production, more of Q_1 is produced when more of Q_2 is produced as P_2 increases. By letting Q_1 be Q and P_2 be P_j, the conclusion follows that $\Delta Q/\Delta P_j > 0$.

Supply Curve of a Complement in Production

When products are complements or joint products in production, a perfectly competitive seller's marginal cost curve of a product is not his supply curve of the product. Instead, his supply curve is the set of (P, Q) numbers determined by the intersection of his shifting marginal cost and marginal (= average) revenue curves. Butter (Q_1) and buttermilk (Q_2) are complements in production: the marginal cost of butter (MC_1) is a decreasing function of the quantity produced of buttermilk; and the marginal cost of buttermilk (MC_2) is a decreasing function of the quantity produced of butter. Thus, as Q_1 increases from Q'_1 to Q''_1 in Figure 11.3a because P_1 has increased from P'_1 to P''_1, MC_2 decreases autonomously of Q'_2 in Figure 11.3b from MC'_2 to MC''_2, thereby shifting the marginal cost curve of Q_2 downward from $MC_2 = C_2(Q_2)'$ to $MC_2 = C_2(Q_2)''$. Since P_2 by assumption has not changed from

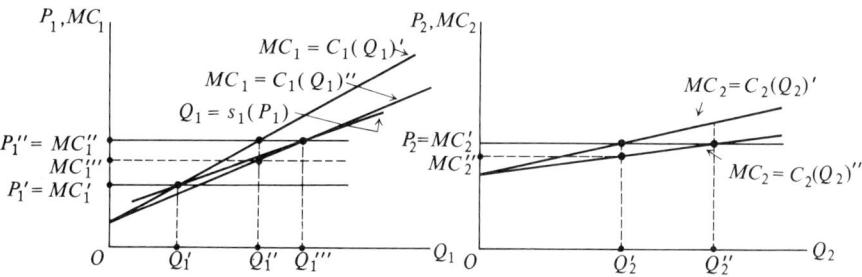

FIG. 11.3a. Hypothetical supply curve of a product of a perfectly competitive seller of complements in production

FIG. 11.3b. Quantity sold of a product is an increasing function of price of a complementary or joint product

P'_2 in Figure 11.3b, Q_2 must increase from Q'_2 to Q''_2 to increase MC_2 from MC''_2 to the equilibrium level $MC'_2 = P'_2$. As Q_2 increases from Q'_2 to Q''_2 in Figure 11.3b, MC_1 decreases autonomously of Q''_1 from MC''_1 to MC'''_1, thereby shifting the marginal cost curve of Q_1 downward from $MC_1 = C_1(Q_1)'$ to $MC_1 = C_1(Q_1)''$. Since P_1 by assumption has not changed from P''_1 in Figure 11.3a, Q_1 must increase from Q''_1 to Q'''_1 to increase MC_1 from MC'''_1 to the equilibrium level $MC''_1 = P''_1$. The seller thus equates P''_1 with MC''_1 on the lower marginal cost curve to determine equilibrium quantity Q'''_1. The curve labeled $Q_1 = s_1(P_1)$ connects the points (P'_1, Q'_1) and (P''_1, Q'''_1); therefore, it is the seller's supply curve of Q_1.

SUMMARY

The quantity of a product a perfectly competitive seller is willing to sell (Q) per unit of time is a function of the price of the product (P), the price of a substitute or rival product (P_r), and the price of a complementary or joint product (P_j), given the parameters of the state of technology and (assuming perfect competition in factor markets) the price of input. The value of Q varies directly with the value of P in accordance with the law of supply of a product of a seller, the rationale of which is the law of increasing marginal cost of a product and the principle of equilibrium of a perfectly competitive seller of products: $\Delta Q/\Delta P > 0$ because $\Delta MC/\Delta Q > 0$ and $P = MC$. The value of Q varies inversely with the value of P_r: $\Delta Q/\Delta P_r < 0$. And Q varies directly with P_j: $\Delta Q/\Delta P_j > 0$.[2]

A perfectly competitive seller's marginal cost curve of a product is his supply curve of the product provided that in the case of a multi-product seller his products are not related in production. If his products are related in production, his supply curve is the set of (P, Q) values determined by the intersection of his shifting marginal cost and marginal ($=$ average) revenue curves. Given the same increase in P, the increase in Q is greater in the case of products that are related in production than in the case of products that are not related in production.

Questions

1. List the principles of the theory of supply of a product that are of primary importance. How do you account for the position of the law of supply of a product of a seller in this list? Verbalize this principle of economics. It is based upon what other principles of economics?

2. Use the equilibrium principle $P = MC$ and the law of increasing marginal cost to analyze the difference quotients $\Delta Q/\Delta P > 0$, $\Delta Q/\Delta P_r < 0$, and $\Delta Q/\Delta P_j > 0$.

3. Analyze the relationship between a supply curve and the corresponding marginal cost curve(s) when (1) products are not related in production; (2) products are substitutes in production; (3) products are complements in production.

NOTES

[1] Further qualifications are stated in footnote 1 of Chapter 10 and are analyzed in Chapter 14.

[2] By definition, marginal cost decreases autonomously of quantity produced of the product with an improvement in the seller's technology or a decrease in the price of (variable) input (W). Therefore, the quantity he is willing to sell (Q) per unit of time increases autonomously of price (P) with an improvement in technology or decrease in price of input. The value of Q may also vary with expected changes in its determinants.

chapter 12

The Market Supply Function of a Product

"The market supply function of a product" is the name of the relation between the aggregate quantity of a product sellers are willing to sell (Q_s) per unit of time and the price of the product (P), the price of a substitute or rival product (P_r), and the price of a complementary or joint product (P_j). The parameters of this function are the state of technology and (assuming perfect competition in factor markets) the price of input. By treating P_r and P_j as parameters, this function is reduced to a relation between Q_s and P, which is depicted by the market supply curve of the product. The market supply curve of a product thus shows how the aggregate quantity of the product sellers are willing to sell (Q_s) per unit of time varies with the price of the product (P) ceteris paribus: $Q_s = S(P)$.

Law of Market Supply of a Product

The market supply curve of a product depicts the law of market supply of a product. According to this law, Q_s varies directly with P: $\Delta Q_s/\Delta P > 0$. In part, the rationale of the law of market supply of a product ($\Delta Q_s/\Delta P > 0$) is

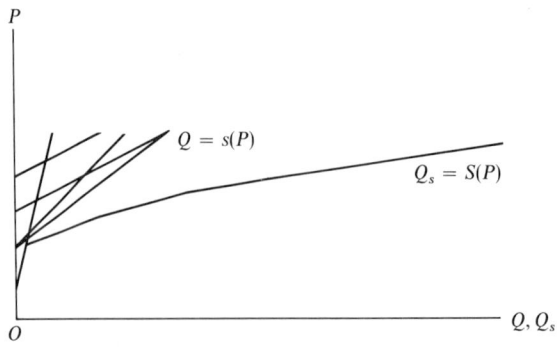

FIG. 12.1. Hypothetical market supply curve of a product

TABLE 12.1: Hypothetical market supply curve of a product

P	Q	Q	Q	Q	Q	Q_s
0						
1	0.00					0.00
2	0.25	0.00	0.00			0.25
3	0.50	1.40	1.00	0.00		2.90
4	0.75	2.70	2.00	2.00	0	7.45
5	1.00	4.00	3.00	4.00	2	14.00

the law of supply of a product of a seller ($\Delta Q/\Delta P > 0$). As seen in Figure 12.1, which depicts hypothetical data presented in Table 12.1, supply curves of individual sellers may be aggregated into the market supply curve by summing the quantity each seller is willing to sell at each specified price of the product, holding P_r and P_j constant. In addition to this rationale, however, aggregate quantity sold varies directly with price if for any reason the *number* of sellers increases as price increases. In particular, price increases may attract high cost sellers into the market who previously had not sold any of the product. In other words, as seen in Figure 12.1, the quantity each seller *currently* in the market is willing to sell increases as the price increases; and the price intercepts of the supply curves of sellers may differ in such a way that the *number* of sellers increases as the price increases.

Change in Supply and Change in Quantity Supplied

The aggregate quantity of a product sellers are willing to sell (Q_s) per unit of time at various prices of the product (P) is called the market supply of the product. A given market supply curve, $Q_s = S(P)$, depicts the aggregate quantity of a product sellers are willing to sell (Q_s) per unit of time at various prices of the product (P). Thus $Q_s = S(P)$ represents a given market supply. For this reason, (1) a change in price of the product (P) does not effect a change in (market) supply of the product, $Q_s = S(P)$. Instead, a change in price of the product (P) is said to effect a change in (market) quantity supplied of the product. Changes in quantity supplied of the product are thus depicted by movements along a given supply curve as price of the product (P) changes. (2) A change in P_r or P_j does effect a change in supply of the product, $Q_s = S(P)$, for at any given value of P a change in P_r or P_j effects a change in Q_s and hence $Q_s = S(P)$. Changes in supply of the product, therefore, are depicted by shifts in the supply curve, $Q_s = S(P)$, as P_r or P_j change.

The conclusion follows from this analysis that Q_s may be called three different things. (1) Q_s is the aggregate quantity of a product sellers are willing to sell. (2) When Q_s changes because of a change in P, holding P_r and P_j constant, Q_s may be called quantity supplied of the product, for quantity supplied is a function of P. (3) When Q_s changes because of a change in P_r or P_j, holding P constant, Q_s may be called supply of the product, for supply is a function of P_r and P_j.

Supply of a Product as a Function of the Price of a Substitute

As seen in Figure 12.2a, the quantity supplied of a product (for example, butter) per unit of time is an increasing function of the price of the product ceteris paribus: $\Delta Q_s/\Delta P > 0$. In this diagram, the price of butter (P) is measured on the vertical axis, and the quantity supplied of butter (Q_s) is measured on the horizontal axis. As seen in Figure 12.2b, the supply of butter (Q_s) per unit of time is a decreasing function of the price of a substitute or rival product in production (for example, milk) ceteris paribus: $\Delta Q_s/\Delta P_r < 0$. In this diagram, the price of milk (P_r) is measured on the vertical axis, and the supply of butter (Q_s) is measured on the horizontal axis. In Figure 12.2b, an increase in the price of milk from P'_r to P''_r induces a decrease in the supply of butter from Q'_s to Q''_s, as depicted by a movement upward along the $Q_s = h(P_r|P')$ curve. In Figure 12.2a, Q'_s and Q''_s are associated with

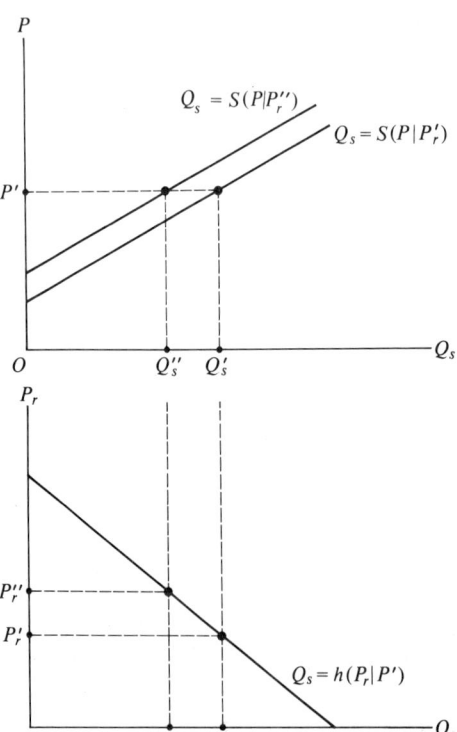

FIG. 12.2a. Quantity supplied of a product varies directly with price of the product

FIG. 12.2b. Supply of a product varies inversely with price of a technical substitute in production

the same price of butter (P'). Thus, as depicted by the $Q_s = S(P|P'_r)$ and $Q_s = S(P|P''_r)$ curves, with the increase in P_r from P'_r to P''_r, the supply curve of butter shifts parallel to itself to the left to portray the decrease in Q_s from Q'_s to Q''_s. To generalize, market supply of a product decreases as the price of a substitute product increases, and increases as the price of a substitute decreases ceteris paribus. The positively-sloped market supply curve of the product thus shifts to the left as the price of a substitute product increases, and to the right as the price of a substitute product decreases.

Supply of a Product as a Function of the Price of a Complement

To repeat, the quantity supplied of butter per unit of time is an increasing function of the price of butter, as depicted also in Figure 12.3a. As seen in Figure 12.3b, the supply of butter (Q_s) per unit of time is an increasing function of the price of a complement or joint product in production (for example, buttermilk) ceteris paribus: $\Delta Q_s/\Delta P_j > 0$. In this diagram, the price of buttermilk (P_j) is measured on the vertical axis, and the supply of butter (Q_s) is measured on the horizontal axis. In Figure 12.3b, an increase in the price of buttermilk from P'_j to P''_j induces an increase in supply of butter from Q'_s to Q''_s as depicted by a movement upward along the $Q_s = i(P_j|P')$ curve. In Figure 12.3a, Q'_s and Q''_s are associated with the same price of butter (P'). Thus, as depicted by the $Q_s = S(P|P'_j)$ and $Q_s = S(P|P''_j)$ curves, with the increase in P_j from P'_j to P''_j, the supply curve of butter shifts parallel to itself to the right to portray the increase in Q_s from Q'_s to Q''_s. To generalize, the supply of a product increases as the price of a complementary product increases, and decreases as the price of a complement decreases ceteris paribus. The positively-sloped market supply curve of the product thus shifts to the right as the price of a complementary product increases, and to the left as the price of a complement decreases.

Elasticity of Market Supply of a Product

The slope of the market supply curve of a product (dQ_s/dP) is a measure of the responsiveness of aggregate quantity supplied (Q_s) to a change in price (P). The price elasticity of market supply of a product, denoted by ε_s (ε = epsilon), which is the percentage change in the dependent variable (Q_s) divided by the percentage change in the independent variable (P), is a related measure of the responsiveness of aggregate quantity supplied to a change in price. When quantity supplied can be varied by discrete amounts, the percentage change in quantity supplied is $\Delta Q_s/Q$; the percentage change in price is $\Delta P/P$; and ε_s is called arc elasticity, since it is calculated by using

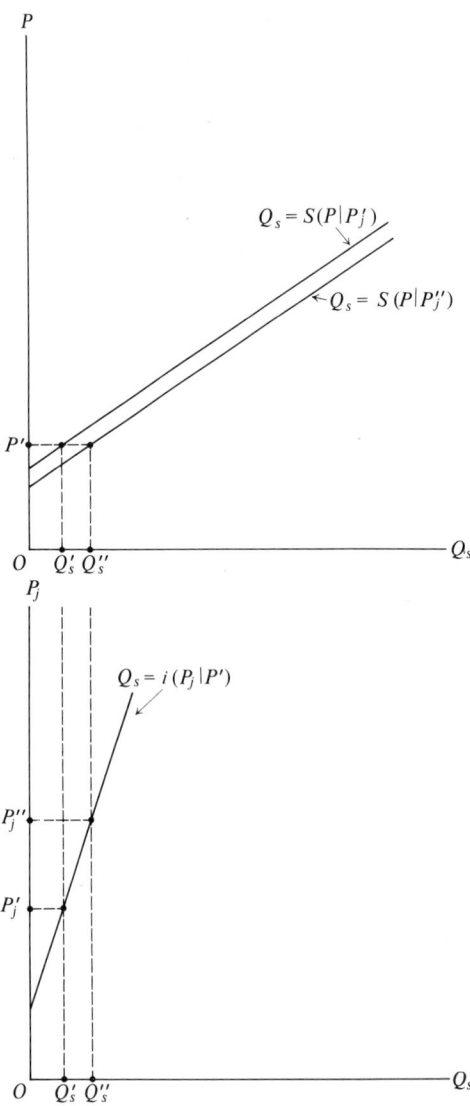

FIG. 12.3a. Quantity supplied of a product varies directly with price of the product

FIG. 12.3b. Supply of a product varies directly with price of a technical complement in production

small finite changes in Q_s and P between two points on the curve. In this context, by dropping the s subscript of Q_s,

$$\varepsilon_s = \frac{\Delta Q/Q}{\Delta P/P} \text{ or } \varepsilon_s = \frac{\Delta Q}{\Delta P} \cdot \frac{P}{Q} \text{ or } \varepsilon_s = \frac{\Delta Q/\Delta P}{Q/P}$$

When quantity supplied is varied by continuous amounts, the percentage change in quantity supplied is dQ_s/Q; the percentage change in price is dP/P; and ε_s is called point elasticity, since it is calculated by using infinitesimally small changes in Q_s and P at a point on the curve. In this context, by dropping the s subscript of Q_s,

(1) $\quad \varepsilon_s = \dfrac{dQ/Q}{dP/P}$ or

(2) $\quad \varepsilon_s = \dfrac{dQ}{dP} \cdot \dfrac{P}{Q}$ or

(3) $\quad \varepsilon_s = \dfrac{dQ/dP}{Q/P}.$

With reference to formula (2), if Q_s is a linear increasing function of P, $Q_s = \pm a + bP$, and $dQ/dP = b$. Hence,

(2') $\quad \varepsilon_s = \dfrac{bP}{bP \pm a}.$

Thus, the value of ε_s varies with price along a linear supply curve, unless $a = 0$; between two linear supply curves of different slopes but same nonzero intercepts; and between two linear supply curves with the same slopes but different intercepts. With reference to formula (3), $\varepsilon_s \gtreqless 1$ according to whether $dQ/dP \gtreqless Q/P$.

Consider curve 1 of Figure 12.4. With reference to (2), since $Q = bP$,

$$\varepsilon_s = \dfrac{bP}{bP} = 1$$

With reference to (3), since $dQ/dP = Q/P$,

$$\varepsilon_s = \dfrac{dQ/dP}{Q/P} = 1.$$

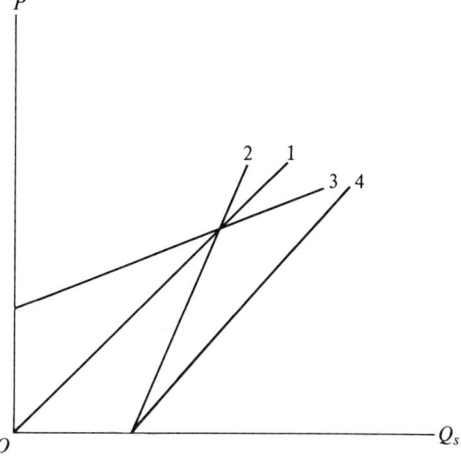

FIG. 12.4. Price elasticity of market supply of a product

Thus, supply is unitary elastic at all price values on a supply curve that is a ray. This is the only case in which elasticity is constant throughout the length of a straight line.

Now, consider curve 2 of Figure 12.4. With reference to (2), since $Q = a + bP$,

$$\varepsilon_s = \frac{bP}{bP + a} < 1$$

But since the importance of a relative to bP decreases as P increases, ε_s approaches unity as P increases. With reference to (3), since $dQ/dP < Q/P$,

$$\varepsilon_s = \frac{dQ/dP}{Q/P} < 1$$

Thus, supply is inelastic if the supply curve is linear and has a positive Q_s intercept; and the value of ε_s approaches unity as P increases.

Now, consider curve 3 of Figure 12.4. With reference to (2), since $Q = -a + bP$,

$$\varepsilon_s = \frac{bP}{bP - a} > 1 \quad (a < bP)$$

But since the importance of a relative to bP decreases as P increases, ε_s approaches unity as P increases. With reference to (3), since $dQ/dP > Q/P$,

$$\varepsilon_s = \frac{dQ/dP}{Q/P} > 1$$

Thus, supply is elastic if the supply curve is linear and has a negative Q_s intercept; and the value of ε_s approaches unity as P increases.

Lastly, compare curves 2 and 4. With reference to (2), since

$$a_4 = a_2 = a \text{ and } b_4 > b_2,$$

$$\frac{b_4 P}{b_4 P + a} > \frac{b_2 P}{b_2 P + a}$$

Thus, $\varepsilon_{s4} > \varepsilon_{s2}$.

SUMMARY

According to the law of market supply of a product, the aggregate quantity of a product sellers are willing to sell (Q_s) per unit of time is an increasing function of the price of the product (P) ceteris paribus. As P increases, other things being equal, the quantity each seller currently in the market is willing to sell per unit of time increases and the number of sellers increases. The relation between Q_s and P is depicted by the market supply curve. Quantity supplied of the product (Q_s) varies directly with its price (P). Supply of the product (Q_s) varies inversely with price of a substitute (P_r) and directly with the price of a complement (P_j). In short, $\Delta Q_s/\Delta P > 0$; $\Delta Q_s/\Delta P_r < 0$; and $\Delta Q_s/\Delta P_j > 0$. The elasticity of Q_s with respect to P (ε_s) is

$$\frac{\Delta Q_s}{\Delta P} \cdot \frac{P}{Q_s}$$

The value of ε_s depends upon the slope and intercept of the supply curve, and the price level.

Questions

1. List the principles of the theory of supply of a product that are of primary importance. How do you account for the position of the law of market supply of a product in this list? Verbalize this principle of economics.

2. What is the rationale of the law of market supply of a product?

3. Distinguish between a change in supply and a change in quantity supplied.

4. Use diagrams to analyze shifts in a market supply curve due to changes in the price of a substitute or rival product.

5. Use diagrams to analyze shifts in a market supply curve due to changes in the price of a joint or complementary product.

6. Define elasticity in general. Why is this concept used in economics? Define price elasticity of market supply of a product. Distinguish between arc and point price elasticity. Show that $\varepsilon_s \gtreqless 1$ according to whether $dQ/dP \gtreqless Q/P$. With reference to $Q_s = \pm a + bP$, show that ε_s is a function of a, b, and P.

PART III

THEORY OF DETERMINATION OF PRICE AND QUANTITY IN A PRODUCT MARKET

The economic theory of determination of price and quantity in a product market consists of two interrelated sets of principles of economics. Each of these principles is an inference drawn from an operation on a set of economic functions. The first set of principles consists of the laws of equilibrium and disequilibrium price and quantity in a competitive product market, and related principles. The subject matter of this set is the human behavior underlying the simultaneous solution of the market supply and demand functions for a product. Thus, these principles are inferences drawn from operations on market supply and demand functions. The principles of this set are presented in Chapter 13.

The second set consists of principles derived from applying the principle of equilibrium of a product seller to different market structures and time periods. The market structures, or degrees of competition, are perfect competition, monopoly, monopolistic competition, and oligopoly. The last three comprise imperfect competition. Market structures are classified by type of revenue function of a product seller (that is, the type of demand curve facing the seller). The time periods are the short run, the very short run, and the long run. Time periods are classified by type of supply curve (cost function) of a seller. Thus, the principles of this set are inferences drawn from operations on cost and revenue functions. The subject matter of this set of principles is the human behavior underlying the pricing and output decisions of a particular type of seller in a market time period, and the inferences that may be drawn from these decisions about price and quantity. The principles of this set are presented in Chapters 14 and 15.

The economic theory of determination of price and quantity in a product market is based on demand and supply curves that represent rationales of human behavior. The demand curve facing a perfectly competitive, monopolistic, or monopolistic-competitive seller is much simpler to derive analytically than is his supply curve. In fact, the primary analytical problem of the theory of determination of price and quantity in these product markets is to derive the supply curve of a seller and to explain why it shifts over time. A seller is in equilibrium with respect to each point on his supply curve. When he is in equilibrium, he has determined that output at which he is maximizing his profit—that is, maximizing the surplus of revenue over cost. Models of human behavior are thus presented in Part III which rationalize the period supply curves of a perfectly competitive, monopolistic, and monopolistic-competitive seller by rationalizing his revenue and period cost functions. The subject matter of this presentation, therefore, is a continuation of the subject matter of Chapter 11—namely, supply functions of a product of a seller. In Chapter 11, a seller's supply curve of a product is rationalized without reference to time period and on the assumption that products may be related in production. From now on, a seller's supply curve of a product is rationalized with reference to time period and on the assumption that products are not related in production, or that a given product is the only product of the seller.

The demand curve facing a perfectly competitive, monopolistic, or monopolistic-competitive seller is much simpler to derive analytically than is the demand curve facing an oligopolistic seller. In fact, the primary analytical problem of the theory of determination of price and quantity in an oligopolistic product market is to derive the demand curve facing a seller and to explain why it shifts over time. The demand curve facing a seller is his average revenue curve (assuming no price discrimination). Thus models of human behavior are presented in Part III which are rationales of the revenue function of an oligopolistic product seller. The subject matter of this presentation, therefore, is a continuation of the subject matter of Chapter 6—namely, revenue functions. These models are classified as classical incapable-of-learning, classical capable-of-learning, modern collusion, and modern non-profit-maximizing models. Only models which directly consider the revenue function of an oligopolistic seller are presented. To present all known oligopoly models would require a textbook in itself.

chapter 13

Equilibrium and Disequilibrium in a Competitive Product Market

The theory of determination of price and quantity in a competitive product market may be presented via the market models of Léon Walras (1834–1910) and Alfred Marshall (1842–1924). Modern versions of the Walrasian and Marshallian market models differ fundamentally in their rationale of human behavior. Consequently, market demand and supply, market equilibrium and disequilibrium, stability of market equilibrium, parameter shifts in market demand and supply curves, and identification of these curves from empirical data may be analyzed in two different ways. Moreover, the analysis of the cobweb theorem is partly Walrasian and partly Marshallian.

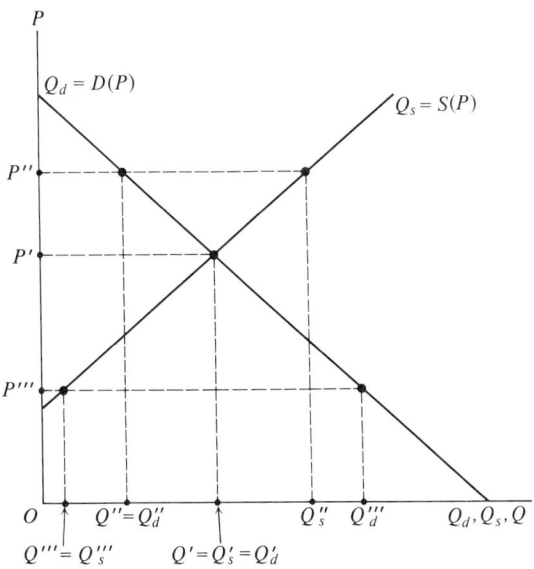

FIG. 13.1. Walrasian market model

Walrasian Market Demand and Supply

According to the modern version of the market model of Léon Walras,[1] market price (P) (the independent variable) is measured on the vertical axis, and quantity demanded (Q_d) and quantity supplied (Q_s) (the dependent variables) are measured on the horizontal axis, of a diagram (see Figure 13.1). The relation between Q_d and P is depicted by the negatively-sloped quantity demanded curve: $Q_d = D(P)$. In this context, demand may be defined as "the aggregate quantity of a product purchasers are willing to purchase (Q_d) per unit of time at various prices of the product (P)." Similarly, the relation between Q_s and P is depicted by the positively-sloped quantity supplied curve: $Q_s = S(P)$. In this context, supply may be defined as "the aggregate quantity of a product sellers are willing to sell (Q_s) per unit of time at various prices of the product (P)."[2]

Walrasian Equilibrium and Disequilibrium Market Price

Since $Q_d = D(P)$ and $Q_s = S(P)$, when P is known Q_d and Q_s are known; and when $Q_d = Q_s$, P satisfies both curves. When quantity demanded equals quantity supplied, the market is in equilibrium; market price remains constant at its current value (P') when the quantity purchasers are willing to purchase (Q'_d) is the same as the quantity sellers are willing to sell (Q'_s) per unit of time. When quantity demanded does not equal quantity supplied, the market is in disequilibrium and searching for a new unique solution to both curves, for market price tends to change when $Q_d \neq Q_s$.

A price (P'') greater than equilibrium price (P') is a disequilibrium price, for at this price the quantity sellers are willing to sell (Q''_s) is greater than the quantity purchasers are willing to purchase (Q''_d) per unit of time—the disequilibrium case called excess quantity supplied (or negative excess quantity demanded), since $Q''_s > Q''_d$ at P''. Unsatisfied willingness of sellers to sell is manifested in undesired increases in their stocks of the product. Price decreases to P' ceteris paribus as sellers try to decrease their stocks by decreasing price of the product. As price decreases, purchasers increase the quantity they are willing to purchase (quantity demanded) and sellers decrease the quantity they are willing to sell (quantity supplied) until the two quantities are equal at P'.

A price (P''') less than equilibrium price (P') is also a disequilibrium price, for at this price the quantity sellers are willing to sell (Q'''_s) is less than the quantity purchasers are willing to purchase (Q'''_d) per unit of time—the disequilibrium case called excess quantity demanded, since $Q'''_s < Q'''_d$ at P'''.[3] Unsatisfied willingness of purchasers to purchase is manifested in undesired decreases in their stocks of the product. Price increases to P'

ceteris paribus as purchasers try to increase their stocks by increasing price of the product. As price increases, purchasers decrease the quantity they are willing to purchase (quantity demanded) and sellers increase the quantity they are willing to sell (quantity supplied) until the two quantities are equal at P'.[4]

The equilibrium price (P') is the only price at which the quantity sellers are willing to sell (Q'_s) is the same as the quantity purchasers are willing to purchase (Q'_d). Thus, it is the price which "clears the market" of the product. At any given price, however, actual quantity sold (Q) is always identically equal to actual quantity purchased (Q). At P', actual quantity purchased and sold (Q') is the same as the quantity purchasers are willing to purchase and sellers are willing to sell: in equilibrium, $Q' = Q'_s = Q'_d$. Since sellers can sell only that quantity which purchasers are willing to purchase, at P'' actual quantity purchased and sold (Q'') is the same as the quantity purchasers are willing to purchase but is less than the quantity sellers are willing to sell: in disequilibrium, when $Q''_s > Q''_d$, $Q'' = Q''_d$. Conversely, since purchasers can purchase only that quantity which sellers are willing to sell, at P''' actual quantity purchased and sold (Q''') is the same as the quantity sellers are willing to sell but is less than the quantity purchasers are willing to purchase: in disequilibrium, when $Q'''_s < Q'''_d$, $Q''' = Q'''_s$.[5]

Walrasian Stable and Unstable Equilibrium

A market is represented by a demand equation and a supply equation. Market equilibrium values of Q and P are determined algebraically by solving these two equations simultaneously. A unique algebraic solution for Q and P exists if the curves of these two equations intersect at only one point. A unique solution is called equilibrium, since Q and P will not change until one of the curves shifts. Economically meaningful solutions are those in which Q and P are nonnegative; and an equilibrium may be stable or unstable in terms of the underlying behavioral assumptions used to explain how people determine Q and P. Market equilibrium is said to be stable when disequilibrium Q and P values become equilibrium Q and P values as purchasers and sellers interact with one another. Conversely, market equilibrium is said to be unstable when disequilibrium Q and P values do not become equilibrium Q and P values. In other words, equilibrium is stable when the market moves from equilibrium to disequilibrium to equilibrium in response to changes in demand and/or supply. Equilibrium is unstable when the market remains in perpetual disequilibrium once equilibrium is disturbed by a shift in the demand and/or supply curves.

The quantity demanded curve of Figure 13.1 is negatively sloped, and the quantity supplied curve is positively sloped. A price higher than equilibrium price (P'') results in excess quantity supplied. Excess quantity supplied decreases to zero as purchasers increase quantity demanded and sellers decrease quantity supplied, as sellers decrease price to its equilibrium level. A price lower than equilibrium price (P''') results in excess quantity demanded. Excess quantity demanded decreases to zero as purchasers decrease quantity demanded and sellers increase quantity supplied, as purchasers increase price to its equilibrium level. Therefore, equilibrium is stable when the quantity demanded curve is negatively sloped, and the quantity supplied curve is positively sloped.

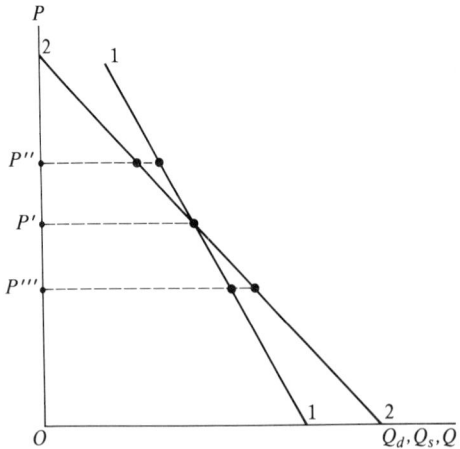

FIG. 13.2. Walrasian stable and unstable equilibrium

The quantity demanded curve of Figure 13.2 is negatively sloped, and the quantity supplied curve is negatively sloped. Let curve 1 be the quantity supplied curve and curve 2 the quantity demanded curve. Then,

$$\left|\frac{\Delta Q_d}{\Delta P}\right| > \left|\frac{\Delta Q_s}{\Delta P}\right| \quad \text{or} \quad \left|\frac{\Delta P}{\Delta Q_d}\right| < \left|\frac{\Delta P}{\Delta Q_s}\right|$$

A price higher than equilibrium price (P'') again results in excess quantity supplied. Excess quantity supplied decreases to zero as purchasers increase quantity demanded more than sellers increase quantity supplied, as sellers decrease price to its equilibrium level. A price lower than equilibrium price (P''') again results in excess quantity demanded. Excess quantity demanded decreases to zero as purchasers decrease quantity demanded more than sellers decrease quantity supplied, as purchasers increase price to its equilibrium level. Therefore, equilibrium is stable when the quantity demanded and supplied curves have negative slopes, and purchasers change quantity demanded more than sellers change quantity supplied, as price changes.

Let curve 1 of Figure 13.2 be the quantity demanded curve and curve 2 the quantity supplied curve. Then,

$$\left|\frac{\Delta Q_d}{\Delta P}\right| < \left|\frac{\Delta Q_s}{\Delta P}\right| \quad \text{or} \quad \left|\frac{\Delta P}{\Delta Q_d}\right| > \left|\frac{\Delta P}{\Delta Q_s}\right|$$

A price higher than equilibrium price (P'') now results in excess quantity demanded. Excess quantity demanded increases as purchasers decrease quantity demanded less than sellers decrease quantity supplied, as purchasers increase price further from its equilibrium level. A price lower than equlibrium price (P''') now results in excess quantity supplied. Excess quantity supplied increases as purchasers increase quantity demanded less than sellers increase quantity supplied, as sellers decrease price further from its equilibrium level. Therefore, equilibrium is unstable when the quantity demanded and supplied curves have negative slopes, and purchasers change quantity demanded less than sellers change quantity supplied, as price changes.

Marshallian Market Demand and Supply

According to the modern version of the market model of Alfred Marshall,[6] demand price (P_d) and supply price (P_s) (the dependent variables) are measured on the vertical axis, and market quantity (Q) (the independent variable) is measured on the horizontal axis, of a diagram (see Figure 13.3).

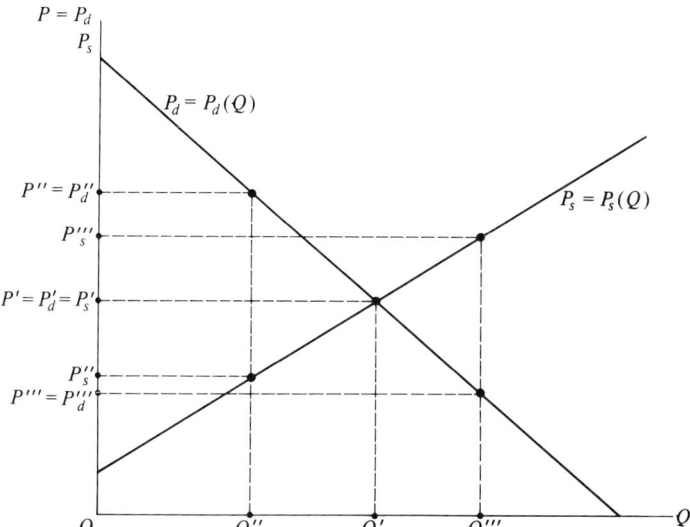

FIG. 13.3. Marshallian market model

The relation between P_d and Q is depicted by the negatively-sloped demand price curve: $P_d = P_d(Q)$. In this context, demand may be defined as "the maximum price purchasers are willing to pay (P_d) for various quantities purchased of a product (Q) per unit of time." Similarly, the relation between P_s and Q is depicted by the positively-sloped supply price curve: $P_s = P_s(Q)$.

In this context, supply may be defined as "the minimum price sellers are willing to continue to accept (P_s) for various quantities sold of a product (Q) per unit of time."

Marshallian Equilibrium and Disequilibrium Market Quantity

Since $P_d = P_d(Q)$ and $P_s = P_s(Q)$, when Q is known P_d and P_s are known; and when $P_d = P_s$, Q satisfies both curves. When demand price equals supply price, the market is in equilibrium; market quantity remains constant at its current value (Q') when the maximum price purchasers are willing to pay (P'_d) is the same as the minimum price sellers are willing to continue to accept (P'_s). When demand price does not equal supply price, the market is in disequilibrium and searching for a new unique solution to both curves, for market quantity tends to change when $P_d \neq P_s$.

A quantity (Q'') less than equilibrium quantity (Q') is a disequilibrium quantity, for at this quantity the minimum price sellers are willing to continue to accept (P''_s) is less than the maximum price purchasers are willing to pay (P''_d)—the disequilibrium case called excess demand price, since $P''_d > P''_s$ at Q''. Since sellers are receiving a higher price than is required for them to produce Q'', they increase market quantity. As quantity increases, purchasers decrease the maximum price they are willing to pay (demand price) and sellers increase the minimum price they are willing to continue to accept (supply price) until the two prices are equal at Q'.

A quantity (Q''') greater than equilibrium quantity (Q') is also a disequilibrium quantity, for at this quantity the minimum price sellers are willing to continue to accept (P'''_s) is greater than the maximum price purchasers are willing to pay (P'''_d)—the disequilibrium case called excess supply price, since $P'''_d < P'''_s$ at Q'''. Since sellers are receiving a lower price than is required for them to continue to produce Q''', they decrease market quantity. As quantity decreases, purchasers increase the maximum price they are willing to pay (demand price) and sellers decrease the minimum price they are willing to continue to accept (supply price) until the two prices are equal at Q'.[7]

Marshallian Stable and Unstable Equilibrium

The demand price curve of Figure 13.3 is negatively sloped, and the supply price curve is positively sloped. A quantity less than equilibrium quantity (Q'') results in excess demand price. Excess demand price decreases to zero as purchasers decrease demand price and sellers increase supply price, as sellers increase quantity to its equilibrium level. A quantity higher than equilibrium quantity (Q''') results in excess supply price. Excess supply price decreases to zero as purchasers increase demand price and sellers decrease supply price, as sellers decrease quantity to its equilibrium level. Therefore, equilibrium is stable when the demand price curve is negatively sloped, and the supply price curve is positively sloped.

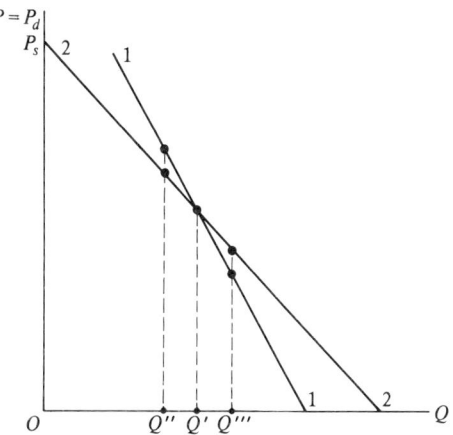

FIG. 13.4. Marshallian stable and unstable equilibrium

Let the negatively-sloped curve 1 of Figure 13.4 be the demand price curve, and let the negatively-sloped curve 2 be the supply price curve. Then,

$$\left|\frac{\Delta P_d}{\Delta Q}\right| > \left|\frac{\Delta P_s}{\Delta Q}\right| \quad \text{or} \quad \left|\frac{\Delta Q}{\Delta P_d}\right| < \left|\frac{\Delta Q}{\Delta P_s}\right|$$

A quantity less than equilibrium quantity (Q'') again results in excess demand price. Excess demand price decreases to zero as purchasers decrease demand price more than sellers decrease supply price, as sellers increase quantity to its equilibrium level. A quantity higher than equilibrium quantity (Q''') again results in excess supply price. Excess supply price decreases to zero as purchasers increase demand price more than sellers increase supply price, as sellers decrease quantity to its equilibrium level. Therefore, equilibrium is stable when the demand and supply price curves have negative slopes, and purchasers change demand price more than sellers change supply price, as quantity changes.

Let curve 1 of Figure 13.4 be the supply price curve and curve 2 the demand price curve. Then,

$$\left|\frac{\Delta P_d}{\Delta Q}\right| < \left|\frac{\Delta P_s}{\Delta Q}\right| \quad \text{or} \quad \left|\frac{\Delta Q}{\Delta P_d}\right| > \left|\frac{\Delta Q}{\Delta P_s}\right|$$

A quantity less than equilibrium quantity (Q'') now results in excess supply price. Excess supply price increases as purchasers increase demand price less than sellers increase supply price, as sellers decrease quantity further from its equilibrium level. A quantity greater than equilibrium quantity (Q''')

now results in excess demand price. Excess demand price increases as purchasers decrease demand price less than sellers decrease supply price, as sellers increase quantity further from its equilibrium level. Therefore, equilibrium is unstable when the demand and supply price curves have negative slopes, and purchasers change demand price less than sellers change supply price, as quantity changes.

Parameter Shifts in Market Demand Curve

A shift to the right of the market quantity demanded curve of Figure 13.1 represents an increase in demand: purchasers are willing to purchase at the same price more units per unit of time than before the parameter change. Conversely, a shift to the left of the market quantity demanded curve represents a decrease in demand: purchasers are willing to purchase at the same price less units per unit of time than before the parameter change. Similarly, a shift upward of the market demand price curve of Figure 13.3 also represents an increase in demand: purchasers are willing to purchase at a higher price the same number of units per unit of time as before the parameter change. Conversely, a shift downward of the market demand price curve represents a decrease in demand: purchasers are willing to purchase at a lower price the same number of units per unit of time as before the parameter change.

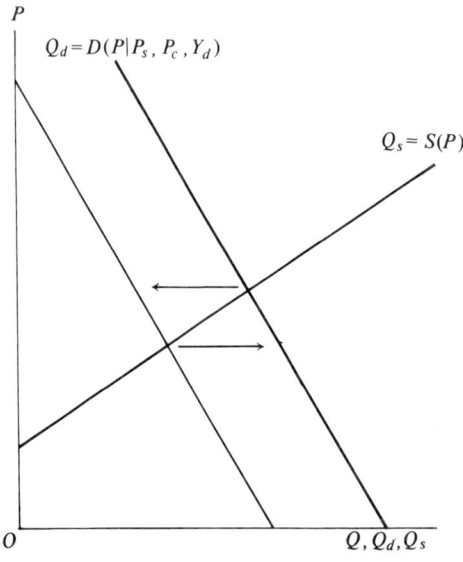

FIG. 13.5. Parameter shifts in market demand curve

Consider the market demand function $Q_d = D(P|P_s, P_c, Y_d)$ of Figure 13.5, which is for a normal product. Let $Q_d = Q_s$, and then let the income of purchasers (Y_d) increase ceteris paribus. The market demand curve shifts to the right since $\Delta Q_d/\Delta Y_d > 0$ for a normal product. The market is in disequilibrium since $Q_s < Q_d$ at the prevailing market price. The new equilibrium price is higher than the initial equilibrium price. Hence, an increase in income of purchasers tends to effect an increase in price of a normal product. Now, let the new equilibrium be disturbed by a decrease in Y_d. Then the market demand curve shifts to the left since $\Delta Q_d/\Delta Y_d > 0$ for a normal product. The market again is in disequilibrium since $Q_s > Q_d$ at the prevailing market price. The new equilibrium price is lower than the previous equilibrium price. Hence, a decrease in income of purchasers tends to effect a decrease in price of a normal product. In short, $\Delta P/\Delta Y_d > 0$ if $\Delta Q_d/\Delta Y_d > 0$.

Again let $Q_d = Q_s$, but this time let the price of a substitute product (P_s) increase ceteris paribus. The market demand curve shifts to the right since $\Delta Q_d/\Delta P_s > 0$. Now, $Q_s < Q_d$ at the prevailing price of the given product. The new equilibrium price is higher than the initial equilibrium price. Hence, an increase in price of a substitute tends to effect an increase in price of a given product. Now, let P_s decrease ceteris paribus. The market demand curve shifts to the left since $\Delta Q_d/\Delta P_s > 0$. At the previous equilibrium price $Q_s > Q_d$. The new equilibrium price is lower than the previous equilibrium price. Hence, a decrease in price of a substitute tends to result in a decrease in price of a given product. In short, $\Delta P/\Delta P_s > 0$ since $\Delta Q_d/\Delta P_s > 0$.

Lastly, let $Q_s = Q_d$, and then let the price of a complementary product (P_c) increase ceteris paribus. The market demand curve shifts to the left since $\Delta Q_d/\Delta P_c < 0$. Now, $Q_s > Q_d$ at the prevailing price of the given product. The new equilibrium price is lower than the initial equilibrium price. Hence, an increase in price of a complement tends to effect a decrease in price of a given product. Now, let P_c decrease ceteris paribus. The market demand curve shifts to the right since $\Delta Q_d/\Delta P_c < 0$. At the previous equilibrium price $Q_s < Q_d$. The new equilibrium price is higher than the previous equilibrium price. Hence, a decrease in price of a complement tends to effect an increase in price of a given product. In short, $\Delta P/\Delta P_c < 0$ since $\Delta Q_d/\Delta P_c < 0$.

Parameter Shifts in Market Supply Curve

A shift to the right of the market quantity supplied curve of Figure 13.1 represents an increase in supply: sellers are willing to sell at the same price more units per unit of time than before the parameter change. Conversely, a shift to the left of the market quantity supplied curve represents a decrease in supply: sellers are willing to sell at the same price less units per unit of time than before the parameter change. Similarly, a shift downward of the market supply price curve of Figure 13.3 represents an increase in supply: sellers are willing to sell at a lower price the same number of units per unit of time as before the parameter change. Conversely, a shift upward of the market supply price curve represents a decrease in supply: sellers are willing to sell at a higher price the same number of units per unit of time as before the parameter change.

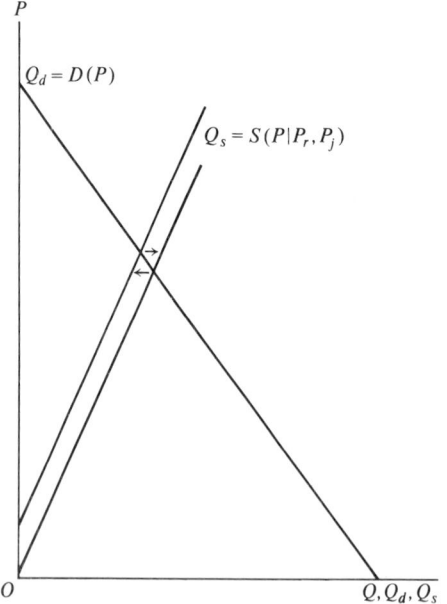

FIG. 13.6. Parameter shifts in market supply curve

Consider the market supply function $Q_s = S(P|P_r, P_j)$ of Figure 13.6. Let $Q_d = Q_s$, and then let the price of a substitute or rival product in production (P_r) increase ceteris paribus. The market supply curve shifts to the left since $\Delta Q_s/\Delta P_r < 0$. Now, $Q_s < Q_d$ at the prevailing price of the given product. The new equilibrium price is higher than the initial equilibrium price. Hence, an increase in price of a substitute tends to effect an increase in price of a given product. Now, let P_r decrease ceteris paribus. The market supply curve shifts to the right since $\Delta Q_s/\Delta P_r < 0$. At the previous equilibrium price $Q_s > Q_d$. The new equilibrium price is lower than the previous equilibrium price. Hence, a decrease in price of a substitute tends to result in a decrease in price of a given product. In short, $\Delta P/\Delta P_r > 0$ since $\Delta Q_s/\Delta P_r < 0$.

Again let $Q_d = Q_s$, but this time let the price of a complementary or joint product in production (P_j) increase ceteris paribus. The market supply curve shifts to the right since $\Delta Q_s/\Delta P_j > 0$. Now, $Q_s > Q_d$ at the prevailing price of the given product. The new equilibrium price is lower than the initial equilibrium price. Hence, an increase in price of a complement tends to effect a decrease in price of a given product. Now, let P_j decrease ceteris paribus. The market supply curve shifts to the left since $\Delta Q_s/\Delta P_j > 0$. At the previous equilibrium price $Q_s < Q_d$. The new equilibrium price is higher than the previous equilibrium price. Hence, a decrease in price of a complement tends to effect an increase in price of a given product. In short, $\Delta P/\Delta P_j < 0$ since $\Delta Q_s/\Delta P_j > 0$.

Identification of Market Supply and Demand Curves

In econometrics, an empirically derived market demand curve for a product is a set of ordered pairs of market quantity (Q) and market price (P) that satisfies the "demand curve." Similarly, an empirically derived market supply curve of a product is a set of ordered pairs of market quantity (Q) and market price (P) that satisfies the "supply curve." A given empirical set of (Q, P) values may be the demand set, the supply set, or a combination of both. If the empirical set of (Q, P) values is the demand set, it may be the Walrasian (Q_d, P) or Marshallian (Q, P_d) demand set. Likewise, if the empirical set of (Q, P) values is the supply set, it may be the Walrasian (Q_s, P) or Marshallian (Q, P_s) supply set. Moreover, a given empirical set of (Q, P) values may be an equilibrium or disequilibrium set.

In mathematics, equilibrium Walrasian supply and demand sets are the same as equilibrium Marshallian supply and demand sets, for each model consists of two equations in the same unknowns of price and quantity, and the simultaneous solution of both equations yields price and quantity values that satisfy both equations. Thus, the equilibrium empirical set implied by the Walrasian model is the same as the equilibrium empirical set implied by the Marshallian model. Consequently, an econometrician using equilibrium data may very well have identified a Walrasian quantity demanded (supplied) curve or a Marshallian demand (supply) price curve—that is, the market demand (supply) curve.

In economics, however, the distinction between Walrasian and Marshallian equilibrium empirical sets is still important, since a mathematical model is more meaningful when it is specified in terms of a rationale of human behavior, either Walrasian or Marshallian or a combination of the two (that is, an eclectic rationale). Moreover, the distinction is crucial to the solution of the "choice of regression" problem of econometrics,[8] for in the Walrasian model quantity is the dependent variable and price is the independent variable, while in the Marshallian model price is the dependent variable and quantity is the independent variable. Furthermore, the distinction is of primary importance in statistical studies of the process whereby price and quantity change.[9] In the Walrasian model, sellers decrease market price in the case of excess quantity supplied at a given price, and purchasers increase market price in the case of excess quantity demanded at a given price. Quantity demanded and supplied then change in response to these price changes until the market is in equilibrium. But in the Marshallian model, sellers increase market quantity in the case of excess demand price at a given quantity, and they decrease market quantity in the case of excess supply price at a given quantity. Demand price and supply price then change in response to these quantity changes until the market is in equilibrium.

Lastly, a disequilibrium Walrasian set may not be the same as a disequilibrium Marshallian set, for in the Walrasian model market price but not market quantity always satisfies both curves, while in the Marshallian model market quantity but not market price always satisfies both curves. Thus, the disequilibrium empirical set implied by the Walrasian model may not be the same as the disequilibrium empirical set implied by the Marshallian model. Consequently, an econometrician using disequilibrium data may have identified, for example, a portion of a Walrasian quantity supplied curve or a portion of a Marshallian demand price curve.

Identification When Market Supply Increases

To be specific, the disequilibrium Walrasian set is the same as the disequilibrium Marshallian set only in the context of an increase in supply. Thus, the disequilibrium empirical set implied by the Walrasian model is the same as the disequilibrium empirical set implied by the Marshallian model only in this context. However, an econometrician using disequilibrium data may have identified a portion of a Walrasian quantity demanded curve or a portion of a Marshallian demand price curve, and hence is faced with the "choice of regression" problem. As seen in Figure 13.7, these conclusions may be substantiated by drawing the Walrasian and Marshallian diagrams, shifting the Walrasian quantity supplied curve to the right and the Marshallian supply price curve downward, and analyzing the resulting Walrasian excess quantity supplied case and the Marshallian excess demand price case, which are paired in the context of an increase in market supply.

As seen in Figure 13.7a, since market quantity satisfies only the demand curve, given market price, in this Walrasian excess quantity supplied case, market price decreases and market quantity increases according to the given demand curve. Thus, the empirical set of disequilibrium (Q, P) values implied by the Walrasian model is the same as the set of (Q_d, P) values lying above the new equilibrium. In disequilibrium, therefore, the demand curve is identified via shifts to the right of the supply curve, the demand curve not shifting.

Similarly, as seen in Figure 13.7b, since market price satisfies only the demand curve, given market quantity, in this Marshallian excess demand price case, market price decreases and market quantity increases according to the given demand curve. Thus, the empirical set of disequilibrium (Q, P) values implied by the Marshallian model is the same as the set of (Q, P_d) values lying above the new equilibrium. In disequilibrium, therefore, the demand curve is identified via shifts downward of the supply curve, the demand curve not shifting.

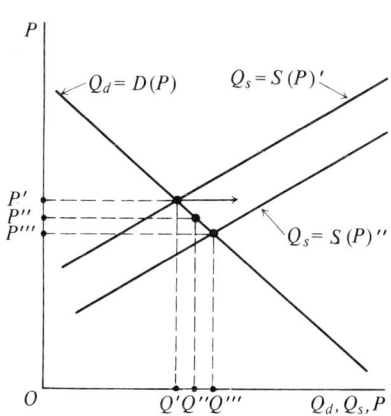

FIG. 13.7a. Excess quantity supplied

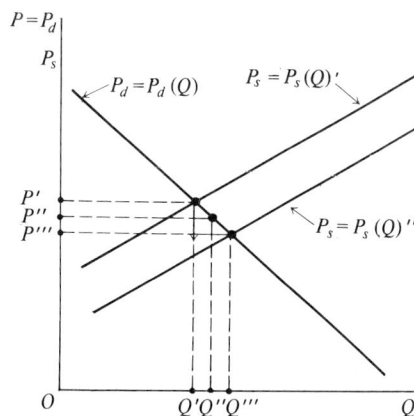

FIG. 13.7b. Excess demand price

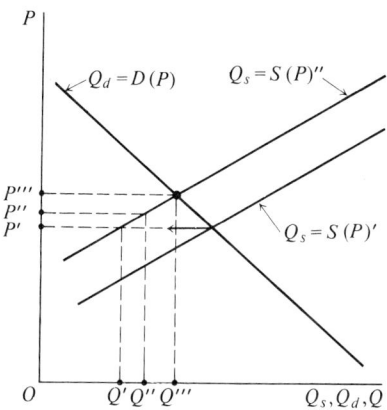

FIG. 13.8a. Excess quantity demanded

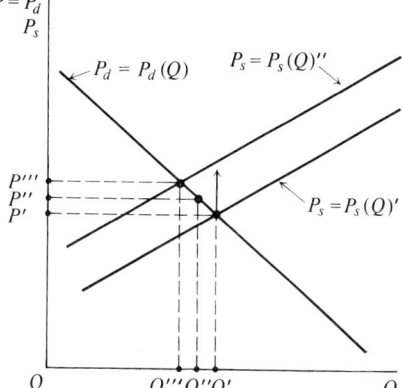

FIG. 13.8b. Excess supply price

Identification When Market Supply Decreases

In the context of a decrease in market supply, the disequilibrium Walrasian set is not the same as the disequilibrium Marshallian set. Thus, the disequilibrium empirical set implied by the Walrasian model is not the same as the disequilibrium empirical set implied by the Marshallian model. Specifically, in the present context, an econometrician using disequilibrium data may have identified a portion of a Walrasian quantity supplied curve or a

222   DETERMINATION OF PRICE AND QUANTITY IN A PRODUCT MARKET

portion of a Marshallian demand price curve. As seen in Figure 13.8, these conclusions may be substantiated by drawing the Walrasian and Marshallian diagrams, shifting the Walrasian quantity supplied curve to the left and the Marshallian supply price curve upward, and analyzing the resulting Walrasian excess quantity demanded case and the Marshallian excess supply price case, which are paired in the context of a decrease in market supply.

As seen in Figure 13.8a, since market quantity satisfies only the new supply curve, given market price, in this Walrasian excess quantity demanded case, market price increases and market quantity first decreases and then increases, but decreases overall, according to that portion of the new supply curve lying below the new equilibrium. Thus, the empirical set of disequilibrium (Q, P) values implied by the Walrasian model is the same as the new set of (Q_s, P) values lying below the new equilibrium. In disequilibrium, therefore, that portion of the new supply curve lying below the new equilibrium is identified via shifts to the left of the supply curve, the demand curve not shifting.

Similarly, as seen in Figure 13.8b, since market price satisfies only the demand curve, given market quantity, in this Marshallian excess supply price case, market price increases and market quantity decreases according to the given demand curve. Thus, the empirical set of disequilibrium (Q, P) values implied by the Marshallian model is the same as the set of (Q, P_d) values lying below the new equilibrium. In disequilibrium, therefore, the demand curve is identified via shifts upward of the supply curve, the demand curve not shifting.

Identification When Market Demand Increases

In the context of an increase in market demand, the disequilibrium Walrasian set again is not the same as the disequilibrium Marshallian set. Thus, again, the disequilibrium empirical set implied by the Walrasian model is not the same as the disequilibrium empirical set implied by the Marshallian model. Specifically, in the present context, an econometrician using disequilibrium data may have identified a portion of a Walrasian quantity supplied curve or a portion of a Marshallian demand price curve. As seen in Figure 13.9, these conclusions may be substantiated by drawing the Walrasian and Marshallian diagrams, shifting the Walrasian quantity demanded curve to the right and the Marshallian demand price curve upward, and analyzing the resulting Walrasian excess quantity demanded case and the Marshallian excess demand price case, which are paired in the context of an increase in market demand.

As seen in Figure 13.9a, since market quantity satisfies only the supply curve, given market price, in this Walrasian excess quantity demanded case, market price and quantity increase according to the given supply curve.

FIG. 13.9a. Excess quantity demanded

FIG. 13.9b. Excess demand price

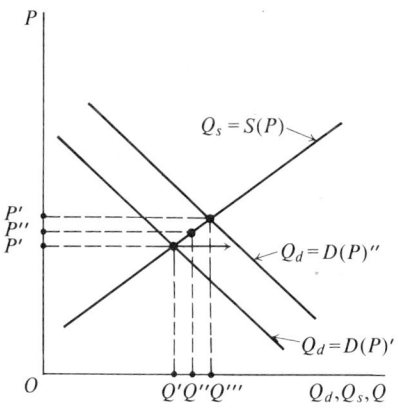

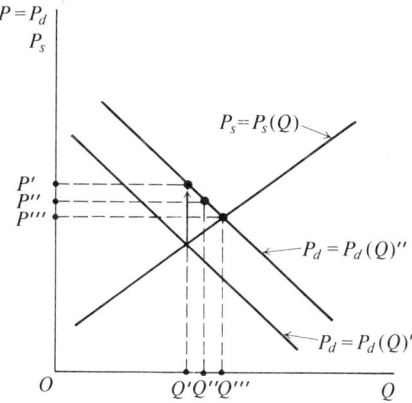

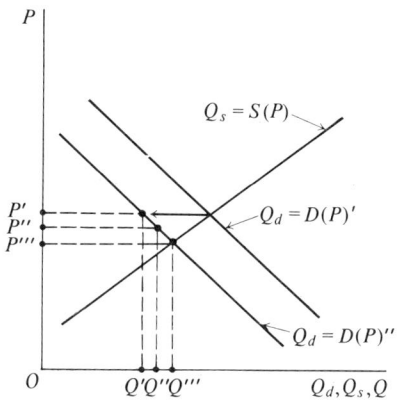

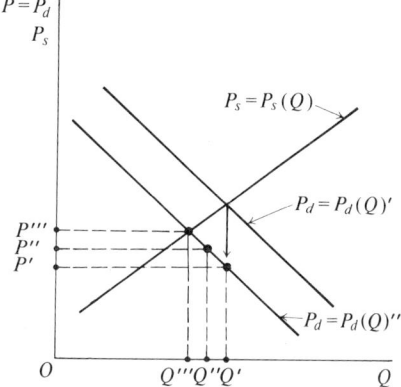

FIG. 13.10a Excess quantity supplied

FIG. 13.10b. Excess supply price

Thus, the empirical set of disequilibrium (Q, P) values implied by the Walrasian model is the same as the set of (Q_s, P) values lying below the new equilibrium. In disequilibrium, therefore, the supply curve is identified via shifts to the right of the demand curve, the supply curve not shifting.

Similarly, as seen in Figure 13.9b, since market price satisfies only the new demand curve, given market quantity, in this Marshallian excess demand price case, market price first increases and then decreases, but increases overall, and market quantity increases according to the new demand curve. Thus, the empirical set of disequilibrium (Q, P) values implied by the Marshallian model is the same as the new set of (Q, P_d) values lying above the new equilibrium. In disequilibrium, therefore, that portion of the new demand curve lying above the new equilibrium is identified via shifts upward of the demand curve, the supply curve not shifting.

Identification When Market Demand Decreases

In the context of a decrease in market demand, the disequilibrium Walrasian set once again is not the same as the disequilibrium Marshallian set. Thus, once again, the disequilibrium empirical set implied by the Walrasian model is not the same as the disequilibrium empirical set implied by the Marshallian model. Specifically, in the present context, an econometrician using disequilibrium data may have identified a portion of a Walrasian quantity demanded curve lying above equilibrium or a portion of a Marshallian demand price curve lying below equilibrium. As seen in Figure 13.10, these conclusions may be substantiated by drawing the Walrasian and Marshallian diagrams, shifting the Walrasian quantity demanded curve to the left and the Marshallian demand price curve downward, and analyzing the resulting Walrasian excess quantity supplied case and the Marshallian excess supply price case, which are paired in the context of a decrease in market demand.

As seen in Figure 13.10a, since market quantity satisfies only the new demand curve, given market price, in this Walrasian excess quantity supplied case, market price decreases and market quantity first decreases and then increases, but decreases overall, according to that portion of the new demand curve lying above the new equilibrium. Thus, the empirical set of disequilibrium (Q, P) values implied by the Walrasian model is the same as the new set of (Q_d, P) values lying above the new equilibrium. In disequilibrium, therefore, that portion of the new demand curve lying above the new equilibrium is identified via shifts to the left of the demand curve, the supply curve not shifting.

Similarly, as seen in Figure 13.10b, since market price satisfies only the new demand curve, given market quantity, in this Marshallian excess supply price case, market price decreases and then increases, but decreases overall, and market quantity decreases according to the new demand curve. Thus, the empirical set of disequilibrium (Q, P) values implied by the Marshallian model is the same as the new set of (Q, P_d) values lying below the new equilibrium. In disequilibrium, therefore, that portion of the new demand curve lying below the new equilibrium is identified via shifts downward of the demand curve, the supply curve not shifting.

Cobweb Theorem

The cobweb theorem is an explanation of cyclical movements in opposite directions of quantity and price of a product, especially agricultural products. Its key assumptions are perfect competition in the product market. Market demand and supply curves do not shift once disequilibrium occurs. Quantity purchased in period t is a function of price in period t. Production is discontinuous over time; and quantity produced and sold in period t is a function of price in period $t-1$. In other words, the farmer plans to increase output along his given supply curve next year according to the price purchasers paid for this year's output. Lastly, price is always set at a level in period t at which quantity demanded equals quantity supplied; that is, the "market is cleared" each period.

The supply function implied by the mathematics of this theorem is the lagged Walrasian market supply function: $Q_{st} = S(P_{t-1})$. The implied demand function is the unlagged Walrasian market demand function: $Q_{dt} = D(P_t)$. But because of the market-clearing assumption the rationale of this theorem is partly Walrasian and partly Marshallian. Specifically, in terms of human behavior, the supply function is the lagged or unlagged Walrasian supply function, and the demand function is the unlagged Marshallian demand function: $Q_{st} = S(P_{t-1})$ or $Q_{st} = S(P_t)$ and $P_{dt} = P_d(Q_t)$. Mathematically, $P_{dt} = P_d(O_t)$ is the same as $Q_{dt} = D(P_t)$, for one is the inverse of the other. But the human behavior underlying these two demand functions is not the same for both functions. To see this, consider Figure 13.11.

The initial equilibrium values of Q and P in Figure 13.11 are Q' and P'. Their new equilibrium values are $Q^{(n)}$ and $P^{(n)}$. With the increase in demand, quantity Q' can be sold at demand price P''—a Marshallian concept. In the Marshallian model, market quantity increases and market price decreases, with or without lags, to equilibrium according to the excess demand price portion of the new demand curve. But the quantity that is sold at P' is quantity supplied Q'—a Walrasian concept. In the Walrasian model, market price and quantity increase, with or without lags, to equilibrium according to the excess quantity demanded portion of the supply curve. Thus, no cycle of Q and P values may be rationalized using either of the two models considered separately from the other, lag or no lag in quantity sold.

However, assume again that the initial values of Q and P are Q' and P'; then assume that excess demand price is followed by excess quantity supplied, which is then followed by excess supply price, followed in turn by excess quantity demanded, which is then followed by excess demand price, etc. Now the cobweb theorem has a rationale, with or without a lag in quantity sold. For analytical purposes, assume a lag in quantity sold. In the first period, quantity supplied Q', which is determined by price P' of the previous period, satisfies the above equilibrium portion of the demand price curve when demand increases. The corresponding demand price P'', which clears the market in the first period, satisfies the above equilibrium portion of the quantity supplied curve in the second period. In the second period, the corresponding quantity supplied, which is determined by price P'' of the first period, satisfies the below equilibrium portion of the demand price curve. The corresponding demand price in the second period, which clears the market in this period, satisfies the below equilibrium portion of the quantity supplied curve in the third period. In the third period, the corresponding quantity supplied satisfies the above equilibrium portion of the demand price curve, etc.

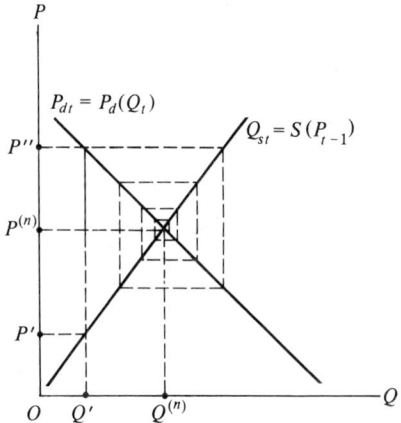

FIG. 13.11. Dampened oscillation

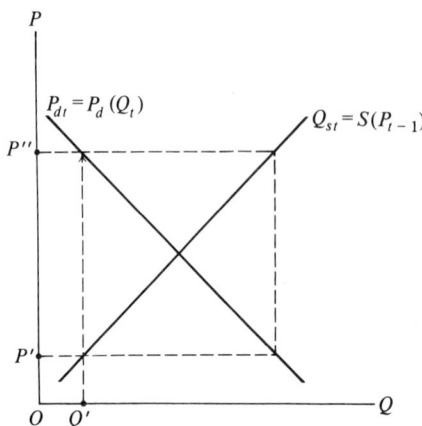

FIG. 13.12. Perpetual oscillation

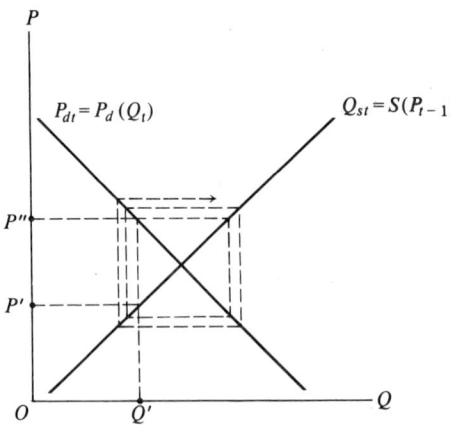

FIG. 13.13. Explosive oscillation

The nature of the cycle depends on the numerical values of the slopes of the two curves relative to one another. In the case of dampened oscillation, price and quantity oscillate toward equilibrium, as seen in Figure 13.11. In this case, the slope of the Walrasian demand curve is greater numerically than the slope of the Walrasian supply curve:

$$\left|\frac{\Delta Q_d}{\Delta P}\right| > \left|\frac{\Delta Q_s}{\Delta P}\right|$$

Conversely, the slope of the Marshallian demand curve is less numerically than the slope of the Marshallian supply curve:

$$\left|\frac{\Delta P_d}{\Delta Q}\right| < \left|\frac{\Delta P_s}{\Delta Q}\right|$$

In the case of perpetual oscillation, price and quantity oscillate perpetually around their equilibrium values, as seen in Figure 13.12. In this case, the demand and supply curves have the same numerical slope values:

$$\left|\frac{\Delta Q_d}{\Delta P}\right| = \left|\frac{\Delta Q_s}{\Delta P}\right| \quad \text{and} \quad \left|\frac{\Delta P_d}{\Delta Q}\right| = \left|\frac{\Delta P_s}{\Delta Q}\right|$$

In the case of explosive oscillation, price and quantity oscillate farther away from equilibrium, as seen in Figure 13.13. In this case, the slope of the Walrasian demand curve is less numerically than the slope of the Walrasian supply curve:

$$\left|\frac{\Delta Q_d}{\Delta P}\right| < \left|\frac{\Delta Q_s}{\Delta P}\right|$$

Conversely, the slope of the Marshallian demand curve is greater numerically than the slope of the Marshallian supply curve:

$$\left|\frac{\Delta P_d}{\Delta Q}\right| > \left|\frac{\Delta P_s}{\Delta Q}\right|$$

SUMMARY

Mathematically, the Walrasian market model is the same as the Marshallian market model. Each model consists of two equations in the same unknowns of price and quantity; and the simultaneous solution of both equations yields price and quantity values that satisfy both equations. Differences between the Walrasian and Marshallian models are thus due (1) to their different definitions of supply and demand and (2) to their different conceptions of the process whereby price and quantity change when the market is in disequilibrium. Specifically, (1) quantity is the dependent variable and price is the independent variable in the Walrasian model. Conversely, price is the dependent variable and quantity is the independent variable in the Marshallian model. (2) In the Walrasian model, sellers decrease market price in the case of excess quantity supplied at a given price, and purchasers increase market price in the case of excess quantity demanded at a given price. Quantity demanded and supplied then change in response to these price changes until the market is in equilibrium. But in the Marshallian model, sellers increase market quantity in the case of excess demand price at a given quantity, and they decrease market quantity in the case of excess supply price at a given quantity. Demand price and supply price then change in response to these quantity changes until the market is in equilibrium.

Thus, the law of equilibrium price and quantity in a competitive product market may be stated in several different ways. Aggregate expenditure on a product remains constant if at its given price the quantity sellers are willing to sell is the same as the quantity purchasers are willing to purchase—if quantity supplied equals quantity demanded. Conversely, aggregate expenditure on a product remains constant if at its given quantity the price sellers are willing to accept is the same as the price purchasers are willing to pay— if supply price equals demand price. A product market is in equilibrium at the intersection of the market supply and demand curves—when price and quantity of the product satisfy both its market supply and demand functions.

The law of disequilibrium price and quantity in a competitive product market may be stated in the same ways. Aggregate expenditure on a product tends to change if at its given price the quantity sellers are willing to sell is not the same as the quantity purchasers are willing to purchase—if quantity supplied is not equal to quantity demanded. Conversely, aggregate expenditure on a product tends to change if at its given quantity the price sellers are willing to accept is not the same as the price purchasers are willing to pay— if supply price is not equal to demand price. A product market is in disequilibrium when either quantity or price of the product does not satisfy both its market supply and demand functions.

The nearest equivalent of the solution concept in economic theory is the concept of equilibrium. But a solution pair of (Q, P) values need not be a stable equilibrium pair, for the conditions for a stable equilibrium are more difficult to satisfy than the conditions for a solution. The static Walrasian and Marshallian models yield a stable equilibrium when the demand curve has a negative slope and the supply curve has a positive slope. However, because of their different behavioral assumptions, the condition for a stable equilibrium of the two models is not the same when both curves are assumed to have negative slopes and slope is defined in the same way in both models. Now, the condition for a stable equilibrium of the Walrasian model is that numerically

$$\left|\frac{\Delta Q_d}{\Delta P}\right| > \left|\frac{\Delta Q_s}{\Delta P}\right| \quad \text{or} \quad \left|\frac{\Delta P}{\Delta Q_d}\right| < \left|\frac{\Delta P}{\Delta Q_s}\right|$$

The condition for a stable equilibrium of the Marshallian model is that numerically.

$$\left|\frac{\Delta P_d}{\Delta Q}\right| > \left|\frac{\Delta P_s}{\Delta Q}\right| \quad \text{or} \quad \left|\frac{\Delta Q}{\Delta P_d}\right| < \left|\frac{\Delta Q}{\Delta P_s}\right|$$

Defining slope in both cases as $\Delta P/\Delta Q$, the Walrasian model thus has a stable equilibrium when the slope of the demand curve is less numerically than the slope of the supply curve. But the Marshallian model has a stable equilibrium when the slope of the demand curve is greater numerically than the slope of the supply curve.

Geometrically, a shift to the right of the quantity demanded curve is the same as a shift upward of the demand price curve. A shift to the left of the quantity demanded curve is the same as a shift downward of the demand price curve. A shift to the right of the quantity supplied curve is the same as a shift downward of the supply price curve, and a shift to the left of the quantity supplied curve is the same as a shift upward of the supply price curve. An analysis of parameter shifts suggests that (for a normal product) $\Delta P/\Delta Y_d > 0$; $\Delta P/\Delta P_s > 0$; $\Delta P/\Delta P_c < 0$; $\Delta P/\Delta P_r > 0$; and $\Delta P/\Delta P_j < 0$.

Since the Walrasian and Marshallian market models are based on different human behavioral assumptions—that is, different definitions of "supply" and "demand" and different conceptions of the process whereby price and quantity change when the market is in disequilibrium—they yield identical sets of disequilibrium (Q, P) values only in the context of an increase in market supply. Thus, the disequilibrium empirical set implied by the Walrasian model is the same as the disequilibrium empirical set implied by the Marshallian model only in the context of an increase in market supply. Consequently, an econometrician using disequilibrium data can uniquely identify only one curve—a given market demand curve. By defining a set of ordered pairs of market (Q, P) values to be a market average revenue (price) curve, in the Marshallian model the market demand curve is the market average revenue curve when the market is in equilibrium or disequilibrium. But in the Walrasian model, (1) the market demand curve is the market average revenue curve in equilibrium if it is not shifting but the supply curve is shifting; (2) the market supply curve is the market average revenue curve in equilibrium if it is not shifting but the demand curve is shifting; (3) the market demand curve is the market average revenue curve in the disequilibrium case of excess quantity supplied; and (4) the market supply curve is the market average revenue curve in the disequilibrium case of excess quantity demanded.

When the demand curve has a negative slope and the supply curve a positive slope, price and quantity oscillate toward their equilibrium values à la cobweb theorem if numerically

$$\left|\frac{\Delta Q_d}{\Delta P}\right| > \left|\frac{\Delta Q_s}{\Delta P}\right| \quad \text{or} \quad \left|\frac{\Delta P_d}{\Delta Q}\right| < \left|\frac{\Delta P_s}{\Delta Q}\right|$$

But P and Q oscillate around their equilibrium values if numerically

$$\left|\frac{\Delta Q_d}{\Delta P}\right| = \left|\frac{\Delta Q_s}{\Delta P}\right| \quad \text{or} \quad \left|\frac{\Delta P_d}{\Delta Q}\right| = \left|\frac{\Delta P_s}{\Delta Q}\right|$$

Lastly, P and Q oscillate away from their equilibrium values if numerically

$$\left|\frac{\Delta Q_d}{\Delta P}\right| < \left|\frac{\Delta Q_s}{\Delta P}\right| \quad \text{or} \quad \left|\frac{\Delta P_d}{\Delta Q}\right| > \left|\frac{\Delta P_s}{\Delta Q}\right|$$

To close, a given expenditure on a product is identically equal to its price times its quantity purchased and sold: $E \equiv PQ$. Price and quantity, and hence expenditure, change with changes in supply and demand. Purchasers and sellers change supply and demand. They change the quantities they are willing to purchase and sell at the given market price. Purchasers and sellers therefore determine the composition of the national expenditure on products. They determine the allocation of resources to the production of products. They determine the allocation of income to the consumption of products. The problem now is to further rationalize this price mechanism which allocates resources by recognizing that supply functions differ according to market time periods and demand functions facing sellers differ according to market structures.

Questions

1. State and compare the Walrasian and Marshallian definitions of supply and demand. How do you explain the convention in economics of measuring price on the vertical axis and quantity on the horizontal axis when price is the independent variable and quantity is the dependent variable?

2. State and compare the Walrasian and Marshallian equilibrium and disequilibrium cases using rationales of human behavior.

3. State and compare the Walrasian and Marshallian stable and unstable equilibrium cases using rationales of human behavior.

4. State and compare the meanings of parameter shifts in the Walrasian and Marshallian demand curves. Use diagrams to prove by analysis that $\Delta P/\Delta Y_d > 0$ if $\Delta Q_d/\Delta Y_d > 0$, that $\Delta P/\Delta P_s > 0$ if $\Delta Q_d/\Delta P_s > 0$, and that $\Delta P/\Delta P_c < 0$ if $\Delta Q_d/\Delta P_c < 0$.

5. State and compare the meanings of parameter shifts in the Walrasian and Marshallian supply curves. Use diagrams to prove by analysis that $\Delta P/\Delta P_r > 0$ if $\Delta Q_s/\Delta P_r < 0$, and that $\Delta P/\Delta P_j < 0$ if $\Delta Q_s/\Delta P_j > 0$.

6. Use diagrams to prove by analysis that in all cases the equilibrium Walrasian sets of (Q_d, P) and (Q_s, P) numbers are the same as the equilibrium Marshallian sets of (Q, P_d) and (Q, P_s) numbers.

7. Use diagrams to prove by analysis that in the case of an increase in supply the disequilibrium Walrasian set of (Q_d, P) numbers is the same as the disequilibrium Marshallian set of (Q, P_d) numbers.

8. Use diagrams to prove by analysis that in all other cases the disequilibrium Walrasian set of numbers is not the same as the disequilibrium Marshallian set of numbers. In each case, what set of numbers is identified? How important is this question?

9. Use diagrams, functions, and rationales of human behavior to explain the cobweb theorem. Prove by analysis that the nature of the cycle depends on the numerical values of the slopes of the market supply and demand curves.

SELECTED READINGS

Jaffé, William. "Walras' Theory of Tâtonnement: A Critique of Recent Interpretations," *The Journal of Political Economy*, LXXIV: 1 (February 1967), pp. 1–19.

Working, E. J. "What Do Statistical 'Demand Curves' Show?" *The Quarterly Journal of Economics*, XLI (1927), pp. 212–235. Reprinted in The American Economic Association. *Readings in Price Theory*. Edited by George J. Stigler and Kenneth E. Boulding. Homewood, Illinois: Richard D. Irwin, Inc., 1952, pp. 97–115.

Makower, Helen and Jacob Marschak, "Assets, Prices, and Monetary Theory," *Economica*. New Series; V (1938), pp. 261–288. Reprinted in The American Economic Association. *Readings in Price Theory, ibid.,* pp. 283–310.

Boulding, Kenneth E. "A Liquidity Preference Theory of Market Prices," *Economica*. New Series; IX (1944), pp. 56–63. Reprinted in The American Economic Association. *Readings in Price Theory, ibid.,* pp. 311–328.

Ezekiel, Mordecai. "The Cobweb Theorem," *The Quarterly Journal of Economics*, LII (February 1938), pp. 255–280. Reprinted in The American Economic Association. *Readings in Business Cycle Theory*. Edited by Gottfried Haberler. Homewood, Illinois: Richard D. Irwin, Inc., 1951, pp. 422–442.

NOTES

[1] Léon Walras, *Elements d'économic politique pure*, 4th ed. (Lausanne, 1900). Translated by William Jaffé, *Elements of Pure Economics* (Homewood, Illinois: Richard D. Irwin, Inc., 1954).

[2] The distinctions between (1) a "change in demand" and a "change in quantity demanded" and (2) a "change in supply" and a "change in quantity supplied" are Walrasian. Concentrate on the distinction between a "change in demand" and a "change in quantity demanded." A "change in demand" is represented by a shift in the demand curve, and a "change in quantity demanded" is represented by a movement along a given demand curve. A "change in demand" induces a change in price, and a change in price induces a "change in quantity demanded." Since a "change in demand" is not a "change in quantity demanded" and a "change in quantity demanded" is not a "change in demand," these two concepts are mutually exclusive. One concept is not a subset of the other concept; one is neither a necessary nor a sufficient condition for the other.

A "change in demand" and a "change in quantity demanded" are not mutually exclusive concepts, however, if the dependent variable of a demand function that relates three or more variables is verbalized as quantity demanded. If Q_d of (say) $Q_d = f(P, Y)$ is verbalized as quantity demanded, then a "change in quantity demanded" occurs with a change in price (P), as represented by a movement along a given demand curve, and with a change in income (Y), as represented by a shift in the demand curve. Thus, a "change in quantity demanded" may be a "change in demand"; and a "change in demand" is a "change in quantity demanded." Consequently, a "change in demand" is a sufficient condition for a "change in quantity demanded"; and a "change in quantity demanded" is a necessary condition for a "change in demand." In short, a "change in demand" is a subset of a "change in quantity demanded," and hence the two concepts are not mutually exclusive.

Similarly, a "change in demand" and a "change in quantity demanded" are not mutually exclusive concepts if the dependent variable of a demand function that relates three or more variables is verbalized as demand. If Q_d of (say) $Q_d = f(P, Y)$ is verbalized as demand, then a "change in demand" occurs with a change in price (P), as represented by a movement along a given demand curve, and with a change in income (Y), as represented by a shift in the demand curve. Thus, a "change in demand" may be a "change in quantity demanded"; and a "change in quantity demanded" is a "change in demand." Consequently, a "change in quantity demanded" is a sufficient condition for a "change in demand"; and a "change in demand" is a necessary condition for a "change in quantity demanded." In short, a "change in quantity demanded" is a subset of a "change in demand," and hence the two concepts are not mutually exclusive.

To conclude, when Q_d changes because of a change in P, Q_d may be verbalized as quantity demanded, for quantity demanded is a function of P: $Q_d = D(P)$. But when Q_d changes because of some other independent variable (such as income), Q_d may be verbalized as demand, for demand is a function of Y in the sense that the demand curve shifts with a change in Y, holding P constant: $Q_d = g(Y)$. But when Q_d changes because of a change in P and Y, Q_d should not be verbalized as quantity demanded or as demand, if a "change in demand" and a "change in quantity demanded" are to be mutually exclusive concepts (see note 5).

[3] The phrases "excess demand" and "excess supply" are incorrect since demand is a schedule relating Q_d to P and supply is a schedule relating Q_s to P. For demand in the schedule sense to be in excess of supply in the schedule sense, the demand curve throughout its length would have to lie to the right of the supply curve; and for supply to be in excess of demand, the supply curve throughout its length would have to lie to the right of the demand curve. Since what is really meant is that at a given price the quantity demanded is not equal to the quantity supplied, these cases should be called excess quantity demanded (not excess demand) and excess quantity supplied (not excess supply). Since demand and supply are schedules, the market is not in (a unique) equilibrium when demand equals supply, but when quantity demanded equals quantity supplied.

[4] To summarize the determination of equilibrium market price,

(1) $\quad Q_d = a_1 - b_1 \cdot P$

(2) $\quad Q_s = -a_2 + b_2 \cdot P$

(3) $\quad Q_d = Q_s$

Therefore,

$$P = \frac{a_1 + a_2}{b_1 + b_2}$$

Conversely, equilibrium market quantity may be determined as follows:

(1) $\quad P_1 = \dfrac{a_1}{b_1} - \dfrac{1}{b_1} \cdot Q$

(2) $\quad P_2 = \dfrac{a_2}{b_2} + \dfrac{1}{b_2} \cdot Q$

(3) $\quad P_1 = P_2$

Therefore,

$$Q = \frac{a_1 b_2 - a_2 b_1}{b_1 + b_2}$$

[5] As implied in note 2, a more general verbalization of Q_d is required when the demand function relates three or more variables. The verbalization must subsume quantity demanded and demand. When Q_d is verbalized as quantity purchased or bought, a change in quantity purchased due to a change in P may be called a "change in quantity demanded"; and a change in quantity purchased due to a change in Y may be called a "change in demand." Thus a "change in quantity demanded" is not a "change in demand"; and a "change in demand" is not a "change in quantity demanded." Consequently, neither is a necessary nor sufficient condition for the other. In short, neither is a subset of the other, and hence the two concepts are mutually exclusive. However, if exchange is permitted when the market is in disequilibrium, the quantity purchased at a price

may not be denoted by the demand curve. Specifically, in the cases of excess quantity supplied and equilibrium, the quantity purchased is denoted by the demand curve; but in the case of excess quantity demanded, the quantity purchased is denoted by the supply curve. The quantity purchasers desire or are willing to purchase, however, is always denoted by the demand curve. To conclude, therefore, Q_d should be verbalized as "quantity purchasers are willing to purchase." Similarly, Q_s should be verbalized as "quantity sellers are willing to sell."

[6] Alfred Marshall, *Principles of Economics*, 8th ed. (London: Macmillan and Co. Ltd., 1920).

[7] To summarize the determination of equilibrium market quantity,

(1) $P_d = c_1 - d_1 \cdot Q$

(2) $P_s = c_2 + d_2 \cdot Q$

(3) $P_d = P_s$

Therefore,

$$Q = \frac{c_1 - c_2}{d_1 + d_2}$$

Conversely, equilibrium market price may be determined as follows:

(1) $Q_1 = \dfrac{c_1}{d_1} - \dfrac{1}{d_1} \cdot P$

(2) $Q_2 = \dfrac{-c_2}{d_2} + \dfrac{1}{d_2} \cdot P$

(3) $Q_1 = Q_2$

Therefore,

$$P = \frac{d_1 c_2 + d_2 c_1}{d_1 + d_2}$$

[8] See H. O. Wold, "Econometrics as Pioneering in Nonexperimental Model Building," *Econometrica*, XXXVII:3 (July 1969), pp. 369–381.

[9] See Otto Eckstein and Gary Fromm, "The Price Equation," *The American Economic Review*, LVIII:5 (December 1968), pp. 1159–1183.

chapter 14

Period Equilibrium of Competitive and Monopolistic Product Sellers

The economic theory of determination of price and quantity in a product market is based on demand and supply curves that represent rationales of human behavior. The demand curve for a product facing a perfectly competitive or monopolistic seller is much simpler to derive analytically than is his supply curve. In fact, the primary analytical problem of the theory of determination of price and quantity in these product markets is to derive the supply curve of a seller and to explain why it shifts over time. A seller is in equilibrium with respect to each point on his supply curve. When he is in equilibrium, he has determined that output at which he is maximizing his profit—that is, maximizing the surplus of revenue over cost. Models of human behavior are thus presented in this chapter which rationalize the period supply curves of a seller by rationalizing his revenue and period cost functions. The subject matter of this chapter, therefore, is a continuation of the subject matter of Chapter 11—namely, supply functions of a product of a seller. In Chapter 11, a seller's supply curve of a product is rationalized without reference to time period, and on the assumption that products may be related in production. In the present chapter, a seller's supply curve of a product is rationalized with reference to time period, and on the assumption that products are not related in production, or that a given product is the only product of the seller.

Short-Run Market Period

The short-run market period may be defined as a time period sufficiently long in duration that a seller varies the input of some factors of production (the variable factors), while holding constant the input of one or more other factors (the fixed factors). Thus, in the short run, total output varies with the input of variable factors, given the input of fixed factors and the state of technology. Several conclusions about cost, equilibrium, and supply follow in sequence from this definition. The cost of fixed factors does not vary with output. Fixed cost is zero for making a decision with respect to number of units of output to produce per unit of time. The short-run total cost curve depicts how total cost varies with output as output varies with the input of variable factors, given the price of each factor and the state of technology. A seller is in short-run equilibrium when he has determined that output at which he is maximizing his profit or minimizing his loss by maximizing his net revenue, which is his total revenue minus his total variable cost. Short-run supply reflects the variable cost of production but not the fixed cost. The short-run supply curve depicts the quantity supplied at various prices as the current rate of output is varied by varying the current rate of input of variable factors to maximize net revenue. Each point on the curve represents the equilibrium solution of the short-run problem of determining the quantity of output to produce and the quantity of variable factors to use per unit of time.

Short-Run Supply Curve of a Perfectly Competitive Seller

As seen in Chapter 6, the demand curve facing a perfectly competitive seller of a product is perfectly elastic, for price is a value determined by market supply and demand that does not vary with his quantity sold. Thus marginal revenue equals average revenue equals price; in short, his total revenue curve is depicted by a ray, which is a positively-sloped line emanating from the point of origin of the revenue diagram. As seen in Chapter 9, his short-run total cost curve has a positive total cost intercept equal to total fixed cost, and is nonlinear. These functions are depicted in Figures 14.1a and 14.1b.

Given price P', profit is maximized at that quantity of output (Q') at which marginal revenue (MR') equals marginal cost (MC').[1] The last unit of quantity Q' adds as much to total revenue (MR') as it adds to total cost (MC'). The slope of the total revenue curve (MR') is the same as the slope of the total cost curve (MC') at Q'. The greatest difference of total revenue (R') over total cost (C') is at Q', given P'. Therefore, (P', Q') is one point on the short-run supply curve. Since $MR' = P' = MC'$ at Q', this point is on the marginal cost curve. Other points such as (P'', Q'') and (P''', Q''') are rationalized in the same way by shifting the revenue curves upward.

The conclusion follows from this analysis that the relevant portion of the short-run marginal cost curve of a perfectly competitive seller represents equilibrium combinations of prices and quantities to him; that is, it represents "optimum" adjustments of quantity produced to changes in price. His short-run supply curve thus is the relevant portion of his short-run marginal cost curve: the properties of his (relevant) short-run marginal cost curve are the properties of his short-run supply curve. The slope of the $Q = s(P)$ curve

FIG. 14.1a. Short-run profit maximization of a perfectly competitive seller of a product

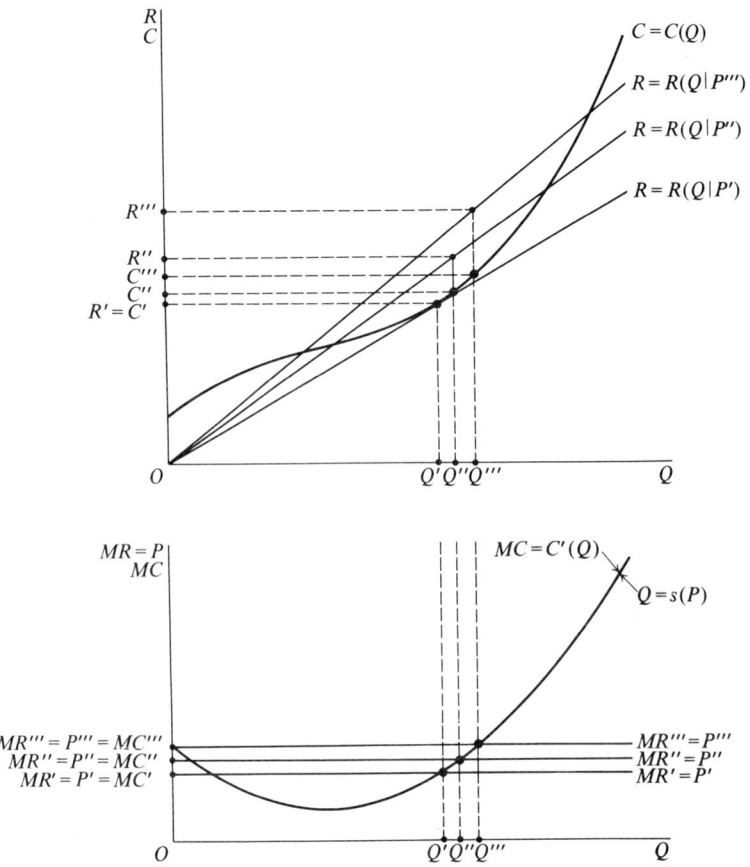

FIG. 14.1b. Short-run supply curve of a product of a perfectly competitive seller

(dQ/dP) is the reciprocal of the slope of the $MC = C'(Q)$ curve (dMC/dQ), since $MC = P$.

The relevant portion of the perfectly competitive seller's short-run marginal cost curve is its positively-sloped portion beginning at its point of intersection with his average variable cost curve.[2] At this point of intersection, his net revenue is zero; above it his net revenue is positive. He continues operation in the short run only if his net revenue is zero or positive.[3] To see this clearly, consider Figures 14.2 to 14.4.

Market price is P' in Figure 14.2a, the short-run market supply and demand diagram. Marginal and average revenue of the seller is the same P' in Figure 14.2b, his short-run price and output diagram. His equilibrium output is Q', for $MR' = P' = MC'$ at Q'. Profit is maximized at Q', given P'. Total revenue

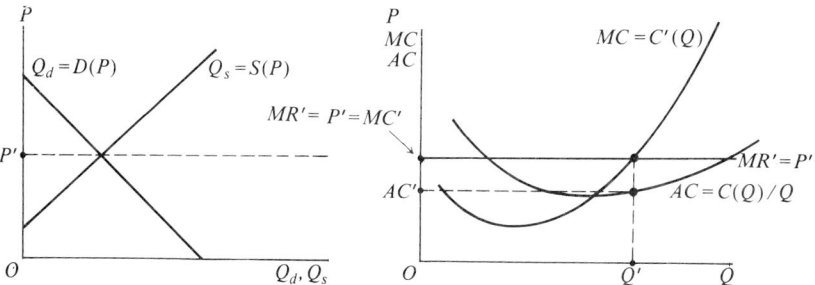

FIG. 14.2a. Short-run market supply and demand

FIG. 14.2b. Positive profit and positive net revenue

from selling Q' at P' is the rectangle $P' \cdot Q'$. Average total cost of producing Q' is AC'. Total cost of Q' is the rectangle $AC' \cdot Q'$. Profit is the rectangle $P' \cdot Q' - AC' \cdot Q'$. No other value of Q yields as large a profit rectangle.

Market price is P'' in Figure 14.3a. Marginal and average revenue of the seller is $MR'' = P''$ in Figure 14.3b. His equilibrium output is Q'', for $MR'' = P'' = MC''$ at Q''. Total revenue is $P'' \cdot Q''$. Average total cost is AC''. Total cost is $AC'' \cdot Q''$. Profit is zero: $P'' \cdot Q'' = AC'' \cdot Q''$. All other values of Q yield negative profits (losses). Average variable cost of Q'' is AVC''. Total variable cost of Q'' is the rectangle $AVC'' \cdot Q''$. Net revenue is the rectangle $P'' \cdot Q'' - AVC'' \cdot Q''$. No other value of Q yields as large a net revenue rectangle.

Market price is P''' in Figure 14.4a. In Figure 14.4b, profit of the seller is negative, but his net revenue is positive: at Q''', $AVC''' < P''' < AC'''$. His total revenue is more than sufficient to cover his total variable cost, but less than sufficient to cover his total cost. Thus, only a portion of his total fixed cost is covered by his total revenue. Nevertheless, his negative profit (loss) is minimized by continuing production in the short run. If he discontinued production, total revenue would decrease to zero, but total cost would decrease only to the level of total fixed cost. Therefore, in the short run, he

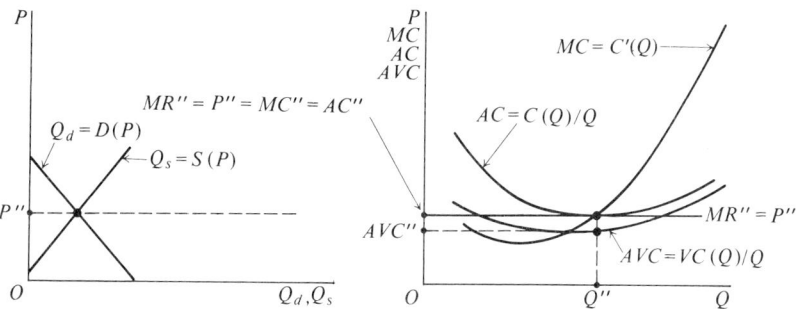

FIG. 14.3a. Short-run market supply and demand

FIG. 14.3b. Zero profit and positive net revenue

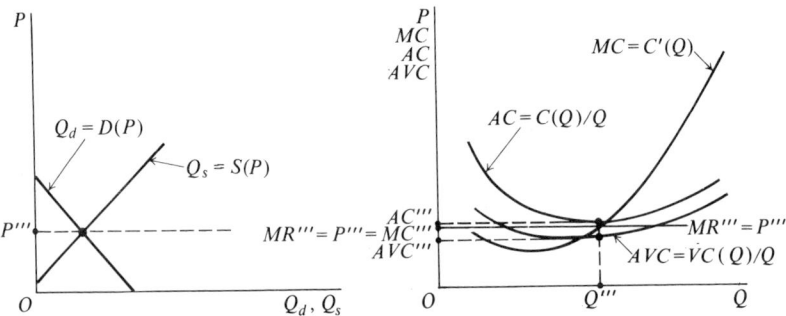

FIG. 14.4a. Short-run market supply and demand

FIG. 14.4b. Negative profit and positive net revenue

continues production of his product if he can cover a portion of his total fixed cost.

His net revenue is zero if $P = AVC$ at equilibrium Q. Total revenue is just sufficient to cover total variable cost. No portion of total fixed cost is covered by total revenue. His negative profit is the same whether he continues or discontinues production. Therefore, in the short run, he is indifferent as to whether to continue production of his product.

His net revenue is negative if $P < AVC$ at equilibrium Q. Total revenue is not sufficient to cover total variable cost. His negative profit is minimized by discontinuing production. Therefore, in the short run, he ceases production of his product if market price is less than average variable cost.

Short-Run "Supply Curve" of a Monopolist

As analyzed in Chapter 6, the demand curve for a product facing a seller denotes the price at which each quantity can be sold; and his average revenue curve denotes the average revenue of each quantity sold. In the case of a non-price-discriminating monopolist, the price of each quantity is its average revenue, for $AR = R/Q = P$ at each quantity. Therefore, the demand curve facing a monopolist, which is the market demand curve, is his average revenue curve. But his average revenue curve is not his marginal revenue curve, for at any given quantity marginal revenue is less than average revenue, and hence his marginal revenue curve lies below his average revenue curve. In short, his total revenue curve has a zero total revenue intercept and is concave downward. As seen in Chapter 9, his short-run total cost curve has a positive total cost intercept equal to total fixed cost, and is nonlinear. These functions are depicted in Figures 14.5 and 14.6.

Given market demand $AR = P(Q)'$, profit is maximized at that quantity of output (Q') at which marginal revenue (MR') equals marginal cost (MC'). The last unit before Q' adds more to total revenue than to total cost, thereby

COMPETITIVE AND MONOPOLISTIC PRODUCT SELLERS 239

FIG. 14.5a. Short-run profit maximization of a monopolist

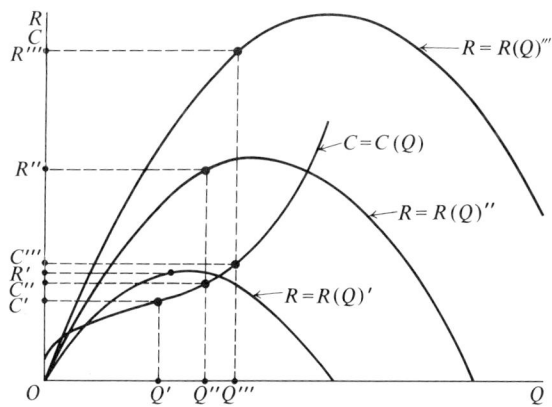

FIG. 14.5b. Short-run "supply curve" of a monopolist

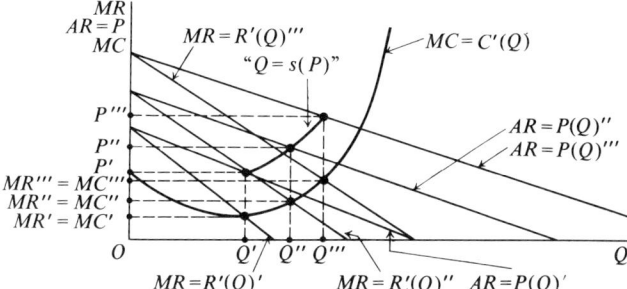

increasing profit. The first unit after Q' adds more to total cost than to total revenue, thereby decreasing profit. The last unit of Q' adds as much to total revenue as it does to total cost, thereby maximizing profit. At Q', the slope of the total revenue curve (MR') is the same as the slope of the total cost curve (MC'). The greatest difference of total revenue (R') over total cost (C') is at Q'. Given Q', the corresponding profit-maximizing price is P'. Therefore, (P', Q') is one point on the monopolist's short-run "supply curve." Other points such as (P'', Q'') and (P''', Q''') are rationalized in the same way by shifting the market demand (average revenue), marginal revenue, and total revenue curves upward as demand increases.

At Q', $P' > MR'$ ($= MC'$). Thus the equilibrium point (P', Q') is not on the monopolist's marginal cost curve. Equilibrium quantity Q' is on his marginal cost curve, but equilibrium price P' is on his average revenue (demand) curve. The same is true of points (P'', Q'') and (P''', Q'''). The set of ordered pairs of P and Q numbers is the monopolist's short-run "supply curve," denoted by $Q = s(P)$. This curve depicts the profit-maximizing

FIG. 14.6a. Short-run profit maximization of a monopolist

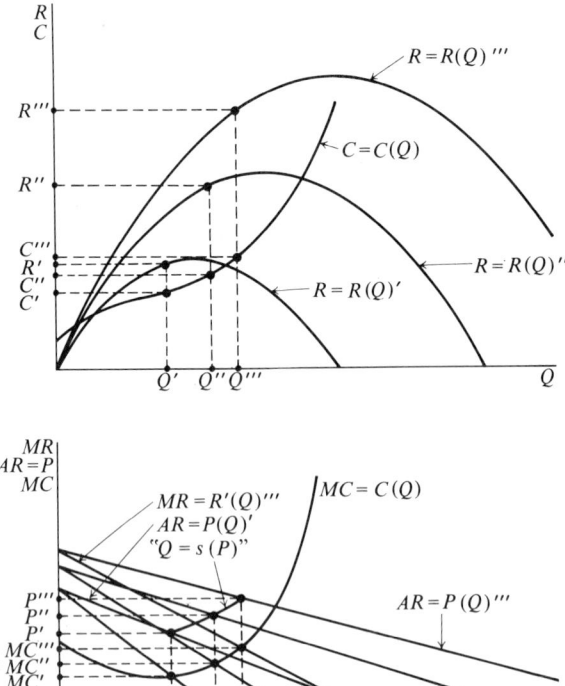

FIG. 14.6b. Short-run "supply curve" of a monopolist

(= equilibrium) prices he charges (P) for various equilibrium quantities sold (Q) per unit of time. Since equilibrium price is greater than marginal cost at equilibrium quantity sold, his marginal cost curve is not his "supply curve."[4]

The slope of his short-run "supply curve" is determined by the relationship between a given set of marginal cost, marginal revenue, and average revenue curves and the pattern of change in the revenue curves. Figure 14.6a depicts the same total cost curve and initial total revenue curve as Figure 14.5a, but a different pattern of change in the total revenue curve. Similarly, Figure 14.6b depicts the same marginal cost curve and initial marginal and average revenue curves as Figure 14.5b, but a different pattern of change in the marginal and average revenue curves. The slope of the "supply curve" of Figure 14.5b is not the same as the slope of the "supply curve" of Figure 14.6b. Thus, a "supply curve" is derived analytically for each pattern of change in demand for the monopolist's product. Change the pattern of demand increases, and the slope of his "supply curve" changes at any given value of equilibrium output. In short, his "supply curve" is not unique; it is a set of curves, one for each pattern of change in his demand curve. Consequently, for a product seller to have a unique supply curve he must be a perfectly competitive seller!

A monopolist continues to produce in the short run only if his total revenue (R) is equal to or greater than his total variable cost (VC)—that is, only if his net revenue $(R - VC)$ is equal to or greater than zero. If $R < VC$ (that is, $R - VC < 0$), he is incurring a loss that can be eliminated in the short run. (However, in the short run he cannot eliminate the loss due to not covering fixed cost.) In Figure 14.7, given market demand $AR = P(Q)'$,

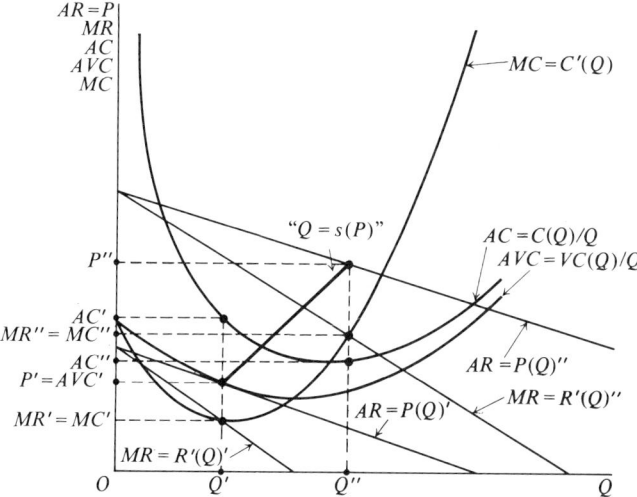

FIG. 14.7. Relevant portion of Short-Run "supply curve" of a monopolist

marginal cost equals marginal revenue at Q'. The price at which Q' can be sold is P'. Total revenue of Q' is the rectangle $P' \cdot Q'$. Average cost of Q' is AC'. Total cost of Q' is the rectangle $AC' \cdot Q'$. Negative profit (loss) is the rectangle $AC' \cdot Q' - P' \cdot Q'$. Average variable cost of Q' is AVC'. Total variable cost of Q' is the rectangle $AVC' \cdot Q'$. Maximum net revenue is zero at Q' since $P' = AVC'$. (The average revenue curve is tangent to the average variable cost curve at Q'.) Minimum negative profit is the amount of fixed cost at Q'—that is, $Q'(AC' - AVC')$. Profit is positive when demand (for example) is $AR = P(Q)''$, for $P'' > AC''$ at equilibrium quantity Q''.

Short-Run Equilibrium of a Multi-Plant Monopolist

In the short run, a monopolist may produce his product in two or more plants, produce a different output in each plant, and incur a different cost per unit for the same plant output. To see this clearly, consider Figures 14.8a and 14.8b. His equilibrium output from all plants is that aggregate output (Q) at which aggregate marginal cost (MC) equals aggregate marginal revenue (MR). His aggregate marginal revenue curve is derived from his aggregate total revenue curve, which is derived from his aggregate average revenue curve, which is the given market demand curve of Figure 14.8b. As seen in Figure 14.8a, his aggregate marginal cost curve is derived by summing his plant marginal cost curves horizontally—by summing, at each marginal cost (mc) value, output (q) of each plant. As seen in Figure 14.8b, given $MC = C'(Q)$, $MR = R'(Q)$, and $AR = P(Q)$, his aggregate equilibrium output is Q', where $MC' = MR'$. The price of Q' is P'.

Aggregate equilibrium output is allocated according to the equimarginal principle that the last unit produced in one plant must add as much to total cost as the last unit produced in every other plant—that marginal cost must be equal in all plants. Thus, plant equilibrium output is that output at which plant marginal cost equals aggregate marginal cost equals aggregate marginal revenue. The marginal cost curves of plants one and two are depicted by $mc_1 = c_1(q_1)$ and $mc_2 = c_2(q_2)$ in Figure 14.8a. The monopolist produces q'_1 units in plant one, where $mc'_1 = MC' = MR'$, and q'_2 units in plant two, where $mc'_2 = MC' = MR'$. At $MR' = MC' = mc'_1 = mc'_2$, $q'_1 = q'_2$. More is produced in plant one than in plant two because at any common output marginal cost (and average cost) is less in one than in two. Thus, as demand decreases, high-cost plants are the first to discontinue operation.

Plant equilibrium average cost is that average cost value corresponding to plant equilibrium output. The average cost curves of plants one and two are depicted by $ac_1 = c_1(q_1)/q_1$ and $ac_2 = c_2(q_2)/q_2$ in Figure 14.8a. Average cost of q'_1 is ac'_1, and average cost of q'_2 is ac'_2: $ac'_1 < ac'_2$.

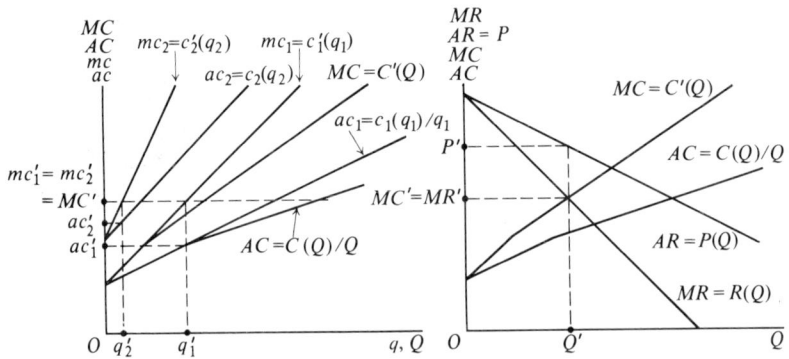

FIG. 14.8a. Short-run equilibrium of a multi-plant monopolist

FIG. 14.8b. Short-run equilibrium of a multi-plant monopolist

Equilibrium of a Multi-Market Monopolist

In the short run and the long run, a monopolist may produce his product for sale in two or more separate markets, sell a different quantity of his output in each market, and charge a different price for the same market quantity. To see this clearly, consider Figures 14.9a and 14.9b. His equilibrium output for all markets is that aggregate output (Q) at which aggregate marginal revenue (MR) equals aggregate marginal cost (MC). Assume that his aggregate marginal cost curve is given, as in Figure 14.9b. As seen in Figure 14.9a, his aggregate marginal revenue curve is derived by summing his market marginal revenue curves horizontally—by summing, at each marginal revenue (mr) value, the quantity sold in each market (q). As seen in Figure 14.9b, given $MR = R'(Q)$, $MC = C'(Q)$, and $AC = C(Q)/Q$, his aggregate equilibrium output is Q', where $MR' = MC'$. The average cost of Q' is AC'.

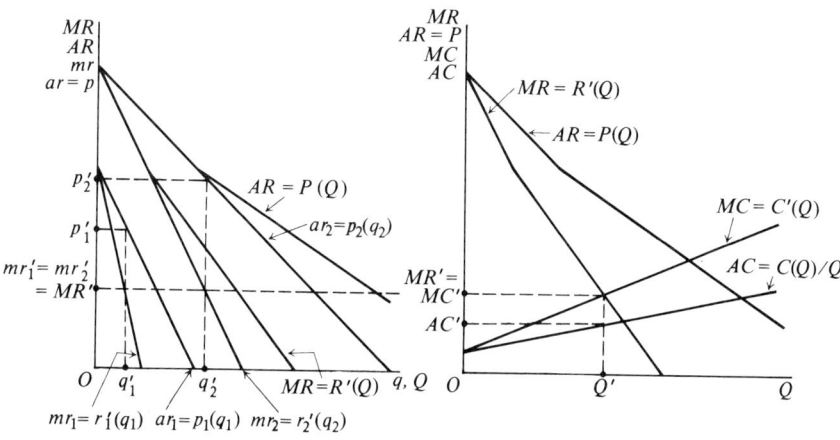

FIG. 14.9a. Equilibrium of a multi-market monopolist

FIG. 14.9b. Equilibrium of a multi-market monopolist

Aggregate equilibrium output is allocated according to the equimarginal principle that the last unit sold in one market must add as much to total revenue as the last unit sold in every other market—that marginal revenue must be equal in all markets. Thus the equilibrium quantity sold in a given market is that quantity at which market marginal revenue equals aggregate marginal revenue equals aggregate marginal cost. The marginal revenue curves of markets one and two are depicted by $mr_1 = r_1(q_1)$ and $mr_2 = r_2(q_2)$ in Figure 14.9a. The monopolist sells q'_1 units in market one, where $mr'_1 = MR' = MC'$, and q'_2 units in market two, where $mr'_2 = MR' = MC'$. At $MC' = MR' = mr'_1 = mr'_2$, $q_1 < q_2$. More is sold in market two than in market one because at any common quantity, demand and hence marginal revenue is greater in two than in one. Thus, as the cost of production increases, low-revenue markets are no longer served.

Market equilibrium price (average revenue) is that demand price corresponding to market equilibrium output. The average revenue curves of markets one and two are depicted by $ar_1 = p_1(q_1)$ and $ar_2 = p_2(q_2)$ in Figure 14.9a. The average revenue of q'_1 is p'_1, and the average revenue of q'_2 is p'_2: $p'_1 < p'_2$.

The fact that $p'_1 < p'_2$ may be rationalized via the concept of price elasticity of demand for a product. Specifically, the coefficient of price elasticity of demand in market one (ε_1) is greater numerically than the same coefficient in market two (ε_2), at any common price value. Thus,

(1) $\qquad mr_1 = p_1\left(1 - \dfrac{1}{|\varepsilon_1|}\right)$

(2) $\qquad mr_2 = p_2\left(1 - \dfrac{1}{|\varepsilon_2|}\right)$

(3) $\qquad mr_1 = mr_2$

(4) $\qquad p_1\left(1 - \dfrac{1}{|\varepsilon_1|}\right) = p_2\left(1 - \dfrac{1}{|\varepsilon_2|}\right) \ (|\varepsilon| \neq 1)$

(5) $\qquad |\varepsilon_1| > |\varepsilon_2|$

(6) $\qquad p_1 < p_2.$[5]

The conclusion follows from this analysis that a monopolist can "discriminate" by charging two different prices in two different markets if he can keep them separate geographically and if the price elasticity of demand is not the same in both markets. Moreover, the greater the numerical value of the coefficient of price elasticity of demand, the lower the price he can charge.

Very Short-Run Market Period

The very short-run market period may be defined as a time period sufficiently short in duration that a seller holds constant the input of all of his factors of production. Thus the output available for sale per unit of time within the immediate market period is a fixed amount called stock (Q_0). Several conclusions about cost, equilibrium, and supply follow in sequence from this definition. The cost of factors does not vary with the number of units sold from stock. Factor cost is a fixed cost. It is zero for making a decision with respect to the number of units to sell per unit of time from stock. A seller is in very short run equilibrium when he has determined that output at which he is maximizing his profit or minimizing his loss by maximizing his total revenue. Very short-run supply does not reflect factor cost. The very short-run supply curve of a seller depicts his quantity supplied at various prices from his stock so as to maximize his total revenue. Each point on this curve, therefore, represents his equilibrium solution of the very short-run problem of determining the quantity of his stock to sell per unit of time. Considered in the aggregate, his solution determines the rationing of a stock among present and future purchasers.

Very Short-Run Market Model

The present very short-run market model is applicable to producers who do not store their goods or services. A producer may not store his goods because they are perishable. Before the advent of refrigeration, perishable goods could not be stored for any appreciable length of time; meats and vegetables had to be sold before they spoiled. Few goods are nonstorable in the United States today. Christmas trees and flowers come to mind as goods that are not stored for sale in a future market once they are cut and placed on the current market. However, they may be cut and stored for a period of time before they are placed on the market. This model as applied to perishable goods, therefore, is important primarily in explaining the determination of price in those areas of the world in which refrigeration is a rarity.

A producer may not store his goods because he does not wish to perform the storage function. Staples such as wheat, corn, and rice are storable goods. They are produced in one period, stored for sale in subsequent periods, and then reproduced ad infinitum. They may not be stored by the producer. For example, a wheat farmer harvests his crop and sells it to a trader. The trader stores it for sale throughout the year, and may have a carry-over for sale in subsequent years. Next year the wheat farmer produces another crop. The cycle repeats itself. According to this tale, therefore, the wheat farmer sells all of his wheat to the trader.[6] Thus, this model may be used to explain the price of a storable good of a producer who sells all of his stock at one time.

A service is nonstorable from one period to the next. It is utilized in a period or it "perishes" from lack of use. It may be reproduced for use during the next period. For example, a hotel manager offers a fixed stock of services yielded by his rooms for the night. His services tonight cannot be stored and added to his services tomorrow night. Tomorrow he offers the same stock of services again. In short, his services are constant per unit of time, are perishable, cannot be stored over time, and are periodically reproduced. Any kind of labor of which the stock is fixed per unit of time is of the same nature —for example, doctors, pilots, teachers, and other professional people. Thus, this model is used to explain the price of a service of which the "stock" is fixed per unit of time.

To conclude, the present model of the very short-run market period is applicable to producers of services and to producers of perishable and nonperishable goods that are not stored by the producer. In each case, the producer has the objective of maximizing his total revenue (profit) from the fixed amount of the product available for sale.

Very Short-Run Supply Curve of a Perfectly Competitive Seller

The competitive seller has no control over his price. Thus, to maximize his total revenue (profit), he sells all of his given stock (Q_0) at the prevailing market price. Since all of his stock is sold at the same price, his very short-run supply curve is perfectly price inelastic (that is, is parallel to the price axis), and his stock curve is the same as his supply curve.

The amount of his stock is identically equal to his current short-run rate of production (quantity produced per unit of time). As seen in Figures 14.10a and 14.10b, the stock curve is depicted by a straight line drawn vertically from the intersection of his marginal revenue and short-run marginal cost curves to the quantity axis of his very short-run supply curve diagram. Similarly, as seen in Figures 14.11a and 14.11b, the stock curve of

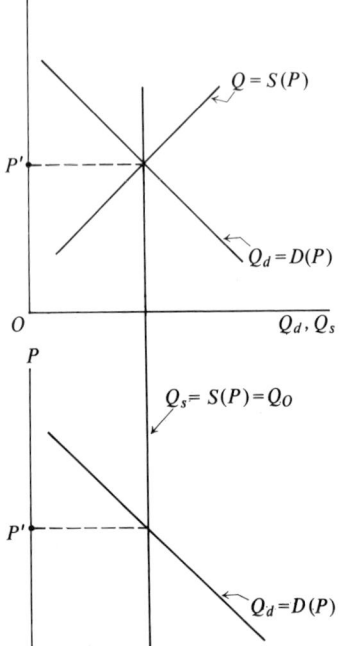

FIG. 14.10a. Short-run supply and demand curves of a perfectly competitive seller

FIG. 14.11a. Short-run market supply and demand curves

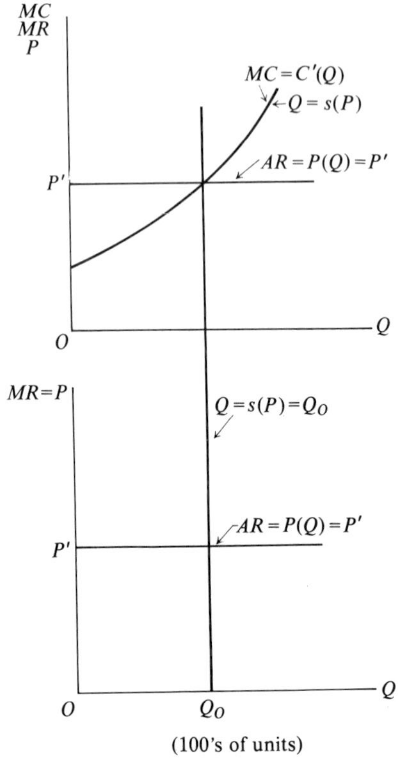

FIG. 14.10b. Perfectly competitive seller's supply curve of a product not stored

FIG. 14.11b. Very short-run market supply curve of a product not stored all sellers of the product is a straight line drawn vertically from the intersection of the short-run market demand and supply curves to the quantity axis of the very short-run market supply curve diagram. In each case, the distance of this line from the origin represents the magnitude of stock (Q_0).

Since market supply is fixed, market price is determined by market demand. As the market demand curve shifts to the right (upward) during the very short-run market period, the marginal revenue curve of a seller shifts upward by increasing its intercept. Each time his marginal revenue (price) curve shifts upward, his total revenue curve shifts upward by increasing its slope. Thus, his very short-run market period profit (= total revenue) is determined solely by market price—that is, by market demand.

Very Short-Run Supply Curve of a Monopolist

Given the demand for his product, the monopolist can vary his price and hence quantity sold from his stock to maximize his total revenue (profit). Assume that his stock is large enough to permit him to sell quantities at which marginal revenue is zero, positive, or negative. He maximizes his total revenue by pricing his product to sell that quantity at which marginal revenue is zero. Marginal revenue is zero at quantity Q' in Figure 14.12. Any quantity less than Q' is sold at a higher price and yields less revenue. Any quantity greater than Q', if it is available, is sold at a lower price and also yields less revenue.

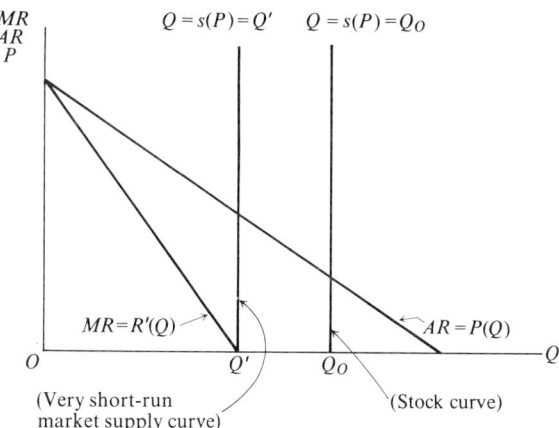

FIG. 14.12. Monopolist's supply curve of a product not stored

The very short-run market supply curve is perfectly inelastic at profit-maximizing quantity sold (Q'). The stock curve is perfectly inelastic at that quantity denoting the short-run rate of production (Q_0). They are the same if the short-run rate of production (stock) is the same as profit-maximizing quantity sold, as in the case of a competitive seller. But the stock of a monopolist may be greater than his very short-run market supply, as in Figure 14.12. Thus, so much may be on hand that to sell it all may result in less than maximum revenue. The "surplus" stock ($Q_0 - Q'$), therefore, may be destroyed if it cannot be stored in anticipation of a profitable future sale.

Long-Run Market Period

The long run may be defined as a time period sufficiently long in duration that a seller varies the input of all of his factors of production. Thus, in the long run, total output varies with the input of all factors, given the state of technology. Several conclusions about cost, equilibrium, and supply follow in sequence from this definition. All factor costs vary with output. All costs are relevant for making a decision with respect to the number of units of output to plan to produce for sale per unit of time in the future. The long-run total cost curve depicts how total cost varies with output as output varies with the input of all factors, given the price of each factor and the state of technology. A seller is in long-run equilibrium when he has determined that output at which he is maximizing his profit, which is his total revenue minus his total cost. Long-run supply reflects all costs of production. The long-run supply curve depicts the quantity supplied at various prices as the planned rate of output is varied by varying the planned rate of input of all factors to maximize profit. Each point on the curve, therefore, represents the equilibrium solution of the long-run problem of determining the quantity of output to plan to produce for sale and the quantity of input to plan to use per unit of time in the future.

Long-Run Supply Curve of a Perfectly Competitive Seller

Hypothetical total revenue and long-run total cost curves of a perfectly competitive seller are presented in Figure 14.13a; and the corresponding marginal and average revenue curves and long-run marginal and average cost curves are presented in Figure 14.13b. Given market price P''', profit is maximized when planned output is Q''', since $MR''' = LMC'''$ at Q'''. Thus (P''', Q''') is one point on his long-run supply curve. Since $MR''' = P''' = LMC'''$ at Q''', this point is also on his long-run marginal cost curve. Other points on his long-run supply curve, such as (P'', Q'') and (P', Q'), may be rationalized and related to his long-run marginal cost curve in the same way by shifting the price (average revenue) and total revenue curves. At the intersection of his long-run marginal and average cost curves, equilibrium output is Q'; and since $P' = LAC'$, his profit is zero. His profit is negative if $P < LAC$ at equilibrium output: total revenue (PQ) is not sufficient to cover total cost ($LAC \cdot Q$). His negative profit is eliminated in the long run by discontinuing production. A perfectly competitive seller's long-run supply curve is thus the positively sloped portion of his long-run marginal cost curve beginning at its intersection with his long-run average cost curve.

Assuming freedom of entry and exit, a seller's long-run supply curve contains *one* stable price and quantity point—the point at which profit is zero. A higher price results in a profit which, through freedom of new sellers, leads to a decrease in price to its zero-profit level. A lower price results in a loss which, through the exit of sellers, leads to an increase in price to its zero-profit level. Since profit is zero in the long run when $MR = P = SMC = SAC = LMC = LAC$, when a perfectly competitive seller is in long-run stable equilibrium, he has built the least-cost plant (absolute minimum long-run average cost) and is operating it at its least-cost level of output (absolute minimum short-run average cost).

This principle may be seen from an analysis of Figures 14.14a and 14.14b. Price P''' in Figure 14.14a is determined by the intersection of the short-run

FIG. 14.13a. Long-run profit maximization of a perfectly competitive seller of a product

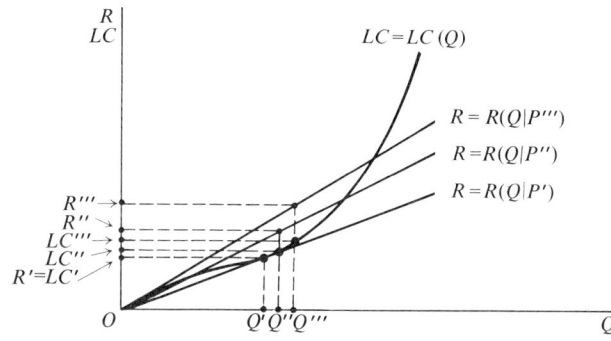

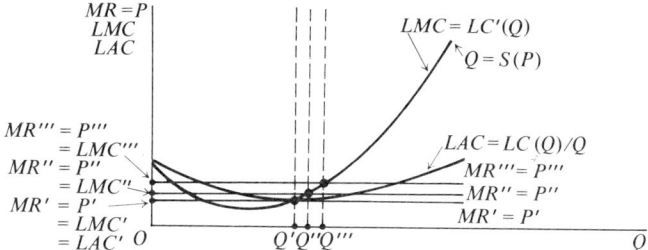

FIG. 14.13b. Long-run supply curve of a product of a perfectly competitive seller

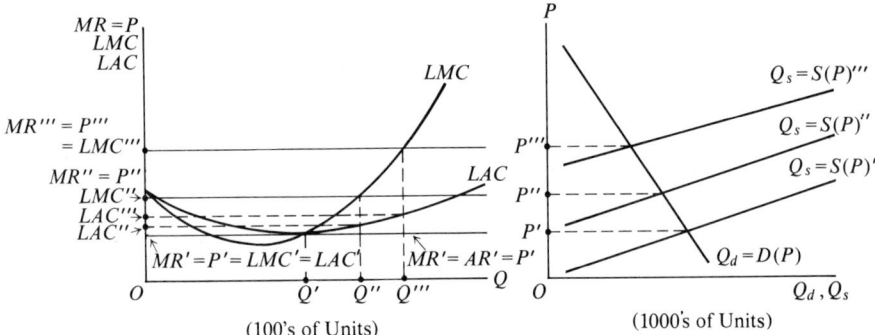

FIG. 14.14a. Long-run supply curve of a product of a perfectly competitive seller

FIG. 14.14b. Short-run market supply and demand

market supply and demand curves of Figure 14.14b. Given P''', the seller makes a maximum profit at Q''', where $MR''' = LMC'''$. Profit per unit of Q''' is $P''' - LAC'''$. Profit induces an increase in the number of sellers in the industry. As a consequence, industry supply increases at the prevailing price (P'''). This increase in supply effects a decrease in market price to (say) P''. The seller still makes a profit: $P'' > LAC''$ at Q''. Market supply increases again via new sellers entering the industry seeking profit. Market price decreases until new sellers have no inducement to enter the industry—that is, until profit is zero at $P' = LAC'$.[7]

Long-Run Supply Curve of a Perfectly Competitive Industry

To repeat, given freedom of entry and exit, a seller in a perfectly competitive industry is in long-run stable equilibrium at that price and output corresponding to the minimum point on his long-run average cost curve (point (P', Q') in Figure 14.14a). Consequently, an industry of n identical sellers is in long-run equilibrium at the same price (P') and at the output ($n \cdot Q'$). Other points on the long-run industry supply curve are derived by increasing market price and ascertaining what happens to long-run stable equilibrium price as industry output increases. As market price increases, industry output increases as more sellers enter the industry (that is, as n increases) in search of the resulting profit. As industry output increases, the price of input may remain constant, increase, or decrease. Thus, long-run stable equilibrium price of a seller may remain constant, increase, or decrease. The long-run supply curve of a perfectly competitive industry, therefore, may have a zero slope (constant-cost industry), positive slope (increasing-cost industry), or negative slope (decreasing-cost industry), assuming freedom of entry and exit.

Constant-Cost Industry

Long-run stable equilibrium price remains constant if the price of input does not change with increases in industry output due to increases in the number of sellers in the industry. In this case, a seller is subject neither to external economies nor to external diseconomies. In other words, his long-run average cost curve does not shift as n increases.

As seen in Figure 14.15b, industry demand curve $Q_d = D(P)'$ intersects short-run industry supply curve $Q_s = S(P)'$ at P'. As seen in Figure 14.15a, a seller is in long-run stable equilibrium at P' producing Q'. Thus, his industry is in long-run equilibrium at P' producing $(n' \cdot Q')$.

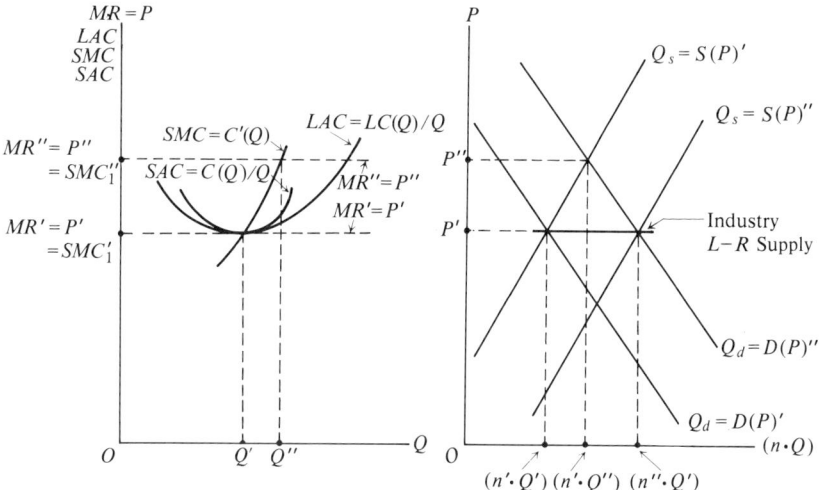

FIG. 14.15a. No external economies or diseconomies

FIG. 14.15b. Long-run supply curve of a constant-cost industry

When industry demand increases to $Q_d = D(P)''$, market price increases to P''. The seller maximizes profit in the short run by increasing output from his present plant, by moving up his short-run marginal cost curve, $SMC = C'(Q)$, from Q' to Q''. As all sellers increase output in the short run, industry output increases along the present industry short-run supply curve, $Q_s = S(P)'$, from $(n' \cdot Q')$ to $(n' \cdot Q'')$. New sellers are attracted to the industry by the profitable price. Supply curve $Q_s = S(P)'$ shifts to the right to become $Q_s = S(P)''$ because of the resulting increase in industry supply. Price decreases to P', where $Q_d = Q_s$. The seller maximizes profit in the short run by decreasing output from his present plant, by moving down his short-run marginal cost curve, $SMC = C'(Q)$, from Q'' to Q'. Profit is zero; no new sellers enter the industry. Long-run equilibrium industry output is $(n'' \cdot Q')$.

The increase in industry output of $(n'' \cdot Q') - (n' \cdot Q')$ is the result of sellers entering the industry because of the initial increase in price. The points of equilibrium are on the zero-sloped industry long-run supply curve.

Increasing-Cost Industry

Long-run stable equilibrium price increases if the price of input increases with increases in industry output due to increases in the number of sellers in the industry. In this case, a seller is subject to external diseconomies. In other words, his long-run average cost curve shifts upward as n increases.

When industry demand increases from $Q_d = D(P)'$ to $Q_d = D(P)''$ in Figure 14.16b, market price initially increases from P' to P''. Consequently, the seller initially increases output from Q' to Q'' in Figure 14.16a. Thus industry output initially increases from $(n' \cdot Q')$ to $(n' \cdot Q'')$. Present sellers make a short-run profit. Therefore, new sellers enter the industry, thereby increasing industry supply. Before market price decreases to P', the price of input increases. Curve $LAC = LC(Q)/Q'$ shifts upward to become $LAC = LC(Q)/Q''$. The new long-run stable equilibrium price is P''', which is greater than P'. Hence the new industry short-run supply curve, $Q_s = S(P)''$, intersects $Q_d = D(P)''$ at P'''. The seller's long-run stable equilibrium output again is Q'. Long-run equilibrium industry output is $(n'' \cdot Q')$. The increase in industry output of $(n'' \cdot Q') - (n' \cdot Q')$ is the result of sellers entering the industry because of the initial increase in price and leaving the industry

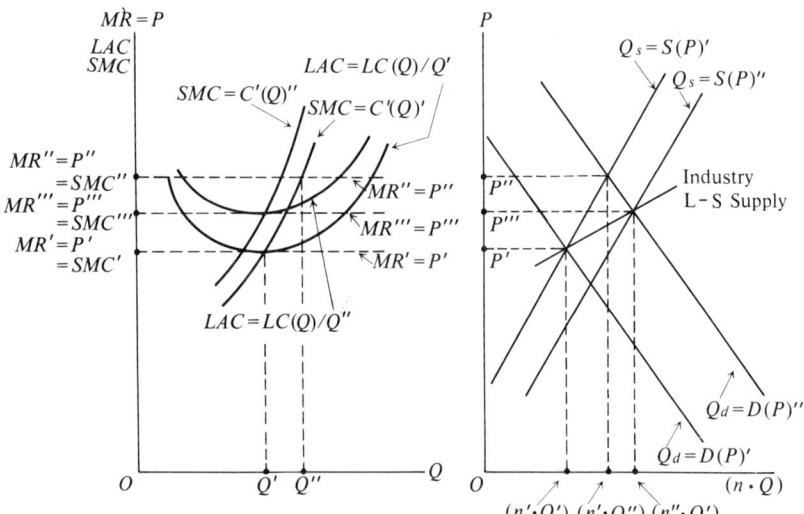

FIG. 14.16a. External diseconomies

FIG. 14.16b. Long-run supply curve of an increasing-cost industry

because of the increase in input costs. The points of equilibrium are on the positively-sloped industry long-run supply curve.

Decreasing-Cost Industry

Long-run stable equilibrium price decreases if the price of input decreases with increases in industry output due to increases in the number of sellers in the industry. In this case, a seller is subject to external economies. In other words, his long-run average cost curve shifts downward as n increases.

When demand increases from $Q_d = D(P)'$ to $Q_d = D(P)''$ in Figure 14.17b, market price initially increases from P' to P''. Consequently, the seller initially increases output from Q' to Q'' in Figure 14.17a. Thus industry output initially increases from $(n' \cdot Q')$ to $(n' \cdot Q'')$. Present sellers make a short-run profit. Therefore, new sellers enter the industry, thereby increasing industry supply. Market price decreases below P', for the price of input decreases. Curve $LAC = LC(Q)/Q'$ shifts downward to become $LAC = LC(Q)/Q''$. The new long-run stable equilibrium price is P''', which is less than P'. Hence the new industry short-run supply curve, $Q_s = S(P)''$, intersects $Q_d = D(P)''$ at P'''. By assumption, the seller's long-run stable equilibrium output again is Q'. Long-run equilibrium industry output is $(n'' \cdot Q')$. The increase in industry output of $(n'' \cdot Q') - (n' \cdot Q')$ is the result of sellers entering the industry because of the initial increase in price and the decrease in input costs. The points of equilibrium are on the negatively-sloped industry long-run supply curve.

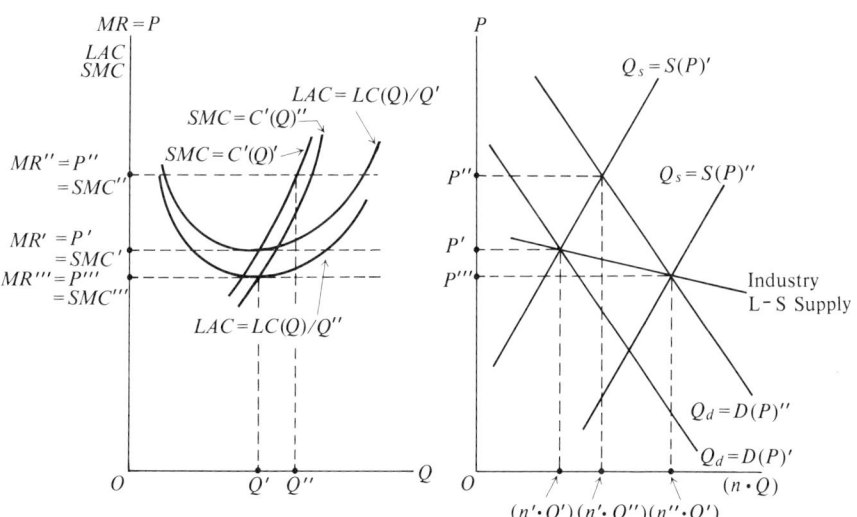

FIG. 14.17a. External economies

FIG. 14.17b. Long-run supply curve of a decreasing-cost industry

Long-Run "Supply Curve" of a Monopolist

Hypothetical total revenue and long-run total cost curves of a monopolist are drawn in Figure 14.18a. Both curves are nonlinear and have zero revenue and cost intercepts. The corresponding marginal and average curves are drawn in Figure 14.18b.

According to Figures 14.18a and 14.18b, given market demand $AR = P(Q)'$, quantity produced is Q' since $MR' = LMC'$ at Q'. Note that at Q' curve SAC_1 is tangent to curve LAC. Thus the optimal plant size to produce Q' is denoted by curve SAC_1. Note also that the price of Q' is P'. Thus, the point (P', Q') is on *a* long-run "supply curve." Other points on *this* long-run

FIG. 14.18a. Long-run profit maximization of a monopolist

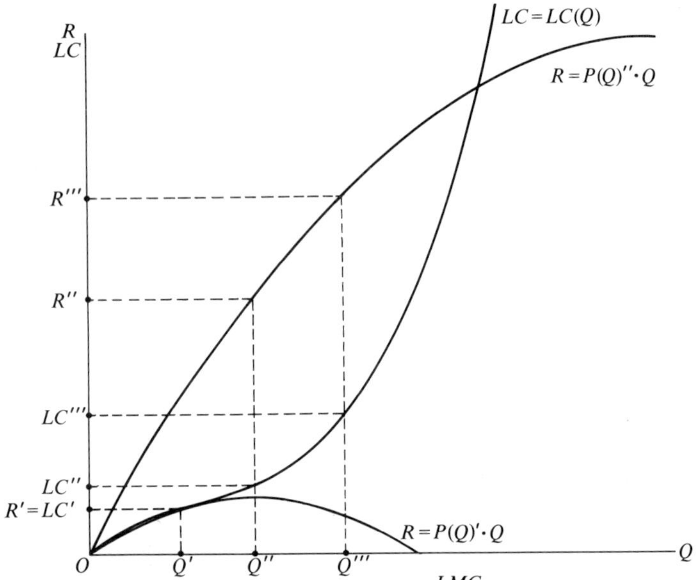

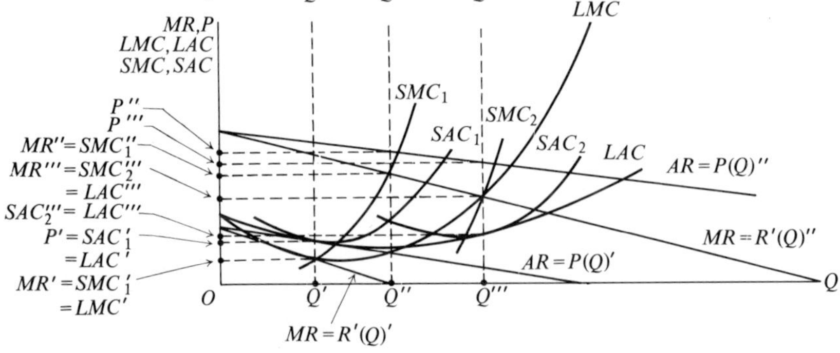

FIG. 14.18b. Long-run "supply curve" of a product of a monopolist

"supply-curve" may be rationalized in the same way as points on a short-run "supply curve"; that is, by shifting the revenue curves upward, ascertaining the Q values at which $MR = LMC$, and then plotting these Q values against the corresponding P values.

In Figure 14.18b, any quantity along market demand curve $AR = P(Q)'$ other than Q' results in a negative profit, a loss. Thus any quantity along a lower market demand curve (not drawn) results in a loss at all output levels and hence a discontinuance of production in the long run.[8] Conversely, as seen in Figure 14.18b, several output levels along a higher market demand curve, such as $AR = P(Q)''$, result in a profit. Given this higher market demand curve, profit is maximized in the short run by producing Q'' from plant SAC_1 since $MR'' = SMC''_1$ at Q''. However, in the long run, profit is maximized by producing output Q''' from plant SAC_2 since $MR''' = LMC''' = SMC'''_2$ at Q'''.

Long-Run Equilibrium of a Multi-Plant Monopolist

Assuming freedom of entry and exit, a perfectly competitive seller is in long-run stable equilibrium at a price and output corresponding to the low point on his long-run average cost curve (see Figure 14.14a). Thus he produces his product at absolute minimum long-run and short-run average cost; his profit is zero. In contrast, a single-plant monopolist may be in long-run equilibrium at an output corresponding to any point on his long-run average cost curve, including (for no particular reason) the low point; his profit may be positive or zero (see Figure 14.18b). In other words, unlike a single-plant monopolist, a perfectly competitive seller tends to build the least-cost plant and to operate it at its least-cost level. However, a multi-plant monopolist who has identical plants tends to do the same thing, for he is in

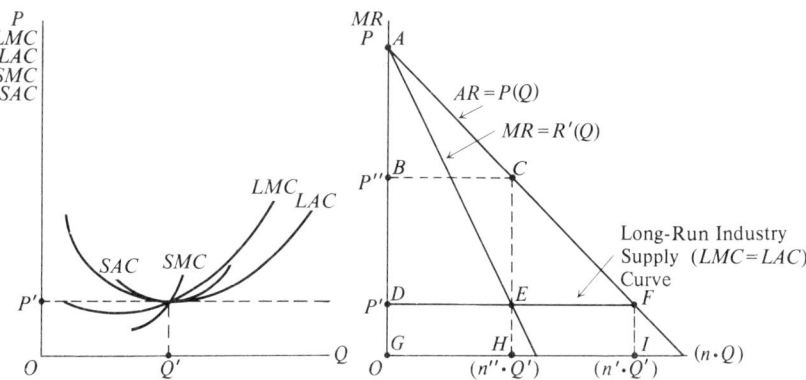

FIG. 14.19a. Long-run equilibrium of a multi-plant monopolist

FIG. 14.19b. Purchasers' and sellers' surplus and welfare loss long-run equilibrium at an output corresponding to the low point on each of his plant long-run average cost curves.

To see this, consider Figure 14.19a, according to which each seller in a perfectly competitive constant-cost industry is in long-run stable equilibrium at (Q', P'). Consequently, as seen in Figure 14.19b, the industry is in long-run equilibrium at $(n' \cdot Q', P')$, since quantity demanded equals quantity supplied at that point. Now, let one seller take control of the n' plants, thereby becoming a monopolist. He still operates each plant at an output corresponding to the low point on its long-run average cost curve. Therefore, each plant is a least-cost plant and is operated at its least-cost level of output. But he operates fewer plants, for he decreases his output from $(n' \cdot Q')$ to $(n'' \cdot Q')$, where long-run marginal cost equals marginal revenue, in order to maximize his profit at price P'' ($> P'$).

SUMMARY

A seller is in equilibrium with respect to each point on his supply curve. When he is in equilibrium, he is maximizing his profit $(R - C)$ or minimizing his loss $(C - R)$. In the short-run market period, his profit is maximized or his loss is minimized when he is maximizing his net revenue $(R - VC)$. Thus his short-run supply curve depicts his quantity supplied at various prices as he varies his current rate of output by varying his current rate of input of variable factors to maximize his net revenue. The short-run supply curve of a perfectly competitive seller is the positively-sloped portion of his short-run marginal cost curve beginning at its intersection with his average variable cost curve. But the short-run marginal cost curve of a monopolist is not his short-run "supply curve," for his equilibrium output is denoted by his short-run marginal cost curve and his equilibrium price is denoted by his (higher) average revenue curve. Moreover, his short-run "supply curve" is not a unique curve, for a "supply curve" is derived analytically for each pattern of change in demand for his product.

Aggregate equilibrium output of a multi-plant monopolist is allocated according to the equimarginal principle that the last unit produced in one plant must add as much to total cost as the last unit produced in every other plant—that marginal cost must be equal in all plants. Similarly, aggregate equilibrium output of a multi-market monopolist is allocated according to the equimarginal principle that the last unit sold in one market must add as much to total revenue as the last unit sold in every other market—that marginal revenue must be equal in all markets.

In the very short-run market period, profit from a product that is not stored is maximized when the seller maximizes his total revenue—that is, sells that quantity of his stock at which his total revenue is a maximum. Thus his very short-run supply curve depicts his quantity supplied at various prices from his stock. The very short-run supply curve of a perfectly competitive seller is the same as his stock curve, which is a straight line drawn vertically from the intersection of his marginal revenue and short-run marginal cost curves to the quantity axis of his very short-run market period diagram to denote his current stock. The stock curve of a monopolist is also a straight line drawn vertically from the intersection of his marginal revenue and short-run marginal cost curves to the quantity axis of his very short-run market period diagram to denote his current stock, but his stock curve is his very short-run supply curve only if the stock level is the same as revenue-maximizing quantity sold.

In the long-run market period, profit is maximized when the seller is maximizing the surplus of revenue over cost. Thus his long-run supply curve depicts his quantity supplied at various prices as he varies his planned rate of output by varying his planned rate of input of all factors to maximize his profit. The long-run supply curve of a perfectly competitive seller is the positively-sloped portion of his long-run marginal cost curve beginning at its intersection with his long-run average cost curve. Assuming freedom of entry and exit, the long-run "supply curve" of a perfectly competitive seller contains *one* stable price and quantity point — the point at which profit is zero. Thus, in this context, a perfectly competitive seller is in stable long-run equilibrium at a price and output corresponding to the low point on his long-run average cost curve; he produces his product in the long run at absolute minimum long-run and short-run average cost. Assuming freedom of entry and exit, the long-run supply curve of an industry is a zero-sloped curve in the case of a constant-cost industry, a positively-sloped curve in the case of an increasing-cost industry, and a negatively-sloped curve in the case of a decreasing-cost industry. The long-run "supply curve" of a monopolist is analyzed in the same way as his short-run "supply curve", except that now the analysis is in reference to his long-run marginal cost curve. A single-plant monopolist may be in long-run stable equilibrium at an output corresponding to any point on his long-run average cost curve, but a multi-plant monopolist who has identical plants is in long-run stable equilibrium at an output corresponding to the low point on each of his plant long-run average cost curves.

Questions

1. Differentiate the short-run, very short-run, and long-run market periods in terms of the period cost curves of a seller—that is, in terms of the period supply curves of a seller.

2. Use diagrams to prove by analysis of the equilibrium principle that the short-run supply curve of a perfectly competitive seller is the relevant portion of his short-run marginal cost curve. What is the "relevant portion"? Why? In your analysis, identify equilibrium price, marginal revenue, average revenue, total revenue, marginal cost, average total cost, total cost, average variable cost, total variable cost, profit, and net revenue.

3. Use diagrams to prove by analysis of the equilibrium principle that the short-run "supply curve" of a monopolist is not his short-run marginal cost curve. Explain in detail why "supply curve" is in quotation marks. In your analysis, identify equilibrium price, marginal revenue, average revenue, total revenue, marginal cost, average total cost, total cost, average variable cost, total variable cost, profit, and net revenue.

4. Use diagrams to prove by analysis of the equimarginal principle that in equilibrium a monopolist may produce his product in two or more plants, produce a different output in each plant, and incur a different cost per unit for the same plant output.

5. Use diagrams to prove by analysis of the equimarginal principle that in equilibrium a monopolist may produce his product for two or more separate markets, sell a different quantity of his output in each market, and charge a different price for the same market quantity.

6. Why might a producer not store his goods? Is a service storable?

7. Use diagrams to prove by analysis of the equilibrium principle that the very short-run supply curve of a perfectly competitive seller is parallel to the price axis and that his stock curve is the same as his supply curve. What determines market price?

8. Use diagrams to prove by analysis of the equilibrium principle that the very short-run supply curve of a monopolist is parallel to the price axis at profit-maximizing quantity sold and that his stock curve may not be the same as his supply curve.

9. Use diagrams to prove by analysis of the equilibrium principle that the long-run supply curve of a perfectly competitive seller is the relevant portion of his long-run marginal cost curve. What is the "relevant portion"? Why?

10. Use diagrams to prove by analysis of the equilibrium principle that, assuming freedom of entry and exit, (a) the long-run supply curve of a perfectly competitive seller contains one stable price and output point and (b) when the seller is in long-run stable equilibrium, he has built the least-cost plant and is operating it at its least-cost level of output.

11. Use diagrams to prove by analysis of the equilibrium principle that the long-run supply curve of a perfectly competitive industry may have (a) a zero slope, (b) a positive slope, or (c) a negative slope, assuming freedom of entry and exit.

12. Use diagrams to prove by analysis of the equilibrium principle that (a) the long-run "supply curve" of a monopolist is not his long-run marginal cost curve and (b) a single-plant monopolist may be in long-run equilibrium at an output corresponding to any point on his long-run average cost curve.

13. Use diagrams to prove by analysis of the equilibrium principle that a multi-plant monopolist whose plants are identical is in long-run equilibrium at an output corresponding to the low point on each of his plant long-run average cost curves.

SELECTED READINGS

Coase, R. H. "The Nature of the Firm," *Economica*, New Series; IV (1937), pp. 386–405. Reprinted in The American Economic Association. *Readings in Price Theory*. Edited by George J. Stigler and Kenneth E. Boulding. Homewood, Illinois: Richard D. Irwin, Inc., 1952, pp. 331–351.

Scitovsky, T. "A Note on Profit Maximization and its Implications," *The Review of Economic Studies*, XI (1943), pp. 57–60. Reprinted in The American Economic Association. *Readings in Price Theory, ibid.*, pp. 352–358.

Hicks, J. R. "Annual Survey of Economic Theory: The Theory of Monopoly," *Econometrica*, III (1935), pp. 1–20. Reprinted in The American Economic Association. *Readings in Price Theory, ibid.*, pp. 361–383.

Kaldor, Nicholas. "Market Imperfection and Excess Capacity," *Economica*, New Series; II (1935), pp. 33–50. Reprinted in The American Economic Association. *Readings in Price Theory, ibid.*, pp. 384–403.

Machlup, Fritz. "Monopoly and Competition: A Classification of Market Positions," *American Economic Review*, XXXVIII (September 1937), pp. 445–451. Reprinted in Kamerschen, D. R. (editor). *Readings in Microeconomics*. Cleveland, Ohio: The World Publishing Company, 1967, pp. 299–306.

Stigler, G. J. "The Statistics of Monopoly and Merger," *The Journal of Political Economy*, XLIV (February 1956), pp. 33–40. Reprinted in Kamerschen, *ibid.*, pp. 332–343.

APPENDIX: Purchaser's and Sellers' Surplus and Net Walfare Loss

In the case of a constant cost industry that is perfectly competitive, the long-run industry supply curve in parallel to the quantity axis. This curve represents constant long-run marginal and average cost of the industry as it adjusts to changes in market demand by changing the number of its single-plant sellers to change its aggregate output. This same curve in the case of a multi-plant monopolist, however, represents constant long-run marginal and average cost of the monopolist as he adjusts to changes in market demand by changing the number of his plants to change his aggregate output. The long-run marginal (= average) cost curve drawn in Figure 14.19b is thus the same for monopoly and perfect competition. The marginal and average revenue curves drawn in Figure 14.19b are also the same for monopoly and perfect competition. These two market structures, therefore, may be compared via Figure 14.19b. The comparison is made via the concepts of purchasers' and sellers' surplus and net welfare loss, which are based upon the Marshallian market model.

Purchasers' Surplus

The maximum amount of money purchasers are willing to pay for a given quantity of a product is equal to the summation of the maximum price they are willing to pay for each unit of the quantity. The market demand curve denotes the maximum price purchasers are willing to pay for each unit of a specified quantity. Thus the area under the market demand curve at a specified quantity represents the maximum amount of money purchasers are willing to pay for that quantity. The amount of money purchasers pay for a specified quantity of a product is equal to that quantity multiplied by the price of that quantity. Thus the area of the price-quantity rectangle at a specified quantity represents the amount of money purchasers pay for that quantity. Purchasers' or consumers' surplus is the difference between the maximum amount of money purchasers are willing to pay and the amount of money they pay for a specified quantity.

In Figure 14.19b (page 255), assuming perfect competition, the specified quantity is $(n' \cdot Q')$ since the market is in long-run equilibrium at that quantity at which quantity demanded equals long-run quantity supplied. The maximum amount of money pur-

260 DETERMINATION OF PRICE AND QUANTITY IN A PRODUCT MARKET

chasers are willing to pay for this quantity is represented by area $AFIG$. And the amount of money purchasers pay for this quantity is represented by area $DFIG$. Thus purchasers' surplus is represented by area AFD ($= AFIG - DFIG$).

But assuming monopoly, the specified quantity is $(n'' \cdot Q')$ since the monopolist is in long-run equilibrium at that quantity at which marginal revenue equals long-run marginal cost. The maximum amount of money purchasers are willing to pay for this quantity is represented by area $ACHG$. And the amount of money purchasers pay for this quantity is represented by area $BCHG$. Thus purchasers' surplus is represented by area ACB ($= ACHG - BCHG$). Since $AFD > ACB$, purchasers lose surplus because of monopoly. The amount of the loss in purchasers' surplus is represented by area $BCFD$ ($= AFD - ACB$).

Sellers' Surplus

The minimum amount of money sellers are willing to accept for a specified quantity of a product is equal to the summation of the minimum price they are willing to accept for each unit of that quantity. The market (or industry) supply curve denotes the minimum price sellers are willing to accept for each unit of a specified quantity. Thus the area under the market supply curve at a specified quantity represents the minimum amount of money sellers are willing to accept for that quantity. The amount of money sellers receive for a specified quantity of a product is equal to that quantity times the price of that quantity. Thus the area of the price-quantity rectangle at a specified quantity represents the amount of money sellers receive for that quantity. Sellers' surplus is the difference between the minimum amount of money sellers are willing to accept and the amount of money they receive for a specified quantity.

In Figure 14.19b, assuming perfect competition, the specified quantity is $(n' \cdot Q')$ since the market is in long-run equilibrium at that quantity at which quantity demanded equals long-run quantity supplied. The minimum amount of money sellers are willing to accept for this quantity is represented by area $DFIG$. And the amount of money sellers receive for this quantity is represented by area $DFIG$. Thus sellers' surplus is zero.

But assuming monopoly, the specified quantity is $(n'' \cdot Q')$ since the monopolist is in long-run equilibrium at that quantity at which marginal revenue equals long-run marginal cost. The minimum amount of money the monopolist is willing to accept for this quantity is represented by area $DEHG$. And the amount of money the monopolist receives for this quantity is represented by area $BCHG$. Thus the monopolist's surplus (profit) is represented by area $BCED$ ($= BCHG - DEHG$). Since $BCED > 0$, the monopolist gains surplus because of his monopoly.

Net Welfare Loss

To summarize, purchasers' surplus is less in a monopolistic market than in a perfectly competitive market. But sellers' surplus is greater in a monopolistic market than in a perfectly competitive market. Specifically, in a perfectly competitive market, the surplus of purchasers is the triangle AFD in Figure 14.19b. But in a monopolistic market, it is the triangle ACB. Thus, under monopoly, purchasers lose the area $BCFD$. Moreover, given a perfectly competitive market and a horizontal supply curve, the surplus of sellers is zero. But given a monopolistic market, the surplus (profit) of the one seller is the rectangle $BCED$, representing the excess of total revenue over total cost. Consequently, under monopoly, the net welfare loss is the triangle CFE; purchasers lose more than the seller's gain.

SUMMARY

The long-run marginal cost curve of a multi-plant monopolist who has identical plants is parallel to the quantity axis. This curve is the same as the long-run industry supply curve of a constant-cost perfectly competitive industry. Thus, since the marginal and average revenue curves are also the same, these two market structures are comparable. Purchasers' or consumers' surplus is the difference between the maximum amount of money purchasers are willing to pay and the amount of money they pay for a specified quantity. Purchasers' surplus is less in a monopolistic market than in a perfectly competitive market. Sellers' surplus is the difference between the minimum amount of money sellers are willing to accept and the amount of money they receive for a specified quantity. Sellers' surplus is greater in a monopolistic market than in a perfectly competitive market. But purchasers lose more than the seller(s) gains, the difference of which is called net welfare loss.

NOTES

[1] The marginal cost curve must intersect the marginal revenue curve from below. If the marginal cost curve intersected the marginal revenue curve from above, negative profit (loss) would be maximized at that quantity at which marginal cost equals marginal revenue.

[2] This definition corresponds to stage II of production (see Chapter 7, pp. 123–124). See O. P. Tangri, "Omissions in the Treatment of the Law of Variable Proportions," *The American Economic Review*, LVI: 3 (June 1966), pp. 484–492, for a discussion of the application of the concept of stages of production to the cost function.

[3] See J. M. Henderson and R. E. Quandt, *Microeconomic Theory* (New York: McGraw-Hill Book Company, 1958), p. 90. Notice that when net revenue is zero or positive the marginal cost curve is intersecting the marginal revenue curve from below.

[4] The monopolist's marginal cost curve depicts the minimum prices imposed upon him that he is willing to continue to accept, called supply price (P_s), for various equilibrium quantities sold (Q). The relation between Q and P_s is called the supply price curve, and is denoted by $P_s = P_s(Q)$. Thus, since supply price equals marginal cost at equilibrium quantity sold, his marginal cost curve is his supply price curve. His supply price curve is therefore a unique curve, but his "supply curve" is not a unique curve, as seen in the next paragraph.

[5] The formula used in (1) and (2) is derived on page 110. To verbalize (1) through (6), the larger the $|\varepsilon|$, the smaller the ratio $|1/\varepsilon|$. The smaller this ratio, the larger the difference $(1 - 1/|\varepsilon|)$. The larger this difference, the larger the product $p(1 - 1/|\varepsilon|)$. Thus, since $(1 - 1/|\varepsilon|)$ is larger on the left side than on the right side of (4), p_2 must be larger than p_1 for $p_1(1 - 1/|\varepsilon_1|)$ to equal $p_2(1 - 1/|\varepsilon_2|)$.

[6] However, the wheat farmer has an alternative; he can store his wheat and trade in it. A trader provides a service by storing wheat. His supply price reflects his per unit cost of obtaining wheat and storing it, if he is a profit maximizer. Assume that cost per unit of storing a given amount of wheat is an increasing function of length of period of storage, that he has no carry-over, and that demand is constant throughout the year. Then market price increases during the year by the amount of the increase in storage cost. If this were not true, traders would incur a loss in holding wheat until it is sold. To decrease this loss, they would sell today rather than tomorrow. The result would be a decrease in today's price and an increase in tomorrow's price,

until the price at which a given quantity is sold reflects its per unit cost of storage over time. Thus, given this set of assumptions, market price during the year is predictable with accuracy. The risk to traders of holding wheat during the year, therefore, is minimal. Assume now that demand changes over time and that wheat is carried over from one harvest to the next. Then price fluctuates over time with changes in market supply and demand. Thus price of a future delivery differs from price of a present delivery because of storage cost and changes in expected market demand and supply between the present and future period. A trader must decide whether to bear the risk of a price change. A trader who does not wish to bear risk hedges against a price change. Specifically, he purchases a spot contract for present delivery of wheat to him at the present market price, and simultaneously he sells a future contract for future delivery of the same quantity of wheat to someone else at the present price plus storage cost. A trader who wishes to bear risk speculates on a price change in his favor by purchasing and selling spot and futures contracts. In this context, a trader may provide two services: he may store wheat and bear the risk of a price change. See the market models of George J. Stigler, *The Theory of Price*, 3rd ed. (New York: The Macmillan Company, 1966), pp. 100–102; and L. G. Telser, "Futures Trading and the Storage of Cotton and Wheat," *Journal of Political Economy*, LXVI (June 1958), pp. 233–255.

Products that are stored and periodically reproduced may be sold in spot and futures markets by speculators. A speculator of a different kind is the holder of stored products that are not periodically reproduced—for example, original paintings, first editions, stamps, coins, and shares of stock. The profit-maximizing holder of such a product equates the marginal return and marginal cost of holding it for a period of time. Its marginal cost during a period is its storage cost plus the amount of money that could be earned on an alternative investment—its opportunity cost. Its marginal return during the period is the utility from holding it plus the increase in its price. (See the market model of Stigler, *op. cit.*, pp. 96–98.)

[7] This paragraph contains a presentation of the freedom of entry case. As an exercise, analyze the freedom of exit case.

[8] However, the seller acts rationally in continuing production in the short run, using plant SAC_1, if net revenue is positive at that output at which $MR = SMC_1$.

chapter 15

Equilibrium of Monopolistic-Competitive and Oligopolistic Product Sellers

Monopolistic-Competitive Seller of a Product

A monopolistic-competitive product market is defined as a market in which many sellers sell differentiated but closely related products. The monopolistic aspect of monopolistic-competition theory is based on the assumption of differentiated products. Since the products are differentiated, each monopolistic-competitive seller has a monopoly of his product. But his product is sold in competition with many similar products of his commodity group. Each product of a commodity group is thus a close substitute for the other products of the group. The competitive aspect of monopolistic-competition theory is based on the assumption of many sellers in a commodity group. The number of sellers in a group is so large that each seller can decrease his price within a certain range of values (and thereby increase his quantity sold as some customers of his competitors switch to his product) while his competitors keep their prices constant. That is, a small change in the price charged by one seller has such a small influence on the quantity sold of each of his large number of competitors that they do not react by changing their prices. Thus the revenue function of one seller is independent of the revenue functions of his competitors.

Demand Curve Facing a Monopolistic-Competitive Seller

Since the number of sellers in a commodity group is so large that each acts independently, the demand curve facing a monopolistic-competitive seller may be drawn. The greater the number and goodness of substitutes, the greater the coefficient of price elasticity of demand for a product at a specified price. The product of a monopolistic-competitive seller has a large number of imperfect but close substitutes; the product of a competitive seller has a large number of perfect substitutes; the product of a monopolistic seller has no close substitutes. Thus the demand curve facing a monopolistic-competitive seller is more elastic at a specified price than is the demand curve facing a monopolistic seller, but is less elastic at a specified price than is the demand curve facing a competitive seller.

Short-Run Equilibrium

Given the assumption that the demand curve facing a seller may be drawn and has a negative slope, in the short run a monopolistic-competitive seller acts as a monopolist seeking equilibrium. He produces and sells his product according to the profit-maximizing principle that the last unit produced should add as much to total revenue as to total cost—that marginal revenue should equal marginal cost. As seen in Figure 14.7 (page 241), given demand curve $AR = P(Q)''$, he sells output Q'' at price P'', making a profit of $(P'' \cdot Q'') - (AC'' \cdot Q'')$. He may attempt to increase his profit via real or fancied changes in the quality of his product, sales promotion campaigns,[1] and changes in distribution and location.[2] In these cases, profit changes with shifts in his revenue and cost curves.

Long-Run Equilibrium

The long-run competitive aspect of monopolistic-competition theory is based on the assumption of freedom of entry and exit. Since sellers are free to enter and leave a market, a monopolistic-competitive seller is in long-run stable equilibrium at an output-price coordinate on the negatively-sloped portion of his long-run average cost curve. To shorten the analysis, assume that the entry of new sellers does not result in external economies or diseconomies for existing sellers. Given this assumption, the long-run average cost curve of an existing seller does not shift with changes in the number of sellers in his group. Figure 15.1 shows that, given demand $AR = P(Q)'$ for a seller's product, he maximizes profit in the long run by producing output Q' since $MR' = LMC'$ at Q'. He sells Q' at his demand price, P'. His profit from Q' is $(P' \cdot Q') - (LAC' \cdot Q')$. His profit induces sellers of differentiated but closely related products to enter his commodity group. The entry of new sellers results in a decrease in demand for his product, for he cannot continue to sell the same quantity at the same price if he loses some of his customers. His demand curve shifts to the left to become $AR = P(Q)''$. Quantity produced now is Q'' since $MR'' = LMC''$ at Q''. Output Q'' is sold at demand price P''. He is in long-run stable equilibrium since profit is zero at Q''—that is, $(P'' \cdot Q'') = (LAC'' \cdot Q'')$. Hence new sellers do not enter his commodity group.

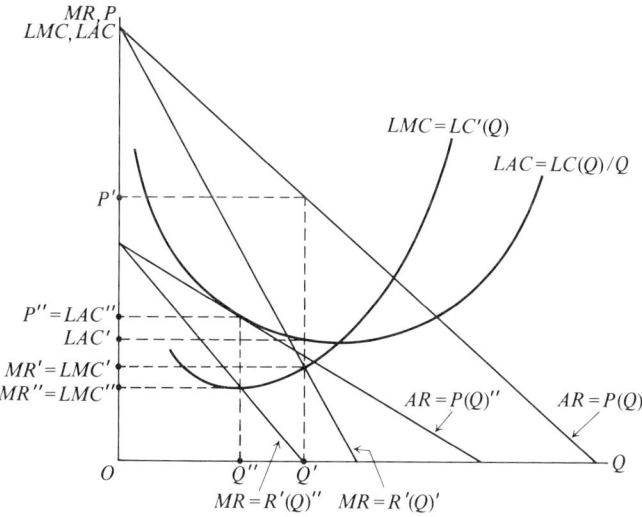

FIG. 15.1. Long-run profit maximization of a monopolistic-competitive seller: freedom of entry case.

Interdependence of Demand Curves Model

The analysis of monopolistic-competition to this point has been based on the assumption that the demand for one seller's product is independent of the demand for products of other existing sellers of his group—that a seller can change his price without the other existing sellers changing their prices. Assume now that the demand for one seller's product is dependent upon the demand for products of other sellers of his group—that a seller cannot change his price as he wishes without the other existing sellers changing their prices.

Specifically, let a seller make a profit by producing Q' at P' in Figure 15.2; and let him make a larger profit by decreasing his price and increasing his quantity according to the curve labeled $ar = p(q)'$. He thinks that $ar = p(q)'$ is his demand curve; thus it is called his subjective demand curve. As he decreases his price, his competitors decrease their prices also to keep all prices of the group in the same proportional relationship to one another. The given seller finds, therefore, that he has not moved down his subjective demand curve. Instead, he finds that he has moved down his proportional demand curve, $AR = P(Q)$. He had hoped to sell more to his present customers per unit of time and to induce customers of other sellers to switch to his product. But the only increase in quantity sold was to his present customers. His profit has not increased but decreased. Assume that he does not learn from this experience, that he still does not recognize that his real demand curve is his proportional demand curve. Let him think that he can increase his profit by decreasing his price and increasing his quantity

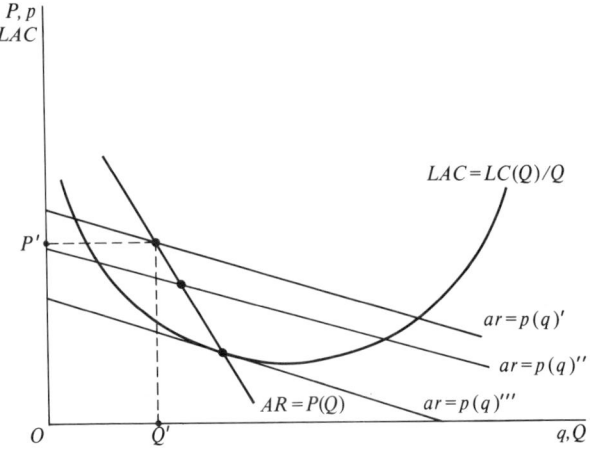

FIG. 15.2. Long-run profit maximization of a monopolistic-competitive seller: interdependence of demand curves case

according to his new subjective demand curve, $ar = p(q)''$. Once again competitors decrease their prices. His subjective demand curve again slides down his proportional demand curve. Profit is decreased once again. Since profit cannot fall below zero in the long run if he is to remain in operation, his long-run stable equilibrium again is a (Q, P) point at which $P = LAC$. Thus short-sighted price cutting results in the same conclusion as freedom of entry.

Oligopolistic Seller of a Product

An oligopolistic product market is characterized by a few sellers of identical or differentiated products considered as a set. The steel industry is an oligopoly of a few sellers selling identical products. The automobile industry is an oligopoly of a few sellers selling differentiated products. The differentiated products of this industry are sufficiently similar to one another that, when they are considered as a set, they may be referred to as a commodity. A Chevrolet, Ford, or Plymouth is a product; an automobile is a commodity. Each oligopolistic seller has some control over the price of his product. He markets his product via advertising and quality rivalry, and administers his price rather than letting it be freely determined by market supply and demand. Entry into an oligopolistic industry (for example, the automobile industry) may be difficult, if not impossible. The essence of oligopoly is that the market is entirely personal to sellers. They are in direct competition with one another. They are potentially intense rivals of one another in the ordinary meaning of the word. They are interdependent with one another.

The revenue function of a seller is nonlinear and interdependent with the revenue functions of other sellers in his industry. His demand (average revenue) curve can be drawn only if the pattern of reaction of other sellers to a price or quantity change on his part is known. When drawn, it is less elastic at any given price than the demand curve of a monopolistic-competitive seller. Oligopoly models that directly consider the revenue function may be classified as classical incapable-of-learning, classical capable-of-learning, modern collusion, and modern non-profit-maximizing models.

Classical Incapable-of-Learning Duopoly Models

A duopoly is an oligopoly of two sellers. The results of a duopoly model supposedly may be extended to three or more sellers without loss of generality. The classical incapable-of-learning duopoly models are those of Augustin Cournot, Joseph Bertrand, and F. Y. Edgeworth. To present their models, assume that each duopolist sells an identical product, such as mineral water from two mineral springs, and that marginal cost of the product is zero. The time period is the very short-run market period. They draw different conclusions about equilibrium price and quantity of the homogeneous product because they make different behavioral assumptions concerning each seller's expectations of the pricing and output policies of the other seller.

Cournot's Model [3]

Cournot assumed that each seller expects the other seller never to change his output, even though he repeatedly observes him do so, and sets his own output so as to maximize his profit by maximizing his revenue. Thus the key policy variable is output. Each seller sets his output to maximize his profit (revenue) and never learns that, by assuming his rival does not change his output, he ends up not maximizing his profit. The end result is that market price decreases and market output increases toward competitive levels. The greater the number of sellers, the closer market price and output approach their competitive levels. Market price and output are stable in equilibrium.

The market for mineral water is depicted by the market demand curve, $AR = P(Q)$, and the market marginal revenue curve, $MR = R'(Q)$, in Figure 15.3. The initial seller (A) acts as a monopolist. To maximize profit, he sells that quantity, $Q' = 500$, at which marginal revenue equals marginal cost equals zero. The price of Q' is P'. The profit (revenue) from Q' is $P' \cdot Q'$. His revenue function initially is the revenue function of a monopolist.

Output Q', where $MR = MC = 0$, is monopoly output. Competitive

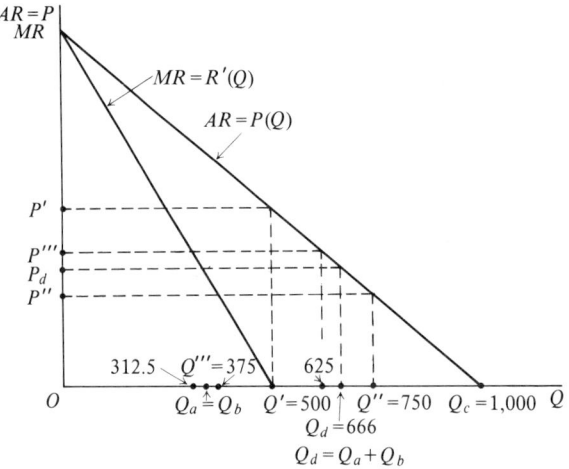

FIG. 15.3. Cournot's model

output is the quantity intercept of the market demand curve, for it is that quantity, $Q_c = 2Q' = 1{,}000$, where demand price = supply price $(MC) = 0$. Thus monopoly output is one-half competitive output. Competitive output is called opportunity output since it is the maximum output a monopolist could sell at a nonnegative price, given the market demand curve.

Seller B is attracted to the mineral industry by its profitability. He opens up a mineral well adjacent to A's well, incurring a fixed cost. He expects A to continue selling $Q' = 500 = \frac{1}{2}Q_c$. Thus he expects to be able to sell any output between Q' and Q_c. His opportunity output when A is selling 500 units is another 500 units. Thus, he maximizes his profit by selling $Q'' - Q' = \frac{1}{2}(Q_c - Q') = 250 = \frac{1}{4}Q_c = Q_c - Q''$. The new market price is P'' since the new market output, $Q'' = \frac{3}{4}Q_c = 750$, can be sold only at P''. So seller B's profit is $P''(Q'' - Q')$, and A's profit is reduced to $P'' \cdot Q'$. In effect, A's revenue curves have shifted downward since $P'' < P'$ at Q'.

Seller A knows that B is selling one-fourth of the opportunity output. He expects B to continue selling the same quantity. Thus he sells one-half of the remaining opportunity output so as to maximize his profit. In effect, he moves along his new total revenue curve from 500 to 375 units, since $375 = \frac{1}{2}Q'' = Q'''$.

Seller B now has to reconsider his output policy. No longer is he maximizing his total revenue by selling $Q'' - Q' = 250$, for total output of $Q''' + (Q'' - Q') = 625$ is sold at P''', not at P''. He knows that, of the opportunity output of $Q_c = 1{,}000$ units, A is selling $Q''' = 375$ units. He expects A to continue selling Q''' units. Thus his profit maximizing output level is $\frac{1}{2}(Q_c - Q''') = 312.5$.

To generalize for A, initially he sells $\frac{1}{2}Q_c = Q' = 500$. Then he decreases his output to $\frac{1}{2}(Q_c - \frac{1}{4}Q_c) = (\frac{1}{2}Q_c - \frac{1}{8}Q_c) = \frac{3}{8}Q_c = 375$—a contraction of $\frac{1}{8}Q_c = \frac{4}{8}Q_c - \frac{3}{8}Q_c$. Then he contracts his output by $\frac{1}{32}$; then by $\frac{1}{128}$, etc. Therefore, his final output is $\frac{1}{3}Q_c = Q_c(\frac{1}{2} - \frac{3}{8} - \frac{1}{32} - \frac{1}{128}\ldots) = 333$.

To generalize for B, initially he sells $\frac{1}{2}(Q_c - Q') = \frac{1}{4}Q_c = 250$. Then he increases his output to $\frac{1}{2}(Q_c - \frac{1}{2}Q'') = \frac{1}{2}(Q_c - \frac{3}{8}Q_c) = Q_c(\frac{1}{2} - \frac{3}{16}) = \frac{5}{16}Q_c = 312.5$, an expansion of $\frac{1}{16}Q_c = \frac{5}{16}Q_c - \frac{4}{16}Q_c$. Then he expands his output by $\frac{1}{64}$; then by $\frac{1}{256}$, etc. Therefore, his final output is $\frac{1}{3}Q_c = Q_c(\frac{1}{4} + \frac{1}{16} + \frac{1}{64} + \ldots) = 333$.

Consequently, equilibrium duopoly output (Q_d) is two-thirds of competitive output (Q_c): $Q_d = \frac{1}{3}Q_c + \frac{1}{3}Q_c = \frac{2}{3}Q_c = 667$. To generalize for n sellers, equilibrium market output is $n/(n + 1)$ times competitive (opportunity) output. In Figure 15.3, A sells Q_a and B sells $(Q_d - Q_a) = Q_b$ units. Duopoly price (P_d) is two-thirds of monopoly price (P'), and duopoly profits are two-thirds of monopoly profit. (Q_a, P_d) is one point on the equilibrium average revenue curve of A, and $(Q_d - Q_a, P_d) = (Q_b, P_d)$ is one point on the equilibrium average revenue curve of B.

Bertrand's Model [4]

Bertrand did not accept Cournot's rationale of human behavior and hence drew different conclusions from his own duopoly model. In the Bertrand model, each seller expects the other seller never to change his price, even though he repeatedly observes him do so, and sets his own price so as to maximize his profit by maximizing his revenue. Thus the key policy variable is price. Each seller sets his price to maximize his profit (revenue) and never learns that, by assuming his rival does not change his price, he ends up not maximizing his profit. The end result is that market price decreases and

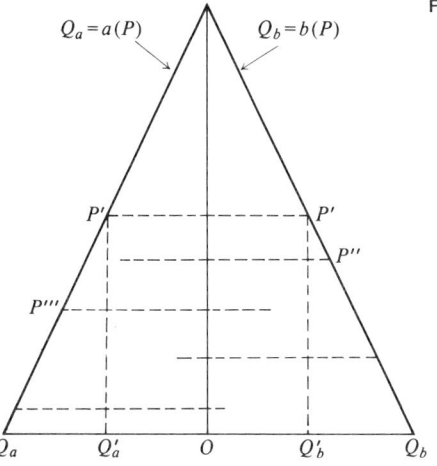

FIG. 15.4. Bertrand's model

market output increases until they reach competitive levels. Market price and output are stable in equilibrium at their competitive levels.

The Bertrand model of the mineral water market is analyzed via a Janus (two-faced) diagram (Figure 15.4). Quantity sold by A at various prices is depicted by the $Q_a = a(P)$ curve. Quantity sold by B at various prices is depicted by the $Q_b = b(P)$ curve. Thus market (joint) quantity sold at various prices is depicted by the combined curves. At $P = MC = 0$, competitive (opportunity) quantity sold is $Q_a + Q_b$. Seller A has the capacity to sell Q_a; and seller B has the capacity to sell Q_b.

Assume first that by chance A and B share the market equally, thereby maximizing their joint (monopoly) profit. Then each seller sells one-fourth of the opportunity output at monopoly price P'. Specifically, A sells $Q'_a = \frac{1}{4}(Q_a + Q_b) = \frac{1}{2}(Q_a)$; and B sells $Q'_b = \frac{1}{4}(Q_a + Q_b) = \frac{1}{2}(Q_b)$. Monopoly output is $Q'_a + Q'_b = Q_a = Q_b = \frac{1}{2}(Q_a + Q_b)$. Assume now that B expects A to keep his price at P', selling Q'_a, and sets his own price so as to maximize his profit. Then B sells all of Q_b at P'', thereby capturing some of A's sales. Seller A now appraises the market situation and assumes that he can sell all of Q_a at P''', thereby capturing some of B's sales. Seller B in turn assumes that he can sell all of Q_b at a price less than P''', etc. The only price at which all of Q_a and Q_b can be sold is zero. Thus price is decreased and quantity sold is increased until price is zero and quantity sold is $Q_a + Q_b$—the competitive stable solution of the oligopoly problem.

Edgeworth's Model [5]

Edgeworth accepted Bertrand's rationale of human behavior but not his assumption that the two sellers jointly could produce the opportunity level of output. Edgeworth assumed instead that their joint capacity output was less than opportunity output. The conclusion follows from his assumptions that market price and output are not stable at their competitive levels but instead oscillate between their monopolistic and competitive levels. The Edgeworth model of the mineral water market is also analyzed via a Janus diagram (Figure 15.5), but this time A has the capacity to produce only Q''_a, and B has the capacity to produce only Q''_b.

Assume again that by chance A and B share the market equally, thereby maximizing their joint (monopoly) profit. Then A sells Q'_a and B sells Q'_b at monopoly price P'. Assume now that B expects A to keep his price at P', selling Q'_a, and sets his own price so as to maximize his profit. Then B sells all of Q''_b at P'', thereby capturing some of A's sales. Seller A now appraises the market situation and assumes that he can sell all of Q''_a at P''', thereby capturing some of B's sales. Seller B in turn assumes that he can sell all of Q''_b at a price lower than P''', etc.

The only price at which all of Q''_a and Q''_b can be sold is $\bar{P}$. But at $\bar{P}$ seller A

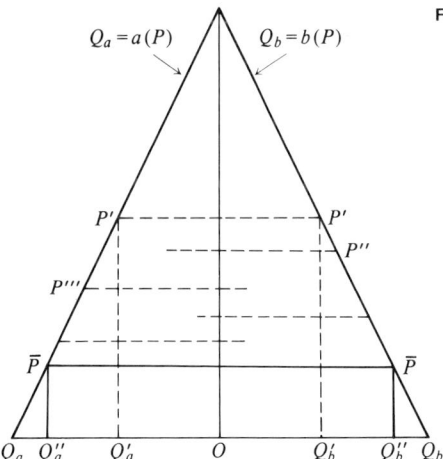

FIG. 15.5. Edgeworth's model

notices that B is selling all of his output, Q_b''. Thus, if B retains price $\overline{P}$, seller A can increase his price to P', sell Q_a'', and increase his profit. But when A increases his price to P', seller B notices that he can increase his price to P'', sell Q_b'', and increase his profit. But then A notices that he can decrease his price to P''', sell Q_a'', and increase his profit, etc. The conclusion follows that this model yields unstable results.

Chamberlin's Mutual Dependence Recognized Model [6]

Two "classical" capable-of-learning models are presented in this chapter. They are Edward Chamberlin's mutual dependence recognized model, first published in 1933, and Paul Sweezy's kinked demand curve model, published in 1939. Chamberlin's model is the same as Cournot's model except for one assumption. In Cournot's model, sellers do not recognize their mutual interdependence. Thus price and quantity sold approach their competitive levels as the number of sellers increases. In Chamberlin's model, sellers recognize their mutual interdependence. Thus price and quantity sold are stable at their monopolistic levels.

The market for mineral water is represented by the market average revenue (demand) curve, $AR = P(Q)$, in Figure 15.6. Seller A first enters the market and as a monopolist maximizes profit (revenue) by selling Q' units at price P'. Seller B now enters the market and maximizes his profit by selling $Q'' - Q'$ units at price P''. Combined profit of both sellers is now $P'' \cdot Q''$. Seller A now recognizes his mutual interdependence with B, and realizes that he can maximize his own profit if he and B share monopoly profit $P' \cdot Q'$ equally. Consequently, A decreases his output to $Q''' = \frac{1}{2}Q'$. Seller B then draws the same conclusion as A. Consequently, B keeps his output at

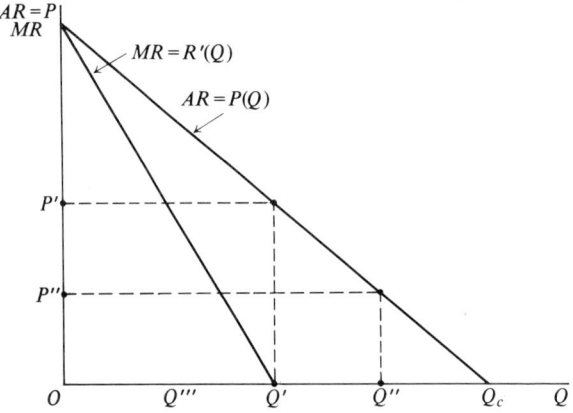

FIG. 15.6. Chamberlin's mutual dependence recognized model

$Q'' - Q' = Q' - Q''' = \frac{1}{2}Q'$. The end result is that combined quantity sold is Q' at price P', with A and B sharing monopoly profit equally. Price and quantity sold are at their monopoly levels and are stable.

Sweezy's Kinked Demand Curve Model[7]

Sweezy created his model to explain the supposed[8] stability of prices of oligopolistic products. It does explain why price of a product may remain at the same level as cost conditions change, but it does not explain how this level is determined. Thus it is an ex post explanation of a given price, rather than an ex ante explanation of determination of that price. Theorists are primarily interested in foresight models, not hindsight models.

Assume that equilibrium quantity sold and price of a product are (Q', P') as denoted by point A in Figure 15.7. The seller's average revenue (demand) curve, $AR = P(Q)$, is kinked at A. He subjectively considers segment PA to be his average revenue curve at prices greater than P' and segment AQ his curve at prices less than P'. He believes that his rivals will not increase their prices if he increases his price above P'; hence he will lose some of his customers if he increases his price. He believes that his rivals will decrease their prices if he decreases his price below P'; hence he will not gain some of their customers if he decreases his price. His rationalization of the market situation, therefore, makes him believe that the elasticity of demand for his product is much greater above than below point A; hence the kink at A.

In effect, segment PA may be considered to be his average revenue curve for all quantity values between zero and Q'. Segment AQ may be considered to be his average revenue curve for all quantity values between Q' and Q. Thus his complete average revenue curve is PAQ. Corresponding to segment

PA is marginal revenue curve PB. Corresponding to segment AQ is marginal revenue curve CD. Thus his complete marginal revenue curve is $PBCD$. Segment BC is on a vertical line drawn from A to Q'. It is the finite discontinuous portion of his complete marginal revenue curve and is determined by the kink in his average revenue curve at A.

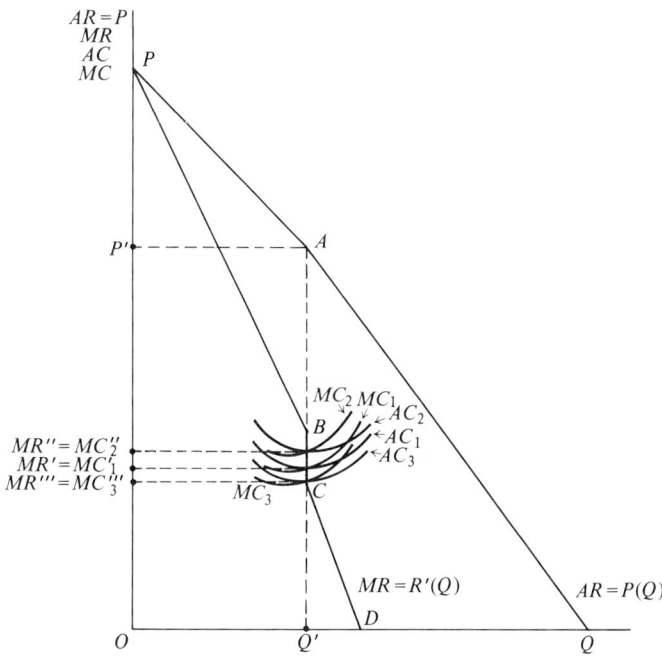

FIG. 15.7. Sweezy's kinked demand curve model

The seller is in equilibrium at (Q', P'), where $MR = MC$. But MR is a set of values depicted by segment BC, and corresponding to each value in the MR set is a corresponding value in the MC set. Given AC_1, he is in equilibrium at (Q', P'), where $MR' = MC'_1$. When the cost of production increases, he is in equilibrium at (Q', P'), where $MR'' = MC''_2$. When the cost of production decreases, he is in equilibrium at (Q', P'), where $MR''' = MC'''_3$. Price tends to be "sticky" since it changes only with relatively large changes in cost and demand.

Monopoly-Cartel Model

The monopoly-cartel model, the equal-shares price-leadership model, and the dominant-seller price-leadership model are three modern collusion models. A cartel is a set of sellers who collude primarily to determine market price and output and to allocate market output between its members, thereby limiting competition. They may openly and explicitly collude via an enforceable contract covering market price and output, shares of market output, and other market variables; or they may secretly collude via a gentlemen's agreement covering these variables; or they may tacitly collude by being members in good standing of trade associations or professional organizations which have the objective of limiting competition.

Assume that a cartel has a monopoly in the production and sale of a homogeneous product. Assume also that the managers of the cartel desire that it be in equilibrium. For it to be in equilibrium, they must maximize its profit in the same way that any monopolist maximizes profit. They must determine that market output and price at which its marginal revenue (MR) equals its marginal cost (MC). The set of equilibrium (P, Q) values derived by setting MR equal to MC is its supply curve. In this context, cartel theory of price and quantity determination is similar to monopoly theory of price and quantity determination.

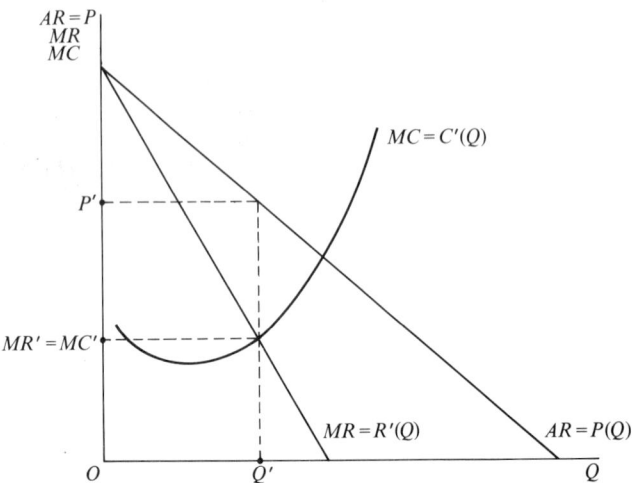

FIG. 15.8. Monopoly-cartel model

Market demand for the cartel's product is depicted by the $AR = P(Q)$ curve of Figure 15.8. The corresponding marginal revenue curve is $MR = R'(Q)$. The marginal cost curve is $MC = C'(Q)$. In simple terms, the marginal cost curve is the horizontal summation of the marginal cost curves of the members of the cartel. The cartel maximizes profit by selling quantity Q', where $MR' = MC'$, at price P'. Price P' is the cartel price at which all sellers must agree to sell their output. Market output Q' is the cartel output which must be allocated to members of the cartel. Since his price is given, a member's share of Q' determines his revenue and hence, in part, his profit. Thus, in the present context, the allocation of market shares is the chief problem of the cartel's management. Its solution of this problem determines the success or failure of the cartel. Shares may be allocated by letting members engage in non-price competition or by setting quotas.

Equal-Shares Price-Leadership Model

In price-leadership models, one seller is recognized as a leader in determining price changes. He announces a price change and his followers change their prices accordingly. Prices are kept equal if all sellers of the price-leadership set sell homogeneous products. However, prices may differ by a standard pattern of differentials if they sell differentiated products.

To describe the present model, assume that two sellers sell homogeneous products. Their combined market demand is depicted by the $AR = P(Q)$ curve of Figure 15.9. Let them agree by either tacit or explicit collusion to

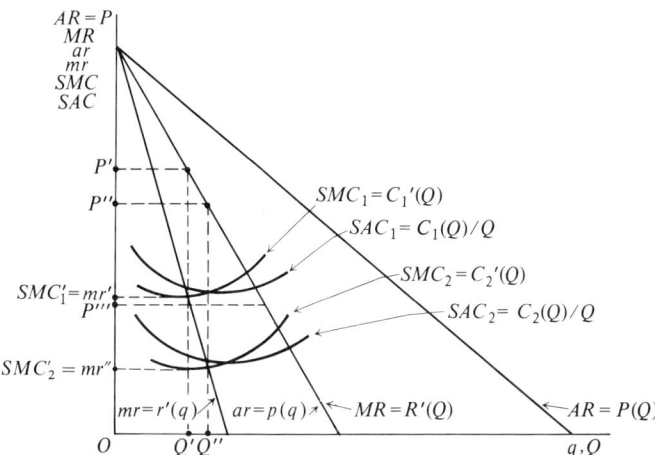

FIG. 15.9. Equal-shares price-leadership model

share the market equally. Then each considers $MR = R'(Q)$ as his average revenue (demand) curve—$ar = p(q)$—and each considers $mr = r'(q)$ as his marginal revenue curve. The first seller's short-run marginal and average cost curves are $SMC_1 = C_1'(Q)$ and $SAC_1 = C_1(Q)/Q$. The second seller's short-run marginal and average cost curves are $SMC_2 = C_2'(Q)$ and $SAC_2 = C_2(Q)/Q$. The second seller is the low-cost seller, for $SAC_1 > SAC_2$ at any common value of output.

The first seller would like to maximize his profit by producing Q', where $SMC_1' = mr'$, and selling it at price P'. The second seller would like to maximize his profit by producing Q'', where $SMC_2'' = mr''$, at price P''. The second seller determines the actual market price for both sellers because of his lower cost of production. He can set his price at its profit-maximizing level of P'' and force the first seller to produce Q'' at P''. The first seller's sales would be zero if he attempted to produce and sell Q' at P', for he would lose all of his customers to the second seller. At P'', market output is $2Q''$.

The present model is not generally given much credence because of its assumption that the dominant (low-cost) seller is willing to share the market equally with his rival(s). In fact, he may wish to have all of the market. He can have all of the market if he sets his price at, say, P''', for then the high-cost seller discontinues production. He might not choose to have all of the market, however, if in doing so he violates his government's antitrust laws. He might decide instead to set a price high enough for the high-cost seller to continue production, but low enough so that he has more than half of the market. In short, in Figure 15.9, the low-cost seller may share the market equally, have all of it, or have over half of it.

Dominant-Seller Price-Leadership Model

The dominant seller in an industry of many small sellers has another option: he can set the market price and permit small sellers to sell all they wish at that price while he satisfies the remainder of market demand. For example, he can sell 2 units at a given price if market demand at that price is 10 units and small sellers sell 8 units. This model is generally given credence empirically. Thus it is generally considered to be a basic price-leadership model.

Each horizontal line in Figure 15.10 depicts a market price set by the dominant seller. Since the small sellers sell all they wish at each given price, each price line depicts their marginal and average revenue curve. Their aggregate marginal cost curve is $MC_1 = C_1(Q_1)$. Given the market price (P), they act in the same way as competitive sellers, equating price with marginal cost to determine their equilibrium output (Q_1). Thus, as analyzed in Chapter 14, their aggregate supply curve is their aggregate marginal cost curve. In short, their supply set of equilibrium (P, Q_1) values is described by $MC_1 = C_1(Q_1)$ since $P = MR_1 = MC_1$.

The marginal cost curve of the dominant seller is $MC_2 = C_2'(Q_2)$ in Figure 15.10. The analytical problem is to determine his average revenue (demand) curve, $AR_2 = P_2(Q_2)$. His marginal revenue curve, $MR_2 = R_2'(Q_2)$, can then be derived from his average revenue curve. His average revenue curve is a set of (Q_2, P) values since $AR_2 = P$. Given market output (Q), as determined by market price (P), output of the dominant seller (Q_2) is $(Q - Q_1)$ since $Q = Q_1 + Q_2$.

The market average revenue (demand) curve is $AR = P(Q)$ in Figure 15.10. At price P', $Q' = Q_1'$, and hence $Q_2' = 0$, since $P' = MR_1' = MC_1'$ at

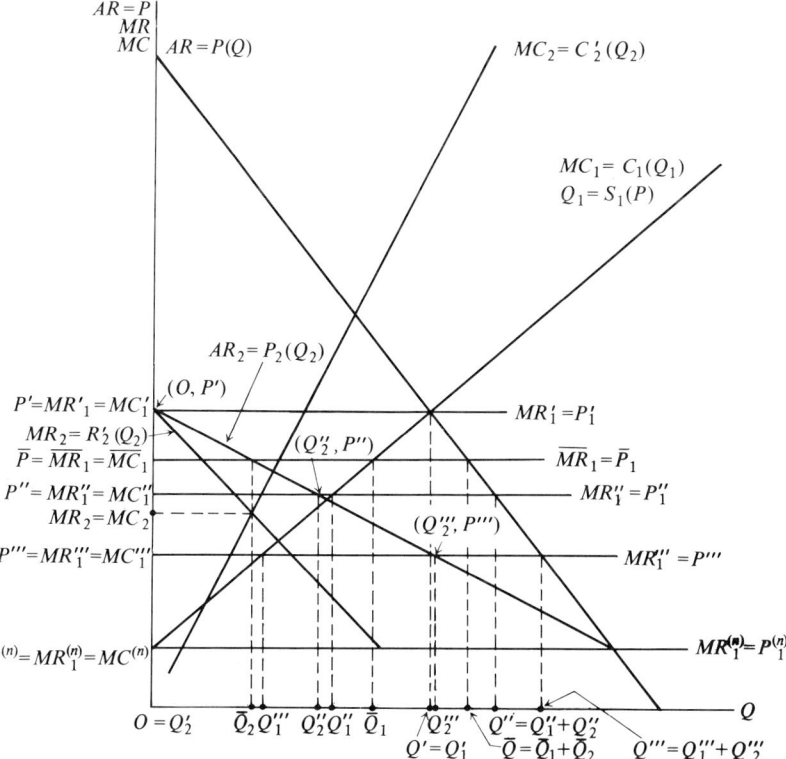

FIG. 15.10. Dominant-seller price-leadership model

Q'. Thus (Q, P') is one point on the average revenue curve of the dominant seller. At price P'', $Q'' = Q_1'' + Q_2''$, and hence $Q_2'' = Q'' - Q_1''$. Thus (Q_2'', P'') is another point on his average revenue curve. Lastly, at price P''', $Q''' = Q_1''' + Q_2'''$, and hence $Q_2''' = Q''' - Q_1'''$. Thus (Q_2''', P''') is a third point on his average revenue curve. His complete demand set of (Q_2, P) values may be rationalized in the same way.

The dominant seller is in equilibrium at that level of output $(\bar{Q}_2)$ at which $MR_2 = MC_2$. He sells $\bar{Q}_2$ at price $\bar{P}$. Given $\bar{P}$, the small sellers are in equilibrium at that level of output $(\bar{Q}_1)$ at which $\bar{P} = \overline{MR}_1 = \overline{MC}_1$. Market output at $\bar{P}$ is $\bar{Q} = \bar{Q}_1 + \bar{Q}_2$.

Baumol's Sales-Maximization Model

The best-known non-profit-maximizing model is probably Baumol's sales-maximization model.[9] In his model, a large seller has the objective of maximizing sales (revenue) subject to a minimum profit. As seen in Figure 15.11, the seller sells output Q' if his objective is solely to maximize profit, for the profit curve, $(R - C) = \pi(Q)$, is at its maximum value at Q'. He sells output Q'' if his objective is solely to maximize revenue, for the revenue curve is at its maximum value at Q''. He sells output Q''' if his objective is to maximize revenue subject to the minimum profit line in Figure 15.11.

How can the total revenue curve be drawn conceptually? The key feature of oligopoly, supposedly, is the interdependence of pricing and output decisions of rival sellers—of revenue functions. But implicit in Figure 15.11

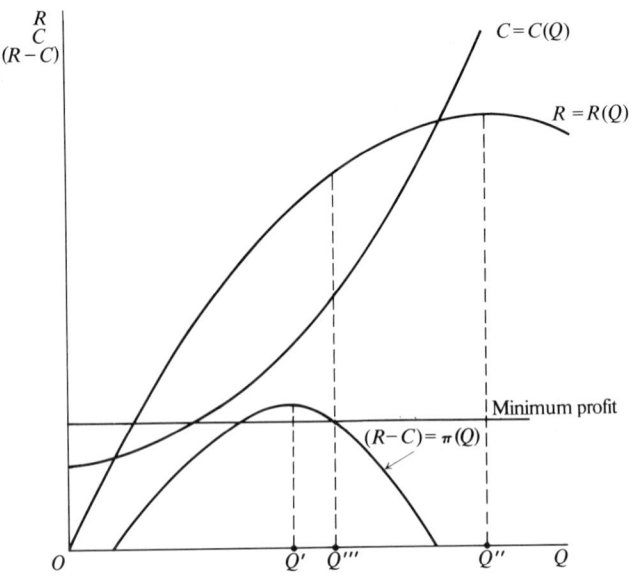

FIG. 15.11. Baumol's sales-maximization model

is the assumption that the seller can vary price and output without being concerned about the reaction of his rivals—that his total revenue curve can be drawn conceptually. Baumol answers this question by drawing on his experience as a business consultant and his study of the decision-making process in large firms. He suggests that managers are slow in making important decisions, have a live-and-let-live attitude, and rely on rules of thumb. Thus anticipated reaction of rivals supposedly plays a small role in making day-to-day decisions on price and quantity sold of a product—in determining the revenue function. But anticipated reaction of rivals plays an important role in making a decision on a major change such as a new advertising campaign or the introduction of a new product.

Why would a seller wish to maximize revenue? The answer is that he might assume a direct relation between revenue and profit. According to a common belief, a business firm grows in size as its revenue increases, and as it grows in size its profit increases. Moreover, purchasers supposedly are attracted to a product that is popular and thus the seller gains distributors and has less trouble in arranging financing.

What is a minimum acceptable profit? The answer supposedly depends on how much money the seller thinks he needs to insure growth, financial security, and payment of dividends.

What role does fixed cost play in determining price and quantity sold? As seen in Chapter 14, a seller who wishes to maximize profit does not consider fixed cost in determining his equilibrium price and quantity. Instead, he considers only marginal cost, which changes with a change in the slope of the total cost curve (that is, a change in variable cost) but not with a change in the intercept of this curve (that is, a change in fixed cost). But in Baumol's model, a seller does consider fixed cost in determining his equilibrium price and quantity, for his profit curve shifts downward as his total cost curve shifts upward by increasing its intercept as fixed cost increases. As his profit curve shifts downward, it is intersected by the given minimum profit line at a smaller equilibrium quantity of output. The smaller output is associated with a higher equilibrium price.

SUMMARY

The demand curve for a product facing a monopolistic-competitive seller is a negatively-sloped curve that may be drawn by assuming that his competitors do not react by changing their prices when he changes his price. It is more elastic at a specified price than is the demand curve facing a monopolist, but is less elastic at a specified price than is the demand curve facing a perfectly competitive seller. In the short run a monopolistic-competitive seller acts as a monopolist seeking equilibrium. The profit of a monopolistic-competitive seller is zero when he is in long-run stable equilibrium; and his price and quantity correspond to a point on the negatively sloped portion of his long-run average cost curve. This conclusion follows from the freedom of entry assumption and from the interdependence of demand curves assumption.

The classical incapable-of-learning models of Cournot, Bertrand, and Edgeworth are based on the assumption that sellers do not recognize their mutual interdependence and act independently of one another. The classical capable-of-learning models of Chamberlin and Sweezy are based on the assumption that sellers recognize their mutual interdependence but still act independently of one another. Edgeworth's model yields an unstable solution of price and quantity sold. The other classical models yield stable solutions of price and quantity sold. Sweezy's model is an ex post explanation of a given price and quantity. The other classical models are ex ante explanations of the determination of price and quantity. Bertrand's model yields perfectly competitive price and quantity equilibrium values. Cournot's model yields price and quantity values that are relatively close to perfectly competitive price and quantity equilibrium values. Chamberlin's model yields monopolistic price and quantity equilibrium values. Present-day economists, in general, give more credence to Chamberlin's model. The other classical models are generally considered to be economic curiosa, useful primarily for teaching students to think analytically and to become familiar with the lingo of economic theory.

Sellers do not have explicit or tacit agreements in the classical models, but they do have such agreements in the modern collusion models. With respect to these models, the monopoly-cartel model yields price and quantity equilibrium values that come closest to monopolistic levels, followed in turn by the equal-shares and then the dominant-seller price-leadership models.

In the modern collusion models, the seller has the objective of maximizing profit. In other modern models, he may have other objectives besides maximizing profit. Specifically, in Baumol's model, the seller has the objective of maximizing revenue subject to a minimum profit. The result of such an assumption is that price and quantity tend to be closer to their perfectly competitive levels.

Questions

1. Differentiate the perfect competition, monopolistic-competition, oligopoly, and monopoly market structures in terms of the revenue function of a seller—that is, in terms of the demand curve facing a seller.

2. What would you have to assume to prove by analysis of the equilibrium principle that in the short run a monopolistic-competitive seller acts as a monopolist seeking equilibrium?

3. Use diagrams to prove by analysis of the (a) freedom of entry assumption or (b) the interdependence of demand curves assumption that a monopolistic-competitive seller is in long-run stable equilibrium at an output–price coordinate on the negatively-sloped portion of his long-run average cost curve.

4. Differentiate the classical incapable-of-learning duopoly models in terms of behavioral assumptions concerning a seller's expectations of the pricing and output policy of his rival.

5. Use a diagram to prove by analysis of the equilibrium principle that in the Cournot model market price decreases and market output increases toward competitive levels as the number of sellers increases and are stable in equilibrium.

6. Use a diagram to prove by analysis of the equilibrium principle that in the Bertrand model market price decreases and market output increases until they reach competitive levels and are stable in equilibrium.

7. Use a diagram to prove by analysis of the equilibrium principle that in the Edgeworth model market price and output are not stable at their competitive levels but, instead, oscillate between their monopolistic and competitive levels.

8. Differentiate the classical incapable-of-learning models and the classical capable-of-learning models in terms of assumptions and conclusions.

9. Use a diagram to prove by analysis of the equilibrium principle that in the Chamberlin mutual dependence recognized model price and quantity sold are stable at their monopolistic levels.

10. Use a diagram to prove by analysis of the equilibrium principle that the Sweezy kinked demand curve model is an explanation of the supposed stability of price in an oligopoly market.

11. Differentiate the classical capable-of-learning models and the modern collusion models in terms of assumptions and conclusions.

12. Use a diagram to prove by analysis of the equilibrium principle that the monopoly-cartel model of price and quantity determination is similar to the monopoly model of price and quantity determination.

13. Use a diagram to prove by analysis of the equilibrium principle that in the equal-shares price-leadership model the lower-cost seller determines market price.

14. Use a diagram to prove by analysis of the equilibrium principle that in the dominant-seller price-leadership model the dominant seller sets the market price and permits smaller sellers to sell all they wish at that price while he satisfies the remainder of market demand.

15. Use a diagram to differentiate Baumol's sales-maximization model from other oligopoly models in terms of assumptions and conclusions.

SELECTED READINGS

Stigler, G. J. "Monopolistic Competition in Retrospect," *Five Lectures on Economic Problems.* New York: The Macmillan Company, 1949, pp. 12–24. Reprinted in Kamerschen, D. R. (editor). *Readings in Microeconomics.* Cleveland, Ohio: The World Publishing Company, 1967, pp. 307–309.

Bishop, R. L. "The Theory of Monopolistic Competition After Thirty Years: The Impact on General Theory," *American Economic Review,* LIV: 3 (May 1964), pp. 33–43. Reprinted in Kamerschen, *ibid.,* pp. 320–331.

Markham, Jesse W. "Market Structure, Business Conduct, and Innovation," *American Economic Review,* LV: 2 (May 1965), pp. 323–332. Reprinted in Kamerschen, *ibid.,* pp. 344–354.

Modigliani, Franco. "New Developments on the Oligopoly Front," *The Journal of Political Economy,* LXVI (June 1958), pp. 215–232. Reprinted in Kamerschen, *ibid.,* pp. 355–378.

Rothschild, K. W. "Price Theory and Oligopoly," *The Economic Journal,* LVII (1947), pp. 299–320. Reprinted in The American Economic Association. *Readings in Price Theory.* Edited by George J. Stigler and Kenneth E. Boulding. Homewood, Illinois: Richard D. Irwin, Inc., 1952, pp. 440–464.

Hotelling, Harold. "Stability in Competition," *The Economic Journal,* XXXIX (1929), pp. 41–57. Reprinted in The American Economic Association. *Readings in Price Theory, ibid.,* pp. 467–484.

Smithies, Arthur. "Optimum Location in Spatial Competition," *The Journal of Political Economy,* XLIX (1941), pp. 423–439. Reprinted in The American Economic Association. *Readings in Price Theory, ibid.,* pp. 485–501.

Hurwicz, Leonid, "The Theory of Economic Behavior," *The American Economic Review*, XXXV (1945), pp. 909–925. Reprinted in The American Economic Association. *Readings in Price Theory, ibid.*, pp. 505–526.

NOTES

[1] For a presentation of sales promotion (advertising) and product quality policies of a profit-maximizing seller, see D. S. Watson, *Price Theory and Its Uses*, 2nd ed. (Boston: Houghton Mifflin Company, 1968), Chapter 18.

[2] See M. L. Greenhut, *Microeconomics and the Space Economy* (Chicago: Scott Foresman and Company, 1963).

[3] Augustin Cournot, *Récherches sur les Principles Mathematiques de la Theories des Richesses* (Paris, 1838); translated by Nathaniel T. Bacon as *Researches into the Mathematical Principles of the Theory of Wealth* (New York: Macmillan and Company, 1897).

[4] Joseph Bertrand, "Theorie Mathematique de la Richesse Sociale," *Journal des Savants* (Paris, 1883), pp. 499–508.

[5] F. Y. Edgeworth, "La Teoria pura del Monopolio," *Giornale degli Economisti*, XV (1897), pp. 13–31; reprinted as "The Pure Theory of Monopoly," in his *Papers Relating to Political Economy* (London: Macmillan and Co. Ltd., 1925), Vol. I, pp. 111–142.

[6] Edward Hastings Chamberlin, *The Theory of Monopolistic Competition*, 7th ed. (Cambridge: Harvard University Press, 1956), Chapter 3.

[7] Paul Sweezy, "Demand Under Conditions of Oligopoly," *The Journal of Political Economy*, XLVII (1939), pp. 568–573; reprinted in The American Economic Association, *Readings in Price Theory* (Homewood, Illinois: Richard D. Irwin, Inc., 1952), pp. 404–409.

[8] See George J. Stigler, "The Kinky Oligopoly Demand Curve and Rigid Prices," *The Journal of Political Economy*, LV (1947), pp. 432–449; reprinted in The American Economic Association, *Readings in Price Theory, op. cit.*, pp. 410–439.

[9] William J. Baumol, *Business Behavior, Value and Growth* (New York: The Macmillan Company, 1959), Chapters 4–8.

PART IV

PRINCIPLES OF THE THEORY OF DEMAND FOR A FACTOR OF PRODUCTION

Seven principles of the economic theory of demand for a factor of production are of primary importance. They are the laws of constant marginal factor cost of a factor of production to a perfectly competitive purchaser of factors, constant marginal revenue of a product to a perfectly competitive seller of products, decreasing marginal (physical) product of a factor to a user (purchaser) who is subject to diminishing marginal returns, decreasing marginal revenue-product of a factor to a purchaser who is subject to diminishing marginal returns, equilibrium of a purchaser, demand for a factor of a purchaser, and market demand for a factor. Each of these principles of economics is a verbalization of an economic function (curve), or an inference drawn from an operation on a set of economic functions (curves). The law of constant marginal factor cost of a factor of production is a verbalization of a marginal factor cost curve of a perfectly competitive purchaser—defined as a purchaser who can purchase all he wishes per unit of time at the prevailing market price ceteris paribus (see Chapter 8). The law of constant marginal revenue of a product is a verbalization of a marginal revenue curve of a perfectly competitive seller—defined as a seller who can sell all he wishes per unit of time at the prevailing market price ceteris paribus (see Chapter 6). The law of decreasing marginal product of a factor of production is a verbalization of a marginal product curve of a user of factors (see Chapter 7). The law of decreasing marginal revenue-product of a factor is a verbalization of a marginal revenue-product curve of a purchaser (see Chapter 16). The principle of equilibrium of a purchaser is an inference drawn from an operation on the marginal factor cost and marginal revenue-product curves of a purchaser (see Chapter 17). The law of demand for a factor of a purchaser is a verbalization of a demand curve of a purchaser (see Chapter 18). And the law of market demand for a factor is a verbalization of a market demand curve (see Chapter 19).

SELECTED READING

Dorfman, Robert. "Mathematical, or 'Linear,' Programming: A Nonmathematical Exposition," *American Economic Review*, XLIII: 5 (December 1953), pp. 797–825. Reprinted in Kamerschen, D. R. (editor). *Readings in Microeconomics*. Cleveland, Ohio: The World Publishing Company, 1967, pp. 547–576.

chapter 16

Revenue-Product Functions

According to the law of decreasing marginal revenue-product of a factor of production to a purchaser (user) who is subject to diminishing marginal returns, the revenue associated with purchasing and/or using an additional unit of a factor varies inversely with quantity purchased and/or used per unit of time. Each additional unit used of a factor per unit of time adds a smaller amount to total revenue-product. Total revenue-product of a factor increases at a decreasing rate as quantity used of the factor per unit of time increases. Marginal revenue-product of a factor is a decreasing function of quantity used of the factor per unit of time.

The revenue-product function of a purchaser of factors of production and seller of products (business firm) is a transformation of his production function from physical output units into monetary revenue units. To see this, think in terms of the output of one product (Q) and the input of one variable factor of production (F). Then, in functional notation form,

(1) $R = R(Q)$ (total revenue function of Chapter 6)
(2) $Q = Q(F)$ (production function of Chapter 7)
(3) $R = R[Q(F)]$ or $R = r(F)$ (total revenue-product function of the present chapter)

The total revenue-product of a factor is thus the money received from the output produced by a quantity of the factor. To generalize, the revenue of input is the revenue of output.

Total Revenue-Product Curve of a Factor of a Perfectly Competitive Seller of a Product

The total revenue-product curve of a factor of production is a set of ordered pairs of input of the factor (F) and revenue (R) having the property that corresponding to each number in the F set of numbers is one number in the

REVENUE-PRODUCT FUNCTIONS 285

R set of numbers: $R = R(F)$. Thus, the total revenue-product curve shows the R value corresponding to each F value and hence how R varies with F per unit of time. The parameters of a total revenue-product curve of a user are the parameters of the corresponding revenue and production functions. As analyzed in Chapter 6, a perfectly competitive seller of a product can sell all he wishes per unit of time at the prevailing price ceteris paribus. As analyzed in Chapter 7, in the short run total product may be said to vary with the input of a variable factor, given the input of fixed factors and the state of technology. Thus, the parameters of a total revenue-product curve of a factor of a perfectly competitive seller of a product are the price of the product ($P = P_0$), the quantity of the fixed factor ($F_f = F_{f0}$), and the state of technology.

The total revenue-product curve of Figure 16.1c is derived by transforming the physical output units of the total product curve of Figure 16.1b into

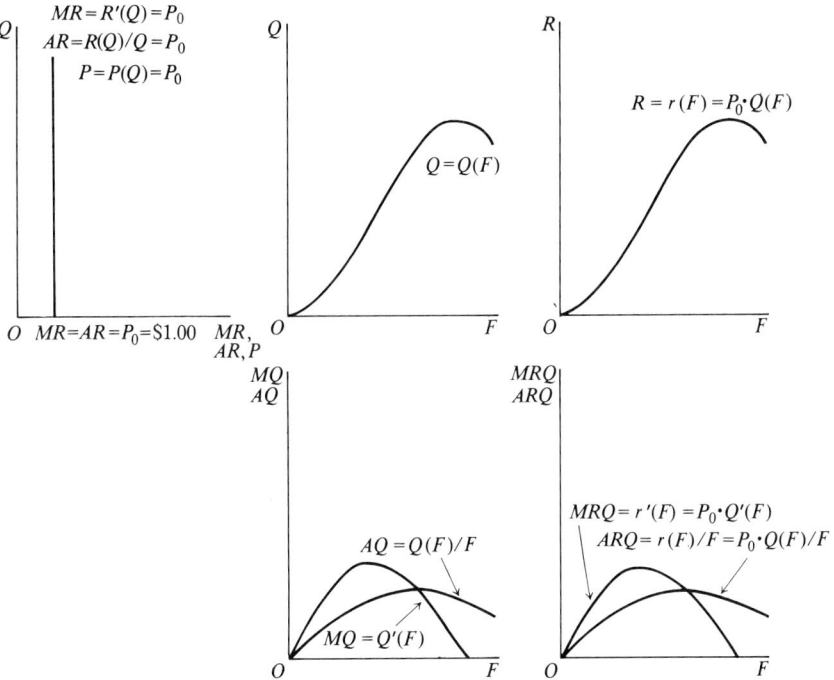

FIG. 16.1a. Hypothetical marginal and average revenue curves of a product of a perfectly competitive seller

FIG. 16.1b. Hypothetical total product curve of a factor

FIG. 16.1c. Hypothetical total revenue-product curve of a factor of a perfectly competitive seller of a product

FIG. 16.1d. Hypothetical marginal and average product curves of a factor

FIG. 16.1e. Hypothetical marginal and average revenue-product curves of a factor of a perfectly competitive seller of a product

TABLE 16.1: Hypothetical revenue-product of a factor to a perfectly competitive seller of a product

(Figure 16.1a)		(Figure 16.1b)		(Figure 16.1c)	
$MR = AR = P = P(Q) = P_0$	Q	$Q = Q(F)$	F	$R = R(F) = P_0 \cdot Q(F)$	F
1	0.000	0.000	0	0.000	0
1	0.384	0.384	1	0.384	1
1	1.536	1.536	2	1.536	2
1	3.168	3.168	3	3.168	3
1	5.370	5.370	4	5.370	4
1	8.000	8.000	5	8.000	5
1	10.944	10.944	6	10.944	6
1	14.112	14.112	7	14.112	7
1	17.408	17.408	8	17.408	8
1	20.736	20.736	9	20.736	9
1	24.000	24.000	10	24.000	10
1	27.104	27.104	11	27.104	11
1	29.952	29.952	12	29.952	12
1	32.448	32.448	13	32.448	13
1	34.496	34.496	14	34.496	14
1	36.000	36.000	15	36.000	15
1	36.864	36.864	16	36.864	16
1	36.992	36.992	17	36.992	17
1	36.288	36.288	18	36.288	18
1	34.656	34.656	19	34.656	19
1	32.000	32.000	20	32.000	20

(Figure 16.1d)			(Figure 16.1e)			
$MQ = Q'(F)$	$AQ = Q(F)/F$	F	$MRQ_c = R'(F)$	$MRQ_d = \Delta R/\Delta F$	$ARQ = R(F)/F$	F
0.000	0.000	0	0.000		0.000	0
0.752	0.384	1	0.752	0.384	0.384	1
1.408	0.736	2	1.408	1.152	0.736	2
1.968	1.056	3	1.968	1.632	1.056	3
2.432	1.344	4	2.432	2.202	1.344	4
2.800	1.600	5	2.800	2.630	1.600	5
3.248	1.824	6	3.248	2.944	1.824	6
3.428	2.016	7	3.428	3.168	2.016	7
3.328	2.176	8	3.328	3.296	2.176	8
3.312	2.304	9	3.312	3.228	2.304	9
3.200	2.400	10	3.200	3.264	2.400	10
2.992	2.464	11	2.992	3.104	2.464	11
2.688	2.496	12	2.688	2.848	2.496	12
2.288	2.496	13	2.288	2.496	2.496	13
1.792	2.464	14	1.792	2.048	2.464	14
1.200	2.400	15	1.200	1.504	2.400	15
0.512	2.304	16	0.512	0.864	2.304	16
0.272	2.176	17	0.272	0.028	2.176	17
−1.152	2.016	18	−1.152	−0.704	2.016	18
−2.128	1.824	19	−2.128	−1.632	1.824	19
−3.200	1.600	20	−3.200	−2.656	1.600	20

monetary revenue units. As seen in Table 16.1, this transformation is effected at each quantity of the factor (F) by multiplying the corresponding quantity of the product (Q) by its price ($P = P_0$). The price at which a quantity of a product can be sold is denoted by the demand curve facing the seller, which in the case of a perfectly competitive seller is denoted by $P = P(Q) = P_0$, as seen in Figure 16.1a. Thus the $R = r(F) = P_0 \cdot Q(F)$ curve of Figure 16.1c is the mathematical product of the $P = P(Q) = P_0$ curve of Figure 16.1a and the $Q = Q(F)$ curve of 16.1b. In short, at each value of F, $R = P_0 \cdot Q$, where $Q = Q(F)$.

With respect to Figure 16.1b, quantity produced of the product (Q) first increases at an increasing rate as input of the factor (F) increases; each additional unit of F adds a larger amount to Q. With respect to Figure 16.1c, total revenue-product (R) first increases at an increasing rate as input of the factor (F) increases; each additional unit of F adds a larger amount to R if it adds a larger amount to Q, given $P = P_0$. To conclude, the slope of the total revenue-product curve increases as input increases if the slope of the total product curve increases as input increases.

Again, with respect to Figure 16.1b, quantity produced (Q) eventually increases at a decreasing rate as input (F) increases; each additional unit of F now adds a smaller amount to Q. With respect to Figure 16.1c, total revenue-product (R) now increases at a decreasing rate as input (F) increases; each additional unit of F adds a smaller amount to R if it adds a smaller amount to Q, given P_0. To conclude, the slope of the total revenue-product curve decreases as input increases if the slope of the total product curve decreases as input increases.[1]

Marginal Revenue-Product Curve of a Factor of a Perfectly Competitive Seller of a Product

When quantity is varied by discrete amounts, discrete marginal revenue-product of a factor (MRQ_d) is the change in R (ΔR) associated with a change of one unit in F ($\Delta F = 1$): $MRQ_d = \Delta R/\Delta F$, where $\Delta F = 1$. In this context, marginal revenue-product is equal to the difference quotient $\Delta R/\Delta F$ of the straight line between two points one F unit apart on the curve. In Table 16.1, the MRQ_d of the tenth unit equals the

$$\lim_{\Delta F \to 1} \frac{\Delta R}{\Delta F} = 3.264$$

Since the total revenue-product curve of Figure 16.1c is nonlinear, the difference quotient is not the same for all changes in quantity, and discrete marginal revenue-product is not the same as continuous marginal revenue-product.[2]

The marginal revenue-product curve of a factor is a set of ordered pairs of input of the factor (F) and (continuous) marginal revenue-product (MRQ) having the property that corresponding to each number in the F set of numbers is one number in the MRQ set of numbers: $MRQ = r'(F)$. Thus, the marginal revenue-product curve shows the MRQ value corresponding to each F value and hence how MRQ varies with F per unit of time. The parameters of a marginal revenue-product curve are the parameters of the corresponding total revenue-product curve that determine the slope of the total curve.

As seen in Figure 16.1c, which depicts hypothetical data presented in Table 16.1, the slope of the total revenue-product curve initially increases as quantity used of the factor increases; initially, each subsequent unit used adds more to total revenue-product than the previous unit. In this context, as seen in Figure 16.1e, a direct relation exists between MRQ and F; the marginal revenue-product curve has a positive slope. Marginal revenue-product (MRQ) is an increasing function of quantity used (F) when total revenue-product (R) increases at an increasing rate as quantity increases.

Eventually, however, as seen in Figure 16.1d, the slope of the total revenue-product curve of a factor attains its highest value. This point on the total revenue-product curve is the inflection point dividing increasing marginal revenue-product from decreasing marginal revenue-product. At this point, the marginal revenue-product curve is at its peak; its slope is zero.

Thereafter, the slope of the total revenue-product curve decreases as quantity used of the factor increases; each subsequent unit used now adds less to total revenue-product than the previous unit. In this context, as seen in Figure 16.1e, an inverse relation exists between MRQ and F; the marginal revenue-product curve has a negative slope. Marginal revenue-product (MRQ) is a decreasing function of quantity used (F) when total revenue-product (R) increases at a decreasing rate as quantity increases.

The marginal revenue-product curve of Figure 16.1e may also be derived by transforming the physical slope values of the marginal product curve of Figure 16.1a into monetary slope values. This transformation is effected at each quantity used of the factor (F) by multiplying the corresponding marginal product (dQ/dF) value by the marginal revenue (dR/dQ) value of the corresponding quantity of the product (Q). The marginal revenue at various quantities of the product is denoted by the marginal revenue curve, which, as seen in Figure 16.1a, is the same as the demand curve of the product facing the perfectly competitive seller: $MR = R'(Q) = P_0$. Thus the $MRQ = r'(F) = P_0 \cdot Q'(F)$ curve of Figure 16.1e is the mathematical product of the $MR = R'(Q) = P_0$ curve of Figure 16.1a and the $MQ = Q'(F)$ curve of Figure 16.1d. In short, at each value of F,

$$MRQ = \frac{dR}{dF} = \frac{dR}{dQ} \cdot \frac{dQ}{dF} \quad \text{or} \quad MRQ = r'(F) = R'(Q) \cdot Q'(F)$$

$$\text{or} \quad MRQ = P_0 \cdot MQ.$$

In terms of discrete marginal revenue-product, marginal revenue-product of a factor is the revenue of a product derived from an additional unit of the factor. In this context, discrete marginal revenue-product ($MRQ = \Delta R/\Delta F$)

is equal to discrete marginal revenue of the product ($MR = \Delta R/\Delta Q$) times discrete marginal product ($MQ = \Delta Q/\Delta F$). Assuming perfect competition in the product market, marginal revenue (MR) is the same as price of the product (P_0). Therefore, the revenue of an additional unit of the factor ($\Delta R/\Delta F$) is the amount of the product produced by that unit ($\Delta Q/\Delta F$) times the price of the product (P_0). In short,

$$MRQ = \frac{\Delta R}{\Delta F} = \frac{\Delta R}{\Delta Q} \cdot \frac{\Delta Q}{\Delta F} = P_0 \cdot \frac{\Delta Q}{\Delta F}.$$

In other words, the addition to total revenue (ΔR) of an additional unit of input (ΔF) is the addition to output (ΔQ) of that unit (ΔF) times the price of output (P_0).[3]

With respect to Figure 16.1d, the marginal product curve first has a positive slope; each additional unit of F adds a larger amount to Q. With respect to Figure 16.1e, the marginal revenue-product curve first has a positive slope; each additional unit of F adds a larger amount to R if it adds a larger amount to Q, given $P = P_0$. To conclude, marginal revenue-product increases if marginal product increases. However, as also seen in Figure 16.1d, the marginal product curve eventually has a negative slope; each additional unit of F now adds a smaller amount to Q. Thus, as seen in Figure 16.1e, the marginal revenue-product curve now has a negative slope; each additional unit of F adds a smaller amount to R if it adds a smaller amount to Q, given $P = P_0$. To conclude, marginal revenue-product decreases if marginal product decreases. In other words, marginal revenue-product varies directly with marginal product.

As seen in Figure 16.1e, a marginal revenue-product curve of a purchaser of factors of production and seller of products who is subject to diminishing marginal returns—decreasing marginal product—is a negatively-sloped curve ($\Delta MRQ/\Delta F < 0$). Marginal revenue-product (MRQ) is a decreasing function of quantity used (F) when total revenue-product (R) increases at a decreasing rate (dR/dF) as quantity used of the factor increases. Thus the law of decreasing marginal revenue-product is a verbalization of a marginal revenue-product curve of a user who is subject to diminishing marginal returns. Since total revenue-product increases at a decreasing rate in this case, and since the phrase "increases at a decreasing rate" is another way of saying "decreasing marginal revenue-product," a total revenue-product curve of a user who is subject to diminishing marginal returns also depicts the law of decreasing marginal revenue-product.

Average Revenue-Product Curve of a Factor of a Perfectly Competitive Seller of a Product

Average revenue-product of a factor of production (ARQ) is the ratio of total revenue-product (R) to quantity used (F): $ARQ = R/F$. Average revenue-product is equal to the difference quotient $\Delta R/\Delta F$ of the ray at a point on the total revenue-product curve. In Table 16.1, the ARQ of the tenth unit equals $24/10 = 2.40$. Since the total revenue-product curve of a factor is not a ray when the user is subject to diminishing marginal returns, the difference quotient varies with F.

The average revenue-product curve of a factor is a set of ordered pairs of input of the factor (F) and average revenue-product (ARQ) having the property that corresponding to each number in the F set of numbers is one number in the ARQ set of numbers: $ARQ = r(F)/F$. Thus the average revenue-product curve shows the ARQ value corresponding to each F value and hence how ARQ varies with F per unit of time. The parameters of an average revenue-product curve are the parameters of the corresponding total revenue-product curve that determine the intercept or the slope of the total curve.

The average revenue-product of the first unit of a factor is the same as its total revenue-product: $ARQ = R/F = R/1 = R$. The total revenue-product curve of Figure 16.1c, which depicts hypothetical data presented in Table 16.1, shows that (by assumption) total revenue-product first increases at an increasing rate and then at a decreasing rate as quantity used of the factor increases. Therefore, average revenue-product first increases and then decreases with quantity used of the factor. The peak of the average revenue-product curve occurs at a quantity of the product that is greater than the quantity at which the marginal revenue-product curve peaks. The average revenue-product curve is intersected at its peak from above by the marginal revenue-product curve; then the rate of decrease of average revenue-product is less numerically than the rate of decrease of marginal revenue-product. The average is determined by all units of a given quantity; the marginal is determined by the last unit. Thus the only way for an average to stop increasing, reach its maximum value, and then decrease is for the marginal to stop increasing first, reach its maximum value first, and then decrease at a rate that is greater numerically than the rate of decrease of the average.

The average revenue-product curve of Figure 16.1f may also be derived by transforming the physical ratio units of the average product curve of Figure 16.1e into monetary ratio units. This transformation is effected at each quantity used of the factor (F) by multiplying the corresponding average product (Q/F) by the average revenue (R/Q) of the corresponding quantity of the product (Q). The average revenue at various quantities of the product is denoted by the average revenue curve, which, as seen in Figures 16.1d, is the same as the demand curve of the product facing the perfectly competitive seller: $AR = R(Q)/Q = P_0$. Thus the $ARQ = P_0 \cdot Q(F)/F$ curve of Figure 16.1f is the mathematical product of the $AR = R(Q)/Q = P_0$ curve of Figure 16.1d and the $AQ = Q(F)/F$ curve of Figure 16.1e. In short, at each value of F,

$$ARQ = \frac{R}{F} = \frac{R}{Q} \cdot \frac{Q}{F} \quad \text{or} \quad ARQ = \frac{R(Q)}{Q} \cdot \frac{Q(F)}{F} \quad \text{or} \quad ARQ = P_0 \cdot \frac{Q}{F}$$

$$\text{or} \quad ARQ = P_0 \cdot AQ$$

Revenue-Product Curves of a Factor of an Imperfectly Competitive Seller of a Product

As analyzed in Chapter 6, the price of a product (P) is not a parameter of a total revenue curve of an imperfectly competitive seller, as exemplified by a monopolist, for now P varies inversely with quantity sold (Q) and hence is a variable: $P = P(Q)$, where $\Delta P/\Delta Q < 0$. Thus P is a variable of the total revenue-product curve of a factor of an imperfectly competitive seller of a product, as seen in Figure 16.2. The $R = r(F) = P(Q) \cdot Q(F)$ curve of Figure

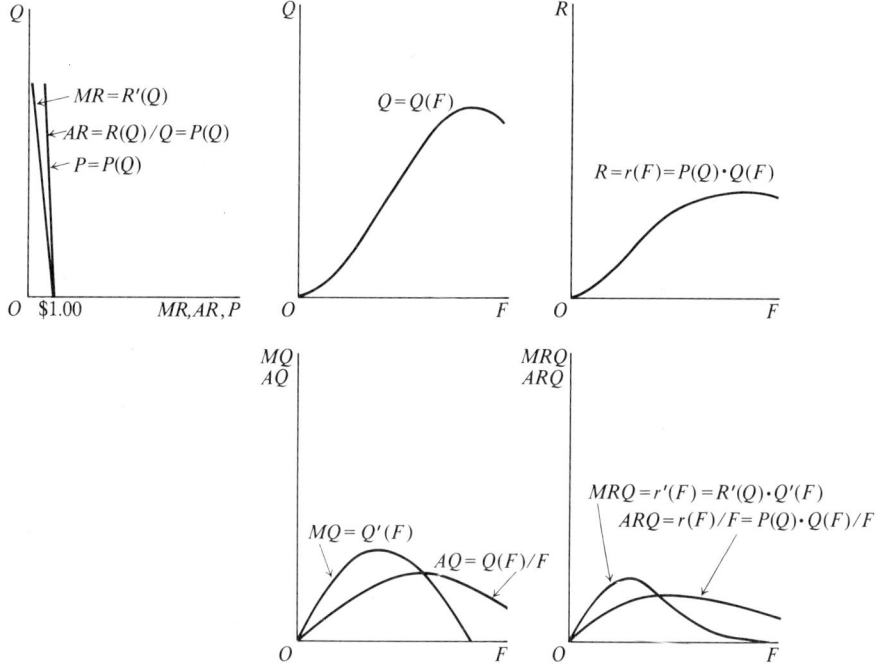

FIG. 16.2a. Hypothetical marginal and average revenue curves of a product of a monopolist

FIG. 16.2b. Hypothetical total product curve of a factor

FIG. 16.2c. Hypothetical total revenue-product curve of a factor of a monopolist in a product market

FIG. 16.2d. Hypothetical marginal and average product curves of a factor

FIG. 16.2e. Hypothetical marginal and average revenue-product curves of a factor of a monopolist in a product market

16.2c is the mathematical product of the $P = P(Q)$ curve of Figure 16.2a and the $Q = Q(F)$ curve of Figure 16.2b. The $MRQ = r'(F) = R'(Q) \cdot Q'(F)$ curve of Figure 16.2e is the mathematical product of the $MR = R'(Q)$ curve of Figure 16.2a and the $MQ = Q'(F)$ curve of Figure 16.2d; and the $ARQ = r(F)/F = P(Q) \cdot Q(F)/F$ curve of Figure 16.2e is the mathematical product of the $AR = R(Q)/Q = P(Q)$ curve of Figure 16.2a and the

$AQ = Q(F)/F$ curve of Figure 16.2d. In other words, at each value of F,

(1) $\quad R = P \cdot Q$, where $P = P(Q)$ and $Q = Q(F)$

(2) $\quad MRQ = \dfrac{dR}{dF} = \dfrac{dR}{dQ} \cdot \dfrac{dQ}{dF} \quad$ or $\quad MRQ = r'(F) = R'(Q) \cdot Q'(F)$

$\quad\quad\quad\quad\quad\quad\quad\quad\quad\quad\quad$ or $\quad MRQ = MR \cdot MQ$

(3) $\quad ARQ = \dfrac{R}{F} = \dfrac{R}{Q} \cdot \dfrac{Q}{F} \quad$ or $\quad ARQ = \dfrac{R(Q)}{Q} \cdot \dfrac{Q(F)}{F} \quad$ or $\quad ARQ = P \cdot \dfrac{Q}{F}$

$\quad\quad\quad\quad\quad\quad\quad\quad\quad\quad\quad$ or $\quad ARQ = P \cdot AQ$

Let output of a product (Q) first increase at an increasing rate as quantity used of a factor (F) increases; then each additional unit of F adds a larger amount to Q. But each additional unit of Q adds a smaller amount to total revenue and hence total revenue-product. Therefore, given the same production function, the rate of increase of total revenue-product as F increases is less in the case of an imperfectly competitive seller than in the case of a perfectly competitive seller of a product. The slope of the total revenue-product curve of Figure 16.2c is less at any given F value than the slope of the total revenue-product curve of Figure 16.1c.

Now, let Q increase at a decreasing rate as F increases; then each additional unit of F adds a smaller amount to Q. But each additional unit of Q adds a smaller amount to total revenue and hence total revenue-product. Therefore, given the same production function, the rate of increase of total revenue-product as F increases is again less in the case of an imperfectly competitive seller than in the case of a perfectly competitive seller of a product. The total revenue-product curve of Figure 16.2c lies below the total revenue-product curve of Figure 16.1c.

Two separate reasons now exist for assuming decreasing marginal revenue-product of a factor of production. The first reason is decreasing marginal product of a factor of production. The second reason is decreasing marginal revenue of a product. Consequently, the marginal revenue-product curve of Figure 16.2e is closer to the horizontal axis than is the marginal revenue-product curve of Figure 16.1e. The value of MRQ at any given value of F is less when both dQ/dF and dR/dQ decrease than when only dQ/dF decreases as F increases. The negatively-sloped portion of the marginal revenue-product curve of Figure 16.2e lies to the left of the negatively-sloped portion of the marginal revenue-product curve of Figure 16.1e.

SUMMARY

The total revenue-product curve of a factor shows how total revenue-product (R) varies with quantity used (input) of the factor (F) per unit of time. The marginal revenue-product curve of a factor shows how the slope of the total revenue-product curve (dR/dF) varies with quantity used of the factor (F) per unit of time. The average revenue-product curve of a factor shows how the ratio of total revenue-product to quantity used (R/F) varies with quantity used of the factor (F) per unit of time. In the case of a user who is subject to diminishing marginal returns, each additional unit used of a factor per unit of time adds a smaller amount to total revenue-product. Total revenue-product (R) therefore increases at a decreasing rate (dR/dF) as quantity used (F) increases. Consequently, marginal revenue-product of the factor ($MRQ = dR/dF$) is a decreasing function of quantity used (F) per unit of time. To generalize, according to the law of decreasing marginal revenue-product of a factor to a user who is subject to diminishing marginal returns, the revenue associated with using an additional unit of a factor varies inversely with quantity used per unit of time.

Marginal and average revenue-product of a factor are increasing when total revenue-product is increasing at an increasing rate as quantity used of the factor increases, and the marginal revenue-product curve lies above the average revenue-product curve. The marginal revenue-product curve is at its maximum value, but average revenue-product continues to increase, at that quantity used of the factor at which total revenue-product begins to increase at a decreasing rate. Eventually, as more units of the factor are used, marginal revenue-product decreases sufficiently to make average revenue-product reach its maximum value. When this happens, the marginal revenue-product curve is intersecting the average revenue-product curve from above. Thereafter, average revenue-product also decreases, and the marginal revenue-product curve lies below the average revenue-product curve. Thus the law of decreasing marginal revenue-product applies to the negatively-sloped portion of the marginal revenue-product curve and to that portion of the total revenue-product curve denoting that total revenue-product is increasing at a decreasing rate. When total revenue-product reaches its maximum value, marginal revenue-product is zero but average revenue-product is some positive value. When total revenue-product decreases, marginal revenue-product is negative. Average revenue-product continues to decrease toward zero and becomes zero when total revenue-product is zero.

When P is a decreasing function of Q, marginal revenue-product decreases as F increases for two different reasons, each reinforcing the other. First, MRQ decreases as F increases because of diminishing marginal returns. Second, MRQ decreases as F increases because of decreasing marginal revenue. Consequently, with respect to negatively-sloped curves, the slope of the marginal revenue-product curve of an imperfectly competitive seller of a product is greater numerically than the slope of the marginal revenue-product curve of a perfectly competitive seller, given the same production function.

Questions

1. List the principles of the theory of demand for a factor that are of primary importance. How do you account for the position of the law of decreasing marginal revenue-product in this list? Verbalize this principle of economics.

2. Define total revenue-product of a factor. What is a total revenue-product curve? Draw a total revenue-product curve and describe its properties. Derive a total revenue-product curve of a perfectly competitive seller of a product from his $Q = Q(F)$ and $P = P(Q)$ curves and describe their relationships. Do the same analysis for an imperfectly competitive seller of a product. What conclusions do you draw from a comparison of the two total revenue-product curves?

3. Define marginal revenue-product of a factor. What is a marginal revenue-product curve? Draw a marginal revenue-product curve and describe its properties. Relate the properties of the total and marginal revenue-product curves. Derive a marginal revenue-product curve of a perfectly competitive seller of a product from his $MQ = Q'(F)$ and $MR = R'(Q)$ curves and describe their relationships. Do the same analysis for an imperfectly competitive seller of a product. What conclusions do you draw from a comparison of the two marginal revenue-product curves?

4. Define average revenue-product of a factor. What is an average revenue-product curve? Draw an average revenue-product curve and describe its properties. Relate the properties of the total and average revenue-product curves, and the marginal and average revenue-product curves. Derive an average revenue-product curve of a perfectly competitive seller of a product from his $AQ = Q(F)/F$ and $AR = R(Q)/Q$ curves and describe their relationships. Do the same analysis for an imperfectly competitive seller of a product. What conclusions do you draw from a comparison of the two average revenue-product curves?

NOTES

[1] Eventually, an additional unit of input adds nothing to output. Thus it adds nothing to revenue. If output is a maximum at some input, revenue is a maximum at the same input. If an additional unit of input reduces output, it also reduces revenue.

[2] When quantity is varied continuously, continuous marginal revenue-product of a factor (MRQ_c) is the instantaneous rate of change of total revenue-product as quantity used of the factor increases or decreases. With respect to the one-factor revenue-product function $R = r(F)$, the instantaneous rate of change is the infinitesimally small change in R (dR) associated with an infinitesimally small change in F (dF): $MRQ_c = dR/dF$. In this context, marginal revenue-product is the slope of the total revenue-product curve of the factor. The slope of the total revenue-product curve is equal to the difference quotient $\Delta R/\Delta F$ of the tangent line at a point on the curve. In Table 16.1, the MRQ_c of the tenth unit equals

$$\frac{dR}{dF} = \lim_{\Delta F \to 0} \frac{\Delta R}{\Delta F} = 3.20$$

[3] Let output price be $1 per unit of output, and let an additional unit of labor add two units to output. Then $MRQ = P \cdot \Delta Q/\Delta F = \$1 \cdot 2 = \$2.00$. The additional unit of labor yielded $2.00 because it yielded 2 units, at $1 per unit, of output.

chapter 17

Equilibrium of a Perfectly Competitive Purchaser of Factors of Production

One of the ultimate aims of a purchaser and user of factors of production is to maximize his profit. Profit equals revenue-product minus factor cost. Factor cost varies with the quantities purchased of factors of production. Revenue-product varies with the quantities used of factors of production. Thus a purchaser-user is faced with the problem of determining the profit-maximizing quantity to purchase and use of each of his factors per unit of time. He is said to be in equilibrium when he has chosen the quantities that maximize his profit. The concern of the economist with this ultimate aim of man is embodied in the so-called "principle of equilibrium of a perfectly competitive purchaser of factors of production," which may be presented in several different ways.[1]

Marginal Revenue-Product Equals Price

Profit $(R - C)$ is maximized at that quantity purchased and used of a factor (F) at which the profit curve, $R - C = r(F) - c(F)$, is at its peak. When the profit curve is at its peak, its slope, $r'(F) - c'(F)$, is zero. Thus profit is maximized at that quantity of the factor (F) at which marginal revenue-product, $r'(F)$, equals marginal factor cost, $c'(F)$. The profit-maximizing quantity of a factor, therefore, may be determined by setting the marginal revenue-product function, $MRQ = r'(F)$, equal to the marginal factor cost function, $MFC = c'(F)$, and solving for F. The principle of equilibrium of a purchaser of factors of production is thus an inference drawn from an operation on the marginal revenue-product and marginal factor cost functions of a purchaser. Assuming perfect competition in the factor market, at each quantity purchased, average factor cost equals marginal factor cost equals price: $AFC = MFC = W = W(F)$. Consequently, when a perfectly competitive purchaser is in equilibrium, he has determined the quantity to purchase and use of each factor at which the marginal revenue-product of a factor (MRQ) equals the price of the factor (W). To elucidate this principle, when a perfectly competitive purchaser is in equilibrium, the amount of money he is willing to accept to use an additional unit of a factor (MRQ) is equal to the amount of money he has to give up to purchase an additional unit of the factor (W):

$$MRQ = W \quad \text{or} \quad \frac{\Delta R}{\Delta F} = \frac{\Delta C}{\Delta F}$$

In other words, the last unit purchased of each factor (ΔF) adds as much to his revenue-product (ΔR) as it adds to his factor cost (ΔC); the "pleasure" of an additional unit (ΔR) is offset exactly by its "pain" (ΔC).

In the two-factors case,

(1) $\quad MRQ_1 = W_1 \quad \text{or} \quad MRQ_1 = MFC_1 \text{ since } W_1 = MFC_1$

(2) $\quad MRQ_2 = W_2 \quad \text{or} \quad MRQ_2 = MFC_2 \text{ since } W_2 = MFC_2$

When two factors are not related in production, the marginal product and hence the marginal revenue-product of one factor do not vary with the quantity used of the other factor. And thus each equation is independent of the other equation: as F_1 changes, MRQ_2 does not change; and as F_2 changes, MRQ_1 does not change.[2] But when two factors are related in production, the marginal product and hence the marginal revenue-product of one factor vary with the quantity used of the other factor. And thus each equation is dependent upon the other equation: as F_1 changes, MRQ_2 changes; and as F_2 changes, MRQ_1 changes.[3]

Equality of the Ratio of Marginal Revenue-Product to Price of Every Factor

Factor cost varies with the quantities purchased of factors of production. Thus, when a purchaser has determined the profit-maximizing quantities to purchase, he has also determined the profit-maximizing factor cost. By dividing both sides of equation (1) by W_1 and both sides of equation (2) by W_2

(1') $\quad \dfrac{MRQ_1}{W_1} = 1$

(2') $\quad \dfrac{MRQ_2}{W_2} = 1$

By setting (1') equal to (2'),

(3) $\quad \dfrac{MRQ_1}{W_1} = \dfrac{MRQ_2}{W_2} (= 1)$

With respect to factors $F_1, F_2, F_3, \ldots, F_n$,

$$(3') \quad \frac{MRQ_1}{W_1} = \frac{MRQ_2}{W_2} = \frac{MRQ_3}{W_3} = \cdots = \frac{MRQ_n}{W_n} (= 1)$$

Therefore, when a perfectly competitive purchaser is in equilibrium, he is allocating his profit-maximizing factor cost in such a way that the last dollar spent on F_1 (W_1) yields the same amount of revenue-product (MRQ_1) as the last dollar spent on $F_2, F_3, \ldots, F_n$—the equimarginal principle of equilibrium of a perfectly competitive purchaser of factors of production.

Equimarginal Principle of Equilibrium of a Perfectly Competitive Purchaser of Factors

The equimarginal principle of equilibrium of a perfectly competitive purchaser of factors may be analyzed via the two-factors case according to the two-faced (Janus) diagram in Figure 17.1. The outlay on factor F_1 begins

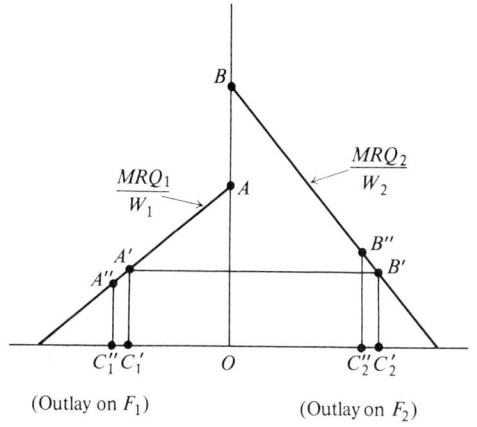

FIG. 17.1. Equimarginal principle of equilibrium of a purchaser of factors of production

with zero at the origin and increases to the left on the horizontal axis. Conversely, the outlay on factor F_2 begins with zero at the origin and increases to the right on the horizontal axis. Thus all values on the horizontal axis are either zero or positive (that is, nonnegative). The marginal revenue-product per dollar of outlay on a factor begins with zero at the origin and increases up the vertical axis. When the outlay on F_1 increases, the quantity purchased of F_1 increases; and as the quantity used of F_1 increases, the marginal revenue-product of F_1 decreases according to the law of decreasing marginal revenue-product of a factor of production. Thus, given W_1, the marginal revenue-product per dollar of outlay on F_1 (MRQ_1/W_1) decreases as the outlay on F_1 increases, as depicted by the curve labeled MRQ_1/W_1.

Similarly, the curve labeled MRQ_2/W_2 depicts the inverse relation between MRQ_2/W_2 and the outlay on F_2.

The purchaser has $C'_1 C'_2$ profit-maximizing dollars to allocate between F_1 and F_2. The marginal revenue-product per dollar of outlay OC'_1 is $C'_1 A'$; therefore the total revenue-product of outlay OC'_1, which is the area under the MRQ_1/W_1 curve at OC'_1, is area $C'_1 A' A O$. Similarly, the marginal revenue-product per dollar of outlay OC'_2 is $C'_2 B'$; and the total revenue-product of outlay OC'_2 is area $C'_2 B' B O$. Since $C'_1 A' = C'_2 B'$, with this allocation the ratio of marginal revenue-product to price is the same for both factors: $MRQ_1/W_1 = MRQ_2/W_2$.

The magnitude $C'_1 C'_2$ is the same as the magnitude $C''_1 C''_2$. Thus the purchaser has $C''_1 C''_2$ profit-maximizing dollars to allocate between F_1 and F_2. The marginal revenue-product per dollar of outlay OC''_1 is $C''_1 A''$; and the total revenue-product of outlay OC''_1 is area $C''_1 A'' A O$. Similarly, the marginal revenue-product per dollar of outlay OC''_2 is $C''_2 B''$; and the total revenue-product of outlay OC''_2 is area $C''_2 B'' B O$. Since $C''_1 A'' < C''_2 B''$, with this allocation the ratio of marginal revenue-product to price is not the same for both factors: $MRQ_1/W_1 < MRQ_2/W_2$.

The combined area when $MRQ_1/W_1 = MRQ_2/W_2$ ($C'_1 A' A O + C'_2 B' B O$) is larger than the combined area when $MRQ_1/W_1 < MRQ_2/W_2$ ($C''_1 A'' A O + C''_2 B'' B O$). To see this, increase the outlay on F_1 from OC'_1 to $OC''_1 (= C''_1 - C'_1)$, thereby increasing total revenue-product by the area $C'_1 A' A'' C''_1$. The outlay on F_2 is decreased from OC'_2 to $OC''_2 (= C'_2 - C''_2)$, thereby decreasing total revenue-product by the area $C'_2 B' B'' C''_2$. The loss in revenue-product ($C'_2 B' B'' C''_2$) is greater than the gain in revenue-product ($C'_1 A' A'' C''_1$). Therefore, when $MRQ_1/W_1 < MRQ_2/W_2$, revenue-product is increased by using more F_2 and less F_1 until $MRQ_1/W_1 = MRQ_2/W_2$. As less F_1 is used, MRQ_1/W_1 increases; and as more F_2 is used, MRQ_2/W_2 decreases, until eventually $MRQ_1/W_1 = MRQ_2/W_2$.

Ratio of Marginal Revenue-Products Equals Ratio of Price

By multiplying both sides of equation (3) by W_1 and dividing both sides by MRQ_2,

(4) $$\frac{MRQ_1}{MRQ_2} = \frac{W_1}{W_2} \left(= \frac{W_1}{MRQ_2}\right)$$

Thus, when a perfectly competitive purchaser is in equilibrium, he is allocating his profit-maximizing factor cost in such a way that the ratio of the marginal revenue-products of any two factors is equal to the ratio of their prices.

Price of Output Equals Marginal Cost

Output varies with the quantities used of factors of production. Thus, when a user has determined the profit-maximizing quantities to use, he has also determined the profit-maximizing output. By setting MRQ_1 equal to $P(\Delta Q/\Delta F_1)$ and MRQ_2 equal to $P(\Delta Q/\Delta F_2)$, equations (1) and (2) are transformed into

$$P(\Delta Q/\Delta F_1) = W_1 \text{ and } P(\Delta Q/\Delta F_2) = W_2$$

which are equivalent to

$$P = W_1(\Delta F_1/\Delta Q) \text{ and } P = W_2(\Delta F_2/\Delta Q)$$

and hence

(5) $\quad P = W_1(\Delta F_1/\Delta Q) = W_2(\Delta F_2/\Delta Q)$

or

$$\frac{\Delta R}{\Delta Q} = \frac{\Delta C_1}{\Delta F_1} \cdot \frac{\Delta F_1}{\Delta Q} = \frac{\Delta C_2}{\Delta F_2} \cdot \frac{\Delta F_2}{\Delta Q}$$

or

$$\frac{\Delta R}{\Delta Q} = \frac{\Delta C_1}{\Delta Q} = \frac{\Delta C_2}{\Delta Q}$$

Therefore, the profit-maximizing output is that output at which the price of output equals the marginal cost of output in the use of each factor:[4] the last unit of output produced by each factor adds as much to revenue as to cost. By dividing equation (5) through by P,

$$\frac{W_1(\Delta F_1/\Delta Q)}{P} = \frac{W_2(\Delta F_2/\Delta Q)}{P} (= 1)$$

which is an alternative form of the equimarginal principle of equilibrium of a perfectly competitive purchaser of factors of production.

Ratio of Marginal Products Equals Ratio of Prices

By setting MRQ_1 equal to $P(\Delta Q/\Delta F_1)$ and MRQ_2 equal to $P(\Delta Q/\Delta F_2)$, equation (4) is transformed into

$$\frac{P(\Delta Q/\Delta F_1)}{P(\Delta Q/\Delta F_2)} = \frac{W_1}{W_2}$$

which is equivalent to

(6) $$\frac{\Delta Q/\Delta F_1}{\Delta Q/\Delta F_2} = \frac{W_1}{W_2} \quad \text{or} \quad \frac{MQ_1}{MQ_2} = \frac{W_1}{W_2}$$

Therefore, when a perfectly competitive purchaser is in equilibrium, he is producing his profit-maximizing output in such a way that the ratio of the marginal products of any two factors is equal to the ratio of their prices.

The ratio W_1/W_2 is a number that denotes the amount of F_2 that a perfectly competitive purchaser has to give up to purchase an additional unit of F_1. Similarly, the ratio MQ_1/MQ_2 is a number that denotes the amount of F_2 he is willing to give up to use an additional unit of F_1. Thus, when a perfectly competitive purchaser is in equilibrium, the amount of F_2 he has to give up to purchase an additional unit of F_1 (W_1/W_2) is equal to the amount of F_2 he is willing to give up to use an additional unit of F_1 (MQ_1/MQ_2).

The ratio W_1/W_2 is the numerical value of the slope of an iso-factor cost curve. The ratio MQ_1/MQ_2 is called the marginal rate of technical substitution of F_1 for F_2. Thus, when a perfectly competitive purchaser is in equilibrium, the numerical value of the slope of an iso-factor cost curve (W_1/W_2) is equal to the marginal rate of technical substitution of F_1 for F_2 (MQ_1/MQ_2). In other words, when a perfectly competitive purchaser is in equilibrium, he is producing his profit-maximizing output in such a way that the ratio of the prices of any two factors is equal to their marginal rate of technical substitution.

The ratio MQ_1/MQ_2 is the numerical value of the slope of an iso-product curve. An iso-product curve depicts all combinations of quantities of two factors (F_1 and F_2) that yield the same level of output to a user. Thus, when a perfectly competitive purchaser is in equilibrium, he has chosen a combination of F_1 and F_2 at which the slope of an iso-factor cost curve is equal to the slope of the iso-product curve that denotes his profit-maximizing output; that is, $-W_1/W_2 = -MQ_1/MQ_2$. In Figure 17.2, assume that iso-product

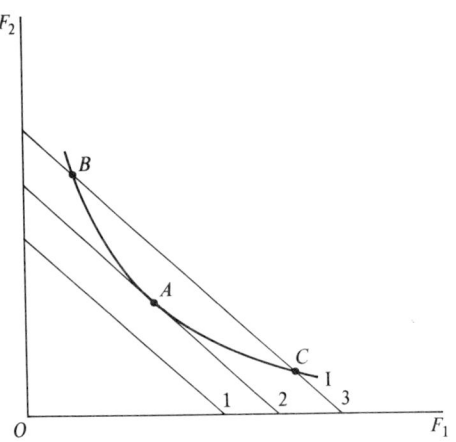

FIG. 17.2. Equilibrium of a perfectly competitive purchaser of factors: ratio of marginal revenue-products equals ratio of prices

curve I represents the profit maximizing output. The slope of iso-factor cost curve 2 ($-W_1/W_2$) is equal to the slope of iso-product curve I ($-MQ_1/MQ_2$) at point A. By multiplying both slopes by -1, $W_1/W_2 = MQ_1/MQ_2$ at point A. Since at point B, $W_1/W_2 < MQ_1/MQ_2$, he is in disequilibrium at B. From B to A, the ratio MQ_1/MQ_2 decreases as more F_1 and less F_2 are used per unit of time until, at A, $W_1/W_2 = MQ_1/MQ_2$. Similarly, at point C, $W_1/W_2 > MQ_1/MQ_2$, and hence he is in disequilibrium. From C to A, the ratio MQ_1/MQ_2 increases as more F_2 and less F_1 are used per unit of time until, at A, $W_1/W_2 = MQ_1/MQ_2$.

An iso-factor cost curve depicts all combinations of quantities of two factors (F_1 and F_2) that may be purchased by a purchaser at a given factor cost. And the higher an iso-factor cost curve lies in the plane, the greater the level of factor cost. Combination A on iso-product curve I and iso-factor cost curve 2, therefore, is preferred to all other combinations that lie on curve 1: it is the combination associated with the lowest level of factor cost per the profit-maximizing level of output. It lies on the lowest attainable iso-factor cost curve, which is curve 2, and is the only attainable combination on this curve. Combination B on iso-product curve I and iso-factor cost curve 3 is attainable but not preferred to A. For by purchasing more F_1 and less F_2, the purchaser can obtain a lower level of factor cost (and therefore a higher profit) and hence a preferred position; that is, he can move onto the lower iso-factor cost curve 2. Similarly, combination C on iso-product curve I and iso-factor cost curve 3 is attainable but not preferred to A. For by purchasing more F_2 and less F_1, the purchaser can attain a lower level of factor cost (and therefore a higher profit) and hence a preferred position; that is, he can move onto the lower iso-factor cost curve 2.

Input Expansion Path

Profit is maximized when the user of factors has chosen the combination of F_1 and F_2 that maximizes the surplus of revenue-product over factor cost. According to equation (5), when he has chosen the profit-maximizing combination,

(5) $\quad P = W_1(\Delta F_1/\Delta Q) = W_2(\Delta F_2/\Delta Q)$

In contrast, cost is minimized when the user has chosen the combination of F_1 and F_2 that minimizes the cost of producing a specified output, which may or may not be the profit-maximizing output. According to equation (6), when he has chosen the cost-minimizing combination,

(6) $\quad \dfrac{\Delta Q/\Delta F_1}{\Delta Q/\Delta F_2} = \dfrac{W_1}{W_2}$

which is equivalent to

$$\frac{\Delta F_2/\Delta Q}{\Delta F_1/\Delta Q} = \frac{W_1}{W_2}$$

which is equivalent to

(6') $\qquad W_1(\Delta F_1/\Delta Q) = W_2(\Delta F_2/\Delta Q)$

or

$$\frac{\Delta C_1}{\Delta F_1} \cdot \frac{\Delta F_1}{\Delta Q} = \frac{\Delta C_2}{\Delta F_2} \cdot \frac{\Delta F_2}{\Delta Q}$$

or

$$\frac{\Delta C_1}{\Delta Q} = \frac{\Delta C_2}{\Delta Q}$$

Therefore, the cost minimizing output is that output at which the marginal cost of output in the use of F_1 equals the marginal cost of output in the use of F_2: the last unit of output produced by each factor adds the same amount to cost.

By comparing equation (5), in which P appears, to equation (6'), in which P does not appear, one may infer that a necessary but not sufficient condition for profit maximization is cost minimization; and a sufficient condition for cost minimization is profit maximization. Cost is minimized when profit is maximized, for cost is minimized per the profit-maximizing level of output. But profit may not be maximized when cost is minimized, for cost is minimized per any specified level of output.

A point on a total cost curve (see pages 155–159) denotes the minimum cost of producing a specified output. Thus, with reference to each point on this curve, the user must determine the combination of F_1 and F_2 that minimizes cost per the specified output. When he has chosen the cost-minimizing combination associated with a specified output, he is on the lowest iso-factor cost curve having a common point with the iso-product curve of the specified output, and hence $W_1/W_2 = MQ_1/MQ_2$. Corresponding to each tangency of an iso-factor cost curve and a specified iso-product curve, therefore, is a point on a total cost curve. Since in this frame of reference a specified output constrains cost, this case is called constrained cost minimization.

Conversely, a point on a total cost curve denotes the maximum output produced at a specified cost. Thus, with reference to each point on this curve, the user must determine the combination of F_1 and F_2 that maximizes the output produced at a specified cost. When he has chosen the output-maximizing combination associated with a specified cost, he is on the highest iso-product curve having a common point with the iso-factor cost curve of the specified cost, and hence $W_1/W_2 = MQ_1/MQ_2$. Corresponding to each tangency of an iso-product curve and a specified iso-factor cost curve, therefore, is a point on a total cost curve. Since in this frame of reference a specified cost constrains output, this case is called constrained output maximization.

Constrained cost minimization and constrained output maximization are depicted graphically in Figure 17.3 by each point of tangency of an iso-product curve and an iso-factor cost curve: with reference to each point, $W_1/W_2 = MQ_1/MQ_2$. The locus (set) of tangencies is called the input expansion path.

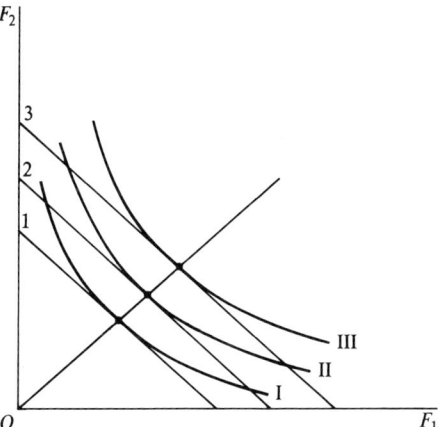

FIG. 17.3. Input expansion path

SUMMARY

One of the ultimate aims of a purchaser and user of factors of production is to maximize his profit. When he is maximizing his profit, he is said to be in equilibrium: he cannot increase his profit by changing the quantities he purchases and uses per unit of time, given the parameters of his factor cost and revenue-product functions. When a perfectly competitive purchaser has determined the profit-maximizing set of factor quantities, in effect he has determined his profit-maximizing factor cost and is allocating it in such a way that (1) the marginal revenue-product of each factor equals its price. (2) The ratio of marginal revenue-product to price is the same for every factor—the equimarginal principle of equilibrium of a perfectly competitive purchaser of factors of production, which is analyzed via a Janus diagram. (3) The ratio of the marginal revenue-products of any two factors equals the ratio of their prices. (4) The price of output equals the marginal cost of output in the use of each factor. (5) The ratio of the marginal-products of any two factors equals the ratio of their prices—which is equivalent to saying that the ratio of the prices of any two factors equals the marginal rate of technical substitution of one factor for the other factor. When a perfectly competitive purchaser has determined a cost-minimizing set of factor quantities, in effect he has determined a cost-minimizing output and is producing it in such a way that the marginal cost of output in the use of one factor equals the marginal cost of output in the use of every other factor. The user is minimizing his cost when he is maximizing his profit, but he may or may not be maximizing his profit when he is minimizing his cost.

Questions

1. List the principles of the theory of demand for a factor of production that are of primary importance. How do you account for the position of the principle of equilibrium of a purchaser of factors in this list?
2. Derive and verbalize the equilibrium principle $MRQ = W$.
3. Derive and verbalize the equimarginal principle of equilibrium of a perfectly competitive purchaser of factors of production for the two factors case and the n-factors case.
4. Analyze this principle in the two-factors case via a Janus diagram.
5. Derive and verbalize the equilibrium principle $MRQ_1/MRQ_2 = W_1/W_2$.
6. Derive and verbalize the equilibrium principle $P = W_1(\Delta F_1/\Delta Q) = W_2(\Delta F_2/\Delta Q)$.
7. Use iso-factor cost and iso-product curves to derive, analyze, and verbalize the equilibrium principle $MQ_1/MQ_2 = W_1/W_2$. (Note: An analysis of equilibrium includes an analysis of disequilibrium). How would the equilibrium principle be stated if you did not accept the concepts of product (that is, revenue-product) and marginal product (that is, marginal revenue-product)?
8. Prove via equations that cost minimization is not necessarily profit maximization, but profit maximization is cost minimization.
9. Analyze the concept of the input expansion path via the concepts of constrained cost minimization and constrained output maximization.

NOTES

[1] The principle of equilibrium of a perfectly competitive purchaser of factors of production is *introduced* in this chapter and is analyzed further in Chapter 23.

[2] In this case, the total revenue-product of one factor is independent of the total revenue-product function of the other factor, and hence the two total revenue-product functions may be added to derive the user's total revenue-product function. In the case of a perfectly competitive purchaser, the total factor cost function of one factor is independent of the total factor cost function of the other factor, and hence the two total factor cost functions may be added to derive the purchaser's factor cost function. In maximizing his profit, the purchaser-user is assumed not to be subject to a factor cost constraint. Given these three assumptions, equilibrium of a multifactor purchaser may be analyzed in exactly the same way as equilibrium of a single-factor purchaser (see Chapter 23).

[3] In this case, the total revenue-product function of one factor is interdependent with the total revenue-product function of the other factor, and hence the two total revenue-product functions may not be added to derive the user's revenue-product function. Equilibrium of a

multi-factor purchaser thus may not be analyzed in exactly the same way as equilibrium of a single-factor purchaser.

[4] Verbalize $W_1(\Delta F_1/\Delta Q)$ as the marginal cost of output in the use of F_1 and $W_2(\Delta F_2/\Delta Q)$ as the marginal cost of output in the use of F_2.

chapter **18**

The Demand Function for a Factor of Production of a Perfectly Competitive Purchaser

"The demand function for a factor of production of a perfectly competitive purchaser" is the name of the relation between the quantity of a factor a purchaser is willing to purchase per unit of time (the dependent variable) and the price of the factor, the price of a substitute factor, and the price of a complementary factor (the independent variables), given the parameters of the state of technology and (assuming perfect competition in product markets) the price of output. The relation between the dependent variable and each of the independent variables is analyzed via the principle of equilibrium of a perfectly competitive purchaser of factors of production. The analysis consists of changing the value of one independent variable, while holding constant the values of the remaining independent variables, and ascertaining the new equilibrium value of the dependent variable. The primary objective of the analysis is to ascertain the sign of each of the difference quotients denoting the change in the dependent variable associated with a change in an independent variable, given the ceteris paribus assumption that in each case "other things are equal" (or are unchanging). When the value of an independent variable is held constant via the ceteris paribus assumption, the variable is called a parameter of the relation being analyzed. Thus the price of a substitute factor, the price of a complementary factor, the state of technology, and the price of output are parameters of the relation between the quantity of a factor a purchaser is willing to purchase per unit of time and the price of the factor.

Demand Curve for a Factor of a Purchaser

The "demand curve for a factor of a purchaser" depicts the relation between the quantity of a factor a purchaser is willing to purchase (F) per unit of time and the price of the factor (W). The relation is denoted by $F = d(W)$. The purchaser is in equilibrium with respect to each ordered pair of W and

DEMAND FUNCTION FOR A FACTOR OF PRODUCTION OF A PURCHASER

F numbers on his demand curve. When he is in equilibrium, in effect he has determined his profit-maximizing factor cost and is allocating it in such a way that the marginal revenue-product of each factor equals its price: $MRQ = W$. A marginal revenue-product curve depicts the relation between marginal revenue-product and quantity used of the factor: $MRQ = r'(F)$. Thus, since $MRQ = W$ at each value of F, a perfectly competitive purchaser's marginal revenue-product curve of a factor, $MRQ = r'(F)$, is his demand curve for the factor, $F = d(W)$—provided that in the case of a multi-factor purchaser his factors are not related in production.[1]

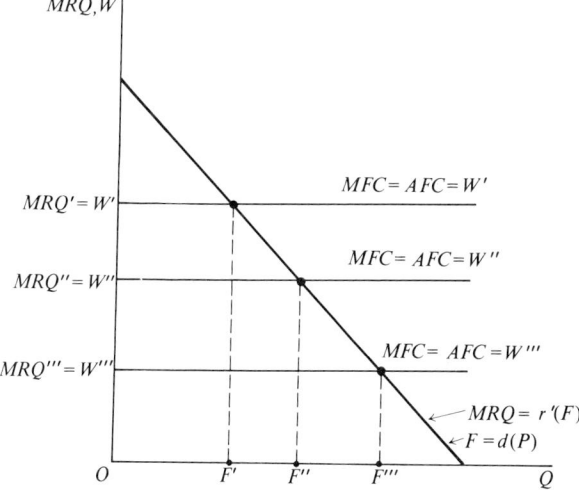

FIG. 18.1. Hypothetical marginal revenue-product and demand curves of a factor of a perfectly competitive purchaser of factors not related in production

A marginal revenue-product curve of a factor and the supply curve of the factor facing a perfectly competitive purchaser are depicted in Figure 18.1. To analyze the equilibrium principle via this figure, given W', the purchaser's profit is maximized at that quantity purchased of the factor (F') at which marginal revenue-product (MRQ') is equal to price (W'). For given W', the revenue-product of the last unit before F' is greater than the factor cost of the same unit ($MRQ > MFC$); hence that unit would increase his profit. Similarly, given W', the revenue-product of the first unit after F' is less than the factor cost of the same unit ($MRQ < MFC$); hence that unit would decrease his profit. But, given W', the revenue-product of the last unit of F' is equal to the factor cost of that unit ($MRQ = MFC$); hence that unit maximizes his profits. Thus (W', F') is one point on the demand curve of the purchaser; and since $MRQ' = W'$ at F', this point is on his marginal revenue-product curve. The same is true of other points such as (W'', F'') and (W''', F'''), which are rationalized in the same way by shifting the supply curve facing the purchaser upward. Consequently, subject to the assumptions already noted, the purchaser's marginal revenue-product curve is his demand curve.

Law of Demand for a Factor of a Purchaser

According to the law of demand for a factor of production of a purchaser, the quantity of a factor a purchaser is willing to purchase (F) per unit of time is a decreasing function of the price of the factor (W): quantity varies inversely with price—$\Delta F/\Delta W < 0$. According to the law of decreasing marginal revenue-product of a factor of production, marginal revenue-product (MRQ) is a decreasing function of quantity used (F): marginal revenue-product varies inversely with quantity—$\Delta MRQ/\Delta F < 0$. According to the principle of equilibrium of a perfectly competitive purchaser, when a purchaser is in equilibrium, the marginal revenue-product of each factor equals its price: $MRQ = W$. Thus the rationale of the law of demand is the law of decreasing marginal revenue-product of a factor and the principle of equilibrium of a perfectly competitive purchaser: a demand curve has a negative slope because the corresponding marginal revenue-product curve has a negative slope and the purchaser-user is assumed to maximize profit.

Price of a Technical Substitute in Production

The quantity of a factor a purchaser is willing to purchase (F) per unit of time is a function of the price of the factor (W): $F = d(W)$. However, F is also a function of the price of a substitute factor in production (W_s). Thus the price of a technical substitute is a parameter of $F = d(W)$.

To ascertain the sign of the difference quotient $\Delta F/\Delta W_s$, consider the equilibrium principle

$$MRQ_1 = W_1 \quad \text{and} \quad MRQ_2 = W_2$$

The purchaser is in disequilibrium when

$$MRQ_1 = W_1 \quad \text{and} \quad MRQ_2 > W_2$$

because of a decrease in W_2. To regain equilibrium, he purchases more of F_2. Aside from the effect on MRQ_2, each additional unit of F_2 induces a decrease in MRQ_1 because of the substitute relationship between F_1 and F_2, and hence

$$MRQ_1 < W_1$$

To be in equilibrium at the given value of W_1, he must increase MRQ_1. According to the law of decreasing marginal revenue-product of a factor,

MRQ_1 varies inversely with F_1. Thus, to regain equilibrium, he purchases less of F_1. Therefore, when F_1 and F_2 are technical substitutes in production, less of F_1 is purchased when more of F_2 is purchased as W_2 decreases. By letting F_1 be F and W_2 be W_s, the conclusion follows that $\Delta F/\Delta W_s > 0$.

Demand Curve for a Technical Substitute in Production

When factors are technical substitutes in production, a perfectly competitive purchaser's marginal revenue-product curve of a factor is not his demand curve of the factor. Instead, his demand curve is the set of (W, F) numbers determined by the intersection of his shifting marginal revenue-product and marginal ($=$ average) factor cost curves. Ditch-digging labor (F_1) and ditch-digging machines (F_2) are technical substitutes in production: the marginal revenue-product of ditch-digging labor (MRQ_1) is a decreasing function of the quantity used of ditch-digging machines; and the marginal revenue-product of ditch-digging machines (MRQ_2) is a decreasing function of the quantity used of ditch-digging labor. Thus, as F_1 increases from F_1' to F_1'' in

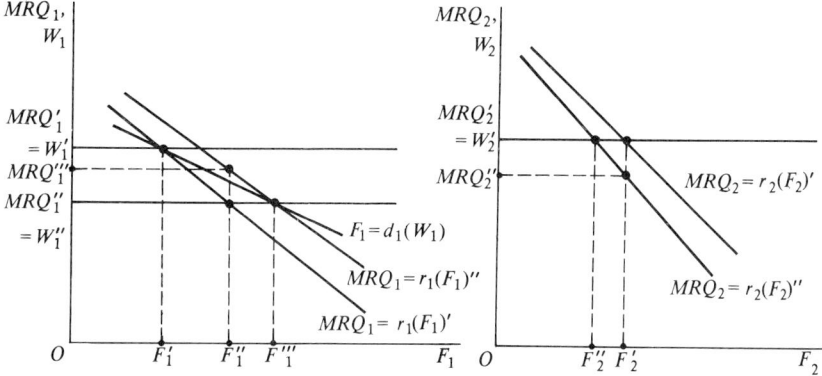

FIG. 18.2a. Hypothetical demand curve for a factor of a perfectly competitive purchaser of substitutes in production

FIG. 18.2b. Demand for a factor is an increasing function of price of a substitute factor

Figure 18.2a because W_1 has decreased from W_1' to W_1'', MRQ_2 decreases autonomously of F_2' in Figure 18.2b from MRQ_2' to MRQ_2'', thereby shifting the marginal revenue-product curve of F_2 downward from $MRQ_2 = r_2(F_2)'$ to $MRQ_2 = r_2(F_2)''$. Since W_2 by assumption has not changed from W_2' in Figure 18.2b, F_2 must decrease from F_2' to F_2'' to increase MRQ_2 from MRQ_2'' to the equilibrium level $MRQ_2' = W_2'$. As F_2 decreases from F_2' to F_2'' in Figure 18.2b, MRQ_1 increases autonomously of F_1'' from MRQ_1'' to MRQ_1''', thereby shifting the marginal revenue-product curve of F_1 upward from $MRQ_1 = r_1(F_1)'$ to $MRQ_1 = r_1(F_1)''$. Since W_1 by assumption has not changed from W_1'' in Figure 18.2a, F_1 must increase from F_1'' to F_1''' to decrease MRQ_1 from MRQ_1''' to the equilibrium level $MRQ_1'' = W_1''$. The purchaser thus equates W_1'' with MRQ_1'' on the higher marginal revenue-product curve to determine equilibrium quantity F_1'''. The curve $F_1 = d_1(W_1)$ connects the points (W_1', F_1') and (W_1'', F_1'''); therefore, it is the purchaser's demand curve for factor F_1.

Price of a Technical Complement in Production

The quantity of a factor a purchaser is willing to purchase (F) per unit of time is a function of the price of the factor (W): $F = d(W)$. However, F is also a function of the price of a technical complement in production (W_c). Thus the price of a technical complement is a parameter of $F = d(W)$.

To ascertain the sign of the difference quotient $\Delta F/\Delta W_c$, consider the equilibrium principle

$$MRQ_1 = W_1 \quad \text{and} \quad MRQ_2 = W_2$$

The purchaser is in disequilibrium when

$$MRQ_1 = W_1 \quad \text{and} \quad MRQ_2 > W_2$$

because of a decrease in W_2. To regain equilibrium, he purchases more of F_2. Aside from the effect on MRQ_2, each additional unit of F_2 induces an increase in MRQ_1 because of the complementary relationship between F_1 and F_2, and hence

$$MRQ_1 > W_1$$

To be in equilibrium at the given value of W_1, he must decrease MRQ_1. According to the law of decreasing marginal revenue-product of a factor of production, MRQ_1 varies inversely with F_1. Thus, to regain equilibrium, he purchases more of F_1. Therefore, when F_1 and F_2 are technical complements in production, more of F_1 is purchased when more of F_2 is purchased as W_2 decreases. By letting F_1 be F and W_2 be W_c, the conclusion follows that $\Delta F/\Delta W_c < 0$.

Demand Curve for a Technical Complement in Production

When factors are technical complements in production, a perfectly competitive purchaser's marginal revenue-product curve of a factor is not his demand curve for the factor. Instead, his demand curve is the set of (W, F) numbers determined by the intersection of his shifting marginal revenue-product and marginal ($=$ average) factor cost curves. Ditch-digging labor (F_1) and hand shovels (F_2) are technical complements in production: the marginal revenue-product of ditch-digging labor (MRQ_1) is an increasing function of the quan-

DEMAND FUNCTION FOR A FACTOR OF PRODUCTION OF A PURCHASER

tity used of hand shovels; and the marginal revenue-product of hand shovels (MRQ_2) is an increasing function of the quantity used of ditch-digging labor.

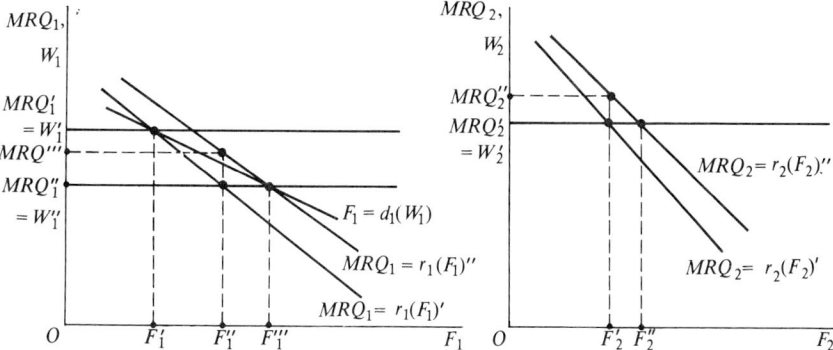

FIG. 18.3a. Hypothetical demand curve for a factor of a perfectly competitive purchaser of complements in production

FIG. 18.3b. Demand for a factor is a decreasing function of price of a complementary factor

Thus, as F_1 increases from F_1' to F_1'' in Figure 18.3a because W_1 has decreased from W_1' to W_1'', MRQ_2 increases autonomously of F_2' in Figure 18.3b from MRQ_2' to MRQ_2'', thereby shifting the marginal revenue-product curve of F_2 upward from $MRQ_2 = r_2(F_2)'$ to $MRQ_2 = r_2(F_2)''$. Since W_2 by assumption has not changed from W_2' in Figure 18.3b, F_2 must increase from F_2' to F_2'' to decrease MRQ_2 from MRQ_2'' to the equilibrium level $MRQ_2' = W_2'$. As F_2 increases from F_2' to F_2'' in Figure 18.3b, MRQ_1 increases autonomously of F_1'' from MRQ_1'' to MRQ_1''', thereby shifting the marginal revenue-product curve of F_1 upward from $MRQ_1 = r_1(F_1)'$ to $MRQ_1 = r_1(F_1)''$. Since W_1 by assumption has not changed from W_1'' in Figure 18.3a, F_1 must increase from F_1'' to F_1''' to decrease MRQ_1 from MRQ_1''' to the equilibrium level $MRQ_1'' = W_1''$. The purchaser thus equates W_1'' with MRQ_1'' on the higher marginal revenue-product curve to determine equilibrium quantity F_1'''. The curve $F_1 = d_1(W_1)$ connects the points (W_1', F_1') and (W_1'', F_1'''); therefore, it is the purchaser's demand curve for factor F_1.

SUMMARY

The quantity of a factor of production a perfectly competitive purchaser is willing to purchase (F) per unit of time is a function of the price of the factor (W), the price of a substitute factor (W_s), and the price of a complementary factor (W_c), given the parameters of the state of technology and (assuming perfect competition in product markets) the price of output. The value of F varies inversely with the value of W in accordance with the law of demand for a factor of a purchaser, the rationale of which is the law of decreasing marginal revenue-product of a factor and the principle of equilibrium of a perfectly competitive purchaser of factors: $\Delta F/\Delta W < 0$ because $\Delta MRQ/\Delta F < 0$ and $MRQ = W$. The value of F varies directly with the value of W_s: $\Delta F/\Delta W_s > 0$. And F varies inversely with W_c: $\Delta F/\Delta W_c < 0$.[2]

A perfectly competitive purchaser's marginal revenue-product curve of a factor is his demand curve for the factor provided that in the case of a multi-factor purchaser his factors are not related in production. If his factors are related in production, his demand curve is the set of (W, F) values determined by the intersection of his shifting marginal revenue-product and marginal ($=$ average) factor cost curves. Given the same increase in W, the increase in F is greater in the case of factors that are related in production than in the case of factors that are not related in production.

Questions

1. List the principles of the theory of demand for a factor that are of primary importance. How do you account for the position of the law of demand for a factor of production of a purchaser in this list? Verbalize this principle of economics. It is based upon what other principles of economics?

2. Use the equilibrium principle $MRQ = W$ and the law of decreasing marginal revenue-product to analyze the difference quotients $\Delta F/\Delta W < 0$, $\Delta F/\Delta W_s > 0$, and $\Delta F/\Delta W_c < 0$.

3. Analyze the relationship between a demand curve and the corresponding marginal revenue-product curve(s) when (1) factors are not related in production; (2) factors are technical substitutes in production; (3) factors are technical complements in production.

NOTES

[1] Further qualifications are stated in footnote 1 of Chapter 17 and are analyzed in Chapter 23.
[2] By definition, marginal revenue-product increases autonomously of quantity used of the factor with an improvement in the purchaser's technology or an increase in the price of output (P). Therefore, the quantity he is willing to purchase (F) per unit of time increases autonomously of price (W) with an improvement in technology or increase in price of output. The value of F may also vary with expected changes in its determinants.

chapter 19

The Market Demand Function for a Factor of Production

The market demand curve for a factor of production shows how the aggregate quantity purchased of the factor (F_d) per unit of time varies with the price of the factor (W) ceteris paribus: $F_d = D(W)$. The parameters of a market demand curve are the price of a substitute factor (W_s) and the price of a complementary factor (W_c). (The state of technology and the price of output are also parameters, unless the latter varies as F_d varies.) The market demand curve for a factor depicts the law of market demand for a factor. According to this law, F_d varies inversely with W: $\Delta F_d/\Delta W < 0$.

Rationale of the Law of Market Demand for a Factor

In part, the rationale of the law of market demand for a factor ($\Delta F_d/\Delta W < 0$) is the law of demand for a factor of a purchaser ($\Delta F/\Delta W < 0$). As seen in Figure 19.1, which depicts hypothetical data presented in Table 19.1, demand curves of individual purchasers may be aggregated into the market demand curve by summing the quantity purchased of each purchaser at each given price of the factor, holding W_s and W_c constant. In addition to this rationale, however, aggregate quantity purchased varies inversely with price if for any reason the *number* of purchasers increases as price decreases. In particular,

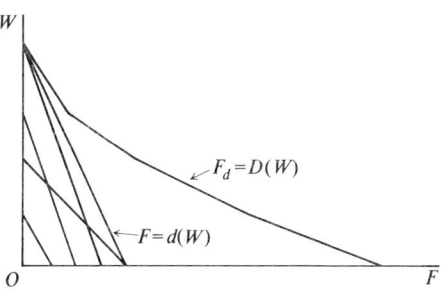

FIG. 19.1. Hypothetical market demand curve for a factor of production

TABLE 19.1: Hypothetical market demand curve for a factor of production

W	F	F	F	F	F	F_d
0	8	4.00	8	2	6.00	28.00
1	7	3.33	6	1	5.25	22.58
2	6	2.67	4	0	4.50	17.17
3	5	2.00	2	0	3.75	12.75
4	4	1.33	0	0	3.00	8.33
5	3	0.67	0	0	2.25	5.92
6	2	0.00	0	0	1.50	3.50
7	1	0.00	0	0	0.75	1.75
8	0	0.00	0	0	0.00	0.00

price decreases may attract high-cost product sellers into the factor market who previously had not purchased any of the factor. In other words, as seen in Figure 19.1, the quantity purchased by each purchaser *currently* in the market increases as the price decreases; and the price intercepts of the demand curves of purchasers may differ in such a way that the *number* of purchasers increases as the price decreases.

Change in Demand and Change in Quantity Demanded

The aggregate quantity purchased of a factor (F_d) per unit of time at various prices of the factor (W) is called the market demand for the factor. A given market demand curve, $F_d = D(W)$, depicts the aggregate quantity purchased of a factor (F_d) per unit of time at various prices of the factor (W). Thus $F_d = D(W)$ represents a given market demand. For this reason, (1) a change in price of the factor (W) does not effect a change in (market) demand for the factor, $F_d = D(W)$. Instead, a change in price of the factor (W) is said to effect a change in (market) quantity demanded of the factor. Changes in quantity demanded of the factor are thus depicted by movements along a given demand curve as price of the factor (W) changes. (2) A change in W_s or W_c autonomously of F_d does effect a change in demand for the factor $F_d = D(W)$; for at any given value of W, an autonomous change in W_s or W_c effects a change in F_d and hence $F_d = D(W)$. Changes in demand for the factor, therefore, are depicted by shifts in the market demand curve, $F_d = D(W)$, as W_s or W_c change.

The conclusion follows from this analysis that F_d may be called three different things. (1) F_d is the aggregate quantity purchased of a factor. (2) When F_d changes because of a change in W, holding W_s and W_c constant, F_d may be called quantity demanded of the factor, for quantity demanded is a function of W. (3) When F_d changes because of a change in W_s or W_c holding

THE MARKET DEMAND FUNCTION FOR A FACTOR OF PRODUCTION 315

W_c constant, F_d may be called demand for the factor, for demand is a function of W_s and W_c.

Aggregate Quantity Purchased of a Factor as a Function of Price of a Technical Substitute in Production

As seen in Figure 19.2a, the aggregate quantity purchased of a factor (for example, ditch-digging labor) per unit of time is a decreasing function of the price of the factor ceteris paribus: $\Delta F_d / \Delta W < 0$. In this diagram, the price of ditch-digging labor (W) is measured on the vertical axis, and the aggregate quantity purchased of this labor (F_d) is measured on the horizontal

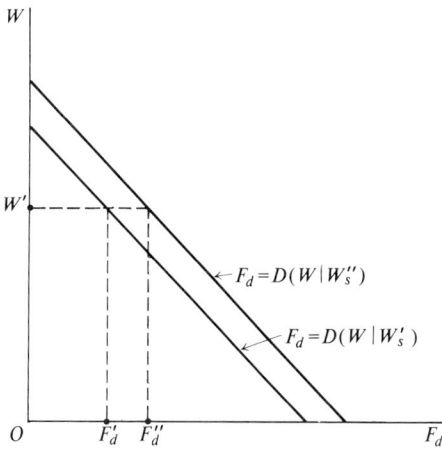

FIG. 19.2a. Quantity demanded of a factor varies inversely with price of the factor

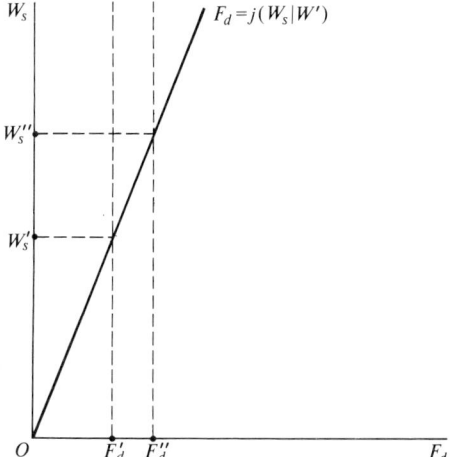

FIG. 19.2b. Demand for a factor varies directly with price of a substitute

axis. As seen in Figure 19.2b, the aggregate quantity purchased of ditch-digging labor (F_d) per unit of time is an increasing function of the price of a technical substitute in production (for example, ditch-digging machines) ceteris paribus: $\Delta F_d/\Delta W_s > 0$. In this diagram, the price of ditch-digging labor (W_s) is measured on the vertical axis, and the aggregate quantity purchased of ditch-digging labor (F_d) is measured on the horizontal axis. In Figure 19.2b, an increase in the price of ditch-digging machines from W'_s to W''_s induces an increase in the quantity purchased of ditch-digging labor from F'_d to F''_d. In Figure 19.2a, F'_d and F''_d are associated with the same price of labor (W'). Thus, with the increase in W_s from W'_s to W''_s, the demand curve for labor has shifted to the right to portray the increase in F_d from F'_d to F''_d. To generalize, market demand for a factor increases as the price of a substitute factor increases and decreases as price of a substitute decreases ceteris paribus. The negatively-sloped market demand curve for a factor shifts to the right as the price of a substitute factor increases and to the left as the price of a substitute decreases.

Aggregate Quantity Purchased of a Factor as a Function of Price of a Technical Complement in Production

To repeat, the aggregate quantity purchased of ditch-digging labor per unit of time is a decreasing function of the price of the labor, as depicted also in Figure 19.3a. As seen in Figure 19.3b, the aggregate quantity purchased of ditch-digging labor (F_d) per unit of time is a decreasing function of the price of a technical complement in production (for example hand shovels) ceteris paribus: $\Delta F_d/\Delta W_c < 0$. In this diagram, the price of shovels (W_c) is measured on the vertical axis, and the aggregate quantity purchased of ditch-digging labor (F_d) is measured on the horizontal axis. In Figure 19.3b, an increase in the price of shovels from W'_c to W''_c induces a decrease in the quantity purchased of ditch-digging labor from F'_d to F''_d. In Figure 19.3a, F'_d and F''_d are associated with the same price of labor (W'). Thus, with the increase in W_c from W'_c to W''_c, the demand curve for ditch-digging labor has shifted to the left to portray the decrease in F_d from F'_d to F''_d. To generalize, the market demand for a factor decreases as the price of a complementary factor increases and increases as the price of a complement decreases ceteris paribus. The negatively-sloped market demand curve for a factor shifts to the left as the price of a complementary factor increases and to the right as the price of a complement decreases.

SUMMARY

According to the law of market demand for a factor of production, the aggregate quantity purchased of a factor (F_d) per unit of time is a decreasing function of its price (W) ceteris paribus. As W decreases, other

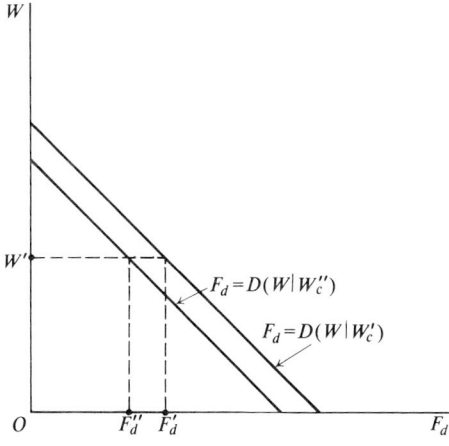

FIG. 19.3a. Quantity demanded of a factor varies inversely with price of the factor

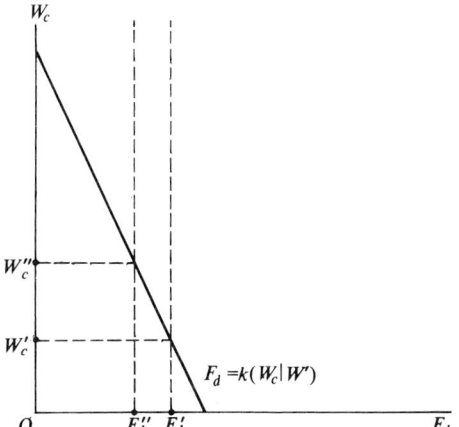

FIG. 19.3b. Demand for a factor varies inversely with price of a complement

things being equal, the quantity purchased of each purchaser currently in the market increases and the number of purchasers increases. The relation between F_d and W is depicted by the market demand curve. Quantity demanded of the factor varies inversely with its price (W). Demand for the factor varies directly with price of a substitute (W_s) and inversely with price of a complement (W_c). In short, $\Delta F_d/\Delta W < 0$; $\Delta F_d/\Delta W_s > 0$; and $\Delta F_d/\Delta W_c < 0$.

Questions

1. List the principles of the theory of demand for a factor that are of primary importance. How do you account for the position of the law of market demand for a factor in this list? Verbalize this principle of economics.

2. What is the rationale of the law of market demand for a factor?

3. Distinguish between a change in demand and a change in quantity demanded.

4. Use diagrams to analyze shifts in a market demand curve due to changes in the price of a substitute factor.

5. Use diagrams to analyze shifts in a market demand curve due to changes in the price of a complementary factor.

APPENDIX: Marginal Physical Productivity Theory of Income Distribution

Assume perfect competition in factor markets F_1 and F_2; then $MFC_1 = W_1$ and $MFC_2 = W_2$. Assume also that all purchasers are in equilibrium; then $MRQ_1 = W_1$ and $MRQ_2 = W_2$. Next, assume perfect competition in product markets; then $P = MR$. Therefore, $MRQ_1 = P \cdot MQ_1$ and $MRQ_2 = P \cdot MQ_2$. Consequently, $MQ_1 = MRQ_1/P = W_1/P$ and $MQ_2 = MRQ_2/P = W_2/P$. Lastly, assume constant returns to scale. Then, in the aggregate,

(1) $\qquad R = PQ = r(F_1, F_2) = W_1 F_1 + W_2 F_2 = MRQ_1 \cdot F_1 + MRQ_2 \cdot F_2$

(2) $\qquad \dfrac{R}{P} = \dfrac{PQ}{P} = Q = \dfrac{W_1}{P} F_1 + \dfrac{W_2}{P} F_2 = MQ_1 \cdot F_1 + MQ_2 \cdot F_2$

In words, the aggregate total revenue-product (R), or aggregate total product (Q), is just sufficient to pay each factor its marginal revenue-product (MRQ), or marginal product (MQ), when the aggregate production function is subject to constant returns to scale. In other words, the sum of income payments ($W_1 F_1 + W_2 F_2$) is just sufficient to exhaust total revenue-product when each factor is paid a price equal to its marginal revenue-product.[1] This theory is called the marginal physical productivity theory of income distribution.

Input-Quantity Ratio as a Function of Input-Price Ratio

Purchasers are in equilibrium with respect to capital (F_2) and labor (F_1) when, in aggregate terms,

$$\dfrac{MRQ_1}{MRQ_2} = \dfrac{W_1}{W_2}$$

assuming perfect competition in factor markets. Corresponding to each equilibrium is a ratio of capital to labor (F_2/F_1). When the price of labor increases relative to the price of capital (when W_1/W_2 increases), capital is substituted for labor (F_2/F_1 increases). As more capital and less labor is used, the marginal revenue-product of capital (MRQ_2) decreases and the marginal revenue-product of labor (MRQ_1) increases until the higher MRQ_1/MRQ_2 is equal to the higher W_1/W_2. Thus $F_2/F_1 = f(W_1/W_2)$, where $\Delta(F_2/F_1)/\Delta(W_1/W_2) > 0$.

Elasticity of Substitution

The curve expressing the relation between F_2/F_1 and W_1/W_2 is called the aggregate substitution curve, for it shows that capital (F_2) is substituted for labor (F_1) when the

THE MARKET DEMAND FUNCTION FOR A FACTOR OF PRODUCTION

price of labor (W_1) increases relative to the price of capital (W_2). The elasticity of F_2/F_1 with respect to W_1/W_2 is called the elasticity of substitution (e_s). The elasticity of substitution (e_s) is defined as the percentage change in the dependent variable (F_2/F_1) divided by the percentage change in the independent variable (W_1/W_2):

$$e_s = \frac{\Delta(F_2/F_1)/(F_2/F_1)}{\Delta(W_1/W_2)/(W_1/W_2)}$$

When applied to the aggregate substitution curve of an economic system, this concept of elasticity is used to analyze changes in the distribution of the national income.

Distribution of National Income

Let $R = PQ$ be the monetary national income. Then labor's relative (percentage) share of the monetary national income is W_1F_1/PQ. Similarly, capital's relative share of the monetary national income is W_2F_2/PQ. The share of labor relative to the share of capital, therefore, is

$$\frac{W_1F_1}{PQ} \div \frac{W_2F_2}{PQ} = \frac{W_1F_1}{W_2F_2}$$

However,

$$\frac{W_1F_1}{W_2F_2} = \frac{W_1}{W_2} \cdot \frac{F_1}{F_2} = \frac{W_1}{W_2} \div \frac{F_2}{F_1}$$

Thus, if the percentage increase in W_1/W_2 along the aggregate substitution curve is greater than the corresponding percentage increase in F_2/F_1, the relative share of labor increases. Conversely, if the percentage increase in W_1/W_2 along the aggregate substitution curve is less than the corresponding percentage increase in F_2/F_1, the relative share of labor decreases. Lastly, if the percentage increase in W_1/W_2 along the aggregate substitution curve is equal to the corresponding percentage increase in F_2/F_1, the relative share of labor remains constant. In short, W_1F_1/W_2F_2 remains constant, increases, or decreases when W_1/W_2 increases according to whether e_s is equal to unity, is less than unity, or is greater than unity.

To see this let $e_s = 1$ and let the wage rate (W_1) increase relative to the interest rate (W_2). Then the increase in the ratio of capital to labor (F_2/F_1) is equal proportionately to the increase in the ratio of the wage rate to the interest rate (W_1/W_2):

$$\frac{\Delta(F_2/F_1)}{(F_2/F_1)} = \frac{\Delta(W_1/W_2)}{(W_1/W_2)} \quad \text{when } e_s = 1$$

For example, let W_1/W_2 increase by 10 percent and let F_2/F_1 increase by 10 percent. Then $W_1/W_2 \div F_2/F_1$ remains constant as W_1/W_2 and F_2/F_1 increase. Thus the relative share of labor remains constant as W_1/W_2 increases if $e_s = 1$.

Next, let $e_s < 1$ and let the wage rate (W_1) increase relative to the interest rate (W_2). Then the increase in the ratio of capital to labor (F_2/F_1) is less proportionately than the increase in the ratio of the wage rate to the interest rate (W_1/W_2):

$$\frac{\Delta(F_2/F_1)}{(F_2/F_1)} < \frac{\Delta(W_1/W_2)}{(W_1/W_2)} \quad \text{when } e_s < 1$$

For example, let W_1/W_2 increase by 10 percent and let F_2/F_1 increase by 5 percent. Then $W_1/W_2 \div F_2/F_1$ increases as W_1/W_2 and F_2/F_1 increase. Thus the relative share of labor increases as W_1/W_2 increases if $e_s < 1$.

Lastly, let $e_s > 1$ and let the wage rate (W_1) increase relative to the interest rate (W_2). Then the increase in the ratio of capital to labor (F_2/F_1) is greater proportionately than the increase in the ratio of the wage rate to the interest rate (W_1/W_2):

$$\frac{\Delta(F_2/F_1)}{(F_2/F_1)} > \frac{\Delta(W_1/W_2)}{(W_1/W_2)} \text{ when } e_s > 1.$$

For example, let W_1/W_2 increase by 10 percent and let F_2/F_1 increase by 15 percent. Then $W_1/W_2 \div F_2/F_1$ decreases as W_1/W_2 and F_2/F_1 increase. Thus the relative share of labor decreases as W_1/W_2 increases if $e_s > 1$.[2]

Technological Progress

In Hicks' classification of technological progress (pp. 127–129), the ratio F_2/F_1 remains constant but the ratio MQ_1/MQ_2 (and hence MRQ_1/MRQ_2) may change with changes in the state of technology. Since in equilibrium $MRQ_1/MRQ_2 = W_1/W_2$, the ratio W_1/W_2 may also change with changes in the state of technology. Therefore, the relative share of labor $(W_1/W_2 \div F_2/F_1)$ may change with changes in the state of technology. Specifically, given F_2/F_1, the ratio MRQ_1/MRQ_2 $(= W_1/W_2)$ remains constant, and hence the relative share of labor remains constant, if technological progress is neutral. But, given F_2/F_1, the ratio MRQ_1/MRQ_2 $(= W_1/W_2)$ decreases, and hence the relative share of labor decreases, if technological progress is capital-using. However, given F_2/F_1, the ratio MRQ_1/MRQ_2 $(= W_1/W_2)$ increases, and hence the relative share of labor increases, if technological progress is labor-using.[3]

NOTES

[1] The aggregate production function must be linearly homogeneous. Euler's theorem concerning this type of function yields the above result. See A. C. Chiang, *Fundamental Methods of Mathematical Economics* (New York: McGraw-Hill Book Company, 1967), p. 373.

[2] Econometric studies suggest that for the American economy, $e_s < 1$ and that W_1/W_2 and W_1F_1/W_2F_2 are increasing. See, for example, J. W. Kendrick and Ryuzo Sato, "Factor Prices, Productivity, and Growth," *The American Economic Review*, LIII: 5 (December 1963), pp. 974–1003.

[3] Some studies suggest that technological progress has been labor-using since World War II. See, for example, C. E. Ferguson, "Substitution, Technical Progress, and Returns to Scale," *The American Economic Review, Papers and Proceedings*, LV: 2 (May 1965), pp. 296–305.

PART V

PRINCIPLES OF THE THEORY OF SUPPLY OF A FACTOR OF PRODUCTION

Products may be classified as goods or services; and factors of production may be classified as labor, capital, or land. However, a stock of real capital consists of intermediate goods (that is, buildings, equipment, and inventories) used to produce other products; and land is a natural resource. Thus, factors of production may also be classified as labor, intermediate goods, or natural resources. An intermediate good such as a tractor is a product output of the capital goods industry that is used as a factor input by a product seller. Similarly, a natural resource such as copper is a product output of the mining industry that is used as a factor input by a product seller. The economic theory of supply of an intermediate good or a natural resource, therefore, may be considered to be the same as the economic theory of supply of a product (see Part III)—leaving labor to be analyzed.

Six principles of the economic theory of supply of labor are of primary importance. They are the laws of constant marginal income of labor to a perfectly competitive seller of labor, decreasing marginal utility and decreasing marginal rate of substitution of leisure for income to a seller who is subject to diminishing marginal returns, equilibrium of a seller, supply of labor of a seller, and market supply of labor. Each of these principles of economics is a verbalization of an economic function or an inference drawn from an operation on a set of economic functions.

Specifically, the law of constant marginal income of labor is a verbalization of the marginal income curve of a perfectly competitive seller—defined as a seller who can sell all he wishes per unit of time at the prevailing market price ceteris paribus (see Chapter 20). The law of decreasing marginal utility of leisure is a verbalization of a marginal utility curve of a seller (see Chapter 2). The law of decreasing marginal rate of substitution of leisure for income is a verbalization of a marginal rate of substitution curve of a seller (see Chapters 2–4). The principle of equilibrium of a seller is an inference drawn from an operation on the income and utility curves of a seller (see Chapter

21). The law of supply of labor of a seller is a verbalization of the supply curve of a seller (see Chapter 22). Finally, the law of market supply of labor is a verbalization of the market supply curve.

The new concepts are leisure and labor. Hours of leisure plus hours of labor equal hours in a day. The price of leisure is an opportunity cost, for it is the wage income given up to obtain an hour of leisure. The price of labor is the wage income received for giving up an hour of leisure. As the wage rate increases, the quantity supplied of labor increases according to the law of supply of labor, and the quantity demanded of leisure decreases according to the law of demand for leisure. Thus the law of supply of labor is the converse of the law of demand for leisure.

SELECTED READINGS

Robbins, Lionel. "On the Elasticity of Demand for Income in Terms of Effort," *Economica*, X (June 1930), pp. 123–129. Reprinted in The American Economic Association. *Readings in the Theory of Income Distribution.* Edited by William Fellner and Bernard F. Haley. Homewood, Illinois: Richard D. Irwin, Inc., 1951, pp. 237–244.

chapter 20

Income Function of a Perfectly Competitive Seller of Labor

According to the law of constant marginal income of labor to a perfectly competitive seller, the income associated with selling an additional unit of labor does not vary with quantity sold per unit of time. Each additional unit sold of labor per unit of time adds the same amount to total income. Total income of labor increases at a constant rate as quantity sold of labor per unit of time increases. Marginal income of labor is a constant function of quantity sold of labor per unit of time.

Total Income Curve of Labor

The total income of labor is the money received from selling a quantity of labor. The total income curve of labor is a set of ordered pairs of quantity sold (F) and income (Y) having the property that corresponding to each

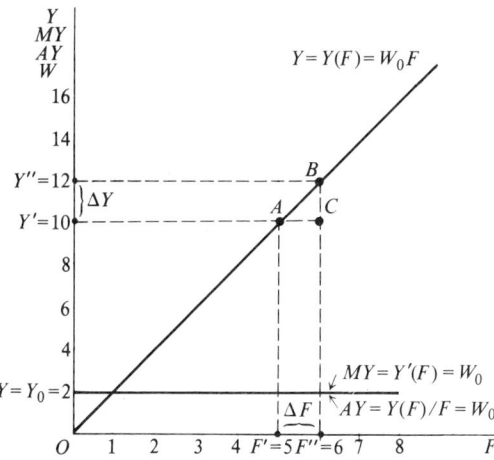

FIG. 20.1. Hypothetical income curves of labor of a perfectly competitive seller

323

number in the F set of numbers is one number in the Y set of numbers: $Y = Y(F)$. Thus the total income curve shows the Y value corresponding to each F value and hence how Y varies with F per unit of time. The parameter of the total income curve of a perfectly competitive seller is the price of the labor, which is the wage rate (W): $W = W_0$.

As seen in Figure 20.1, which depicts hypothetical data presented in Table 20.1, the total income curve of a perfectly competitive seller is a ray, the

TABLE 20.1: Hypothetical income of labor to a perfectly competitive seller

$AY = Y/F = W_0$	F	$Y = W_0 F$	$MY_d = \Delta Y/\Delta F$	$MY_c = dY/dF$
2	0	0		2
2	1	2	2	2
2	2	4	2	2
2	3	6	2	2
2	4	8	2	2
2	5	10	2	2
2	6	12	2	2
2	7	14	2	2
2	8	16	2	2

equation of which is $Y = W_0 F$. The curve has a zero total income intercept because total income of labor is zero when quantity sold is zero: $Y = W_0 \cdot 0 = 0$. It is linear because each successive unit is sold at the same price ($W_0 = 2$); hence each successive unit sold adds the same amount ($2) to total income. The slope of $Y = Y(F)$ therefore remains constant as quantity sold increases.

Marginal Income Curve of Labor

When quantity sold is varied by discrete amounts, discrete marginal income of labor (MY_d) is the change in Y (ΔY) associated with a change of one unit in F ($\Delta F = 1$): $MY_d = \Delta Y/\Delta F$, where $\Delta F = 1$. In this context, marginal income is equal to the difference quotient ($\Delta Y/\Delta F$) of the straight line between two points one F unit apart on the curve. In Figure 20.1, between points A and B on $Y = Y(F)$,

$$MY_d = \lim_{\Delta F \to 1} \frac{\Delta Y}{\Delta F} = \frac{Y'' - Y'}{F'' - F'} = \frac{CB}{AC} = \text{slope of line } AB = 2$$

Since the total income curve of a perfectly competitive seller is linear, the difference quotient is the same for all changes in quantity sold, and hence discrete marginal income equals continuous marginal income.[1]

The marginal income curve of labor is a set of ordered pairs of quantity sold (F) and (continuous) marginal income (MY) having the property that corresponding to each number in the F set of numbers is one number in the MY set of numbers: $MY = Y'(F)$. Thus the marginal income curve shows the MY value corresponding to each F value and hence how MY varies with F per unit of time. The parameters of a marginal income curve of a perfectly competitive seller are the parameters of the market demand and supply curves.

As seen in Figure 20.1, which depicts hypothetical data presented in Table 20.1, the marginal income curve of a perfectly competitive seller is a zero-sloped (horizontal) straight line ($\Delta MY/\Delta F = 0$), the equation of which is $MY = W_0$. The curve is a horizontal straight line because each successive unit is sold at the same price ($W_0 = \$2$); hence each successive unit sold adds the same amount (\$2) to total income. Marginal income, therefore, remains constant as quantity sold increases.

To conclude, marginal income (MY) is a constant function of quantity sold (F) when total income (Y) increases at the constant rate W_0 as quantity increases. Thus the law of constant marginal income is a verbalization of the marginal income curve of a perfectly competitive seller. Since total income increases at a constant rate, and since the phrase "increases at a constant rate" is another way of saying "constant marginal income," the total income curve of a perfectly competitive seller also depicts the law of constant marginal income.

Average Income Curve of Labor

The average income of labor (AY) is the ratio of total income (Y) to quantity sold (F): $AY = Y/F$. Average income is equal to the difference quotient ($\Delta Y/\Delta F$) of the ray at a point on the total income curve. In Figure 20.1, at point A on $Y = Y(F)$,

$$AY = \frac{F'A}{OF'} = \text{slope of line } OA = 2$$

Since the total income curve of a perfectly competitive seller is a ray, the difference quotient is the same at each point on the curve.

The average income curve of labor is a set of ordered pairs of quantity sold (F) and average income (AY) having the property that corresponding to each number in the F set of numbers is one number in the AY set of numbers: $AY = Y(F)/F$. Thus the average income curve shows the AY value corresponding to each F value and hence how AY varies with F per unit of time. The parameters of the average income curve of a perfectly competitive seller are the parameters of the market demand and supply curves.

As seen in Figure 20.1, which depicts hypothetical data presented in Table 20.1, the average income curve of a perfectly competitive seller is a zero-sloped (horizontal) straight line ($\Delta AY/\Delta F = 0$), the equation of which is $AY = W_0$. The curve is a horizontal straight line because each quantity is sold at the same price ($W_0 = \$2$); hence each quantity sold has the same average income (\$2). Average income, therefore, remains constant as quantity sold increases.

Demand Curve for Labor Facing a Seller

The demand curve for labor facing a seller shows the price at which each quantity can be sold. A perfectly competitive seller can sell all he wishes per unit of time at the prevailing price ceteris paribus. Thus the demand curve for labor facing him is a horizontal straight line that depicts the given price. Moreover, at each F value, average income equals marginal income equals price: $AY = MY = W = W(F) = W_0$. Consequently, the demand curve facing a perfectly competitive seller is his average income curve, which is the same as his marginal income curve. To conclude, average income and marginal income are equal and are constant functions of quantity sold when the demand curve facing the seller is a horizontal straight line.

Iso-Wage Curve

The iso-wage of income and leisure is the constant (equal) wage rate associated with various combinations of income and leisure. An iso-wage curve of income and leisure is a set of ordered pairs of quantities of income (Y) and leisure (Q) having the properties that (1) corresponding to each number in the Q set of numbers is one number in the Y set of numbers and (2) each pair of numbers of the function is associated with the same wage rate: $Y = W_0(Q)$. Thus an iso-wage curve shows the Y value corresponding to each Q value and hence how Y varies with Q per unit of time, holding the wage rate constant. In other words, *an iso-wage curve depicts all combinations of quantities of income and leisure associated with the same wage rate.* The parameters of an iso-wage curve are the parameters of the demand curve for labor facing the seller. The parameters of the demand curve facing a perfectly competitive seller, $AY = W(F) = W_0$, are the parameters of the market demand and supply curves of labor, for W_0 changes with shifts in these curves.

As seen in Figure 20.2, an iso-wage curve of a perfectly competitive seller is a negatively-sloped straight line "anchored" on the horizontal axis at 24 hours, the equation of which is $Y = W_0 H - W_0 Q$. It is negatively sloped because labor (F) and leisure (Q) are rivals for the hours of a day (H); a worker may devote more time to leisure by devoting less time to labor, and vice versa. Thus his income ($Y = W_0 F$) varies directly with his labor (F)

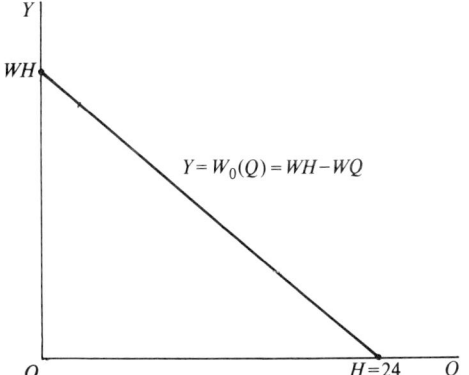

FIG. 20.2. Iso-wage curve of a perfectly competitive seller of labor

and inversely with his leisure (Q), given his wage rate (W_0). If he uses all of his time for labor, his income is $W_0 H$; if he uses all of his time for leisure his income is zero. The curve is "anchored" at 24 hours because the maximum number of hours of leisure ($=$ minimum number of hours of labor) in a day is 24, regardless of the wage rate. Since its horizontal intercept is a constant the curve shifts with changes in W by changing its slope and vertical intercept.[2]

The slope of an iso-wage curve is denoted by dY/dQ and is equal to the negative of the wage rate: $dY/dQ = -W$. By multiplying both sides by -1, $-dY/dQ = W$. The $-dY/dQ$ notation and the W notation denote numerical values and are verbalized as the amount of Y that a seller must give up (ΔY) to purchase an additional unit of Q (ΔQ) while keeping the wage rate constant. If $W = \$2$, the purchaser of leisure must give up two dollars of income to purchase an additional unit of leisure.

The higher the wage rate, the higher the level of income at any given quantity of leisure and hence the farther away from the point of origin lies the curve—that is the higher the income intercept. Thus an iso-wage curve may be drawn in Figure 20.2 for each level of the wage rate facing a seller. Two curves which depict two different wage rates cannot intersect; for if the two curves intersected, the same combination of quantities of income and leisure would be associated with two different wage rates, which is inconsistent with the income function $Y = Y(F) = W_0 \cdot F$. According to this function, an income is associated with one wage rate.

Iso-Real-Wage Curve

The real income of a person is the physical quantity of products (y) that his money income (Y) enables him to purchase. Since his real income (y) is equal to the ratio of his money income (Y) to an index of product prices (P), his real income increases with an increase in Y, holding P constant, or with a

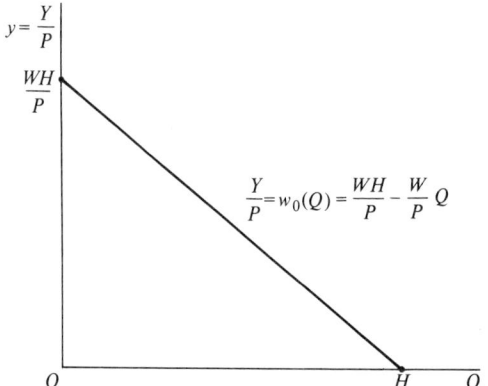

FIG. 20.3. Iso-real-wage curve of a perfectly competitive seller of labor

decrease in P, holding Y constant. Similarly, the real wage rate of a person is the physical quantity of products (w) that his money wage rate (W) enables him to purchase. Since his real wage rate (w) is equal to the ratio of his money wage (W) to an index of product prices (P), his real wage rate increases with an increase in W, holding P constant, or with a decrease in P, holding W constant. An iso-real-wage curve (see Figure 20.3) is a transformation of an iso-wage curve from monetary units to physical units. This transformation is effected by dividing both sides of the iso-wage equation by P:

(1) $\qquad Y = WH - WQ \qquad$ iso-wage equation

(1') $\qquad Q = H - \dfrac{1}{W} Y \qquad$ inverse of iso-wage equation

(2) $\qquad \dfrac{Y}{P} = y = \dfrac{WH}{P} - \dfrac{W}{P} Q \qquad$ iso-real-wage equation

(2') $\qquad Q = H - \dfrac{P}{W} y \qquad$ inverse of iso-real-wage equation

Thus the slope of an iso-real-wage curve is equal to $-W/P$; its vertical intercept is WH/P; and its horizontal intercept is H.

SUMMARY

Dropping the zero subscript and thinking in terms of a perfectly competitive seller, total income of labor of a seller (Y) is equal to its price (W) times its quantity sold (F): $Y = WF$. The curve expressing the relation between Y and F is called the total income curve of labor of a seller. The price of labor to a seller (W) is equal to his average income from the labor (AY), since each is the ratio of his total income (Y) to his quantity sold (F): $AY = Y/F = W$. The curve expressing the relation between $AY\ (= W)$ and

F is called the average income curve of labor of a seller. Lastly, marginal income of labor may be defined as the infinitesimally small change in Y (dY) associated with an infinitesimally small change in F (dF), or as the addition to total income (ΔY) of one additional unit of labor ($\Delta F = 1$): $MY_c = dY/dF$ and $MY_d = \Delta Y/\Delta F$, where $\Delta F = 1$. The curve expressing the relation between dY/dF and F is called the marginal income curve of labor of a seller of labor.

Average income (= price) is the same as marginal income in the case of perfect competition from the seller's side in the labor market, for in this case, the seller can sell all he wishes per unit of time at the prevailing price ceteris paribus. Hence each additional unit sold per unit of time adds the same amount (equal to price) to total income. Total income (Y) therefore increases at the constant rate W as quantity sold of labor (F) increases. Consequently, marginal income of labor ($MY = W$) is a constant function of quantity sold (F) per unit of time. To generalize, according to the law of constant marginal income of labor to a perfectly competitive seller, the income associated with selling an additional unit of labor does not vary with quantity sold per unit of time.

The demand curve for labor facing a perfectly competitive seller is a horizontal straight line that depicts the given price. This curve is his average (= marginal) income curve. His total income curve is derived from his average income curve by multiplying each quantity by price.

An iso-wage curve depicts all combinations of quantities of income (Y) and leisure (Q) associated with the same wage rate (W). An iso-wage curve may be drawn for each level of W. The greater the value of W, the higher the curve lies in the OQY plane, while still being "anchored" at 24 hours (H). No two curves intersect. An iso-wage curve of a perfectly competitive seller is a negatively-sloped straight line; its Q intercept is equal to H. The numerical value of the slope of an iso-wage curve is denoted by $-dY/dQ$ or W and is verbalized as the amount of Y that a purchaser of leisure must give up ($-\Delta Y$) to purchase an additional unit of Q (ΔQ) while keeping the money wage rate constant. An iso-real-wage curve depicts all combinations of quantities of real income (y) and leisure (Q) associated with the same real wage rate (w).

Questions

1. List the principles of the theory of supply of labor that are of primary importance. How do you account for the position of the law of constant marginal income in this list? Verbalize this principle of economics.

2. Define total income of labor of a seller. What is a total income curve? Draw a total income curve of a perfectly competitive seller of labor and describe its properties.

3. Define marginal income of labor of a seller. What is a marginal income curve? Draw a marginal income curve of a perfectly competitive seller of labor; describe its properties; and relate the properties of the total and marginal income curves.

4. Define average income of labor of a seller. What is an average income curve? Draw an average income curve of a perfectly competitive seller of labor; describe its properties; and relate the properties of the total and average income curves, and the marginal and average income curves.

5. What is the demand curve for labor facing a perfectly competitive seller? Relate this curve to the corresponding income curves.

6. Define the iso-wage of income and leisure. What is an iso-wage curve? Draw an iso-wage curve of a perfectly competitive purchaser of leisure; describe its properties; and relate marginal income and the slope of an iso-wage curve.

7. Prove that an iso-real-wage curve is a transformation of an iso-wage curve from monetary units to physical units.

NOTES

[1] When quantity sold is varied continuously, continuous marginal income of labor (MY_c) is the instantaneous rate of change of total income as quantity sold of labor increases or decreases. With respect to the function $Y = Y(F)$, the instantaneous rate of change is the infinitesimally small change in Y (dY) associated with an infinitesimally small change in F (dF): $MY_c = dY/dF$. In this context, marginal income is the slope of the total income curve of labor. The slope of the total income curve is equal to the difference quotient ($\Delta Y/\Delta F$) of the tangent line at a point on the curve. In Figure 20.1, at point A on $Y = Y(F)$,

$$MY_c = \frac{dY}{dF} = \lim_{\Delta F \to 0} \frac{\Delta Y}{\Delta F} = \frac{CB}{AC} = \text{slope of line } AB = 2.$$

[2] The slope of an iso-wage curve is $-W$; its Y intercept is WH; and its Q intercept is H:

(1) $\quad H = F + Q$
(2) $\quad F = H - Q$
(3) $\quad Y = WF$
(4) $\quad Y = W(H - Q)$
(5) $\quad Y = WH - WQ$
(6) $\quad \dfrac{dY}{dQ} = -W$
(7) $\quad Y \text{ intercept} = WH$
(8) $\quad Q = H - \dfrac{1}{W}Y$
(9) $\quad Q \text{ intercept} = H$

chapter **21**

Equilibrium of a Perfectly Competitive Seller of Labor

According to the principle of equilibrium of a seller of labor, when a seller is in equilibrium, he cannot improve his utility by changing the quantity he sells per unit of time, given the parameters of his income and utility functions. To present this principle, assume that the money wage rate (W) is the same as the real wage rate ($w = W/P$), by letting an index of product prices have a value of one ($P = 1$). Then, when a perfectly competitive seller has determined the equilibrium quantity of his labor, in effect he is allocating a given amount of time in such a way that (1) the ratio of the marginal utility of leisure to the marginal utility of income equals the price of leisure. In other words, the marginal rate of substitution of leisure for income equals the price of leisure. (2) The marginal utility of leisure equals the marginal utility of income times the price of leisure. In other words, the marginal utility of leisure equals the marginal utility of labor. (3) The ratio of the marginal utility of leisure to the price of leisure equals the marginal utility of income. Assume now that the money wage rate is not the same as the real wage rate. Then, when a perfectly competitive seller is in equilibrium, (4) the ratio of the marginal utility of leisure to the marginal utility of income equals the ratio of the price of leisure to the price of products.

Marginal Rate of Substitution of Leisure for Income Equals the Price of Leisure

When a seller of labor has determined the equilibrium quantity of his labor, in effect he is maximizing his utility subject to his income; this is constrained (limited) by his wage rate, which is the price of labor and the opportunity cost (price) of leisure. An iso-utility curve of income and leisure depicts all combinations of quantities of income (Y) and leisure (Q) that yield the same level of utility to a seller of labor, given the parameter of the curve, which is his taste for income and leisure. Similarly, an iso-wage curve depicts all combinations of quantities of income (Y) and leisure (Q) associated with the same wage rate (W) given the parameters of the curve, which in the case of a perfectly competitive seller of labor are the parameters of the market demand and supply curves of the labor which determine W. The conclusion follows that, when a seller is in equilibrium, he has chosen that combination of Y and Q at which the slope of the highest attainable iso-utility curve ($dY/dQ = -MU/\lambda$, where MU is marginal utility of leisure and λ is marginal utility of money income) is equal to the slope of the iso-wage curve ($dY/dQ = -W$) denoting his given wage: $-MU/\lambda = -W$.

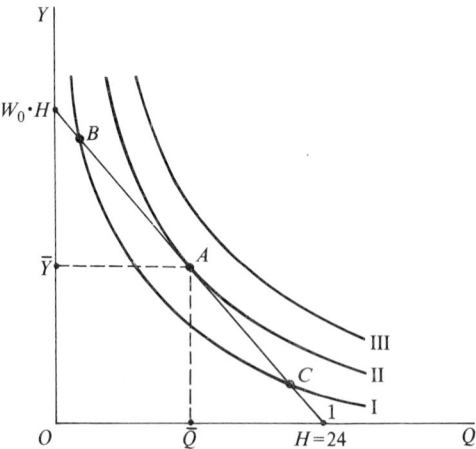

FIG. 21.1. Equilibrium of a perfectly competitive seller of labor: marginal rate of substitution of leisure for income equals the price of leisure

To see this, consider Figure 21.1. Combinations of Y and Q beyond iso-wage curve 1 are not attainable with the given wage represented by this curve. Combinations of Y and Q on and below iso-wage curve 1 are attainable with the given wage. The highest attainable combination of Y and Q ($\bar{Y}, \bar{Q}$) is on an iso-utility curve (curve II) that is tangent to iso-wage curve 1 at one unique point. At this point of tangency (point A), the slope of iso-utility curve II ($-MU/\lambda$) is equal to the slope of iso-wage curve 1 ($-W$). Therefore, by multiplying both slopes by -1, when he is in equilibrium, in effect he is choosing a combination of Q and Y such that

$$\frac{MU}{\lambda} = W$$

Point B on iso-wage curve 1 and iso-utility curve I in Figure 21.1 is attainable but not preferred to A; for by having more leisure (Q) and less income (Y), the seller of labor can attain a higher level of utility and hence a preferred position; that is, he can move onto the higher iso-utility curve II. He is in disequilibrium at B, since

$$\frac{MU}{\lambda} > W$$

and in equilibrium at A, since

$$\frac{MU}{\lambda} = W$$

From B to A, the ratio MU/λ decreases as more Q and less Y are taken per unit of time.

Similarly, point C on iso-wage curve 1 and iso-utility curve I in Figure 21.1 is attainable but not preferred to A; for by having more Y and less Q, the seller of labor can attain a higher level of utility and hence a preferred position; that is, he can move onto the higher iso-utility curve II. He is in disequilibrium at C, since

$$\frac{MU}{\lambda} < W$$

and in equilibrium at A, since

$$\frac{MU}{\lambda} = W$$

From C to A, the ratio MU/λ increases as more Y and less Q are taken per unit of time.

To conclude, when a perfectly competitive seller of labor and purchaser of leisure is in equilibrium, the amount of income he is willing to give up to purchase an additional unit of leisure $(-dY/dQ = MU/\lambda)$ is equal to the amount of income he has to give up to purchase an additional unit of leisure $(-dY/dQ = W)$. That is, when he is in equilibrium, the marginal rate of substitution of leisure for income (MU/λ) on the highest attainble iso-utility curve is equal to the numerical value of the slope of the iso-wage curve (W) denoting his constant wage rate. In short, when a perfectly competitive seller of labor and purchaser of leisure has determined the equilibrium quantity of his labor and hence leisure, in effect he is allocating a given amount of time in such a way that the marginal rate of substitution of leisure for income equals the price of leisure, or the ratio of the marginal utility of leisure to the marginal utility of income equals the price of leisure.

Marginal Utility of Leisure Equals Marginal Utility of Labor

By multiplying $MU/\lambda = W$ by λ, when a perfectly competitive seller has determined the equilibrium quantity of his labor, in effect he is allocating a given amount of time (H) in such a way that the marginal utility of leisure (MU) equals the marginal utility of income (λ) times the price of leisure (W):

$$MU = \lambda W \quad \text{or} \quad \frac{\Delta U}{\Delta Q} = \frac{\Delta U}{\Delta Y} \cdot \frac{\Delta Y}{\Delta Q}$$

But λW is also the (marginal) utility of the income derived from the last hour of labor, called the marginal utility of labor ($\Delta U/\Delta F$):

$$\frac{\Delta U}{\Delta F} = \frac{\Delta U}{\Delta Y} \cdot \frac{\Delta Y}{\Delta F}, \text{ where } \lambda = \frac{\Delta U}{\Delta Y} \text{ and } W = \frac{\Delta Y}{\Delta F}$$

Thus, in equilibrium, the marginal utility of leisure ($\Delta U/\Delta Q$) equals the marginal utility of labor ($\Delta U/\Delta F$):

$$\frac{\Delta U}{\Delta Q} = \frac{\Delta U}{\Delta F} \quad \text{or} \quad MU = \lambda W$$

In other words, when a perfectly competitive seller of labor and purchaser of leisure is in equilibrium, he is allocating a given amount of time in such a way that the last hour allocated to leisure (ΔQ) yields the same amount of utility (ΔU) as the last hour allocated to labor (ΔF)—the equimarginal principle of equilibrium of a seller of labor.

Equimarginal Principle of Equilibrium of a Seller of Labor

The equimarginal principle of equilibrium of a seller of labor may be analyzed according to the two-faced (Janus) diagram in Figure 21.2. The quantity of time (H) allocated to leisure (Q) begins with zero at the origin and increases to the left on the horizontal axis. Conversely, the quantity of time (H) allocated to labor (F) begins with zero at the origin and increases to the right on the horizontal axis. Thus all values on the horizontal axis are either zero or positive (that is, nonnegative). The marginal utility of leisure or labor begins with zero at the origin and increases up the vertical axis. As leisure increases, the marginal utility of leisure ($\Delta U/\Delta Q$) decreases according to the law of

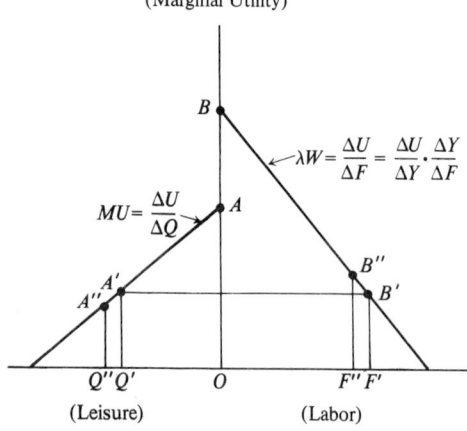

FIG. 21.2. Equimarginal principle of equilibrium of a perfectly competitive seller of labor

decreasing marginal utility of a product (leisure), as depicted by the curve labeled

$$MU = \frac{\Delta U}{\Delta Q}$$

Similarly, as labor increases, the marginal utility of labor ($\Delta U/\Delta F$) decreases according to the law of decreasing marginal utility of a product (income), as depicted by the curve labeled

$$\lambda W = \frac{\Delta U}{\Delta F} = \frac{\Delta U}{\Delta Y} \cdot \frac{\Delta Y}{\Delta F}$$

The seller of labor has $Q'F'$ hours to allocate between Q and F. The marginal utility of leisure OQ' is $Q'A'$; therefore, the total utility of leisure OQ', which is the area under the MU curve at OQ', is area $Q'A'AO$. Similarly, the marginal utility of labor OF' is $F'B'$, and the total utility of labor OF' is area $F'B'BO$. Since $Q'A' = F'B'$, with this allocation the marginal utility of leisure equals the marginal utility of labor: $MU = \lambda W$.

The magnitude $Q'F'$ is the same as the magnitude $Q''F''$. Thus the seller has $Q''F''$ hours to allocate between Q and F. The marginal utility of leisure OQ'' is $Q''A''$, and the total utility of leisure OQ'' is area $Q''A''AO$. Similarly, the marginal utility of labor OF'' is $F''B''$, and the total utility of labor OF'' is area $F''B''BO$. Since $Q''A'' < F''B''$, with this allocation the marginal utility of leisure is less than the marginal utility of labor: $MU < \lambda W$.

The combined area when $MU = \lambda W$ ($Q'A'AO + F'B'BO$) is larger than the combined area when $MU < \lambda W$ ($Q''A''AO + F''B''BO$). To see this, increase the quantity of time allocated to leisure from OQ' to OQ'' ($= Q'' - Q'$), thereby increasing total utility by the area $Q'A'A''Q''$. Because of the restriction that $H = Q + F$, the quantity of time allocated to labor is decreased from OF' to OF'' ($= F' - F''$), thereby decreasing total utility by the area $F'B'B''F''$. The loss in utility ($F'B'B''F''$) is greater than the gain in utility ($Q'A'A''Q''$). Therefore, when $MU < \lambda W$, utility is increased by increasing labor (F) and decreasing leisure (Q) until $MU = \lambda W$. As leisure (Q) decreases, MU increases; and as labor (F) increases, λW decreases, until eventually $MU = \lambda W$.

Marginal Utility Per Dollar of Leisure Equals Marginal Utility of Income

By dividing $MU = \lambda W$ by W, when a perfectly competitive seller of labor has determined the equilibrium quantity of his labor, in effect he is allocating a given amount of time in such a way that the ratio of the marginal utility of leisure to the price of leisure equals the marginal utility of income:

$$\frac{MU}{W} = \lambda \quad \text{or} \quad \frac{\Delta U}{\Delta Q} \div \frac{\Delta Y}{\Delta Q} = \frac{\Delta U}{\Delta Y}$$

Thus, if the sale of one hour of leisure yields \$1 (if $\Delta Q = W = \Delta Y = 1$), when he is in equilibrium, the utility of the dollar received for giving up one hour of leisure ($\Delta U/\Delta Y = \Delta U$) equals the utility of the hour given up ($\Delta U/\Delta Q = \Delta U$). In other words, when he is in equilibrium, the marginal utility per dollar of leisure equals the marginal utility of money income.

Ratio of Marginal Utilities Equals Ratio of Prices

The slope of the highest attainable indifference curve is equal to $-MU/\lambda$. The slope of the iso-real-wage curve denoting a given real wage is equal to $-W/P$. When a perfectly competitive seller of labor is in equilibrium:

$$\frac{MU}{\lambda} = \frac{W}{P} \quad \text{or} \quad \frac{MU}{W} = \frac{\lambda}{P}$$

SUMMARY

When a seller of labor is in equilibrium, in effect he is maximizing the utility of his time, which is allocated to labor and leisure. Assuming that $W = w$, when a perfectly competitive seller is in equilibrium,

(1) $\quad \dfrac{MU}{\lambda} = W$

By multiplying both sides of (1) by λ, when he is in equilibrium,

(2) $\quad MU = \lambda W$

By dividing both sides of (2) by W, when he is in equilibrium,

(3) $\quad \dfrac{MU}{W} = \lambda$

When $W \neq w$, he is in equilibrium when

(4) $\quad \dfrac{MU}{\lambda} = \dfrac{W}{P} \quad \text{or} \quad \dfrac{MU}{W} = \dfrac{\lambda}{P}$

Questions

1. List the principles of the theory of supply of labor that are of primary importance. How do you account for the position of the principle of equilibrium of a seller of labor in this list? Verbalize this principle of economics.

2. Use iso-wage and iso-utility curves to derive, analyze, and verbalize the equilibrium principle $MU/\lambda = W$. (Note: an analysis of equilibrium includes an analysis of disequilibrium.) How would the equilibrium principle be stated if you did not accept the concepts of utility and marginal utility?

3. Derive and verbalize the equilibrium principle $MU = \lambda W$.

4. Derive, verbalize, and analyze via a Janus diagram the equimarginal principle of equilibrium of a seller of labor.

5. Derive and verbalize the equilibrium principle $MU/W = \lambda$.

6. Use iso-real-wage and iso-utility curves to derive, analyze, and verbalize the equilibrium principle $MU/\lambda = W/P$.

chapter 22

The Supply Function of Labor of a Perfectly Competitive Seller

The supply curve of labor of a seller (laborer) is a set of ordered pairs of W and F numbers having the properties that (1) corresponding to each number in the W set of numbers is one number in the F set of numbers and (2) each pair of numbers represents equilibrium of the seller: $F = s(W)$. Thus the supply curve of labor of a seller shows how the quantity of his labor he is willing to sell (F) per unit of time varies with the price of the labor (W) ceteris paribus. In general, a seller's supply curve of labor depicts the law of supply of labor of a seller. According to this law, F varies directly with W: $\Delta F/\Delta W > 0$. The parameters of the supply curve of a perfectly competitive seller are the price of products (P) and his taste for products and leisure (T).

Law of Demand for Leisure of a Purchaser (Consumer)

A seller of labor is a purchaser of leisure, and the law of supply of labor is the converse of the law of demand for leisure: as the wage rate (= price of labor = price of leisure) increases, the quantity supplied of labor increases, according to the law of supply of labor, and the quantity demanded of leisure decreases, according to the law of demand for leisure. Thus the supply curve of labor of a seller may be constructed from his demand curve for leisure. This construction consists of plotting $F = H - Q$ against W, where $H = H_0 = 24$ hours (or some other time period), and Q and W are given by his demand curve for leisure. The analytical problem, therefore, is the derivation of the demand curve for leisure of a purchaser.

A purchaser of leisure is in equilibrium with respect to each point on his demand curve for leisure, and movement from one point to another point (à la law of demand for leisure of a purchaser) is rationalized via the principle of equilibrium of a purchaser of leisure. As analyzed in Chapter 21, when a perfectly competitive purchaser of leisure is in equilibrium, in effect he is

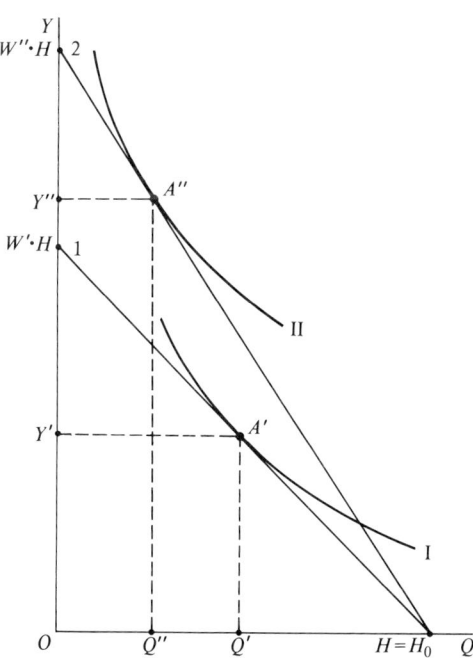

FIG. 22.1a. Equilibrium of a perfectly competitive purchaser of leisure: marginal rate of substitution of leisure for income equals the price of leisure

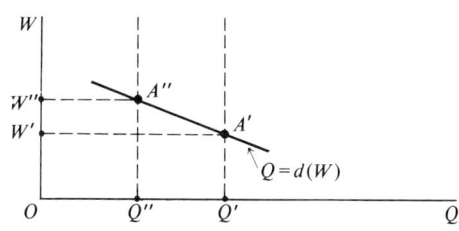

FIG. 22.1b. Hypothetical demand curve for leisure of a perfectly competitive purchaser

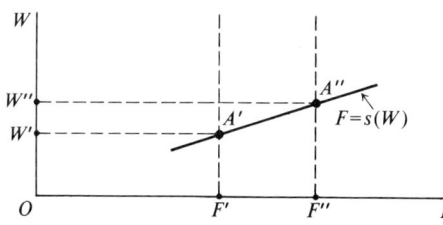

FIG. 22.1c. Hypothetical supply curve of labor of a perfectly competitive seller

allocating a given amount of time in such a way that the marginal rate of substitution of leisure for income equals the price of leisure. Thus, in Figure 22.1a, the purchaser is in equilibrium at A' and A'', for at both points

$$\frac{MU}{\lambda} = W$$

Points A' and A'' therefore represent equilibrium pairs of W and Q values (also W and Y values). The (W, Q) equilibrium pairs of values appear in Figure 22.1b as points A' and A'' on the demand curve for leisure of a purchaser. Specifically, point A' in Figure 22.1b denotes the equilibrium pair (W', Q'); and point A'' denotes the equilibrium pair (W'', Q''). The corresponding (W, F) equilibrium pairs of values appear in Figure 22.1c as points A' and A'' on the supply curve of labor of a seller. Specifically, point A' in Figure 22.1c denotes the equilibrium pair (W', F'), where $F' = H_0 - Q'$; and point A'' denotes the equilibrium pair (W'', F''), where $F'' = H_0 - Q''$.

As seen in Figures 22.1a and 22.1b, the equilibrium pair (W'', Q'') is obtained by increasing W from W' to W'' and ascertaining the new equilibrium value of Q (Q''). Specifically, the increase in W effects a shift of iso-wage curve 1 until it is tangent to a higher iso-utility curve (curve II); that is, curve 1 becomes curve 2. With the increase in W, the Y intercept and the numerical value of the slope of the iso-wage curve increase, while the Q intercept remains the same. At the new point of equilibrium (A''), the slope of iso-utility curve II equals the slope of iso-wage curve 2. In this case, the increase in W to W'' induces a decrease in Q to Q''—the law of demand for leisure of a purchaser (consumer) of leisure. Other equilibrium pairs of (W, Q) values along the demand curve for leisure of a purchaser may be rationalized in the same way.

Law of Supply of a Seller of Labor

The law of supply of labor of a seller may also be rationalized directly, without the use of the law of demand for leisure of a purchaser, via the total income of labor, $Y = Y(F) = W_0 F$, and the iso-utility curve of income and labor, $Y = U_0(F)$, drawn in Figure 22.2a. The total income curve of labor is explained in Chapter 20. The iso-utility curve of income and labor is constructed from the iso-utility curve of income and leisure. Specifically, according to the iso-utility curve of income and leisure, $dY/dQ < 0$; thus, according to the iso-utility curve of income and labor, $dY/dF > 0$, for decreasing leisure (Q) to increase income (Y) is the same as increasing labor (F) to increase income. Similarly, dY/dQ increases numerically as Q decreases; thus dY/dF increases as F increases. Therefore, the iso-utility curve of income and labor is positively-sloped and concave from above a tangent line because the iso-utility curve of income and leisure is negatively-sloped and concave from above a tangent line.

A seller of labor is in equilibrium with respect to each point on his supply curve of labor, and movement from one point to another point (à la law of supply of labor of a seller) is rationalized via the principle of equilibrium of a seller of labor. As analyzed in Chapter 21, when a perfectly competitive seller

FIG. 22.2a. Equilibrium of a perfectly competitive seller of labor: relative marginal utility equals price

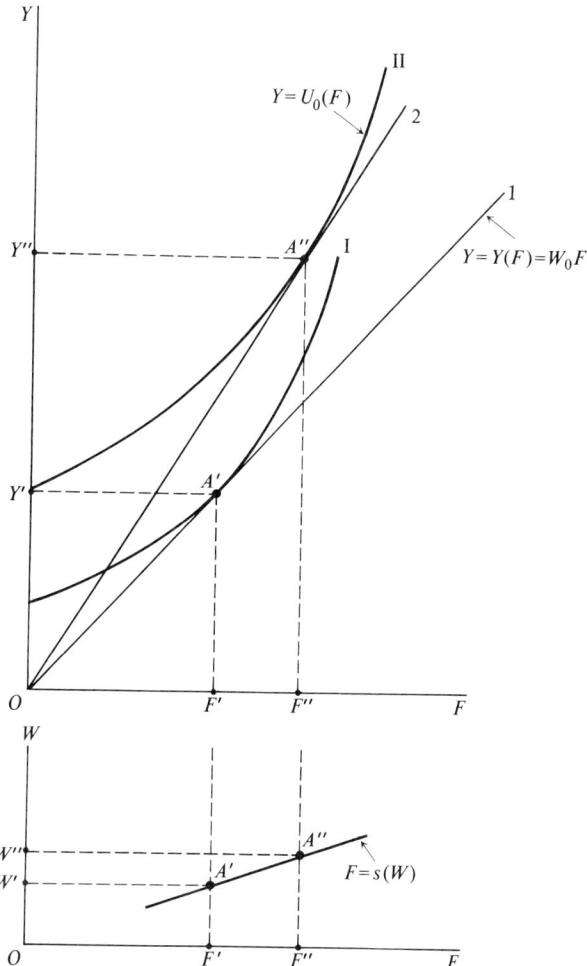

FIG. 22.2b. Hypothetical supply curve of labor of a perfectly competitive seller

of labor is in equilibrium, in effect he is allocating a given amount of time in such a way that the marginal rate of substitution of leisure for income equals the price of leisure. Thus, in Figure 22.2a, the seller is in equilibrium at A' and A'', for at both points

$$\frac{MU}{\lambda} = W$$

Points A' and A'', therefore represent equilibrium pairs of F and W values (also Y and W values). The (W, F) equilibrium pairs of values appear in

Figure 22.2b as points A' and A'' on the supply curve of labor of a seller. Specifically, point A' in Figure 22.2b denotes the equilibrium pair (W', F'); and point A'' denotes the equilibrium pair (W'', F'').

As seen in Figures 22.2a and 22.2b, the equilibrium pair (W'', F'') is obtained by increasing W from W' to W'' and ascertaining the new equilibrium value of F (F''). Specifically, the increase in W effects a shift of the total income curve of labor (curve 1) until it is tangent to a higher iso-utility curve (curve II); that is, curve 1 becomes curve 2. With the increase in W, the slope of the total income curve increases, while the Q intercept (which is zero) remains the same. At the new point of equilibrium (A''), the slope of iso-utility curve II equals the slope of the new total income curve of labor (curve 2). In this case, the increase in W to W'' induces an increase in F to F''—the law of supply of labor of a seller. Other equilibrium pairs of (F, W) values along the supply curve of labor of a seller may be rationalized in the same way.

Substitution and Income Effects

The total effect on leisure (Q) of a change in the price of leisure (W) is the substitution effect plus the income effect, which analytically is distinct from the substitution effect. The substitution effect on leisure of a change in the money wage rate (W) is the result of the corresponding change in the price of leisure relative to the price of products (that is, the change in the ratio W/P of the iso-real-wage curve). The income effect on leisure of a change in the money wage rate is the result of the corresponding change in the worker's money income and hence real income, which in effect is a change in the absolute price of products (that is, a change in the ratio Y/P of the iso-real-wage curve). In terms of indifference curve analysis, according to the substitution effect principle, as the price of leisure increases relative to the price of products, the quantity purchased of leisure decreases and the quantity purchased of products increases, while the overall level of utility associated with leisure and products remains constant. Thus the substitution effect on leisure of an increase in the money wage rate is a movement up a given iso-utility curve as leisure decreases and products (real income) increases. According to the income effect principle, the purchaser's real income increases when the money wage rate increases, and hence he can purchase more leisure and products to increase his utility or preference. Therefore, the income effect on leisure of an increase in the money wage rate is a movement to a higher iso-utility curve.

To see this, consider Figure 22.3. In this figure, the purchaser is in equilibrium initially at A', where iso-real-wage curve 1 is tangent to iso-utility curve I. Then the price of leisure increases, and he is in equilibrium at A''', where curve 2 is tangent to curve II. The income effect may be eliminated by reducing his money income and leisure so that he is in equilibrium at a

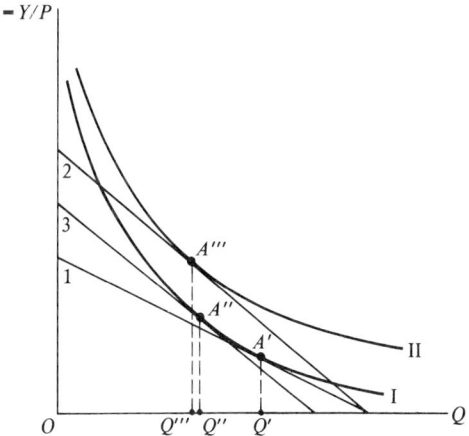

FIG. 22.3. Income effect strengthens substitution effect

higher point on his initial iso-utility curve. Iso-real-wage curve 3 represents the various attainable combinations of leisure and real income after they have been reduced to eliminate the income effect. It is parallel to iso-real-wage curve 2, since leisure and real income are exchanged at the new price ratio, and it is tangent to iso-utility curve I, since his adjusted real income and leisure are just sufficient for him to be on curve I. The total decrease in leisure (increase in labor) due to the increase in the money wage rate is $Q''' - Q'$. The substitution effect is $Q'' - Q'$; and, in this case, the income effect is $Q''' - Q''$.

The substitution effect on leisure of a change in the money wage rate is always negative: an increase in the real wage rate due to an increase in the money wage rate induces a decrease in leisure. Thus the substitution effect on labor of a change in the money wage rate is always positive: an increase in the real wage rate due to an increase in the money wage rate induces an increase in labor. By definition, leisure and real income are substitutes in consumption when the marginal utility of leisure is a decreasing function of real income and the marginal utility of real income is a decreasing function of leisure.

The income effect on leisure of a change in the money wage rate is negative if leisure and real income are substitutes: an increase in real income due to an increase in the money wage rate induces a decrease in leisure. Thus the income effect on labor of a change in the money wage is positive if leisure and real income are substitutes: an increase in real income due to an increase in the money wage rate induces an increase in labor. Therefore, if leisure and real income are substitutes, the income effect strengthens the substitution effect (see Figure 22.3).

By definition, leisure and real income are complements in consumption when the marginal utility of leisure is an increasing function of real income and the marginal utility of real income is an increasing function of leisure. The income effect on leisure of a change in the money wage rate is positive if leisure and real income are complements: an increase in real income due to an increase in the money wage rate induces an increase in leisure. Thus the income effect on labor of a change in the money wage rate is negative if leisure and real income are complements: an increase in real income due to an increase in the money wage rate induces a decrease in labor. Therefore, if leisure and real income are complements, the income effect weakens the substitution effect (see Figure 22.4).

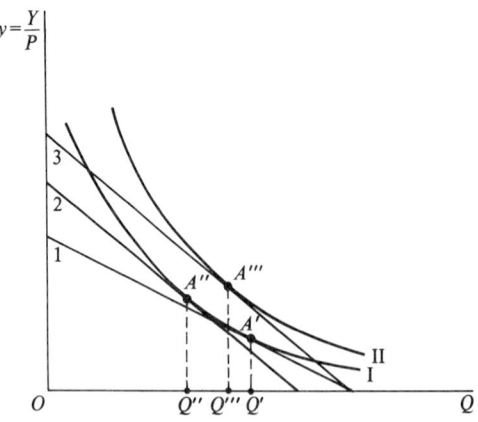

FIG. 22.4. Income effect weakens substitution effect

The greater the percentage of a given quantity of time allocated to labor, the greater the income effect of a change in the money wage rate. Conceivably, if labor accounts for a relatively large percentage of a worker's time and if leisure and real income are complements in consumption, the negative income effect on labor may be greater than the positive substitution effect on labor. The total effect, then, is that F varies inversely with W (see Figure 22.5).

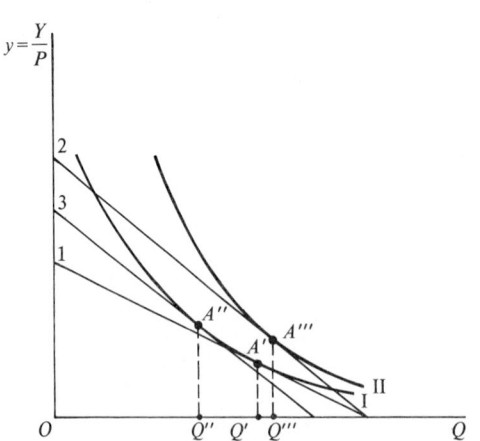

FIG. 22.5. Income effect greater than substitution effect

A worker may consider leisure and real income to be substitutes when he considers his real income to be low. Thus, as his money wage rate increases, he may work more hours per day and have fewer hours of leisure in order to have more income than he would have if he maintained the same hours of labor. But he may consider leisure and real income to be complements once a desired level of real income has been attained via increases in the money wage rate and hours worked. Thus, as his money wage rate continues to increase, he may work fewer hours per day and have more hours of leisure, while maintaining the same level of desired real income. In this case, to induce him to work more hours per day, his money wage rate must be decreased, or the price of products must be increased, or he must be induced to consider leisure and real income as substitutes—be made to feel that his real income is low.

In other words, according to the law of supply of labor, an increase in the price of labor (W) induces an increase in the quantity sold of labor (F). But as seen in Figure 22.6a, the law of supply of labor may hold only for a given set of (W, F) values. Eventually, increases in W increase real income and labor to an extent that labor may decrease if W increases further—the backward-bending supply curve of labor. Similarly, according to the law of demand for leisure, an increase in the price of leisure (W) induces a decrease in the quantity purchased of leisure (Q). But as seen in Figure 22.6b, the law

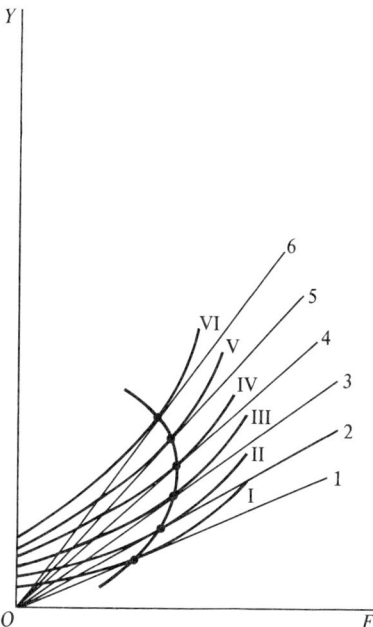

FIG. 22.6a. Backward-bending supply curve of labor

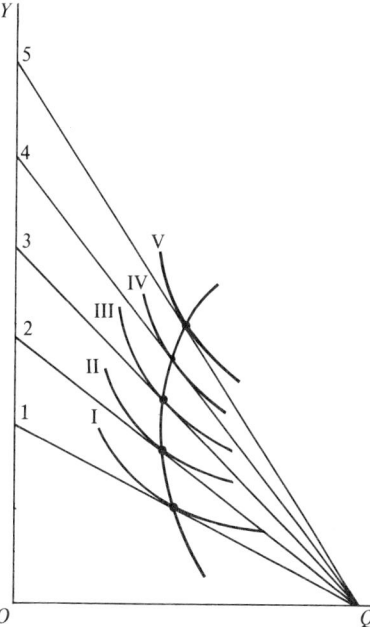

FIG. 22.6b. Forward-bending demand curve for leisure

of demand for leisure may hold only for a given set of (W, Q) values. Eventually, increases in W increase real income and decrease leisure to an extent that leisure may increase if W increases further—the forward-bending demand curve for leisure.

Quantity Sold of Labor as a Function of the Price of Products

The supply curve of labor of a seller shows that the quantity of his labor he is willing to sell (F) per unit of time varies with the price of the labor (W) ceteris paribus: $F = s(W)$. However, his labor is also a function of the price of products (P), as denoted by an index of product prices; thus P is a parameter of $F = s(W)$. As already noted, the supply curve of labor of a seller may be constructed from his demand curve for leisure. Thus, to analyze the relation between F and P, given W, think in terms of a worker's demand curve for leisure.

The total effect on leisure (Q) of a change in the price of products (P) is the substitution effect plus the income effect, which analytically is distinct from the substitution effect. The substitution effect on leisure of a change in the price of products is the result of the corresponding change in the price of leisure relative to the price of products (that is, the change in the ratio W/P of the iso-real-wage curve). The income effect on leisure of a change in the price of products is the result of the corresponding change in the absolute price of products (that is, the change in the ratio Y/P of the iso-real-wage curve), which changes the purchaser's real income (that is, changes the purchasing power of his money income). In terms of indifference curve analysis, according to the substitution effect principle, as the price of products decreases relative to the price of leisure, the quantity purchased of products increases and the quantity purchased of leisure decreases, while the overall level of utility associated with leisure and products remains constant. Thus the substitution effect on leisure of a decrease in the price of products is a movement up a given indifference curve as leisure decreases and products (real income) increases. According to the income effect principle, the purchaser's real income increases when the price of products decreases, and hence he can purchase more leisure and products to increase his utility or preference. Therefore, the income effect on leisure of a decrease in the price of products is a movement to a higher indifference curve.

To see this, consider Figure 22.3. In this figure, the purchaser is in equilibrium initially at A', where iso-real-wage curve 1 is tangent to indifference curve I. Then the price of products decreases, and he is in equilibrium at A''', where curve 2 is tangent to curve II. The income effect may be eliminated by reducing his money income and leisure so that he is in equilibrium at a higher point on his initial indifference curve. Iso-real-wage curve 3 represents the various attainable combinations of leisure and real income after they have been reduced to eliminate the income effect. It is parallel to iso-real-wage curve 2, since leisure and real income are exchanged at the new price ratio, and it is tangent to indifference curve I, since his adjusted real income and leisure are just sufficient for him to be on curve I. The total decrease in leisure (increase in labor) due to the decrease in the price of products is $Q''' - Q'$. The substitution effect is $Q'' - Q'$; and, in this case, the income effect is $Q''' - Q''$.

The substitution effect on leisure of a change in the price of products is always positive: an increase in the real wage rate due to a decrease in the price of products induces a decrease in leisure. Thus the substitution effect on labor of a change in the price of products is always negative: an increase in the real wage rate due to a decrease in the price of products induces an increase in labor.

The income effect on leisure of a change in the price of products is positive if leisure and real income are substitutes: an increase in real income due to a decrease in the price of products induces a decrease in leisure. Thus the income effect on labor of a change in the price of products is negative if leisure and real income are substitutes: an increase in real income due to a decrease in the price of products induces an increase in labor. Therefore, if leisure and real income are substitutes, the income effect strengthens the substitution effect (see Figure 22.3). Consequently, the quantity sold of labor, at any given value of the money wage rate, varies inversely with the price of products: $\Delta F/\Delta P < 0$.

The income effect on leisure of a change in the price of products is negative if leisure and real income are complements; an increase in real income due to a decrease in the price of products induces an increase in leisure. Thus the income effect on labor of a change in the price of products is positive if leisure and real income are complements: an increase in real income due to a decrease in the price of products induces a decrease in labor. Therefore, if leisure and real income are complements, the income effect weakens the substitution effect (see Figure 22.4). But, if the income effect is less than the substitution effect, the quantity sold of labor, at any given value of the money wage rate, still varies inversely with the price of products: $\Delta F/\Delta P < 0$.

The greater the percentage of a given quantity of time allocated to labor, the greater the income effect of a change in the price of products. Conceivably, if labor accounts for a relatively large percentage of a worker's time and if leisure and real income are complements in consumption, the positive income effect on labor may be greater than the negative substitution effect on labor (see Figure 22.5). The total effect then is that the quantity of labor, at any given value of the money wage rate, varies directly with the price of products: $\Delta F/\Delta P > 0$.

SUMMARY

The quantity of his labor a seller is willing to sell (F) per unit of time is a function of the price of the labor (W) and the price of products (P), given the parameters of his taste for leisure and real income. (Alternatively, the quantity of labor (F) is a function of the real wage rate (W/P).) The relation between the dependent variable (F) and each of its independent variables (W, P) is analyzed via the principle of equilibrium of a seller of labor. The analysis consists of changing the value of one independent variable, while holding constant the value of the other independent variable, and ascertaining the new equilibrium value of F. The primary objective of the analysis is to ascertain the sign of the difference quotients $\Delta F/\Delta W$ and $\Delta F/\Delta P$, given the ceteris paribus assumption that in each case "other things are equal" (or are unchanging). When the value of an independent variable is held constant via the ceteris paribus assumption, the variable is called a parameter of the curve being analyzed. Thus P is a parameter of the supply curve of labor of a perfectly competitive seller, denoted by $F = s(W)$.

According to the law of supply of labor of a seller, the quantity of his labor a seller is willing to sell (F) per unit of time varies directly with its price (W): $\Delta F/\Delta W > 0$. The total effect on F of a change in W is the substitution effect plus the income effect. The substitution effect on F of a change in W is always consistent with the law of supply of labor of a seller. The income effect on F of a change in W is consistent with this law if leisure and real income are substitutes, and inconsistent with it if they are complements. The law is violated if leisure and income are complements and the income effect is greater than the substitution effect.

Similarly, the total effect on the quantity of his labor a seller is willing to sell (F) per unit of time of a change in the price of products (P) is the substitution effect plus the income effect. The substitution effect on F of a change in P is always negative. The income effect on F of a change in P is also negative if leisure and real income are substitutes, but it is positive if they are complements. Thus the total effect on F of a change in P is negative unless they are complements and the income effect is greater than the substitution effect, in which case F varies directly with P.

Questions

1. List the principles of the theory of supply of labor that are of primary importance. How do you account for the position of the law of supply of labor of a seller in this list? Verbalize this principle of economics.

2. Use iso-wage and iso-utility curves to analyze the law of demand for leisure of a purchaser and the law of supply of labor of a seller. In each analysis, derive the demand curve for leisure and the supply curve of labor.

3. Use iso-wage and iso-utility curves to analyze substitution and income effects in three different frames of reference.

4. Use iso-wage and iso-utility curves to derive, analyze, and verbalize the backward-bending supply curve of labor and the forward-bending demand curve for leisure.

5. Define the marginal rate of substitution of leisure for money income. Based upon pages 342–347, draw and explain the most important property of a marginal rate of substitution of leisure for money income curve. Of what value would this curve be? Would it be the same as the demand curve for leisure of a purchaser?

6. Use iso-real-wage and iso-utility curves to analyze the relation between F and P. In your analysis, identify the substitution, income, and total effects on quantity purchased of leisure of a change in the price of (other) products, and show that the total effect may or may not be consistent with the substitution effect.

PART VI

THEORY OF DETERMINATION OF PRICE AND QUANTITY IN A FACTOR MARKET

The economic theory of determination of price and quantity in a factor market consists of two interrelated sets of principles of economics. Each of these principles is an inference drawn from an operation on a set of economic functions. The first set of principles recognizes the similarities between factors and products. Specifically, the service of labor may be considered to be a product, and other factors may be considered to be the product outputs of the capital goods and mining industries. In short, commodities may be classified as products, labor, intermediate products, or natural resources. Thus this set is the same as the laws of equilibrium and disequilibrium price and quantity in a competitive product (commodity) market (Chapter 13) and of product (commodity) sellers (Chapters 14 and 15).

The second set of principles recognizes the dissimilarities between factors and products. Specifically, the demand for a factor is derived from the demand for the product it produces; and the product may be sold in perfectly competitive or imperfectly competitive markets. Similarly, the factor may be purchased in perfectly competitive or imperfectly competitive markets. Thus the principle of equilibrium of a factor purchaser may be applied to various market structures. The principles of this set are presented in Chapter 23. The subject matter of this set is the human behavior underlying the pricing and input decisions of a particular type of purchaser and the inferences that may be drawn from these decisions about market price and quantity.

chapter 23

Structural Equilibrium of a Factor Purchaser

The economic theory of determination of price and quantity in a factor market is based on demand and supply curves that represent rationales of human behavior. The supply curve of a factor facing a purchaser of the factor is his average factor cost curve, assuming no price discrimination. The average factor cost curve of a perfectly competitive or monopsonistic purchaser is much simpler to derive analytically than his demand curve. A purchaser is in equilibrium with respect to each point on his demand curve. When he is in equilibrium, he has determined that input at which he is maximizing his profit (or minimizing his loss). Models of human behavior are thus presented in this chapter which rationalize the demand curve facing a purchaser by rationalizing his revenue-product and factor cost functions. The subject matter of this chapter therefore is a continuation of the subject matter of Chapter 18—namely, demand function for a factor of production of a purchaser. In Chapter 18, a purchaser's demand curve for a factor is rationalized on the assumption that factors may be related in production. In the present chapter, a purchaser's demand curve for a factor is rationalized on the assumption that factors are not related in production, or that a given factor is the only variable factor.

Perfect Competition in Product and Factor Markets

As seen in Chapter 8, the supply curve facing a perfectly competitive purchaser of a factor of production is perfectly elastic, for price is a value determined by market supply and demand that does not vary with his quantity purchased. Thus marginal factor cost equals average factor cost equals price; in short, his total factor cost is depicted by a ray, which is a positively-sloped line emanating from the point of origin of the factor cost diagram. As seen in Chapter 16, his total revenue-product curve has a zero total revenue-product intercept and is concave downward.[1] These functions are depicted in Figures 23.1a and 23.1b.

FIG. 23.1a. Profit maximization of a perfectly competitive purchaser of a factor of production

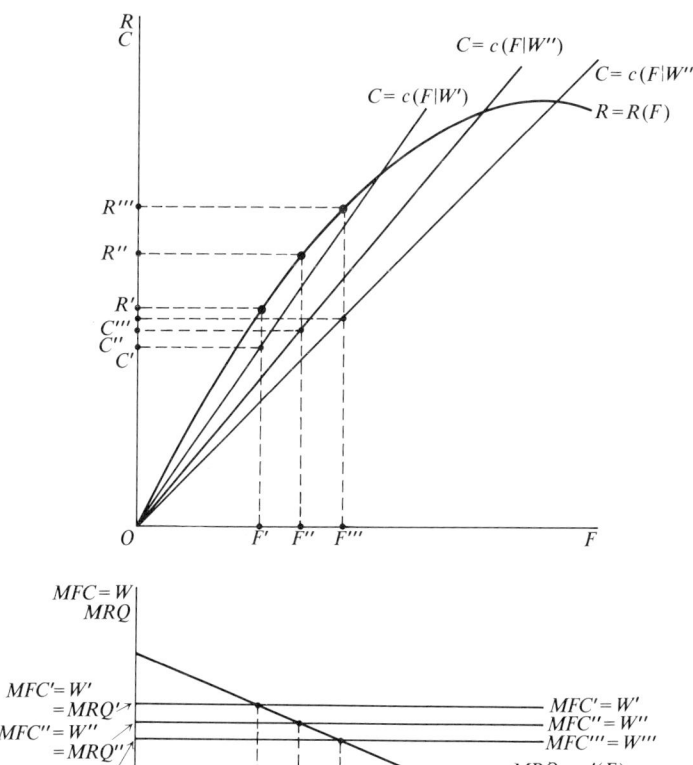

FIG. 23.1b. Demand curve for a factor of production of a perfectly competitive purchaser

Given price W', profit is maximized at that quantity of input (F') at which marginal revenue-product (MRQ') equals marginal factor cost (MFC').[2] The last unit of F' adds as much to total revenue-product (MRQ') as it adds to total factor cost (MFC'). The slope of the total revenue-product curve (MRQ') is the same as the slope of the total factor cost curve (MFC') at F'. The greatest difference of total revenue-product (R') over total factor cost (C') is at F', given W'. Therefore, (F', W') is one point on his demand curve. Since $MFC' = W' = MRQ'$ at F', this point is on his marginal revenue-product curve. Other points such as (F'', W'') and (F''', W''') are rationalized in the same way by shifting the factor cost curves downward.

The conclusion follows from this analysis that the marginal revenue-product curve of a perfectly competitive purchaser represents equilibrium combinations of prices and quantities to him; that is, it represents "optimum" adjustments of quantity purchased to changes in price. His demand curve is thus his marginal revenue-product curve: the properties of his marginal revenue-product curve are the properties of his demand curve. The slope of the $F = d(W)$ curve (dF/dW) is the reciprocal of the slope of the $MRQ = r'(F)$ curve $(dMRQ/dF)$ since $MRQ = W$.

Monopoly in Product Market—Perfect Competition in Factor Market

For analytical purposes, let the seller of a product be a monopolist, the sole seller of the product; and in his role of purchaser of a factor, let him be a perfectly competitive purchaser—one of many purchasers of the factor. Then a distinction may be made between sales value of the marginal product $(SVMQ)$ and marginal revenue-product (MRQ) of a factor of production. Specifically, the (discrete) marginal revenue-product of a factor may be defined as the revenue derived from using an additional unit of the factor per unit of time: $MRQ = \Delta R/\Delta F$. In this context, MRQ is the addition to revenue (ΔR) of an additional unit of the factor (ΔF). By definition, MRQ is equal to the marginal revenue of a product $(MR = \Delta R/\Delta Q)$ times the marginal product of the factor $(MQ = \Delta Q/\Delta F)$: $MRQ = MR \cdot MQ$. If $P = MR$, the addition to revenue (ΔR) of an additional unit of a factor (ΔF) is the addition to output (ΔQ) of that unit (ΔF) times the price of output (P): $MRQ = P \cdot MQ$. This definition of MRQ is also the definition of $SVMQ$: $SVMQ = P \cdot MQ$. To repeat, $SVMQ = MRQ$ if $P = MR$—that is, in the case of perfect competition from the seller's side in a product market. However, in the case of monopoly, $P > MR$ at a value of Q. Therefore, in this case, $SVMQ > MRQ$ at a value of F. Consequently, the $SVMQ = P \cdot MQ = f(F)$ curve of a monopolist (see Figure 23.2) lies above his $MRQ = MR \cdot MQ = r'(F)$ curve in the same way that his average revenue curve lies above his marginal revenue curve.

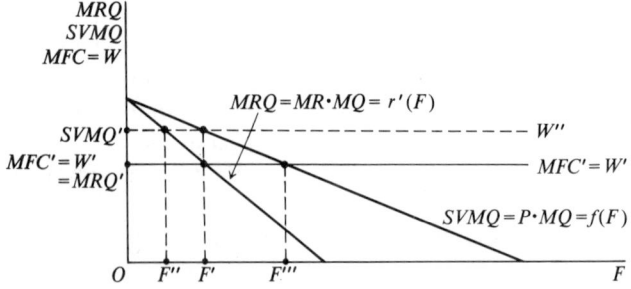

FIG. 23.2. Monopolistic exploitation

Monopolistic Exploitation

As seen in Figure 23.2, at equilibrium quantity (F'), a product monopolist pays the factor a price (W') less than the sales value of its marginal product ($SVMQ'$). To see this, assume that a monopolist is in equilibrium when he has 100 workers, that output per hour of the hundredth worker is one unit, that the (marginal) revenue of this unit is $2.00, and that the price per unit of the total output of all 100 workers is $3.00. Then $MRQ = \$2.00$, but $SVMQ = \$3.00$: the hundredth worker produces a unit of output valued at $3.00 but he is paid only $2.00, since $MRQ = W < SVMQ$. Some economists[3] infer from this analysis that a worker is being "exploited" since his wage is less than his sales value of the marginal product. However, other economists ask, if each factor of production is paid less than its $SVMQ$, and if both labor and capital are paid according to the same principle, how meaningful is the idea that labor is being "exploited" because it is paid less than its $SVMQ$? Also, as seen in Figure 23.2, if the wage is increased (say, by government) so that it equals $SVMQ$, the profit-maximizing monopolist decreases his employment (to F'') until $W = MRQ$, thereby again making $W < SVMQ$ (at F''); thus the net effect is a loss of input and output.

Perfect Competition in Product Market— Monopsony in Factor Market

For analytical purposes, let the seller of a product be a perfectly competitive seller—one of many sellers of the product—and in his role of purchaser of a factor, let him be a monopsonist—the sole purchaser of the factor. As analyzed in Chapter 8, the supply curve of a factor facing a purchaser denotes the price at which each quantity can be purchased; and his average factor cost curve denotes the average factor cost of each quantity purchased. In the case of a non-price-discriminating monopsonist, the price of each quantity is its average factor cost, for $AFC = C/F = W$ at each quantity. Therefore, the supply curve facing a monopsonist, which is the market supply curve, is his average factor cost curve. But his average factor cost curve is not his marginal factor cost curve, for at any given quantity marginal factor cost is greater than average factor cost, and hence his marginal factor cost curve lies above his average factor cost curve. In short, his total factor cost curve has a zero total factor cost intercept and is concave upward. As seen in Chapter 16, his total revenue-product curve has a zero total revenue-product intercept and is concave downward. These functions are depicted in Figures 23.3a and 23.3b.

Given market supply $AFC = W(F)'$, profit is maximized when quantity purchased is F'. The last unit before F' adds more to total revenue-product than to total factor cost, thereby increasing profit. The first unit after F'

FIG. 23.3a. Profit maximization of a monopsonist

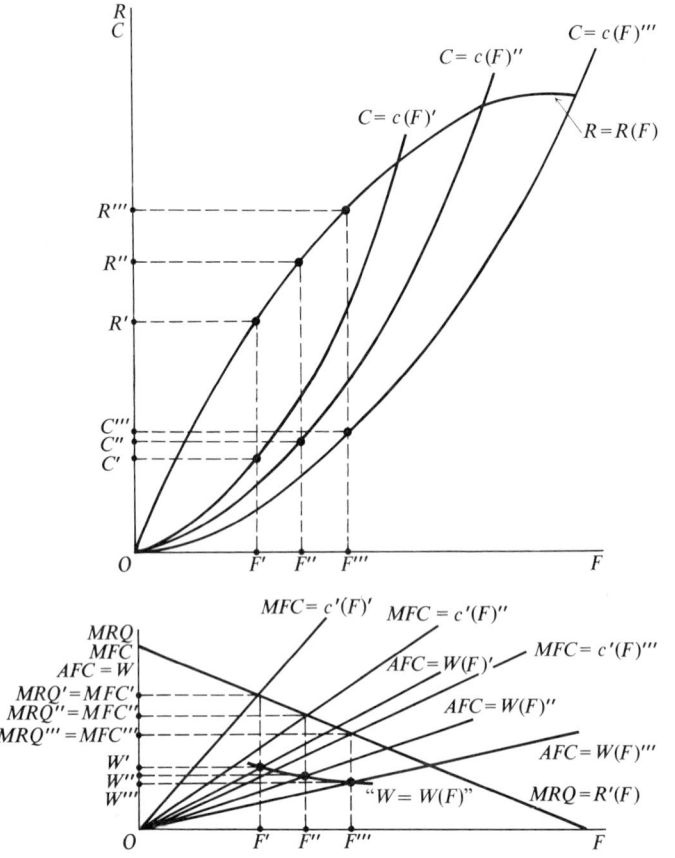

FIG. 23.3b. "Demand curve" of a monopsonist

adds more to total factor cost than to total revenue-product, thereby decreasing profit. The last unit of F' adds as much to total revenue-product as it adds to total factor cost, thereby maximizing profit. At F', the slope of the total revenue-product curve (MRQ') is the same as the slope of the total factor cost curve (MFC'). The greatest difference of total revenue-product over total factor cost is at F'. Given F', the corresponding equilibrium price is W'. Therefore, (F', W') is one point on the monopsonist's "demand curve" for the factor. Other points such as (F'', W'') and (F''', W''') are rationalized in the same way by shifting the market supply (average factor cost), marginal factor cost, and total factor cost curves downward as supply increases.

At F', $W' < MRQ'$ ($= MFC'$). Thus the equilibrium point (F', W') is not on the monopsonist's marginal revenue-product curve. Equilibrium quantity F' is on his marginal revenue-product curve, but equilibrium price

THE THEORY OF DEMAND FOR A FACTOR OF PRODUCTION 357

W' is on his average factor cost (supply curve). The same is true of points (F'', W'') and (F''', W'''). The set of ordered pairs of F and W numbers is the monopsonist's "demand curve," denoted by "$W = W(F)$." This curve depicts the profit-maximizing ($=$ equilibrium) prices he pays (W) for various equilibrium quantities purchased (F) per unit of time. Since equilibrium price is less than marginal revenue-product at equilibrium quantity purchased, his marginal revenue-product curve is not his "demand curve."[4]

The slope of his "demand curve" is determined by the relationship between a given set of marginal revenue-product, marginal factor cost, and average factor cost curves and the pattern of change in the average factor cost (supply) curve. Thus a "demand curve" is derived analytically for each pattern of change in supply of the factor. Change the pattern of supply increases, and the slope of his "demand curve" changes at any given value of equilibrium input. In short, his "demand curve" is not unique; it is a set of curves, one for each pattern of change in his supply curve. Consequently, for a factor purchaser to have a unique demand curve he must be a perfectly competitive purchaser!

Monopsonistic Exploitation

As seen in Figure 23.3b, when a monopsonist is in equilibrium with respect to a factor (at F'), he is paying it a price (W') less than its marginal revenue-product (MRQ')—the case of monopsonistic exploitation. Unlike monopolistic exploitation, in the present case, government or a labor union may impose a higher wage without effecting a decrease in employment. In fact, an external force may increase the wage rate and the level of employment. Specifically, in Figure 23.4, the monopsonist initially is in equilibrium at F', paying a wage rate of W'. Now, assume that the wage rate is set at W'', where $W'' = MRQ' = MFC'$, by some external force. Since each unit of the quantity F' is now paid the same wage rate (W''), marginal factor cost and

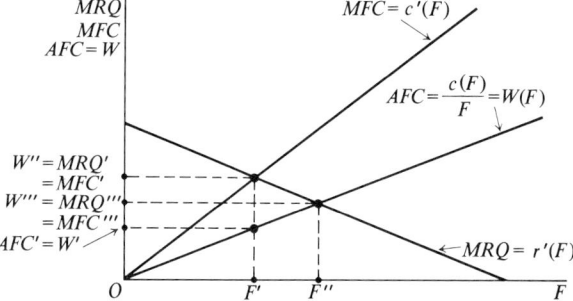

FIG. 23.4. Monopsonistic exploitation

average factor cost are the same value (W'') up to and including F' employment. Thus equilibrium employment stays at F' when the wage rate is set at W''. Assume now that the wage rate is set at W''', where $W''' = MRQ''' = MFC'''$, by some external force. Since each unit of the quantity F'' is now paid the same wage rate (W'''), marginal factor cost and average factor cost are the same value (W'') up to and including F'' employment. Thus equilibrium employment increases to F'' when the wage rate is set at W'''.

Monopoly in Product Market— Monopsony in Factor Market

For analytical purposes, let the seller of a product be a monopolist in the product market and a monopsonist in a factor market. Then a distinction may be made between equilibrium $SVMQ$, MRQ, and W. Specifically, as seen in Figure 23.5, at equilibrium input F', $SVMQ' > MRQ' > W'$—the case of monopolistic and monopsonistic exploitation.

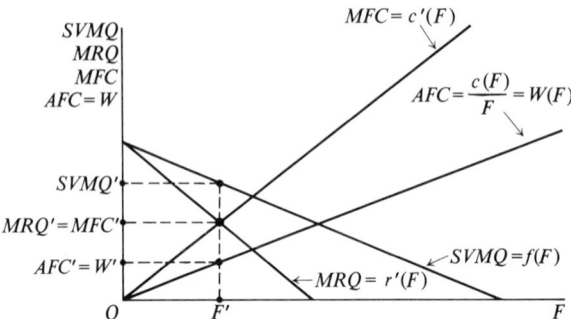

FIG. 23.5. Monopolistic and monopsonistic exploitation

Bilateral Monopoly

Implicit in the preceding models is the assumption of perfect competition between sellers. Now, let a market consist of one purchaser and one seller. The sole purchaser is called the monopsonist and the sole seller is called the monopolist. The analysis of the determination of price and quantity in this type of market is referred to as the model of bilateral monopoly. Although it is applicable to any product or factor market, this model is most often applied by economists to a labor market. In this context, it consists of the labor monopsonist (the business firm) and the labor monopolist (the labor union).

Preferred Equilibrium of Monopsonist (Business Firm)

The monopolist's (labor union's) supply price curve of labor is depicted in Figure 23.6 by the curve labeled $W_s = W_s(F)$. Assuming no price discrimination, this curve is the monopsonist's (business firm's) average factor cost

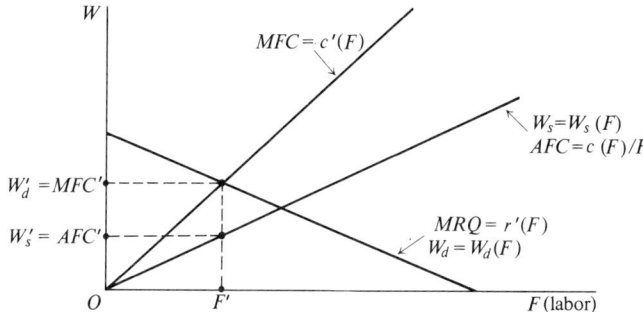

FIG. 23.6. Preferred equilibrium of monopsonist

curve, $AFC = c(F)/F$, since $AFC = W_s$. Corresponding to the business firm's average factor cost curve is its marginal factor cost curve, $MFC = c'(F)$. The business firm's marginal revenue-product curve, $MRQ = r'(F)$, is also depicted in Figure 23.6. This curve is the business firm's demand price curve, $W_d = W_d(F)$, since $MRQ = W_d$. To maximize its profit, the business firm prefers (1) to purchase that quantity determined by the intersection of its demand price (marginal revenue-product) and marginal factor cost curves at (2) the price determined by the corresponding point on its average factor cost curve, which is the labor union's supply price curve. This preference is satisfied if the labor union is willing to let the business firm determine quantity and hence price—that is, if the labor union is willing to permit each of its members to act as a perfectly competitive seller of labor. Given this assumption, the business firm chooses market quantity F', where $W'_d = MFC'$, to be purchased (sold) at market price W'_s, where $W'_s = AFC'$, thereby making a maximum profit of $(W'_d - W'_s)F'$.

Preferred Equilibrium of Monopolist (Labor Union)

The monopsonist's (business firm's) demand price curve for labor is depicted in Figure 23.7 by the curve labeled $W_d = W_d(F)$. Assuming no price discrimination, this curve is the monopolist's (labor union's) average income curve, $AY = Y(F)/F$, since $AY = W_d$. Corresponding to the labor union's average income curve is its marginal income curve, $MY = Y'(F)$. The labor union's supply price curve, $W_s = W_s(F)$, is also depicted in Figure 23.7. To maximize its profit, the labor union prefers (1) to sell that quantity determined by the intersection of its supply price and marginal income curves at (2) the price

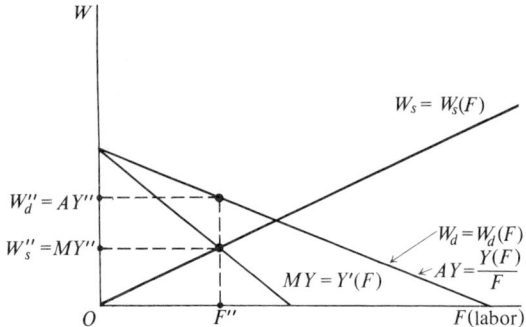

FIG. 23.7. Preferred equilibrium of monopolist

determined by the corresponding point on its average income curve, which is the business firm's demand price curve. This preference is satisfied if the business firm is willing to let the labor union determine quantity and hence price—that is, if the business firm is willing to act as if it were a perfectly competitive purchaser of labor, one of many purchasers rather than the only purchaser. Given this assumption, the labor union chooses market quantity F'', where $W_s'' = MY''$, to be sold (purchased) at market price W_d'', where $W_d'' = AY''$, thereby making a maximum profit of $(W_d'' - W_s'')F''$.

Indeterminacy of Market Equilibrium

The equilibrium preferred by the monopsonist (business firm), as based upon its supposed marginal and average factor cost functions, is not the same as the equilibrium preferred by the monopolist (labor union), as based upon its supposed marginal and average income functions. To see this, superimpose Figure 23.6 upon Figure 23.7, as in Figure 23.8. The business firm prefers to be in equilibrium at (F', W'), but the labor union prefers to be in equilibrium at (F'', W''). The price preferred by the seller (W'') is higher than the price preferred by the buyer (W'). The quantity preferred by the seller (F'') is greater than the quantity preferred by the buyer (F'). Consequently, price and quantity are said to be indeterminate in the bilateral monopoly model of a market. The market is indeterminate only in the sense, however, that the economist needs more data (or assumptions) than inconsistent factor cost and income functions to predict market price and quantity. Factor cost and income functions set the outer limits within which the purchaser and seller, via collective bargaining, determine price and quantity.

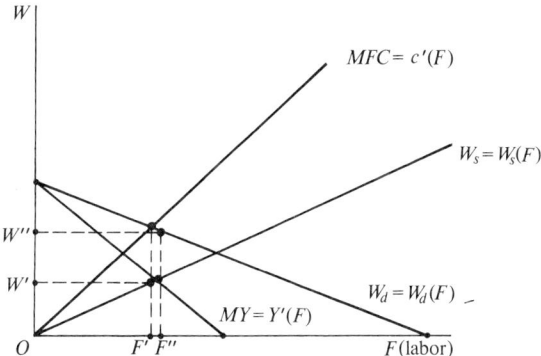

FIG. 23.8. Indeterminancy of equilibrium

SUMMARY

A purchaser is in equilibrium with respect to each point on his demand curve. When he is in equilibrium, he is maximizing his profit. The demand curve of a perfectly competitive purchaser is his marginal revenue-product curve, since $W = MRQ$ at equilibrium F. However, if a perfectly competitive factor purchaser is an imperfectly competitive product seller, his sales value of the marginal product curve lies above his marginal revenue-product curve; hence he pays the factor a price less than the sales value of its marginal product—a situation called monopolistic exploitation. The marginal revenue-product curve of a monopsonist in the factor market is not his "demand curve," for his equilibrium input is denoted by his marginal revenue-product curve, and his equilibrium price is denoted by his (lower) average factor cost curve. Moreover, his "demand curve" is not a unique curve, for a "demand curve" is derived analytically for each pattern of change in supply of the factor. Since at equilibrium input the monopsonist pays the factor a price less than its marginal revenue-product, he is said to engage in monopsonistic exploitation. In the case of monopolistic and monopsonistic exploitation, at equilibrium input, $SVMQ > MRQ > W$. Determinate solutions of price and quantity are based upon the assumption of perfect competition between sellers of a factor. In the case of bilateral monopoly, however, one purchaser is bargaining with one seller, each seeking inconsistent solutions, with the result that the actual solution requires more data.

Questions

1. Use diagrams to prove by analysis of the equilibrium principle that the demand curve for a factor of a perfectly competitive purchaser is his marginal revenue-product curve.

2. Differentiate between $SVMQ$ and MRQ.

3. Use a diagram to present and analyze monopolistic exploitation. Why might the "cure" for monopolistic exploitation be less acceptable than the "pain"?

4. Use diagrams to prove by analysis of the equilibrium principle that the "demand curve" of a monopsonist is not his marginal revenue-product curve. Explain in detail why "demand curve" is in quotation marks.

5. Explain the meaning and possible "cure" of monopsonistic exploitation.

6. Use a diagram to present the case of monopoly in a product market and monopsony in a factor market.

7. Use diagrams to present and analyze the bilateral monopoly model, discussing in particular the preferred equilibrium of the monopsonist, the preferred equilibrium of the monopolist, and the indeterminacy of market equilibrium.

SELECTED READINGS

Kaldor, Nicholas. "Alternative Theories of Distribution," *The Review of Economic Studies*, XXIII: 2 (1955–1956), pp. 83–100. Reprinted in Kamerschen, D. R. (editor). *Readings in Microeconomics*. Cleveland, Ohio: The World Publishing Company, 1967, pp 381–406.

Hirshleifer, Jack. "An Exposition of the Equilibrium of the Firm: Symmetry Between Product and Factor Analysis," *Economica*, XXIX (August 1962), pp. 263–268. Reprinted in Kamerschen, *ibid.*, pp. 407–413.

Reder, Melvin W. "Alternative Theories of Labor's Share." From *The Allocation of Economic Resources: Essays in Honor of Bernard Francis Haley*. Edited by Moses Abramovitz and others (Stanford University Press, 1959). Reprinted in Kamerschen, *ibid.*, pp. 414–441.

Liebhafsky, E. E. "A 'New' Concept in Wage Determination: Disguised Productivity Analysis," *Southern Economic Journal*, XXVI (October 1959), pp. 141–146. Reprinted in Kamerschen, *ibid.*, pp. 443–452.

Weston, J. Fred. "The Profit Concept and Theory: A Restatement," *The Journal of Political Economy*, XLIV (April 1954), pp. 152–170. Reprinted in Kamerschen, *ibid.*, pp. 453–479.

Worcester, Dean A., Jr. "A Reconsideration of the Theory of Rent," *The American Economic Review*, XXVI (June 1946), pp. 258–277. Reprinted in Kamerschen, *ibid.*, pp. 480–500.

Robertson, Dennis H. "Wages-Grumbles," *Economic Fragments*. London: P. S. King and Son, Ltd., 1931, pp. 42–57. Reprinted in The American Economic Association. *Readings in the Theory of Income Distribution*. Edited by William Fellner and Bernard F. Haley. Homewood, Illinois: Richard D. Irwin, Inc., 1951, pp. 221–236.

Bloom, Gordon F. "A Reconsideration of the Theory of Exploitation," *Quarterly Journal of Economics*, LV (1940–1941), pp. 413–442. Reprinted in The American Economic Association. *Readings in the Theory of Income Distribution*, *ibid.*, pp. 245–277.

Reynolds, Lloyd G. "Relations between Wage Rates, Costs and Prices," *The American Economic Review*, XXXII: supplement (1942), pp. 275–289. Reprinted in The American Economic Association. *Readings in The Theory of Income Distribution*, *ibid.*, pp. 294–313.

Lerner, A. P. "The Relation of Wage Policies and Price Policies," *The American Economic Review*, XXIX: supplement (1939), pp. 158–169. Reprinted in The American Economic Association. *Readings in The Theory of Income Distribution, ibid.*, pp. 314–329.

NOTES

[1] In Chapter 16, the total revenue-product curve is drawn with its initial portion concave upward.

[2] The marginal revenue-product curve must intersect the marginal factor cost curve from above.

[3] For example, see Joan Robinson, *Economics of Imperfect Competition* (London: Macmillan and Co. Ltd., 1933), pp. 281–291.

[4] The monopsonist's marginal revenue-product curve depicts the maximum prices imposed upon him that he is willing to pay, called demand price (W_d), for various equilibrium quantities purchased (F). The relation between F and W_d is called the demand price curve and is denoted by $W_d = W_d(F)$. Thus, since demand price equals marginal revenue-product at equilibrium quantity purchased, his marginal revenue-product curve is his demand price curve. His demand price curve, therefore, is a unique curve, but his "demand curve" is not a unique curve, as seen in the next paragraph.

PART VII

PARTIAL AND GENERAL EQUILIBRIUM THEORY

It is a magnificent feeling to recognize the unity of a complex of phenomena which appear to be things quite apart from the direct visible truth.
(Albert Einstein, quoted by Ronald W. Clark in *Einstein: The Life and Times*)

Consider an economic system of households and business firms interacting in product and factor markets. A product market is in equilibrium when quantity supplied of the product equals quantity demanded. A factor market is in equilibrium when quantity supplied of the factor equals quantity demanded. A household is in general equilibrium when it is in equilibrium with respect to its purchases of products and sales of labor. A business firm is in general equilibrium when it is in equilibrium with respect to its sales of goods (including capital goods) and services and purchases of factors of production. Each product and factor market is in equilibrium when each household and business firm is in general equilibrium. The economic system is in general equilibrium when each of its product and factor markets is in equilibrium. It is in partial equilibrium when a market that for analytical purposes is considered in isolation from other markets is defined to be in equilibrium. Partial equilibrium theory is presented in Chapters 1–23. General equilibrium theory is presented in Chapter 24.

chapter 24

General Equilibrium Theory

The approach to a more profound knowledge of ... basic principles ... is tied up with the most intricate mathematical methods.
(Albert Einstein, quoted by Ronald W. Clark in *Einstein: The Life and Times*)

General equilibrium theory consists of three interrelated sets of principles of economics. The first set consists of principles regarding the optimum allocation of a given amount of products (resources) among households as they compete to attain preferred positions. The second set consists of principles regarding the optimum allocation of a given amount of factors (resources) in the production of various products—that is, among business firms as they compete to attain preferred positions. The third set consists of principles regarding general equilibrium of all markets, in which case each person has attained a position that is preferred, given his command over resources and the prices of resources. This presentation of general equilibrium theory is based on the assumption of perfect competition in all markets. Thus, no purchaser or seller can directly influence any price. Instead, prices are determined by market supply and demand, and are given values to individual purchasers and sellers. In short, prices are parameters to households and business firms.

General Equilibrium of Households

For analytical purposes, assume that each household consists of one individual, that a given amount of products is held by individuals, and that each individual purchases and sells products until he is in equilibrium. For an economic system to be in general equilibrium, product quantities, product prices, factor quantities, and factor prices must be mutually consistent with one another. Let the word "commodity" denote a "product" or a "factor." Then commodity quantities and prices are mutually consistent

GENERAL EQUILIBRIUM THEORY

when they satisfy all supply and demand equations representing the economic system. The equilibrium set of quantity and price values that satisfies all equations is determined by solving the system of equations simultaneously. A system of equations is consistent with equilibrium when the number of equations equals the number of variables—the essential feature of general equilibrium theory.[1] The present model consists of mn variables and equations, given $m - 1$ market prices.

Consider first the number of variables. Let x be the final quantity of a commodity held by an individual; $\bar{x}$ be the initial quantity of a commodity held by an individual; p be the market price of a commodity; r differentiate between commodities; m be the total number of commodities; i differentiate between individuals; n be the total number of individuals; and u denote the marginal utility of a commodity. According to this notation, in an economic system of m commodities, r takes the values $1, 2, ..., m$; that is, $r = 1, 2, ..., m$. With n individuals, i takes the values $1, 2, ..., n$; that is, $i = 1, 2, ..., n$. Thus, x_{ri} is the final quantity of the rth commodity held by the ith individual. And $\bar{x}_{ri}$ is the initial quantity of the rth commodity held by the ith individual. The market price of the rth commodity is p_r. The mth commodity is the *numeraire*, and hence $p_m = 1$. The marginal utility of the rth commodity to the ith individual is u_{ri}. Given this notation, the present model consists of m commodities purchased and sold by n individuals at $m - 1$ market prices. Therefore, given $m - 1$ prices p_r (for $r = 1, 2, ..., m - 1$), the present model explains mn variables x_{ri} (for $r = 1, 2, ..., m$ commodities and $i = 1, 2, ..., n$ individuals).

Consider now the number of equations. This model is based on the assumption that each individual holds an initial quantity of one or more commodities and purchases and sells quantities until he has the desired amount of each commodity—that is, until he is in equilibrium. When an individual is in equilibrium with respect to m products (including leisure),

$$\frac{MU_1}{p_1} = \frac{MU_2}{p_2} = ... = \frac{MU_{m-1}}{p_{m-1}} = MU_m$$

But $MU_r = u_r$. Thus,

(1) $$\frac{u_1}{p_1} = \frac{u_2}{p_2} = ... = \frac{u_{m-1}}{p_{m-1}} = u_m$$

or

$$\frac{u_r}{p_r} = u_m \quad (r = 1, 2, ..., m - 1)$$

which is equivalent to

(1') $$\frac{u_r}{u_m} = p_r \quad (r = 1, 2, ..., m - 1)$$

When applied to all individuals, this equilibrium condition becomes

(1″) $\dfrac{u_{ri}}{u_{mi}} = p_r \ (r = 1, 2, \ldots, m - 1)$ and $(i = 1, 2, \ldots, n)$

To verbalize, when an individual is in equilibrium, the marginal utility per dollar of expenditure on one product equals the marginal utility per dollar of expenditure on every other product, according to equation (1). Alternatively, according to equation (1′), the ratio of the marginal utility of the rth commodity (u_r) to the marginal utility of the mth commodity (u_m) equals the ratio of the price of the rth commodity (p_r) to the price of the mth commodity ($p_m = 1$). In other words, according to equation (1′), the marginal rate of substitution of the rth commodity for the mth commodity ($-dx_m/dx_r = u_r/u_m$) equals the ratio of the price of the rth commodity (p_r) to the price of the mth commodity ($p_m = 1$).

When an individual is in equilibrium, he is maximizing his utility subject to his expenditure, which is constrained by his income. In effect, he is balancing his budget, for then his expenditure equals his income. His expenditure on a commodity is $p_r x_r$; his expenditure on all commodities is $\sum_r p_r x_r$; his income from a commodity is $p_r \bar{x}_r$; and his income from all commodities is $\sum_r p_r \bar{x}_r$. Consequently, when his budget is balanced,

(2) $\sum_r p_r x_r = \sum_r p_r \bar{x}_r$

or

(2′) $\sum_r p_r (x_r - \bar{x}_r) = 0$

When applied to all individuals, this equilibrium condition becomes

(2″) $\sum_r p_r (x_{ri} - \bar{x}_{ri}) = 0 \quad (i = 1, 2, \ldots, n)$

To conclude, each individual has $m - 1$ equilibrium equations in (1′) and one balanced budget equation in (2′), a total of m equations: $(m - 1) + 1 = m$. Thus, the total number of equations for n individuals is mn, which is equal to $(m - 1)n$ in (1″) plus n in (2″): $(m - 1)n + n = mn$. Consequently, the number of variables equals the number of equations. The model is consistent with general equilibrium of households.

Optimum Allocation of Products

The general equilibrium of households model provides a rationale of why trading between individuals may result in an optimum allocation of products (resources) among them. To see this, consider the equimarginal principle of equilibrium of a purchaser of products, which may be stated algebraically as $u_r/u_m = p_r/p_m$. According to this principle of economics, an individual has an optimum allocation of his income when the marginal rate of substitution of any two products is equal to the ratio of their prices. An iso-utility (indifference) curve diagram is used to present this principle. Similarly, two indifference curve diagrams may be merged into one diagram, called the Edgeworth–Bowley box, which then may be used to present the equimarginal principle of general equilibrium of households, which may be stated algebraically as $u_{ri}/u_{mi} = p_r/p_m$. According to this principle of economics, an economic system has an optimum allocation of products (resources) when, for all individuals, the marginal rate of substitution is the same between every pair of products.

To construct the Edgeworth–Bowley box, let the equimarginal principle of general equilibrium of households be applied to two individuals A and B, who jointly own two products, X_1 and X_2, in fixed amounts. Think in terms of preference ordering theory.[2] Let the set of indifference curves in Figure 24.1a depict the preference ordering between X_1 and X_2 of individual A,

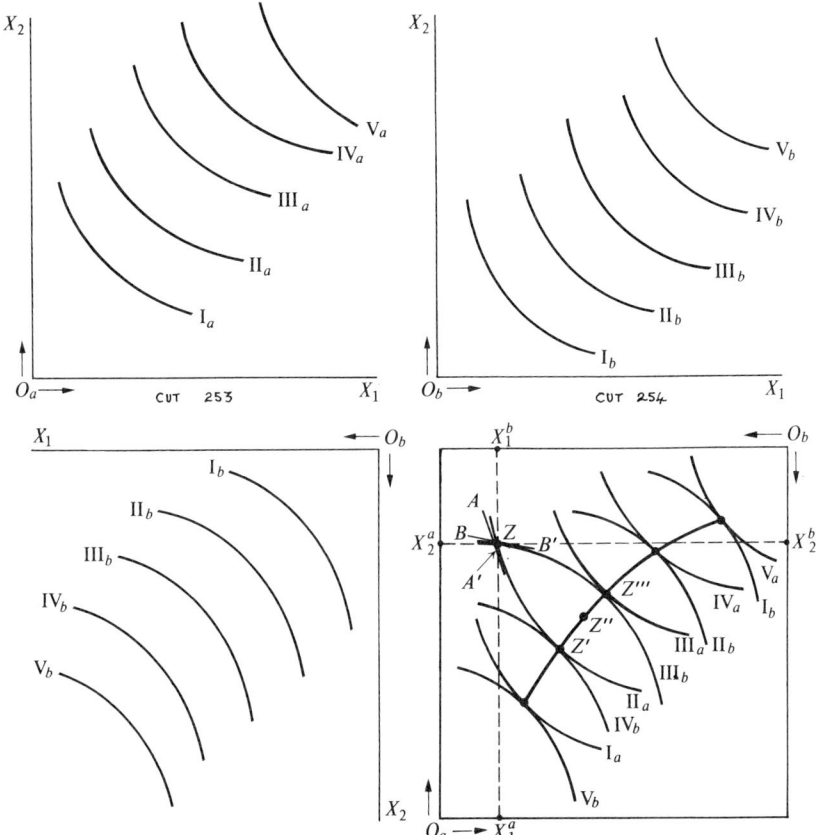

FIG 24.1a. Preference ordering of individual A
FIG. 24.1b. Preference ordering of individual B
FIG. 24.1c. Preference ordering of individual B
FIG. 24.1d. Optimum allocation of products

and let the set of indifference curves in Figure 24.1b depict the preference ordering between X_1 and X_2 of individual B. Rotate the origin of Figure 24.1b to the left by 180°, as in Figure 24.1c, and then superimpose Figure 24.1c on Figure 24.1a, as in Figure 24.1d. The result is the Edgeworth–Bowley box of Figure 24.1d, the dimensions of which represent the fixed amounts of X_1 and X_2 owned jointly by A and B.

Let the initial allocation of X_1 and X_2 between A and B be according to point Z in Figure 24.1d. Then the initial allocation of X_1 is X_1^a units to A and X_1^b units to B; and the initial allocation of X_2 is X_2^a units to A and X_2^b units to B. At point Z, A's marginal rate of substitution of X_1 for X_2 (denoted by the slope of AA') is greater numerically than B's (denoted by the slope of BB'). Thus, the amount of X_2 that A is willing to give up to obtain an additional unit of X_1 is greater than the amount of X_2 that B is willing to give up to obtain an additional unit of X_1. Conversely, B's marginal rate of substitution of X_2 for X_1 is greater than A's. Thus, the amount of X_1 that B is willing to give up to obtain an additional unit of X_2 is greater than the amount of X_1 that A is willing to give up to obtain an additional unit of X_2. Consequently, A is willing to give X_2 to B, and B is willing to give X_1 to A, until the marginal rate of substitution is the same for both A and B. The two rates approach equality as A gives up X_2 for X_1 and B gives up X_1 for X_2.

The marginal rate of substitution is the same for both A and B at points Z', Z'', and Z''' in Figure 24.1d. A is indifferent to moving from Z to Z', by giving up X_2 to obtain X_1, because he stays on the same indifference curve (II_a) and hence his real income does not change. But A prefers to move from Z to Z''', by exchanging products according to B's indifference curve III_b, for then A would be giving up a smaller amount of X_2 and obtaining a larger amount of X_1. Thus A would be increasing his real income while B's real income remained the same. Similarly, B is indifferent to moving from Z to Z''', by giving up X_1 to obtain X_2, because he stays on the same indifference curve (III_b) and hence his real income does not change. But B prefers to move from Z to Z', by exchanging products according to A's indifference curve (II_a), for then B would be giving up a smaller amount of X_1 and obtaining a larger amount of X_2. Thus B would be increasing his real income while A's real income remained the same.

In short, A and B are in conflict. A would like to move from Z to Z''' by exchanging products according to B's indifference curve III_b, but B would like to move from Z to Z' by exchanging products according to A's indifference curve II_a. Because of this conflict, the set (locus) of points of tangency of the indifference curves of A and B—that is, the set of points at which $u_{ri}/u_{mi} = p_r/p_m$ holds true—is called the conflict curve. A would like to move to higher indifference curves by moving up the conflict curve from left to right, while B would like to move to higher indifference curves by moving down the conflict curve from right to left.

The conflict between A and B leads to bargaining as each tries to increase his real income. The result of bargaining may be a contract in which both benefit from trade. Relative to point Z, both benefit if the contract calls for an allocation of products according to point Z'' (or any other point between Z' and Z''' on the conflict curve). Since both may gain via a contract, the conflict curve is also called the contract curve: A and B contract to exchange products until the marginal rate of substitution is the same for both in order to increase their real income. In short, they have a common interest in moving to the contract curve, and a conflict of interest in moving along the conflict curve.

Relative to point Z, A would lose real income if the new allocation was according to a point on the conflict curve to the left of point Z', and B would lose real income if the new allocation was according to a point on the conflict curve to the right of point Z'''. Thus, both A and B gain real income if they exchange products until their marginal rates of substitution are the same and if the new allocation point is within the set of points on the conflict curve bounded by their initial indifference curves. In other words, every point not on the conflict curve (point Z) is "inferior" to a set of points on the curve (points Z' ... Z'''). But every point on the conflict curve is not "superior" to every point not on the curve.

General Equilibrium of Business Firms

For analytical purposes, assume that a given amount of factors of production is held by business firms and that each firm purchases and sells factors until it is in equilibrium. The present model consists of mN variables and equations, given $m - 1$ market prices. Again let the word "commodity" denote a "product" or a "factor."

Consider first the number of variables. Let x be the output of a commodity if it is a positive value; x be the input of a commodity if it is a negative value; p be the market price of a commodity; r differentiate between commodities; m be the total number of commodities; j differentiate between business firms; N be the total number of business firms; and q denote the marginal product of an input. According to this notation, in an economic system of m commodities, r takes the values $1, 2, ..., m$; that is, $r = 1, 2, ..., m$. With N business firms, j takes the values $1, 2, ..., N$; that is, $j = 1, 2, ..., N$. Thus, positive x_{rj} is the output of the rth commodity by the jth firm, and negative x_{rj} is the input of the rth commodity by the jth firm. The market price of the rth commodity is p_r. The market price of the mth commodity by hypothesis is one: $p_m = 1$. From the input side, q_{rj} denotes the marginal product of the rth factor in the output of the jth firm. From the output side, q_{rj} denotes the marginal product of input in the production of the rth product of the jth firm. Given this notation, the present model consists of m commodities purchased and sold by N firms at $m - 1$ market prices. Therefore, given $m - 1$ prices p_r (for $r = 1, 2, ..., m - 1$), the present model explains mN variables x_{rj} (for $r = 1, 2, ..., m$ commodities and $j = 1, 2, ..., N$ firms).

Consider now the number of equations. This model is based on the assumption that each firm holds an initial quantity of one or more commodities and purchases and sells quantities until it has the desired amount of each commodity—that is, until it is in equilibrium. Let a firm's set of m commodities x_r ($r = 1, 2, ..., m$) consist of k factors x_s ($s = 1, 2, ..., k$) and $(m - k)$ products x_t ($t = k + 1, k + 2, ..., m$). Then two separate systems of equations may be considered, one for the input side and one for the output side of the firm.

With respect to the input side, when a firm is in equilibrium with respect to k factors,

$$\frac{MRQ_1}{W_1} = \frac{MRQ_2}{W_2} = \cdots = \frac{MRQ_{k-1}}{W_{k-1}} = \frac{MRQ_k}{W_k}$$

But $W_s = p_s$ since a factor is defined to be a commodity. Moreover, with respect to factor s, given the price of output of the firm (P_j), $MRQ_s = P_j \cdot MQ_s$ and $MQ_s = q_s$. Therefore, by replacing W_s by p_s and by dividing through by P_j,

(3) $$\frac{q_1}{p_1} = \frac{q_2}{p_2} = \cdots = \frac{q_{k-1}}{p_{k-1}} = \frac{q_k}{p_k}$$

or

$$\frac{q_s}{p_s} = \frac{q_k}{p_k} \quad (s = 1, 2, ..., k)$$

which is equivalent to

(3') $$\frac{q_s}{q_k} = \frac{p_s}{p_k} \quad (s = 1, 2, ..., k)$$

When applied to all firms, this equilibrium condition becomes

(3'') $$\frac{q_{sj}}{q_{kj}} = \frac{p_s}{p_k} \quad (s = 1, 2, ..., k) \quad \text{and} \quad (j = 1, 2, ..., N)$$

To verbalize, when a firm is in equilibrium, the marginal product of one factor in output per dollar of cost of the factor equals the marginal product per dollar of cost of every other factor, according to equation (3). Alternatively, according to equation (3'), the ratio of the marginal product of the sth factor in output (q_s) to the marginal product of the kth factor in output (q_k) equals the ratio of the price of the sth factor (p_s) to the price of the kth factor (p_k). In other words, according to equation (3'), the marginal rate of technical substitution of the sth factor for the kth factor ($-dx_k/dx_s =$

q_s/q_k) equals the ratio of the price of the sth factor (p_s) to the price of the kth factor (p_k).

With respect to the output side, a firm is in equilibrium with respect to $(m - k)$ products when

$$\frac{p_{k+1}}{MC_{k+1}} = \frac{p_{k+2}}{MC_{k+2}} = \ldots = \frac{p_{m-1}}{MC_{m-1}} = \frac{p_m}{MC_m}$$

or

$$\frac{MC_{k+1}}{p_{k+1}} = \frac{MC_{k+2}}{p_{k+2}} = \ldots = \frac{MC_{m-1}}{p_{m-1}} = \frac{MC_m}{p_m}$$

But $p_m = 1$ by hypothesis. Moreover, with respect to product t, given the price of (variable) input of the firm (W_j), $MC_t = W_j/MQ_t$ and $MQ_t = q_t$. Therefore, by letting $p_m = 1$ and by dividing through by W_j,

(4) $$\frac{1/q_{k+1}}{p_{k+1}} = \frac{1/q_{k+2}}{p_{k+2}} = \ldots = \frac{1/q_{m-1}}{p_{m-1}} = 1/q_m$$

or

$$\frac{1/q_t}{p_t} = 1/q_m \quad (t = k + 1, k + 2, \ldots, m - 1)$$

which is equivalent to

(4′) $$\frac{q_m}{q_t} = p_t \quad (t = k + 1, k + 2, \ldots, m - 1)$$

When applied to all firms, this equilibrium condition becomes

(4″) $$\frac{q_{mj}}{q_{tj}} = p_t \quad (t = k + 1, k + 2, \ldots, m - 1) \quad \text{and} \quad (j = 1, 2, \ldots, N).$$

To verbalize, when a firm is in equilibrium, the reciprocal of the marginal product of input in the production of one product per dollar of revenue of the product equals the reciprocal of the marginal product per dollar of revenue of every other product, according to equation (4). Alternatively, according to equation (4′), the ratio of the marginal product of input in the production of the mth product (q_m) to the marginal product of input in the production of the tth product (q_t) equals the ratio of the price of the tth product (p_t) to the price of the mth product ($p_m = 1$). In other words, according to equation (4′), the marginal rate of transformation of the tth product for the mth product ($-dx_m/dx_t = q_m/q_t$) equals the ratio of the price of the tth product (p_t) to the price of the mth product ($p_m = 1$).

Underlying (3′) and (4′), and hence (3″) and (4″), is the production function of a firm, which is the basis of the marginal products of its factors. Since the

jth firm may produce more than one product with more than one factor, its production function is stated in implicit form as

(5) $\quad f_j(x_{1j}, x_{2j}, ..., x_{mj}) = 0 \quad (j = 1, 2, ..., N)$.

Thus, each firm has a production equation in (5) and $m - 1$ equilibrium equations in (3′) and (4′), a total of m equations: $1 + (m - 1) = m$. The total number of equations for N firms therefore is mN, which is equal to $(m - 1)N$ in (3″) and (4″) plus N in (5): $(m - 1)N + N = mN$. Consequently, the number of variables equals the number of equations. The model is consistent with general equilibrium of business firms.

Optimum Allocation of Factors of Production

The general equilibrium of business firms model provides a rationale of why trading between firms may result in an optimum allocation of factors (resources) among them. To see this, consider the equimarginal principle of equilibrium of a purchaser of factors of production, which may be stated algebraically as $q_r/q_m = p_r/p_m$. According to this principle of economics, a business firm has an optimum allocation of an outlay of money when the marginal rate of technical substitution of any two factors is equal to the ratio of their prices. An iso-product curve diagram is used to present this principle. Similarly, two iso-product curve diagrams may be merged into one diagram, called the Edgeworth–Bowley box, which then may be used to present the equimarginal principle of general equilibrium of business firms, which may be stated algebraically as $q_{rj}/q_{mj} = p_r/p_m$. According to this principle of economics, an economic system has an optimum allocation of factors (resources) when, for every business firm, the marginal rate of technical substitution is the same between every pair of factors.

To construct the Edgeworth–Bowley box, let the equimarginal principle of general equilibrium of business firms be applied to two business firms, A and B, who jointly own two factors, X_1 and X_2, in fixed amounts. Figure 24.2a depicts a set of firm A's iso-product curves, and Figure 24.2b depicts a set of firm B's iso-product curves. Rotate the origin of Figure 24.2b to the left by 180°, as in Figure 24.2c, and then superimpose Figure 24.2c on Figure 24.2a, as in Figure 24.2d. The result is the Edgeworth–Bowley box of Figure 24.2d, the dimensions of which represent the fixed amounts of X_1 and X_2 owned jointly by A and B.

Let the initial allocation of X_1 and X_2 between A and B be according to point Z in Figure 24.2d. Then the initial allocation of X_1 is X_1^a units to A and X_1^b units to B; and the initial allocation of X_2 is X_2^a units to A and X_2^b units to B. At point Z, A's marginal rate of technical substitution of X_1 for X_2 (denoted by the slope of AA') is greater numerically than B's (denoted by the slope of BB'). Thus, the amount of X_2 that A is willing to give up to obtain an

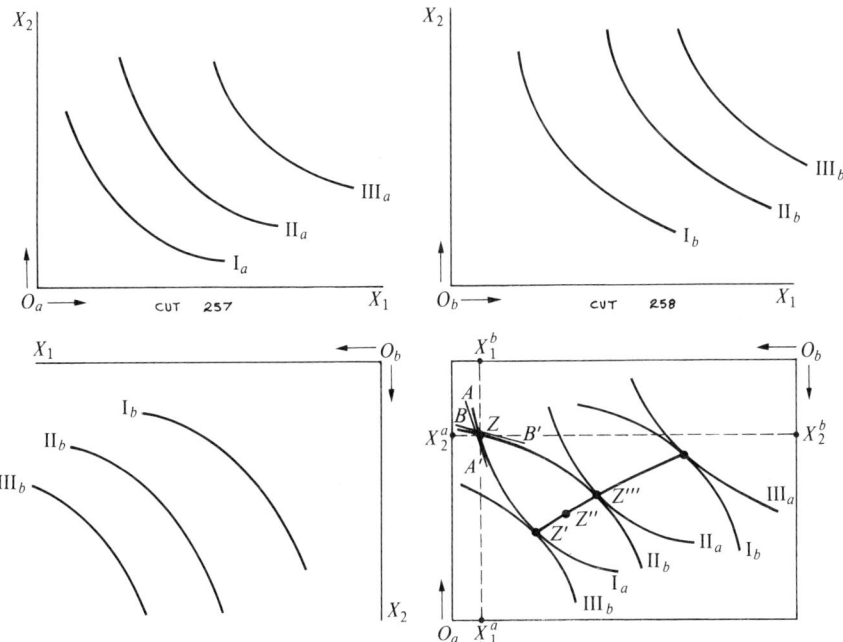

FIG. 24.2a. Iso-revenue-product curves of firm A
FIG. 24.2b. Iso-revenue-product curves of firm B
FIG. 24.2c. Iso-revenue-product curves of firm B
FIG. 24.2d. Optimum allocation of factors of production

additional unit of X_1 is greater than the amount of X_2 that B is willing to give up to obtain an additional unit of X_1. Conversely, B's marginal rate of technical substitution of X_2 for X_1 is greater than A's. Thus the amount of X_1 that B is willing to give up to obtain an additional unit of X_2 is greater than the amount of X_1 that A is willing to give up to obtain an additional unit of X_2. Consequently, A is willing to give X_2 to B, and B is willing to give X_1 to A, until the marginal rate of technical substitution is the same for both A and B. The two rates approach equality as A gives up X_2 for X_1 and B gives up X_1 for X_2.

The marginal rate of technical substitution is the same for both A and B at points Z', Z'', and Z''' in Figure 24.2d. A is indifferent to moving from Z to Z', by giving up X_2 to obtain X_1, because he stays on the same iso-product curve (I_a) and hence his product does not change. But A prefers to move from Z to Z''', by exchanging factors according to B's iso-product curve II_b, for then A would be giving up a smaller amount of X_2 and obtaining a larger amount of X_1. Thus, A would be increasing his product while B's product remained the same. Similarly, B is indifferent to moving from Z to Z'', by giving up X_1 to obtain X_2, because he stays on the same iso-product curve (II_b) and hence his product does not change. But B prefers to move from Z

to Z', by exchanging factors according to A's iso-product curve I_a, for then B would be giving up a smaller amount of X_1 and obtaining a larger amount of X_2. Thus, B would be increasing his product while A's product remained the same.

In short, A and B are in conflict. A would like to move from Z to Z''' by exchanging factors according to B's iso-product curve II_b, but B would like to move from Z to Z' by exchanging factors according to A's iso-product curve I_a. Because of this conflict, the set (locus) of points of tangency of the iso-product curves of A and B—that is, the set of points at which $q_{rj}/q_{mj} = p_r/p_m$ holds true—is called the conflict curve. A would like to move to higher iso-product curves by moving up the conflict curve from left to right, while B would like to move to higher iso-product curves by moving down the conflict curve from right to left.

The conflict between A and B leads to bargaining as each tries to increase his product. The result of bargaining may be a contract in which both benefit from trade. Relative to point Z, both benefit if the contract calls for an allocation of factors according to point Z'' (or any other point between Z' and Z''' on the conflict curve). Since both may gain via a contract, the conflict curve is also called the contract curve: A and B contract to exchange factors until the marginal rate of technical substitution is the same for both in order to increase their product. In short, they have a common interest in moving to the contract curve, and a conflict of interest in moving along the conflict curve.

Relative to point Z, A would lose product if the new allocation was according to a point on the conflict curve to the left of point Z'; and B would lose product if the new allocation was according to a point on the conflict curve to the right of point Z'''. Thus, both A and B (and hence the economy) gain product if they exchange factors until their marginal rates of technical substitution are the same and if the new allocation point is within the set of points on the conflict curve bounded by their initial iso-product curves. In other words, every point not on the conflict curve (point Z) is "inferior" to a set of points on the curve (points $Z' \ldots Z'''$), but every point on the conflict curve is not "superior" to every point not on the curve.

General Equilibrium of Markets in an Exchange Economy

A general equilibrium model consists of two sets of conditions for general equilibrium: each household (individual) and business firm must be in equilibrium, and each product and factor market must be in equilibrium. Consider first an economic system consisting solely of households (individuals) who exchange a given amount of products until each is in equilibrium. To repeat, when the households are in general equilibrium,

(1″) $\dfrac{u_{ri}}{p_r} = u_{mi}$ ($r = 1, 2, ..., m - 1$) and ($i = 1, 2, ..., n$)

(2″) $\sum_r p_r(x_{ri} - \bar{x}_{ri}) = 0$ ($i = 1, 2, ..., n$)

A market is in equilibrium when quantity supplied equals quantity demanded —that is, when excess quantity demanded is zero. Define quantity demanded of a product of an individual as x_r; then market quantity demanded of the same product of all individuals is $\sum_i x_{ri}$. Define quantity supplied of a product of an individual as $\bar{x}_r$; then market quantity supplied of the same product from all individuals is $\sum_i \bar{x}_{ri}$. Thus, all markets are in equilibrium when

(6) $\sum_i (x_{ri} - \bar{x}_{ri}) = 0$ ($r = 1, 2, ..., m - 1$)

General Equilibrium of Markets in a Production and Exchange Economy

Consider now an economic system consisting of households and business firms in which production and exchange of commodities takes place. To repeat, when the households are in general equilibrium,

(1″) $\dfrac{u_{ri}}{p_r} = u_{mi}$ ($r = 1, 2, ..., m - 1$) and ($i = 1, 2, ..., n$)

(2″) $\sum_r p_r(x_{ri} - \bar{x}_{ri}) = 0$ ($i = 1, 2, ..., n$)

And when the business firms are in general equilibrium,

(3″) $\dfrac{q_{sj}}{q_{kj}} = \dfrac{p_s}{p_k}$ ($s = 1, 2, ..., k$) and ($j = 1, 2, ..., N$)

(4″) $\dfrac{q_{mj}}{q_{tj}} = p_t$ ($t = k + 1, k + 2, ..., m - 1$) and ($j = 1, 2, ..., N$)

(5) $f_j(x_{1j}, x_{2j}, ..., x_{mj}) = 0$ ($j = 1, 2, ..., N$)

Households supply commodity r if

$\sum_i (x_{ri} - \bar{x}_{ri}) < 0$

Conversely, households demand commodity r if

$\sum_i (x_{ri} - \bar{x}_{ri}) > 0$

Similarly, business firms supply commodity r if

$\sum_j x_{rj} > 0.$

Conversely, business firms demand commodity r if

$\sum_j x_{rj} < 0$

Consequently, when all commodity markets are in equilibrium, the economic system's $m - 1$ commodity prices satisfy

(7) $$\sum_j x_{rj} = \sum_i (x_{ri} - \bar{x}_{ri}) \qquad (r = 1, 2, ..., m - 1)$$

SUMMARY

An axiom of microeconomic theory is that an individual seeks to maximize his utility (or preference) subject to his income ($=$ expenditure). Assume perfect competition in all product markets. Then product price ratios are the same for every individual, and when an individual is maximizing his satisfaction subject to his income, his marginal rate of substitution for every pair of products equals the common ratio of prices—the equimarginal principle of equilibrium of a purchaser (consumer) of products. Thus, given common product price ratios (that is, perfect competition), when every individual is in equilibrium, the marginal rate of substitution between every pair of products is the same for every individual—the equimarginal principle of general equilibrium of households.

Another axiom of microeconomic theory is that a business firm seeks to maximize its profit. Assume perfect competition in all factor markets. Then factor price ratios are the same for every business firm, and when a business firm is maximizing its profit, its marginal rate of technical substitution for every pair of factors equals the common ratio of prices—the equimarginal principle of equilibrium of a purchaser of factors of production. Thus, given common factor price ratios (that is, perfect competition), when every business firm is in equilibrium, the marginal rate of technical substitution between every pair of factors is the same for every business firm—the equimarginal principle of general equilibrium of business firms.

According to the equimarginal principles of general equilibrium of households and business firms, an economic system has an optimum allocation of products and factors when all individuals and business firms are in equilibrium. A general equilibrium allocation is said to be Pareto optimal or efficient: any other allocation makes at least one individual or business firm "worse off" in terms of preferred position. In other words, an allocation of "resources" or "commodities" is not Pareto optimal if another allocation makes no one "worse off" and someone else "better off" in terms of preferred position. The conflict curves of households and business firms are Pareto optimal loci, for they depict allocations that are Pareto optimal.

SELECTED READING

Bator, F. M. "The Simple Analytics of Welfare Maximization," *The American Economic Review*, XLV: 11 (March 1957), pp. 22–59. Reprinted in Kamerschen, D. R. (editor). *Readings in Microeconomics*. Cleveland, Ohio: The World Publishing Company, 1967, pp. 503–544.

Questions

1. Use a line of attainable combinations and iso-utility (that is, indifference) curves to derive, analyze, and verbalize the equilibrium principle $u_r/u_m = p_r$ $(r = 1, 2, \ldots, m-1)$. How would this principle be stated if you did not accept the concepts of utility and marginal utility? What would be the question and your answer if the mth product was not money and the rth product was not leisure? What if the mth product was money income and the rth product was leisure?

2. Use an Edgeworth–Bowley box diagram to derive, analyze, and verbalize the equilibrium principle $u_{ri}/u_{mi} = p_r$ $(r = 1, 2, \ldots, m-1$ and $i = 1, 2, \ldots, n)$. How would this principle be stated if you did not accept the concepts of utility and marginal utility?

3. Use iso-product and iso-factor cost curves to derive, analyze, and verbalize the equilibrium principle $q_s/q_k = p_s/p_k$ $(s = 1, 2, \ldots, k)$. How would this principle be stated if you did not accept the concepts of output and marginal product?

4. Use an Edgeworth–Bowley box diagram to derive, analyze, and verbalize the equilibrium principle $q_{sj}/q_{kj} = p_s/p_k$ $(s = 1, 2, \ldots, k$ and $j = 1, 2, \ldots, N)$. How would this principle be stated if you did not accept the concepts of output and marginal product?

5. Use iso-revenue and iso-input (that is, transformation) curves to derive, analyze, and verbalize the equilibrium principle $q_m/q_t = p_t$ $(t = k+1, k+2, \ldots, m-1)$. How would this principle be stated if you did not accept the concepts of cost (that is, input) and marginal cost (that is, marginal product)?

6. State, analyze, and verbalize the conditions for general equilibrium of markets in an exchange economy.

7. State, analyze, and verbalize the conditions for general equilibrium of markets in a production and exchange economy.

NOTES

[1] For a solution to be meaningful, equilibrium prices and quantities must be positive or zero—that is, nonnegative.

[2] See the appendix to Chapter 2.

Index

Aggregate supply and demand, 7
Allocation of factors, 374–376
Allocation of products, 368–371
Average cost, 161–163
Average expenditure, 18–19
Average factor cost curve
    of a monopsonist, 148
    of a perfectly competitive purchaser, 142
Average income, 325–326
Average product, 116–117
Average revenue
    of a monopolist, 101–102
    of a perfectly competitive seller, 95–96
Average revenue-product, 289–290

Baumol's model, 277–279
Bertrand's model, 269–270
Bilateral monopoly, 358
Business firm, 4–5

Cardinal versus ordinal, 40
Chamberlin's model, 271–272
Circular flow of income, 1–2
Cobweb theorem, 224–227
Combinations, ranking of, 40
Competitive market, 209–233
Competitive purchaser, 13–26, 44–52
Competitive seller, 92–93, 99, 263
Complement, price of a, 62–63, 194–195
Complements, in consumption, 34, 36–37, 71–74
    in production, 121–122, 173–175, 195–196
Constant cost industry, 251–257
Constant marginal expenditure, 17–18

Consumption
    substitutes in, 34–36
    complements in, 34, 36–37, 71–74
Cost
    average, 161–163
    functions, 155–179
    long-run, 166–169
    marginal, 159–161
    monetary and real, 169
    short-run, 155–166
    total, 155–159
Cournot's model, 267–269

Demand, change in, defined, 69–70, 314–315
    for a factor, 283–320, 347–358
    for a product, 11–87
    for output, 7
Demand curve, interdependency of, 265–266
Distribution theory, 4
Dominant-seller model, 276–277
Duopoly models, classical, 267

Edgeworth's model, 270–271
Effects, 55–56
Elasticity
    and aggregate expenditure, 75–76
    cases, 78–82
    cross, 82
    of market demand, 74–75, 83
    of market supply, 201–204
    and price-consumption curve, 85–87
    price, geometry of, 76–78
    and total revenue, 104–105
Equilibrium
    of business firm, 371–374
    and disequilibrium, 209–233

Equilibrium (*cont.*)
  of a factor purchaser, 347–358
  general, 5, 366–379
  of households, 366–368
  long-run, 225
  of markets, 376–379
    indeterminancy of, 351–352
  Marshallian, 214–216
  of monopolist (labor union), 354–5
  of monopolistic-competitive sellers, 263–266
  of monopsonist (business firm), 356
  of multi-market monopolist, 242, 244
  of multi-plant monopolist, 241–242, 255
  of oligopolistic sellers, 266–279
  partial, 5
  of a perfectly competitive purchaser,
    of factors, 295
    of products, 44–52
  of a perfectly competitive seller, of
    labor, 331
    of products, 180–190
  theory, 5–6, 356
  Walrasian, 211–213
Equality of the ratio of
  marginal revenue-product to price, 296–297
  marginal utility to price, 48–49
  price to marginal cost, 181–182
Equal-shares model, 275–276
Equimarginal principle of equilibrium
  of a perfectly competitive purchaser
    of factors, 297–298
    of products, 49–50
  of a perfectly competitive seller
    of labor, 334–335
    of products, 182–183
Exchange economy, 376–377
Expansion path
  input, 301–302
  output, 186–187
Expenditure
  average, 18–19
  on factors, 2–4
  function, 13
  iso-, 20–23
  law of constant marginal, 17–18
  marginal, 16–17
  on a product, 75–76
  on products, 2–3
  total, 13–15
Exploitation
  monopolistic, 346
  monopsonistic, 348–349

Factor cost
  average, 142, 148
  function, 139
  iso-, 143–145, 149–150
  marginal, 141–142, 147–148
  total, 140, 146–147
Factor market
  monopoly in, 345
  monopsony in, 355
  perfect competition in, 352–354
Function
  cost, 155–179
  demand, 53–87, 306–320
  expenditure, 13–26
  factor cost, 139–154
  income, 323–330
  marginal rate of substitution, 37, 57–60
  of an economic system, 3–5
  production, 111–138
  revenue, 92–110
  revenue-product, 284–294
  supply, 191–205
  utility, 27–43

Hicks, 67n, 129
Household, theory of, 4–5

Identity
  national income, 6–7
  national product, 6
Imperfectly competitive purchaser of a factor, 145–146
Imperfectly competitive seller of a product, 99, 291–292

Income
  average, 325-326
  circular flow of, 1-2
  curve of labor, 324-326
  effect, 55-56, 340
  elasticity, 82-83
  function, 323
  identity, 6-7
  marginal, 324-325
  of purchaser, 73-74
  purchaser's money, 63-65
  total, 323-324
Income-consumption curve, 64-65
Indifference
  map, 41
  relation, 40-41
Industry cost, 251-253
Input expansion path, 301-302
Iso-expenditure, 20-23
Iso-factor cost, 143-145, 149-150
Iso-input, 170-175
Iso-product, 117-122
Iso-real-wage, 327-328
Iso-revenue, 96-98, 105-106
Iso-utility, 32-34
Iso-wage, 326-327

Janus diagram, 49-50, 182-193, 297, 334

Labor
  backward-bending supply curve, 341
  demand curve facing a seller, 326
  equilibrium of a seller of, 331
  income function of a seller of, 323
  marginal income curve of, 324-326
  total income curve of, 323-324
Law
  of constant marginal expenditure, 17-18
  of decreasing marginal utility, 31-32
  of demand, for a factor of a purchaser, 308
    for a product of a purchaser, 61
  of market demand, for a product, 68-69
    for a factor, 313-314
  of market supply, of a product, 198-199
  of supply, of a product of a seller, 192-193
Leisure, 338
Long-run cost, 166-167
Long-run equilibrium, 255, 264-265
Long-run market period, 248
Long-run supply, 249-250, 254-255

Macroeconomic theory, 7-8
Map, indifference, 41
Marginal cost equals price, 180, 299
Marginal expenditure, 16-18
Marginal factor cost, 141-142, 147-148
Marginal income, 324-325
Marginal product, 114-116
Marginal rate of substitution, 37-38, 46-47, 57-61, 331-333
Marginal returns to variable input, 124-126
Marginal revenue, 94-95, 101
Marginal revenue-product, 287-289
Marginal revenue-product equals price, 184, 295-296
Marginal utility, 30-32, 47-48, 333-336
Market
  demand for a product, 68-69, 74-75, 82-83, 104-105, 216-217, 222-224
  equilibrium, 360
  long-run, 248
  price, 210-211
  quantity, 214
  short-run, 234-235
  supply, 198-204, 217-222
Marshallian model, 213-214
Microeconomics theory, 3
Model
  Baumol's, 277-279
  Bertrand's, 269-270

384 INDEX

Model (*cont.*)
   Chamberlin's, 271–272
   Classical duopoly, 267
   Cournot's, 267–269
   dominant-seller price-leadership, 276–277
   of an economic system, 2
   Edgeworth's, 270–271
   equal-shares price-leadership, 275–276
   interdependence of demand curves, 265–266
   monopoly cartel, 273–275
   Sweezy's, 272–273
   very short-run market, 245
Monetary and real costs, 169
Money, 37–38, 60–61
Money income, 63–65, 73–74
Monopolist, 99–110, 254–255, 350–351
   multi-market, 244
Monopolistic competition theory, 263–264
Monopolistic exploitation, 355
Monopoly, 273–275, 354–355, 358
Monopsony, 355–358
Monopsonist, 146–153, 359
Monopsonistic exploitation, 357–358

National income, 6–7
National product, 6

Oligopolistic seller, 263, 266–267
Optimum allocation, 368–371, 374–376
Ordering theory, 39
Output, 7, 186–188

Parameter shifts, 216–219
Partial equilibrium theory, 5–6, 365
Perfect competition, 352–357
Perfectly competitive industry, 250
Perfectly competitive purchaser, 53, 139–145, 306, 338
Perfectly competitive seller, 92–98, 180–197, 235–238, 246–247, 248–250, 284–289, 355
Period equilibrium, 234
Preference ordering theory, 39–42
Preferred equilibrium, 359–360
Price
   elasticity, 74–82, 85–87, 104–105
   equals marginal cost, 180–181, 299
   equals marginal revenue-product, 295–296
   of a complement, 62–63, 71–73, 194–195, 201
   of input, 184
   of a substitute, 62, 70–71, 193, 200
   of a technical complement, 310
   of a technical substitute, 308–309
Price and quantity, determination of
   in a factor market, 346–358
   in a product market, 207–208
Price-consumption curve, 55, 85–87
Price-discrimination, 108–109, 152–153
   first degree monopolist, 108–109
   first degree monopsonist, 152–153
Price-leadership model, 276–277
Principles
   of equilibrium of a perfectly competitive purchaser, of factors, 295–305, 347–357
     of products, 44–52
   of equilibrium of a perfectly competitive seller, of labor, 331–337
     of products, 180–190, 234–280
   of the theory, of demand for a factor, 283
     of demand for a product, 11
     of supply of a factor, 321–322
     of supply of a product, 89–90
Product
   average, 116–117
   curves, of capital, 134–137
     of labor, 133–137
   Giffen, 56–57
   identity, 6

INDEX 385

inferior, 56–57
iso-, 117–126
marginal, 114–116
normal, 56–57
total, 111–114
Production function, 111–138
Products, allocation of, 359–365
Progress, 127–129
Proportions, 124–126
  fixed, 126–127
Purchaser, of factors, 283–322
  of products, 11–91

Ranking of combinations, 40
  ordinal, 40
Rate, *see* marginal rate of substitution
Ratio, *see* equilibrium
Rationale, *see* law
Real cost, 169
Region of production, economic, 123–124
Relation, 40–41
Returns to scale, 126–127
Revenue
  average, 95–96, 101–104
  functions, 92–110
  iso-, 96–98, 105–106
  marginal, 94–95, 101–104
  total, 93–94, 99, 102, 104
Revenue-product
  average, 289
  function, 284
  of an imperfectly competitive seller, 291
  marginal, 287
  total, 284–286

Seller, of factors, 321–341
  of products, 89–205, 234–282
Scale, 126–127
Short-run, 124–126, 155–169, 234–242, 264
  very, 244–248
Stages of production, 132–137
Structural equilibrium, 352–362

Substitutes in consumption, 34–36, 62
  in production, 119–121, 172–173, 193
Substitution and income effects, 55–56
  see also marginal rate of substitution
Supply
  change in, defined, 199–200
  of a factor, 321–349
  of a product, 19–20, 89–205, 234–282
  of output, 7
Supply curve, backward-bending, 341
Supply and demand, identification of, 219–224
Sweezy's model, 272–273
Symmetry of stages of production, 132–137
System, model of an economic, 2

Technical complements and substitutes, 308–311, 315–316
Technological progress, 127–139
Theorem, cobweb, 224–227
Theory
  of business firm, 4–5
  of demand for a product, 11–87
  of price and quantity in a factor market, 351–355
  product market, 207-282
  distribution, 4
  of demand for a factor, 283–320
  general equilibrium, 5–6, 366–379
  of households, 4–5
  macroeconomic, 7–8
  microeconomic, 3
  partial equilibrium, 5–6, 365
  preference ordering, 39–42
  of supply, of factor, 321–341
    of a product, 89–205, 234–282
  value, 3
Total
  expenditure, 13–15
  factor cost of a monopsonist, 146–147
  of a perfectly competitive purchaser, 140–141

Total (*cont.*)
   income, 323–324
   product, 111–114
   revenue of a monopolist, 99–101
   perfectly competitive seller, 93–94
   revenue-product, 284–287
   utility, 27–30

Utility
   function, 27
   law of decreasing marginal, 31–32
   iso-, 32–37
   marginal, 30–31
   total, 27–30

Variable proportions, 124–126
Value theory, 3

Wage curve, iso-, 326–327
Walrasian model, 210–213